KILLER ROADS: FROM CRASH TO VERDICT

Contemporary Litigation Series

Consulting Editors for the
CONTEMPORARY LITIGATION SERIES

Professor Stephen A. Saltzburg
University of Virginia Law School

Professor Kenneth R. Redden
University of Virginia Law School

KILLER ROADS: FROM CRASH TO VERDICT

RICHARD S. KUHLMAN

*Law Firm of Foss, Schuman,
Drake and Barnard
Chicago, Illinois*

THE MICHIE COMPANY
Law Publishers
CHARLOTTESVILLE, VIRGINIA

Library of Congress Catalog Card No. 85-82597
ISBN 0-87215-896-9

TABLE OF CONTENTS

TABLE OF CONTENTS

NOTE ON ROAD DESIGN STANDARDS

Road design standards referred to in this book come in two basic categories: guidance systems and design standards. The guidance systems standards apply to all the information systems on the road. These information systems usually consist of signs, painting on the pavement, guardrails, reflectors, and similar *additions* to the basic "ribbon of concrete." The engineering criteria for those guidance systems are found in the Manual on Uniform Traffic Control Devices (sometimes referred to in the following pages as "MUCTD"), which each state (and Federal) Highway Department updates and issues every few years. For transportation negligence cases dealing with defects in the guidance systems of the road such as broken warning signs or missing striping, recourse must be had to the issue of the relevant jurisdiction's Manual on Uniform Traffic Control Devices that was in effect *at the time of the crash.*

Road design standards deal with the actual geometrics of the road, such as how long and sharp the horizontal curves can be, whether vertical curves should start within horizontal curves, and how many things the road should be doing to the driver at the same time. The most definitive road design standards in the United States have, for several decades, been found in the Red, Blue and Yellow Books issued by the American Association of State Highway Transportation Officials, which is sometimes referred to herein as "AASHO" or "AASHTO," depending on whether the word "Transportation" had been added to the title at the relevant time. AASHO became AASHTO in 1973. For crashes dealing with negligence in the design of a roadway, recourse must be had to the AASHTO design standards in effect *at that point in the past* when (as Defendants will argue) the road was designed and built, or (as Plaintiffs will argue) when the road should have been updated and improved prior to the time the Plaintiff received his injuries.

INTRODUCTION — THE ORIGIN OF THE KILLER ROADS

The killer roads of the United States originated, and continue to draw sustenance from an amalgam of technological progress and human greed. All human institutions, including technology, change through tradeoffs: for every new thing obtained there is a corresponding lose of something previously held. The supporters of the change, not surprisingly, invariably derive some advantage, usually economic in our society, from the new thing while the opponents of the change usually have nothing to gain, and often something economic to lose, from an alteration of the *status quo.* The issue of whether a technically possible change will be made depends on a value judgment weighing the corresponding bottom line viewpoints of the winner and losers about the change. It is only when those who will gain from the change reach a sufficient preponderance over those who will not gain from it that the change itself, now classified as "progress," takes place. Almost all the moving and shaking in human history has been substantially motivated by the search for an answer to the fundamental question: "Where's mine?"

The origin of modern roads, and how they degenerated into killers, offer excellent examples of how this process works.[1]

---

1. History abounds with other, less immediately relevant, situations where technically possible developments were delayed for substantial periods until an economic motivation for their implementation developed. Jean Turdin designed viable plans for gas lighting in 1618, some two centuries before it was commercially adopted. Schwenter set out the principles of the electric telegraph in 1635. Bushnell invented the submarine in 1775, Newcomen invented the steam engine in 1711, but it was ignored for 30 years until a commercial application was first found for it in mining. F. Braudel, *The Structures of Everyday Life: Civilization and Capitalism,* at 434 (1979).

In the year 9 A.D. the Roman legions of Augustus Caesar, supported by the latest technology of that era, were pushing east over the Rhine River in a mighty effort to extend "civilization" over western Germany.[2] If this invasion had succeeded almost two thousand years of subsequent history, and at least two world wars, would probably have been very different. The invasion failed when the three legions of Quintilius Varus were surprised and destroyed in the Teutoberg Forest,[3] but it left behind a silent legacy: some of the finest and longest lasting roads in the history of the world.[4]

On June 24, 1812, almost two thousand years later, the Grand Army of Napoleon invaded Russia, using many of those Roman roads for logistical support, but the soldiers of Napoleon could march only about 100 kilometers in twenty-four hours on those roads, the same speed that the legions of Augustus could travel.[5]

The price paid for keeping the same roads in use for 1,803 years was the limitation of movement on those roads to a relatively slow and unchanging velocity. The capability to improve both the construction of those roads and the velocity of travel upon them existed for a long time before the birth of Napoleon.[6] The value judgment to uproot a static society by quickening the rate of overland travel was not made until the Industrial Revolution of 1830, however, because there was no economic motivation for such a change prior to that time.[7]

---

2. W. Durant, *Caesar and Christ,* at 218 (1944).

3. *Id.*

4. M. Grant, *History of Rome,* at 264-65 (1978); M. Grant, *The Army of the Caesars,* at 307 (1974).

5. Braudel, *supra* note 1, at 424.

6. *Id.* at 27.

7. "Transportation improvements after 1830 were simply the consequence of large scale investments of deliberate, systematic improvement, because the economic growth of the time made them both profitable and necessary." *Id.* at 428.

Indeed, perhaps the single most revolutionary aspect of the entire Industrial Revolution was the recognition it gave to the previously generally overlooked fact that technological developments, such as modern roads, could *have* economic consequences that were worth seeking.[8] Before this recognition, western society was as static as India, China, and Islam.[9] Without this elevation of greed and gain, science could never have progressed from its non-material origins as an abstract philosophy in classic Greece and Rome[10] into a practical, profit-oriented instrument superbly adept at developing and drawing economic benefits from the mass market of consumers through such new technologies as modern roads and faster vehicles.[11]

This is not to say, of course, that previous technological breakthroughs did not receive appropriate rewards. The first person to develop the torch, or the bow and arrow was, in all likelihood, rewarded with massive quantities of food,

---

8. D. Spengler, *The Decline of the West,* Vol. II, at 300-01 (Knopf, 1980).

9. Braudel, *supra* note 1, at 316-17.

10. A.N. Whitehead, *Science and the Modern World,* at 7 (1953).

11. The economic origins of modern science are clear and unique. The ancient Greeks had no interest in using science as a source of profit. M.I. Finley, *Economy and Society in Ancient Greece,* at 186, 188 (1981). Indeed, they consciously rejected the social and political changes that usually follow new technology. J. Landels, *Engineering in the Ancient World,* at 186-87 (1978). These non-material values were accepted by the sciences of most of the leading pre-industrial societies, including India (see Spengler, Vol. II, *supra* note 8, at 12-13, 133, 137-38); China (J. Gernet, *A History of Chinese Civilization,* at 485, 489 (1982)); and Islam (Braudel, *supra* note 1, at 449-50). By comparison, western science was seeking to expand profit and commerce as early as 1484, when King John III of Portugal appointed commissions of mathematicians to aid the maritime trade of his nation by developing a new technology to find latitude at sea, and by the Sixteenth Century both governmental and private bodies in England were financing scientific research to promote commercial activity and profit. A. Smith, *Science and Society,* at 39-45 (1972).

money, and members of the opposite sex. What was truly revolutionary about the science and technology that produced the Industrial Revolution and modern roads in the western world was the realization that the desire for economic gain could motivate unceasing efforts to build a better mousetrap. Modern science ceased to be an abstract philosophy and became the market force that generated modern technology only after society decided that economic profit for its own sake would be the basis of law and morality. The vast social forces spawning modern jurisprudence and the killer roads began when political and economic power passed from those who believed peasants should be hitched to plows and went over to those who realized it was more profitable for all concerned to let peasants earn and spend money, thereby creating consumers and "citizens."[12]

NEGLIGENCE THEORY — THE FIRST LICENSE TO KILL

All of these divergent elements melded in the crucible of the Industrial Revolution to produce the negligence theory — the first license to kill. The Industrial Revolution was a revolution in politics and economics as well as in industry and technology. In addition, because it did new things in

---

12. A similar commercialization of society produced a remarkable series of technological breakthroughs in China long before the European Industrial Revolution. Chinese iron masters developed blast furnaces fueled with coke in the Eleventh Century, producing in 1078 A.D. 40% more iron than England and Wales generated in 1788. During this era China also created canals, coinage, banking, paper money, and deep sea cross oceanic expansion long before similar processes matured in Europe. All this new technology was based upon the commercialization of Chinese society, giving people a motive to create these things, and the process stopped when Chinese society rejected and subordinated its mercantile entrepreneurs. *See* William H. McNeill, *The Pursuit of Power,* at 24-54 (University of Chicago Press, 1982).

all these fields, it was also a revolution in law, resulting in society issuing at least two licenses to kill that directly relate to the problem of killer roads.

The first legal problem faced by the new industrial system of Nineteenth Century Europe was that the profit-oriented developers creating the new technology did not want to pay for all the damages, deaths and mutilations their new railroads, steamboats, and factories were going to cause. This was a very serious problem because before the Industrial Revolution a property owner was held strictly liable for all the damages people suffered on, or because of, his property. This strict liability standard would have destroyed the Industrial Revolution before it began because a movement growing out of a new and revolutionary importance given to the profit incentive could hardly have prospered by bankrupting the early developers and manufacturers seeking to achieve those profits through new technology.

To solve this problem, the common law called once again upon its inexhaustible ability to create good things for people who can pay their lawyers and came up with a legal revolution known as the negligence theory. This was really a license to kill dressed up in powdered wigs and fancy words, because it meant that the new industrial technology could kill and maim virtually at will, provided only that the developers of these new machines could show they were using "reasonable care,"[13] two words that promptly became an annuity for lawyers because no two lawyers being paid

---

13. About the year 1825, negligence began to be recognized as a separate and independent basis of tort liability. Its rise [replacing earlier strict liability concepts] coincided in a marked degree with the Industrial Revolution; and it very probably was stimulated by the rapid increase in the number of accidents caused by industrial machinery. Prosser, *Law of Torts,* p. 140 (4th ed. 1971). *See also* 2 Harper & James, *The Law of Torts,* p. 747 (1956); Winfield, "The History of Negligence in the Law of Torts," 42 Law Q. Rev. 184 (1926).

by different clients have ever agreed on what those words mean.

The fact that the negligence theory and the Industrial Revolution began at about the same time has had at least one consequence directly applicable to transportation negligence issues. Defendants have always argued that they were using reasonable care (and were therefore not negligent) if they were following industry custom and were at least no worse than most other people who were doing what they did at the time they did it.[14] Defendants in road negligence cases can use this argument to great effect because it is often very difficult to argue that any given road, no matter how terrible, is much worse than most other roads.

In the first place, most roads were created before they *could* have been done negligently because they were built before national standards on road design and safety emerged. Thus, in 1977, roughly 90% of the road mileage in the United States[15] had been built prior to 1950, when national standards began to emerge.[16]

Prior to 1916 there were few, if any, national road, highway, or crossing standards. In 1916 the federal govern-

---

14. Industry custom is not conclusive on the issue of what constitutes reasonable care at the time, but it is admissible in court on the issue of what was feasible, what the Defendants' peers considered to be minimum standards, and what far reaching consequences might strike the industry if higher standards were not required. Darling v. Charleston Community Mem. Hosp., 33 Ill. 2d 326, 211 N.E.2d 253 (1965); Williams v. Brown Mfg. Co., 93 Ill. App. 2d 334, 236 N.E.2d 125 (1968), *rev'd,* 45 Ill. 2d 418, 261 N.E.2d 305 (1970); Murphy v. Messerschmidt, 41 Ill. App. 3d 659, 355 N.E.2d 78 (1976), *aff'd,* 68 Ill. 2d 79, 368 N.E.2d 1299 (1977).

15. Some 3,313,000 miles out of a total of 3,867,000 miles of rural and municipal highways were in use. *See The Statistical Abstract of the United States,* United States Department of Commerce, Bureau of the Census, at 638 (1979).

16. R. Kuhlman, *Transportation Negligence 1984,* at 1-15.

ment, under the Federal Aid Highway Act, began providing the states with funds to build roads, but the states were still free to set, or not to set, their own safety and design standards. National road design criteria relevant to safety issues had not really begun to evolve prior to the 1950's, when the American Association of State Highway and Transportation Officials (AASHTO) began publication of their increasingly definitive design standards known as the "Red Book" (A Policy on Design of Urban Highways and Arterial Streets, published in 1957 and updated in 1973 by AASHTO,[17] and the "Blue Book" (A policy on Geometric Design of Rural Highways, published in 1954 and 1965 by AASHO.)[18] Even these works were not generally accepted by many governments and corporations in charge of road and rail transportation facilities for many years after they were published. See *The Law and Roadside Hazards,* pp. 44-45, published by the Insurance Institute for Highway Safety, 1974. Even today, no federal legislation exists to mandate AASHTO standards upon states, counties, or towns, and most states required the marking, signing, and other safety criteria in the Manual on Uniform Traffic Control Devices only for state transportation facilities, excluding county and local facilities.

The fact that most roads and crossings were built before authoritative design and safety standards existed, not surprisingly, resulted in the creation of a large number of transportation facilities that were dangerous when built. This situation was aggravated by the fact that most road and highway departments channeled the maximum amount of their annual appropriations into politically advantageous new construction, ignoring or seriously slighting maintenance of existing facilities. As a consequence, the national transportation facilities became more dangerous and lethal with each passing year.

---

17. *Id.*
18. *Id.*

LITIGATING CHRONOLOGICAL STANDARDS OF CARE

There are a large number of dangerous transportation facilities in this country that were not created negligently in a legal sense, because the standards of design and safety existing at that time were lax or even nonexistent. To establish liability against a defendant in charge of such a facility, it is necessary for plaintiff's counsel to examine the (usually) long period of time subsequent to the creation of the facility and to find some action or inaction of the defendant during that period that can support a negligence verdict.

Initially, it is somewhat difficult to establish the concept that a facility such as a highway not negligently created somehow became negligent, even though it remained substantially intact and merely failed to receive upgrading from postcreation progress in state of the art technology. A large part of this difficulty stems from the static origin and nature of the negligence theory, which began along with modern technology in the early Industrial Revolution.

With the simultaneous origin of modern technology and the negligence theory, there was a combined operation to free industrial development from the crushing burdens of strict liability for all the injuries created by technology. Conversely, however, as state of the art technology had no time to develop when negligence emerged as a distinct cause of action, it was inevitable that the law would view technology-oriented negligence as a chronologically static concept. A defendant's conduct was either negligent or not negligent as of a fixed and frozen moment in time, and no subsequent events could alter that determination.

This concept of chronologically fixed negligence (or lack thereof), insulated from subsequent events traditionally unrelated to the issue of whether there was a breach of duty, is reflected in the following language from the *Restatement (Second) of Torts* § 4 (1965):

> The breach of a duty, as the word is used in the Restatement of this Subject, does not make the actor liable. It merely subjects him to liability. . . . Whether he is liable or not depends on matters which are usually beyond his control. Thus, whether or not he is liable depends upon whether his breach of duty results in an injury to someone to whom the duty is owing in such as manner as to make the breach of the duty a legal cause of the injury, *and this depends upon the course of events subsequent to the actor's breach of his duty, a matter over which the actor has no effective control.* [Emphasis added.]

Similar formulations of negligence as a chronologically fixed concept impervious to subsequent events may be found in *Strapelli v. City of Chicago,* 295 Ill. App. 469, 14 N.E.2d 986, 988 (1938), as follows: "Ordinary care must necessarily be such care as relates to the facts and circumstances which exist *at the time of its required use.*"

And, again, it is found in *Chicago, Burlington & Quincy R.R. v. Owen,* 21 Ill. App. 339, 343 (1886), as follows: "Whether a given act is negligent or improper is to be determined by the surroundings and conditions existing *at the time and which were or ought to have been known to the party sought to be charged.*"

Obviously, the adroit defendant can base at least part of his defense on the contention that, just as subsequent events cannot relieve him of liability after he has breached his duty, so the subsequent events (or nonevents) of failing to upgrade to meet evolving technology cannot impose liability upon an originally nonnegligent creation of the transportation facility, or other artifact, at issue.

The transportation facility negligence situation is usually factually unique not only because it seeks a somewhat retroactive application of negligence that cuts against the grain of chronologically fixed negligence theory, but also because the defendant will usually be in charge of large numbers of virtually fungible facilities. The control exercised by a railroad over the vast numbers of crossings or by a highway department over the thousands of road miles it has created immediately distinguishes these cases from the traditional "products" or strict liability situation, where the defendant manufacturer quickly gives up control over its products to the distribution chain and can escape liability if the products were not defective or unreasonably dangerous when they left the manufacturer's control. See § 402A of the *Restatement of Torts* (4th ed. 1971).

Product liability theory, then, does not actually cover chronological technological negligence situations. Initially, this is simply because many injury generating areas of technology, such as roads, highways, railroad crossings, houses, and buildings, have not been held, to our knowledge, to be "products" at all within the scope of that doctrine. In *Hunt v. Blasius,* 74 Ill. 2d 203, 384 N.E.2d 368 (1978), the plaintiffs were occupants of an auto that struck a sign that had allegedly been defectively anchored next to the road. The court dismissed the strict liability action against the contractor who installed the sign because:

> there [was] no allegation [by plaintiff] of a defect in the post which affected its intended or actual use — to safely support the sign. The risks which inhered in the collision with the post were the same risks which attend all collisions between motorists and stationary objects which align the highway. In the absence of any facts which would indicate that the post, in supporting the sign, subjected motorists to any unreasonable or unexpected risks, we cannot sustain plaintiffs' action in strict liability. 384 N.E.2d at 372.

The implication in this reasoning from *Hunt* is that a strict liability action might lie for a defect in a transportation facility that did subject motorists to unreasonable and unexpected risks. In *Maddan v. R.A. Cullinan & Son, Inc.,* 88 Ill. App. 3d 1029, 411 N.E.2d 139 (1980), where plaintiff motorist was denied a strict liability action against the contractor that installed a roadside guardrail, the Court said:

> Classify a guardrail as a product and the courts will next be confronted with the assertion that State planted trees, culverts, bridges, and highways themselves are products. We do not believe that the doctrine of products liability . . . was ever intended to encompass such items. 411 N.E.2d at 140-41.

On a deeper level of analysis, however, it is clear that the situation in which the defendant's technology is not negligently substandard when first put into public use, but rather became substandard through the defendant's failure to upgrade in the light of subsequent technical developments, will not really fit the products liability doctrine, "products are defective which are dangerous because they fail to perform in the manner reasonably to be expected in light of their nature and intended function." *Dunham v. Vaughan & Bushnell Mfg. Co.,* 42 Ill. 2d 339, 247 N.E.2d 401, 403 (1969). Under this test, and that of § 402A of the Restatement, a product is only "unreasonably dangerous" if it is somehow defective, and it is only defective if it fails to perform in the manner reasonably to be expected, and such defects do not really exist if the defendant's technology is capable of performing in the expected manner when the defendant puts it into public use.

The astronomical number of units under a transportation defendant's control is also highly significant. If the defendant is a highway department, the fungible units will be (usually millions of) road miles. If the defendant is a railroad operating over a wide area, the fungible units will be (hundreds, perhaps thousands of) similar crossings, particularly if the crossing at issue is, as most are, at grade, nonelectrified, and passively protected.

The relevance of the vast number of facilities controlled by the defendant is the "reasonableness" of the defendant's failure to upgrade such facilities to meet postcreation advances in technology. The defendant often will be able to argue that it could not determine in advance where the plaintiff would be injured, and while it might be reasonable to require the defendant to upgrade its facility if it had only a few, it would be grossly unreasonable to require the defendant to go bankrupt through constant upgrading of its vast number of facilities to incorporate every advance in technology.

To meet these issues, the plaintiff must establish, usually over the defendant's objections, a relevant chronological point in measuring state of the art technology through "red flagging" of the particular facility at issue.

Many transportation facility negligence cases hinge on the time period from which to select the state of the art technology against which the defendant's conduct will be measured. Defendants invariably argue for chronologically earlier and technologically lower standards. Plaintiffs seek chronologically later and technologically higher standards.

"The whole theory of negligence," as Professor Prosser observed long ago, "presupposes some uniform standard of behavior." *The Law of Torts,* p. 124 (2d ed. 1955). The uniform standard, of course, is that of reasonable or ordinary care (65 C.J.S. Negligence § 1(4) (1966)), and under this standard our law has defined negligence as ". . . a failure to do what the reasonable man would do under the same or similar circumstances." Prosser, *supra* at 125.

Under these concepts, the presence or absence of negligence in a given case must be determined by measuring the defendant's conduct against generally accepted standards of reasonable care under the particular circumstances involved. The search for negligence, then, like any other exercise in measurement, will ultimately depend upon the measuring standard selected. The outcome of negligence cases in the area of transportation facility design and maintenance, medical malpractice, automotive design, or anything else involving extensive technological development over a long period of time, may rest on the initial decision of what point in time is to be selected and examined for the state of the art technology that constitutes the standard of reasonable care under the circumstances. (Industry custom is not conclusive on the issue of what constitutes reasonable care at the time, but it is highly relevant as illustrating what is feasible, what defendant's peers consider to be minimum standards, and what far-reaching consequences may strike the industry if higher standards are required.) *Darling v. Charleston Community Memorial Hosp.,* Ill. 2d 326, 211 N.E.2d 253 (1965); *Williams v. Brown Mfg. Co.,* 93 Ill. App. 2d 334, 236 N.E.2d 125 (1968), *rev'd,* 45 Ill. 2d 418, 261 N.E.2d 305 (1970); *Murphy v. Messerschmidt,* 41 Ill. App. 3d 659, 355 N.E.2d 78 (1976), *aff'd,* 68 Ill. 2d 79, 368 N.E.2d 1299 (1977).

The basic issue underlying the selection of an appropriate chronological standard of care in any negligence case where the artifact or instrumentality at issue has been in general use for a long time, during which technology has substantially progressed beyond the initial standards, is what duty, if any, the defendant has to upgrade previously created items in light of current developments.

Cases involving the allegedly negligent design, construction, and/or maintenance of a transportation facility usually present chronological negligence issues in a fairly pure form, for the relevant periods of time from which standards of care may be selected, ranging from the creation of the facility to the crash at issue, are quite long. The crucial issue in such cases will often be at what chronological point to select the relevant state of the art technology to measure against the defendant's conduct.

A defendant charged with negligently designing, building, or maintaining a transportation facility can generally argue with a great deal of support that, in order to meet its particular burden of reasonable care, it need only satisfy the design and safety criteria, if any, existing in the distant past when the facility was created. Defendants in transportation facility negligence cases make great efforts to have the factfinder adopt the earlier, and lower, industry design and safety standards because once such a ruling is made, the defendant can presumably (although not always) show it met this standard, if not later and stricter ones. The defendant can then argue that the common usage of a business or occupation is a test of care or negligence and is a proper matter for consideration in determining whether or not sufficient care has been exercised in a particular case. Such conformity to industry standards may even afford a sufficient basis for an argument that proper care was exercised in the absence of evidence tending to show that the custom did not involve reasonable care. 65 C.J.S. Negligence, § 16 (1966). See also Prosser, *The Law of Torts,* p. 135 (2d ed. 1955).

Defendants can bolster their claim for the earlier measuring standard of care not only by citing the legal precedents for chronologically fixed negligence cited above but also by going into great detail to establish how rapidly the relevant technology has improved since the facility in question was created. This is obviously done to show, again, how much it would cost to put the unending flood of new improvements into its astronomical number of facilities. In the field of transportation engineering, for example, standards on median barriers, stopping sight distances, reflex-reaction times, and many similar matters that were only "recommended" in the 1950's had become requirements by the 1960's and 1970's. Similarly, in recent years an increasing number of states have been adopting the increasingly strict railroad and traffic sign control criteria in the updated editions of the *Manual of Uniform Traffic Control Devices.* Even the techniques of locating hazardous and dangerous areas on transportation facilities have developed increasing complexity and sophistication in recent years, as evidenced by Report FHWA-RD-77-83, *Identification of Hazardous Locations,* published in December 1977 by the Federal Highway Administration Offices of Research and Development.

The final gloss on this defense argument is then often provided, as it was in many of our cases, by the fact that the successive American Association of State Highway and Transportation Officials' design and safety manuals apply only prospectively — specifically exempting preexisting transportation facilities from their scope.

These defense arguments, bolstered by common sense and authoritative literature, are obviously very powerful. Judges and juries are not likely to hold a defendant to a standard of care that would inevitably force it into bankruptcy and ruin, and the inescapable fact is that few defendants could afford to upgrade all their facilities to current safety levels.

One effective way for plaintiffs to deflect these defense arguments is to establish, where possible, that the defendant did not meet the relevant design or safety standards in effect when the facility was created. Plaintiffs who can do this can avoid the burden of establishing the need to impose a later, higher standard of care. In this respect, it should be remembered that most authoritative publications, including the AASHTO design and safety standards, reflect, rather than create, professional consensus. Generally speaking, before AASHTO standards are adopted, they are subjected to nationwide testing and study. The results of these tests and studies are generally published in other authoritative works long before they are published in AASHTO standards. Thus, the most currently accepted design, perception, reaction, visibility, and safety standards were generally accepted among designers and transportation engineers before they were published by AASHTO. Competent expert testimony can therefore sometimes establish that a given transportation facility should have been designed or built under criteria the profession had generally accepted but which AASHTO had not yet officially adopted.

Alternatively, it may be possible to show that the defendant failed to meet the relevant industry standards existing when the facility was created through proof that the defendant relied upon a negligent custom of ignoring available scientific safeguards for financial reasons. Since highway departments and railroads have been chronically under-financed, there are many areas of scientific development, such as reaction time formulas and sight distance calculations, that highway departments have been slow in adopting, even after AASHTO had published them. A plaintiff who can establish that higher safety criteria were known, accepted, reasonably cheap, and otherwise available when the facility was created, can condemn the defendant's stingy conservatism in neglecting to build that higher standard into the facility with the following language from the Restatement of Torts, § 295A:

> No group of individuals and no industry or trade can be permitted, by adopting careless and slipshod methods to save time, effort, or money, to set its own uncontrolled standard at the expense of the rest of the community. If the only test is to do what has always been done, no one will ever have any great incentive to make any progress in the direction of safety.

In many transportation facility negligence cases, however, it will not be possible to show that the defendant failed to meet the standard of care existing when the facility was created. This is because many of our existing facilities were built when safety criteria were either nonexistent, unsettled, or pathetically low. To prevail in the majority of these cases, the plaintiff must show that prior to plaintiff's accident, the particular facility involved in his case should have been upgraded to meet a higher standard of care that would have prevented the crash. To do this, plaintiff must gather all the available evidence of prior crashes, complaining letters, recommendations for improvement, applicable safety statutes, governmental warnings, crash rates, death rates, and anything else establishing that the dangers of this particular facility should have been "red flagged" to the defendant before the plaintiff was injured.

If the factfinder accepts this singling out of the facility at issue, the defendant will lose much of the "common sense" force behind its argument that it would be financially destroyed if required to constantly upgrade all of its facilities after they are built. The same evidence establishing that the defendant should have upgraded this particular dangerous facility, of course, will then simultaneously establish that the defendant was negligent in not making such improvements and also that the defendant's negligence should be measured against the design and safety standards existing at the time the defendant should have upgraded the facility.

Evidence that the defendant knew or should have known of the defect at issue before the plaintiff's injury is required to establish most negligence cases. There is, however, a decisive difference concerning the applicable standard of care between the case where the defendant should have known of the defect because it had actual notice through concrete things (such as complaining letters, the presence of a safety device, or police reports) and the case where the plaintiff can only argue that the defendant had constructive notice of a defect just because it had existed for a long time. The plaintiff's ability to invoke a higher postconstruction standard of care is somewhat related to the defendant receiving actual notice of the defect sufficient to create the clear duty to repair or improve the facility. Evidence of constructive notice of defects, even when not specifically barred by statute (see Ill. Rev. Stat. ch. 85, § 3-102), often cannot substitute for this "actual notice" of defects required to invoke a later and higher standard of care against a defendant. Simply put, the defendant will invariably attempt to blend the facility at issue into all its other similar facilities to support its claim for the older, lower standard of care which is premised on the ruinous cost of constantly upgrading everything.

SOVEREIGN IMMUNITY — THE SECOND LICENSE TO KILL

Louis XIV apparently never uttered the famous claim attributed to him to be the state ("L'etat, c'est moi"),[19] but that motto and the arrogance associated with it, have been the operative philosophy of far too many individuals and governmental entities charged with the design, construction, and maintenance of modern roads. Through the legal device known as "sovereign immunity," most people and governmental bodies that worked on the public roads have been, until recently, immune from civil liability for failure to use reasonable care. The consequences of this insulation, which most states have abolished over the past decade, was a pernicious encouragement of shoddy work. The Supreme Court of Illinois expressed the general judicial dislike for highway departments believing themselves to be soul brothers of dead French kings in the following terms: "The rule of (governmental) tort immunity is unjust, unsupported by any valid reason, and has no rightful place in modern society."[20]

The combination of the lack of standards when most roads were created, and the sovereign immunity enjoyed by the creators of those roads, produced a result similar to that produced by blending nitroglycerin and acid.

In recent years most states[21] and legislatures[22] have at-

19. W. & A. Durant, *The Age of Louis XIV,* at 15 (1963). The quotation, of course, translates as "I am the state," an opinion generally restricted to dead kings and I.R.S. agents.

20. Molitor v. Kaneland Community Unit Dist. No. 302, 18 Ill. 2d 11, 163 N.E.2d 89, 96 (1959). Edwin Borchard expressed the idea thusly:

> The common law and the political theory underlying both British and American constitutional law have been regarded as a bulwark of protection to the individual in his relations with the government. The "rule of law" which Dicey and others extol is designed by judicial control to restrict within the counts of legality the operation of the governmental machine in its contact with the citizen. Borchard, "Governmental Liability in Tort," 34 Yale L.J. 1 (1942).

21. Over thirty states have, by judicial decision, either completely or partially abolished sovereign immunity in the tort field.

22. The Illinois Constitution of 1970, in art. XIII, § 4, provides that:

tempted to undo part of the damage created by this unfortunate mixture of elements by repealing sovereign immunity, particularly in the road design and maintenance areas. Under these new

---

In 1983, the Ohio Supreme Court abolished sovereign immunity and the Mississippi Supreme Court prospectively abolished sovereign immunity — both Courts holding that governmental immunity should fall because innocent victims of governmental maladministration should have a remedy against public tortfeasors and that stare decisis does not require perpetuation of demonstrable error. Enghauser Mfg. Co. v. Eriksson Eng'g, 451 N.E.2d 228 (Ohio 1983); and Pruett v. City of Rosedale, 421 So. 2d 1046 (Miss. 1983).

In 1984, the Oklahoma Supreme Court outlawed sovereign immunity as a rule "no longer supportable in reasons, justice, or in the light of the overwhelming trend against its recognition." Vanderpool v. State, 672 P.2d 1153 (Okla. 1983).

Other jurisdictions abolishing this pernicious immunity in tort include the District of Columbia. *See* Carter v. Carlson, 447 F.2d 358 (1971), *rev'd on other grounds sub nom.* District of Columbia v. Carter, 409 U.S. 418, 93 S. Ct. 602, 34 L. Ed. 2d 613 (1973); Spencer v. General Hosp., 425 F.2d 479 (D.C. Cir. 1969); City of Foley v. Terry, 278 Ala. 30, 175 So. 2d 461 (1965); Scheele v. City of Anchorage, 385 P.2d 582 (Alaska 1963); City of Fairbanks v. Schaible, 375 P.2d 201 (Alaska 1962); Stone v. Arizona Hwy. Comm'n, 93 Ariz. 384, 381 P.2d 107 (1963); Muskopf v. Corning Hosp. Dist., 55 Cal. 2d 211, 359 P.2d 457, 11 Cal. Rptr. 89 (1961), *modified sub nom.* Corning Hosp. Dist. v. Superior Court, 57 Cal. 2d 488, 370 P.2d 325, 20 Cal. Rptr. 621 (1962); Evans v. Board of County Comm'rs, 174 Colo. 97, 482 P.2d 968 (1971); Colorado Racing Comm'n v. Brush Racing Ass'n, 136 Colo. 279, 316 P.2d 582 (1957); Murphy v. Ives, 151 Conn. 259, 196 A.2d 596 (1963); Hargrove v. Town of Cocoa Beach, 96 So. 2d 130 (Fla. 1957); Smith v. State, 93 Idaho 795, 473 P.2d 937 (1970); Molitor v. Kaneland Community Unit Dist. No. 302, 18 Ill. 2d 11, 163 N.E.2d 89 (1959), *cert. denied,* 362 U.S. 968 (1960); Perkins v. State, 252 Ind. 549, 251 N.E.2d 30 (1969); Klepinger v. Board of Comm'rs, 143 Ind. App. 155, 239 N.E.2d 160 (1968); Brinkman v. City of Indianapolis, 141 Ind. App. 662, 231 N.E.2d 169 (1967); Carroll v. Kittle, 203 Kan. 841, 457 P.2d 21 (1969); Haney v. City of Lexington, 386 S.W.2d 738 (Ky. 1964); Board of Comm'rs v. Splendour Shipping & Enters. Co., 273 So. 2d 19 (La. 1973); Hamilton v. City of Shreveport, 247 La. 784, 174 So. 2d 529 (1965); Morash & Sons v. Commonwealth, 363 Mass. 612, 296 N.E.2d 461 (1973); Myers v.

standards, governmental entities and their employees, while not

---

Genesee County Auditor, 375 Mich. 1, 133 N.W.2d 190 (1965); Williams v. City of Detroit, 364 Mich. 231, 111 N.W.2d 1 (1961); Spanel v. Mounds View School Dist. No. 621, 264 Minn. 279, 118 N.W.2d 795 (1962); Johnson v. Municipal Univ. of Omaha, 184 Neb. 512, 169 N.W.2d 286 (1969); Brown v. City of Omaha, 183 Neb. 430, 160 N.W.2d 805 (1968); Rice v. Clark County, 79 Nev. 253, 382 P.2d 605 (1963); Merrill v. City of Manchester, 114 N.H. 722, 332 A.2d 378 (1974); Willis v. Department of Conservation & Economic Dev., 55 N.J. 534, 264 A.2d 34 (1970); McAndrew v. Mularchuk, 33 N.J. 172, 162 A.2d 820 (1960); Hicks v. State, 88 N.M. 588, 544 P.2d 1153 (1975); Kitto v. Minot Park Dist., 224 N.W.2d 795 (N.D. 1974); Ayala v. Philadelphia Bd. of Pub. Educ., 453 Pa. 584, 305 A.2d 877 (1973); Becker v. Beaudoin, 106 R.I. 562, 261 A.2d 896 (1970); Kelso v. City of Tacoma, 63 Wash. 2d 913, 390 P.2d 2 (1964); Long v. City of Weirton, 214 S.E.2d 832 (W. Va. 1975); Holytz v. City of Milwaukee, 17 Wis. 2d 26, 115 N.W.2d 618 (1962); Town of Douglas v. York, 445 P.2d 760 (Wyo. 1968). For an expanded discussion of the sovereign immunity doctrine, see Harley & Wasinger, "Governmental Immunity: Despotic Mantle or Creature of Necessity," 16 Washburn L.J. 12 (1976); Van Alstyne, "Governmental Tort Liability: A Decade of Change," U. Ill. L.F. 919 (1966); Comment, "Judicial Abrogation of Governmental Sovereign Immunity: A National Trend with a Pennsylvania Perspective," 78 Dick. L. Rev. 365 (1973); Comment, "The State As A Party Defendant: Abrogation of Sovereign Immunity In Tort In Maryland," 36 Md. L. Rev. 653 (1977).

"Except as the General Assembly may provide by law, sovereign immunity in this state is abolished."

The General Assembly subsequently responded to the 1970 Constitution by granting certain governmental entities that limited tort immunity in the Tort Immunity Act, Ill. Rev. Stat., ch. 85, § 1-101 *et seq.,* but generally, under both the Immunity Act and the common law, governmental entities in Illinois must design, construct, and maintain their roads, highways, and crossings with reasonable care.

In a few states, liability for defective highways has been statutorily imposed. *See* Conn. Gen. Stat. § 13a-144 (1977); Kan. Stat. Ann. § 68-419(a) (Cum. Supp. 1977); Mass. Gen. Laws Ann. Ch. 81, § 18 (Michie/Ann. § 3.996, 102-04 (Callaghan 1977)); S.C. Code Ann. § 57-5-1810 (Law. Co-op. 1976). Such provisions for liability may not succeed where the state constitution prohibits suits against the state. *See* Arkansas State Hwy. Comm'n v. Nelson Bros., 191 Ark. 629, 87 S.W.2d 394 (1935).

insurers of public safety,[23] can be held liable in damages for failure to use reasonable care in the design, construction, or maintenance of public roads and road shoulders.[24]

---

23. Electrical Prods. Corp. v. County of Tulare, 116 Cal. App. 2d 147, 253 P.2d 111 (1953).

24. For Arizona law, see Rodney v. City of Phoenix, Maricopa County Superior Court No. C-387927, May 29, 1981, reported at 24 A.T.L.A. L. Rep. 366; Hernandez v. State of Arizona, Pima County Superior Court No. 168611, August 21, 1981, reported at 25 A.T.L.A. L. Rep. 123.

For California law, see Reel v. City of South Gate, 340 P.2d 276, 171 Cal. App. 2d 49 (1959). California by statute imposes civil liability for foreseeable injuries on public property. West Ann. Gov. Code § 835; Weddle v. State, 191 Cal. Rptr. 819 (Cal. App. 1983). Public officials in California can also be held civilly liable for negligent performance of official duties. Ness v. City of San Diego, 144 Cal. App. 2d 668, 301 P.2d 410 (1956); Schilling v. Casper, Sacramento County Superior Court No. 268963, August 27, 1982, reported at 26 A.T.L.A. L. Rep. 64-65.

For Illinois law, see Kobylanski v. Chicago Bd. of Educ., 63 Ill. 2d 165, 347 N.E.2d 705 (1976); Lansing v. County of McLean, 45 Ill. App. 3d 91, 359 N.E.2d 165 (1976); Holda v. County of Kane, 88 Ill. App. 3d 522, 410 N.E.2d 552 (1980); Collins v. School Dist. No. 189, St. Clair County, 115 Ill. App. 3d 100, 450 N.E.2d 387 (1983); the common law holds that:

> The State owes a duty to those using its streets and highways to keep those roads in a reasonably safe condition. *Shuck v. State of Illinois,* 25 Ill. Ct.Cl. 209 (1965). This duty extends to properly maintaining the shoulders of a highway for the use for which they are reasonably intended. *Parkinson v. State of Illinois,* 31 Ct.Cl. 99, 101 (1976);

See also Kolski v. State of Illinois, 31 Ct.Cl. 307, 312 (1976), where the court held: "The State of Illinois is charged with maintaining its highways in a reasonably safe condition and with using reasonable diligence in doing so." The State's duty of due and reasonable care extends to maintenance of the shoulder of roadways for the use for which they are reasonably intended.

For Indiana law in accord, see State v. Thompson, 385 N.E.2d 198, at 205 (Ind. App. 1979); Indiana State Hwy. Comm'n v. Clark, 371 N.E.2d 1323, at 1327 (Ind. App. 1978); Elliott v. State, 342 N.E.2d 674, at

The widespread nature of the killer roads and the carnage they cause has led certain states and governmental bodies to limit, as a policy matter, the civil liability they will accept in this

---

676-77 (Ind. App. 1976).

For Massachusetts law, see Scholl v. New England Power Serv. Co., 340 Mass. 267, 163 N.E.2d 279 (1960); Eklon v. City of Chelsea, 223 Mass. 213, 111 N.E. 866 (1916); Flynn v. Hurley, 322 Mass. 182, 124 N.E.2d 810 (1955).

For Michigan law, see Grinis v. Michigan Dep't of State Hwys., Court of Claims No. 6693, January 20, 1982, reported at 25 A.T.L.A. L. Rep. 214.

For New York law, see Atkinson v. County of Oneida, 77 A.D.2d 257, 432 N.Y.S.2d 970 (1980); Scott v. State, 19 A.D.2d 574, 240 N.Y.S.2d 279 (1963).

Ohio, reflecting the more liberal general modern trend abolishing or severely limiting sovereign immunity, has enacted statutes vitiating the immunity defense for counties (Ohio Code Supplement, § 305-12) and for the State (Ohio Code Supplement, § 2743.02). Case law has further established that other governmental entities, whose immunity defenses were not specifically abrogated by statute, must still follow the duty of maintaining highways and bridges with reasonable care. Basham v. Jackson, 51 Ohio App. 2d 100, 367 N.E.2d 66, *aff'd* 54 Ohio St. 2d 366, 377 N.E.2d 491 (1977).

Pennsylvania similarly abrogated the immunity. Tilli v. County of Northhampton, 370 F. Supp. 459 (E.D. Pa. 1974).

Texas, reflecting a minority view, held in Gates v. City of Fort Worth, 567 S.W.2d 871 (Tex. App. 1978), that governmental immunity still existed in Texas jurisprudence and, in Villarreal v. City of San Antonio, 657 S.W.2d 175 (Tex. App. 1983), that failure of a city to erect barricades at the end of a dead end street was a governmental function covered by the immunity provisions of the State Tort Claim Act. In City of Wichita Falls v. Ramos, 596 S.W.2d 654 (Tex. Civ. App. 1980), however, Texas mitigated this strict view, holding that cities generally have a duty to exercise ordinary care in maintaining streets and sidewalks in a reasonably safe condition. The defendant's liability in Texas, even after a breach of this duty, is not unconditional. In City of Beaumont v. Henderson, 349 S.W.2d 301 (Tex. Civ. App. 1961), the court held that Texas cities must exercise ordinary care in constructing reasonably safe sidewalks and streets and in maintaining them, but they are not insurers of the safety of such places. It is only where a defect is such that

area. One form this limitation policy takes is the enactment of a direct statute imposing limits on governmental civil liability.[25] Other states have imposed limited public liability for transportation facility negligence cases by relegating such actions to administrative agencies or boards of claims.[26]

---

reasonably prudent men would not permit it to continue that liability exists.

25. Six of the 19 states which have enacted a general tort immunity law also have statutory limitations on the amount of recovery. In fact, 16 of the 24 states which allow for general liability of governmental agencies by an "open-ended" statute also impose statutory limitations on recovery of damages.

Examination of these limitations shows a wide range. On the average, however, most states provide statutory limitations of $300,000 per accident. The following states provide statutory limitations on damages recoverable from governmental agencies: Alabama (§ 11-93-2 of the Code of Alabama, 1975); Colorado (§ 24-10-111 of the Colorado Revised Statutes Annotated); Delaware (§ 4013 of the Delaware Code Annotated); Florida (§ 768.28(5) of the Florida Statutes Annotated); Indiana (§ 34-4-16.5-4 of the Indiana Statutes Annotated); Kansas (§ 75-6105 of the Kansas Statutes Annotated); Maine (§ 8105 of the Maine Revised Statutes Annotated); Maryland (Maryland Tort Claims Act); Massachusetts (Massachusetts Annotated Laws, Chapter 258 §§ 2, 10); Minnesota (§ 466.04 of the Minnesota Statutes Annotated); Montana (§ 2-9-104 of the Montana Code Annotated); Nevada (§ 41.035 of the Nevada Revised Statutes); New Hampshire (New Hampshire Revised Statutes Annotated and Estate of Cargill v. City of Rochester, 406 A.2d 704 (N.H. 1979)); New Mexico (§ 41-4-19 of the New Mexico Statutes Annotated); North Dakota (§ 32-21.103 of the North Dakota Code Annotated); Oklahoma (154, Chapter 5, Volume 47-51 of the Oklahoma Statutes Annotated); Oregon (§ 30.70 of the Oregon Revised Statutes); Pennsylvania (§ 8553 of the Pennsylvania Consolidated Statutes Annotated, Title 42); Rhode Island (§ 9-31-3 of the General Laws of Rhode Island, 1956); South Carolina (§ 5-7-70 of the South Carolina Tort Claims Act); Texas (§ 2, Article 6252-19 of the Texas Civil Statutes), and Wyoming (§ 1-39-118 of the Wyoming Statutes).

26. *See* Ala. Code §§ 41-9-61 to 73 (1975); Ark. Stat. Ann. §§ 13-1401 to 1406 (1968); Ill. Ann. Stat. ch. 37, §§ 439.1-.8 (Smith-Hurd 1972); Ky. Rev. Stat. §§ 44.040-.160 (1971); N.C. Gen. Stat. §§ 143-291 to 300 (1978); S.D. Compiled Laws Ann. §§ 21-32-1 to 14 (1967); Tenn. Code

Whatever form it takes, abrogation or limitation of the sovereign immunity defense will produce better roads, as well as fairer lawsuits. It is probably a sad commentary on our species, but history demonstrates conclusively that we rarely produce excellence in any field without incentives to do so.[27] In general recognition of these facts, most states where limited sovereign immunity now exists strictly construe that immunity on the grounds that it is contrary to public policy and unknown at common law. See *Bennett v. City of Lansing,* 52 Mich. App. 289, 217 N.W.2d 54 (1974); *Smith v. Lancaster County Tax Bureau,* 23 Pa. D. & C. 3d 734 (1982); *Hennigs v. Centreville Twp.,* 56 Ill. 2d 151, 306 N.E.2d 287 (1973).

Ohio Accord: Strohofer v. City of Cincinnati, 6 Ohio 3d 118, 451 N.E.2d 787 (1983), held that without a specific statute granting immunity, the defense of sovereign immunity will not

---

Ann. §§ 9-801 to 812 (1973); W. Va. Code §§ 14-2-1 to 29 (1972); Wis. Stat. § 16.007 (1975). The state constitutions of Alabama, Arkansas, Illinois and West Virginia prohibit suits against the state in courts of general jurisdiction. Kentucky, South Dakota, Tennessee and Wisconsin have constitutional provisions which enable the legislature to prescribe the manner of suit.

Administrative claims boards have been justified as relieving the courts from the burden of governmental tort litigation; providing assurance that tort claims against governmental entities will be decided from a uniform point of view divorced from local prejudices and attitudes; and developing a degree of expertise in adjudicating such claims which may be expected to come through specialization.

27. Modern technology, for example, developed only when European merchants, traders and manufacturers received sufficient financial incentives to justify the effort of constant invention and marketing of new products. Before these incentives, western technology had remained static for over a thousand years. S. Smiles, "The Engineers and the Industrial Revolution," printed in *The Development of Western Technology Since 1500,* at 82-83 (1964). These economic incentives to new technology that entered our culture in the Eighteenth Century were unique: no other society has ever used, or rewarded, technology purely for finding only the best, most efficient, and most economical solution for a given problem. J. Elliel, *The Technological Society,* at 70 (1964). Other societies, like highway departments with immunity, produced shoddy technology when incentives for better performance were lacking.

block a tort suit against a municipality. *Cado Business Sys. of Ohio, Inc. v. Board of Educ.,* 8 Ohio App. 3d 385, 457 N.E.2d 939 (1983) further clarified that the courts must strictly construe immunity statutes where they do exist. *Zents v. Board of Comm'rs of Summit County,* 9 Ohio St. 3d, 204, 459 N.E.2d 881 (1984), held that counties may only be held liable for harms that are torts preserving sovereign immunity in many other fields.

Texas Accord: Texas held in *Schultz v. City of Houston,* 551 S.W.2d 494 (Tex. App. 1977), that the statutory immunity provision requiring notice of claim to a city within set time periods, was in derogation of common law and should be construed strictly in favor of the claimant. Texas courts further strictly construed their Tort Claims Act limited immunity in *Norton v. Brazos County,* 640 S.W.2d 690 (Tex. App. 1982) and in *Turvey v. City of Houston,* 602 S.W.2d 517 (1980).

An analysis of particular areas involved in immunity litigation follows, but of course the statutes and case law of the particular jurisdiction at issue should be investigated early in any crash case work up.

The general rule is that, where blanket sovereign immunity has been abolished, the governmental entity can be civilly liable, even if its individual agents and employees are granted immunity. *Horton v. City of Ottawa,* 40 Ill. App. 3d 544, 352 N.E.2d 23 (1976); *Mora v. State of Illinois,* 369 N.E.2d 868 (1977); *Novoa v. County of Ventura,* 133 Cal. App. 3d 137, 183 Cal. Rptr. 736 (1982).

California: Bell v. City of Palos Verdes Estates, 224 Cal. App. 2d 257, 36 Cal. Rptr. 424 (1964). Both a government employee and the entity which employs him are liable for employee's negligence in the performance of his duties. *Widdows v. Koch,* 263 Cal. App. 2d 228, 69 Cal Rptr. 464 (1968). The judicial test as to whether a governmental employee can be held responsible in damages for injuries resulting from his acts or failure to act, or whether he will be granted immunity under the discretionary exclusion rule, will hinge on whether his act or omission was "discretionary" or "ministerial."

The general rule, even where some form of sovereign immunity still exists, is that the immunity does not apply to road design, construction, and maintenance activities.

Massachusetts: Valade v. City of Springfield, 7 Mass. App. 13, 384 N.E.2d 1256 (1979). City was liable from liability for injuries and damage caused when the plaintiff, riding his motorcycle on a dark night, hit a raised manhole in street. Liability was premised on the argument that construction and maintenance of city sewers were not revenue-providing activities.

Michigan: Central Advertising Co. v. City of Novi, 91 Mich. App. 303, 283 N.W.2d 730 (1979). Exceptions by statute to general grant of immunity included the failure to keep highways reasonably maintained and safe for travel.

New York: Under New York law, the governmental entities, even if they have discretionary immunity from formulating traffic control plans, can be negligent in failure to review and re-evaluate the plans in light of actual operation. *Atkinson v. County of Oneida,* 77 A.D.2d 257, 432 N.Y.S.2d 970 (1980). In *Ewen v. City of New York,* Queens County Supreme Court No. 13829-75, June 11, 1980, reported at 23 A.T.L.A. L. Rep. 366, a settlement of $1.5 million for injuries were awarded plaintiff, an auto passenger, who sustained injuries when his car hit water standing in a road and hydroplaned and careened off into a tree. The water was standing on the road because Defendant City had an improper maintenance of roadway drainage resulting in dangerous driving conditions. No immunity allowed. New York Thruway Authority, which failed to adequately inspect escarpment, was liable for damages resulting from accident which occurred when truck struck boulders which had fallen to the highway from the escarpment, see also *Waddingham v. State,* 90 A.D.2d 855, 456 N.Y.S.2d 843 (1982).

Ohio: The defense of sovereign immunity was denied to municipalities in tort suits alleging negligent design and placement of traffic signals. *Strohofer v. City of Cincinnati,* 6 Ohio St. 3d 118, 451 N.E.2d 787 (1983). Ohio courts also held in *Roberts v. City of Fairborn,* 102 Ohio App. 91, 141 N.E.2d 297 (1956), that a city's statutory duty to keep its streets open, in repair, and free from nuisances is an exception to the general common law rule immunizing a municipality from the consequences of the negligence in the discharge of its governmental functions.

Pennsylvania: 42 Pa. C.S.A. § 8542 imposes local governmental civil liability for:

> (b)(6)(i) A dangerous condition of streets owned by the local agency, except that the claimant to recover must establish that the dangerous condition created a reasonably foreseeable risk of the kind of injury which was incurred and that the local agency had actual notice or could reasonably be charged with notice under the circumstances of the dangerous condition at a sufficient time prior to the event to have taken measures to protect against the dangerous condition.

COST OF THE KILLER ROADS

The fact that most roads and crossings were built before authoritative design and safety standards existed not surprisingly resulted in the creation of a large number of transportation facilities that were dangerous or defective when built. This situation was aggravated by the fact that most road and highway departments channeled the maximum amount of their annual appropriations into politically advantageous new construction, ignoring or seriously slighting maintenance of existing facilities. As a consequence, the national transportation facilities became more dangerous and lethal with each passing year. Today, every practicing lawyer in this country will have, statistically, at least one client involved in a serious crash substantially caused by defective road maintenance or design and one baby out of every forty born this year is going to die in such a crash.[28]

By 1965, Ralph Nader called national attention to the carnage on our national road system as follows:[29]

> A transportation specialist, Wilfred Owen, wrote in 1946 "There is little question that the public will not tolerate for long an annual traffic toll of 40-50,000 fatalities." Time has shown Owen to be wrong. Unlike aviation, marine, or rail transportation, the highway transport system can inflict tremendous casualties and property damage without in the

---

28. Claybrook, "Auto Safety Standard Compliance," at 27, 58 *Trial* (May 1981).

29. R. Nader, *Unsafe at Any Speed,* at vii-viii (1965).

> least affecting the viability of the system. Plane crashes, for example, jeopardized the attraction of flying for potential passengers and therefore strike at the heart of the air transport economy. They motivate preventive efforts. The situation is different on the roads. Highway accidents were estimated to have cost this country in 1964 $8.3 billion in property damage, medical expenses, lost wages, and insurance overhead expenses. Add an equivalent sum to compromise roughly the indirect costs and the total amounts to over 2 percent of the gross national product.

In 1967 and 1974, the American Association of State Highway and Transportation Officials published the "Yellow Book" (Highway Design and Operational Practices Related to Highway Safety), calling for a "crash program" to stop the national mass murder on public roads and railroad crossings. This publication noted that between 1900 and 1967 approximately 1.7 million Americans died in crashes, which is more than twice the number of Americans that were killed in all wars in which the United States was involved since 1776.[30]

In 1970 alone, nationwide, 54,845 people died in motor vehicle accidents. Since 1970, the slaughter on the killer roads of the United States has reached consistently ghastly proportions. In 1979, motor vehicle crashes killed 52,800 people, and in 1980, crashes killed 52,600 people. Thus, within a margin of fluctuation of approximately 2,000 deaths per year (or roughly 5 percent of the 1970 statistics), the mortality on the national road and crossing network achieves inexplicable uniformity. Between 1973 and 1977, some 245,428 people were killed in motor vehicle accidents.[31] In addition, between 1970 and 1977, an additional 14,778 people were killed and 284,852 were injured at railroad crossings.[32] In comparison, approximately 54,000 Americans were killed and 303,706 were injured during the Korean War,

---

30. The State of the Art of Traffic Safety (Arthur D. Little, Inc., June 1966); National Highway Safety Standards, United States Department of Transportation (1967).

31. Statistical Abstract of the United States, at 643-44.

32. *Id.* at 661.

while 57,000 were killed and 303,706 were injured in Vietnam from 1961 through May 7, 1975.[33] Thus, between 1970 and 1977, roads and railroad crossings witnessed the slaughter of some 315,000 people, a figure roughly six times larger than the number of American soldiers killed in either Korea or Vietnam. Indeed, during each of those years, the number of people dying on American roads was roughly equal to the number of American soldiers killed during the entire Korean conflict. The April 18, 1980 edition of the Chicago Sun Times reported, at page 48, that auto accidents are now the leading cause of death for children under 14 in the United States — and the chances of a child in this age group being killed by a car crash are almost twice that of dying of cancer, the second ranked killer of these children.

In the "cold" figures of dollars and cents, the cost of this carnage is massive. *Automotive News* (October 26, 1981, p. 8) reported that the financial cost of road and crossing crashes in 1979 alone was $36 billion, and the cost of such crashes in 1980 was $39.3 billion. This makes road crashes a more financially costly health problem than coronary heart disease. Indeed, among major diseases in the United States, only cancer takes a greater financial toll than the killer roads.[34]

Money, of course, is not the most appropriate medium in which to measure the cost of the killer roads. In our country today a motor vehicle crash is reported every five seconds, and those crashes are causing a substantial injury every nine seconds and one death every eleven minutes. Every one of the 146 million drivers in the United States can, statistically, expect to be in a crash once a decade.[35] Current crashes injure 3.5 million people per year; 250,000 of these require hospitalization, and over 3,000 are crippled for life.[36]

This mayhem cannot be dismissed as mere bad driving. Bad transportation facilities are slaughtering good drivers and making bad drivers worse.

---

33. *Hammond Almanac,* at 728-31 (1980).

34. The Chicago Sun Times, October 7, 1981, at 72.

35. Todd, "How Traffic Laws Provoke Accidents," *Trial,* at 70 (Jan. 1982).

36. The Wall Street Journal, April 14, 1982, at 1, col. 6.

Thus, state of the art engineering generally recognizes that defective roads are a major proximate cause of this slaughter.

"It is seldom that an accident results from a single cause. There are usually several influences affecting the situation at any given time. These influences can be separated into three groups: the human element; the vehicle element; and the highway element." *AASHO, A Policy On Geometric Design of Rural Highways,* 122 (1965).

The problem, of course, is that few drivers, or lawyers, or voters, read things like the *AASHO Policy On Geometric Design of Rural Highways.* Bad driving and bad vehicles cannot account for the problem of the carnage on the killer roads because too many accidents are taking place on roadways or railroad crossings that were defectively constructed, marked, or maintained.[37] No motorist involved in a crash on a defective area of roadway reached the scene of the crash by parachute: every one of them managed somehow to drive himself, however sleepy or stupified, and his vehicle, however broken down, to the substandard location of the crash.

The killer roads are, in all probability, the most generally overlooked cause of mass death currently active in this country: they substantially contribute to the fact we inflict the equivalent of the Vietnam War upon ourselves every year. The time has come to solve this problem eating away at all of us. Lawsuits, however masterfully developed, cannot bring about this solution because crashes must occur *before* a lawsuit can be brought. What we need is a *better* program to correct the killer roads before they kill again, as well as competent legal services for those injured or killed until the corrections are in place. In the words of Ralph Nader written twenty years ago: "The true mark of a humane society must be what it does about prevention of accident injuries, not the cleaning up of them afterward."[38]

---

37. R. Kuhlman, "Legal Problems Created by the Killer Roads of the United States," *The Forum,* Vol. 19, No. 2, at 269 (Winter 1984).

38. Nader, *supra* n. 29, at viii.

CHAPTER 1

TRANSPORTATION FACILITY NEGLIGENCE

In order to aid the attorney in determining whether transportation facility negligence exists[1] and what type of expert, if any, should be employed, the following items are sensitization devices to alert attorneys to situations where they may need an expert witness, such as, an engineer, to analyze a transportation facility.

First, the on-sight crash investigation must be prompt. Evidence begins to alter, even disappear, immediately after a crash as other vehicles travel the road obliterating evidentiary matters. In addition, repair crews may descend upon the scene within hours of the crash, to clean, paint, post signs, and conduct other activities that change the evidence.

Second, the on-sight crash location should be memorialized on video tape or film. Photographic evidence will preserve the positive evidence, such as, skid marks, missing signs, debris, etc. Even though you may not know what the relevant issues are at this time, the photographs will be the evidentiary record you will need.[2]

§ 1-1. Visibility.

Note the visibility at the time of the crash. Transportation facility negligence has less chance to be the cause of a crash occurring in good visibility because the drivers involved have better chances to avoid the negligence in the facility if they can see it in advance. One very sad case referred to the author involved a station wagon full of children. The station wagon was rammed at high speed in

---

1. Mulvaney v. City of Worcester, 293 Mass. 32, 199 N.E. 405 (1935). City was held liable for negligent lighting of a street. The city's liability was based on a negligence, rather than a nuisance theory.

2. *See* Cameron v. State, 7 Cal. 3d 318, 497 P.2d 777, 102 Cal. Rptr. 305 (1972), photographs of dirt shoulder taken promptly after crash were crucial evidence establishing that there was a rut in shoulder of road which caused crash.

broad daylight on a negligently designed curve by an uninsured, indigent, intoxicated driver. The driver did not survive the crash. Expert analysis revealed that an action would have been appropriate against the transportation facility if the crash had occurred at night or in other reduced visibility circumstances. The fact that the crash occurred in full daylight, however, deprived the injured children of an action against the facility because the offending driver could have seen, and therefore should have avoided, the dangers built into the road. Good visibility reduces the prospects of transportation facility causal negligence. Remember, entities maintaining a transportation facility must not only use due care to make the facility itself safe but must also "warn motorists of those hazards which are incident to that portion of a highway which remains under [defendant's] maintenance jurisdiction." *Janssen v. City of Springfield,* 79 Ill. 2d 435, 438, 404 N.E.2d 213, 219 (1980).

§ 1-1(A). Weather.

Note the weather at the time of the crash. Defects in the design, construction, or maintenance of the facility have a greater chance of being the proximate cause of a crash when rain or snow makes the traveling surfaces wet and slippery, thus increasing requisite braking distances. The reasonable speed at which trains and vehicles may operate is directly related to visibility: the less you can see, the slower you should travel. If a vehicle was operating at or near maximum speed under reduced visibility conditions, be alert to the fact that this not only may indicate a viable action against the driver but may also aggravate visibility restrictions and other defects created by the negligent design or maintenance of the facility. These considerations are particularly acute in the analysis of train/car crashes at grade crossings because the railroad speed limits are set for good visibility conditions. Trains often fail to slow down when poor weather reduces visibility. "After all," as an engineer, whose train had obliterated a car, told the jury, "we had the right of way and drivers had to look out for us." This engineer drove a train that had the word "kills" painted on the cab of the engine.

§ 1-1(B). Straight or Curved Road.

Did the crash occur on a straight road or on a curve? It is difficult to be negligent in designing or maintaining a straight road. Like boiling water, it is possible to make a mess of it, but you have to really try hard to do so. On a curve, however, negligent maintenance is more likely to exist, and it may be the proximate cause of a crash.

§ 1-1(B)(1). Vertical Curve.

There are two types of curves in roads. One type is the vertical curve — it curves up and down; the other type is the horizontal curve — it curves from side to side.

A vertical curve going up is a crest vertical curve. A vertical curve going down is a sag vertical curve. Even a "straight" section of a road can have many vertical curves that may not be exposed in the police report or aerial photograph. Vertical curves are most significant in crashes occurring at night under reduced visibility because motorists on the ascending side of a vertical curve lose a good deal of their ability to see what is happening on the other side of the vertical curve. They are like drivers going up a hill, unable to see the descending slope. In fact, the 1965 AASHO Blue Book states authoritatively that motorists ascending a vertical curve at night will have a 54 percent sight reduction. Any failure to properly place signs, mark the road, post approximate speed limits or guardrails may constitute a proximate cause of a crash occurring at night on or near a crest vertical curve.

§ 1-1(B)(2). Horizontal Curve.

If a crash occurred on a horizontal curve, the length and sharpness of the curve is important. If the curve is very sharp, it is likely to be dangerous and warrants signs giving advance notice to motorists that they are approaching something unusual, especially if it is not preceded by many other curves. The AASHO Blue Book, p. 103 (1954) states: "Where curves are flatter than 3 degrees, the accident rate does not vary with the frequency of the curves. For 3- to 6-degree curves, the accident rate is nearly double that for the less than 3-degree curves when they occur infrequently." Page 105 states: "The introduction of a relatively sharp curve in a section on which curves are infrequent, presents a hazard several times that of the same curve in a section where curves are frequent."

The length of horizontal curves is important because the sharper they are, the longer they should be, to allow the motorist "run on" and "run off" space within which he can become oriented to entering and leaving the curve. Horizontal curves with higher accident rates than surrounding road sections are prime targets to warrant signs alerting approaching motorists of the curve. They also may warrant lower speed limits than surrounding road sections. Reflectors and lighting should also be considered if the accident rate on the curve is markedly higher at night. As stated in *Evaluation of Criteria for Safety Improvements on the Highway* (Roy Jurgensen and Associates Research Analysts, Inc., p. 48 (1966)): "Accidents on curves are reduced when the driver is made aware of the curve. The delineation of curves tends to reduce accidents."

§ 1-2. Painting and Marking of Road.

Closely examine the painting on the road. Most jurisdictions have adopted the Uniform Manual on Traffic Control

Devices, which warrants that there should be striping of some color on the outer edges and up the middle of the road. Most versions of the Manual also call for painting any curbing running down the center of the road. Failure to comply with these marking criteria may constitute proximate cause of crashes occurring at night or in bad visibility. Failure to post warranted signs, failure to post warranted signs in the correct location, or failure to properly maintain posted signs may establish a failure of due care. *Martin v. Ann Arbor R.R.,* 76 Mich. App. 41, 255 N.W.2d 763 (1977).

In addition, the issue of improper signing where it is appropriate to raise that issue is a hardy variety of claim, particularly impervious to summary judgment, and usually left to the jury. *Salvati v. Department of State Hwys.,* 415 Mich. 708, 330 N.W.2d 64 (1982).

§ 1-3. Police Report.

Obtain a copy of the police report. Examine it carefully. It contains the relevant information you will need, such as, visibility, weather, road condition, and signing condition that will be recorded by the reporting officer. By the time of trial the reporting officer may remember little about the case. He will, however, defend his report.

§ 1-4. Obstacle Near Roadside.

If the crash involves a vehicle striking an obstacle near the roadway, determine how close the obstacle was to the road and whether it was painted or marked. As the 1965 Blue Book states at p. 221: "Physical obstructions in or near the roadway that may constitute a hazard to traffic should be adequately marked." If your expert feels that even good visibility would not remove all the confusion and dangers posed by the defective facility, however, the courts may be very liberal in supporting a plaintiff's case. Thus, in *Bentley v. Saunemin Twp.,* 83 Ill. 2d 10, 413 N.E.2d 1242 (1980), the Illinois Appellate and Supreme Courts reversed, as a matter of law, a jury verdict that a driver who had a good advance view in broad daylight of an intersection guarded by a negligently obscured stop sign was the sole proximate cause of a crash in the intersection. The nature of the intersection would be unclear to the driver, justifying the holding under traditional law, but the case also comes close to adopting the new maxim, long recognized by engineers, that crashes are foreseeable on bad facilities because bad facilities generate bad driving.

§ 1-5. Warning and Safety Devices.

If a jurisdiction elects to install safety devices such as lights, warning signs, or guardrails, the universal rule is that they must be reasonably maintained. *Johnston v. City of East Moline,* 405 Ill. 460, 91 N.E.2d 401 (1950); *Baran v. City of Chicago Heights,* 43 Ill. 2d 177, 251 N.E.2d 227 (1969). If a crash occurs at or near a light that was not working or a warning sign that had fallen down, there are excellent prospects that a transportation facility negligence case exists.

§ 1-5(A). Median Barrier.

In crashes caused by one vehicle crossing the centerline into the opposite lane of traffic, there is always the possibility that failure of the responsible entity to provide a center or median barrier for the road may be considered transportation facility negligence. The volume of traffic, width of lane separation, posted speeds, and prior accident history of the road will be relevant to this issue.

The volume of traffic is important because median barriers, like lighting, are expensive major improvements usually warranted on only high volume facilities. As a general rule of thumb, median barriers will not be appropriate for cost effectiveness reasons on two-lane facilities and would be only remotely reasonable for four-lane facilities with a very high accident rate. As the 1967 AASHO Yellow Book expressed the interrelationship between traffic volumes, width of separation, and posted speed, at page 32: "Effective median barriers should be installed on all existing and proposed high volume, high speed divided highways with narrow medians where traffic engineering studies establish the need."

§ 1-5(B). Lighting.

Like median barriers, lighting is an expensive safety measure that is warranted normally only on high traffic volume facilities. Thus, most rural roads are normally unlit.

If the jurisdiction has adopted a statute similar to Ill. Rev. Stat., ch. 85, § 3-104(a), immunizing the initial design decision not to provide safety measures, even if warranted, the defense may contend that all technical state of the art lighting warrants are irrelevant if lighting has never been provided. Of course, lighting installed and negligently maintained will usually establish liability under *Johnston v. City of East Moline,* 405 Ill. 460, 91 N.E.2d 401 (1950). Conversely, however, statutes such as Ill. Rev. Stat., ch. 85, § 3-104(b) allow a plaintiff to attack a failure to provide warranted lighting (or medians or other safety devices) after the facility opened to traffic, and the safety device "was necessary to warn of a condition which endangered the safe movement of traffic, and which would not be reasonably apparent to or anticipated by a person in the exercise of due care."

Under the warrants, lighting should be considered for any facility of even moderate traffic volume that has a markedly higher accident rate at night than during daylight.

As the 1968 Indiana Manual on Uniform Traffic Control Devices (which is repeated and adopted in virtually identical form in most other states) expresses the point at page 184: "At night, when clarity and distance of vision are sharply curtailed, adequate artificial lighting is needed to call attention to indicate the actual location of obstructions and hazards."

According to the 1954 AASHO Blue Book at page 184: "Statistics indicate that the nighttime accident rate is higher than during daylight hours which to a large degree may be attributed to impaired visibility."

Lack of lighting, where lighting was warranted, has an excellent chance of constituting a proximate cause of a nighttime crash because, as established through research and published, among other places, in the Dec. 1971/Jan. 1972 edition of ROBOT, by the highly efficient South African Road Safety Council, page 6 — 60 percent of drivers suffer from some degree of night blindness.

Transportation facility negligence may exist in an otherwise fault-free situation where the motorist must, due to the design of the facility, be doing many things at the same time. This is a particularly sensitive matter during reduced visibility conditions when the motorist must concentrate on both operating his vehicle and studying the road ahead. The point is potentially even more important under reduced visibility conditions at passively protected grade railroad crossings where the motorist must pay attention to the operation of his vehicle, the road ahead, and the tracks to one or both sides of the road. The issue may become still more acute if the road also is a climbing (crest vertical curve), a dipping (sag vertical curve), a twisting (horizontal curve), or a tipping (technically, the superelevation normally connected with the run on, or approach, and the run off, or exit area, of a horizontal curve).

The more things a motorist has to pay attention to at the place of the crash, the greater the chances are for transportation facility negligence because of the standard enunciated in the 1965 AASHO Blue Book, page 22, that:

> An error in perception or judgment or a faulty action on the part of the driver can easily lead to an accident. Highways should be designed so that a driver needs to make only one decision at a time and is never surprised by an unexpected situation where he must make a decision but does not have enough time. Accidents are more likely to occur where there are a number of things the driver must observe and react to simultaneously.

§ 1-5(C). Confusing or Surprising Road Area.

Roads should not confuse or surprise drivers. When this happens, drivers do not know what to do and often decide incorrectly, causing crashes. Drive the road under circumstances similar to the crash and look for surprising or confusing geometrics, optical illusions, etc. Where present, road confusion or road surprises strongly indicate possible transportation facility negligence. See *Roundey v. City of Phoenix,* Maricopa County Superior Court No. C-387927, May 29, 1981, reported at 24 A.T.L.A. L. Rep. 366. In *Roundey,* the defendant was held liable for failure to warn of a sudden road surprise where the pavement narrowed.

Bear in mind on proximate cause issues, that such surprises are usually far more lethal at night and under reduced visibility.

In order to prevent these surprises, some cases require highway departments to provide "clear vision areas even beyond the improved portions of the road." See *Cryderman v. Soo Line R.R.,* 78 Mich. App. 465, 260 N.W.2d 135 (1977).

§ 1-5(D). Guardrail.

The "Guide for Selecting, Locating and Designing Traffic Barriers," published by AASHTO in 1977, states at page 5: "Guardrail issues must be evaluated on an individual basis and, in the final analysis, must usually be solved by engineering judgment."

Hence, those issues hinging on the presence or absence of guardrails require an academic transportation engineer or a practical engineer for analysis.

§ 1-5(E). Signs.

For issues hinging on whether a warranted sign had not been posted, consult the jurisdiction's current edition of the Uniform Manual on Traffic Control Devices and, if possible, retain either an academic transportation engineer or a practical transportation engineer.

Signing is usually required to warn of danger points on the road. *Estate of Klaus v. Michigan State Hwy. Dep't,* 90 Mich. App. 277, 282 N.W.2d 805 (1979).

Note, however, that good signing cannot cure other design defects. As the 1973 AASHTO Red Book notes at page 416: "Good signing cannot cure the ills of poor highway design."

§ 1-5(F). Ditches.

If the case involves vehicles that have fallen into ditches, consultation with an academic transportation engineer or a practical engineer will be required. These issues are quite complex, involving the propriety of guardrails, angles of front and back slope, shape of bottom, drainage patterns, and other matters.

Note generally, as stated in *National Cooperative Highway Research Program, Report 118, Location, Selection, and Maintenance of Highway Traffic Barriers,* published by the Highway Research Board in 1971, at page 4: "Ditches near roadways can be a severe hazard if their cross sections are such that they cannot be successfully traversed by errant vehicles."

§ 1-5(G). Reflectors and Delineators.

In situations where the road direction is confusing, particularly at night or in reduced visibility conditions, there may be a need for reflectors or delineators. There are few clear professional criteria on the issue and, again, you will need an appropriate engineering opinion. The absence of reflectors or delineators along a confusing section of road where a crash occurred at night or under reduced visibility conditions may suggest possible transportation facility negligence. The suggestion, of course, will be even stronger if the target defendant had installed these devices prior to the crash and then failed to properly maintain them. The 1965 AASHO Blue Book at page 243 states: "Locations frequently are encountered where many drivers are confused regarding the direction of the road, particularly at night. Guide posts or delineators generally are used at such places."

State of the Art on Roadway Delineation Systems, published in 1976 by the United States Department of Transportation, Federal Highway Administration, Office of Research and Development at page 41 states: "Increased emphasis should be placed on the use of post delineators on rural two-lane roads. Sudden changes of alignment and uncertainty of the roadway path are more prevalent on the two-lane roads."

§ 1-5(H). Seat Belts.

Under Illinois law, a failure to wear seat belts is not contributory negligence as a matter of law. *Old Second Nat'l Bank v. Baumann,* 86 Ill. App. 2d 547, 408 N.E.2d

224 (1980). This is the majority view. A small body of cases allow the seat belt issue to bear on liability itself. *Curry v. Moser,* 89 A.D.2d 1, 454 N.Y.S.2d 311 (1982) *contra Spier v. Barker,* 35 N.Y.2d 444, 323 N.E.2d 164, 363 N.Y.S.2d 916 (1974). Failure to fasten available automobile seat belts may not constitute contributory negligence as a matter of common law. See *King Son Wong v. Carnation Co.,* 509 S.W.2d 385 (Tex. App. 1974); and *Lafferty v. Allstate Ins. Co.,* 425 So. 2d 1147 (Fla. App. 1982), where evidences of motorist's failure to wear a seat belt, which an expert testified would have prevented plaintiff's injuries, was inadmissible both as defense on liability and as limitation on damages in personal injury action.

§ 1-6. Lay Opinions.

Usually, the prior crash history of the facility cannot be obtained before a suit is filed, but often insight can be obtained by talking to local people and local police and by reading old copies of local newspapers. If the facility is referred to as "the killer" or "the widowmaker," there will usually be a design or maintenance defect justifying the name. As a general rule, people only notice and apply nicknames to defective transportation facilities. As Shakespeare said, it is only the evil that lives on.

Under *Delany v. Badame,* 49 Ill. 2d 168, 274 N.E.2d 353 (1971), lay witnesses may state whether vehicles they observed were going fast or slow, but they may not state that the vehicle was going too fast or slow. For that opinion, an appropriate expert will be needed. See also Cleary and Graham, *Handbook of Illinois Evidence,* § 701.1 (4th ed. 1984).

Similarly, under *Deaver v. Hickox,* 121 Ill. App. 2d 465, 256 N.E.2d 866 (1970), a police officer without additional expertise in the field of physics or engineering may testify to where skid marks were but may not estimate vehicle speed from those skid marks.

In any event, be mindful of the following engineering fact:

> Several tests have been conducted which indicate that most drivers, even those with good vision, are unable to accurately judge the speed of on-coming vehicles, or the closing rate, when executing a passing maneuver. Other tests have shown the driver's inability to estimate passing and over-taking distance in similar situations.

See *Traffic Engineering Theory and Practice,* by Louis J. Pignataro, (1973), at page 14, note 16, and studies noted therein.

§ 1-7. Ownership and Maintenance of Road.

The early factual investigation of a crash case often discloses that several governmental and private entities have been involved with the road in question over a period of time. Thus, one governmental body aided by various private consultants may have designed the road, another entity may have constructed it, and yet another set of public and private entities may have held maintenance jurisdiction over the road between the time it opened to traffic and the time of the crash at issue.

In order to determine which of these public and private entities are really going to be target defendants, the plaintiff's attorney must develop his theory of the case to ascertain if the cause of action rests, singularly or collectively, on negligence in design, construction, or maintenance. Particular care should then be exercised to properly serve notices, complaints, and other required documents upon the entities who had responsibilities for the areas *where* plaintiff will contend the negligence took place *at the time* that plaintiff contends the negligence took place. Conversely, defense lawyers should inquire, at the earliest stages of a crash case, into the question of whether the entity they represent had responsibility for the defect at issue at a relevant time.

The universal rule of law supporting this requirement is that a governmental body cannot be held liable for a dangerous or defective road condition unless it had the ability, directly (by its own agents) or indirectly (by warnings to another entity) to remedy the condition. *Gillespie v. City of Los Angeles,* 36 Cal. 2d 553, 225 P.2d 522 (1950).

The meticulous care plaintiffs must use in joining the appropriate defendant was demonstrated in *Dixon v. City of Chicago,* 101 Ill. App. 3d 453, 428 N.E.2d 542 (1981). In *Dixon* the plaintiff was a pedestrian injured on a defective curb, suing the city for negligent maintenance of defective streets and sidewalks. The court granted summary judgment to the defendant, irrespective of the conditions of the defendant's streets and sidewalks, because the plaintiff alleged the accident was caused by a defective "curb," and at this location the curbs were under the maintenance jurisdiction of the State of Illinois.

Similarly, in *Tunk v. Village of Willow Springs,* 120 Ill. App. 3d 800, 458 N.E.2d 1132 (1983), the defendant village was awarded summary judgment because the plaintiff sued it for negligent maintenance of a road within the maintenance jurisdiction of the state.

California: *Bartlett v. State,* 145 Cal. App. 2d 50, 301 P.2d 985 (1956), State Highway Patrol not negligent for failure to replace warning sign within exclusive maintenance jurisdiction of local government; Cal. Code § 831.3, nondedicated road; grading, maintenance or repair; reasonable care; condition; duty. Neither a public entity nor a public employee is liable for any injury occurring because of the grading or the performance of other maintenance or repair on any road which has not officially been accepted as part of the road system under the public entity; *Peterson v.*

City of Vallejo, 259 Cal. 2d 757, 66 Cal. Rptr. 776 (1968), city was not liable for wrongful death of decedent as a result of an accident allegedly caused by defective condition of a street where the city was neither in possession nor in control of the street; *Gillespie v. City of Los Angeles,* 36 Cal. 2d 553, 225 P.2d 522 (1950).

Illinois: Agreement between city and state for city to repair and maintain streets and intersection under jurisdiction and control of state did not render city liable for failure to warn driver of dangerous intersection. *Heintz v. Vorwerk,* 115 Ill. App. 3d 899, 451 N.E.2d 551 (1983).

Louisiana: State of Louisiana, through Department of Transportation and Development, could not be held liable for automobile accident which occurred on road that was not part of state highway system and was not maintained by Department. *Kappel v. State Through Dep't of Hwys.,* 430 So. 2d 1084 (La. App. 1983).

State Department of Transportation and Development was liable for injuries sustained by motorist in intersection collision caused by sequence malfunction of traffic light even though city had agreed to "maintain" light under contract. Sequence malfunction caused opposing lights at intersection to indicate green at same time. *Jones v. Winston,* 437 So. 2d 889 (La. App. 1983).

Michigan: *Potes v. Department of State Hwys.,* 128 Mich. App. 765, 341 N.W.2d 210 (1983). Since roadway at issue was a county road, statute providing that it was the duty of county to keep its roads in reasonable repair was applicable. *Hargis v. City of Dearborn Heights,* 34 Mich. App. 594, 192 N.W.2d 44 (1971). Design of bridge, constructed by county which relinquished jurisdiction to city, was such as to permit pedestrians to take shortcut by stepping off sidewalk onto terrace forming wall of foundation of bridge, both city and county were liable for damages arising from death of minor who fell into drain while taking shortcut across bridge. County's failure to correct defect in design of bridge constructed by county which relinquished jurisdiction to city did not insulate city from liability for its negligence in failing to correct defect.

Missouri: City, though it was charter first-class city, had no authority to assume control over state highway within city limits. Thus, city was not liable for injuries sustained as result of defects in highway. *Crofton v. City of Kansas City,* 660 S.W.2d 709 (Mo. App. 1983).

New York: *Ossmer v. Bates,* 97 A.D.2d 871, 469 N.Y.S.2d 273 (1983). Defendant town should have been granted summary judgment dismissing third-party complaint and cross-claim of county in action for wrongful death and conscious pain and suffering arising out of automobile accident that occurred on county highway which was owned, designed, maintained, repaired, and controlled by county. *Santos v. City of New York,* 86 A.D.2d 796, 452 N.Y.S.2d 572 (1982). In action brought by injured workman who alleged that defendant city was negligent in permitting pavement to be defective and remain in a defective and hazardous condition and in failing to install a ramp or other safe means of egress for loaded hand trucks at accident site, copy of the lease and official map of the premises in question were relevant to the issue of whether defendant city was in effective control of the premises and was responsible for maintenance. See also *Barber v. Town of Northumberland,* 121 Misc. 2d 655, 468 N.Y.S.2d 827 (1983).

Ohio: In *Ballard v. Board of Comm'rs,* 31 Ohio App. 224, 167 N.E. 404 (1928), the court held that an intercounty highway surveyed by state highway department was a county road where no actual construction was done by the state. In *Wickham v. City of Upper Arlington,* 51 N.E.2d 739 (Ohio App. 1942), where a realty company had abruptly lowered the grade of city street extensions running through its development, the court held that the developer bore sole responsibility for the grade lowering and the only theory under which the city could be held liable was for failure to erect a barrier or warning of the approaching grade drop. Note that Illinois adopted this theory, that an entity must post barricades or warnings on its road to protect motorists, where reasonably necessary, of approaching dangers on roads it does not control directly. See *Janssen v. City of Springfield,* 79 Ill. 2d 435, 404 N.E.2d 213 (1980). Under Ohio law, on the issue of whom to sue for a road defect, the court in *Starcher v. Logsdon,* 66 Ohio St. 2d 57, 419 N.E.2d 1089 (1981), dismissed a complaint against county commissioners for negligent bridge maintenance causing a crack because the defendants did not have primary responsibility to do the maintenance work at issue.

Pennsylvania: Township was not responsible for injuries sustained by driver and passengers when automobile struck pothole on state highway. Commonwealth had exclusive responsibility for repair and maintenance of state roads. *Medina v. Township of Falls,* 454 A.2d 674 (Pa. Commw. 1983). *Litwinko v. Gray,* 267 Pa. Super. 541, 407 A.2d 42 (1979). In view of the fact that city ordinance invested city with ultimate responsibility for selecting street car stops and city was responsible for erecting safety island to facilitate disembarkation of passengers at dangerous intersections, evidence made question for jury on plaintiff's theory that both city authority and transportation authority were negligent in maintaining intersection that was intently dangerous. *Thompson v. Collins,* 8 Lycoming 1 (1961); *Heinlein v. Allegheny County,* 374 Pa. 496, 98 A.2d 36 (1953). In *Heinlein,* a county and a borough erected a bridge pursuant to an agreement requiring the county to maintain the bridge, which then became a part of a boulevard, which was itself then incorporated by statute as a state highway. The court held that, insomuch as the statute did not exclude bridges from the commonwealth's maintenance duty, the county was not responsible for maintaining the bridge. The county, consequently was not responsible as a matter of law for injuries, fatalities or damages caused by defective bridge maintenance.

Texas: *Gabbert v. City of Brownwood,* 176 S.W.2d 344 (Tex. App. 1943). Under a charter giving city of Brownwood exclusive jurisdiction over its streets and highways, city had jurisdiction over state highway running through the city, and it was the city's nondelegable duty to keep that highway in repair. Therefore, the city was liable for injuries to an employee of a truck owner who, while attempting to get into a truck which had stopped at night on the highway, was injured by stepping into open, unguarded end of a culvert.

§ 1-8. Insurance.

Insurance is a pivotal question in many jurisdictions that still allow full or partial sovereign immunity. Some jurisdictions hold that such insurance waives the immunity. *Kobylanski v. Chicago Bd. of Educ.,* 63 Ill. 2d 165, 347 N.E.2d 705 (1976); *Lansing v. County of McLean,* 45 Ill. App. 3d 91, 359 N.E.2d 165 (1976). Other jurisdictions hold that the immunity takes precedence over the insurance. Michigan Code, *Liability Insurance,* § 3.996 (109); Mich. Comp. Laws § 691.1409.

§ 1-9. Design.

With certain variations, most jurisdictions impose liability for negligent design of roads under circumstances where defendants know or should know that such design defects make damages similar to the plaintiff's reasonably foreseeable. This format often withdraws immunity from a design after the design goes into use and the defendant, through actual or constructive notice, knows or should know of the defect.

California: *Cameron v. State,* 7 Cal. 3d 318, 497 P.2d 777, 102 Cal. Rptr. 305 (1972). State liable for negligent superelevation design of roadway. *Contra,* see *Levin v. State,* 146 Cal. App. 3d 410, 194 Cal. Rptr. 223 (1983).

State's creation of a six-foot wide shoulder on highway exit ramp was not reasonable. Thus, state was not entitled to design immunity defense in suit seeking damages for death of motorist, who was hit by car while changing tire on shoulder. *Weddle v. State,* 191 Cal. Rptr. 819 (Cal. App. 1983).

Florida: State Department of Transportation was immune from suit for actions in designing and allegedly failing to upgrade and improve bridge on which automobile accident occurred. The Department was not immune from suit, however, with respect to placement of warning signs in order to warn of known dangerous condition. *Perez v. Department of Transp.,* 435 So. 2d 830 (Fla. 1983). Similarly, in *City of St. Petersburg v. Collom,* 419 So. 2d 1082 (Fla. 1982) the Court held that when a governmental entity designs a road with a curve too sharp for the speed limit, the entity cannot be liable for building the road because that decision was taken at the judgmental planning level. However, the court continued, if the entity knows during the construction stage or learns after the road opens that automobiles cannot negotiate the curve at applicable speeds, then an operational-level duty arises to warn motorists of the hazard. Thus, while the design stage of the road building process may be immunized, actual experience with traffic is not.

Illinois: Under Illinois Revised Statutes, Chapter 85, Section 3-103, a local governmental entity is basically not liable for negligent design. "The local public entity is liable, however, if after the execution of such plan or design it appears from its use that it has created a condition that is not reasonably safe."

Michigan: *Stremler v. Michigan Dep't of State Hwys.,* 58 Mich. App. 620, 228 N.W.2d 492 (1975). Defendant's defective highway design may lead to continuing obligation to correct such defects.

New York: New York Court held in *Mullahey v. City of New York,* Queens County Supreme Court No. 365-79, April 26, 1982, that municipal bodies must maintain a reasonable height for their guardrail and that no design immunity can countervent this requirement. 25 A.T.L.A. L. Rep. 366. *Weiss v. Fote,* 7 N.Y.2d 579, 200 N.Y.S.2d 409 (1960), limited municipal liability for judgmental error in planning highway design, but recognized a continuing obligation to review such a plan in light of its actual operation. It did not, however, exclude all liability even for initial planning, for there we said that "liability for injury arising out of the operation of a duly executed highway safety plan may . . . be predicted on proof that the plan either was evolved with adequate study or lacked reasonable basis" (7 N.Y.2d at 589).

Ohio: A county is allowed immunity for acts or omissions undertaken pursuant to an executive or planning function or design requiring official judgment or discretion. However, after the design has been built and the road is open, the county may be held liable for the negligence of its agents in carrying out the design. *Zents v. Board of Comm'rs,* 9 Ohio St. 3d 204, 459 N.E.2d 881 (1984).

Texas: A city is not liable for construction of an improvement in accordance with a reasonable plan or design. The city may, however, be liable for negligent operation and maintenance of the road after it opens. *Dilley v. City of Houston,* 148 Tex. 191, 222 S.W.2d 992 (1949).

§ 1-10. Maintaining Existing Structures.

The clear standard in both law and engineering is that governmental entities must use reasonable care to maintain road safety features they put in, and liability will attach for negligent maintenance, even if those features did not have to be put in.

§ 1-10(A). Street Lights.

Although lights are rarely specifically warranted under express language in engineering texts and M.U.T.C.D.'s, a series of other defects may warrant them, and when provided they must be reasonably maintained. *Baran v. City of Chicago Heights,* 43 Ill. 2d 177, 251 N.E.2d 227 (1969); *Johnston v. City of East Moline,* 405 Ill. 460, 91 N.E.2d 401 (1950); *City of Chicago v. Powers,* 42 Ill. 169 (1866); *City of Freeport v. Isbell,* 83 Ill. 440 (1876).

Bunker v. City of Glendale, 111 Cal. App. 3d 325, 168 Cal. Rptr. 565 (1980). Although absence of traffic control signals or signs does not itself make a condition a dangerous one, when a dangerous condition exists which would not be reasonably apparent to, or anticipated by, exercising due care, a sign is necessary to warn of the condition, and public entity's failure to provide such a sign may provide a basis for imposition of liability.

§ 1-10(B). Electric Signals.

Electric signals, once installed, must be reasonably maintained. *Porter v. City of Decatur,* 16 Ill. App. 3d 1031, 307 N.E.2d 440 (1974).

Bakity v. County of Riverside, 12 Cal. App. 3d 24, 90 Cal. Rptr. 541 (1970). Notwithstanding statutes providing that public entity may not be held liable for failure to install traffic signs or signals public entity may be liable for installing traffic signs when it does so in manner constituting trap (citing: Gov't Code §§ 830, 830.4, 830.8).

§ 1-10(C). Warning Signs.

California: *Briggs v. State,* 14 Cal. App. 3d 489, 92 Cal. Rptr. 433 (1971). Where state undertook to place warning signs in area of mud slide, it was obligated to place signs properly and should have to answer for any inadequate or deceptive warning proximately contributing to accident.

Illinois: Warning signs, once installed, must be reasonably maintained. *Smith v. Godin,* 61 Ill. App. 3d 480, 378 N.E.2d 218 (1978).

Michigan: *Salvati v. Department of State Hwys.,* 415 Mich. 708, 330 N.W.2d 64 (1982).

§ 1-10(D). Sidewalks.

Sidewalks must be reasonably maintained after they are initially provided.

Illinois: *Dziewatkowski v. City of Chicago,* 109 Ill. App. 2d 405, 248 N.E.2d 734 (1969); *Jones v. City of Rock Island,* 101 Ill. App. 2d 174, 242 N.E.2d 302 (1968); *Livings v. City of Chicago,* 26 Ill. App. 3d 98, 392 N.E.2d 716 (1979).

Massachusetts: *Jakobsen v. Massachusetts Port Auth.,* 520 F.2d 810 (1st Cir. 1975). The mere natural accumulation of ice or snow on a sidewalk did not preclude a finding of negligence against a defendant responsible for maintaining the sidewalk.

Michigan: *Griswold v. City of Ludington,* 116 Mich. 401, 74 N.W. 663 (1898).

§ 1-10(E). Ditches.

Governmental bodies must reasonably maintain, and board over, ditches they create in streets. *Village of Jefferson v. Chapman,* 127 Ill. 438, 20 N.E. 33 (1889); *City of Chicago v. Seben,* 165 Ill. 371, 46 N.E. 244 (1897).

§ 1-10(F). Barriers.

When barriers are put in, they must be reasonably placed and maintained. *Erfurt v. State,* 141 Cal. App. 3d 837, 190 Cal. Rptr. 569 (1983): Defendant liable for negligent placement of abutment guardrail.

§ 1-10(G). Missing Signs, Warnings, and Devices.

Signs, warnings, and safety devices required under the standard of due care must generally be provided, even if no specific warrant on that particular device exists in an applicable engineering or maintenance authority. Again, of course, the law of the particular jurisdiction should be consulted.

§ 1-10(H). Covering for Slippery Road.

Slippery road surfaces generally require covering or treatment under due care warrant. *Kitto v. Wattleworth,* 24 Ill. App. 2d 484, 164 N.E.2d 817 (1960).

§ 1-10(I). Warnings.

Missing warnings required in the exercise of due care must generally be provided, even if not specifically required by a particular warrant.

Illinois: *Osborne v. City of Harvey,* 16 Ill. App. 3d 740, 306 N.E.2d 601 (1973); *Ohms v. State,* 30 Ct. Cl. 410 (1975).

Louisiana: *Holmes v. Christopher,* 435 So. 2d 1022 (La. App. 1983).

New York: *Koester v. State,* 90 A.D.2d 357, 457 N.Y.S.2d 655 (1982) (missing signs); *Humphrey v. State,* 90 A.D.2d 901, 456 N.Y.S.2d 861 (1982) (missing marking).

§ 1-10(J). Barricades.

Missing barricades required in the exercise of due care must generally be provided, even if not specifically required by a particular warrant.

Illinois: *Koehler v. State,* 27 Ill. Ct. Cl. 384 (1972); *Stanley v. State,* 22 Ill. Ct. Cl. 438 (1957); *Garrett v. State,* 22 Ill. Ct. Cl. 343 (1956).

CHAPTER 2

ENGINEERING STANDARDS

§ 2-1. Origin.[1]

Public roads in the United States were largely financed and maintained by local entities prior to 1891, when New Jersey began providing state aid money to its counties for rural roadbuilding. These innovations were followed by a few other states prior to 1900, and all states were providing aid to counties by 1917.

In 1893 Massachusetts became the first state to authorize the construction of state highways, a practice followed shortly thereafter by a few other states.

By 1900 there were 8,000 automobiles running on American roads, none of these roads had really been designed for motor vehicles. In that same year, Vermont enacted a law requiring every motorist to employ "a person of mature age" to walk one-eighth of a mile ahead of him bearing a red flag.[2]

---

1. For much of the engineering material in this section, the author is largely indebted to Dr. Gary Long and his article "Transportation Design, Control and Safety Standards," published in Transportation Negligence 1984, Illinois Institute for Continuing Legal Education, at page 7-1 *et seq.* (1984).

2. W. Leuchtenburg, *The Perils of Prosperity, 1914-32,* University of Chicago press, at 185, 1958.

In 1901 there was still not a single filling station in the entire country.[3]

In 1902, San Francisco, Cincinnati, and Savannah still maintained speed limits of eight miles an hour.[4]

By 1904 the number of vehicles increased to 55,000[5] (a 700% rise in four years). The automobile entered mass production in 1908, when Henry Ford first introduced a simple standardized car manufactured on a moving assembly line. By 1929, America was producing 4,800,000 autos per year and 28 million vehicles were on the road.[6]

By 1910 about half the states had set up highway departments when the popularity of the motor car roared to even higher levels with the invention of the self-starter.[7]

In 1914 the American Association of State Highway Officials (AASHO), the most authoritative promulgator of road design standards in this country was formed.[8]

In 1916 the federal government, which had vigorously supported and subsidized railroads throughout the Nineteenth Century, first expressed an interest in seriously supporting road improvement through passage of the Federal Aid Road Act, authorizing $75 million over five years for rural highway improvements, beginning the policy of providing grants in aid to the states to share in road building costs. The form of this federal involvement, from its inception, was carefully crafted to insulate the federal government from civil liability in road design and maintenance cases. The federal role has generally been to passively provide funds to the states for the states to use in the design and maintenance of federal and designated state

---

3. *Id.* at 186.

4. *Id.*

5. Long, *supra* note 1, at 7-6.

6. Leuchtenburg, *supra* note 2, at 186.

7. Long, *supra* note 1, at 7-6.

8. *Id.*

roads crossing the state. Courts have generally protected the federal government from civil liability, based on these facts, when the states use federal funds in a negligent road design or maintenance project, even on federal roads.[9]

By 1920, all states were providing some aid to counties for road building, and most states either had or were developing highway agencies capable of carrying out the duties required for receiving federal aid. This is when automobile transportation emerged as the dominant mode of travel in America.[10]

Most of the present day roadway routes were in existence by now, but they were largely unpaved, unsuited to all weather travel by automobiles, and generally not intended for use by motor vehicles. One root of the killer-road problem, thus, is the fact that the automobile inherited, and had to make do with, a road system created for other means of transportation.[11] This difficulty was magnified by

---

9. Mahler v. United States, 306 F.2d 713 (3d Cir. 1962); Delgadillo v. Elledge, 337 F. Supp. 827 (E.D. Ark. 1972). 28 U.S.C. § 2680(a) grants the federal government immunity for "any claim based upon the exercise or performance or the failure to exercise or perform discretionary function or duty . . . whether or not the discretion involved be abused." In Daye v. Commonwealth, 344 F. Supp. 1337, 1349 (E.D. Pa. 1972), *aff'd,* 483 F.2d 294, 299 (3d Cir. 1973), the Third Circuit held that the Highway Safety Act, 23 U.S.C. § 40 *et seq.,* did not create an implied cause of action for personal injuries sustained as a result of a violation of the standards set forth therein.

10. Long, *supra* note 1, at 7-7.

11. The process whereby new technology takes over the supporting instrumentalities of its predecessors is bumpy, but not unique. To give highway departments due credit, they have ample precedent, but not justification, for their present problems. Arnold Toynbee described the process:

> One source of disharmony between the institutions of which a society is composed is the introduction of new social forces — aptitudes or emotions or ideas — which the existing set of institutions was not originally designed to carry . . . *Vis inertiae* tends at all times to keep most parts of the social structure as they

the operations of our political system, which has always given charismatic new road construction a disproportionate claim on available highway funds over maintenance efforts.[12]

In 1920, the Highway Research Board was established as part of the National Academy of Sciences. The Board has developed into the principal medium for distribution of research findings on highway technology.

In 1924, states began providing some substantial amounts of financial support for city streets.

In that same year, as motor vehicle travel continued to expand, Secretary of Commerce Herbert Hoover, convened the First National Conference on Street and Highway Safety. This conference recognized the lack of uniformity in traffic laws nationwide and also established the basic framework wherein individual states would have sovereign power to regulate and control traffic activities.[13]

---

are, in spite of their increasing incongruity with new social forces constantly coming into action. In this situation the new forces . . . perform their creative work either through new institutions that they have established for themselves or through old institutions that they have adapted to their purpose . . . [The new forces] enter indiscriminately into any institutions which happen to be in their path." A. Toynbee, *A Study of History,* at 279-80 (1947).

12. "Changing vehicular technology has antiquated the design of some of our older roadways. Roadways designed when cars attained a top speed of 40 m.p.h. could have sharper curves and turns than are acceptable for today's vehicles. Rather than upgrade obsolete design features, there has always been a tendency to prefer to spend limited highway funds to build new roadways. Politicians certainly receive more favorable visibility cutting ribbons on new facilities than inconveniencing motorists with detours as old ones are reworked. Furthermore, limited state and local funds show more accomplishment when used to pay only 10 percent, 30 percent, or 50 percent of the cost of new construction projects (with federal aid making up the remainder) than when used to pay 100 percent of the cost of maintenance or corrective actions on old facilities not on the federal aid system." Long, *supra* note 1, at 7-25.

13. *Id.* at 7-8 *et seq.*

In 1927, AASHO published its *Manual of Uniform Standards For Traffic Control on Rural Highways.* This did not include urban streets since state highway officials had no responsibilities within urban areas.

It was not until 1928 that every state had finally built up an engineering organization that was capable of discharging the highway duties falling upon the states. It was also in 1928 when the first edition of the *Model Traffic Ordinance* was published. This was intended as a model for adoption by municipalities as a supplement to state law. The "Rules of the Road" from the *Uniform Vehicle Code* were not repeated in the *Model Traffic Ordinance* because the state code was to be embedded by reference. The *Model Traffic Ordinance* has been revised and published in conjunction with the *Uniform Vehicle Code* since its creation.

The Third National Conference on Street and Highway Safety in 1930 resulted in the production of the *Manual of Uniform Standards for Traffic Control on Urban Streets,* which complemented the AASHO manual for rural highways. The Fourth National Conference in 1934 resulted in a joint effort with AASHO to consolidate rural and urban traffic control devices into the 1935 *Manual on Traffic Control Devices* published by AASHO, which was the first edition of the present manual.

Between 1938 and 1944 seven separate policies on the geometric design of rural highways were formulated by AASHO. These became the standards for design in later decades. During this interval, a federal reorganization in 1939 transferred the Bureau of Public Roads from the Department of Agriculture to the Federal Works Agency and renamed it the Public Roads Administration. This reflected a recognition that rural public roads were serving functions beyond those primarily of agricultural transportation. Thereafter, the first edition of the *Handbook of the*

Institute of Traffic Engineers was published in 1941. This handbook contained a compilation of state-of-the-art information on traffic engineering.

World War II brought attention to the role of highways in national defense. As a result of this and studies of nationwide routes begun by the Public Roads Administration in 1939, Congress included the designation of a new system of highways in the Federal Aid Highway Act of 1944, the National System of Interstate Highways. However, funding was not provided until 1952. Congress also included another new highway system in its 1944 legislation, the Federal Aid Secondary System. This system was to be composed of principal secondary routes. The 1944 Act also provided separate funds for the first time for extension of the rural federal aid systems into urban areas.

In 1945 AASHO adopted a separate set of design standards for secondary and feeder roads. These standards were presented as a single table of numerical values for various design elements to supplement the primary highway geometric standards. They were not superseded until 1961.

The second edition of the *Manual of Uniform Traffic Control Devices* (MUTCD) was published in 1948. It began to stress uniformity across all jurisdictions.

The year 1950 brought the publication of the first edition of the *Highway Capacity Manual* by the Highway Research Board, the second edition of the *Traffic Engineering Handbook,* with a new title, by the Institute of Traffic Engineers, and the *Policies on Geometric Highway Design* by AASHO. This latter publication was nothing more than a compilation of the seven original policies bound together in a single volume, but unchanged.

The Federal Aid Highway Act of 1952 for the first time included a specific authorization of funds for construction of the National System of Interstate Highways. The funds were very limited but were greatly increased in 1954.

In 1954 AASHO integrated the seven policies on geometric highway design and expanded the material into a comprehensive treatise in the first edition of *A Policy on Geometric Design of Rural Highways.* This book was published in a blue cover and became widely known within the transportation profession as the "Blue Book" because of its cumbersome title.

The first textbook in the transportation field, *Traffic Engineering,* by Matson, Smith and Hurd, appeared in 1955. This book became a classic and continued to be used over the next decade and a half without revision.

In 1957 AASHO published its first edition of *A policy on Arterial Highways in Urban Areas.* This served as a companion to the Blue Book for use in urban areas, and became known as the "Red Book" because of its red cover.

In 1958 Congress repealed the Federal Aid Road Act of 1916, and all succeeding amendments and supplements, and codified highway provisions into Title 23 of the United States Code.

The first session of the 86th Congress in 1959 brought House Document No. 93, "Federal Role in Highway Safety," to national attention. This was prepared in response to the 1956 Highway Act, and it pointed out the need for more transportation research and stepped-up implementation programs.

The third edition of the *Manual on Uniform Traffic Control Devices* was released in 1960 and adopted by the Bureau of Public Roads in 1961 in accordance with 23 U.S.C. § 109(d). Also, in 1961, AASHO published *Geometric Design Standards for Highways Other Than Freeways,* which superseded the secondary and feeder road standards and established a single set of combined values for use on both primary and secondary highways. These combined standards served for nearly a decade until AASHO once again decided that certain features unique to local roads were not adequately treated by combined standards.

In 1964 the federal government initiated a Spot Safety Improvement Program that provided funds for small projects to correct localized safety problems. Three years later this program evolved into the "Traffic Operations Program to Improve Capacity and Safety" (known as TOPICS) and was very highly regarded in the transportation profession for the immediate safety benefits that resulted.

The second edition of the AASHO Blue Book was published in 1965. Although nearly two decades have since passed, it has still not been superseded.

The second edition of the *Highway Capacity Manual* was published by the Highway Research Board in 1965. Except for an interim report (1980 TRB Circular 212) it, too, has not been superseded.

Two other works that were published in 1965 were the third edition of the *Traffic Engineering Handbook* of the Institute of Traffic Engineers, and Ralph Nader's book, *Unsafe at Any Speed.* Nader's book represented the beginning of emphasis on vehicular elements as factors in highway crashes.

Public Law No. 89-139 (1965), referred to as the Baldwin Amendment, began an era of active involvement of the federal government in highway safety. The Baldwin Amendment stipulated that each state should have a highway safety program in accord with uniform standards approved by the Secretary of Commerce, although such a program was not mandatory. The following year, however, the federal government actively entered the highway safety field with the Highway Safety Act of 1966, which amended Title 23 of the U.S. Code. Section 402(a) required each state to have a highway safety program. Section 402(b) made the governors responsible and extended the programs to include all political subdivisions and provide funding for each governmental level. Section 402(c) authorized funds and set penalties for failure to comply. Section 402(e) established that uniform standards were to be set. Some of the more noteworthy standards are —

Standard 6, Codes and Laws. — Each state was to develop a plan to assure uniformity of the traffic codes and laws within its jurisdictions and these were to be consistent with the uniform rules of other states. It was later proposed that this standard be modified to require strict adherence to the "Rules of the Road" in Chapter 11 of the *Uniform Vehicle Code,* but this action was stayed by the Gray Amendment of 1973.

Standard 9, Identification and Surveillance of Accident Locations. — "To identify specific locations or sections of streets and highways which have high or potentially high accident experience, as a basis for establishing priorities for improvements, selective enforcement or other operational practices that will eliminate or reduce the hazards at locations so identified."

Standard 12, Highway Design, Construction and Maintenance. — "To assure: (a) that existing streets and highways are maintained in a condition that promotes safety, (b) that capital improvements either to modernize existing roads or to provide new facilities meet approved safety standards, and (c) that appropriate precautions are taken to protect passing motorists as well as highway workers from accident involvement."

Standard 13, Traffic Engineering Service (originally titled Traffic Control Devices). — To assure the full and proper application of traffic engineering principles and uniform standards for traffic control to reduce the likelihood and severity of traffic accidents.

Standard 14, Pedestrian Safety (highway oriented). — To emphasize pedestrian safety in all aspects of highway transportation.

Along with the Highway Safety Act of 1966, Congress also passed the National Traffic and Motor Vehicle Safety Act. This legislation authorized the establishment of safety standards for motor vehicles and prohibited the manufacture or import of any vehicle failing to conform to the standards. In response to this authorization, over 50 motor vehicle standards were promulgated during the next nine years.

A book prepared by a private research firm and published by the Automobile Manufacturers Association, Inc., entitled *The State of the Art in Traffic Safety,* brought attention in 1966 to the concept of loss reduction rather than just accident prevention. It suggested more emphasis should be focused on vehicle design, occupant restraint systems, roadside obstacle removal or protection, and emergency medical services.

One of the most significant safety publications was prepared in 1966 by AASHO. Officially released in 1967 and entitled *Highway Design and Operational Practices Related to Highway Safety,* it became known in the transportation profession as the "Yellow Book" due to the color of its cover. This first edition of the Yellow Book contained 34 specific recommendations and conclusions in two major subject areas: roadside design and appurtenances; and traffic operations. It was adopted as federal policy through Instructional Memorandum ("IM") 21-11-67 for all projects with design speeds of 50 m.p.h. or higher, and the states were asked to apply it to the extent practical on all other completed federal-aid roadways. The Yellow Book focused on the alarmingly high percentage of traffic fatalities associated with "single-vehicle accidents" (35 percent) and the accident causes. It triggered a change in philosophy that roadways not only must be safe for a motorist who makes no error in driving but also must be kept in repair and free from hazards in the event that a driver exhibits a human trait and makes an error. It called for an intensive concerted effort in the shortest possible time to remove roadside hazards on streets and highways throughout the nation.

During 1968 the Federal Highway Administration released the first edition of its safety publication *Handbook of Highway Safety Design and Operating Practices.* This handbook focused primarily on corrective treatments for high-type highway facilities suffering design and operating problems.

In 1969 AASHO revised and published a second edition of the *Geometric Design Standards for Highways Other Than Freeways.* Although this publication was intended to refer to both primary and secondary roadways, an effort was underway to establish separate standards for secondary roadways.

In 1970 the Highway Users Federation for Safety and Mobility published the first edition of its *Maintenance and Highway Safety Handbook.* This publication focused on good and bad maintenance operations.

Also in 1970, Congress amended the 1966 Highway Safety Act and formed the National Highway Traffic Safety Administration (NHTSA) within the United States Department of Transportation. This newly formed department was for the administration of 23 U.S.C. § 402 and other safety programs. The predecessor for NHTSA was the National Highway Safety Bureau, created in the Highway Safety Act of 1966. As a part of this legislation, a special bridge replacement program was created, and a rail crossing demonstration program was initiated. Another important change in the 1970 legislation was to create a separate system of urban roadways for federal aid funding beyond the extensions of rural federal aid roads into urban areas. The 1970 Act also created the National Highway Institute for training governmental employees and raised the federal share of funding for the primary, secondary and urban systems to 70 percent beginning in 1973.

In 1970, AASHO published a *Geometric Design Guide for Local Rural Highways,* which differentiated some of the standards from those pertaining to primary highways, similar to the bifurcation that existed prior to 1961. Standards for urban local roads and streets were completed a few months later, and the two sets of standards were published together by AASHO in 1971 entitled *Geometric Design Guide for Local Streets and Roads.* This publication was divided into two parts: one for rural facilities and the other for urban facilities. It pertained to rural and urban roads of the local and collector functional types. While the publication presented minimum design values, it recommended the use of more liberal values wherever economically feasible.

In 1971 AASHO re-examined and revised its stopping sight distance standards and published *A Policy on Design Standards for Stopping Sight Distance.* This amended AASHO's *Geometric Design Guide for Local Roads and Streets* that was barely off the press, as well as the 1965 Blue Book and 1969 "nonfreeway" standards. In its reconsideration AASHO decided to supplement, not replace, its original minimum standards with "desirable" standards, based upon re-examining human perception and reaction time, coefficients of friction on wet pavements, drivers' eye heights in modern passenger cars, heights of objects, and initial vehicle speeds related to design speed. Use of desirable standards, not minimum standards, was recommended.

The fourth edition of the *Manual on Uniform Traffic Control Devices* was published by FHWA in 1971. This represented the new standards that were supposed to be substantially consistent in all states and on all roadways.

In 1973 the second editions of the AASHTO Red Book and FHWA's *Handbook of Highway Safety Design and Operating Practices* were both published. FHWA expanded the scope of the handbook for the second edition to include all highways.

Congressional concern in highway safety, design, and operation became clear when the report on a series of hearings by subcommittees of the House Committee on Public Works was published in 1973 subtitled "The Need for a Safer Driving Environment" (Committee Print 93-7, 93rd Congress, First Session). The final section of the report asserts clearly that it is the responsibility of government and its agencies to assure that "maximum safety is incorporated into our motor vehicle transportation system." This accompanied the Highway Safety Act of 1973, which provided for some significant highway safety construction programs with funding for the first time for construction improvements not on the federal aid systems:

23 U.S.C. § 203. Availability of funds.
23 U.S.C. § 151. Pavement marking demonstration program.
23 U.S.C. § 152. Hazard elimination program.

As an example, § 203 required each state to maintain a survey of all railroad-highway crossings and identify those that may require separation, relocation, or protective devices. The Act provided 90 percent federal aid funding for safety improvements to railroad-highway crossings on any federal aid highway system except interstate and required at least half of the funds to be available for protective devices. As a minimum, each state shall provide signs for all railroad-highway crossings.

The Federal Aid Highway Act of 1973 signaled the beginning of a raid on the Highway Trust Fund. It made it possible for local officials in urban areas to decide not to use revenues from the Highway Trust Fund for road improvements but to receive instead an equal amount from the general fund for mass transit.

The Federal Aid Highway Amendments of 1974, Pub. L. No. 96-643, established a uniform national maximum speed limit on public highways of 55 m.p.h., increased the maximum permissible vehicle weight restrictions that states may impose on the interstate highway system, and authorized carpool, bikeway and rural transit programs.

As part of the Highway Safety Improvement Program, in 1974 FHWA 6-8-2-1 specified that all highways were in the program elements. Among the items stipulated were a process for identification of safety needs, including a reference system for accurately locating accidents, a traffic records system, a procedure for identifying and reporting hazardous locations, elements and sections, engineering surveys of grade crossings, roadside obstacles, locations with low skid resistance, and locations with hazardous conditions associated with narrow bridges; also a process for systematic correction of identified safety needs, including establishment of priorities, and implementation of countermeasures.

During the period from about 1972 to 1976, many of the professional organizations in the highway field elected to change their names in recognition of the broadening transportation interests of their constituencies. The changes were also stimulated by the restructuring of federal, state, and local governments, creating several modal administrations under a general transportation department. The Highway Research Board (HRB) became the Transportation Research Board (TRB); the Institute of Traffic Engineers became the Institute of Transportation Engineers (ITE); the American Road Builders Association (ARBA) became the American Road and Transportation Builders Association (ARTBA); and the American Association of State Highway Officials (AASHO) became the American Association of State Highway and Transportation Officials (AASHTO).

In 1974, AASHTO published the second edition of the Yellow Book. This version expanded and updated the material of the first edition and contained a commentary urging the application of optimum design standards rather than minimum design standards. It also asserted that "the highway should offer no surprises to the driver, in terms of either geometrics or traffic controls. The violation of driver expectancies . . . is undoubtedly a large factor in accident causation and thus a situation to be avoided."

A very significant publication entitled *Positive Guidance in Traffic Control* was released by FHWA in 1975. It was the first of a series focusing on increased attention to driver expectancy and human factors in transportation design and control as a means for improving safety.

FHWA released a new shortcourse in 1975 emphasizing safety aspects of roadway design entitled *Dynamic Design for Safety.* Another FHWA publication released in 1975 was the *Traffic Control Devices Handbook: An Operating Guide.* This was developed as an operational guide to supplement the *Manual on Uniform Traffic Control Devices.*

The *Transportation and Traffic Engineering Handbook* was published by the Institute of Traffic Engineers in 1976. Although this was the first edition with this title, it was actually the fourth edition of the ITE handbook.

The Highway Safety Act of 1976 amended 23 U.S.C. § 203 and authorized funds for railroad grade crossing improvements for locations not on the federal aid highway systems. The Federal Aid Highway Act of 1976 authorized funds for safety improvements for locations not on the federal aid highways systems for correction of safety hazards, elimination of high hazard locations, removal of roadside obstacles, etc., replacing a demonstration program from the 1973 Highway Safety Act.

Another significant feature of the Federal-Aid Highway Act of 1976 was the recognition by Congress that the states were not keeping up with their maintenance responsibilities in preserving and repairing the federal-aid roadways that were already in existence. Widespread concern over the deteriorating condition of the nation's highway system led Congress to create the Federal-Aid RRR Program for the resurfacing, restoration, and rehabilitation of existing roadways. This was a major reversal of policy since federal-aid funds for highways had always been restricted to new construction. The RRR program authorized funds to preserve and repair existing federal-aid primary, secondary and urban pavement surfaces as well as enhance highway safety by upgrading deficient roadway geometric features of the older facilities such as narrow lanes, shoulders, clear recovery areas, bridges, sharp curves, steep grades, cross slopes, restricted sight distances. Extensive improvements do not qualify as RRR projects and are considered under the separate category of reconstruction. A controversy promptly erupted over how the RRR funds should be split between roadway surface repairs and geometric improvements and what highway geometric standards should apply for these minor improvement projects. Upgrading to the geometric standards for new construction projects would often be extraordinarily expensive and not a minor project. It was feared that this would concentrate funds on only a small number of improvement projects and leave unattended many miles of federal-aid roadways that were badly in need of pavement repair, which would satisfy neither repair nor safety objectives. AASHTO and FHWA both proposed standards that were considerably less stringent than the standards for new construction, and other perspectives were advanced by safety organizations and state highway agencies. Laxer standards were argued as compromising safety and violating legislative mandates which make safety a primary objective of all federal-aid highway programs, including RRR. Overall, most RRR spending has been for road surface repairs without geometric improvements. To resolve this dilemma, in the Surface Transportation Assistance Act of 1982 Congress requested that the Transportation Research Board study the issues and recommend minimum RRR standards.

The second edition of the *Maintenance and Highway Safety Handbook* was prepared by the Highway Users Federation for Safety and Mobility and published by FHWA in 1977. Also in 1977 a valuable synthesis of the growing information on traffic barriers entitled *Guide for Selecting, Locating, and Designing Traffic Barriers* was published by AASHTO.

The following year, 1978, the third edition of the *Handbook of Highway Safety Design and Operating Practices* was published by FHWA. This edition contained more material pertaining to lower type highways and a new introductory chapter with a quantitative treatment of the highway safety problem to put specific safety concerns into perspective with all others. This volume was promoted as a reference guide illustrating the various fundamental principles of safety in the design and operation of existing as well as new roadways of all categories.

The fifth edition of the *Manual on Uniform Traffic Control Devices* (MUTCD) was published in 1978. It contained an expanded treatment on traffic controls for railroad crossings and bicycle facilities, and incorporated all of the addenda issued for the 1971 edition of the manual.

The *Railroad-Highway Grade Crossing Handbook* was published by FHWA in 1978. Due to the color of its cover, it quickly became known as the "Green Book" and pertained to the state of technology for railroad and highway crossings at the same elevation.

The 1978 federal legislation brought several changes. It continued funding for off-system safety improvements. It increased funding for hazard elimination and pavement markings. It substantially increased funding for railroad-highway grade crossing improvements for any public road, with the federal share at 90 percent. At least 50 percent of the grade crossing funds were reserved for protective devices. It revised the hazard elimination program, 23 U.S.C. § 152: "Each state shall conduct and systematically maintain an engineering survey of all public roads to identify hazardous locations, sections, and elements, including roadside obstacles and unmarked or poorly marked roads, which may constitute a danger to motorists and pedestrians, assign priorities for the correction of such locations, sections and elements, and establish and implement a schedule of projects for their improvement." Each state was to establish an evaluation process approved by the Secretary of Transportation and develop cost-benefit data for various types of corrections and treatments that were to be used in setting priorities for highway improvement projects. The 1978 legislation also allowed states to transfer apportionments between the primary and other federal-aid highway systems and introduced penalties for states that failed to enforce effectively the national 55 m.p.h. speed limit or to carry out an effective vehicle weight enforcement program. It also increased emphasis on the replacement and rehabilitation of bridges and required that at least 20 percent of each state's apportionment for the primary and secondary systems be used for the restoration, rehabilitation, and resurfacing of existing highways.

In 1979 the first set of revisions for the 1978 MUTCD was released. Some of the rulings included a compliance date by which the particular revision is to be fully implemented.

In 1979 FHWA published its training course entitled *Safety Design and Operational Practices for Streets and Highways.* This was followed in 1981 by FHWA's four-volume, 11-week graduate level training program, entitled *A Highway Safety and Traffic Study Program.*

In 1981 FHWA published its *Synthesis of Safety Research Related to Traffic Control and Roadway Elements.* This consisted of a two-volume set of reports covering each of 17 traffic safety research subject areas.

The second edition of the *Transportation and Traffic Engineering Handbook* was published by ITE in 1982.

The second edition of the *Traffic Control Devices Handbook* was published by FHWA in 1983. Also in 1983 the second set of revisions for the 1978 MUTCD was released. Another set of 19 amendments to the 1978 MUTCD was published in 1984.

§ 2-2. Law and Engineering.

Lawyers and engineers rarely come into contact with one another, and generally fail to understand that both professions operate largely, although not entirely, on the basis of prior precedents (which are called "warrants" in engineering). In the area of roadway design, construction, and maintenance both law and engineering have established a large number of relevant precedents. Knowledge of these standards is essential to every stage in the prosecution or defense of a transportation facility negligence case, including what to look for at the scene of a crash. A great number of the legal and engineering rules, in fact, overlap and can therefore be used in coordinated procedures.

The issue of what legal and engineering standards apply to a crash case does, however, involve at least one major difference between the two. The legal standards, generally, will all be current as of the date of the crash on trial. The engineering standards to be used, however, may be current, ancient, or somewhere in between. (See the Introduction section on Litigating Chronological Standard of Care.) Cases can easily be won or lost depending on what time period is chosen to measure relevant state of the art design and safety technology. For this reason, both plaintiff and defense counsel must be familiar with at least the general status of those standards over a broad period of time.

§ 2-3. Road Features and Faults.

The following constitutes an attempt to gather together engineering standards on road features and faults. I have not compiled this material with the thought of turning lawyers and laymen into engineers. The material is offered solely to sensitize lawyers and laymen to cases where transportation facility negligence may exist and where it may be worthwhile to call in engineers for a detailed, extensive, and usually expensive work-up.

§ 2-3(A). Emphasis on Safety in Design and Maintenance.

Every crash case involving death or serious injury will not necessarily present a cause of action for negligent road design or maintenance. Filing specious lawsuits without any merit prostitutes our profession and should be avoided at all cost. If, however, there are genuine issues raising a possible lack of care in the design or maintenance of a road or crossing, consideration should be given to using the increasing state of the art emphasis on safety features as the dispositive element in the decision to proceed. Certainly, safety has been all too neglected in the design and maintenance problems discussed previously. Plaintiffs could also invoke these safety standards if defendants claim that the road or crossing at issue had not killed or injured enough people prior to the crash at issue to warrant upgrading that would have prevented that crash. There is something disturbingly irrelevant (at least to an old plaintiff's lawyer) about the often repeated defense argument that transportation facilities are to be evaluated on the basis of body counts.[14]

Plaintiffs in crash cases can, in fact, often argue that increasing state of the art emphasis on safety warranted the defendant finding and correcting the defect at issue, irrespective of other notice, before the plaintiff's injury. Technical support for this emphasis on safety, rather than notice, includes the following standards:

1. The 1954 AASHO Blue Book at page 102:

> The geometric features of highways are designed to serve the traveling public. Toward this end — among considerations of mobility, convenience and economy in operation — safety is of primary concern. Highway safety can be bettered through the application of present engineering technology. The proved safety features applicable to a given type or class of highway within the limit of available funds, should be built into the highway during the construction stage.

2. A policy on Geometric Design of Rural Highways, published by AASHO in 1965 (The 1965 Blue Book) at pages 121-22:

> For safe operation highways should be designed with the application of the latest engineering technology available. Safety features applicable to a given type of highway should be built into the highway during the original construction. High design standards generally result in low accident rates.

---

14. In one of my plaintiff crash cases, a defense expert argued that three years of carnage on a killer curve did not constitute "notice" to the defendant of dangers in the curve at issue because the defendant should wait for five years to see if the first three years were a fluke. The jury rewarded this approach with a multi-million dollar plaintiff's verdict.

And at page 127: "It is well to recognize that highway accidents will happen and highways should be designed so that they are as safe as possible."

3. Highway Design and Operational Practices Related to Highway Safety, published by AASHO in 1967 (the 1967 Yellow Book) at pages 1-2:

> In the development of plans for highway improvements, all elements of design should be reviewed to insure that any feature likely to be associated with injury or accident to the highway user is eliminated or minimized in its effect. An intensive crash program to remove roadside hazards on existing streets and highways and to engineer the roadsides of new facilities with safety as a major criterion should have a paramount place in the highway program of each state. Only in this way will the motorist who inadvertently leaves the traveled way have adequate protection against death or injury. Design standards more liberal than the minimums prescribed will often increase safety. Constant field checks of the operating conditions with existing and new designs are recommended for evaluation of their effectiveness and cost efficiency.

And at page 15: "Typical examples of the application of improved design include: sight distances greater than the minimum, [and] flattening side slopes sufficiently to eliminate the need for guardrail."

4. The Need for Highway Safety Consciousness, by Rep. John A. Blantni, Chairman, Special Subcommittee on the Federal-Aid Highway Program, of the Committee on public Works, of the United States House of Representatives, published in *Roadside Hazards,* edited by the Eno Foundation for Highway Traffic Control, Inc. (1968), at page 2: "Safety is the most essential ingredient of the highway."

5. A Policy on Design of Urban Highways and Arterial Streets, published by AASHTO in 1973 (the 1973 Red Book) at page 23:

> Designing a highway to compensate for poor driving behavior is one of the highway engineer's major problems. The more that is learned of driver behavior the better the highway can be designed to accommodate the myriad types of persons with ever changing attitudes that drive the highways. Thus, the interest and cooperation of behavioral scientists should be solicited and encouraged by the highway engineer. Highways should be designed to accommodate all drivers in relative safety, including reasonable provisions for those whose driving competence has been seriously impaired regardless of whether it be due to emotional problems, alcohol, or other factors.

6. Highway Design and Operation Practices Related to Highway Safety, published by AASHTO in 1974 (the 1974 Yellow Book, updating the 1967 Yellow Book), at page 8:

> The July 1973 Report of the Subcommittees of the House Committee on Public Works Dealing with Highway Safety, Design and Operations, states: "Whose responsibility is it to see that maximum safety is incorporated into our motor vehicle transportation system?" On this, the Subcommittee is adamant. It is the responsibility of Government and specifically those agencies that, by law, have been given that mandate.

7. The Guide for Selecting, Locating and Designing Traffic Barriers, published by AASHTO in 1977 at page 3:

> Existing highways should be upgraded when feasible to eliminate hazardous conditions. . . . An extensive effort has been made in recent years to improve highway safety. To accomplish this, a major emphasis has been placed on the elimination of hazardous roadside conditions and on the improvement of traffic barriers to shield those hazards that can not be eliminated.

8. "From the total roadside slope safety aspect, design decisions must be influenced by the most critical expected occurrence . . . ." *National Cooperative Highway Re-*

search Program Report 158, "Selection of Safe Roadside Cross Sections," published by Transportation Research Board, National Research Council, at page 11 (1975).

9. "Because human performance varies from individual to individual, consideration must be given to atypical, or nonaverage, characteristics." *Traffic Engineering Theory and Practice,* Louis J. Pignataro, at page 11 (1973).

See Chapter 3, § 3-1, Reasonable Care of Roads.

§ 2-3(B). Sight Distance and Design Minimums.

AASHTO explains the sight distance element in road design as follows:[15]

> Ability to see ahead is of the utmost importance in the safe and efficient operation of a highway. Rolling stock on a railroad is confined to a fixed path, yet block signal systems and trained operators are necessary for safe operation. On the other hand, the path and speed of motor vehicles on the open highway are subject to the control of drivers whose training largely is elementary. If safety is to be built into highways the designer must provide sight distance of sufficient length in which drivers can control the speed of their vehicles so as to avoid striking an unexpected obstacle on the traveled way. Also, at frequent intervals and for a substantial portion of their length, 2-lane highways should be open to view a sufficient distance to enable drivers to occupy the opposing traffic lane to pass overtaken vehicles without hazard.
>
> Sight distance is the length of highway ahead visible to the driver. The minimum sight distance available on a highway should be sufficiently long to enable a vehicle traveling at or near the likely top speed to stop before reaching an object in its path. While greater length is desirable, sight distance at every point along the highway should be at least that required for a below average operator or vehicle to stop.

---

15. *A Policy on Geometric Design of Rural Highways,* published by AASHO, at 134 (1965).

> Minimum stopping sight distance is the sum of two distances: one, the distance traversed by a vehicle from the instant the driver sights an object for which a stop is necessary, to the instant the brakes are applied; and the other, the distance required to stop the vehicle after the brake application begins.

One problem with this sight distance concept is that modern vehicles are lower than the older vehicles used as design models when the sight distances used by road designers were set. The change in vehicles lowering the drivers eye level and reducing what he can see ahead has changed many previously adequate curves into dangerous areas, raising various interesting chronological negligence issues. Dr. Gary Long explains the issue:[16]

> Due care requires road designers to pay appropriate attention to future needs. The driver's eye height is a good example.
>
> Drivers' eye heights affect stopping and passing sight distances. Based on the vehicles on the road at the time, the 1954 Blue Book adopted a value of 4.5 feet from the pavement to the driver's eye for use in roadway design. The auto industry, however, was at work making lower and lower cars. Research around 1958 indicated that the eye heights of most motorists on the road were well under 4.5 feet, implying that they had less advance view than was assumed in the standard. When the 1965 edition of the Blue Book was published, a value of 3.75 feet was adopted. This could have created a problem for roads designed during the interim if the designers ignored this changing phenomenon and merely applied minimum standards. It also creates a problem for old roads that were designed when vehicles were higher.
>
> The driver's eye height example can be examined further. The 1960's decade brought an increase in popularity of two-passenger sports cars and small

16. Long, *supra* note 1, at 7-23, 7-24.

> foreign passenger cars having driver eye heights lower than 3.75 feet. When AASHO issued its revised stopping sight distance policies in 1971, it examined this issue but decided not to reduce the driver's eye height for design and merely recognized that some "low-slung vehicles" with lower drivers' eye heights existed. Of course, these vehicles have become very prevalent now, and American automobile manufacturers are even producing them. As a consequence, the 1984 amendments to the MUTCD finally included a change to a driver's eye height of 3.5 feet for use in computing no-passing zones on two-lane roadways. Public agencies were given five years to fully implement the new standard.
>
> The change in no-passing zone markings to compensate for roadway designs applying minimum standards based on a higher driver's eye height is an illustration of the interrelationship between design and operations. If the roadway were designed for a lower driver's eye height, a change in no-passing zones would not be necessary. Design shortcomings are often difficult and costly to upgrade and tend to exist for a long time. Sometimes they can be adequately compensated for by traffic control devices, but as stated in the 1974 Yellow Book, "Often the safety deficiencies generated by minimum design are impossible to correct by any known traffic device or appurtenance. A warning sign is a poor substitute for adequate geometric design."

The fact that sight distances on many curves are inadequate for modern vehicles makes a very strong argument that *maintenance* must make up the difference if design will not: thus, speed limits must be lowered (a maintenance issue) and warning signs erected (again a maintenance issue) if design factors do not lengthen these curves and make them gentler in curvature. At bottom is the emerging state of the art engineering position that road and crossing safety features must *exceed* minimum standards.[17] This is particularly true for the added dangers

17. *Highway Design and Operational Practices Related to Highway Safety,* published by AASHTO, at 15 (1974).

that inadequate sight distances create at night, when visibility is reduced even further. For relatively few dollars, upgraded signing and marking can noticeably reduce these dangers. As AASHTO states:

> A disproportionately high number of accidents occur in hours of darkness compared to daylight hours. Although many of the factors which make nighttime travel hazardous are difficult to cope with, every effort must be made to improve the situation as much as possible. Responsible officials must give added attention to improvements and better maintenance of lighting, signing, marking, and delineation in order to make night driving as safe as possible. What looks like a good sign during daylight hours can be completely ineffective at night. Regular cleaning and inspection to identify failing reflective surfaces are imperative. *Highway Design and Operational Practices Related to Highway Safety*— AASHTO, at 62-63 (1974).

§ 2-3(C). The Hazardous Roadside.

When a vehicle leaves the road and strikes a roadside obstacle such as a pole or ditch, transportation facility negligence may be involved because, since at least 1967, there has been a major engineering effort to make the roadsides safer for vehicles that must leave the pavement. The length of the required "clear zone" may fluctuate under local standards depending on such factors as traffic flow and road classification, but for most roads the minimum clear zone should be 30 feet. Warrants for this minimum width include the following:

1. "For warranting purpose, a 30-ft. zone adjacent to the traveled way is recommended as the minimum for being clear of roadside obstacles; a zone of more than 30-ft. width is desirable. If the 30-ft. zone cannot be cleared of roadside obstacles, due to practical or economic reasons, guardrail may be warranted for the roadside areas." *National Cooperative Highway Research Program Report 54,* "Loca-

tion, Selection and Maintenance of Highway Guardrails and Median Barriers," Highway Research Board, at page 4 (1968).

2. "Nontraversable hazards located within 30 feet of the traveled way warrant a longitudinal traffic barrier." *National Cooperative Highway Research Program Report 118,* "Location, Selection, and Maintenance of Highway Traffic Barriers," published by The Highway Research Board, The National Research Council, The National Academy of Sciences, and The National Academy of Engineering, at page 5 (1971).

In any event, alarm bells should go off in the minds of plaintiffs and defense attorneys when vehicles strike objects dangerously close to the road.

Technical authority for this safe roadside movement include the following:

1. "A coordinated effort to provide a forgiving roadside must be made in design, construction, maintenance, and traffic control stages of project development if there is to be success in reducing the sizable number of fatal and other serious accidents which occur each year off the roadway." *Highway Design and Operational Practices Related to Highway Safety*— AASHTO, at 37 (1974).

2. *The Guide for Selecting, Locating and Designing Traffic Barriers,* published by AASHTO in 1977, at page 3:

> Existing highways should be upgraded when feasible to eliminate hazardous conditions. . . . An extensive effort has been made in recent years to improve highway safety. To accomplish this, a major emphasis has been placed on the elimination of hazardous roadside conditions and on the improvement of traffic barriers to shield those hazards that cannot be eliminated.

3. "Objects in or near the roadway that constitute serious hazards to traffic, including installations designed for the control of traffic, should be adequately marked." *A*

Policy on Geometric Design of Rural Highways — AASHO, at 126 (1965).

4. "Objects on the side of the road frequently contribute to accidents. In most cases when a vehicle leaves the roadway the driver does not have the ability to fully control the vehicle. Any object in or near the path of the vehicle becomes a contributing factor in the severity of the accident." *A Policy on Geometric Design of Rural Highways* — AASHO, at 126 (1965).

5. "Physical obstructions in or near the roadway that may constitute a hazard to traffic should be adequately marked. Such object markings by painting or use of other high visibility material pertains to obstructions such as structure piers, abutments, parapets, poles, sign posts, and guardrails, as well as curbs and other objects utilized in conjunction with islands or installations designed for the control of traffic." *A Policy on Geometric Design of Rural Highways* — AASHO, at 221 (1965).

6. "Nearly one-third of all highway fatalities occur when vehicles inadvertently leave the roadway and strike a roadside obstacle. Removal of these obstacles, thus providing traversable roadsides, would give drivers of errant vehicles the opportunity to regain control of their cars." *National Cooperative Highway Research Program Report 118,* "Location, Selection, and Maintenance of Highway Traffic Barriers," published by The Highway Research Board, The National Research Council, The National Academy of Sciences, and the National Academy of Engineering, at 4 (1971).

7. "Culvert headwalls, utility poles, large trees, inlets in medians, sign supports, luminaire standards, guardrails, curbs, bridge piers and similar features should be placed an adequate distance from the main lanes of travel or shielded from errant vehicles. These factors, which are the "fixed objects" of all too many single-vehicle accidents, deserve

special treatment." *Highway Design and Operational Practices Related to Highway Safety* — AASHTO, at 40 (1974).

8. "The significance of the roadside in the highway safety problem is apparent from the National Safety Council's statistics. Year after year, between 30 and 35 percent (12,000 to 13,000) of the highway fatalities in the United States occur in noncollision accidents, most of which involve the vehicles leaving the roadway." "*Roadside Design for Safety*" by K.A. Stonex — Assistant Director, General Motors Proving Ground, in Highway Research Board Proceedings, Volume 39, at 120, note 1 (1969).

§ 2-3(D). Confusing or Multiple Decisions.

Two related and basic rules of road design and maintenance are that a driver should always be able to understand the road situation ahead, and the driver should only have to do one thing at a time. If the driver does not know what he is supposed to do, or if he must do several things at once, the chances are very good that he will take too long to decide, or execute his decision badly. Road situations presenting drivers with confusing or multiple decision situations raise strong possibilities that transportation facility negligence may exist. Engineering warrants for these rules include the following:

> 1. An error in perception or judgment or a faulty action on the part of the driver can easily lead to an accident. *Highways should be designed so that a driver needs to make only one decision at a time. Accidents are more likely to occur where there are a number of things the driver must observe and react to simultaneously.* Standardization plays an important role toward this end, as by this means the driver becomes aware of what to expect on a certain type of highway. *A Policy on Geometric Design of Rural Highways* — AASHO, at 122 (1966).

2. Accidents are likely to occur where drivers are called upon to make decisions under circumstances where their vehicles are unable to respond properly as, for example, where a truck is ascending a grade. It would be logical to expect more accidents on grades and curves than on level tangent highways where decisions are called for less frequently and vehicles are fully responsive. *On Geometric Design of Rural Highways* — AASHO, at 127 (1965).

3. The safety of all highway users is dependent on the driver's visual comprehension of the highway and its appurtenances and his visual awareness of other vehicles on and approaching the highway. *A Policy on Design of Urban Highways and Arterial Streets* — AASHTO, at 12 (1973).

4. The driver consciously or subconsciously locates the environment's principle features and orients himself in relation to them. A driver who is unable to orient himself becomes confused and a confused driver is likely to be a hazardous one. The location of a highway can help keep the driver oriented by directing the vehicle in such a way that prominent landmarks, either manmade or natural, frequently appear within the driver's natural line of vision. *A Policy on Design of Urban Highways and Arterial Streets* — AASHTO, at 13 (1973).

5. The stimulation of the visual, auditory, and tactual senses influences the decisions concerning highway design. The response time needed by a driver depends upon the particular sense or senses that are stimulated. The design of curbs, center islands, or bridge piers should be highly visible to decrease the driver response time. Whenever the driver is confronted with a complex traffic or highway situation and is required to make choices, judgments, and decisions, his response time may increase to 2, 3, or even 5 seconds. Multiple signs and signals at intersections may present discrimination problems to drivers and should, whenever possible, be simplified. *A Policy on Design of Urban Highways and Arterial Streets* — AASHTO, at 23-24 (1973).

§ 2-3(E). The Impaired Driver.

Drivers with alcohol, drugs, and similar unpleasantries in them do not, of course, make ideal plaintiffs and may well have no valid cause of action if they get into crashes. It is possible, however, for driver and road fault to combine as proximate causes of a crash. Such a situation, for example, might exist when a drunken driver at night leaves the unlit road, and promptly falls into a hidden deep ditch lurking immediately adjacent to the pavement. In such cases, bear in mind that road safety standards do require consideration for the impaired driver. Thus, *A Policy on Design of Urban Highways and Arterial Streets,* AASHTO (1973) states at page 24: "Highways should be designed to accommodate all drivers in relative safety, including reasonable provisions for those whose driving competence has been seriously impaired regardless of whether it be due to emotional problems, alcohol, or other factors." And again at page 280:

> Highways should be designed to accommodate all drivers in relative safety, including reasonable provisions for those whose driving competence has been seriously impaired regardless of whether it be due to emotional problems, alcohol, or other factors. Design features which are particularly important for the safety of low competence drivers include the following: wide and smooth, clear roadside areas; break-away supports for signs and lights; fixed source lighting; clear pavement striping; guardrail and median barrier; impact absorbing devices at gores; . . . .

§ 2-3(F). Sharpness of Curves.

The sharper the curve, the more important it is that all warranted design and maintenance features be in place. This is because crashes are more likely to happen on sharp curves. According to *The Handbook of Highway Safety Design and Operating Practices,* published in 1978 by the

United States Department of Transportation and the Federal Highway Administration, Introduction, Note 2:

> Another example of isolating areas of concern is a 1976 report by the Insurance Institute for Highway Safety "Priorities for Roadside Hazard Modification." This study showed that more than 26 percent of fatal accident sites had curvature greater than 6 degrees and a down grade of 2 percent or more. Half of the fatal accidents occurred at curves greater than 6 degrees regardless of grade. The major conclusion was that top priority should be given to correction of hazards at or near curves greater than 6 degrees.

CHAPTER 3

LEGAL STANDARDS ON ROAD FEATURES

Due to the abrogation of sovereign immunity, governmental entities entrusted with the design, construction, and maintenance of roads and highways are now literally encrusted with legal duties of care that may become relevant in a crash case. Some of these are listed below, but the laws of the particular jurisdiction involved should always, of course, be consulted.

§ 3-1. Reasonable Care of Roads.

Governmental entities must design, construct, and maintain roads and highways with reasonable care. For an interesting case covering the field on these issues, see

Merling v. Commonwealth, 468 A.2d 894 (Pa. Commw. 1983). In *Merling,* the defendant was liable for injuries sustained by a motorist who was injured when, in attempting to avoid colliding with a disabled truck blocking his lane of travel, he drove his vehicle onto a berm which gave way and the vehicle tumbled into a ditch. The truck had become disabled as a result of striking a pothole, and the guardrails were in a state of disrepair.

California: Cal. Code § 835; *Ness v. City of San Diego,* 144 Cal. App. 2d 668, 301 P.2d 410 (1956). California law recognizes negligent road design and maintenance as a cause of action. *Schilling v. Casper,* Sacramento County Superior Court No. 268963, August 27, 1982, 26 A.T.L.A. L. Rep. 64-65. (A.T.L.A. is the Association of Trial Lawyers of America.)

It is the duty of a municipality to keep its streets and sidewalks in a safe condition and to provide against dangers by the use of care as to the means of travel and other purposes for which the road may be used. *Campbell v. City of Palm Springs,* 218 Cal. App. 2d 12, 32 Cal. Rptr. 164 (1963).

Florida: *Welsh v. Metropolitan Dade County,* 366 So. 2d 518 (Fla. 1979). It is a duty of a municipality to keep streets in a safe condition and to place warnings of known dangerous conditions.

Illinois: For state duty, see *Kolski v. State,* 31 Ill. Ct. Cl. 307, 312 (1976). For city duty, see *Kobylanski v. Chicago Bd. of Educ.,* 63 Ill. 2d 165, 347 N.E.2d 705 (1976). For county duty, see *Lansing v. County of McLean,* 45 Ill. App. 3d 91, 359 N.E.2d 165 (1976); *City of Highland Park v. County of Cook,* 37 Ill. App. 3d 15, 344 N.E.2d 665 (1975); *Hennigs v. Centreville Twp.,* 56 Ill. 2d 151, 306 N.E.2d 287 (1973).

Indiana: For governmental liability in transportation facility negligence cases, see *Campbell v. State,* 259 Ind.

55, 284 N.E.2d 733 (1972); *State v. Thompson,* 385 N.E.2d 198 (Ind. App. 1979); *Indiana State Hwy. Comm'n v. Clark,* 371 N.E.2d 1323, 1327 (Ind. App. 1978).

Kansas: The Kansas Supreme Court held that state engineers making annual inspections of roads must use reasonable care in those inspections. *Ingram v. Howard-Needles-Tammen & Bergendoff,* 234 Kan. 289, 672 P.2d 1083 (1983).

Note: This is an important point because all highway departments must use some inspection services, and if they missed your defect, that could be negligence right there.

Massachusetts: For transportation facility negligence, see *Eklon v. City of Chelsea,* 223 Mass. 213, 111 N.E. 866 (1916).

Michigan: For transportation facility negligence, see *Quinlivan v. Great Atl. & Pac. Tea Co.,* 395 Mich. 244, 235 N.W.2d 732 (1975); *Hall v. State,* 109 Mich. App. 592, 311 N.W.2d 813 (1981); *Endykiewicz v. State Hwy. Comm'n,* 414 Mich. 377, 324 N.W.2d 755 (1982). A statute requiring all governmental entities with jurisdiction over a highway to maintain that highway as a thoroughfare reasonably safe and convenient for public travel need not, after the abrogation of sovereign immunity at common law, be strictly construed as being in derogation of common law. A highway liability statute exists to provide reasonable redress from government for those injured through negligent road maintenance.

New York: See *Gutelle v. City of New York,* 55 N.Y.2d 794, 432 N.E.2d 124, 447 N.Y.S.2d 422 (1981); *Bodner v. Steinhardt,* 71 A.D.2d 702, 418 N.Y.S.2d 484 (1979), holding governmental bodies have a duty to use reasonable care in road patching and road design under New York law. The State "is under a continuing duty to review road design in light of actual operation and to take reasonable steps to minimize the risks of danger." *Baily v. State,* N.Y.

Court of Claims No. 61903, August 13, 1981 reported at 25 A.T.L.A. L. Rep. 166.

Under New York law, the governmental entities even if they have discretionary immunity from formulating traffic control plans, can be negligent in failure to review and re-evaluate the plans in light of actual operation. *Atkinson v. County of Oneida,* Oneida County Supreme Court No. 78-1304, July 13, 1981, reported at 25 A.T.L.A. L. Rep. 28.

Pennsylvania: *Palmer v. Penn-Ohio Rd. Materials, Inc.,* 470 F. Supp. 1199 (W.D. Pa. 1979); *Drew v. Laber,* 477 Pa. 297, 383 A.2d 941, *appeal after remand,* 277 Pa. Super. 419, 419 A.2d 1216 (1978).

A municipality must design and maintain its highways so as to protect motorists from dangers which reasonably careful design and maintenance could prevent. *Mitchell v. Borough of Rochester,* 395 Pa. 373, 150 A.2d 338 (1959). *Gerr v. Emrick,* 283 F.2d 293 (3d Cir. 1960), *cert. denied,* 365 U.S. 817, 81 S. Ct. 698, 5 L. Ed. 2d 695 (1961). Under Pennsylvania law, governmental entities may be sued for negligent road maintenance.

See Chapter 2, § 2-3(A), Emphasis on Safety in Design and Maintenance.

§ 3-1(A). Duty Not to Increase Dangers.

As an adjunct to their duty to use reasonable care, governmental bodies must not create or increase dangers to the public.

California: California Court holds State must use reasonable care in issuing vehicle permits to oversized vehicles along routes using low overpasses. *Hill v. People,* 91 Cal. App. 3d 426, 154 Cal. Rptr. 142 (1979) reported at 22 A.T.L.A. L. Rep. 317 (1975). The Court held that "a public entity has no discretion to create a dangerous condition on its property." 22 A.T.L.A. L. Rep. 318.

Illinois: Danger from defective street maintenance plan: *City of Chicago v. Seben,* 165 Ill. 371, 46 N.E. 244 (1897); *Baran v. City of Chicago Heights,* 43 Ill. 2d 177, 251 N.E.2d 227 (1969). Danger from defective traffic light: *Porter v. City of Decatur,* 16 Ill. App. 3d 1031, 307 N.E.2d 440 (1974). Danger from defective security service at public housing location: *Cross v. Wells Fargo Alarm Servs.,* 82 Ill. 2d 313, 412 N.E.2d 472 (1980).

Louisiana: Markings created impression that shoulder was a traffic lane. *Rivet v. State,* 434 So. 2d 436 (La. App. 1983).

Ohio: *Fisher v. City of Wooster,* 4 Ohio App. 3d 250, 448 N.E.2d 514 (1982), held a city had created a nuisance for which it was responsible in damages when it allowed its streets to become unsafe for ordinary modes of travel.

§ 3-1(B). Design and Maintenance of Road Shoulders.

Governmental entities must use reasonable care in design and maintenance of road shoulder areas adjacent to the pavement.

California: California Court in *Weddele v. State,* Riverdale County Supreme Court No. 113-721, May 1983, reported at 26 A.T.L.A. L. Rep. 363, held Defendant State liable for inadequate width of road shoulder. See also *Gibson v. Garcia,* 216 P.2d 119 (Cal. App. 1950), where a transit company maintaining a defective pole along a road shoulder was held liable to a pedestrian injured when the unsafe pole rotted out by termites was struck by a negligent motorist and fell on plaintiff.

Alderson v. Santa Clara County, 124 Cal. App. 2d 334, 268 P.2d 792 (1954). A county is held liable for injuries when defects and/or obstructions that are close to the highway are hidden from view. However, it must be proven that the driver of the vehicle was not negligent in leaving the highway.

Florida: *City of Tamarac v. Garchar,* 398 So. 2d 889 (Fla. App. 1981), held municipalities have a general duty to use due care to remove roadside hazards.

Hawaii: The Hawaii Court in *Anders v. State,* 590 P.2d 564 (Hawaii 1979) holds that the State must use reasonable and ordinary care in maintaining not only the highways, but also the shoulders of the road.

Illinois: *Parkinson v. State,* 31 Ill. Ct. Cl. 99, 101 (1976); *Kolski v. State,* 31 Ill. Ct. Cl. 307, 312 (1976); *Welch v. State,* 25 Ill. Ct. Cl. 270 (1966); *Berry v. State,* 26 Ill. Ct. Cl. 377 (1968).

Massachusetts: In a recent Massachusetts case, an electric utility company was held liable for negligently erecting an uncrashworthy electric light pole on a road shoulder in a busy shopping area having reason to know that the pole was insufficiently resistant to withstand foreseeable and expectable low velocity impacts from cars. The Court held in the Massachusetts case that there have been many prior crashes involving the pole, invoking the duty on defendant to make the pole more resistant to foreseeable future crashes. *Bernier v. Boston Edison Co.,* 403 N.E.2d 391 (Mass. 1980).

Michigan: Jogger injured stepping on broken traffic signal left as stake in shoulder. *Pate v. Department of Transp.,* 339 N.W.2d 3 (Mich. App. 1983).

Michigan Court in *McKee v. Michigan State Hwy. Dep't,* Wayne County Circuit Court No. 75-064190, March 6, 1981, reported at 24 A.T.L.A. L. Rep. 172, found defendant negligent for posting a light standard 6′3″ away from the roadway. Plaintiff's car hit water, hydroplaned, went off the pavement, and smashed into the pole. Plaintiff's expert established that at the time the pole was placed, engineering standards required that freeways have a 10′ clear roadside.

Michigan Court in the case of *Santo v. State,* Michigan Court of Claims, No. 5638, January 29, 1980, reported at 23 A.T.L.A. L. Rep. 271, says State must use reasonable care to maintain road shoulders whether improved or not improved.

New Hampshire: In the New Hampshire case of *Vanasee v. New England Tel. & Tel. & Exeter-Hampton Elec. Co.,* New Hampshire, Strafford County Superior Court Civil No. 11-578, June 11, 1981, reported in 25 A.T.L.A. L. Rep. 151-52, a utility company was held negligent for placing a utility pole near the traveled roadway in an area where it was foreseeable that vehicles would leave the road at night and hit the negligently mispositioned, unlighted, and unmarked utility pole. Expert testimony under the *National Electric Safety Code* required that utility poles shall be placed and installed and maintained so as to make the pole safe "as far as practicable." Case held that the obligation of utilities under that code in the placement of poles may well require a searching out for more effective precautions than those already in place. The section from the National Electric Safety Code is actually called the "American National Standard Electric Safety Code" (1973 Edition) Section 21, 211. It states "all electric supply communication lines and equipment shall be installed and maintained so as to reduce hazards to life as far as practicable."

New York: Shoulder too loose. *Rouse v. State,* 97 A.D.2d 962, 468 N.Y.S.2d 756 (1983).

Culvert only four feet from pavement was negligence. *Terwilliger v. State,* 96 A.D.2d 688, 466 N.Y.S.2d 792 (1983).

Ohio: *Adkins v. Village of Ontario,* 8 Ohio St. 3d 45, 457 N.E.2d 317 (1983), ditch in shoulder. *Dickerhoof v. City of Canton,* 6 Ohio St. 3d 128, 451 N.E.2d 1193 (1983), held a city liable for injuries caused by its failure to maintain a road shoulder in a condition reasonably safe for normal travel.

Pennsylvania: *Bowman v. Columbia Tel. Co.,* 406 Pa. 455, 179 A.2d 197 (1962). Defendant liable for negligent maintenance of telephone pole that fell on Plaintiff's car.

Virgin Islands: The Virgin Island's Court in *Hodge v. Monsanto,* 592 F.2d 184 (3d Cir. 1979), held that the government of the Virgin Islands was liable for injuries sustained when plaintiff's vehicle hit a tree stump within a few inches of the paved surface of the road and was deflected into oncoming traffic.

Washington: *Brown v. Blankenbaker,* Cause No. 14707, Mason Superior Court, Washington, November 1983.

See Chapter 2, § 2-3(C), The Hazardous Roadside.

§ 3-2. Railroads' Duty to Use Reasonable Care.

Illinois: Railroads must exercise reasonable care in operating trains and maintaining crossings. *Illinois State Trust Co. v. Terminal R.R. Ass'n,* 440 F.2d 497 (7th Cir. 1971); *Illinois Cent. R.R. v. Chicago Title & Trust Co.,* 79 Ill. App. 623 (1899).

Indiana Accord: *Pennsylvania R.R. v. Mink,* 138 Ind. App. 311, 212 N.E.2d 784 (1966); *New York Cent. R.R. v. Wyatt,* 135 Ind. App. 205, 184 N.E.2d 657 at 670 (1962); *Minninger v. New York Cent. R.R.,* 123 Ind. App. 338, 109 N.E.2d 104 (1952); *Pennsylvania R.R. v. Huss,* 96 Ind. App. 71, 180 N.E. 919 (1932). Trains must be operated at speeds that are not unreasonable in view of the weather, visibility, and all other relevant conditions. *New York Cent. R.R. v. Milhiser,* 231 Ind. 180, 108 N.E.2d 57 (1952).

Under Indiana law, motorists approaching a railroad crossing are entitled to assume that the railroad has used due care in maintaining the crossing and has obeyed all applicable statutes, ordinances, and regulations concerning warning signs at the crossing and train operations over the crossings. *Chicago S.S. & S.B.R.R. v. Luca,* 91 Ind. App. 521, 170 N.E. 564 (1930); and *Southern I.R.R. v. Drennen,* 44 Ind. App. 14, 88 N.E. 724 (1909), and *Lake Erie & W.R.R. v. McFarren,* 188 Ind. 113, 122 N.E. 330 (1919).

Under Indiana law a railroad crossing may be extra-hazardous for motorists either because of its permanent features or because of temporary circumstances, such as weather and visibility affecting the crossings used at a particular time. *Central Ind. R.R. v. Anderson Banking Co.,* 252 Ind. 270, 247 N.E.2d 208 (1969); and *Indianapolis Union Ry. v. Walker,* 1-573188, Court of Appeals of Indiana, 1st Dist., Nov. 12, 1974, Indiana decisions 439-42.

A railroad's duty of care is higher in places where harm is more likely to ensue if the railroad is negligent, and track road intersections are such places. *Indianapolis Union Ry. v. Boettcher,* 131 Ind. 82, 28 N.E. 551 (1891).

Texas: In *State Hwy. Dep't v. Pinner,* 531 S.W.2d 851 (Tex. App. 1975), the jury excused a driver's failure to comply with a statute requiring vehicles to come to a stop before a railroad crossing. The jury found that the driver was unable to stop at the crossing, and could not avoid a collision with a train, for reasons not caused by the driver's own negligence.

§ 3-3. Duty to Maintain.

The general rule is that governmental bodies providing facilities must reasonably maintain them, even though roads and/or safety or marking devices are not mandated.

§ 3-3(A). Roads.

Once a governmental entity elects to provide a road, it must be maintained and built in a reasonably safe condition.

Illinois: *Baran v. City of Chicago Heights,* 43 Ill. 2d 177, 251 N.E.2d 227 (1969).

New York: The Court of Appeals has recently commented in a relevant case, *Bottalico v. State,* 59 N.Y.2d 302, 451 N.E.2d 454 (1983) as follows: "In providing a roadway itself, the State has a duty to maintain it in a reasonably safe condition (see *Gutelle v. City of New York,* 55 N.Y.2d 794, 795, 447 N.Y.S.2d 422, 432 N.E.2d 124; *Tomassi v. Town of Union,* 46 N.Y.2d 91, 97, 412 N.Y.S.2d 842, 385 N.E.2d 581; *Annino v. City of Utica,* 276 N.Y. 192, 196, 11 N.E.2d 726)." *Alva S.S. Co. v. City of New York,* 405 F.2d 962 (2d Cir. 1969), held that while a city often is under no duty to undertake an act in the first instance, once it decides to do that act it must be done reasonably, with due care for those who will be immediately affected by its actions.

§ 3-3(B). Lights and Signals.

Once lights and electric signals are provided, they must be reasonably maintained.

California: *Hoel v. City of Los Angeles,* 136 Cal. App. 2d 295, 288 P.2d 989 (1955). Defendant liable on failure to fix broken electric signal. *Mathews v. State,* 82 Cal. App. 3d 116, 145 Cal. Rptr. 443 (1978). Malfunctioning intersection traffic control signals can create dangers for intersection traffic. The governmental entities with maintenance jurisdiction over such traffic controls face liability in damages to those injured in the intersection thereby.

Hawaii: City was liable for injuries sustained by pedestrian at intersection where traffic signals were malfunctioning. *Wong v. City & County of Honolulu,* 665 P.2d 157 (Hawaii 1983).

Illinois: *Johnston v. City of East Moline,* 405 Ill. 460, 91 N.E.2d 401 (1950); *City of Chicago v. Powers,* 42 Ill. 169 (1866); *City of Freeport v. Isbell,* 83 Ill. 440 (1876).

Texas: A City may be liable for failure to barricade, light, or post warnings about dangers and defects in the streets. *Gabbert v. City of Brownwood,* 176 S.W.2d 344 (Tex. App. 1943), error refused.

§ 3-3(C). Intersections.

California: *Zamarripa v. City of Coachella,* 193 Cal. Rptr. 358 (Cal. App. 1983).

Florida: The Florida Court in *Cirslip v. City of Fort Pierce,* St. Lucie County, 19th Judicial Circuit Court No. 77-563, Oct. 8, 1982 — the Florida Court of Appeals reversed the trial court and the Appellate Court held that it was not proper for the trial court to give the defendant summary judgment in a case where two cars collided in an intersection and one passenger in one vehicle was knocked through the windshield, flew through the air and landed on a spike projecting out of a utility pole defendant city had placed in the intersection. The Appellate Court held that it was a fact issue for which the city could be held liable if the jury found they had negligently placed the spike in the pole under circumstances where it was foreseeable that "some person would come in dangerous contact with the spike in some manner." That case is reported at 26 A.T.L.A. L. Rep. 123 (1982).

Louisiana: *Holt v. Singletary,* 441 So. 2d 330 (La. App. 1983).

New Mexico: *Grano v. Roadrunner Trucking, Inc.,* 656 P.2d 890 (N.M. App. 1982).

§ 3-3(D). Median Strips.

Florida: *Town of Belleair v. Taylor,* 425 So. 2d 669 (Fla. App. 1983). *City of Tamarac v. Garchar,* 398 So. 2d 889 (Fla. App. 1981), was an action by a motorist against a city for injuries caused by the plaintiff's collision with a boulder placed on the median strip of a city road. The city knew that such boulders created dangers for motorists, but the city allowed said condition to exist, endangering automobiles driving on the median in order to protect the median grass. Under traditional "balancing of interests" analysis the Court condemned such unreasonable action which protected grass by endangering life. The Court held the city owed a duty of due care to people, not to vegetation.

Louisiana: *Lewis v. State,* 436 So. 2d 1305 (La. App. 1983). Plant Lovers Beware!

§ 3-3(E). Potholes.

Reasonable care, of course, mandates removal of dangerous potholes upon reasonable notice.

Illinois: *Parson v. City of Chicago,* 117 Ill. App. 3d 383, 453 N.E.2d 770 (1983).

New York: *Baily v. State,* N.Y. Court of Claims No. 61903, August 13, 1981, reported at 25 A.T.L.A. L. Rep. 166.

Texas: In *County of Harris v. Eaton,* 573 S.W.2d 177 (Tex. 1978), the plaintiff was injured when his automobile struck a large hole in the County road. The Court held the hole in the road had existed for such a sufficiently long enough time that the defendant knew or should have known about it.

§ 3-3(F). Drop-Offs.

Various jurisdictions have condemned drop-offs of varying height between the pavement and the road shoulder. The drop-off may cause a vehicle to go out of control when leaving the pavement, or may prevent a return to the pavement.

California: Two to three inch drop-off condemned — *Zeppi v. State,* 345 P.2d 33 (Cal. 1959).

Louisiana: Unreasonable drop condemned — *Pitre v. Aetna Life & Cas. Co.,* 434 So. 2d 191 (La. App. 1983). Six to eight-inch drop condemned — *Payne v. Louisiana Dep't of Transp. & Dev.,* 424 So. 2d 324 (La. App. 1982);

Thornhill v. Louisiana Dep't of Transp. & Dev., 424 So. 2d 331 (La. App. 1982); *Everett v. Louisiana Dep't of Transp. & Dev.*, 424 So. 2d 336 (La. App. 1982). Four to six-inch drop condemned — *Scott v. Louisiana Dep't of Transp. & Dev.*, 424 So. 2d 284 (La. App. 1982).

Michigan: Unreasonable drop condemned — *Karrar v. Board of Rd. Comm'rs*, 339 N.W.2d 653 (Mich. App. 1983).

New York: Unreasonable drop condemned — *Bottalico v. State*, 451 N.E.2d 454, 464 N.Y.S.2d 707 (1983). Three to four-inch drop-off condemned — *Raynor v. State*, 98 A.D.2d 865, 470 N.Y.S.2d 810 (1983).

§ 3-3(G). Marking and Signing.

Most states must follow marking and signing rules in the current Manual for Uniform Traffic Control Devices. Lower level political entities may be bound to follow the manual by statute or case law. Even where the manual is not binding, reasonable care must be taken to maintain marking and signing provided. Bear in mind that signing and warning are generally required where reasonably necessary to warn drivers of approaching danger. *Mullins v. County of Wayne*, 16 Mich. App. 365, 168 N.W.2d 246 (1969).

Arizona: Arizona Court held in *Roundey v. City of Phoenix*, Maricopa County Superior Court No. C-387927, May 29, 1981, reported at 24 A.T.L.A. L. Rep. 366, that governmental bodies must use reasonable care in road signing and the defendant city was guilty of negligence for failing to properly sign and warn of a road narrowing situation.

California: *Mittenhuber v. Herrera*, 142 Cal. 3d 1, 190 Cal. Rptr. 694 (1983). The natural topography of public property will require a warning sign when it is unreasonably deceptive or dangerous for those using the property with due care.

Irwin v. Padelford, 127 Cal. App. 2d 135, 273 P.2d 539 (1954). Motorist driving automobile on through street is entitled to rely on controlling government agency obeying law and properly marking intersecting streets.

Indiana: Under Indiana law, the State must follow the Indiana Uniform Manual on Traffic Control Devices. *State v. Thompson,* 385 N.E.2d 198 (Ind. App. 1979).

Louisiana: The State and a contractor were liable for injuries resulting from an automobile crash caused by a temporary application of white reflective striping on the highway in such a manner as to create the impression that the shoulder was, in fact, an additional traffic lane. *Rivet v. State,* 434 So. 2d 436 (La. App. 1983).

Michigan: Negligent Sign Placement. *Gorelick v. Michigan Dep't of State Hwys.,* 339 N.W.2d 635 (Mich. App. 1983).

New York: Defendant could be liable for negligent placement of stop sign. *Sanchez v. Lippincott,* 89 A.D.2d 372, 455 N.Y.S.2d 457 (1982).

§ 3-4. Duty to Provide Barriers and Guardrails.

Barriers and guardrails along the roadside, and median barriers down the road center must be provided when required by due care.

California: California law holds governmental entities must provide guardrails and barriers where due care requires them. *Meneses v. Tracey,* Santa Clara Superior Court No. 492051, Dec. 8, 1982, reported at 26 A.T.L.A. L. Rep. 207. Median barriers — *Ducey v. Argo Sales Co.,* 25 Cal. 707, 602 P.2d 755 (1979), Defendant liable for not erecting needed barrier; *Harland v. State,* 75 Cal. App. 3d 475 (1977), State liable for negligent barrier design. *Morris v. State,* 89 Cal. App. 3d 962, 153 Cal. Rptr. 117 (1979). Defendant could be liable on failure to keep median barrier in proper repair. *Erfurt v. State,* 141 Cal. App. 3d 837, 190

Cal. Rptr. 569 (1983). Defendant liable for negligent guardrail placement and locations.

Connecticut: Median barriers — *D'Arcy v. Commissioner of Transp.,* Waterbury Superior Court, No. 44172, June 17, 1982, reported in 26 A.T.L.A. L. Rep. 22.

Florida: Median barriers — *Ferla v. Metropolitan Dade County,* 374 So. 2d 64 (Fla. App. 1979).

Illinois: Guardrail — *Osborne v. City of Harvey,* 16 Ill. App. 3d 740, 306 N.E.2d 601 (1973); *Koehler v. State,* 27 Ill. Ct. Cl. 384 (1972). Median barrier — *Chapman v. Checker Taxi Co.,* 43 Ill. App. 3d 699, 357 N.E.2d 111 (1976).

Indiana: *City of Indianapolis v. Moss,* 74 Ind. App. 129, 128 N.E. 857 (1920).

Iowa: Median barrier — *Lewis v. State,* 256 N.W.2d 181 (1977).

Kentucky: Guardrail — *Commonwealth, Dep't of Hwys. v. Automobile Club Ins. Co.,* 467 S.W.2d 326 (Ky. App. 1971).

Louisiana: *Rue v. State, Dep't of Hwys.,* 372 So. 2d 1197 (La. 1979).

Maine: Defendant liable for negligent maintenance, allowing snow and ice to pile up on guardrail. *Goodine v. State,* 468 A.2d 1002 (Me. 1983).

Massachusetts: *Flynn v. Hurley,* 322 Mass. 182, 124 N.E.2d 810 (1955).

Michigan: Median barrier — *Arnold v. Michigan Dep't of State Hwys.,* Michigan Court of Claims, No. 4939, January 23, 1980, reported at 23 A.T.L.A. L. Rep. 118 (April 1980); *Hall v. Michigan Dep't of Hwys.,* Michigan Court of Claims No. 4606, November 29, 1979, reported at 23 A.T.L.A. L. Rep. 123; *Detroit Bank & Trust Co. v. State,* 55 Mich. App. 131, 222 N.W.2d 59 (1974); defendant could be liable for installing wrong kind of median barrier. Guardrails — *Grinis v. Michigan Dep't of State Hwys.,*

Michigan Court of Claims No. 6693, January 20, 1982 reported at 25 A.T.L.A. L. Rep. 214.

Minnesota: Median barrier — *MOMO v. Bradley,* Hennepin County District Court, No. 747807, decided November 9, 1979, reported in 23 A.T.L.A. L. Rep. 123 (April, 1980).

Montana: Government has a duty to use reasonable care to maintain guardrails and shoulders under the case of *Johnson v. United States,* U.S. Dist. Court for the Dist. of Montana, No. 78-186-H, September 16, 1981, reported at 25 A.T.L.A. L. Rep. 166.

New York: Median barrier — *Lattanzi v. State,* New York Court of Claims No. 58288, decided June 1, 1978, reported at 21 A.T.L.A. L. Rep. 321 (September 1978); *Bodner v. Steinhardt,* 418 N.Y.S.2d 484 (1979). Guardrails — *Wingerter v. State,* 58 N.Y.2d 848, 446 N.E.2d 776, 460 N.Y.S.2d 20 (1983); *Zalewski v. State,* 53 A.D.2d 781, 384 N.Y.S.2d 545 (1976); *Warren v. New York State Thruway Auth.,* 51 A.D.2d 679, 378 N.Y.S.2d 530 (1976); *Hall v. State,* 28 A.D.2d 1203, 285 N.Y.S.2d 330 (1967).

New York law on guardrail height — New York Court held in *Mullahey v. City of New York,* Queens County Supreme Court No. 365-79, April 26, 1982, that municipal bodies must maintain a reasonable height for their guardrail and that no design immunity can countervent this requirement. 25 A.T.L.A. L. Rep. 366 (1982).

New York law on guardrail material — New York Court holds wood to be an unreasonable guardrail material in *Horton v. East Hudson Parkway Auth.,* U.S. Dist. Court for the Southern Dist. of New York, No. 78 CIV. 4339, May 15, 1981, reported at 24 A.T.L.A. L. Rep. 414. A $2 million plus jury verdict for below the knee leg amputation of a 25-year-old housewife caused when a wooden guardrail penetrated her car and cut off her leg. Plaintiff driver swerved her car to avoid an animal, and sideswiped the wooden guardrail which speared the car.

Oklahoma: *Terry v. Edgin,* 598 P.2d 228 (1979).

Pennsylvania: *Black v. City of Philadelphia,* Philadelphia County Court of Common Pleas, No. 4590, decided March 29, 1978, reported at 21 A.T.L.A. L. Rep. 225 (June, 1978); *Palmer v. Penn-Ohio Rd. Materials, Inc.,* 470 F. Supp. 1199 (W.D. Pa. 1979). *Rosa v. City of Chester,* 175 F. Supp. 11 (E.D. Pa. 1959), *rev. on other grounds,* 278 F.2d 876 (3d Cir. 1960), defendant liable for failure to erect needed guardrail. *Wensel v. North Versailles Twp.,* 136 Pa. Super. 485, 7 A.2d 590 (1939), defendant could be liable for failure to install needed guardrail.

Washington State: General duty on barriers — *Bartlett v. Northern Pac. Ry.,* 74 Wash. 2d 881, 447 P.2d 735 (1969); Guardrails — *Raybell v. State,* 6 Wash. App. 795, 496 P.2d 559 (1972).

§ 3-5. Duty to Provide Warning.

Warnings to motorists must be provided when required by due care.

California: Statutory duty to post needed warnings and signals, see Cal. Vehicle Code §§ 21350 and 21351. See also *Weddle v. State,* 191 Cal. Rptr. 819 (Cal. App. 1983).

Florida: *Perez v. Department of Transp.,* 435 So. 2d 830 (Fla. 1983). The Court held that the state's placement of road warning signs did not constitute "placement" of "traffic control devices" for which the Department was immune from suit. The Court rejected the defendant's claim that placement of such devices was within a governmental entity's police power and was a judgmental planning level function to which sovereign immunity was attached.

Illinois: Warning of danger on adjacent roadway — see *Janssen v. City of Springfield,* 79 Ill. 2d 435, 404 N.E.2d 213 (1980). Warning signs — *Osborne v. City of Harvey,* 16 Ill. App. 3d 740, 306 N.E.2d 601 (1973). Flagman needed —

Ohms v. State, 30 Ill. Ct. Cl. 410 (1975). Flares needed — *Stanley v. State,* 22 Ill. Ct. Cl. 438 (1957). Lights needed to warn of defect in road — *Garrett v. State,* 22 Ill. Ct. Cl. 343 (1956). General duty to warn of known danger — *Hout v. State,* 25 Ill. Ct. Cl. 301 (1966); *Linneen v. City of Chicago,* 310 Ill. App. 274, 34 N.E.2d 100 (1941).

Louisiana: *Garrick v. Washington Parish,* 440 So. 2d 787 (La. App. 1983).

Massachusetts: *Scholl v. New England Power Serv. Co.,* 340 Mass. 267, 163 N.E.2d 279 (1960).

Texas: In *State v. McBride,* 601 S.W.2d 552 (Tex. App. 1980), the State was held liable for failure to properly warn of a known road danger. The State had posted barricades and signs to slow down, but had not warned drivers that, even at slower speeds, they would encounter serious road danger from slick and muddy road surfaces that drivers could not have known about without warning signs. *Jezek v. City of Midland,* 605 S.W.2d 544 (Tex. 1980), held that where the city maintains an intersection in such a manner that the vision of motorists is obstructed, the city must warn of, or remove, the dangers blocking visibility. In *State v. Nichols,* 609 S.W.2d 571 (Tex. App. 1980), the plaintiff's injuries were sustained when his automobile ran into a "washout" or sunken-in portion of highway. The Court allowed the plaintiff a right of recovery against the State under a statute providing that the State shall be liable for personal injuries caused by the negligence of a State employee acting within the scope of his employment or office when such injuries are caused by some condition or use of tangible real or personal property. The Court reasoned the washout arose from a condition or "washout" in the road. The case shows how courts twist to avoid strict immunity statutes (see Introduction, *supra,* Sovereign Immunity — The Second License to Kill).

§ 3-6. Bridges.

Reasonable care must be used in designing, building, and maintaining bridges.

Louisiana: State was liable for failure to use due care in creating surface of a bridge that was defective and unreasonably dangerous. *Campbell v. State Dep't of Hwys.,* 439 So. 2d 1175 (La. App. 1983); *Holmes v. Christopher,* 435 So. 2d 1022 (La. App. 1983).

Missouri: *Hall v. County of New Madrid,* 645 S.W.2d 149 (Mo. App. 1982).

New Jersey: Municipalities held liable for failure to post "Bridge Freezes Before Road" signs. During winter the road was wet, but the bridge the road led into was already icy and plaintiff went off the bridge without warning. *Baker v. Heckman,* N.J. Middlesex County Superior Court No. L-11846-80, Feb. 23, 1983, cited at 26 A.T.L.A. L. Rep. 306.

New York: *Sandford v. State,* 94 A.D.2d 857, 463 N.Y.S.2d 595 (1983).

§ 3-7. Depressions in Roadway.

Reasonable care generally precludes dangerous depressions in roadway Defendant knew or should have known about.

California: *Ulwelling v. Crown Coach Corp.,* 206 Cal. App. 2d 96, 23 Cal. Rptr. 631 (1962). Dangers and defects in the street are conditions within the purview of Public Liability Act for which liability may be imposed on city.

New York: *Marcus v. County of Nassau,* 95 A.D.2d 846, 464 N.Y.S.2d 205 (1983).

§ 3-8. Slippery Substances on Road.

Reasonable care generally precludes slippery substances on a road if sufficient time exists to reasonably alert the governmental entity it should remove the substance.

Arizona: In *Hernandez v. State,* Pima County Superior Court No. 168611, August 21, 1981, reported at 25 A.T.L.A. L. Rep. 123, the Defendant was held guilty of negligent road maintenance for putting the wrong kind of surface onto a road which caused an oil "bleed" which when mixed with rainwater created a dangerously slippery surface.

District of Columbia: Water — *Roberts v. District of Columbia,* District of Columbia Superior Court No. 928-78, Feb. 16, 1982, reported at 25 A.T.L.A. L. Rep. 269.

Louisiana: Oil — *Naylor v. Louisiana Dep't of Pub. Hwys.,* 423 So. 2d 674 (La. App. 1982).

§ 3-9. Roadside Vegetation.

Governmental entities, in exercise of reasonable maintenance functions, must cut roadside vegetation obscuring the vision of motorists.

Alabama: Defendant liable for crash caused by elm tree obscuring stop sign. *City of Scottsboro v. Johnson,* 436 So. 2d 859 (Ala. 1983).

Indiana: *Hurst v. Board of Comm'rs,* 446 N.E.2d 347 (Ind. App. 1983).

Massachusetts: *Miles v. Commonwealth,* 288 Mass. 243, 192 N.E. 488 (1934). Encroaching tree obscured road, establishing negligent maintenance.

Michigan: *Moerman v. Kalamazoo County Rd. Comm'n,* 129 Mich. App. 584, 341 N.W.2d 829 (1983). Defendant liable for tree encroaching onto roadway.

Texas: Obstruction of traffic sign by trees or bushes is "condition" of such sign, exposing municipality to liability under Tort Claims Act for negligent failure to keep view of sign unobstructed. *Kenneally v. Thurn,* 653 S.W.2d 69 (Tex. App. 1983).

§ 3-10. Speed Limits.

Reasonable care must be used in setting speed limits that provide minimum stopping sight distance. Even if that is present, bear in mind that the speed limit may have been set for daylight visibility and may not be adequate at night. Inquiry should also be made into the height of drivers' eye level assumed in setting the speed limit, as modern cars are lower, and drivers can see less, than in many earlier design models used to set stopping sight distance. Keep in mind the relationship between speed limits and stopping sight distance.

Michigan: Michigan Court holds State failed to use reasonable care in posting speed limit for speedway exit ramp. *Blankenship v. State,* Michigan Court of Claims No. 6704, Oct. 26, 1982, cited in 26 A.T.L.A. L. Rep. 123.

See Chapter 2, § 2-3(B), Sight Distance and Design Minimums.

§ 3-11. Curves.

There are two basic kinds of road curves. Horizontal curves go from side to side. Vertical curves go up and down. Curves are generally the most dangerous part of a road. If the crash occurred on a horizontal (side to side) curve, the length and sharpness of the curve may be important. If the curve is very sharp, it is likely to be dangerous and warrant signs giving advance notice to motorists that they are approaching something unusual, especially if it is not preceded by many other curves. The AASHO Blue Book, as early as 1954, pointed out (at page 103): "Where curves are flatter than 3 degrees, the accident rate does not vary with the frequency of the curves. For 3 to 6 degree curves, the accident rate is nearly double that for the less than 3 degree curves when they occur infrequently." Again, the 1954 Blue Book states at page 105: "The introduction of a relatively sharp curve in a section on which curves are infrequent, presents a hazard several times that of the same curve in a section where curves are frequent."

The length of horizontal curve is important because, generally, the sharper they are the longer they should be to allow the motorist "run on" and "run off" space within which he can become oriented to the curve. A sharp, short horizontal curve without a warning sign where a crash occurred in reduced visibility could well indicate a transportation facility negligence case.

Similarly, horizontal curves with higher accident rates than surrounding road sections are prime targets to warrant signs alerting approaching motorists of the curve. They also may warrant lower speed limits than surrounding road sections. Reflectors and lighting should also be considered if the accident rate on the curve is markedly higher at night. As stated in *Evaluation of Criteria for Safety Improvements on the Highway* (Roy Jurgensen & Associates Research Analysts, Inc., 1966, at 48): "Accidents on curves are reduced when the driver is made aware of the curve. The delineation of curves tends to reduce accidents."

Louisiana: The Louisiana Court in *Rouseel v. State,* St. James Parish, 23rd Judicial District Court No. 13, 587 Decided June 6, 1983, cited at 26 A.T.L.A. L. Rep. 363, held Defendant State negligent for the improper design of a road curve for having improper degree of angle, slope, and contour for use of contour, for use of substandard materials, and for inadequate warnings.

See Chapter 2, § 2-3(F), Sharpness of Curves.

§ 3-12. Slopes.

The slopes of the off shoulder area must be traversable by a vehicle to provide the forgiving roadside for which engineers are calling. If the slopes are too steep, or littered with obstacles, so that a vehicle leaving the pavement cannot reasonably be expected to return, a guardrail is probably warranted. A non-traversable slope not protected by a guardrail may very strongly indicate a lack of due care.

Michigan: Michigan Court in *Scruggs v. State,* Wayne County Circuit Court No. 80-036-206 NI, November 3rd, 1983, reported at 27 A.T.L.A. L. Rep. 175, held the defendant state negligent for designing a road slope to have the improper grade, violating AASHTO Standards, causing undue icing during winter months which caused a crash.

See Chapter 2, § 2-3(C), The Hazardous Roadside.

§ 3-13. Road Width.

If the road is not wide enough to meet design criteria, particularly at curves and other places calling for vehicle maneuver, a failure to use due care in design or maintenance may exist.

Arizona: Arizona Court in *Hull v. Greenlee County,* Gila County Superior Court No. 21,779-B, Nov. 29, 1980, reported at 24 A.T.L.A. L. Rep. 219, reports a jury verdict of $2.363 million, total for three men injured when their car slipped off a soft road shoulder and rolled down a mountainside because the road they were on was not wide enough to meet the rural roadway standards set out by the AASHO 1965 and 1970 publications.

CHAPTER 4

NOTICE

One of the crucial disputed issues in virtually every crash case, under case law or statute, is whether the defendant had sufficient notice of the defect at issue before the Plaintiff's crash to be held liable for a lapse in due care for not making timely corrections that would, more probably than not, have prevented the plaintiff's injuries. Without this notice, defendants can use the chronological defense, cited earlier, that it would go bankrupt if it were required to constantly upgrade all of its road miles or crossings. From initial field inspection through discovery and trial, the most important question in these cases for both sides is invariably: why should the place of this crash have stood out to defendant before the crash?

A good example of the importance of this notice element to the plaintiff's claim can be found in *Presley v. City of*

Norwood, 36 Ohio St. 2d 29, 303 N.E.2d 81 (1973). In *Presley,* the plaintiff sued a city for injuries sustained when he slipped and fell in a puddle of grease which was on the city's premises. It was held to be error when the trial court failed to charge the jury concerning the necessity of finding the city had notice of the hazard.

This Notice must be of reasonably foreseeable harm from the defect.[1] Such Notice comes in two basic forms: actual notice (what defendant or its agents actually knew) and constructive notice (what defendant or its agents should have known).[2] Once either form of notice is established, the defendant, unless only one form of Notice is specified by statute, will have great difficulty escaping liability for failure to upgrade or correct the defect. *Hout v. State,* 25 Ill. Ct. Cl. 301 (1966); *Linneen v. City of Chicago,* 310 Ill. App. 274, 34 N.E.2d 100 (1941); *Barrett v. City of Claremont,* 41 Cal. 2d 70, 256 P.2d 977 (1953). Bear in mind, however, that local statutory requirements for a written Notice of Claim to be filed on defendant within a certain period after a crash are dispositive of the right to sue usually unless the plaintiff is a minor or incompetent. See *Commercial Carrier Corp. v. Indian River County,* 371 So. 2d 1010, on remand, 372 So. 2d 1022, on remand, *Cheney v. Dade County,* 372 So. 2d 1182 (Fla. 1979), appeal after remand, 398 So. 2d 488 (Fla. 1981). See also *City of San*

---

1. *Moran v. Aken,* 93 Ill. App. 3d 774, 417 N.E.2d 846 (1981).

2. Beamon v. City of Highland Park, 85 Mich. App. 242, 271 N.W.2d 187 (1978).

Hilts v. County of Solano, 265 Cal. App. 2d 161, 71 Cal. Rptr. 275 (1968), in establishing liability of county for maintaining an intersection in a defective condition, it must be shown that county had actual or constructive notice of alleged dangerous condition of intersection.

City was liable for injuries sustained in collision of automobile with protruding manhole cylinder in street. Cylinder was protruding at dangerous level which was either known to city or should have been known by city. City of Jackson v. Locklar, 431 So. 2d 475 (Miss. 1983).

Antonio v. Esquivel, 163 Tex. 222, 353 S.W.2d 410 (1961), requiring a city to have actual or constructive notice of defects in the city sidewalks or streets. Note further *City of Houston v. Torres,* 621 S.W.2d 588 (Tex. 1981), where Texas courts held that compliance with a statute requiring notice of an injury in writing within 90 days of injury is mandatory and is a condition precedent to maintenance of a suit against a city for such injury.

The reason for such strict rules was exemplified in *Artco-Bell Corp. v. City of Temple,* 616 S.W.2d 190 (Tex. 1981), where the Texas Court articulated that the reason for such notice requirements of tort claims against a municipality is to provide the municipality with a chance to investigate an accident while facts are fresh and the evidence remains substantially intact, enabling a municipality to guard against unfounded claims, to settle claims, and to prepare for trial.

Failure to comply with such requirements will bar suit, despite evidence the defendant had actual or constructive notice of the defect. *Holt v. Tioga County,* 95 A.D.2d 934, 464 N.Y.S.2d 278 (1983); *Shaddox v. Melcher,* 270 Cal. App. 2d 598, 76 Cal. Rptr. 80 (1969); *Viles v. State,* 423 P.2d 818, 56 Cal. Rptr. 666 (1967). The statutory form of written notice must also be complied with. Sometimes, however, the plaintiff can survive failure to comply with strict statutory Notice of Claim requirements. Courts upon occasion excuse timely service of Notice upon the wrong agent of the defendant. This happened in *Chaulsett v. City of Fort Lauderdale,* 272 So. 2d 163 (Fla. 1973) where the Florida court held that if plaintiff gave actual as well as written notice of accident and injury to the city, such notice was sufficient, even if not given to a member of the class of officials delineated in the notice statute, if, as alleged, an insurance adjuster acting on behalf of the city conducted an investigation which resulted in plaintiff being advised by such adjuster that the city would not be held responsible and that the insurer was going to decline payment. This is a good example of the non-divisible defendant acting through all its agents.

Courts have also excused a plaintiff's failure to serve required Notice of Claim where the failure is attributable to physical or mental incapacity (*City of Houston v. Torres,* 621 S.W.2d 588 (Tex. 1981); or its conduct of defendants' agents, such as the city attorneys in *City of Houston v. Block,* 571 S.W.2d 496 (Tex. 1978)).

Without either actual or constructive notice of the defect, the defendants should be able to invoke the general common law rule that, "In order for an act or omission to be negligent, the person charged therewith must generally have, or be reasonably chargeable with knowledge that it involved danger to another." 65 C.J.S. *Negligence,* § 5(1) (1966).

The presence or absence of such notice, even if only based on road geometrics, can be a material fact issue precluding summary judgment.[3]

Notice of a defect may also be used to establish liability against a party that would otherwise not be liable for the fault of another. Thus, in *Coudry v. City of Titusville,* 438 So. 2d 197 (Fla. 1983), it was held that a defendant governmental entity might be liable for defective work of an independent contractor, for which the city would not otherwise be liable, if the city knew or should have known of the defects and failed to correct them.

It is part of the plaintiff's burden to establish this notice element during plaintiff's case in chief. *Briggs v. State,* 14 Cal. App. 3d 489, 92 Cal. Rptr. 433 (1971). The thing that plaintiff must prove defendant had adequate notice of is

---

3. Bond v. Inhabitants of Billerica, 235 Mass. 119, 176 N.E. 281 (1920); Paulin v. John R. Jurgensen Co., 7 Ohio App. 3d 273, 455 N.E.2d 524 (1982); Bowen v. Riverton City, 656 P.2d 434 (Utah 1982).

also often in dispute. Thus, in *Spelbring v. Pinal County,* 662 P.2d 458 (Ariz. App. 1983), the plaintiff established that the defendant had known for a long time that rocks could roll down a 60-degree slope onto a road. The defendant escaped liability, however, by showing it did not have notice of the actual 12-inch rock that rolled off that slope onto that road, causing plaintiff's crash. See also *Matts v. City of Phoenix,* 137 Ariz. 116, 669 P.2d 94 (1983); *Norris v. City of New Orleans,* 433 So. 2d 392 (La. App. 1983).

If the defendant does have adequate actual or constructive notice of particular road hazards that caused crashes, it is generally held liable for failure to correct them. *Naylor v. Louisiana Dep't of Pub. Hwys.,* 423 So. 2d 674 (La. App. 1982); *Adams v. Town of Bolton,* 297 Mass. 459, 9 N.E.2d 562 (1937).

§ 4-1. Self-Made Defects.

One body of widely accepted law holds that a defendant needs no notice of transportation defects it has created and should therefore assume responsibility for. This was the concept behind the teaching of *Porter v. City of Decatur,* 16 Ill. App. 3d 1031, 307 N.E.2d 440 (1974), in which the defendant was held liable for dangers created by a negligently maintained traffic light because: "[T]he [defendant] is bound to take notice of the dangerous character of that which it causes to be done . . . [and] when a [defendant] creates a hazardous condition and someone is injured as a consequence it must respond in damages, just as others are required to do." 307 N.E.2d at 443-44.

This concept was further clarified in *Cross v. Wells Fargo Alarm Servs.,* 82 Ill. 2d 313, 412 N.E.2d 472 (1980), in which the defendant Public Housing Authority was held liable for increasing the risk of attack upon inhabitants of the buildings by providing guard services that terminated at 1:00 a.m. (The plaintiff was attacked at 1:15 a.m.)

This theory of notice is closely related to the doctrine that the defendant must not, by its actions, increase the dangers of its streets, as exemplified by *City of Chicago v. Seben,* 165 Ill. 371, 46 N.E. 244 (1897), where the two concepts were blended thusly:

> Where the [defendant] has adopted a plan, and created an existing condition in a street in pursuance thereof, and that condition renders the street unsafe, the city must go further, and perform the duty cast upon it, growing out of the statute, to exercise ordinary care to make the street thus encumbered with the product of its plan reasonably safe for public travel. 46 N.E. at 247.

See also *Tuttle v. Department of State Hwys.,* 397 Mich. 44, 243 N.W.2d 244 (1976). In *Tuttle,* the State was held negligent when, after determining that a stop control at a new intersection was not sufficiently noticeable, it failed to carry out its own work orders to make the control more visible.

California Accord: *Pritchard v. Sully-Miller Contracting Co.,* 178 Cal. App. 2d 246, 2 Cal. Rptr. 830 (1960). Where a municipality deliberately set certain automatic traffic signals in such a manner that a dangerous condition was created for traffic; the plaintiff did not have to show the defendant had particular notice or knowledge of the defect.

Notice and failure of exercise reasonable care ordinarily are essential to show culpability on the part of any defendant, even a city, but where the city itself created the dangerous condition, it is per se culpable and without notice.

Wood v. County of Santa Cruz, 133 Cal. App. 2d 713, 284 P.2d 923 (1955). Here, a motorcyclist brought suit against a county for personal injuries, alleging that trimming of trees along a road had been done by a county road crew and that branches had been permitted to lie on the paved portion of the road for about two weeks before the accident. The Court held no further proof was necessary to charge the county with knowledge of the dangerous condition it had created. See also *Reel v. City of South Gate,* 171 Cal. App. 2d 49, 340 P.2d 276 (1959).

New York Accord: A local requirement of prior written notice of alleged highway defects prior to filing of a civil action against a town was not applicable to a suit against the town which created the condition complained of or committed affirmative acts of negligence. The town knew what it had done. *Haviland v. Smith,* 91 A.D.2d 764, 458 N.Y.S.2d 11 (App. Div. 1982).

If a city created a dangerous condition by placing a cover on a water valve box located in the street bed on an inadequate and unsuitable support, the city would be liable for a pedestrian's injuries from the box, even though prior written notice of the defect in the box or cover had not been provided. The pedestrian injured his heel when he stepped upon the cover, the cover tipped, and the heel entered the box. *Barrett v. City of Buffalo,* 96 A.D.2d 709, 465 N.Y.S.2d 376 (1983).

Matter of Rouse v. State, 97 A.D.2d 962, 468 N.Y.S.2d 756 (1983). Because the State created a hazardous condition by placing stone and gravel on highway two weeks prior to accident, claimant was not required to establish notice as prerequisite for recovery. See also *Henry Muszynski v. City of Buffalo,* 29 N.Y.2d 810, 327 N.Y.S.2d 368, 277 N.E.2d 414 (1971), holding city not entitled to written notice of road defect it created.

Florida Accord: *City of St. Petersburg v. Collom,* 419 So. 2d 1082 (Fla. 1982), held that when a governmental entity creates, and knows of, a dangerous condition which is not readily apparent to persons who could be injured by the condition, a duty is imposed on the entity to warn the public of, or protect the public from, the known danger and failure to fulfill such operational-level duty can sustain an action against the governmental entity.

§ 4-2. Constructive Notice.

Constructive notice of the defect will, of course, sustain a negligence case because a defendant is chargeable with notice of dangerous, unsafe, or hazardous conditions on its highways where these conditions are of such a nature that the defendant could reasonably have ascertained their existence and corrected them. *Board of Comm'rs v. Briggs,* 167 Ind. App. 96, 337 N.E.2d 852, 867 (1975). Similarly, "one who negligently fails to remedy a dangerous condition on his property may be held liable for an injury suffered by another in consequence thereof, although he was not aware of the peril of such other person in time to avoid the injury." 65 C.J.S. *Negligence,* § 5(1)(1966).

Case law in all jurisdictions clearly delineates the universal grounding of the constructive notice doctrine. Thus, *City of Waco v. Witt,* 126 S.W.2d 1002 (Tex. App. 1939) held that constructive notice may exist or be implied when a defect has existed so long that a municipality, by the exercise of ordinary care, should have discussed it. Similarly, *Leon v. City of Miami,* 312 So. 2d 518 (Fla. 1975) held that a governmental entity is liable for injuries resulting from defects which have been in existence so long that they could have been discovered and repaired in the exercise of reasonable care.

The criteria against which the facts of a given case will be measured to determine whether a governmental entity has constructive notice of a road defect were enunciated in *Palermo v. City of Chicago Heights,* 2 Ill. App. 3d 1004, 276 N.E.2d 470 (1971):

> Constructive notice is present where a defective condition exists for such a length of time that public authorities, by the exercise of reasonable care and

> diligence, might have known of the condition. Baker v. City of Granite City, 311 Ill.App. 586, 37 N.E.2d 372. Factors to be considered are the conspicuity of the defect and the length of time it existed. Trojan v. City of Blue Island, 10 Ill.App.2d 47, 50, 134 N.E.2d 29. The issue is generally one for the trier of fact and becomes a question of law only if "all of the evidence, when viewed in its aspect most favorable to [the plaintiff here] that . . . so overwhelmingly favors [the defendant] . . . no contrary [finding] . . . based on that evidence could ever stand." Pedrick v. Peoria & Eastern R.R. Co., 37 Ill.2d 494, 510, 229 N.E.2d 504, 513, 276 N.E.2d at 473.

The length of time a defect must exist where it can be seen and corrected in order to hold a governmental entity to constructive notice of its existence will, of course, vary substantially from case to case.

Thus, in *Duewel v. Lahman,* 103 Ill. App. 3d 220, 430 N.E.2d 662 (1981), the defendant county was held to have constructive notice that a stop sign had been missing from its post for 8-1/2 hours. On the other hand, in *Kolski v. State,* 31 Ill. Ct. Cl. 307 (1976), the court was on less controversial ground in holding the defendant to have constructive notice of a broken guardrail that had existed for one month.

The time period a defendant must know of a defect to be held to "constructive notice" of it really depends on how long it would reasonably take to correct the defect. As Wigmore put it, "The interval of time to which any inference will be allowable must depend upon the nature of the thing and the circumstances of the particular case." 2 Wigmore, *Evidence,* § 437, at page 513. Thus, while 8-1/2 hours is sufficient time to replace a post or sign, (see *Duewel v. Lahman supra*), the Court held in *Electrical Prods. Corp. v. County of Talare,* 116 Cal. App. 2d 147, 253 P.2d 111 (1953) that the defendant did not have constructive (or actual) notice of defects it learned of hours before a crash because it would have taken a long time to correct those defects. See also *Loewen v. City of Burbank,* 124 Cal. App. 2d 551, 269 P.2d 121 (1954). Liability requires Notice plus a failure to take such action as may be reasonably necessary within the available time. See also *Garber v. City of Los Angeles,* 226 Cal. App. 2d 349, 38 Cal. Rptr. 157 (1964). In an alternative approach, some statutes create a time period defining the period of time after which a defendant will have notice. *Beamon v. City of Highland Park,* 85 Mich. App. 242, 271 N.W.2d 187 (1978) (defendant has constructive notice of road defects it knew or should have known of for thirty days).

These cases actually rest on a proximate cause analysis: if the time between the moment the defendant obtained notice of the defect and the moment of the crash would not have been sufficient for reasonable corrections to have removed the danger, then the defendant's failure to correct the defect after obtaining notice did not cause the crash on the Plaintiff's injuries.

On this basis, the defendant was held liable in *Kelson v. Buckley,* 429 So. 2d 477 (La. App. 1983) for failure to warn of malfunctioning lights it had known of for over two months, a period long enough to fix the lights or post the warnings. Similarly, Michigan holds that a governmental entity cannot be held liable for a road defect unless the entity:

> knew, or in the exercise of reasonable diligence should have known, of the existence of the defect (*and had a reasonable time to repair the defect before the injury took place*). Knowledge of the defect and time to repair the same shall be conclusively presumed when the defect existed so as to be readily apparent to an ordinarily observant person for a period of 30 days or longer before the injury took place. (MC. § 691.1403.) (Emphasis Added.)

See also *Potere v. City of Philadelphia,* 380 Pa. 581, 112 A.2d 100 (1955), where the defendant was held to have had actual notice of a dangerous cave-in beneath a street two days before a crash. The time period of notice would have sufficed to warn or repair.

In *Rodgers v. Shaler Twp.,* 164 Pa. Super. 558, 67 A.2d 806 (1949), the Court held that constructive notice or negligence might reasonably have been found in that, for a period of five months, the township had failed to repair a hole in that part of the road intended for and used by pedestrians and vehicular travel, thus allowing a finding of constructive notice and negligence.

Similarly, in *Williams v. City of Dallas,* 636 S.W.2d 222 (Tex. App. 1982), an action for personal injuries was sustained when a pedestrian fell into a storm sewer, became aware of evidence that the drain cover had been missing for a period of *four months.* This was held sufficient to raise a fact issue as to the city's negligence in failing to discover and remedy the defect.

It should be noted that a constructive notice may be based upon the emphasis the defendant should be giving to safety inspections of its own transportation facilities.

Constructive Notice may also be based upon the obvious dangers presented, over a reasonable time period, by the road geometrics. *Levine v. City of Los Angeles,* 68 Cal. App. 3d 481, 137 Cal. Rptr. 512 (1977); *Rush v. Wilkes-Barre City,* 54 Luz. L. Reg. 119 (Pa. Com. Pl. 1964). In *Chappell v. Dwyer,* 611 S.W.2d 158 (Tex. App. 1981), the state was found to know of, and therefore held liable for, an arroyo running parallel to a dirt road in a state park.

California Definition: A public entity has constructive notice of a defect if the condition existed for such a period of time and was of such an obvious nature that the public entity, in the exercise of due care, should have discovered the condition and its dangerous character. Cal. Gov't Code

§ 835.2. But see, *Van Dorn v. City & County of San Francisco,* 103 Cal. App. 2d 714, 230 P.2d 393 (1951): To charge a city with constructive notice of a defect in a sidewalk or street, some element must be shown of conspicuousness or notoriety so as to put city authorities on inquiry as to existence of the defect or its condition and its dangerous character.

Pennsylvania Definition: Murray v. Siegal, 413 Pa. 23, 195 A.2d 790 (1963). A city or an abutting property owner is not liable for injuries due to the dangerous condition of a sidewalk, unless its notice of the condition, whether actual or constructive, is established.

To establish such constructive notice, it is necessary to show that the defect could have been discovered and corrected because it existed for quite some time.

§ 4-3. Origin of Actual Notice of Danger and Defects.

Anything that could, and should have called the defendant's attention to the need for correcting the defect at issue prior to the plaintiff's crash can constitute actual notice.

Forms of actual Notice can include, but are certainly not limited to, the following:

§ 4-3(A). The Non-Divisible Defendant.

Governmental entities, railroads, and others running transportation facilities are single entities. The highway department, the police department, the fire department ambulances, and any other tentacles of the defendant, act, see, and learn on behalf of the whole entity. It is uncommon for a transportation facility to escape periodic visits from various arms of the defendant: police cars and maintenance crews and grass mowers and similar groups of agents are generally "making the rounds" all year long, and indeed the defendant may be liable for failure to maintain a reasonable inspection service if this is not the case. Certainly, few defendants will admit that they just throw vast numbers of roads or crossings out for public use and then ignore what is happening on those facilities until lawsuits start raining down on them. Under the unitary defendant theory, what each agent of the defendant sees, the defendant itself sees, and the defendant, being omnipotent should be able to draw the correct inferences from facts its agents see and know.[4]

The defendant should, in most jurisdictions, be chargeable with the knowledge of its agents under the universal doctrine that "a principal is generally charged with notice received by an agent within the scope of the agency." West's Indiana Law Encyclopedia, Agency, § 91. The same concept is in Federal Rules of Evidence 801(d)(2). Thus, in *Duewel v. Lahman,* 103 Ill. App. 3d 220, 430 N.E.2d 662 (1981), the court held the defendant county had sufficient notice of a stop sign that had fallen down 8-1/2 hours before the plaintiff's crash and was held liable for failure to fix the sign before the crash. The court based its finding that the defendant had adequate notice because it had mowers and police patrols on the scene before the crash, and notice to these agents was notice to the county under the authority of *Doyle v. Teas,* 5 Ill. 202, 243 (1843).

---

4. California holds public entities to the standard that they "should know" the dangers of defects their agents have actual knowledge of, even if those agents do not realize those dangers. Cal. Gov't Code, § 835.23.

Massachusetts holds public entities liable for failure to cure roadway railing defects they "have notice of or, by the exercise of proper care and diligence, might have had reasonable notice of." Mass. Gen. Laws Ann. Ch. 84, § 15.

Michigan holds public entities to knowledge of highway defects that "should have been discovered and repaired in the exercise of reasonable diligence." Beamon v. City of Highland Park, 85 Mich. App. 242, 271 N.W.2d 187 (1978).

If, however, the defendant can establish that it had a reasonable inspection policy, which failed to detect the defect, some jurisdictions will excuse the failure. *Demoruelle v. State Dep't of Transp. & Dev.,* 423 So. 2d 1202 (La. App. 1983); *Marino v. Tuolumme County,* 118 Cal. App. 2d 675, 258 P.2d 540 (1953). The factual issue in such instances is often whether an inspection procedure can be operated with due care if it failed to detect defects it should have noticed over a reasonable time period. Thus in *Anderson v. City of Thousand Oaks,* 65 Cal. App. 3d 82, 135 Cal. Rptr. 127 (1976), the Court held the defendant city could not establish immunity for itself merely because a requested investigation conducted by the County Traffic Security counsel failed to disclose reasons for lowering speed restrictions on a new road section. The *Anderson* court stated the city could still be liable if it failed to remove dangers it had actual or constructive notice of. Thus, merely looking and not seeing does not, and should not, grant absolution barring a statute saying it does.

In a related area, Discovery, governmental entities joined as defendants in a lawsuit based on a road crash often improperly contend that only the Highway Department is a party, and that other branches of the entity, such as the Police Department and Fire Department, are non-parties whose records must be separately subpoenaed and whose employees are not agents of the entity as a whole. These contentions should be summarily dismissed.

§ 4-3(B). Crashes.

Police crash reports involving the road area at issue (a point often in dispute) may concern "prior crashes" (before the instant crash) or "subsequent crashes" (after the instant crash). Generally, only prior crashes can be admitted as notice of danger to the defendant, but, under similar circumstances, both prior and subsequent crashes can be admitted as evidence of how the plaintiff's crash happened, or of the existence of a dangerous condition in the roadway area.

§ 4-3(B)(1). Prior Crashes.

The general rule regarding prior crashes in the relevant road area[5] was stated by Judge Weinstein:

> Evidence of other accidents in the same place . . . is generally admissible, not because it shows that Defendant has a general tendency to be negligent, but because it tends to prove either (1) the existence of a dangerous or defective condition . . . or (2) that Defendant knew or should have known of the dangerous or defective condition.[6]

In addition to notice and the existence of a dangerous condition, prior crashes may also be relevant to the issue of how the crash at issue happened, by showing other drivers (before or after the crash) came to grief[7] under relevant similar circumstances because of the same road defects allegedly causing the plaintiff's injury.[8]

---

5. Defendants often argue for the narrowest possible road area to search for prior crashes, and plaintiffs usually seek the opposite. The "relevant" road area by industry custom is a *minimum* of 1/4 mile, for most highway departments keep records of road problems in sections that are larger.

6. *Weinstein's Evidence,* § 404 (20) at page 404-120. See also Johnston v. County of Yolo, 274 Cal. App. 2d 46, 79 Cal. Rptr. 33 (1969) (Evidence of prior similar crashes admitted).

7. Wells v. Village of Kenilworth, 228 Ill. App. 332 (1923); Central Amusement Co. v. Van Nostran, 85 Ind. App. 476, 154 N.E. 390 (1926).

8. If a proper foundation can be established, the substantially similar prior crashes can be used not only to show that the defendant had notice of the defect, but also to show that the plaintiff's crash was caused (in whole or in part) by the same defect that caused the prior crashes. Thus, in Cleary & Graham, *Handbook of Illinois Evidence,* § 401.15, pp. 140-41 (4th ed. 1984) the authors state:

§ 4-3(B)(1)(a). Notice.

If the prior crashes are offered to show the defendant had notice of the road defects at issue, most jurisdictions do not require an exact similarity of circumstances with the plaintiff's crash.[9] This is because highway departments should be looking to the clustering of crashes of all kinds in particular road areas to obtain knowledge of where road faults exist.[10] No segregation of crashes into particular types of causation classifications is possible at this stage when defendant should be held to notice of road faults under the "knew or should have known" standard. There are at least two reasons for this. In the first place, a given road fault (such as inadequate sight distance on a horizontal curve) can cause many different kinds of crashes, (cross median, plowing into cars ahead, single vehicles leaving

---

Evidence of similar happenings is admissible to prove the effect resulting from certain conditions. *Cooper v. Randall,* 59 Ill. 317 (1871). . . . The logic of *Bloomington v. Legg,* 151 Ill. 9, 13, 37 N.E. 696 (1894), as to both negligence and strict liability cases, seems unassailable: "Where an issue is made as to the safety of any machinery or work of man's construction which is for practical use, the manner in which it has served that purpose, when put to that use, would be a matter material to the issue, and ordinary experience of that practical use, and the effect of such use, bear directly upon such issue."

9. "If the prior accident is offered to prove notice, a lack of exact similarity of conditions will not cause exclusion provided the accident was of a kind which should have served to warn the defendant." *Weinstein's Evidence,* § 401 (10) at p. 401-54. See also Hilts v. County of Solano, 265 Cal. App. 2d 161, 71 Cal. Rptr. 275 (1968); Campus Sweater & Sportswear Co. v. M.B. Kahn Constr. Co., 515 F. Supp. 64, 88-91 (D.S.C. 1979), *aff'd,* 644 F.2d 877 (4th Cir. 1981); Rucker v. Norfolk & W. Ry., 77 Ill. 2d 434, 396 N.E.2d 534 (1979).

10. See the Appendix to this chapter for discussion, and citation, of how police departments should collect, and learn from, crash data to find defective road areas. See also Garber v. City of Los Angeles, 226 Cal. App. 2d 349, 38 Cal. Rptr. 157 (1964). The evidence of defects or dangerous conditions is, in fact, gathered by previous accidents.

the pavement), under substantially different circumstances (night, rain, fog, ice). In the second place, all the governmental entity should be doing at this stage is sticking pins in a map, or some equally mechanical activity, to indicate crashes and then noting where the pins pile up.

Thus, in *Von Tagen v. United States,* 557 F. Supp. 256 (N.D. Cal. 1983), the defendant was not allowed to show details, (the contributory fault of drivers involved), in prior crashes offered to show defendant had notice of the defect.

If the number of crashes and/or the number of deaths and/or the number of injuries substantially exceed statewide averages for similar facilities, the defendant will generally be held to have notice of the danger.[11]

§ 4-3(B)(l)(b). Causation and Existence of Defect.

Where prior crashes are introduced to show causation or the existence of a dangerous condition, substantial similarity conditions with the crash at issue must generally be shown, for the evidence is offered for a much more precise basis of relevancy than notice evidence.[12]

Care must be taken to distinguish the type of road danger that evidence of prior crashes is introduced to confirm. If the prior crashes are introduced to show the

11. Identification of Hazardous Locations, December 1977, Final Report by the Federal Highway Administration, Office of Research and Development.

12. Henderson v. Illinois Cent. Gulf R.R., 114 Ill. App. 3d 754, 449 N.E.2d 942 (1983); City of Chicago v. Jarvis, 226 Ill. 614, 80 N.E. 1079 (1907); Shepard v. City of Aurora, 5 Ill. App. 2d 12, 124 N.E.2d 584 (1955); Newton v. Meissner, 76 Ill. App. 3d 479, 394 N.E.2d 1241 (1941); Hecht Co. v. Jacobsen, 180 F.2d 13, 17 (D.C. Cir. 1950). The circumstances must not all be identical, and substantial similarity of relevant factors is sufficient. P.B. Mutrie Motor Transp., Inc. v. Interchemical Corp., 378 F. Supp. 447 (D. Mass. 1967).

existence in the past of the particular road defect allegedly causing plaintiff's crash, then prior crashes must have substantially similar circumstances to the crash at issue to make certain that extraneous factors did not cause the prior crashes. Evidence of the details of the prior crashes would be both admissible and essential foundation for such evidence. *Hecht Co. v. Jacobsen,* 180 F.2d 13, 17 (D.C. Cir. 1950); *Potter v. Natural Gas Co.,* 183 Pa. 575, 39 A. 7 (1898); *Ft. Worth & D.C. Ry. v. Looney,* 241 S.W.2d 322 (Tex. Civ. App. 1951); *Malone v. Hawley,* 46 Cal. 409 (1873).

Similarly, if prior similar crashes are offered to support the proposition that the instant crash had the same cause, the details of the prior crashes would be appropriate and crucial evidence to test the validity of that proposition. *Stormer v. Alberts Constr. Co.,* 401 Pa. 461, 165 A.2d 87 (1960).

If however, the prior crashes are only offered to show that the defendant should have had notice of the generally dangerous nature of the road crossing, the only relevant factor is the number and location of the crashes. Evidence of the details of the prior crashes would be neither relevant nor proper to support such evidence. As the Court noted in *Henderson v. Illinois Cent. Gulf R.R.,* 114 Ill. App. 3d 754, 449 N.E.2d 942 at 945 (1983): "The proponent may not, however, introduce details of the prior accidents when he is offering the evidence only to show the generally hazardous nature of the site. Those details are irrelevant; they unfairly prejudice the jury against the defendant; and their introduction is grounds for reversal."

Care must also be taken to introduce prior crashes under a theory of negligence to which they are relevant. In *Plough v. Baltimore & Ohio R.R.,* 164 F.2d 254 (2d Cir. 1947), for example, the plaintiff alleged that defendant railroad had improperly operated a train that did not give whistle warnings over a crossing. Plaintiff alleged no negligence in the design, maintenance, or signing of the crossing, or of the speed limits set for the train, or even of the train speed. Under such a limited negligence theory the Court did not allow plaintiff to introduce evidence of prior crashes at that crossing because prior crashes are rarely admissible only on the basis that a previously negligent party was negligent again,[13] and plaintiff had pled no other grounds to support the prior crash evidence.

The prior conduct admitted should also be such that defendant could reasonably be expected to learn of defects in the road or crossing from it. Thus, in *Johnson v. Grand Trunk W.R.R.*, 58 Mich. App. 708, 228 N.W.2d 795 (1975), the Court allowed evidence of prior train-car crashes at the crossing at issue, but excluded evidence of previous near misses or close calls there.

§ 4-3(B)(2). Absence of Prior Crashes.

Both sides, but particularly the defendant, must be very careful, when seeking to introduce evidence that there were not any prior crashes. Evidence of this type is far more dangerous to a defendant than it appears to be (and, indeed, it does not appear to be dangerous to a defendant lucky enough to find such evidence).

The danger, and it can be mortal to a defendant, presented by such evidence is that the absence of prior crashes is not even relevant unless it can first be shown

13. Evidence of prior negligence similar to that alleged at the time of the crash may be allowed under a "continuing course of conduct" theory on the issue of the existence of a dangerous defect at the time of plaintiff's injuries. Thus in Larsen v. Vigliarolo Bros., 77 A.D.2d 562, 429 N.Y.S.2d 273 (1980), where the plaintiff motorcyclist alleged the city allowed the road to remain covered with spilled debris, causing his crash, evidence was admitted of prior spillage of debris and accidents at that location.

that the defects causing the plaintiff to crash also *existed* in the same condition during all the earlier time periods during which there were no prior crashes. This rule, on reflection, makes perfectly good sense. If the plaintiff crashed due to a pothole in a road that existed for a week before the crash, there would be no point in showing that there were no crashes at that location during the years before the pothole existed. Accordingly, *Tracy v. Village of Lombard,* 116 Ill. App. 3d 563, 451 N.E.2d 992 (1983) stated: "Evidence of history of no accidents is permissible for the limited purpose of showing absence of notice of a dangerous condition, provided that the proof shows that the condition had been unchanged. (*Wolczek v. Public Service Co.* (1930), 342 Ill. 482, 174 N.E. 577; *Robinson v. Southwestern Bell Telephone Co.* (1960), 26 Ill. App. 2d 139, 167 N.E.2d 793; *see discussion in* E. Cleary and M. Graham, Handbook of Illinois Evidence § 401.15 (3d ed. 1979).) 451 N.E.2d at 1000." See also *Grubaugh v. City of St. Johns,* 82 Mich. App. 282, 266 N.W.2d 791 (1978). In *Grubaugh,* evidence of the absence of previous accidents was not admitted to prove an absence of negligence. The Court reasoned that evidence of the absence of accidents has less probative value than evidence of the existence of previous accidents, since evidence of prior accidents involves positive proof directly tending to establish the existence of a defect. It is always harder to prove a negative than a positive. Evidence of prior crashes raises the defendant's standard of care to that of a person aware of the defect; whereas evidence of the absence of accidents usually involves generally unreliable negative evidence, which does not tend directly to prove the absence of the negligence. It's easier to show a crash was in your road area than why it wasn't there.

The difficulty a defendant faces in introducing evidence of the absence of prior crashes was shown in *Parson v. City of Chicago,* 117 Ill. App. 3d 383, 453 N.E.2d 770 (1983). In *Parson,* the defendant was not allowed to introduce evidence that there had been no prior crashes during the time the pothole had existed. The *Parson* court reasoned that:

> In any event as the trial court noted there was no evidence of the angle, the condition of the vehicle, familiarity of drivers with the potholes, and other factors. Generally evidence of the absence of prior accidents is proper only if the offering party lays a proper foundation by establishing that such absence took place under conditions substantially similar to those surrounding the accident sued upon. (*Smith v. Verson Allstell Press Co.* (1979), 74 Ill.App.3d 818, 30 Ill.Dec. 562, 393 N.E.2d 598, *leave to appeal denied.*) Absent such proof the trial court did not abuse its discretion in refusing to admit the evidence, particularly since "evidence of absence of accidents has less probative value than evidence of previous accidents, and thus is more easily outweighed by the factor that the collateral issue will result in jury confusion. . . . Evidence of absence of accidents usually involves generally unreliable negative evidence . . . and does not tend directly to prove absence of negligence." *Grubaugh v. City of St. Johns* (1978), 82 Mich.App. 282, 288, 289, 266 N.W.2d 791, 794, *leave to appeal denied.*
>
> Furthermore it is difficult to see how evidence of lack of prior accidents could establish proper maintenance, although it might be relevant to the issues of causation or constructive notice, neither of which was argued by the city of appeal. That the pothole existed was undisputed. Proper maintenance includes the filling of potholes and the repairing of deteriorated portions of the roadway. (*Harding v. Chicago Park District* (1975), 34 Ill.App.3d 425, 339 N.E.2d 779, leave to appeal denied.) Even if the precise type of accident which did occur was unexpected, it is not unforeseeable that accidents can be caused by potholes. And the jury did determine that the pothole did in fact cause the accident. 453 N.E.2d at 774-75.

Any defendant seeking to introduce evidence of the absence of prior crashes, irrespective of the difficulty presented in laying a proper foundation to satisfy the *Parson* rule, should seriously reflect on whether the game is worth the candle. In order to get such evidence admitted, the defendant will have to show the defects allegedly causing the plaintiff's crash have existed during the entire period of time during which no prior crashes took place. A court admitting evidence of the absence of prior crashes without a showing of such longevity for the road defects at issue would be committing clear error. Moreover, a defendant introducing evidence of such long-lasting defects might be cutting its own throat: Such evidence could strike the jury as the equivalent of a guilty plea on liability and would also invoke the rule of *Palermo v. City of Chicago Heights,* 2 Ill. App. 3d 1004, 276 N.E.2d 470 (1971) that: "Constructive notice is present where a defective condition exists for such a length of time that public authorities, by the exercise of reasonable care and diligence, might have known of the condition. 276 N.E.2d at 473.

In short, in order to show it lacked notice of the defect because there were no prior crashes, the defendant may be required to show the defects at issue had existed for so long that the defendant should have known about them anyway.

§ 4-3(B)(3). Subsequent Crashes.

Crashes subsequent to the crash at issue cannot charge the defendant with notice of a dangerous condition that allegedly caused plaintiff's injuries. Subsequent crashes under similar circumstances have, however, ". . . as much probative value as evidence of prior accidents, on the question of whether the condition was 'dangerous and naturally calculated to cause accidents.'" *Eisenbraun v.*

City of New York, 2 Misc. 2d 98, 159 N.Y.S.2d 73, 74 (1955).[14]

Most jurisdictions allow subsequent crashes to show danger and causation, but not notice.

Subsequent crashes may also be used to attack the credibility of a defendant claiming no prior crashes exist,[15] if the number of subsequent crashes renders the assertion highly unlikely. Of course, the subsequent crashes must have occurred under similar circumstances, and there

---

14. See also Veit v. State, 78 N.Y.S.2d 336 at 338 (1948); Hoyt v. New York, L.E. & W.R.R., 118 N.Y. 399, 405, 23 N.E. 565 (1890); Henwood v. Chaney, 156 F.2d 392, 397 (8th Cir 1946); Laitenberger v. State, 57 N.Y.S.2d 418, 422 (Ct. Cl. 1945); *Richardson on Evidence,* § 166, p. 140 (7th ed.).

In Galieta v. Young Men's Christian Ass'n, 32 A.D.2d 711, 300 N.Y.S.2d 170, at 173 (1969) the Court noted:

> Evidence of a subsequent accident occurring under conditions similar to those existing at the time of the accident complained of is admissible and of probative value on the issue of whether a dangerous condition existed, but cannot charge the defendant with notice of such a condition (Masters v. City of Troy, 50 Hun 485, aff'd, 123 N.Y. 628, 25 N.E. 952; Wilson v. Town of Spafford, 57 Hun 589; Eisenbraun v. City of New York, 2 Misc.2d 981, 159 N.Y.S.2d 73; Richardson, Evidence [9th ed.] § 201; 41 N.Y.Jur., Negligence, § 101).

15. "Generally speaking, any evidence which tends to contradict or discredit the testimony of a witness may be introduced for consideration by the jury." Kelly, *Blackfield's Automobile and Practice,* University of Missouri, § 421.3 at 288. See also Newcomb v. Frink, 278 A.D. 998, 105 N.Y.S.2d 704 (1951); Singer v. Walker, 39 A.D.2d 90, 331 N.Y.S.2d 823 (1972); Note St. Louis S.W. Ry. v. Jackson, 242 Ark. 858, 416 S.W.2d 273 (1967), *appeal after remand* 246 Ark. 268, 438 S.W.2d 41 (1969) (interoffice memorandum prepared by highway department employees, referring to observations of danger at crossing, proposed measures, and additional observations to study measures that might be taken by railroad, was admissible to impeach testimony of employees that signal lights were visible at considerable distance and that they had made no recommendations); Missouri Pac. Transp. Co. v. Sharp, 194 Ark. 405, 108 S.W.2d 579 (1937) (proof of dates of certain events disputing witness' testimony on bus on date of plaintiff's alleged injury).

must be a genuine issue concerning the existence of the prior crashes, such as plaintiff lacking independent access to the prior crash records.

§ 4-3(C). Road Condition.

The mere existence of road defects for long enough to reasonably allow discovery and cure can put the defendant on notice of the danger if defendant's agents see the defect (actual notice) or should have seen it (constructive notice). As Wigmore states: "Direct exposure to the senses . . . [is] of course always [a] legitimate mode of evidencing knowledge of the dangerous condition of a machine or place." 2 Wigmore, *Evidence,* § 252, at p. 76.

Road condition evidence, like crash evidence, may consist of proof the road was in a certain state before or after the plaintiffs' crash. Such evidence is, of course, offered for the proposition that the road was in a similar condition at the time of the crash. The road condition evidence offered may be of the same defects that allegedly caused the plaintiffs' crash, or of other defects.

§ 4-3(C)(1). Other Defects.

The theory behind the admission of evidence of road defects existing before the instant crash other than the defects causing that crash is that the defendant should have made timely discovery of those other defects, and had it done so the defects that did cause the crash would also have been detected, and presumably cured. The rule on when evidence of these other defects is admissible, consequently, is that they, ". . . should be so closely associated with the defect in question that the discovery of the former would naturally lead to the discovery of the latter or would warn of its existence." 2 Wigmore, *Evidence,* § 252, at pp. 77-82.[16]

§ 4-3(C)(2). Prior Defects.

"The condition of a place or thing at the time of an injury," Wigmore wrote, "may always be evidenced by showing its condition before or after that time, provided no substantial change has occurred . . . even if this necessarily involves mention of repairs." 2 Wigmore, *Evidence,* § 283, at p. 186.[17]

Thus, in *Fritsky v. City of Pittsburgh,* 340 Pa. 217, 16 A.2d 422 (1940), where the Plaintiff's auto went out of control on an icy street, evidence was admitted to show that for several winters water had been coming down from a hill and freezing on that street, giving defendant notice of the icy conditions existing at the time of the crash.[18] Cases involving evidence of road conditions prior to the instant crash have covered time periods ranging from 45 minutes or less before the crash, *Clement v. Cummings,* 212 Or. 161, 317 P.2d 579 (1957), to a year or more before the crash. *Hunt v. City of Dubuque,* 96 Iowa 314, 65 N.W. 319 (1895).

---

16. See Osborne v. City of Detroit, 32 F. 36 (C.C.E.D. Mich. 1886) (Court allowed evidence of defects in sidewalks near defect causing injury); District of Columbia v. Disney, 81 F.2d 272 (C.A.D.C. 1935) (Evidence of holes in sidewalk 25 to 30 feet from hole at issue admitted); Reil v. State, 4 Wash. App. 976, 484 P.2d 1150 (1971). (General condition of 12-mile road area admitted on issue of condition at the scene); Conrod v. Town of Ellington, 104 Wis. 367, 80 N.W. 456 (1899) (General bad condition of road area two days before crash admitted); Cleveland, C.C. & I. Ry. v. Newell, 104 Ind. 264, 3 N.E. 836 (1885) (Evidence admitted that shortly before crash, a rail broke near the rail at issue).

17. City of Phoenix v. Boggs, 1 Ariz. App. 370, 403 P.2d 305 (1965); Barrenberg v. Boston, 137 Mass. 231 (1884).

18. See also R. v. Burdett, 4 B & Ald. 95, 124 (1820); Bogardus v. Trinity Church, 4 Sandf. Ch. 633, 744 (N.Y. 1847).

§ 4-3(C)(3). Subsequent Defects.

Road defects existing after the alleged crash may be admitted for the proposition that they existed before[19] and/or at the time of[20] the instant crash,[21] provided no change in relevant conditions has taken place since the instant crash.[22]

Cases allowing evidence of road defects after the instant accident have ranged from subsequent time periods of a few hours or less,[23] a few days,[24] a few weeks[25] to over a year.[26] The crucial factor is that the defects be relevant to the road condition at the time of the crash, be relevant to the causal factors of the crash, and be essentially similar in surrounding circumstances.[27]

§ 4-3(D). Public Complaints.

Complaining letters from motorists about the facility written prior to the plaintiff's injuries are evidence of notice. Such complaints were admissible in *State v. Thompson,* 385 N.E.2d 198 (Ind. App. 1979) and similar

---

19. On the theory of notice.

20. On the theories of causation and dangerous nature of the place.

21. 2 Wigmore, *Evidence,* § 437, at 514.

22. Tuckel v. City of Hartford, 118 Conn. 334, 172 A. 222 (1934); Commonwealth v. Billings, 97 Mass. 405, 407 (1867); Thayer v. Thayer, 101 Mass. 111, 113 (1869); Broderick v. City of New York, 255 A.D. 875, 7 N.Y.S.2d 809 (1938).

23. DeCarion v. Washington, 36 N.Y.S.2d 93 (1942); Fuller v. Jackson, 92 Mich. 197, 52 N.W. 1075 (1892).

24. Link v. Philadelphia & R.R., 165 Pa. 75, 30 A. 820, 822 (1895); Herrick v. Town of Holland, 83 Vt. 502, 77 A. 6 (1910).

25. Gauss v. Carducci, 37 Ill. App. 2d 181, 185 N.E.2d 285 (1962); Williams v. City of Lansing, 152 Mich. 169, 115 N.W. 961 (1908).

26. Big Apple Super Markets of Peachtree, Inc. v. W.J. Milner & Co., 111 Ga. App. 282, 141 S.E.2d 567 (1965).

27. Dean v. Town of Sharon, 72 Conn. 667, 45 A. 963 (1900); Bailey v. City of Centerville, 108 Iowa 20, 78 N.W. 831 (1899).

cases. Many highway departments and other large corporate defendants routinely collect such complaints and they have a devastating impact on the jury.

Conversely, the defendant can cite the lack of such prior complaints as evidence it lacked notice. See *Clarke v. Michals,* 4 Cal. App. 3d 364, 84 Cal. Rptr. 507 (1970). In *Clarke,* the evidence was that no prior complaint about ice on the bridge at issue had ever been received by the city prior to the time the plaintiff's vehicle skidded on that ice. No representative of the city was aware that the bridge was in an icy condition on the day of the accident until after the accident had taken place. This established that the city was not liable for having failed to take measures to protect against icy conditions on the bridge. The lack of knowledge again proved a formidable defense. No defendant will be required in negligence law to defend against dangers it did not, in the exercise of due care, know of.

§ 4-3(E). Internal Recommendations.

Recommendations to improve the facility from the defendant's own personnel may amply establish the defendant's actual notice of defects. A large construction or manufacturing project may receive input from many different sources, particularly if outside contractors and/or federal funds are involved. The final decisions implemented usually strike a balance somewhere between maximum safety and minimum cost expense. The defendant's files, as in the civil Ford Pinto cases, may memorialize the opinions of "inside" experts who put the defendant on notice that the balance had swung too far away from safety considerations. Such recommendations were admissible in *Travelers Ins. Co. v. Eviston,* 110 Ind. App. 143, 37 N.E.2d 310 (1941) and *Ohio & M. Ry. v. Stein,* 133 Ind. 243, 31 N.E. 180 (1892).

In *Copeland v. Louisiana Dep't of Transp. & Dev.,* 428 So. 2d 1251 (La. App. 1983), the State was held liable for injuries caused by a defective intersection because the state had determined those defects existed, and had prepared corrective plans, several years previously.

It should also be noted that a defendant admits the need for an improvement once it orders that improvement, and due care must be exercised by the defendant to secure the effectuation of such an improvement within a reasonable time. Thus, in *Grof v. State,* 337 N.W.2d 345 (Mich. App. 1983), the State, which had prepared and approved work authorization in December of 1974 calling for installation of four-way stop signs at intersection, was liable for injuries and death arising from intersectional automobile collision in September of 1975, prior to installation of signs. Although already controlled, the intersection sustained a high incidence of severe injury accidents prior to collision, and the State gave no reason for delay in installation of signs.

§ 4-3(F). Reputation of the Road.

The defendant, as part of the community, may be held to actual or constructive notice of the fact a road area has a terrible and dangerous reputation under Wigmore's formulation that: "The reputation of the place or machine, and the fact that its dangerousness or the existence of the defect was reputed or generally talked about would be relevant as showing the probable carrying of information by someone to the person charged." 2 Wigmore, *Evidence,* § 252, at pp. 76-77.

Supporting Wigmore, the Court held in *Chase v. City of Lowell,* 151 Mass. 422, 426, 24 N.E. 212 (1890) that:

> [T]he fact that [the highway defect] was generally talked about in the community is a circumstance which may properly be considered. In such a case,

> notoriety derives its force as evidence, not merely from its suggestion that the defect was of such a kind that the authorities would have been likely to discover it in the first instance with their own eyes, but quite as much from the probability that their attention would have been brought by others to a matter which was generally talked about and in which they were interested.

See also *Chicago & A. Ry. v. Shannon,* 43 Ill. 338 (1867) (admitting reputation of the unsafeness of a boiler).

§ 4-4. Notice of Plaintiff.

Drivers and pedestrians, even if they are familiar with streets and sidewalks containing defects, need not memorize the precise location of danger spots and are not guilty of contributory fault merely because they do not avoid such dangers. *Claytor v. Durham,* 417 A.2d 1196, 273 Pa. Super. 571 (1980).

It is also highly foreseeable to defendants that drivers and pedestrians will be thinking and talking about other things as they travel, or will become lulled by travel into a condition called "road hypnosis", and will not pay precise attention to where they are at any particular moment.

California Accord: *Barrett v. City of Claremont,* 41 Cal. 2d 70, 256 P.2d 977 (1953). In a lawsuit for negligent road maintenance, a plaintiff, who cannot know that municipality had *actual* notice of the condition, may rely upon constructive notice imputed to the municipality by the passage of time. The rationale was that if the municipality had performed its duty of conducting a reasonable inspection for defects, it would have had actual knowledge of the existence of dangerous defect. This merely substitutes a slightly more "active" rationale for the usual "passive" reasoning for imputing constructive notice, namely, that the defect was just lying out there for so long that the defendant should have found it.

APPENDIX

HOW GOVERNMENTAL ENTITIES SHOULD USE CRASH DATA TO LOCATE PROBLEM ROAD AREAS

REFERENCE ONE:

EVALUATION OF CRITERIA FOR SAFETY IMPROVEMENTS ON THE HIGHWAY, Prepared by Roy Jorgensen and Associates for U.S. Dept. of Commerce, Bureau of Public Roads, Office of Highway Safety — 1966

PART 1: IDENTIFICATION OF HAZARDOUS LOCATIONS

° With the data presently available, hazardous locations — points, intersections, sections of highway — best can be determined by number of accidents as related to traffic volume exposure. This requires the determination of accident experience for all locations.

° Individual accidents should be identified accurately as to location to permit groupings of accidents by individual locations or segments of the highway.

° Accident data should be obtained over a sufficient period of time to insure statistical reliability. Analytical procedures should provide for measure statistical reliability.

° The most reliable methods currently in use for identifying hazardous locations are (1) the number-rate method, and (2) the rate quality-control method.

Methods of identifying hazardous locations should use criteria that measure both accident numbers and traffic volume exposure. Two methods, number-rate and rate quality-control, fulfill this requirement. If other methods of hazard identification, now in a developmental state, prove to be more effective they should be adopted.

In order to provide the necessary data for identifying hazardous locations, the accident records system should be established to provide (1) the number and accurate location of accidents, (2) traffic volumes at the locations, and (3) locality and highway features-urban land use and number of lanes.

RECOMMENDATION: To insure full utilization of hazardous location identification, a highway agency policy should be established which sets objectives, assigns responsibilities, and requires procedures to be developed for (1) field investigation of identified locations, (2) selection of possible hazard-reducing improvements, and (3) cost-effectiveness analysis. (PAGE V NOTE # 1)

REFERENCE TWO:

"HIGHWAY GEOMETRIC DESIGN CONSISTENCY RELATED TO DRIVER EXPECTANCY" Volume II Research Report — April 1981 — Final Report, by C. Messer, J. Mounce, R. Brackett, of Texas A & M Research Foundation, Published April 1981, Published by Federal Highway Administration.

Traffic engineers in most states collect accident records by highway locations. If the accidents for a given site become too numerous, that site is examined by design engineers to determine if the design is faulty. (PAGE 28 NOTE # 4)

REFERENCE THREE:

SAFETY DESIGN AND OPERATIONAL PRACTICES FOR STREETS AND HIGHWAYS — MAY, 1980. Published by U.S. Department of Transportation and Federal Highway Administration. Prepared by Texas Institute — N.J. Rowan & D.L. Woods

---

The Highway Safety Improvement program for each state shall consist of three components:

° PLANNING

° IMPLEMENTATION

° EVALUATION

The planning component consists of:

° A process for collecting and maintaining a record of accident, traffic and highway data,

° A process for analyzing available data to identify highway locations of features determined to be hazardous on the basis of accident experience or potential,

° A process for conducting engineering studies of hazardous locations and features to develop proposed highway safety improvements, and

° A process for establishing priorities for implementing proposed safety improvements.

The implementation component consists of a process for programming and implementing safety improvements.

The evaluation component consists of a process for determining the effect that safety improvements have in reducing the number and severity of accidents and potential accidents. To be included in this process are:

° The cost of, and the safety benefits derived from, the various means and methods used to mitigate or eliminate hazards,

° A record of accident experience before-and-after the implementation of safety improvement, and

° A comparison of accident number, rates and severity observed after the implementation of a safety improvement had not been made. (PAGE 2.1-2 NOTE # 3)

REFERENCE FOUR:

SAFETY DESIGN AND OPERATIONAL PRACTICES FOR STREETS AND HIGHWAYS — MAY, 1980. Published by U.S. Department of Transportation and Federal Highway Administration. Prepared by Texas Institute — N.J. Rowan & D.L. Woods

---

2.1.36 Use of Accident Data

Currently, federal policy requires that identification of hazardous locations be based on analysis of accident experience. Four different analysis techniques commonly are used:

° Number of accidents method (frequency)

° Rate of accidents method

° Number-rate method

° Rate-quality control method (PAGE 2.1-3 NOTE # 4)

REFERENCE FIVE:

HANDBOOK OF HIGHWAY SAFETY DESIGN AND OPERATING PRACTICES — 1978. Published by U.S. Department of Transportation and Federal Highway Administration.

One critical problem is to isolate those sections of highway which have unusually high accident rates compared to the rest of the system. (PAGE — INTRODUCTION NOTE # 1)

REFERENCE SIX:

TRAFFIC ENGINEERING THEORY AND PRACTICE

Louis J. Pignataro (1973)

Complete accident records are essential to analyzing accidents and planning accident prevention measures through engineering, education and enforcement. (PAGE 275 NOTE # 13)

Reporting accurate locations of accidents is essential for later studies of high accident locations and the implementation of remedial action. (PAGE 276 NOTE # 14)

ACCIDENTS AND CHARACTERISTICS OF TRAFFIC OPERATION AND HIGHWAY DESIGN FEATURES. To plan any kind of corrective measures related to traffic regulations and operation and physical features of roadways, it is essential for engineers to understand the relationship between highway design features, operating characteristics, and accident occurrence. (PAGE 282 NOTE # 17)

TRAFFIC ACCIDENT RATES. Since accident reporting laws and their interpretations differ widely, it is usually necessary to confine comparisons between cities or states to traffic fatalities. Within an area where reporting is uniform, a traffic accident rate may be based separately on deaths or injuries or on a combination of deaths and injuries. Total accidents may also be used, but care must be taken when injuries or property damage accidents are used to be certain that reporting is comparable. Computation of any of these rates will reflect the accident exposure of an entire area. (PAGE 278 NOTE # 15)

Accident statistics are normally compiled on a yearly basis, but analysis is required more often if remedial measures are to be effective. (PAGE 281 NOTE # 16)

CHAPTER 5

CAUSES OF ACTION—WHO TO SUE AFTER A CRASH

§ 5-1. Ownership of the Road.

Assuming that you represent parties who have sustained serious injuries in a crash on a negligently designed, constructed, or maintained transportation facility, you must still be careful to sue the proper governmental body responsible for the negligence you allege. Failure to serve the proper defendant with notice of claim or complaint within the required time period may constitute professional negligence and will certainly do your case no good.

The meticulous care plaintiffs must use in joining the appropriate defendant was demonstrated in *Dixon v. City of Chicago,* 101 Ill. App. 3d 453, 428 N.E.2d 542 (1981), where the case turned on the difference between "streets," "sidewalks," and "curbs." In *Dixon* the plaintiff was a pedestrian injured on a defective curb. The plaintiff sued defendant city for negligent maintenance of defective "streets and sidewalks." The court awarded summary judgment to the defendant because, even if the defendant's "streets and sidewalks" were defective, the accident was caused by a defective "curb," and at this location the "curbs" were under the maintenance jurisdiction of the State of Illinois.

Similarly, in *Tunk v. Village of Willow Springs,* 120 Ill. App. 3d 800, 458 N.E.2d 1132 (1983), the defendant village was awarded summary judgment because the plaintiff sued it for negligent maintenance of a road within the maintenance jurisdiction of the state.

The moral of the story is clear: be sure you find out the defendant responsible for the negligence you allege caused the plaintiff's injury. For defense lawyers the converse is true: make sure when you receive a notice of claim or complaint that your client was in fact responsible for the defect that the plaintiff alleges caused the crash.[1]

It can be that two defendants will share jurisdiction and responsibility for a given road defect. In such cases great

---

1. *California Accord:* Avey v. County of Santa Clara, 257 Cal. App. 2d 708, 65 Cal. Rptr. 181 (1968), held that city and county could not be held liable for dangerous conditions of shrubbery on state controlled road island.

Florida Accord: County's adoption of master plan for control of traffic in both unincorporated and incorporated areas of county relieved other governmental entities of responsibility for damages resulting from faulty or defective traffic control devices. Jaramillo v. City of Coral Cables, 436 So. 2d 1087 (Fla. App. 1983).

Michigan Accord: Contracts to do maintenance work cannot supplant the legal responsibility for maintenance, commonly called "maintenance foundation." Thus, where the state had statutory jurisdiction over all state trunkline highways, the State, rather than the city, therefore was the proper party to respond in damages for the death of a motorist on the highway. Beyer v. Fraternal Order of Eagles, 333 N.W.2d 314 (Mich. App. 1983). See also Phardel v. State, 120 Mich. App. 806, 328 N.W.2d 108 (1982).

New York Accord: A school was not liable for injuries sustained by a motorcyclist, who was struck by a vehicle exiting from school driveway. There was no evidence that school obstructed highway or interfered with its use. Matthews v. Scotia-Glenville School Sys., 94 A.D.2d 912, 463 N.Y.S.2d 629 (1983); Pontonero v. DaPrano, 24 A.D.2d 546, 261 N.Y.S.2d 425 (1965). Where a county had maintenance jurisdiction of that portion of a road in a town, the town was not liable for damage from an accident resulting from improper maintenance; Burcroff v. County of Orleans, 114 Misc. 2d 16, 450 N.Y.S.2d 651 (1982) — Town may not be

care must be taken to sue the proper defendant under an appropriate theory. In *Hodges v. City of Winter Park,* 433 So. 2d 1257 (Fla. App. 1983), for example, where the city may have negligently constructed a manhole and the county may have negligently uncovered it during construction work, the Court held factual negligence issues precluded summary judgment for either entity. Again, in *Ingram v. Howard-Needles-Tammen & Bergendoff,* 234 Kan. 289, 672 P.2d 1083 (1983), a truck driver killed in an accident caused by hole in turnpike bridge was entitled to recover from the turnpike authority and from consulting engineers that performed annual inspection.

§ 5-2. Possible Causes of Action.

The following sections list possible causes of action that may arise out of a crash. In general, of course, any person of entity involved, from the designer of the road to the rescue ambulance team, may be liable for a failure to use due care. The plaintiffs' lawyer must ensure through appropriate pre-filing investigation that the defendants joined were, in fact, guilty of negligence. Crashes that took place despite a party's best efforts to prevent them are not negligence cases and should not be brought.[2] On the other hand, any party guilty of action or inaction making crashes reasonably foreseeable may validly be joined as a defendant.[3]

held liable for damages arising out of defective condition of county road. The town did not maintain, inspect, repair or pave the road, and the town did not owe the county any duty to advise it of a defect in the road.

2. Sech v. Rogers, 6 Ohio St. 3d 462, 453 N.E.2d 705 (1983). A driver was not liable for death of county employee who was struck in chest by piece of guardrail while working on removal of guardrails on side of highway.

3. *Roadside Object Placement:* Billboard advertiser, Phillip Morris Co., held liable for negligently placing a billboard where it would block the view of motorists driving out of defendant's store premises, thereby

In *Karle v. Cincinnati Street Ry.*, 69 Ohio App. 327, 43 N.E.2d 762 (1942), a plaintiff motorist was allowed to sue both a city and a street car company for injuries sustained

---

making crashes foreseeable. Gordon v. Phillip Morris, Inc., Vermont, Chittenden County Superior Court Ho. S 797-82, Oct. 24, 1983, reported at 27 A.T.L.A. L. Rep. 113.

California Court holds telephone company liable to user of telephone booth for harm resulting from negligent placing of booth too close to major roadway, thereby foreseeably increasing risk from drunken driver veering off pavement and into telephone booth. Bigbee v. Pacific Tel. & Tel. Co., 192 Cal. Rptr. 857, 665 P.2d 947 (1983).

Note in the New Hampshire cases of Vanasee v. New England Tel. & Tel. and Exeter-Hampton Elec. Co., New Hampshire, Strafford County Superior Court Civil No. 11-578, June 11, 1981, reported in 25 A.T.L.A. L. Rep. 151-52, a utility company was held negligent for placing a utility pole near the travelled roadway in an area where it was foreseeable that vehicles would leave the road at night and hit the negligently mis-positioned, unlighted, and unmarked utility pole. Expert testimony under the National Electric Safety Code required that utility poles shall be placed and installed and maintained so as to make the pole safe "as far as practicable." Case held that the obligation of utilities under the code in the placement of poles may well require a searching out for more effective precautions than those already in place. The section from the National Electric Safety Code is actually called the "American National Standard National Electric Safety Code (1973 Edition) Sections 21, 211. It states "all electric supply communication lines and equipment shall be installed and maintained so as to reduce hazards to life as far as practicable."

NOTE: This relates to a recent Massachusetts case where an electric utility company was held liable for negligently erecting an uncrashworthy electric light pole in a busy shopping area having reason to know that the pole was insufficiently resistant to withstand foreseeable and expectable low velocity impacts from cars. The Court held in the Massachusetts case that defendant would have to make the pole more resistant to foreseeable future crashes. Bernier v. Boston Edison Co., 403 N.E.2d 391 (Mass. 1980). See also Gibson v. Garcia, 216 P.2d 119 (Cal. App. 1950), where a transit company maintaining a defective pole along a highway was held liable to a pedestrian injured when the unsafe pole rotted out by termites was struck by a negligent motorist and fell on plaintiff.

when his automobile struck tracks negligently constructed by both defendants. Again, in *Lattea v. City of Akron,* 9 Ohio App. 3d 118, 458 N.E.2d 868 (1982) the state supervisors and inspectors for bridge repair project, knew or should have known of the risk that a sidewalk would collapse when reinforcement bars were cut. The state had the power to protect the public by stopping the negligent contractor's work until adequate safety precautions were taken, but failed to do so. The state was therefore in pari delicto with the contractor in the actual commission of his negligence. The plaintiff could therefore recover for injuries caused by the contractor's negligence from both the contractor and from the state that should have found and corrected that negligence.

§ 5-2(A). The Emergency Vehicle.

When an emergency vehicle is involved in a crash, the governmental entity responsible for that vehicle, as well as its crew, is not necessarily immune from suit.

Police and emergency vehicles on an emergency call may proceed past a red light or stop signal, but only after slowing down as may be required for safe operation. The vehicle must proceed with due regard for the safety of all persons. *Mayfield v. City of Springfield,* 103 Ill. App. 3d 1114, 432 N.E.2d 617 (1982).

Obscuring vegetation on adjoining ground: Morales v. Costa, 427 So. 2d 297 (Fla. App. 1983).

Medical prescriptions: Texas Court of Appeals holds that a person injured in a crash may sue the driver's doctor for failure to warn him that one of the effects of prescribed drug, Quaaludes, might be a foreseeable decrease in the driver's ability to control his vehicle. Gooden v. Tips, 651 S.W.2d 364 (Tex. App. 1983).

Vehicle Air Wakes: In Marks v. Mobil Oil Corp., 562 F. Supp. 759 (E.D. Pa. 1983), the jury held that a large oil tanker going at an excessive speed created a negligently induced air wake that pushed plaintiff's small Volkswagen Beetle off the road injuring plaintiff.

Malfunctioning signals make crashes foreseeable. Williams v. State Hwy. Dep't, 44 Mich. App. 51, 205 N.W.2d 200 (1972).

§ 5-2(B). Adjoining Owners.

If your client, at the moment he or she earns the right to be the "plaintiff," is in a vehicle that leaves the road at a place where such action is foreseeable and crashes into an obstacle alongside the road, an action may lie against the owner of the land adjoining the road where the obstacle was located. *Morales v. Costa,* 427 So. 2d 297 (Fla. App. 1983). (Landowner whose tree obscured stop sign liable for crash.)

One criteria for such an action is that it must have been reasonably foreseeable that vehicles would leave the road where your client's vehicle did. Without this foreseeability (which can be established, among other things, by prior crashes or engineering studies by your expert) the court may hold that neither the party responsible for the road, nor the party responsible for the shoulder and surrounding area, breached any duty to your client. *Hoffman v. Vernon Twp.,* 97 Ill. App. 3d 721, 423 N.E.2d 519, 522 (1981). On this issue, the *Hoffman* court stated:

> Also pertinent is section 368 of the Restatement (Second) of Torts, which states the general rule of law applicable to factual situations similar to this one, involving artificial conditions near a highway:
>
> A possessor of land who creates or permits to remain thereon an excavation or other artificial condition so near an existing highway that he realizes or should realize that it involves an unreasonable risk to others accidentally brought into contact with such condition while traveling with reasonable care upon the highway, is subject to liability for physical harm thereby caused to persons who
>
> (a) are traveling on the highway, or
>
> (b) foreseeably deviate from it in the ordinary course of travel. (Restatement (Second) of Torts § 368 (1965).)
>
> The official comments to the Restatement further illustrate the applicability of this rule:

[The rule] applies also to those who reasonably and expectably deviate from the highway and enter upon the abutting land in the ordinary course of travel. The possessor is required to anticipate the possibility of such deviations and to realize, where a reasonable man would do so, that the traveler so deviating may encounter danger. The public right to use the highway carries with it the right to protection by reasonable care against harm suffered in the course of deviations which may be regarded as the *normal incidents of travel.* (emphasis added) (Restatement (Second) of Torts § 368, comment e, at 269-70 (1965).)

In determining where the condition is one which creates an unreasonable risk of harm to persons lawfully traveling on the highway and deviating from it, the essential question is whether it is so placed that travelers may be expected to come in contact with it in the course of a deviation reasonably to be anticipated in the ordinary course of travel. Distance from the highway is frequently decisive, since those who deviate in any normal manner in the ordinary course of travel cannot reasonably be expected to stray very far. . . . Distance is important, however, only as it affects the recognizable risk; and other factors, such as the nature of the condition itself, its accessibility and the extent and character of the use of the highway, must be taken into account. Restatement (Second) of Torts § 368, comment h, at 271 (1965).

Note that the same doctrine may place the duty to maintain reasonably safe ingress to and egress from another person's property or adjoining owners. Thus, in Laufenberg v. Golab, 108 Ill. App. 3d 133, 438 N.E.2d 1238 (1982), the court stated:

It is correct, as plaintiff urges as a matter of law, that the duty of the owner of property may be extended by the facts in a particular case so as to require the furnishing of reasonably safe means of ingress and egress to invitees. This is carefully expressed in cases such as *McDonald v. Frontier Lanes, Inc.* (1971), 1 Ill.App.3d 345, 272 N.E.2d 369. There, plaintiff was a patron of a tavern. She was injured in attempting to leave. She left the exit door and crossed a sidewalk

> between parked cars. She fell as a result of stepping into an artificial hole in the parkway. As pointed out by this court, there is a legal duty to provide invitees "with reasonably safe means of ingress and egress" and "within limitations dictated by the facts of the case, beyond the precise boundaries of such premises." 1 Ill.App.3d 345, 351, 272 N.E.2d 369.

The citator leads us to *Harris v. Union Stock Yard & Transit Co. of Chicago* (1975), 29 Ill. App. 3d 1072, 331 N.E.2d 182. This case states the same rule and uses the same language (29 Ill. App. 3d 1072, 1076, 331 N.E.2d 182):

> Plaintiff has alleged that defendants owed him a duty to provide a safe means for him to travel from the Amphitheatre to his automobile after completing work on February 8 1969. Defendant Union agrees that there is a duty to provide an invitee with a reasonably safe means of ingress and egress, both within the premises owned or controlled by the inviter, and, within limitations dictated by the facts of the case, beyond the precise boundaries of the premises. [Citations.]
>
> The important language to be noted there is that "the facts of the case" dictate the extent of the duty "beyond the precise boundaries of the premises." 438 N.E.2d at 1240-41.

Ohio: *Hay v. Norwalk Lodge No. 730,* B.P.O.E., 92 Ohio App. 14, 109 N.E.2d 481 (1951) held that the owner of property adjoining a rural road does not have to inspect his trees and vegetation to determine whether they are a threat to motorists on the road. However, an adjoining owner who acquires knowledge, either actual or constructive, of a condition of his plants which may result in injury to a traveler must exercise reasonable care to correct that danger.

Texas: Owner or occupant of premises abutting highway has a duty to exercise reasonable care not to endanger safety of people using highway as means of travel. An adjoining owner or occupant is liable for any injury that proximately results from his negligence, and attempted delegation of this duty to an independent contractor does not relieve the owner or occupant of liability for his own negligence. *Alamo Nat'l Bank v. Kraus,* 616 S.W.2d 908 (Tex. 1981).

Do not lose sight of the fact that the entity responsible for maintaining the road may have a duty, in the exercise of due care, to warn of dangers on adjoining property reasonably posing a danger to motorists on the road itself.[4]

---

4. The engineering warrants for the road maintenance entity removing or warning of reasonably foreseeable danger on the adjoining property go back at least to the work *Highway Design and Operational Practices Related to Highway Safety,* published by AASHO in 1967, popularly referred to by engineers as "the 1967 Yellow Book," which stated, at pages 1 and 2 that:

> An intensive crash program to remove roadside hazards on existing streets and highways and to engineer the roadsides of new facilities with safety as a major criterion should have a paramount place in the highway program of each State. Only in this way will the motorist who inadvertently leaves the traveled way have adequate protection against death or injury.
>
> . . . .
>
> To increase safety when vehicles leave the pavement, a clear recovery area, free of physical obstruction, should be provided along the roadway 30 feet or more from the edge of the traveled way in rural areas. Corrective programs should be undertaken at once to eliminate from the roadside or to relocate to protected positions such hazardous fixed objects as trees, drainage structures, massive sign supports, utility poles, and other ground-mounted obstructions that are now exposed to traffic. Where this is impracticable, an adequate guardrail or other type of protection should be provided.
>
> . . . .
>
> The use of appurtenances along the roadside must be reviewed continually to minimize the number of such objects that can be struck by vehicles. Each jurisdiction should periodically review its signing and retain only the essential signs. The continuing demands for additional nonessential highway signs must be firmly resisted.

While the duty of a governmental entity to maintain its road is

§ 5-2(C). The Road Contractor.

If your client is involved in a crash on an area of road under construction, remember many statutes impose strict liability on contractors who violate their provisions. Ill. Rev. Stat. ch. 121, § 314.1 *et seq.* (1981); *Binge v. J.J. Borders Constr. Co.,* 95 Ill. App. 3d 238, 419 N.E.2d 1237 (1981); *Vegich v. McDougal Hartmann Co.,* 84 Ill. 2d 461, 419 N.E.2d 918 (1981); and *Dodson v. Shaw,* 113 Ill. App. 3d 1063, 448 N.E.2d 188 (1983).

The contractor also has a nondelegable[5] common law duty to "protect the traveling public from dangerous conditions created by its construction activities." *Dodson v. Shaw, supra,* at 448 N.E.2d 192-93.[6]

---

distinct from the duty of the adjoining owner to maintain his property, Piearski v. Club Overlook Estates, Inc., 281 Pa. Super. 162, 421 A.2d 1198 (1980), many cases impose the duty upon the entity charged with road maintenance responsibility to remove or warn of adjoining hazards. Janssen v. City of Springfield, 79 Ill. 2d 435, 404 N.E.2d 213 (1980) (dangerous adjoining road); Briggs v. State, 14 Cal. App. 3d 489, 92 Cal. Rptr. 433 (1971); Armas v. Metropolitan Dade County, 429 So. 2d 59 (Fla. App. 1983) (adjoining foliage blocking vision on road); Marinelli v. Montour R.R., 278 Pa. Super. 403, 420 A.2d 603 (1980) (governmental entities responsible for making road reasonably safe must abate dangerous conditions existing on private lands abutting the highways); Frangis v. Duquesne Light Co., 122 P.L.J. 197 (Pa. Com. Pl. 1974), aff'd, 335 A.2d 796, 232 Pa. Super. 420 (1975). Possessors of land near a highway have a duty not to create or permit an artificial condition to exist which can reasonably be foreseen to involve an unreasonable risk to others accidentally brought in contact with such condition.

5. The contractor's duty to use reasonable care, like the governmental entities, is non-delegable:

Pennsylvania: Walsh v. City of Pittsburgh, 379 Pa. 229, 108 A.2d 769 (1954). Street contractor liable for negligence of a watchman it hired to warn of excavation.

6. Boyer v. Tenn Tom Constructors, 702 F.2d 609 (5th Cir. 1983). A driver was injured when his vehicle struck a road contractor's machine. The driver was allowed to invoke the road work contract requiring the contractor to use reasonably necessary precautions in its work. Leija v.

Contractors or private designers may also have been retained by governmental entities to design or inspect road areas, and liability may attach for their failure to use due care. *Ingram v. Howard-Needles-Tammer & Bergendoff,* 234 Kan. 289, 672 P.2d 1083 (1983). Often, this rule creates conflicting claims or defenses between contractors.[7] Governmental knowledge or approval of the defect

---

Materne Bros., 34 Wash. App. 825, 664 P.2d 527 (1983).

Florida Accord: The same common law duty of reasonable care attaches to contractors concerning road areas they build and then leave behind. Note Echols v. Hammett Co., Florida, Palm Beach County Circuit Court No. 78-4039, Nov. 14, 1983, reported at 27 A.T.L.A. L. Rep. 114. In Echols, the plaintiff was injured in a crash he did not remember. He was allowed, under hypnosis, to testify that his car hit a bump, went off the road, and was not allowed to get back on the road from the shoulder because of a drop-off between the road and shoulder. Plaintiff then brought in engineers and reconstruction experts to establish that the road contractor who worked on that road section used inadequate stabilizing material which caused the rate of soil erosion on the shoulder to accelerate. There were no witnesses who remembered the crash, and due to heavy vegetation, easy detection of the defect had not been possible. See also Higgs v. Holland Paving Co., 438 So. 2d 112 (Fla. App. 1983).

Massachusetts Accord: Catania v. Town of Barnstable, 3 Mass App. 321, 329 N.E.2d 140 (1975). The plaintiff motorist was driving down road which was being repaired. She came to a spot where the pavement had been removed. As her wheels struck the drop caused by the removal of the pavement, she ran off the road and struck a tree. The court sustained a verdict in favor of motorist against the construction company which had not placed any warning signs at the point where the pavement was removed.

7. Evidence that excavating contractor, whose contract required it to temporarily pave site, failed to do so. Asphalt paving contractor, whose contract required permanent paving of site, was delayed in commencing performance by weather conditions. The record was sufficient to impose full liability on excavating contractor and to absolve asphalt contractor for injuries sustained by party who fell in hole in roadway. Ashkinazy v. City of New York, 98 A.D.2d 737, 469 N.Y.S.2d 437 (1983).

may immunize the contractor.[8]

The duty to design, construct, or maintain a road is nondelegable, and the governmental entity charged with that duty is therefore negligent when a contractor it has hired to perform such a function fails to use due care, rendering the road unsafe. *Van Arsdale v. Hollinger,* 68 Cal. App. 2d 245, 437 P.2d 508, 66 Cal. Rptr. 20 (1968).[9]

Florida: *Dickerson, Inc. v. Buckley,* 261 So. 2d 570 (Fla. 1972). A driver involved in an intersection collision sued a paving contractor, alleging the contractor had removed a controlling stop sign. The action was lost because the plaintiff could not prove the contractor had removed the sign.

---

8. *Florida:* Contractor, which constructed road and which was sued, along with Department of Transportation, for damages sustained in accident allegedly caused by defect in road, was entitled to instruction to effect that contractor was not liable if Department was aware of defect. Echols v. Hammet Co., 423 So. 2d 923 (Fla. App. 1982).

Massachusetts: Mahoney v. Walter Reed Corp., 12 Mass. App. Dec. 80 (1956). In action for property damage to plaintiff's automobile which collided with an island dividing the highway, against the contractor who constructed the island under a contract with the Metropolitan District Commission, a public authority, the contractor was not negligent in failing to provide safety precautions, since at time of accident, the road had been opened to public use by the said Commission and the contractor was no longer in control and owed no duty to third persons using the way. Note, however, that contractor may not be immunized for following obviously unreasonable or defective plans, even if provided or approved by a governmental entity. Hunt v. Blasius, 74 Ill. 2d 203, 384 N.E.2d 368 (1978). In addition, the contractor may not be immunized if it fails to follow plans, even if the governmental entity responsible for the road negligently approves the work. Hunt v. Blasius, supra; Boddie v. Litton Unit Handling Sys., 118 Ill. App. 3d 520, 455 N.E.2d 142 (1983).

9. *Michigan Accord:* State, whose project engineer had duty of overseeing contractor and construction engineer, was liable for injuries sustained by driver who drove into roadway excavation which was not adequately marked. Phardel v. State, 120 Mich. App. 806, 328 N.W.2d 108 (1982).

Pennsylvania: *Serego v. C.W. Good, Inc.,* 193 F.2d 741 (3d Cir. 1952). A contractor improving a highway had a duty to post reasonably visible barricades, detour signs, lights or other warnings the road was closed.

Texas: In *Rash v. Ross,* 371 S.W.2d 109 (Tex. App. 1963), the court found that a Plaintiff motorist was contributorily negligent in driving to left of the center line, could not recover against a road construction contractor who had not provided warning signs, flares, and warning flags designating the proper path for traffic. Note that such a harsh ruling overlooks the fact bad roads can cause crashes, and can "create" driver fault. Note also that comparative negligence, which most states now have, would preclude such a harsh outcome.

§ 5-2(D). The Negligent or Reckless Vehicle Entruster.

Many states recognize a cause of action against persons and entities who improperly entrust motor vehicles to people who are incompetent and/or unfit drivers. This cause of action sounds in both negligence[10] and in wilful and wanton misconduct.[11]

---

10. *Negligent entrustment recognized:*

Illinois: Seward v. Griffin, 116 Ill. App. 3d 749, 452 N.E.2d 558 (1983).

Georgia: Evans v. Hyde Oldsmobile, Georgia, Cobb County State Court No. 82 A-3154, Nov. 29, 1983, reported at 27 A.T.L.A. L. Rep. 112.

Michigan: Worth v. Dortman, 94 Mich. App. 103, 288 N.W.2d 603 (1979). The basis of the theory of negligent entrustment is that an owner or lender of a motor vehicle has the duty not to put it in the control of a known unfit or incompetent driver, for operation on public highways. See also Monig v. Alfono, 400 Mich. 425, 254 N.W.2d 759 (1977).

Texas: Connor v. Dye Trucking Co., Texas, 219th Judicial District Court, No. 219-034-82, Dec. 12, 1983, reported at 27 A.T.L.A. L. Rep. 160.

11. *Wilful and wanton entrustment recognized:* Lockett v. Bi-State Transit Auth., 94 Ill. 2d 66, 445 N.E.2d 310 (1983).

The main difference between the two actions lies in how obvious it should have been to a "reasonable man" that the vehicle owner should not have entrusted the vehicle to the person who was driving it when the plaintiff was injured. On this issue, the plaintiff can introduce evidence of the driver's prior driving record and employment record.[12] Indeed, even one prior crash involving the driver is sufficient to raise the fact issue that the vehicle may have been wilfully and wantonly entrusted to him. *Burlington N.R.R. v. JMC Transport, Inc.,* 567 F. Supp. 389 (N.D. Ill. 1983).

Ohio: *Rogers v. Kazee,* 10 Ohio App. 3d 139, 460 N.E.2d 1149 (1983), held that liability for negligent entrustment arises from the act of entrusting a motor vehicle, with permission to operate the same, to one whose incompetency, inexperience or recklessness is known or should have been known by the owner. In Rogers, the defendant mother entrusted her car to her daughter. The mother had no reason to believe her daughter would allow her husband to operate the automobile while the husband was intoxi-

---

12. *Driver's past record admitted:*

District of Columbia: Defendant city liable for entrusting municipal garbage truck to a driver with 15 previous accidents, records of which came into evidence. Bernon v. District of Columbia, D.C. Superior Court No. 15190-81, May 9, 1983, cited in 26 A.T.L.A. L. Rep. 447.

Florida: Hernandez v. Alturas Packing Co., Florida, Polk County Circuit Court No. GCG 80-740, Nov. 21, 1980, at 24 A.T.L.A. L. Rep. 156.

Illinois: Lockett v. Bi-State Transit Auth., 94 Ill. 2d 66, 445 N.E.2d 310 (1983).

Michigan: Buschlen v. Ford Motor Co., 121 Mich. App. 113, 328 N.W.2d 592 (1982). To prove negligent entrustment, plaintiff must show that defendant knew or would have been on notice that entrustee was not to be trusted.

Texas: Connor v. Dye Trucking Co., Texas, 219th Judicial District Court, No. 219-034-82, Dec. 12, 1983, reported at 27 A.T.L.A. L. Rep. 160.

cated. There could, thus, be no liability imposed against the mother for negligent entrustment by the daughter.

Texas: The Court in *Garza v. Wirsing,* 604 S.W.2d 391 (Tex. App. 1980), found for a defendant charged with negligent entrustment when the defendant established he had not entrusted his vehicle to anyone, a classic defense to the negligent entrustment suit. See also *Green v. Texas Elec. Wholesalers, Inc.,* 651 S.W.2d 4 (Tex. App.), *reh'g denied,* 647 S.W.2d 1 (1982), which underscored the importance of the entrustment element of this cause of action. *Green* held that the basis of responsibility under the doctrine of negligent entrustment is an owner's own negligence in knowingly permitting his motor vehicle to come under the control of an incompetent or reckless driver. Note further, under Texas law for this cause of action, the case of *Fidelity & Guaranty Ins. Underwriters, Inc. v. McManus,* 633 S.W.2d 787 (Tex. 1982), which sets out other necessary elements.

§ 5-2(E). Interior and Exterior of Vehicle.

The work of Ralph Nader documented in *Unsafe At Any Speed* and the Ford Pinto droptank cases have created a substantial amount of public awareness that the vehicle manufacturer and distribution chain may be the basis for lawsuits if the vehicle behaves unusually, such as bursting into flames after a very soft "fender bender" tap. Similarly, the tire manufacturer can be sued if the tires burst or the mechanic who put the tires on could be liable if the tires fall off.

The possible causes of action that can be generated from the vehicle are not yet exhausted, however. Recent decisions, such as *Bean v. Volkswagenwerk Aktiengesellschaft,* 109 Ill. App. 3d 333, 440 N.E.2d 426, 428-29 (1982), require the interior of vehicles to be sufficiently crashworthy to prevent death or serious injury to the occupants of vehicles in a "second collision," which is "the collision between a passenger and an interior part of the vehicle following the initial impact" between two vehicles. As the *Bean* court pointed out, "Under this theory, the plaintiff does not allege that the particular design defect caused the accident. Rather, he alleges that the [interior] defect enhanced those injuries he would already have sustained by virtue of the initial impact." See also *MacCuish v. Volkswagenwerk,* A.G. Massachusetts, Middlesex County Superior Court No. 80-2586, March 15, 1984, 27 A.T.L.A. L. Rep. 203. (Volkswagen passenger sued vehicle manufacturer for aggravation of injuries caused when defective seat and window caused passenger to be ejected after low speed two-vehicle crash).

This modern jurisprudence undermines earlier decisions such as *Evans v. General Motors Corp.,* 359 F.2d 822 (7th Cir. 1966), which held that a manufacturer had no duty to provide for safety in the event of a collision. The Eighth Circuit, in *Larsen v. General Motors Corp.,* 391 F.2d 495 (8th Cir. 1968), took a position more in line with modern cases, requiring a manufacturer to provide a reasonably safe and "crashworthy" vehicle in which to travel.

The Seventh Circuit abandoned the *Evans* rule, and came into line with the *Larsen* rule in *Huff v. White Motor Corp.,* 565 F.2d 104 (7th Cir. 1977).

The issue then will be what level of proof the plaintiff must establish to show injuries caused or enhanced by the "second collision" with the vehicle interior. Obviously if the plaintiff cannot establish any injuries attributable to the second collision, he cannot sustain a case against the manufacturer for lack of crashworthiness. *Curtis v. General Motors Corp.,* 649 F.2d 808 (10th Cir. 1981). Most courts, however, merely require the plaintiff to show injuries "probably" caused or enhanced by the second collision. *Bean v. Volkswagenwerk Aktiengesellschaft, supra; Richardson v. Volkswagenwerk A.G.,* 552 F. Supp. 73 (W.D. Mo. 1982).

How, then, should the actual damages be apportioned between the first and second crashes? The correct rule is probably found in the *Restatement (Second) of Torts,* § 433B (1965), which provides:

> (2) Where the tortious conduct of two or more actors has combined to bring about harm to the plaintiff, and one or more of the actors seeks to limit his liability on the ground that the harm is capable of apportionment among them, the burden of proof as to the apportionment is upon each such actor.
>
> (3) Where the conduct of two or more actors is tortious, and it is proved that harm has been caused to the plaintiff by only one of them, but there is uncertainty as to which one has caused it, the burden is upon each such actor to prove that he has not caused the harm.

Cases applying this Restatement rule include *Smith v. Fiat-Roosevelt Motors, Inc.,* 556 F.2d 728 (5th Cir. 1977); *Seattle First Nat'l Bank v. Shoreline Concrete Co.,* 91 Wash. 2d 230, 588 P.2d 1308 (1978), and *Lahocki v. Contee Sand & Gravel Co.,* 398 A.2d 490 (Md. 1979). Indeed, the uniform rule of the cases is that each defendant who caused some of the plaintiff's damages is liable for all of those damages if he cannot apportion out the particular harm he alone caused. See *Mitchell v. Volkswagenwerk A.G.,* 669 F.2d 1199 (8th Cir. 1982), where the first and second impacts caused the plaintiff passenger to sustain the nonapportionable injury of paraplegia, for which both defendant driver and defendant car manufacturer were held fully liable.[13]

---

13. *Alabama Accord:* Edwards v. General Motors Corp., Alabama, Circuit Court of Jefferson County, Sept. 27, 1983, reported at 26 A.T.L.A. L. Rep. 392-93.

Massachusetts Accord: Elias v. Ford Motor Co., U.S. District Court for

§ 5-2(F). Emotional Injury.

In *Rickey v. Chicago Transit Auth.*, 98 Ill. 2d 546, 457 N.E.2d 1 (1983), the Illinois Supreme Court abolished the old Illinois rule requiring a physical impact before a plaintiff could sue for the negligent infliction of emotional harm. The new Illinois rule is this:

> The standard that we substitute for the one requiring contemporaneous injury or impact is the standard which has been adopted in the majority of jurisdictions where this question of recovery by a bystander for emotional distress has been examined. (See, *e.g.*, *Niederman v. Brodsky*) (1970), 436 Pa.Super. 401, 261 A.2d 84; *Owens v. Childrens Memorial Hospital* (8th Cir.1973), 480 F.2d 465 (applying Nebraska law); *Robb v. Pennsylvania R.R. Co.* (Del.1965), 210 A.2d 709; *Stadler v. Cross* (Minn.1980), 295 N.W.2d 552; *Tobin v. Grossman* (1969), 24 N.Y.2d 609, 301 N.Y.2d 609, 301 N.Y.S.2d 554, 249 N.E.2d 419; *Whetham v. Bismarck Hospital* (N.D.1972), 197 N.W.2d 678; *Shelton v. Russell Pipe and Boundary Co.* (Tenn.1978), 570 S.W.2d 861; *Guilmette v. Alexander* (1969), 128 Vt. 116, 259 A.2d 12.) That standard has been described as the zone-of-physical-danger rule. Basically, under it a bystander who is in a zone of physical danger and who, because, of the defendant's negligence, has reasonable fear for his own safety is given a right of action for physical injury or illness resulting from emotional distress. This rule does not require that the bystander suffer a physical impact or injury at the time of the negligent act, but it does require that he must have been in such proximity to the accident in which the direct victim was physically injured that there was a high risk to him of physical impact. 457 N.E.2d at 5.

---

the District of Mass., Civil Action No. 78-2609-Z, April 14, 1982, reported at 25 A.T.L.A. L. Rep. 204.

Michigan Accord: Bahlman v. Hudson Motor Car Co., 290 Mich. 683, 288 N.W. 309 (1939).

Third Circuit Accord: Seese v. Volkswagenwerk, 648 F.2d 833 (3d Cir. 1981).

New York cases are in accord with the Illinois standard. New York now allows persons in the zone of physical danger from a crash who watch it, to recover for emotional injuries they suffer from watching the crash — plaintiff mother and daughter who were within the zone of physical danger imperiled by a negligent driver were allowed to recover for emotional injuries from seeing that the defendant had struck and seriously injured their husband/father in his car. *Bovsum v. Sanperi* and *Kugle v. Mid-Westchester Indus. Park, Inc.,* both reported at 27 A.T.L.A. L. Rep. 0153.

Other jurisdictions reject the requirement plaintiffs alleging emotional injury prove they were within a zone of physical danger.

California: *Dillon v. Legg,* 68 Cal. App. 2d 728, 441 P.2d 912, 69 Cal. Rptr. 72 (1968).

Florida: Florida seems still to be following the old requirement of a physical impact before an action may be brought for emotional distress arising out of a crash. Thus, in *Cadillac Motor Div., Gen. Motors Corp. v. Brown,* 428 So. 2d 301 (Fla. App. 1983), there was no impact upon which damages for mental distress could be awarded. A judgment awarding damages for mental distress in favor of plaintiff was, therefore, reversed. In *Stewart v. Gilliam,* 271 So. 2d 466 (Fla. App. 1972), however, the court held that the plaintiff could recover for *physical* consequences of mental or emotional disturbances caused by a negligent act without a physical impact. The "impact rule" was rejected. putting *Stuart* and the *Cadillac Motor* cases together, and making due allowance for the fact *Cadillac Motor* was decided eleven years after *Stuart,* we find Florida allowing recovery for physical, but not mental injuries flowing from emotional distress caused by crashes where the plaintiff does not sustain a physical impact. Next, they'll be asking Florida lawyers to stack angels on pinheads!

Michigan: *Daley v. LaCroix,* 384 Mich. 4, 179 N.W.2d 390 (1970).

New Mexico: *Ramirez v. Armstrong,* 100 N.M. 538, 673 P.2d 822 (1983).

Ohio: Ohio will not allow recovery for emotional injury from crashes unless the plaintiff suffers a physical impact. *Paugh v. Hanks,* 6 Ohio St. 3d 72, 451 N.E.2d 759 (1983).

Pennsylvania: The Pennsylvania Supreme Court rejecting the zone of danger rule in allowing recovery for emotional distress for a mother who, from a vantage point of safety, sustained great emotional trauma from witnessing her daughter's death through the negligence of a defendant driver. *Sinn v. Burd,* 486 Pa. 146, 404 A.2d 672 (1979), cited in 22 A.T.L.A. L. Rep. 290. However, in *Banyas v. Lower Bucks Hosp.,* 293 Pa. Super. 122, 437 A.2d 1236 (1980). The Court held that under Section 436A of the Restatement (Second) of Torts governing negligence resulting in emotional disturbance, a negligent person is not liable when his conduct results in *emotional* trauma alone. Thus, the *Sinn v. Burd* decision and the *Banyas* decision put Pennsylvania law into the same gridlock on this issue that we saw earlier in Florida.

Texas: *Cavitt v. Jetton's Greenway Plaza Cafeteria,* 563 S.W.2d 319 (Tex. App. 1978), held that where an emotional shock results in an impairment of use or control of physical structures of the body, a compensable injury results. This inverts the old rule that a physical impact must precede and cause emotional harm. Here, the emotional shock precedes and causes the physical effect.

CHAPTER 6

PROXIMATE CAUSE ISSUES IN TRANSPORTATION FACILITY NEGLIGENCE CASES

§ 6-1. Introduction.

Causation in law is different from causation in the rest of the world. In a philosophical sense, everything is part of the cause of all that comes after it. Arnold Toynbee wrote, in *A Study of History* that the Peloponnesian War between Athens and Sparta doomed classic civilization, rendering inevitable the rise and fall of Rome, a causal relationship Gibbon overlooked in *The Decline and Fall.* Sartre denied that there could be innocent victims in war, because any soldier who did not desert was a cause of the subsequent harm done by and to him. The American Civil Rights movement summed all this up concisely with the truism that, "If you're not part of the solution, you're part of [and a cause of] the problem."

In law, cause becomes an issue of policy and not an instrument of factual analysis. The issue in law is whether, as a policy decision, the defendant should be held liable for the plaintiff's injuries, and the resolution of that issue in a crash case depends on whether the plaintiff's crash was a reasonably foreseeable result of the defendant's negligence.

Traffic crashes are often the result of many convergent streams of negligence. Thus, a two-car, head-on crash on a curving road may involve negligent driving by one or both drivers, negligent failure by the passengers (if any) to warn of dangers, negligent road design by engineers, and negligent failure by some governmental entity to sign, mark, and otherwise maintain the road. These factors are recognized by transportation engineering technology, which holds that, "It is seldom that an accident results from a single cause. There are usually several influences affecting the situation at any given time. These influences can be separated into three groups: the human element, the vehicle element, and the highway element."[1]

---

1. *A Policy on Geometric Design of Rural Highways,* p. 122 (AASHTO, 1965).

Due to the fact that crash cases usually involve complex interaction of multiple causal factors, the cases require far more mastery of proximate cause rules than simple recognition of the rule that "what is the proximate cause of an injury is ordinarily a question of fact to be determined by a jury from a consideration of all of the evidence."[2] This is because different jurisdictions have given wildly fluctuating interpretations to the complex fact issues in crash cases, usually using proximate cause as the filter through which disfavored fact patterns are dismissed out of the judicial system.[3]

Most jurisdictions now hold that any event that was a "substantial factor" in causing an event or any injury[4] is a

---

2. Davis v. Marathon Oil Co., 64 Ill. 2d 380, 356 N.E.2d 93 (1976).

3. Proximate cause formulations are the traditional sphincter through which the legal system eliminates cases where, as a policy matter, it would not be appropriate for liability to attach. As Prosser describes it, "proximate cause is merely the limitation which the courts have placed upon the actors' responsibility for the consequences of the actors' conduct. . . . As a practical matter, legal responsibility must be limited to those causes which are so closely connected with the result and of such significance that the law is justified in imposing liability. Some boundary must be set to liability for the consequences of any act, upon the basis of some idea of justice or policy." Keeton, Prosser and Keeton on Torts, at 264 (5th ed. 1984).

On the other hand, again as a policy matter, some jurisdictions use the proximate cause concept as a vehicle to extend liability, or at least make it easier to establish. New York does this by lowering the quantum of proof required to establish causation in a death case. Wingerter v. State, 58 N.Y.2d 848, 446 N.E.2d 776, 460 N.Y.S.2d 20 (1983).

4. Foreseeable harmful consequences are not insulated by "intervening" cause. In Central Union Tel. Co. v. Sokola, 34 Ind. App. 429, 73 N.E. 143 (1905), the defendant Telephone Co. negligently allowed its broken and insulated wires to remain on its poles for several months. Then the wires fell down on plaintiff for unknown reasons, killing him. Defendant argued that a prior storm was the proximate cause of the

legally relevant proximate cause of that event,[5] even if

death. The Court rejected this argument: "It is true the storm concurred to produce the injury, but appellant's prior negligence contributed to the injury, and this negligence cannot be said to be a remote cause, for the reason that whatever it did contribute it contributed at the time and place of the injury. The intervening storm and the defective condition of the wires were concurrent causes of the injury, and were both present and active in the result. . . . It is . . . not necessary . . . that the precise injury which in fact did occur should have been foreseen. It is sufficient if it was to be reasonably expected that injury might occur to some person engaged in exercising a legal right in an ordinarily careful manner." 73 N.E. at 145.

Note under Washington law, the case of Close v. Workman, Kitsap County Superior Court No. 80-0031-6, cited at 24 A.T.L.A. L. Rep. 354. A police officer who was injured when his police car was struck in the side by defendant's speeding car, developed chronic pain syndrome and depression after all other symptoms and injuries had been successfully removed by medical treatment. The chronic pain syndrome and resultant depression were sustained as elements of damages for which the jury could award compensation.

Florida: Gray v. Break, 440 So. 2d 1297 (Fla. App. 1983). In order to maintain a negligence tort action, plaintiff must show that injury or damage to plaintiff was proximately caused by defendant's failure to conform to a standard of conduct designed for the protection of others.

Stahl v. Metropolitan Dade County, 438 So. 2d 14 (Fla. App. 1983). But for the negligence or omission the injury would not have occurred is reasonably voiced when the sequence between the negligent act or omission and plaintiff's injury is direct and continuous.

Michigan: Abel v. Eli Lilly & Co., 418 Mich. 311, 343 N.W.2d 164 (1984) stated:

> This principle was also developed in Holloway v. General Motors Corp. (On Rehearing), 403 Mich. 614, 626, 628, 271 N.W.2d 777 (1978), in which the question arose whether a plaintiff in a products liability action must establish the specific cause of the defect among alternative possible causes. In that case, testimony showed that the break in a ball-joint assembly may have been due to a defect in design, material, assembly, or a combination of design and material. The Court found that greater specificity in identifying the defect was not required for two reasons: (1) the purpose of tort law is to compensate injured persons (not merely to deter the manufacture of a specific product defect, a goal which would place a premium on defect identification), and (2) plaintiff was not at fault in her inability to produce more specific evidence of the defect and had not been deficient in her duty to prove the particular defect by the most

5. Anderson v. Minneapolis, S.P. & S.S.M. Ry., 146 Minn. 430, 179

other things were also substantial factors, and therefore

accurate evidence reasonably available. The Court recognized that the situation was analogous to the theory of alternative liability expressed in Summers v. Tice, 403 Mich. 625, fn. 15, 271 N.W.2d 777.

Ohio: Strother v. Hutchinson, 67 Ohio St. 2d 282, 423 N.E.2d 467 (1981). Injury complained of must be foreseen or anticipated in order to be the result of a negligent act.

Baum v. Augenstein, 10 Ohio App. 3d 106, 460 N.E.2d 701 (1983). Trial court was wrong in directing a verdict in favor of a defendant where differences could occur on issue of proximate cause. The jury could reasonably conclude that defendant and another were concurrent tortfeasors.

Texas: Strakos v. Gehring, 360 S.W.2d 787 (Tex. 1962). All persons whose acts contributed to an injury are liable. One's negligence does not excuse the negligence of the other. Missouri Pac. R.R. v. American Statesman, 552 S.W.2d 99 (Tex. 1977). When a negligent act or omission is a factor in causing an injury is an element of proximate cause, means that the negligent act or omission was a substantial factor in bringing about the injury and without it no harm would have been incurred.

N.W. 45 (1920). Accord: Johnson v. Bender, 369 N.E.2d 936 (Ind. App. 1977); Tabor v. Continental Baking Co., 110 Ind. App. 633, 38 N.E.2d 257 (1941). Subsequent cases citing the general acceptance of the substantial factor test for proximate cause include: Carney v. Goodman, 38 Tenn. App. 55, 270 S.W.2d 572 (1954); Walton v. Blauert, 256 Wis. 125, 40 N.W.2d 545 (1949); New Orleans & N.E.R.R. v. Burge, 191 Miss. 303, 2 So. 2d 825 (1941); Dunham v. Village of Canisteo, 303 N.Y. 498, 104 N.E.2d 872 (1952); Edgecomb v. Great Atl. & Pac. Tea Co., 127 Conn. 488, 18 A.2d 364 (1941); Restatement (Second) of Torts, §§ 431, 433. See Note, 15 West. Res. L. Rev. 807 (1964).

Of the two terms, "substantial" is of more legal importance than "factor." Any road defect at a crash location may well have been a causal factor, and the real issue is whether the danger posed by the defect was foreseeable and grave enough to elevate it, as a matter of legal policy, to the level of a "substantial" factor. The resolution of this issue often depends upon how responsive the Court is to new legal causes of action, such as transportation facility negligence. "The question," Prosser emphasizes, "is primarily not one of causation, and never arises until causation has been established. It is rather one of the fundamental policy of the law, as to whether the Defendants' responsibility should

concurring proximate causes,[6] of that event. Road defects are therefore generally given to jury deliberations[7] as

---

extend to such results." Keeton and Prosser, *op. cit.,* at 280-81.

Thus, complex and changeable policy issues underlie the apparently immutable legal formulation that: "'Proximate cause' is that which, in a natural and continuous sequence, unbroken by an efficient intervening cause, produces the injury, and without which the result would not have occurred." Coyne v. Pittsburgh Rys., 393 Pa. 326, 141 A.2d 830 (1958).

6. "If the defendant's conduct was a substantial factor in causing the plaintiff's injury, it follows that he will not be absolved from liability merely because other causes have contributed to the result, since such causes, innumerable, are always present. In particular, however, each defendant who is not relieved of liability is also a contributing cause, and that person, too, is to be held liable. Thus where two vehicles collide and injure a bystander, or a passenger in one of them, each driver may be liable for the harm inflicted. The law of joint tortfeasors rests very largely upon recognition of the fact that each of two or more causes may be charged with a single result." Prosser and Keeton, *op. cit.* at 282.

California Accord: Harland v. State, 75 Cal. App. 3d 475, 142 Cal. Rptr. 201 (1977). The State is not exonerated from liability since it negligently maintained the highway in a dangerous condition and a third party negligently used the highway. The negligence of both parties was the proximate cause of injury.

Michigan Accord: Kirby v. Larson, 400 Mich. 585, 256 N.W.2d 400 (1977). There may be two or more proximate causes of injury which are actionable. Recovery is not limited to one proximate cause.

7. Proximate cause is a jury issue and courts should leave the jury decision undisturbed if there is even a reasonable doubt on the issue. Chicago I. & L.R.R. v. Carter, 149 Ind. App. 585, 274 N.E.2d 537 (1971).

It is for the jury to decide whether plaintiff has met his burden of proof. If either side has grounds for a proximate cause finding in their favor, then this issue must be decided by the jury.

Stevens v. Jefferson, 436 So. 2d 33 (Fla. 1983). The trier of fact must decide the foreseeability issue and whether an intervening cause is foreseeable.

Glover v. City of Houston, 590 S.W.2d 799 (Tex. 1979). The question for the jury to decide was whether the alleged negligence of city to properly maintain streets and to warn motorists of dangerous condition resulting therefrom was a proximate cause of injuries sustained by motorist.

possible causes, among other causes of crashes, unless the fact pattern of the crash is so unusual or bizarre that the Court, as a policy matter, will grant defendant summary judgment on the ground that this crash was not a foreseeable consequence[8] of the road defects.[9] Juries usually do,

---

Friedan v. Pan Tex Hotel Corp., 653 S.W.2d 365 (Tex. App. 1983). Question of law is when circumstances are such that reasonable minds could not arrive at different conclusion. Proximate cause is question of fact.

8. In determining whether intervening force is a superseding cause, the test is whether intervening conduct was so extraordinary as not to have been reasonably foreseeable, or whether it was reasonable to be anticipated. Bleman v. Gold, 431 Pa. 348 (1968).

East Tex. Theatres Inc. v. Rutledge, 453 S.W.2d 466 (Tex. 1970). (1) Cause-in-fact, a cause which produces an event and without which event would not have occurred; and (2) foreseeability, are essential elements of proximate cause.

Hart v. Van Zandt, 399 S.W.2d 791 (Tex. 1965). Whether natural and unbroken chain of events leads directly and proximately to reasonably foreseeable injury or result was set in motion by alleged negligence is the most important question for proximate cause.

9. The issue of whether a consequence should be held foreseeable enough for liability to attach to the defendants' negligence has raged since Palsgraf v. Long Island R.R., 248 N.Y. 339, 162 N.E. 99 (1928), and now fills entire libraries. See Dias, The Duty Problem in Negligence, 13 Camb. L. J. 198 (1955); Dias, The Breach Problem and the Duty of Care, 30 Tulane L. Rev. 377 (1956); Fleming, The Passing of Polemis, 39 Canadian Bar Rev. 489 (1961); Goodhart, The Imaginary Necktie and the Rule in Re Polemis, 68 Law Q. Rev. 514 (1952); Goodhart, Liability and Compensation, 76 Law Q. Rev. 567 (1960); Green, Foreseeability in Negligence Law, 61 Columbia Law Rev. 1401 (1961); Payne, The "Direct" Consequences of a Negligence Act, 5 Current Legal Problems 189 (1952); Payne, Foreseeability and Remoteness of Damage in Negligence, 25 Mod. L. Rev. 1 (1962); Williams, The Risk Principle, 77 Law Q. Rev. 179 (1961); Wilson and Slade, A Re-Examination of Remoteness, 15 Mod. L. Rev. 458 (1952); Wright, Re Polemis, 14 Mod. L. Rev. 393 (1951).

Perhaps because nobody really knows what "foreseeability" means, in the abstract, the virtually universal rule is that "questions of proximate

and should, decide these cases because defectively designed or maintained roads will foreseeably and predictably cause crashes.[10]

The proper analysis of proximate cause issues is essential at every level of a transportation facility negligence analysis if prohibitive expense is to be avoided and if necessary actions such as sending claim notices, are to be taken promptly. When the case is first referred to an attorney, for example, the issues should be subjected promptly to proximate cause filtering to determine whether the negligence of each target defendant could constitute a proximate cause of the crash.

Many otherwise excellent cases may be filtered out through this initial proximate cause screening. A recent referral, for example, involved a private corporation that designed guardrails for an elevated roadway in the late 1960's (when guardrail technology was largely experimental), a major governmental institution that installed and maintained the guardrails until the late 1970's and a plaintiff who sustained massive injuries in the late 1970's

---

cause are for the court only in plain and undisputed cases, and if there is any reasonable doubt as to proximate cause, it is a question of fact to be determined by the jury." Chicago, I. & L.R.R. v. Carter, 149 Ind. App. 585, 274 N.E.2d 537 (1971); Wroblewski v. Grand Truck W.R.R., 29 Ind. Dec. 277, 276 N.E.2d 567 (1971).

Indiana Accord: Under Indiana law, defendants who negligently create or maintain dangerous places will be held liable for foreseeable injuries sustained by others in that place, even if the victims do not know, or can no longer remember, precisely why they were injured there. New York Cent. R.R. v. Cavinder, 141 Ind. App. 42, 211 N.E.2d 502 (1965).

10. *Indiana Accord:* Under Indiana law, defectively designed and maintained roads will foreseeably and predictably cause crashes. Campbell v. State, 259 Ind. 55, 284 N.E.2d 733 (1972); Elliott v. State, 342 N.E.2d 674 (Ind. App. 1976); Indiana State Hwy. Comm'n v. Clark, 371 N.E.2d 1323 (Ind. App. 1978); and State v. Thompson, 385 N.E.2d 198 (Ind. App. 1979).

when her automobile struck the guardrail and was promptly catapulted into orbit by the guardrail, which had been designed, installed and/or maintained in such a manner as to function as a take-off ramp for vehicles coming into contact with it. Initial expert analysis of the case revealed that the design of the guardrails may have been deficient, even under the experimental state-of-the-art technology in the late 1960's. The main culprit, however, was clearly the governmental unit that had exercised exclusive jurisdiction over the guardrails during the years after the design plans were approved. The attorney who originated the case had not made a timely diagnosis of possible transportation facility negligence, and notices of claim required to preserve causes of action against the governmental entity had not been filed. The only remaining potential defendant was the private contractor that had prepared the initial design, but the case was refused due to proximate cause filtering, which established the probability that the governmental entity's years of exclusive control, during which upgrades reflecting technical improvements should have been made, would more probably than not constitute an intervening cause, insulating whatever negligence the private contractor may have been guilty of.

Conversely, however, many seemingly hopeless cases can be resurrected through timely diagnosis of transportation facility negligence, coupled with appropriate presentation of proximate cause principles to the jury. Thus, when an uninsured, indigent, drunken teenager crossed the center line at night on an unlit road and collided with our client in a head-on crash, we were able to secure a substantial verdict against the governmental entity in charge of the facility on the theory that one proximate cause of the crash was the government's negligent failure to install a required median barrier down the center of the road. The plaintiff's closing argument to the jury centered largely on the dual proximate cause rule, and the defense's attempt to direct the jury's attention to the negligence of the judgment-proof teenager could be negated through the counter-procedure of pointing out that the teenager could not have penetrated into the plaintiff's lane, even if the teenager was the most negligent driver in history, if the required median barrier had been in place.

The crucial importance that proximate cause elements can have in these cases is pointed out by the fact that the teenager might well have constituted an intervening cause relieving the governmental entity from liability if the very same crash had occurred in broad daylight. The proximate cause analysis that always works powerfully for defendants accused of transportation facility negligence connected with crashes occurring in good visibility is that the parties to the crash, or at least one of them, should have seen the dangers in the facility in time to avoid them.

Appropriate proximate cause filtration may exclude on the grounds of relevance, or at least detoxify, many harmful evidentiary items. Thus, in *Chapman v. Checker Taxi Co.,* 43 Ill. App. 3d 699, 357 N.E.2d 111 (1976), where a speeding taxi hit a lane divider and then hit a police car, the court minimized and questioned the relevance of the fact that the cab was speeding at the time because "this factor might not necessarily have affected the accident because it would have occurred even absent [the speeding]." 357 N.E.2d at 119.

Similarly, *State v. Thompson,* 385 N.E.2d 198, 205 (Ind. App. 1979), holds road defects a proximate cause for subsequent crashes also involving the negligence of third parties: "When a Defendant has been shown to have knowledge that independent and intervening forces might occur and result in damage or injury due to the effects of the Defendant's negligence, he cannot escape liability by claiming that the specific manner in which the damage or injury occurred was unforeseeable."[11]

§ 6-2. All Foreseeable Substantial Causes Are Proximate Causes.

The essential test for legal proximate cause is this: The injury must be the natural and probable result of the negligent act or omission and be of such a character as an ordinary prudent person ought to have foreseen as likely to occur as a result of negligence, although it is not essential that the person charged with the negligence should have foreseen the precise injury that results from his acts. *Cunis v. Brennan,* 7 Ill. App. 3d 204, 287 N.E.2d 207 (1982).[12] On the other hand, most jurisdictions hold that an intervening efficient cause is a new and independent force which breaks the causal connection between the original wrong and the injury and itself becomes the direct and immediate cause of the injury.[13] The intervention of independent concurrent or intervening forces will not break causal connection if the intervention of such forces was itself probable or foreseeable.[14]

---

11. "Where harmful consequences are brought about by intervening independent forces the operation of which might have been reasonably foreseen, then the chain of causation extending from the original wrongful act to the injury is not broken by the intervening and independent forces and the original wrongful act is treated as a proximate cause." Ortho Pharmaceutical Corp. v. Chapman, 388 N.E.2d 541 (Ind. App. 1979).

12. See also Neering v. Illinois Cent. R.R., 383 Ill. 366, 50 N.E.2d 497 (1943); Illinois Cent. R.R. v. Oswald, 338 Ill. 270, 170 N.E. 247 (1930); and Hartnett v. Boston Store, 265 Ill. 331, 106 N.E. 837 (1914).

13. Illinois Cent. R.R. v. Oswald, 338 Ill. 270, 170 N.E. 247 (1930); Pullman's Palace Car Co. v. Laack, 143 Ill. 242, 32 N.E. 285 (1892).

14. Wintersteen v. National Cooperage & Woodenware Co., 361 Ill. 95, 197 N.E. 578 (1935); Sycamore Preserve Works v. Chicago & N.R.R., 66 Ill. 11, 7 N.E.2d 740 (1930). Green v. City of Chicago, 73 Ill. 2d 100, 382 N.E.2d 1205 (1978).

Under all these formulations, each aspect of negligence that is a substantial, or reasonably foreseeable, factor in causing a crash and injuries is a legal proximate cause of that crash.[15]

A crash may be "proximately caused" by several convergent areas of negligence. Thus, in *Millette v. Radosta,* 84 Ill. App. 3d 5, 404 N.E.2d 823 (1980), one defendant negligently manufactured an automobile that another defendant negligently drove into the plaintiff's truck. The jury found both defendants negligent, and the defendant driver argued that the jury finding against the defendant manufacturer mandated a finding that the defendant driver could not also have been a proximate cause of the crash. In rejecting this contention, the court held: "It is fundamental in the law of negligence that there may be more than one proximate cause of injury and that one is liable for negligent conduct whether it contributed in whole or in part to the plaintiff's injury, so long as it was one of the proximate causes of injury." 404 N.E.2d at 838.[16]

---

15. Davelis v. Central Eng'g Co., 86 Ill. App. 3d 593, 408 N.E.2d 218 (1980). See also William Prosser, The Law of Torts, § 41 (4th ed. 1971).

Indiana Accord: Johnson v. Bender, 369 N.E.2d 936, 939-40 (Ind. App. 1977); "[I]f the defendant's negligence is a substantial factor in producing plaintiff's injury, and if the particular injury suffered is one of a class that was reasonably foreseeable at the time of the defendant's wrongful act, then there is causal relation in fact as well as legal cause."

Pennsylvania Accord: In Kravinsky v. Glover, 396 A.2d 1349 (Pa. Super. 1979), the Court ruled that a behavioral therapist's testimony that a crash was a significant cause of the plaintiff's driving phobia was sufficient to establish proximate cause linking the crash and the phobia.

16. See also Nelson v. Union Wire Rope Corp., 31 Ill. 2d 69, 199 N.E.2d 769 (1964), and Buehler v. Whalen, 70 Ill. 2d 51, 374 N.E.2d 460 (1977), where plaintiff passenger was allowed to recover against the concurrent negligence of both the manufacturer that negligently produced the vehicle plaintiff rode in and the negligent driver of a second vehicle that struck plaintiff's vehicle, causing it to burst into flames.

§ 6-3. Foreseeable and Non-Foreseeable Intervening Causes.

Even in jurisdictions that have adopted comparative negligence, "[t]he law remains that if the conduct of a defendant is found not to be the proximate cause of the injury, no liability arises." *Nunley v. Village of Cahokia,* 115 Ill. App. 3d 208, 450 N.E.2d 367 (1983). Similarly, "Even under the comparative negligence doctrine . . . the jury cannot be required to find only one proximate cause." *Dodson v. Shaw,* 113 Ill. App. 3d 1063, 448 N.E.2d 188 (1983). Thus, where a driver admits that he was not paying any attention to the road, and concedes that he could have avoided the crash by tending to his driving, it would be difficult to find other negligent parties concurring proximate causes of the resultant crash.[17]

Outside of such extreme cases, however, governmental entities are usually held responsible to foresee, and provide roads reasonably safe for bad drivers, who are therefore generally not intervening proximate causes in transportation facility negligence cases.[18]

---

17. See Jeanguenat v. Zibert, 78 Ill. App. 3d 948, 397 N.E.2d 1235 (1979).

18. In Bak v. Burlington N., Inc., 93 Ill. App. 3d 269, 417 N.E.2d 148 (1981), the plaintiff slipped and fell in the defendant's train station, sustaining injuries. Nine months later the plaintiff died from an overdose of painkillers necessitated by pain from the fall-related injuries. The trial court gave defendant a summary judgment on the apparent lack of proximate cause and the appellate court reversed:

> To constitute probable cause an injury "must be the natural and probable result of the negligent act or omission and be of such a character as an ordinarily prudent person ought to have foreseen as likely to occur as a result of the negligence, although it is not essential that the person charged with negligence should have foreseen the precise injury which resulted from his act." (Neering v. I.C.R.R. Co., 383 Ill. 366, 380, 50 N.E.2d 497 (1943).) The intervention of a new, independent intervening cause does not necessarily relieve one of responsibility for a negligent act "when the intervening cause of an injury is anticipated, . . .". (Neering at 381, 50

§ 6-3(A). Bad Driving Is a Foreseeable Result of Road Faults.

Bad roads will foreseeably turn good drivers into bad

N.E.2d 497). Thus, for example, it has been uniformly held that negligent treatment by a physician is reasonably foreseeable and the original tortfeasor is liable for aggravation of the original injury caused by the negligent treatment. (Chicago City Ry. Co. v. Saxby, 213 Ill. 274, 277, 72 N.E. 755 (1904). See, generally, Annot., 100 A.L.R.2d 808 (1965).) Proximate cause is ordinarily a question of fact and to escape liability a defendant "must demonstrate that the intervening event was unforeseeable as a matter of law." Davis v. Marathon Oil Co., 64 Ill. 2d 380, 395, 1 Ill. Dec. 93, 356 N.E.2d 93 (1976).

Whether an intervening cause, the overdose considered as accidental, was a natural and probable consequence of defendant's primary acts alleged to have caused the original injury may be best addressed by analogy to other "second injury" cases. There are a number of cases in which an injured plaintiff's conduct after the first injury has produced an aggravation of the injury or a new injury. In a class of cases characterized as the "crutches" cases, a general rule has evolved that where an injured party non-negligently is using crutches and falls, the original tortfeasor is liable for those injuries as well. (See, generally, Annot. 31 A.L.R.3d 1000, 1010-1015 (1970); Devlin v. Chicago City Ry. Co., 210 Ill. App. 7, 9 (Abst. 1918). See, also, Swanson v. Williams & Co., 278 A.D. 477, 106 N.Y.S.2d 61, 63-66 (1951).) Recovery has also been allowed where plaintiff became dizzy because of an original concussion and fell through a window, (Millman v. United States Mortgage & Title Guar. Co., 121 N.J.L. 28, 1 A.2d 265, 269-270 (1938)); where a plaintiff suffered an eye injury and 15 months later was chopping wood and got a splinter in his eye which necessitated the removal of the organ, (City of Port Arthur v. Wallace, 141 Tex. 201, 171 S.W.2d 480, 483 (1943)); and where plaintiff suffered a brain concussion and three weeks later fell off a ladder during a dizzy spell, (Eli Witt Cigar & Tobacco Co. v. Matatics, Fla., 55 So.2d 549, 551 (1951).) Causation, however is rejected where either the injured party acts negligently or incurs another injury through an instrumentality or activity which is not causally linked to the treatment of the first injury. (See, e.g., Brown v. New York Training School for Girls, 285 N.Y. 37, 32 N.E.2d 783, 784 (1941).) In Brown, the decedent by mistake swallowed a mercury tablet which had not been prescribed for the injury thinking it was a sedative tablet which had been prescribed. Here the Darvon was prescribed as a result of the primary injury. Brown was so distinguished by the later New York case of Swanson v. Williams & Co., 278 A.D. 477, 106 N.Y.S.2d at 65-66.

A motion for summary judgment and its supporting documents must be strictly construed and must leave no question of the

drivers and bad drivers into killers. The law will not allow

---

movant's right to judgment. (Littrell v. Coats Co., 62 Ill. App. 3d 516, 519-20, 19 Ill. Dec. 629, 379 N.E.2d 293 (1978).) Here a material question of fact is raised as to whether the overdose was a negligent act of decedent, a non-negligent accidental overdose, or a voluntary suicide. Another question for the fact finder is the ultimate one of whether defendant's alleged primary negligent act was the proximate cause of decedent's death. 417 N.E.2d at 149-150.

Florida Accord: Cooper v. IBI Sec. Serv., 281 So. 2d 524 (Fla. App. 1973). Concurrent causes are when foreseeable acts of third person are combined with tortfeasor's negligence which brings harm to innocent party.

State Dep't of Transp. v. Eades, 383 So. 2d 973 (Fla. App. 1982). A police officer who fell through drainage grading on shoulder of state public highway while writing an accident report was allowed to recover from state for injuries sustained.

Rex Utils., Inc. v. Gaddy, 413 So. 2d 1232 (Fla. App. 1982). Trial court did not err in preventing defendant from introducing evidence and then later in the trial arguing to the jury that plaintiff's decedent was guilty of comparative negligence when he failed to wear protective headgear while riding the motorcycle at time of accident. Not wearing protective headgear is in violation of statute and no evidence was presented that the violation of statute was proximate cause of injuries sustained by decedent.

Ohio Accord: Pugh v. Akron-Chicago, Transp. Co., 64 Ohio App. 479, 28 N.E.2d 1015, aff'd, 137 Ohio St. 164, 28 N.E.2d 501 (1940). An actor should realize that a third person might intervene in his negligent conduct even though the intervention is negligent or done in a negligent manner. This does not make it a superseding cause of harm to another, even though the negligent conduct is a substantial factor in causing harm to another.

Clauss v. Fields, 29 Ohio App. 2d 93, 278 N.E.2d 677 (1971). A combined negligence becomes the proximate cause of injury when the negligence of two or more persons produce a single invisible injury. These people are liable, both jointly and severally.

Texas Accord: City of Houston v. Hagman, 347 S.W.2d 355 (Tex. App. 1961). City was liable for injuries sustained when motorist's automobile skidded on mud washed by rain from an adjoining embankment into the street and struck a concrete pillar and then was struck by a following car. The embankment was left by city as a result of construction and

defendants to argue that there is an unpredictable relationship between road faults and bad driving, particularly since both engineering and medicine now document clearly that sudden confrontation with serious danger tends to slow or paralyze the human reaction mechanism. (See Chapter 7 on the reactions of the reasonable man.)[19]

---

such collision was within the limits of foreseeability.

Clark v. Waggoner, 452 S.W.2d 437 (Tex. 1970). First wrongdoer is not excused by intervention of third person which contributes to injurious effect of first negligence, if such intervention should have been foreseen.

Jezek v. City of Midland, 605 S.W.2d 544 (Tex. 1980). It is foreseeable if dangerous obstruction is not corrected that a motorist using the roadway in a motor vehicle will sustain injury.

19. *California Accord:* Lorincie v. San Diego Gas & Elec. Co., 247 Cal. App. 2d 765, 56 Cal Rptr. 47 (1967). It must be taken into account the probable actions of other people, of vehicles, and natural causes which may make the presence of the obstruction more hazardous, or create another hazard in considering whether a subsequent event should have been reasonably foreseen at time of placement of stationary obstacle upon highway.

Florida: Stabile v. Lamb, 226 So. 2d 347 (Fla. App. 1969). Plaintiff's lawful stop was not an unexpected stop caused by change in traffic signal so as to constitute contributing cause of rear-end collision.

Warning Safety Lights, Inc. v. Gallor, 346 So. 2d 92 (Fla. App. 1977). Question for jury whether misplacement of cones or failure to anchor them was cause of injury to motorist who ran into median while trying to avoid hitting cones was made by evidence in action against highway repair contractor and subcontractor employed to place and maintain work barriers.

Lee v. Dunnigan, 384 So. 2d 165 (Fla. App. 1980). Driver who struck car ahead of her following that car's collision with pick-up truck had to prove that unexpected or extraordinary event was sole cause of accident in order to avoid liability.

Nunziato v. P & L Auto Parts, Inc., 403 So. 2d 1031 (Fla. App. 1981). Driver was not liable to decedent's estate for wrongful death action because conduct of other driver with which he collided was traveling at 60 m.p.h. in 30 m.p.h. zone, crossed center line into other lane where collision occurred and in dozing off was an intervening cause even though he, himself, was negligent in driving with high blood-alcohol

California Law on Bad Roads Causing Bad Driving: *Irvin v. Padelford,* 127 Cal. App. 2d 135, 273 P.2d 539 (1954). (Failure to erect an intersection stop sign caused a two-vehicle crash and the city was not relieved by the negligence of the second driver, who should have yielded right of way to first driver). See also *Hilts v. County of Solano,* 265 Cal. App. 2d 161, 71 Cal. Rptr. 275 (1968) (Even if eastbound motorist was negligent and his negligence contributed to a collision with a northbound motorist, the county would nevertheless be liable if the dangerous condition of the intersection was a concurring proximate cause of the crash; *Kechter v. City of Downey,* 265 Cal. App. 2d 877, 71 Cal. Rptr. 844 (1968)). (Where defendant city created road defects, the plaintiff could recover for damages sustained in an automobile accident caused by those defects even though negligence of another driver had concurred with that of city in causing the crash).

Illinois Law on Bad Roads Causing Bad Driving: In *Bentley v. Saunemin Twp.,* Docket No. 52873, Agenda 24,

---

level and in speeding.

Ohio: Cascone v. Herb Kay Co., 6 Ohio St. 3d 155, 451 N.E.2d 815 (1983). An intervening act breaks the causal connection between negligence and injury depending upon whether the cause is a responsible agency which could have eliminated the hazard, and whether the intervening act is reasonably foreseeable by the one who is guilty of the negligence. This relieves one of liability for his negligence.

Fannin v. Cubric, 21 Ohio App. 2d 99, 255 N.E.2d 270 (1970). Where an original act is wrongful or negligent and its natural and continuous sequence produces an effect which would not have taken place without the act, proximate cause is established, and fact that some other act joins with the original act to cause injury does not prevent the original act from being proximate cause of the injury.

Texas: Southwest Forest Indus. Inc. v. Bauman, 659 S.W.2d 702 (Tex. App. 1983). Foreseeability does not require anticipation of how injury will grow out of dangerous condition which his negligence created.

decided September 1980, where the court affirmed an appellate court decision reversing a jury verdict against a plaintiff passenger and in favor of a defendant local government entity that had negligently maintained a stop sign. The jury had found the negligent driving of the driver of plaintiff's vehicle to be the sole proximate cause of the crash. The Supreme Court held it appropriate to reverse the jury, even under the very pro-jury verdict standards of *Pedrick v. Peoria & E.R.R.,* 37 Ill. 2d 494, 229 N.E.2d 504 (1967), because defendants should have foreseen the failure of the driver, without the benefit of the stop sign, to recognize other indications of an approaching hazard. Hence, the court held that it could not be said that the driver's negligence was the sole proximate cause of plaintiff's death. There may be more than one proximate cause of any injury. In *Duewel v. Lahman,* 103 Ill. App. 3d 220, 430 N.E.2d 662 (1981), the court held that negligent driving was a foreseeable consequence of the defendant county's failure to properly maintain an intersection stop sign. Again, in *Sears v. Kois Bros. Equip., Inc.,* 110 Ill. App. 3d 884, 443 N.E.2d 214 (1982), a truck negligently loaded by one defendant was negligently driven by a second defendant on a road negligently maintained by a third defendant, and crashed into plaintiff. The defendant responsible for the road was not able to convince the court that the negligent loading and driving of the truck were nonforeseeable intervening causes of the crash that was also caused by defective road maintenance. 443 N.E.2d at 219. Again, in *Lemings v. Collinsville School Dist. No. 10,* 118 Ill. App. 3d 363, 454 N.E.2d 1139 (1983), the defendant negligently placed a dumpster so that it blocked the view pedestrians would have of oncoming cars. Due to this obstructed view, the plaintiff, a ten-year-old child, walked into the street and was struck by a car. The defendant responsible for placing the dumpster was not allowed to argue that the negligence of the car driver was an intervening cause of the plaintiff's injuries. The court held that negligent driving and negligent walking into the street were foreseeable consequences of the negligent placement of the dumpster.

Indiana Law on Bad Roads Causing Bad Driving: *Johnson v. Bender,* 369 N.E.2d 936 (Ind. App. 1977).

Louisiana Law on Bad Roads Causing Bad Driving: *Rue v. State, Dep't of Hwys.,* 372 So. 2d 1197 (La. 1979).

New York Law on Bad Roads Causing Bad Driving: *Bodner v. Steinhardt,* 71 A.D.2d 702, 418 N.Y.S.2d 484 (1979).

§ 6-3(B). Governmental Entities Must Foresee Bad Driving.

Foreseeable events cannot be intervening causes. *Davis v. Thornton,* 384 Mich. 138, 180 N.W.2d 11 (1970).

Engineering standards clearly foresee that drunken, exhausted, and otherwise substandard drivers are going to be on the road, and require that the roads be maintained in a reasonably safe condition for such impaired drivers. The law, similarly requires governmental entities to maintain roads reasonably safe for substandard drivers. The foreseeable negligence of a third party is not an intervening proximate cause, and bad driving is foreseeable. *Wilborg v. Denzell,* 359 Mass. 279, 268 N.E.2d 855 (1971); *Dillon v. Tamminga,* 64 Mich. App. 305, 236 N.W.2d 718 (1975).

California Accord: *Curreri v. City & County of San Francisco,* 262 Cal. App. 2d 603, 69 Cal. Rptr. 20 (1968). (Negligence of automobile driver whose vehicle struck plaintiff would not preclude possibility of a finding that a dangerous road condition was permitted to exist by city and that the road condition was a concurring proximate cause of the injury so as to permit recovery by plaintiff against city.)

Pennsylvania Accord: *Grainy v. Campbell,* 493 Pa. 88, 425 A.2d 379 (1981). The liability of contractor and gas company who forced pedestrian traffic into the street by obstructing an entire berm, was not relieved by intervening negligent act of truck driver who struck boy scout who was forced to walk on roadway.

§ 6-3(C). Drunk Driving Is Foreseeable.

Perhaps the most common form of impaired driver involved in crashes is the drunk driver. There is no doubt that drunken plaintiffs (or plaintiffs' decedents) do not have a great deal of jury appeal and, particularly in contributory negligence jurisdictions, may be denied any recovery at all due to massive contributory fault. Bear in mind, however, that it is possible for road faults and drinking to be concurring proximate causes of a crash, and a substantial body of law precludes governmental entities from claiming drunken drivers were unforeseeable intervening causes insulating the governmental entity from liability for its own negligence.

California Accord on Drunk Drivers Being Foreseeable: See *Bigbee v. Pacific Tel. & Tel. Co.,* 192 Cal. Rptr. 857, 665 P.2d 947 (1983).

Illinois Accord on Drunk Drivers Being Foreseeable: In *Thorsen v. City of Chicago,* 74 Ill. App. 3d 98, 392 N.E.2d 716 (1979), the defendant city had negligently removed sidewalks, forcing plaintiff to walk in the street, where a drunk driver hit him. The defendant city argued that the intervention of the drunk driver should insulate their defendants whose negligence had "set the stage" for the crash, from liability. In *Thorsen,* however, it was not established, at least not by an in-court admission, that the drunk driver could have avoided the crash by better driving. The *Thorsen* court consequently ruled against the city, holding:

> While the City argues that it could not have foreseen that a drunk driver would swerve and strike plaintiff, since the City's conduct was a substantial factor in bringing about harm to the plaintiff, the fact that it might not have foreseen the exact manner in which the harm occurred does not prevent the City from being liable. Restatement (Second) of Torts § 435(1)(1965). 392 N.E.2d at 724.

Thorsen hinges on the concept that transportation facility negligence constitutes a substantial factor in subsequent crashes, even if the exact manner in which those crashes occur was not foreseeable. The underlying *Thorsen* rationale is that defendants guilty of transportation facility negligence should be liable for subsequent crashes because those crashes were, at least in general, very predictable from the defendant's negligence. This reasoning seems persuasive.

The *Thorsen* reasoning, moreover, was also followed by the Illinois Supreme Court in *Greene v. City of Chicago,* 73 Ill. 2d 100, 382 N.E.2d 1205 (1978). In *Greene,* the defendant city negligently maintained a street by allowing the street lights to go out. Plaintiff's car stalled in this negligently darkened street one night and, while plaintiff was out of his car making repairs, another car struck plaintiff's vehicle and injured him. The court rejected the city's argument that the second driver's negligence constituted an intervening cause insulating the city from liability because:

> The rule that the causal connection between a person's negligence and an injury is broken by the intervention of a new, independent, efficient and intervening cause so that the negligence is not actionable, is subject to the qualification that if the intervening cause was foreseen by the wrongdoer, his negligence may be considered the proximate cause of the injury and he may be held liable notwithstanding the intervening cause. The intervening act of a third person does not

> necessarily relieve the author of an earlier negligent or wrongful act from responsibility when the intervening cause of an injury is of such nature as could reasonably have been anticipated, in which case the earlier negligent act, if it contributed to the injuries, may be regarded as the proximate cause. 382 N.E.2d at 1211.

The *Greene* court concluded:

> the intervention of a criminal act [intoxicated driving], however, does not necessarily interrupt the relation of cause and effect between [earlier transportation facility] negligence and an injury. If at the time of the [earlier] negligence, the criminal act might reasonably have been foreseen, the causal chain is not broken by the intervention of such act. 382 N.E.2d at 1211.

See also *Ray v. Cock Robin, Inc.,* 57 Ill. 2d 19, 310 N.E.2d 9 (1974), and *Felty v. New Berlin Transit, Inc.,* 71 Ill. 2d 126, 374 N.E.2d 203 (1978).

Louisiana Accord on Drunk Drivers Being Foreseeable: State transportation department was liable for death of passenger in accident caused by curve and existence of six to eight inch dropoff between shoulder and paved roadway. Fact that driver was intoxicated did not relieve department of liability. *Everett v. Louisiana Dep't of Transp. & Dev.,* 424 So. 2d 336 (La. App. 1982).

§ 6-3(D). Crashes Aggravating Prior Injuries.

Most jurisdictions hold clearly that governmental entities are liable when their road faults cause crashes that aggravate prior injuries.

Illinois: *Kolakowski v. Voris,* 94 Ill. App. 3d 404, 418 N.E.2d 1003 (1981).

§ 6-3(E). Road Defects Held Causes of Crashes.

The following citations on specific holdings causally linking road defects with crashes should be read in conjunction with the corresponding sections of Chapter 3, "Legal Standards on Road Features."

§ 6-3(E)(1). Shoulder Drop-Off.

California: *Drummond v. City of Redondo Beach,* 255 Cal. App. 2d 715, 63 Cal. Rptr. 497 (1967).

Louisiana: Evidence sustained finding that condition of highway was causative factor in head-on collision. Travel surface was higher than shoulder which pulled vehicle when driver attempted to reenter highway after going on to shoulder to avoid another vehicle. *Clark v. Aetna Cas. & Sur. Co.,* 427 So. 2d 907 (La. App. 1983); *Murphy v. Louisiana Dep't of Transp. & Dev.,* 424 So. 2d 336 (La. App. 1982).

Michigan: *Karrar v. Board of Rd. Comm'rs,* 339 N.W.2d 653 (Mich. App. 1983).

New York: Pavement drop-off of 3½ inches between state road and median at point at which motorcyclist lost control after leaving road due to his inattentiveness constituted a hazard. Thus, state was liable for 20% of damages resulting from death of motorcycle passenger. *Penzell v. State,* 120 Misc. 2d 600, 466 N.Y.S.2d 562 (1983).

§ 6-3(E)(2). Sharp Curves (Curve Design).

California: *Johnston v. County of Yolo,* 274 Cal. App. 2d 46, 79 Cal. Rptr. 33 (1969).

Indiana: *State v. Edgman,* 447 N.E.2d 1091 (Ind. App. 1983).

§ 6-3(E)(3). Inadequate Warnings and Signings.

California Law: *Johnston v. County of Yolo,* 274 Cal. App. 2d 46, 79 Cal. Rptr. 33 (1969). *Cameron v. State,* 7 Cal. 3d 318, 497 P.2d 777, 102 Cal. Rptr. 305 (1972). The state's failure to properly warn of dangerous "S" curves and superelevations was an independent, separate concurrent cause of injuries sustained when plaintiff's vehicle failed to negotiate curve and crashed into hillside.

Florida Law: *Department of Transp. v. Neilson,* 419 So. 2d 1071 (Fla. 1982). Failure to exercise reasonable maintenance jurisdiction over existing devices and roads may support liability against the governmental entity with such maintenance jurisdiction.

Indiana Law: *State v. Edgman,* 447 N.E.2d 1091 (Ind. App. 1983).

Louisiana Law: State was liable for damages sustained by truck driver when truck rig overturned as result of driver attempting to avoid vehicle which was ahead of driver. State had failed to adequately warn of repair crew present on highway. *Stephens v. State Dep't of Transp. & Dev.,* 440 So. 2d 920 (La. App. 1983); .17% blood alcohol level at time of fatal accident, evidence sustained finding that State was 60% liable for one-vehicle accident on dead-end segment of highway. State had failed to give adequate warnings of conditions on highway.

Required warnings, if not provided, can be causes of crashes, even if the driver's ability to respond to the warnings was impaired by alcohol. *Humphrey v. State,* 60 N.Y.2d 742, 457 N.E.2d 767, 469 N.Y.S.2d 767 (1983).

Ohio: *Moore v. City of Columbus,* 139 N.E.2d 656 (Ohio 1956). The condition of a "Dead End" sign could be considered in determining whether the municipality had violated a statute requiring streets to be kept free from nuisances.

Pennsylvania Law: *Hawk v. Trumbull Constr. Co.,* 401 Pa. 570, 166 A.2d 41 (1960). (Failure to warn of traffic route changes during road construction.)

§ 6-3(E)(4). Inadequate Curbs.

California: *Curreri v. City & County of San Francisco,* 262 Cal. App. 2d 603, 69 Cal. Rptr. 20 (1968).

§ 6-3(E)(5). Inadequate Sight Distance.

California: *Feingold v. County of Los Angeles,* 254 Cal. App. 2d 622, 62 Cal. Rptr. 396 (1967). (Plaintiff's were passengers in a westbound truck, which ran a stop sign and blocked an intersection until their truck was struck by a southbound automobile. Plaintiffs argued that regardless of whether their truck driver heeded the stop sign, both drivers were unable to see each other until both drivers were committed to intersection, due to defendant's negligent maintenance. The Court held that stated a cause of action against the county on theory of dangerous condition of property.)

Louisiana: *Wilkinson v. Department of Transp. & Dev.,* 434 So. 2d 1155 (La. App. 1983).

§ 6-3(E)(6). Design of Bridge.

Idaho: *Leliefeld v. Johnson,* 104 Idaho 357, 659 P.2d 111 (1983).

Louisiana: *Wilkinson v. Department of Transp. & Dev.,* 434 So. 2d 1155 (La. App. 1983).

§ 6-3(E)(7). Improper Driving Surface.

Louisiana: *Campbell v. State Dep't of Hwys.,* 439 So. 2d 1175 (La. App. 1983).

Massachusetts: *Tosches v. Town of Sherborn,* 341 Mass. 310, 169 N.E.2d 901 (1960) (Tar negligently spread on road).

§ 6-3(E)(8). Negative Superelevation and Improper Banking.

Louisiana: Adverse crown and existence of low shoulder on curve established prima facie case of negligence against Department of Transportation. *Murphy v. Louisiana Dep't of Transp. & Dev.,* 424 So. 2d 344 (La. App. 1982).

New York: *Merrill Transp. Co. v. State,* 97 A.D.2d 921, 470 N.Y.S.2d 764 (1983) (improper banking caused crash.)

§ 6-3(E)(9). Inadequate Pavement Marking.

Indiana: *State v. Edgman,* 447 N.E.2d 1091 (Ind. App. 1983).

§ 6-3(E)(10). Encroaching Vegetation.

New York: *McKenna v. State,* 91 A.D.2d 1066, 458 N.Y.S.2d 675 (1983).

Texas: *Kenneally v. Thurn,* 653 S.W.2d 69 (Tex. App. 1983). Failure to keep an unobstructed view of traffic sign exposing municipality to liability under Tort Claims Act.

Ohio: *Royce v. Smith,* 68 Ohio St. 2d 106, 429 N.E.2d 134 (1981). A statute providing that the county engineer had control of all trees and shrubs in county and that the board of township trustees has control of all trees and shrubs in township roads was only to apportion the respective responsibilities of board of township trustees and county engineers concerning the maintenance of roadside vegetation. The adjoining owners were not therefore relieved of liability for their dangerous vegetation.

§ 6-3(E)(11). Improper Snow Removal From Road.

New Jersey: *Paternoster v. New Jersey Dep't of Transp.,* 190 N.J. Super. 11, 461 A.2d 759 (1983).

Ohio: *Mills v. City of Springfield,* 142 N.E.2d 859 (Ohio App. 1956). A statute imposing the duty upon a municipality to keep its streets open, in repair, and free from nuisance, does not change the rule that a property owner is not immune from suit for injuries resulting from normal and natural accumulation of snow and ice on his streets and sidewalks. The statute created a new affirmative duty.

However, a different rule is applied where ice or snow has accumulated wholly or in part through the fault of the city.

§ 6-3(E)(12). Roadside Obstacles.

Placing obstacles in the path of where people will foreseeably travel constitutes negligence. *Riley v. New England Tel. & Tel. Co.,* 234 N.E.2d 746 (Mass. 1968).

§ 6-3(E)(12)(a). Poles.

Fact issues existed as to whether utility pole, which was located six inches outside curb line of street, was a defect in the street for which the city could be held liable if it had notice of the defect. A bus passenger sustained injury when the passenger's arm, which was propped in open bus window, was apparently wedged between the bus window frame and a power pole as the bus was going forward. Although there was no evidence of actual notice, the pole was maintained in the same location for 24 years and bore scrape marks from passing vehicles. *Kicklighter v. Savannah Transit Auth.,* 167 Ga. App. 528, 307 S.E.2d 47 (1983).

Austin v. City of Mt. Dora, 417 So. 2d 807 (Fla. App. 1982). Decision by city to erect lines from its power plant to transmit power along a street and an avenue leading to the intersection where plaintiff was injured constituted a planning function based on basic policy judgments. The location of individual poles and guy wires to support those powerlines was, however, an implementation of that policy and, hence, an operational function outside of the city's governmental tort immunity.

§ 6-3(E)(12)(b). Ditches.

Fact question existed as to whether highway shoulder, which adjoined unmarked ditch, was defectively maintained and played a role in the accident. A vehicle left the paved portion of the highway due ostensibly to driver error, traveled along the road's shoulder and abutting ditch, and crashed into a culvert. *Pontello v. County of Onondaga,* 94 A.D.2d 427, 464 N.Y.S.2d 891 (1983).

§ 6-3(E)(12)(c). Telephone Booth.

California Court holds telephone company liable to user of telephone booth for harm resulting from negligent placing of booth too close to major roadway, thereby foreseeably increasing risk from drunken driver veering off pavement and into telephone booth. The car left the road, jumped the curb and sidewalk, and struck the plaintiff trapped inside the booth. The court on appeal held it was error to grant Summary Judgment for defendant. It is a jury question and requires re-submission for trial whether a negligently driven car might veer off the adjacent roadway and crash into the phone booth as a reasonably foreseeable risk. Foreseeable, culpable, intervening causes will not supersede the original negligent tortfeasors liability. Foreseeability does not mean probably. *Bigbee v. Pacific Tel. & Tel. Co.,* 192 Cal. Rptr. 857, 665 P.2d 947 (1983).

§ 6-3(E)(12)(d). Billboards.

Billboard advertiser, Phillip Morris Co., was held liable for negligently placing a billboard where it would block the view of motorists driving out of defendant's store premises, thereby making crashes foreseeable. *Gordon v. Phillip Morris, Inc.,* Vermont, Chittenden A.T.L.A. L. Rep. 113.

§ 6-3(E)(12)(e). Fire Hydrants.

St. Germain v. City of Fall River, 177 Mass. 550, 59 N.E. 447 (1901), the plaintiff was injured when a wheel of his vehicle hit a hydrant standing near the curb. Plaintiff's knowledge of the existence of the hydrant will not defeat his recovery. He may never have noted any of its details: he may never have been near enough to observe that it was so erected as to be hit by the rim of a wheel coming near the curbstone.

§ 6-3(E)(13). Sidewalk Defects.

Massachusetts: *Slunimsky v. City of Springfield,* 37 Mass. App. Dec. 18 (1967). There was a defect in sidewalk which caused plaintiff to fall and in part was attributable to her accident, although ice and snow may have contributed also to her injuries in part and there could be liability.

§ 6-3(E)(14). Holes and Hollows in Road.

Massachusetts: *Adams v. Town of Bolton,* 297 Mass. 459, 9 N.E.2d 562 (1937). Passengers in automobile sued Defendant town for injuries sustained when their automobile struck a hollow in the highway. The town knew or should have known of defective condition of highway prior to date of accident, and, in the exercise of reasonable care, the town should have foreseen that there was danger of the accident and should have taken adequate measures to prevent it.

Texas: *Sutton v. State Hwy. Dep't,* 549 S.W.2d 59 (Tex. App. 1977). A depression in the highway was a "premises defect" within Tort Claims Act.

§ 6-3(E)(15). Improper Guardrail and No Barrier.

Illinois: *Chapman v. Checker Taxi Co.,* 43 Ill. App. 3d 699, 357 N.E.2d 111 (1976). Defendant City of Chicago held liable for negligent design and maintenance of automatic median divider.

Kentucky: *Commonwealth, Dep't of Hwys. v. Automobile Club Ins. Co.,* 467 S.W.2d 326 (Ky. App. 1971). Defendant liable for failure to provide warranted guardrails on "S" curve. Court noted defendants duty to maintain roads with due care ". . . includes the duty to erect or maintain barriers or guardrails at dangerous places on the highway. . . ." 467 S.W.2d at 328.

Michigan: *Arnold v. Michigan Dep't of State Hwys.,* Michigan Court of Claims No. 4939 (1980), Reported 23 A.T.L.A. L. Rep. 118 (April 1980), State liable for failure to provide warranted median barrier; *Hall v. Michigan Dep't of Hwys.,* Court of Claims No. 4606 (1979), cited in 23 A.T.L.A. L. Rep. 123 (April 1980), defendant liable for negligent design and maintenance of blunt end median.

Minnesota: *Momo v. Bradley,* Hennepin County District Court No. 747807, decided November 9, 1979, reported at 23 A.T.L.A. L. Rep. 123 (April 1980), defendant county held liable for improper design and maintenance of median barrier.

New York: *Lattanzi v. State,* 53 N.Y.2d 1045 (1981), aff'd, 74 A.D.2d 378 (1980). State did not properly design and test the guardrail system prior to its installation and the inferior capabilities of the guardrail were the proximate cause of the claimant's injuries. See also *Humphrey v. State,* 60 N.Y.2d 742, 457 N.E.2d 767, 469 N.Y.S.2d 767 (1983), negligently placed barrier was a cause of crash, although driver was impaired by alcohol. See also *Hall v. State,* 28 A.D.2d 1203, 285 N.Y.S.2d 330 (1967), defendant liable when plaintiff's vehicle went through negligently maintained guardrail. In *Warren v. New York State Thruway Auth.,* 51 A.D.2d 679, 378 N.Y.S.2d 530 (1976), the defendant was liable for failure to install warranted guardrail. In *Zalewski v. State,* 53 A.D.2d 781, 384 N.Y.S.2d 545 (1976), the State was held liable when plaintiff's vehicle penetrated negligently installed and maintained guardrail.

Ohio: *Hunter v. City of Cleveland,* 46 Ohio St. 2d 91, 346 N.E.2d 303 (1976). City had notice that barricades and lanterns it put around excavation were regularly taken away, leaving the excavation unguarded. The City was liable for foreseeable injuries received by child who fell trying to jump over the unmarked excavation.

Pennsylvania: *Walsh v. City of Pittsburgh,* 379 Pa. 229, 108 A.2d 769 (1954). Where a barricade around a street excavation consisted only of light weight planking, and was so placed in the road that it would foreseeably be removed by traffic, the excavation could have been better guarded. The negligence of some unknown driver, who struck and removed barricade, did not exonerate the contractor from liability for injuries to guest in automobile that fell into excavation.

See also *Thompson v. City of Philadelphia,* 466 A.2d 1349 (Pa. Super. 1983). Truck driver's negligence was not an intervening cause that could bar recovery from city with road maintenance jurisdiction for death which occurred when truck drove through guardrail and crashed into decedent's vehicle.

See also *Black v. City of Philadelphia,* (1978) reported at 21 A.T.L.A. L. Rep. 225 (June 1978), where the City was held liable for failure to install a warranted barrier along a dangerous curve.

Washington: *Bartlett v. Northern Pac. Ry.,* 74 Wash. 2d 881, 447 P.2d 735 (1968), held, "[Defendant] *may* be chargeable with negligence for failure to maintain warning signs or barriers *if the situation along the highway is inherently dangerous or of such character as to mislead a traveler exercising reasonable care.*" 447 P.2d at 736; *Raybell v. State,* 6 Wash. App. 795, 496 P.2d 559 (1972), State liable for failure to maintain warranted guardrails on deceptive and dangerous road.

§ 6-3(E)(16). Defective Signals.

Michigan: *Tuttle v. Department of State Hwys.,* 397 Mich. 44, 243 N.W.2d 244 (1976). The Department of State Highways was negligent when, after determining that a stop control was too hard to see, it failed to carry out its own work orders to correct that condition.

§ 6-3(E)(17). Crossing Guards.

Armstrong v. City of Ann Arbor, 58 Mich. App. 359, 227 N.W.2d 343 (1975). It was a fact issue for the jury whether the negligence of a city-employed school-crossing guard was the proximate cause of an accident where a child collided with the side of a truck.

§ 6-3(E)(18). Passing Signals.

Wilfong v. Batdorf, 6 Ohio St. 3d 100, 451 N.E.2d 1185 (1983). Jury issue if failure to give available signal while passing another vehicle caused crash.

§ 6-3(E)(19). Intersection Design.

California: *Newson v. City of Oakland,* 37 Cal. App. 3d 1050, 112 Cal. Rptr. 890 (1974).

§ 6-4. Notice and Foreseeability.

The more notice a defendant has of the dangers posed by a road defect, obviously, the more foreseeable future crashes in that road area are, and the less likely it is that the negligence of third parties, usually negligent driving, will be construed as an intervening cause. Thus, in *Heffler v. State,* 96 A.D.2d 926, 466 N.Y.S.2d 370 (1983), the State's statistics on prior crashes showed a particular intersection to be dangerous and future crashes to be likely. For these reasons, the negligent driving of a drunken driver whose vehicle collided with the plaintiff's vehicle was not an intervening act severing the State's liability for its own negligence.

CHAPTER 7

REACTIONS OF A REASONABLE MAN

§ 7-1. Introduction.

Let us assume that on some future rainy night one of your clients is driving at a reasonable speed around a horizontal road curve. Suddenly, the car hits a pothole created by negligent maintenance, or a hidden lake of impounded water that has accumulated in the road because of defective drainage, and the car goes out of control, skidding into an oncoming lane of traffic, where it causes a crash with another vehicle.

The law may presume from the fact that your client was skidding out of control that he or she was guilty of negligent driving. *O'Dell v. Dowd,* 102 Ill. App. 3d 189, 429 N.E.2d 548 (1981); *Calvetti v. Seipp,* 37 Ill. 2d 596, 227 N.E.2d 758 (1967). If you are not able to rebut this presumption, the other parties to the ensuing lawsuit will be entitled to judgment against your client as a matter of law. *O'Dell v. Dowd, supra,* at 552.

Now let us suppose engineers calculate that, based on sight distances, visibility angles, and other good stuff, your client could have seen the road defect three and one-half or four seconds before impact if he was traveling at the posted speed. Would this information help or hurt your case? The answer to this question is twofold:

1. the evidence itself will usually be of more benefit to the party most familiar with the medical and engineering aspect of human reaction under stress; and
2. if your opponent is familiar with the mechanism of reaction and you are not, your case may very well be pulverized.

In order to do well in this area of litigation, you must know the documentation establishing that people do not react to sudden danger with the speed or certainty of computers. Indeed, if the danger is severe or sudden enough, the reasonable man may not be able to react at all.

The concept of the reasonable man, like many other glittering generalities, covers so many areas that it establishes nothing. To state that a party is negligent if he or she fails to react as a reasonable man would react does not advance the inquiry very far if we do not know how reasonable or even average people are supposed to react. Juries and attorneys who lack any evidence of predictable human reaction patterns based on current legal, engineering, or medical study must be seriously handicapped in their abilities to determine whether legal fault can be attributed to decisions and actions taken with little or no prior warning in an emergency situation.

These issues often become crucial in transportation facility negligence situations and in many other cases in which the presence or absence of both negligence and contributory negligence may depend upon whether people acting under a sudden emergency situation took an unreasonably long time to react to that situation.

§ 7-2. Using the Defendant's Negligence to Increase the Plaintiff's Reasonable Reaction Time.

Plaintiffs caught in sudden emergency situations caused by the defendant's negligence cannot be expected to react as swiftly and calmly as persons under normal situations. This "sudden peril" rule was enunciated as follows in *Laflin v. Estate of Mills,* 53 Ill. App. 3d 29, 368 N.E.2d 522, 527 (1977):

> It is a fundamental principle of negligence law that when judging the quality of an individual's conduct the standard to which an individual will be held will be influenced by the circumstances within which that individual is acting. *Lawson v. Belt Ry. Company of Chicago* (1975), 34 Ill. App. 3d 7, 339 N.E.2d 381. Thus, where an individual finds himself in a perilous position caused by an agency beyond his control, he need not exercise the same degree of coolness, self-possession and judgment necessary under ordinary circumstances. He must be judged by the standard of conduct of a prudent person acting under similar circumstances. (*Darby v. Checker Cab Co.,* 6 Ill. App. 3d at 194, 285 N.E.2d 217.)

To invoke this rule to justify an increase in the appropriate reaction time, a party must show that he acted under sudden peril for which he had no responsibility, control or advance warning. *Brackensick v. Chicago Motor Coach Co.,* 4 Ill. App. 2d 84, 123 N.E.2d 350 (1954); *McLaren v. Byrd,* 296 Ill. App. 345, 15 N.E.2d 993 (1938). The actor will also be required to establish that he was proceeding with normally computed due care prior to the emergency. *Hawbaker v. Danner,* 226 F.2d 843 (7th Cir. 1955); *Jines v. Greyhound Corp.,* 46 Ill. App. 2d 364, 197 N.E.2d 58 (1964), *rev'd on other grounds,* 33 Ill. 2d 83, 210 N.E.2d 562 (1965).

This legal doctrine, of course, offers the plaintiff an excellent strategic opportunity to focus the factfinder's attention on the alleged negligence of the defendant as a rebuttal to any allegations of contributory negligence.

The application of this doctrine to railroad crossing crashes was clearly stated in *Pearson v. Baltimore & Ohio R.R.,* 200 F.2d 569 (7th Cir. 1952), in which the court noted that motorists approaching a crossing may safely assume that the railroad would obey all applicable laws and safety regulations concerning train operations, crossing design and crossing maintenance. If the railroad negligently violated these obligations, the court reasoned this would not relieve the motorist from the burden of exercising reasonable care for his own safety, but: "[T]he amount of care necessary [for motorists] to meet the standard of reasonableness [is] thereby diminished . . . . [T]he defendant's prior negligence may be a factor in determining whether [the motorist] has used due care." *Pearson v. Baltimore & Ohio R.R., supra,* at 573.

Additional Illinois decisions applying this "sudden peril" rule include *Johnson v. Gallatin County,* 418 F.2d 96 (7th Cir. 1969), and *Lester v. Hennessey,* 20 Ill. App. 2d 479, 156 N.E.2d 247 (1959).

Indiana Law on Sudden Peril Rule: Under Indiana law, the defendant's prior negligence creating a dangerous road situation into which a motorist drives will lower the motorist's standard of care on the issue of what is reasonably required from that motorist. *Pearson v. Baltimore & Ohio R.R.,* 200 F.2d 569 (7th Cir. 1952). See also *Grand Rapids & Indiana R.R. v. Cox,* 8 Ind. App. 29, 35 N.E. 183 (1893), where the court said at 34, 35, "The Defendant's prior negligence may be a factor in determining whether the motorist has used due care." See also *New York Cent. R.R. v. Wyatt,* 135 Ind. App. 205, 184 N.E.2d 657, *transfer denied,* 244 N.E. 373 and 193 N.E.2d 63 (1962), where the court held that the defendant's creating a sudden danger for a motorist "may have an important bearing on the question of whether the motorist was using due care." 184 N.E.2d at 667-68.

Massachusetts Law on Sudden Peril Rule: In determining whether conduct is negligent toward another, the fact that an actor is confronted with a sudden emergency which requires rapid decision is a factor in determining the reasonable character of his choice of action. In an emergency, the law does not require one to take the most prudent course that could have been taken. *Birch v. Strout,* 303 Mass. 28, 20 N.E.2d 429 (1939), held that proper conduct in emergency is no defense to one who by negligence created the emergency.

Michigan Law on Sudden Peril Rule: *Manning v. Cheboygan Area Schools,* 76 Mich. App. 700, 257 N.W.2d 222 (1977), held that when a plaintiff asserts the doctrine of sudden emergency, the facts must be viewed in the light most favorable to the defendant. To assert the doctrine of sudden emergency, the facts must indicate that the circumstances attending the accident were either "unusual," such as a blizzard, or "unexpected," meaning a suddenly revealed and totally unexpected peril.

Moskalik v. Dunn, 392 Mich. 583, 221 N.W.2d 313 (1974), held that the existence of an emergency is but one of many factors to be taken into consideration on the issue of whether the person acted reasonably under the circumstances.

New York Law on Sudden Peril Rule: *Rossman v. La Grega,* 28 N.Y.2d 300, 270 N.E.2d 313, 321 N.Y.S.2d 588 (1971), held that when confronted with an emergency not created by his own negligence, a person is governed by the standard that would apply under pressure of such an emergency, and not by what would be proper or reasonable if one had time for reflection and deliberate judgment.

Ferrer v. Harris, 55 N.Y.2d 585, 434 N.E.2d 231, 449 N.Y.S.2d 162, amended, 56 N.Y.2d 737, 436 N.E.2d 1342, 451 N.Y.S.2d 740 (1982), stated that when a sudden and unexpected event or combination of events leaves little or no time for reflection or deliberate judgment, this itself may be a significant circumstance which, realistically as well as conceptually, should enter into determination of reasonableness of choice of action pursued.

Under *McGloin v. Austin,* 89 A.D.2d 583, 452 N.Y.S.2d 243, aff'd, 58 N.Y.2d 731, 445 N.E.2d 207, 459 N.Y.S.2d 243 (1982), it was a jury question whether the defendant was negligent in failing to stop when suddenly confronted by plaintiff's car, which had stopped while blocking the left lane of the roadway.

In *Hayes v. State,* 80 Misc.2d 385, 362 N.Y.S.2d 994 (1975), the Court held a failure of judgment in not reacting soon enough to an emergency so sudden and immediate that seconds made a difference was not negligence.

Ohio Law on Sudden Peril Rule: For purposes of the sudden emergency doctrine, a "sudden emergency" is defined as a sudden and unexpected occurrence of a transitory nature which demanded immediate action without time for reflection or deliberation and did not comprehend a static condition which lasted over a period of time. *Heidbreder v. Northampton Twp. Trustees,* 64 Ohio App. 2d 95, 411 N.E.2d 825 (1979).

Pennsylvania Law on Sudden Peril Rule: *Troutman v. Tabb,* 285 Pa. Super 353, 427 A.2d 673 (1981), held that negligence may not be implied because of failure to perform a duty that arose so quickly and unexpectedly that there was no chance to apprehend the situation or react deliberately.

Where one finds himself in a position of danger which is not a result of his negligence, he is not responsible if he makes a mistake in judgment in getting out; an honest exercise of judgment is all that is required of him even if he could have done better had he had time to deliberate.

Texas Law on Sudden Peril Rule: A person will not be relieved of the legal consequences of unreasonable and imprudent conduct when confronted with a sudden emergency, but the fact finder may conclude that conduct which in other circumstances would be reasonable or imprudent is not so in emergency situations. *Del Bosque v. Heitmann Bering-Cortes Co.,* 468 S.W.2d 522 (Tex. App. 1971).

§ 7-3. Mechanics of Reaction — PIEV Theory.

The foregoing legal concepts of increased or decreased reaction time will remain meaningless without reference to current medical and engineering standards on the mechanics of human reaction.

Reaction to stress situations is largely under the control of the brain, and medical science knows very little about that organ. We do not know what all the functional properties of the separate lobes are (Gardner, *Fundamentals of Neurology* (University of California Press (1973)); or how information is stored (Rose, *The Conscious Brain,* pp. 260-61 (Oxford University Press, 1973)); or what all the brain cells do (*The Conscious Brain, supra* at 70). Most important for present purposes is the fact that we have only tentative clues as to the impact of experience on brain structure and organization. Mork & Ervin, *Violence and the Brain,* p. 33 (1970). In short, we do not know what goes on inside the brain when it is responding to stress (or doing almost anything else):

> Psychology has been defined as the study of consciousness. By this is meant the mental life of an individual — feelings, sensations, thoughts and whatever else it is that goes on within our skulls every day. The brain scientist cannot explain the workings of the "mind" . . . yet. The sum total of our consciousness — of our "mind" — is the product of very complicated brain processes. We are only now beginning to learn how the brain works in performing simple tasks such as responding to sensory information and generating movement. The brain scientist is still at a loss when it

> comes to explaining desires, ambitions, or other feelings in terms of brain mechanisms. This does not mean that these feelings are not the result of brain activity — they most certainly are. The brain mechanisms associated with them are simply poorly understood at this time. Teyler, *A Primer of Psycho Biology — Brain and Behavior,* pp. 123-24 (1975).

From these facts, appropriate direct testimony or cross examination can establish that nobody can predict how any individual brain will react to any particular stress situation. Tables and charts of reaction times, some of which are discussed below, are relevant only as generalities.

How, then, does the reasonable man react? The basic answer seems to be that, in general, he reacts with amazing speed in most situations. Sir John C. Eccles, the double Nobel laureate who was one of the greatest experts on the human brain, stated that "the brain operates at levels of complexity transcending any human evaluation." Eccles, *Facing Reality,* p. 162 (1975).

Current transportation engineering standards agree with this conclusion. Most standard works, including the AASHTO Blue Books and Red Books, break human reactions down into the four-stage process of perceiving the problem, having the intellectual thought generation about it, having an emotional response to it, and taking volitional action to solve the problem. The four-stage "PIEV" (perception, intellect, emotion, volitional act) reaction process was definitively expounded in the basic text, Matson, Smith and Hurd, *Traffic Engineering,* pp. 20-21, as follows:

> Regardless of which sensory perceptions are involved, the road user's response to the stimulus of a particular traffic situation takes time. The time required for a response such as putting on the brake is taken up by the psychological process of perception, intellection, emotion and volition.

> "Perception" means the road user does not have a simple reflect response to the stimuli he encounters under most traffic conditions. In nearly every case, he must perceive a complex and involved situation before he can react, and as the complexity of the situation increases, the time required to perceive conditions increases.
>
> "Intellection" is the forming of new thoughts and ideas. The time required for comparing, regrouping and registering new sensations is the intellection time. "Emotion" means the emotion may vitally influence or affect the final message which is sent to the muscles to be carried out.
>
> Behavior growing out of fear or anger is not unusual in traffic accidents. "Volition" is the will to take some action.

Contemporary medical research is increasing the "normal reaction times" accepted as engineering standards for nonemergency situations, based upon continuing discoveries of how complex the decision and reaction process is. Thus, *A Policy on Geometric Design of Rural Highways,* published by AASHO in 1965, assumed at page 135 a two and one-half second normal, nonemergency reaction time, whereas *A Policy on Design of Urban Highways and Arterial Streets,* published by AASHTO in 1973, assumed at page 277 that "in general, a driver's perception time varies from about 0.5 seconds for simple situations to as much as 3 or 4 seconds for more complex situations." The 1973 work then adds additional time elements for intellection, emotion response and volitional action, concluding, at page 277, that "for passing another vehicle [a standard simple reaction standard under nonstress circumstances] the perception-reaction initial maneuver time used is about 3.5 to 4.5 seconds." By way of comparison, *Traffic Engineering Theory and Practice,* by Louis Pignataro, assumes a standard PIEV nonstress reaction time of 0.5 seconds to four seconds. *Highway Engineering,* by Oglesby, assumes that most standard PIEV reactions should take three seconds or less.

The effect of the reaction standards employed can be devastating. A vehicle traveling at 50 m.p.h. will cover 220 feet in three seconds. If the driver or operator of that vehicle has 220 feet of road or track from the point at which the danger is perceived to the point of impact, each second spent in the PIEV reaction process will obviously be very important to the issues of whether the impact was avoided, and whether a failure to avoid the impact was negligent.

These calculations could be even more devastating if one side of the litigation is armed with the appropriate authorities and expert witnesses on the relevant reaction time issues and the other side is unprepared for the contest.

§ 7-4. Mechanics of Reaction — Increasing PIEV Time.

Design defects in the transportation facility may, like bad weather, increase the time required to perceive a situation. AASHTO has prepared the following partial listing of facility design elements affecting perception time at page 278 of the 1973 Red Book:

> 1. Visual, auditory and tactual impressions of highway characteristics will produce a faster driver response than feeling the effect of curvature from unbalanced lateral friction or pull upon the steering wheel.
> 2. Touch and sound sensations from highway surface roughness or from rough center dividers are relatively efficient in terms of perception-reaction time.
> 3. Use of visual indication to signal the driver has a slight disadvantage in speed of response compared to auditory and tactual stimuli in simple responses.

However, a visual means, for instance a sign, can be located some distance ahead of the vehicle and thus offset this disadvantage.

4. A warning based on a particular sensation should be located a sufficient distance ahead of the hazard to permit complex judgment responses to take place.

5. Warning and guide signs should be placed to take advantage of the faster eye movement and avoid the slower movement of turning the head.

6. To ensure prompt comprehension, destination names on signs should be kept to a minimum.

7. Any design of curbs, center islands, bridge piers, or other highway features which makes them other than highly visible will increase the difficulty of the driver's task, and will lengthen driver response time and likelihood of error.

8. Whenever the driver is confronted with a complex traffic or highway situation and is required to make choices, judgments, and decisions, his response time may increase to 2, 3, or even 5 seconds. Such judgments may occur in passing, at multiple ramps, at complicated intersections, and other similar conditions. It is desirable to design interchanges and intersections so that there will be only simple two-choice channels or otherwise the smallest number possible. Distance between choices must be sufficient for response time.

9. Multiple signs and signals at intersections may present discrimination problems to drivers and should, whenever possible, be simplified.

10. Drivers perform best when required to do only one thing at a time. It is important in freeway design to avoid situations where multiple decisions are required or where decisions on future actions may distract drivers from an immediate situation requiring all of their attention.

In addition, international medical and physiological research has clearly established that many persons suddenly confronted with unexpected dangers have their normal reactions slowed or paralyzed. This factor can be advantageously offset from the standard PIEV reaction times through cross-examination that brings out that the PIEV figures are obtained from safe, clearly explained, simple tests on essentially prewarned subjects in antiseptic laboratories. Thus, the adroit cross-examiner can bring out how the dirty, disgusting, confusing conditions at the transportation facility in question when the crash occurred render all the PIEV statistics irrelevant.

The known tendency of people to lose much of their normal reaction capacities under sudden emergencies should directly require increased safety features in the design (and maintenance) of the facility, under the rule that "Highways should be designed to accommodate all drivers in relative safety, including reasonable provisions for those whose driving competence has been seriously impaired." 1973 AASHTO Red Book, p. 280.

Some of the medical sources establishing the slowing of reaction time under sudden stress include:

Driver Reaction Time in Traffic, by G.M. McKay of the University of Birmingham in December-January, 1967-1965, volume of *New Zealand Road Safety,* p. 18, "In cases of extreme emotional stress, a pathological situation may arise in which the normal response to traffic may be suspended."

Preliminary Investigation into a Psychological Assessment of Driving Stress, by Dr. T.J. Hunt, published by the Division of Human Psychology, Institute for Medical Research, Medical Research Council, London, England, July 1968, p. 36,

> As a result of exposure (to sudden startle) a driver may continue in a state of apprehension and/or uncertainty for a minute — or even longer — following the actual incident which initiated the danger. Incorrect decision making may therefore continue for some time after unexpected incident, and any accident or error in driving occurring during that period may be occa-

sioned by the continuing effects of startle, rather than as a direct result of the incident itself.

Psychology and Behavior of Drivers in the Causation of Accidents, by E.C. Poulton, Assistant Director of the Medical Research Council, Applied Psychology Research Unit, Cambridge, England, Vol. 14, No. 4, *International Road Safety and Traffic Review,* p. 16.

> One of the most interesting pieces of experimental research carried out at the British Road Research Laboratory concerns overtaking on a two-lane road (Crawford, 1960; Road Research Laboratory, 1963, pp. 110-118). The driver was following a car, and there was a car ahead coming in the opposite direction. At a given signal he had to decide whether or not to overtake. Decision times ranged from an average of about 1.0 second when the driver had four seconds to spare after overtaking, to about 2.0 seconds when the driver had no time to spare. Thus the decision times reflected the difficulty of the decisions. When the driver should have started to overtake at once if he was to do so at all, because he had little or no time to spare, his maneuver was delayed owing to the difficulty of deciding whether or not to overtake. Clearly, drivers should not need to find themselves in such a difficult and dangerous situation.

Operator Response Factors in the Location and Control of Foot Pedals, ROBOT, published by the South African Road Safety Council, September-October 1976, p. 23: "Reaction time has been demonstrated to be closely related to the number of alternative possible stimuli; that is, perpetual uncertainty."

The complexity of the situation confronting the subject may also increase reaction time, as established by the following:

National Co-Operative Highway Report 50 — *Factors Influencing Safety at Highway-Rail Grade Crossings,* prepared by the Highway Research Board, National Research

Council, National Academy of Sciences — National Academy of Engineering, p. 84:

> Response time to visual stimuli increases with an increasing complexity or number of stimuli. The more complex the visual field, the more things one has to attend to, the longer it takes for any one thing to be reacted to. Response time also increases as the stimuli become less distinct and/or more ambiguous.
>
> Essen (47) has shown that reaction times to lights increase as the lights are placed farther from the observer. The results suggest that reaction times obtained at near point must be increased if they are to be applied to the driver in motion, whose attention is directed farther and farther down the road as his speed increases. Finally, response time increases with increasing angular displacement of the stimulus from the direct line of sight.

Of course, the medical tendency of human reaction time to increase under unexpected stress dovetails nicely into the legal "Sudden Peril" doctrine.

§ 7-5. Legal Concepts of Fault and the Mechanisms of Reaction.

In addition to the issue present in virtually every crash case of whether drivers reacted "reasonably" to sudden peril, there are other legal issues related to the human reaction mechanism with which attorneys and engineers should have some familiarity.

§ 7-5(A). Road Defects and Legal Reaction Standards.

The very fact that the road has a defect raises the issue that such a defect could have slowed or even stopped the reaction mechanism of unsuspecting drivers or passengers. Thus, *Huffman v. City of Holyoke,* 386 Mass. 582, 436 N.E.2d 952, 954 (1982), defined the road defects: "A defect on a public way constitutes anything in the condition or state of the roadway which renders it unsafe or inconvenient for ordinary travel."

Such "unsafe" or "inconvenient" features, when suddenly confronted, especially under reduced visibility conditions, will foreseeably increase reaction times, even for drivers familiar with the road, under the medical studies documenting the PIEV Theory. See *Daigneault v. Town of Auburn,* 357 Mass. 612, 259 N.E.2d 574 (1970).

Similarly, *Salinas v. Kahn,* 2 Ariz. App. 181, 407 P.2d 120, 127 (1965), held that a motorist can rely on outward appearances of the road and motorists are not bound by unposted signs or the unexpressed opinions of engineers. Suddenly appearing road defects destroying the safe outward road appearance motorists are relying on will increase reaction times predictably.

§ 7-5(B). Following Too Closely.

Most states follow the general rule that "[a] driver of an automobile must use every reasonable precaution to avoid a collision with the automobile ahead. *Ryon v. Javior,* 69 Ill. App. 3d 946, 952, 387 N.E.2d 936 (1979). A driver approaching from the rear has the duty to keep a safe lookout and must take into account the prospect of having to stop his vehicle suddenly." *Snedden v. Lavenka,* 92 Ill. App. 3d 979, 416 N.E.2d 1097, 1102 (1981).

New York Accord: *DeMartino v. United States,* 558 F. Supp. 1188 (E.D.N.Y. 1938) held that under New York law, a driver is required to drive his car at a sufficient distance behind the car ahead so as to be able to stop without a collision if the preceding automobile is stopped with due cause.

Tenczar v. Milligan, 47 A.D.2d 773, 365 N.Y.S.2d 272 (1975), held that a motorist is bound to see what he should have seen with proper use of his senses.

Ohio Accord: *State v. Ward,* 105 Ohio App. 1, 150 N.E.2d 465 (1958), held that an automobile driver must watch everything and everybody in front of him and on sides and in rear so far as possible.

Bird v. Hart, 2 Ohio St. 2d 9, 205 N.E.2d 887 (1965), stated that when a following driver hit a preceding driver, the following driver had violated an assured clear distance ahead statute and was guilty of negligence per se unless his conduct had some legal excuse.

Pennsylvania Accord: Anticipation by driver must include sudden slowing or stopping of vehicle. *Bohner v. Stine,* 463 A.2d 438 (Pa. Super. 1983).

Texas Accord: It is the duty of anyone driving on a road to maintain such clear distance behind the preceding vehicle so that he will be able to slow down or even stop without colliding with preceding vehicle. *Texas Hwy. Dep't v. Broussard,* 615 S.W.2d 326 (Tex. App. 1981).

The fact, however, is that attorneys properly informed about road defects and their impact upon the human reaction mechanism may be able to show that poor driving, such as following too close, may have been due to road design, construction, or maintenance defects reducing the motorists' stopping right distance. Thus, *Lucas v. Carson,* 38 Mich. App. 552, 196 N.W.2d 819 (1972), enunciated that the rule against following too closely by the test of due or ordinary care must be reasonably construed in light of attending conditions.

Indeed, a "rear ender" crash may have been caused not by the fault of the driver in the rear, as the law generally presumes, but by the fault, or act, of the driver in front who stopped suddenly without affording adequate reaction time to the driver in the rear. *Edwards v. Houston Transit Co.,* 342 S.W.2d 787 (Tex. App. 1961).

The basic legal standards for drivers assume fact situations that allow normal control and visibility for the motorist. Thus, erratic driving, such as skidding out of the proper lane, usually raises the rebuttable presumption of negligence. *O'Dell v. Dowd,* 102 Ill. App. 3d 189, 429 N.E.2d 548 (1981). Similarly, motorists should not ignore that which is plainly visible. *Golleher v. Herrera,* 651 S.W.2d 329 (Tex. App. 1983). Rules can be made to work fairly with adequate knowledge of road defects and their impact on a driver's control, vision, and reactions.

§ 7-5(C). Choice of Alternatives.

"The fact that a party has not chosen the safest course of conduct (*Allen v. Dhuse,* 104 Ill. App. 3d 806, 809, 60 Ill. Dec. 559, 433 N.E.2d 356 (1982)), or that the course of conduct chosen entails certain hazards, is not proof of negligence as a matter of law unless the less-safe course of action is unreasonable." (*Connolly v. Melroy,* 63 Ill. App. 3d 850, 853-854, 20 Ill. Dec. 654, 380 N.E.2d 863 (1978).)" *Reuter v. Kocan,* 113 Ill. App. 3d 903, 446 N.E.2d 882, 885 (1983).

This, when coupled with the "Sudden Peril" Rule, establishes that a party reacting under stress can follow any course of conduct reasonable or foreseeable *under the emergency circumstances.* Other safer alternatives may not even be relevant.

There can be no issue of liability if following other courses of conduct would have produced the same result. Thus, in *Szarat v. City of Chicago,* 117 Ill. App. 3d 809, 454 N.E.2d 68 (1983), a plaintiff pedestrian who fell on defendant's sidewalk could not be guilty of contributory fault by failing to keep a proper lookout because the defects causing the fall were covered with snow and not readily visible. Similarly, if a driver is inattentive, or even drunk, contributory fault may not be present if the driver crashes due to road defects that could not be detected and avoided within the reaction time of a reasonable man. Thus, the argument would be that, because an alert and sober driver could not have reasonably avoided the deathtrap, the driver's negligence, although he was lying in a drunken stupor on the floor of his car, was not the proximate cause of the crash.

On the other hand, of course, it is a very strong defensive position if the defendant can show that the plaintiff's injuries resulted from an "unavoidable accident" that would have happened irrespective of the defendant's negligence. *Kasper Instruments, Inc. v. Maurice,* 394 So. 2d 1125 (Fla. App. 1981). Thus, in *Lemos v. Montex,* 659 S.W.2d 145 (Tex. App. 1983), a party not keeping a proper lookout before a crash was excused because several cars parked at the corner of the intersection at issue would have blocked the view of an ordinary person who was looking. See also *Yarborough v. Berner,* 467 S.W.2d 188 (Tex. App. 1971) and *Airline Motor Coaches, Inc. v. Fields,* 140 Tex. 221, 166 S.W.2d 917 (1942).

Of course, the fact that other alternatives would have produced no better, or different, result must usually be established by expert witnesses working from physical evidence and road geometrics in the record. As a general rule, a witness may not directly testify about what he or she would have done differently (as a driver or passenger) had the situation been different from what it actually was. *Elyria-Lorain Broadcasting Co. v. Lorain Journal Co.,* 298 F.2d 356 (6th Cir. 1961).

Generally, neither negligence nor contributory negligence can exist when a party took action either reasonable under the circumstances (including reactions from sudden peril), or where the party really had no better alternatives.

Thus, in *State Farm Mut. Auto Ins. Co. v. Shoaf,* 4 Ohio App. 2d 122, 446 N.E.2d 824 (1982), the Court held that the action of plaintiff's insured in accelerating his automobile to try to swerve away from defendant's horse, which came running out from an intersecting road, was not unreasonable and was not a basis for establishing contributory negligence on the part of plaintiff's insured.

Similarly, a great body of case law holds that motorists are not negligent, absent speeding, drinking, sleeping behind the wheel, or other unusual factors, if they crash into vehicles that suddenly turn in front of them; or cross the center line and smash into them.

Turn Cases

Ohio: *Powell v. Montgomery,* 27 Ohio App. 2d 112, 272 N.E.2d 906 (1971). Evidence supported direction of verdict in crash case in favor of northbound motorist, who alleged that, without warning, southbound motorist turned his vehicle left and partially into the path in which northbound motorist was traveling, causing collision.

Texas: *Beacon Nat'l Ins. Co. v. Burleson,* 484 S.W.2d 109 (Tex. App. 1972). A driver of motor vehicle upon a highway and making a right turn into her driveway did not need to keep a proper lookout to the rear of her car.

Center Line Cross-Overs

Kralik v. Martin, 659 S.W.2d 136 (Tex. App. 1983). The Defendant's vehicle crossed the center line without warning and for no reason. The reasonable inference from the evidence sufficiently supported trial court's findings of both negligence per se and negligence on the part of the Defendant and her negligence was the proximate cause of accident and of plaintiff's damages.

The point to be noted in these sudden turn and cross-over cases is that they are usually based merely on an analysis of the conduct of the drivers involved, and often overlook how negligent road design, marking or signing could have proximately caused the crash by reducing sight distances, establishing too high a speed limit, maintaining too high a shoulder drop off, or suddenly confronting a terrified driver with some unexpected road hazard.

§ 7-5(D). Violation of Statutes.

Violation of traffic and safety ordinances and statutes is usually evidence, but not conclusive proof, of negligence. *deJesus v. Seaboard Coast Line R.R.*, 281 So. 2d 198 (Fla. 1973); *St. Louis-San Francisco Ry. v. Burlison,* 262 So. 2d 280 (Fla. App. 1972). Parties accused of such statutory violations may counter that the violations were not due to their negligence due to unavoidable factors, such as suddenly appearing road defects slowing down their reactions.

§ 7-5(E). Negligence Inferred From Crash.

The universal rule is that neither negligence nor contributory negligence can be inferred from the mere fact there was a crash. See *Kenyon v. State,* 21 A.D.2d 851, 250 N.Y.S.2d 1007 (1964), where a motorist's car skidded and went out of control, but contributory negligence could not be inferred from this fact alone.

CHAPTER 8

STANDARD OF CARE ISSUES AMONG DRIVERS, PASSENGERS, AND THIRD PARTIES

§ 8-1. General Principles.

Litigators must understand the different duties, standards of care, and proximate cause standards for drivers, passengers, and pedestrian third parties. The driver is generally held to a higher standard of care than the passenger, and passenger contributory negligence, if any, is more easily removed from the case by proximate cause analysis than is driver negligence. Thus, in single-vehicle crashes, while it is rarely possible for the driver to sue the passenger, it is often possible for the passenger to sue the driver. Defense attorneys generally attempt to link the passenger to the driver and thus impose the driver's higher standard of care upon the passenger through a theory of joint venture or agency.

In crash cases where one represents both a passenger and a driver, it is therefore prudent to bear in mind the differing legal standards applicable to each client. The potential conflict inherent between drivers and passengers in the same vehicle involved in the same crash should also be resolved, with full disclosure to each client, early in the representation.

In crash cases where a passenger brings an action against his driver and a defective road, there are usually two main issues on contributory fault: (1) whether the passenger should have entered the vehicle at all, and (2) whether the passenger should have attempted to take control of the vehicle prior to the crash.

§ 8-2. Identifying the Driver.

§ 8-2(A). Legal Assumption the Owner Was Driving.

When a vehicle containing two or more occupants is involved in a high-speed crash, it is often impossible to resolve from the wreckage the crucial issue of who was driving, or even who used to be who. The law of most states presumes that the owner was driving, in the absence of contrary evidence. In *Anderson v. Launer,* 13 Ill. App. 2d 503, 142 N.E.2d 838, 840 (1957), the court stated: "Proof of ownership raises the presumption that the car was under the [owner] defendant's control at the time of the accident and the burden of rebutting this inference then passes to the defendant." See also *Winston v. Sears, Roebuck & Co.,* 88 Ill. App. 2d 358, 233 N.E.2d 95, 98-99 (1967); *Tolefree v. March,* 99 Ill. App. 3d 1011, 425 N.E.2d 1247 (1981).

State Laws on Owner-Driver Presumptions

Florida: *Carrazana v. Coca Cola Bottling Co.,* 375 So. 2d 345 (Fla. App. 1979). Here a visible name implied ownership. There was a rebuttable presumption that the vehicle was owned by the defendant because the defendant's name appeared on a commercial vehicle involved in an accident. The Court further presumed that the operator of the vehicle was an employee of the defendant, and was, at the time of accident, engaged in the scope of his employment.

Slitkin v. Avis Rent A Car System, 382 So. 2d 883 (Fla. App. 1980). The plaintiff has the burden of proving that automobile was being operated with the owner's knowledge and consent.

Michigan: *Ensign v. Crater,* 41 Mich. App. 477, 200 N.W.2d 341 (1972). Where the owner of an automobile produced evidence sufficient to rebut the presumption of consent and knowledge of operation of his automobile by third person, the burden shifted to plaintiff to show by a preponderance of the evidence that the car was being operated with the owner's express or implied consent or knowledge at the time of accident.

Roberts v. Posey, 386 Mich. 656, 194 N.W.2d 310 (1972). The presumption of the owner's consent or knowledge of driving arises upon proof of owner's permission to use his automobile. After the owner's permission is established, the burden shifts to the owner to show that his vehicle was not thereafter being driven with his consent or implied consent or knowledge. Mich. Comp. Laws Ann. § 257.401.

Thomas v. Checker Cab Co., 66 Mich App. 152, 238 N.W.2d 558 (1975). Evidence establishing that taxicab company's name and colors were upon the taxicab created a prima facie case that the company had custody and control of the vehicle whether the company actually did or not. This presumption was sufficient to carry an action to the jury; this rule attracts only the burden of going forward with the evidence and is not the ultimate burden of proof, which is still on the injured party.

Fout v. Dietz, 401 Mich. 403, 258 N.W.2d 53 (1977). Rebuttable common-law presumption that operator was driving vehicle with consent of owner, whether expressed or implied, arises when the operator is not a member of family of owner.

Ohio: *Cincinnati Transit, Inc. v. Tapley,* 28 Ohio App. 2d 26, 273 N.E.2d 906 (1971). A prima facie case of liability against the defendant was established with the introduction of evidence showing the name of defendant on the side of the truck that was operated by the negligent driver.

Clauss v. Fields, 29 Ohio App. 2d 93, 278 N.E.2d 677 (1971). Where owner of a car driven by another is inside the car, a rebuttable presumption arises as to the owner's control and whether the driver is acting as his agent in operating the car; but a jury question of agency arises where the evidence is such that reasonable minds might differ as to whether the owner-passenger actually had right of control at the time of injury.

Pennsylvania: *Feagles v. Sullivan,* 32 D. & C. 47 (1938). A minor who borrowed his father's automobile and allowed a companion to drive it while he sat beside him was liable for the companion's negligence, not only on the basis of respondeat superior but also on the ground that he has such a high degree of control over the driver that the negligence of the driver is legally his.

Sweeney v. City of Pittsburgh, 348 Pa. 80, 34 A.2d 67 (1943). The presence of defendant's name on a commercial vehicle raises a "rebuttable presumption" that the vehicle is owned by defendant and that the driver of the vehicle is acting within the scope of his employment; such a presumption is sufficient to take the case to jury, even though the defendant produces uncontradicted evidence that the driver was not its employee, or produces evidence that the defendant did not own the vehicle in question.

Husin v. Spring Garden Brick & Clay Products Co., 62 York 157 (Pa. Com. Pl. 1949). When the defendant's name is on a commercial vehicle being driven in traffic, the presumption arises that the driver is acting within the scope of his employment. This presumption is overcome only in the following instances: (a) where the owner shows that the vehicle was not being used in the scope of the employment; or (b) where there are uncontradictable physical facts which make it mathematically impossible for the vehicle to have been so used; (c) where there is undisputed documentary evidence which makes it impossible for the vehicle to have been so used.

Moser v. McCarty, 9 Lycoming 77 (Pa. Com. Pl. 1963). Proof that the owner permitted another to use his vehicle may be expressed or implied. Implied permission may be proven by circumstances surrounding the use of a motor vehicle prior to the date of the accident.

Smalish v. Westfall, 440 Pa. 409, 269 A.2d 476 (1970). The fact that a vehicle owner is present or a passenger while the vehicle is being negligently driven by someone else does not *necessarily* make the owner liable for an injury caused thereby, or impute to him the driver's negligence, or create a presumption of a master-servant relationship. On the other hand, the driver's presence under these circumstances is sure to raise fact issues that will go to the jury that the owner would prefer not to see raised at all. A famous defense lawyer once told a prospective juror, "You understand the mere fact my client has been indicted does not raise any presumption he is guilty?" "Well," answered the juror, "it's a hell of a character reference."

Texas: *Better Beverages, Inc. v. Meschwitz,* 643 S.W.2d 502 (Tex. App. 1982). Under the "branded-car doctrine," evidence that the name of the defendant is printed on the side of a vehicle raises a presumption that the identified party is the owner of the vehicle. Such evidence is not conclusive and can be rebutted by evidence to the contrary. As a practical matter, rebutting such evidence will usually be virtually impossible.

Hunsucker v. Omega Industries, 659 S.W.2d 692 (Tex. App. 1983). Once the plaintiff proved ownership of the commercial vehicle at issue, such proof raised the presumption that the vehicle was being operated by an employee of the owner in the course and scope of his employment.

§ 8-2(B). Driver Identity Issue Renders Plaintiff's Careful Driving Habits Admissible.

When the crash wreckage raises an issue concerning the identity of the driver of plaintiff's vehicle, plaintiffs may introduce various forms of evidence that might not otherwise be admissible.

Evidence that the plaintiff was a good driver may be admitted under these circumstances if there is any issue that plaintiff's vehicle was improperly operated. This evidence of plaintiff's good driving is then relevant to establish that plaintiff must have been a passenger, and not the driver, of his vehicle. Thus, in *Hall v. Kirk,* 13 Ill. App. 3d 656, 300 N.E.2d 600 (1973), the estate of a person killed in a two-car collision brought a wrongful death action against the estate of the other occupant of plaintiffs' decedent's vehicle and the driver of the second vehicle. The other occupant of plaintiffs' decedent's vehicle had been driving the vehicle at the time of the crash. Neutral eyewitnesses testified that the vehicle containing plaintiffs' decedent had been speeding at the time of the crash. (It should be noted in passing that the stricture of *Plank v. Holman,* 46 Ill. 2d 465, 264 N.E.2d 12, 15 (1970), that "reconstruction testimony may not be used as a substitute for eyewitness testimony" would not apply here as no eyewitness could establish the identity of the person driving the vehicle containing plaintiffs' decedent.) Under the circumstances, the *Hall* court approved of plaintiff's introducing evidence that plaintiff's decedent had been a careful driver "for the purpose of showing that the plaintiff was not the driver of the vehicle. We believe that this was correct since there was no direct evidence as to who was driving the vehicle." 300 N.E.2d at 603.

Similarly, in *Robinson v. Workman,* 9 Ill. 2d 420, 137 N.E.2d 804 (1956), the estate of a person killed in a car crash brought a wrongful death action against the owner and other occupant of the car plaintiffs' decedent had occupied. Both decedent plaintiff's and decedent defendant's bodies were found in the car, and other witnesses testified that the car occupied by defendant and plaintiffs' decedent had been weaving all over the road before the crash. There was thus no doubt that the car occupied by plaintiffs' decedent and defendant had been negligently operated and the issue was the identity of the driver of that car. In order to establish that plaintiffs' decedent had not been the driver, the plaintiffs were allowed to admit evidence of plaintiffs' good driving habits. The jury found for plaintiffs. The appellate court reversed the verdict, feeling that there was no evidence in the record as to who the driver had been, and plaintiffs had therefore failed to meet their burden of proof. The Illinois Supreme Court reversed the appellate court, holding that the record had ample evidence plaintiffs' decedent had not been the driver and that this evidence included the properly admitted evidence of plaintiffs' decedent's good driving habits. The Supreme Court, in fact, specifically noted that one reason for overruling the appellate court was that "in this case, the Appellate Court . . . [said], in effect, that [plaintiffs' decedent] abandoned his usual careful habits . . ." 137 N.E.2d at 808. See also *Dwinelle v. Union Pacific R.R.,* 104 Colo. 545, 92 P.2d 741 (1939), cited at 32 A.L.R.2d 992 (1953), where it was also held that the estate of one of two occupants of a vehicle could bring in evidence of the decedent's careful driving habits when both occupants were killed in a collision.

In *Hawbaker v. Danner,* 226 F.2d 843, 847-48 (7th Cir. 1955), the plaintiffs' decedent was an occupant in a car that drove onto a bridge where a collision had just taken place. The car containing plaintiffs' decedent proceeded to smash into the cars already littering the bridge, and plaintiffs' decedent was killed. In an action against the driver of the car that caused the first collision, plaintiffs were allowed to introduce evidence of the careful driving habits of the driver of the car carrying plaintiffs' decedent, although eyewitnesses had testified to seeing plaintiffs' decedent's car for several seconds before it crashed into the other cars. (These witnesses also saw the actual collision of plaintiffs' decedent's car into the other cars.) In sustaining the admission of evidence of the careful driving habits of the driver of plaintiffs' decedent's car, the court noted that the car was confronted by a sudden emergency situation when it drove onto the bridge, there was no eyewitness testimony as to how that driver had been operating his car before he drove onto the bridge, and there was consequently no eyewitness testimony about why that driver had allowed his vehicle to be placed in such a position of peril. The court therefore concluded: "The testimony of what [the driver of plaintiffs' decedent's car] did to escape injury was not proof that he was using reasonable care to avoid being placed in a position of danger. The careful driving habits were material." 226 F.2d at 848.

Thus, evidence of careful driving habits, just like expert testimony on the issue of who the driver was, will be admitted even if there are eyewitnesses to the crash so long as the eyewitnesses do not know who was driving the vehicle at issue when the crash occurred. *Noonan v. Maus,* 197 Ill. App. 103 (1915).

§ 8-2(C). Driver Identity Issue May Enhance Admissibility of Crash Photos.

Crash photos, particularly if they show the interior of vehicles, are often quite gory. High speed impacts between vehicles of sufficient weight can crush, or even liquify, significant portions of the human body. Pictures of such scenes are not pretty, but the folk wisdom of lawyers has invariably held that plaintiffs will gain, and defendants will correspondingly be held more accountable, if the jury is permitted to see such pictures.

The weak points about these photos, for their proponents, is that they are usually cumulative and prejudicial. Once oral testimony of eyewitnesses or experts (or both) has established the events of the crash, the photos of the carnage become duplicative for the most part. This substantially weakens the probative value of the photos and may lead the trial court to grant an exclusionary motion pointing out the high prejudicial impact of the photos under the rationale of Rule 403 of the Federal Rules of Evidence that "[Even] relevant evidence may be excluded if its probative value is substantially outweighed by the danger of unfair prejudice, confusion of the issues, or misleading the jury."

If, however, there is an issue about the identity of the driver of plaintiff's vehicle, the crash photos clearly become much more relevant if they can shed light on that issue. Even where there is no issue about the driver's identity raised by defendants, the plaintiffs can consider offering crash photos showing who the driver was on the theory that he, or she, can introduce all evidence relevant and material to their theory of the case. *Schneider v. Kirk,* 83 Ill. App. 2d 170, 226 N.E.2d 655 (1967).

Cases allowing the introduction of photos showing bodies inside, or even lying around outside a crashed vehicle are common and the photos can offer some evidence of the driver's identity. See *Hanson v. Rand,* 344 Ill. App. 418, 101 N.E.2d 119 (1951); *MacGregor v. Bradshaw,* 193 Va. 787, 71 S.E.2d 361 (1952); *Shaughnessy v. Morrison,* 116 Conn. 661, 165 A. 553 (1933), cited at 32 A.L.R.2d 994 (1953).

§ 8-2(D). Other Reasons to Admit Crash Photos.

Admissibility is less clear if the crash photos cannot shed light on the driver's identity. The prejudicial impact of such photos may outweigh their probative value if no other evidentiary use may be made of the photos. Some suggested additional points of relevance we have found to justify introducing crash photos that do not identify the driver are discussed below.

Warning Time. If there is an issue about how much warning time the occupants of plaintiff's vehicle had, then crash photos showing bodies inside the vehicle may be relevant by showing that the occupants did not have enough time to leave the vehicle. This point would be particularly important if the occupants could have left the vehicle, given enough warning time before the crash. Such arguments are appropriate for the occupants of vehicles parked or slowly going over railroad tracks when struck by trains. Such arguments are not appropriate for the occupants of vehicles colliding at high pre-crash speed. Photos showing no occupants in the vehicle are not appropriate to support an alleged adequate warning time, since the bodies may have been thrown out of the vehicle after impact.

Speed. If speed of either or both vehicles involved in the crash is relevant, crash photos may be offered under the argument that the presence or absence of carnage and wreckage is one basis from which the jury can infer the speed, and perhaps even the angle, of the impacting vehicles.

Death of Occupant. Crash photos may also be offered to establish the fact of death, which is certainly a relevant and material issue in a wrongful death action. Such a rationale was cited to support the introduction of crash photos in *Godvig v. Lopez,* 202 P.2d 935, 937 (Or. 1949), where the court noted: "The more modern decisions . . . uphold the admissibility of photographs showing the physical condition of injured persons, or even the appearance of deceased persons if they tend to show the circumstances or cause of death."

Pain and Suffering. Juries are allowed to see the more gruesome personal injuries "in the flesh," even after they have been completely described in oral testimony. Thus, in *LeMaster v. Chicago Rock Island & Pacific R.R.,* 35 Ill. App. 3d 1001, 343 N.E.2d 65 (1976), plaintiff was allowed to present to the jury his own testimony about the loss of his left leg and left hand, medical testimony about those amputations, photographs of his stumps taken during the healing process, and photographs of the stumps taken while he was dressing. Even after all that evidence, plaintiff was still allowed to show the jurors his actual stumps in person.

Ohio Accord on Pain and Suffering Photos: *Reeves v. City of Springfield,* 111 Ohio App. 387, 171 N.E.2d 178 (1961). When the plaintiff fell on a public sidewalk and the extent of injuries was before the jury, there was no abuse of discretion in admitting photographs taken of plaintiff's face while in the hospital.

Michigan Accord on Pain and Suffering Photos: *Taylor v. Michigan Power Co.,* 45 Mich. App. 453, 206 N.W.2d 815 (1973). Admission of gruesome photographs of a decedent was proper where photographs were relevant to the issue of whether or not there had been conscious pain and suffering prior to death.

Details of Crash Scene. Many courts admit crash photos showing gory injuries if the photos also establish relevant details about the crash scene.

Massachusetts: *Podolsky v. LaForge,* 92 F.2d 954 (1st Cir. 1937). In action for death and conscious suffering of plaintiff motorist who collided with truck, pictures of the scene of the accident were properly introduced through a witness who testified he was at the place of the accident within ten minutes after it occurred and who would say the photos accurately depicted the accident scene.

Ohio: *Bailey v. Greeley General Warehouse Co.,* 83 N.E.2d 244 (Ohio 1948). Posed accident reconstruction photographs are admissible if such photographs are identified as fair and accurate representations of conditions as the witness saw such conditions.

Booksbaum v. Christian, 202 N.E.2d 205 (Ohio App. 1936). Photographs were identified by cross-examining a witness who could not properly identify one automobile in the photo. The court nevertheless held there was a sufficient identification to allow admission of photos where the only purpose served was to show point of contact between the automobiles, and where extent of damage to the automobiles was not a jury question.

Pennsylvania: *Vanic v. Ragni,* 435 Pa. 26, 254 A.2d 618 (1969). For a photograph showing conditions different from those conditions at time of accident to be admissible, any changes must be specifically pointed out, and capable of being clearly understood by jury.

An argument for admission of crash photos in death cases should not only include the foregoing elements, but should also include a direct attack on the undue screening of evidence from juries in civil death cases. The exclusion of evidence that, in terms of Federal Rule of Evidence 401, "has any tendency to make the existence of any fact that is of consequence to the determination of the action more probable or less probable," simply because of an undue concern to treat jurors as children to be shielded from the facts of life was condemned soundly by Wigmore. See Wigmore, *Evidence in Trials at Common Law,* Vol. 4, § 1158, at 350 (Chadbourn rev. 1972).

§ 8-3. Passenger's Contributory Negligence Based on Joint Venture.

Defendants often seek to reduce a passenger's award by attempting to hold a plaintiff passenger to the higher standard of care of a driver by arguing that the driver's contributory negligence adheres to the passenger because both were involved in a joint venture at the time of the crash. This argument requires the defendant to establish that plaintiff and the defendant had joined in a common enterprise, had a community of interest in performing the common enterprise, had a common right to direct and control the policy of the venture, and had a right to share in profits and losses. *Russell v. Klein,* 33 Ill. App. 3d 1005, 339 N.E.2d 510 (1975); *Richton v. Farina,* 14 Ill. App. 3d 697, 303 N.E.2d 218 (1973).

More important for transportation facility negligence cases, *Andes v. Lauer,* 80 Ill. App. 3d 411, 399 N.E.2d 990 (1980), has held that related co-workers traveling to work in a common vehicle owned by one of them were not engaged in a joint venture. The court reasoned that:

> A joint enterprise can exist only in a business relationship (*Smith v. Bishop* (1965), 35 Ill.2d 380, 205 N.E.2d 461), and the relation between two employees is not to be so labeled. As between co-employees, there is no sharing of profits, no shared proprietary interest and no right to direct the conduct of the other. As between co-employees in a car pool, there is no joint enterprise that will support the imputation of vicarious contributory negligence. 399 N.E.2d at 993.

The *Andes* rationale would seem to vitiate a passenger-driver joint enterprise agreement arising from many relationships.

§ 8-4. The Passenger's Duty of Care.

"It is a matter of common experience that passengers in a vehicle trust to the driver to avoid the ordinary dangers of the road, and [passengers are not required] to tender advice, unless conscious of the driver's ignorance or want of care." *Zank v. Chicago, Rock Island & Pacific R.R.,* 17 Ill.

2d 473, 161 N.E.2d 848, 853 (1959). Consequently, it is ordinarily not contributory negligence or contributory willful and wanton misconduct for a passenger to fall asleep absent circumstances (which the opposition must prove) of an obvious danger, raising a duty in the passenger (breach of which the opposition must prove) to warn the driver. *Ramirez v. Deters,* 41 Ill. App. 3d 935, 938-39, 357 N.E.2d 546 (1976); *Smith v. Solfest,* 65 Ill. App. 3d 779, 382 N.E.2d 831 (1978).

In *Schultz v. Whitney,* 87 Ill. App. 3d 676, 410 N.E.2d 186 (1980), the plaintiff was a passenger in a car being driven by an intoxicated driver when a two-vehicle crash occurred. The jury was instructed that the issue of the contributory negligence of plaintiff's driver did not apply to the plaintiff's passenger in her action against the other driver.

Similarly, a plaintiff pedestrian run down by a vehicle containing both an intoxicated driver and a passenger was held to have no right to sue the passenger in *Fugate v. Galvin,* 84 Ill. App. 3d 573, 406 N.E.2d 19 (1980). The passenger in *Fugate* was absolved from responsibility for the driver's negligence, although the passenger knew the driver was intoxicated:

> Where the passenger does not own the car . . . the final decision to permit an intoxicated driver to take the car upon the road is never the passenger's, and so there can be no duty on him.
>
> The decision to take to the road in an intoxicated condition remained the driver's alone. 405 N.E.2d at 21-22.

The passenger's lower duty of care was further underscored in *Davelis v. Central Engineering Co.,* 86 Ill. App. 3d 593, 408 N.E.2d 218, 222 (1980), where the court noted: "A passenger is under no duty to warn the driver of a danger which the driver sees." An even more comprehensive enunciation of the passenger's lower standard of care is found in *Andes v. Lauer,* 80 Ill. App. 3d 411, 399 N.E.2d 990, 992-93 (1980), which quotes Mizra & Applemen, *Illinois Tort Law and Practice* § 4.7:

> At one time one or more of the Appellate Districts embraced rules which proved to be absurdities, in that they required substantially the same duty of the occupant as was required of the motorist in driving the automobile. . . . Since every approaching automobile constitutes a potential hazard in view of the possibility that it might swing across the center line, particularly in a line of oncoming cars where one might attempt to pass another, and considering that an automobile might be approaching from an intersecting road or from a driveway, to give true service to such a rule would require a constant harassment of the driver by the passenger seeking to comply with the law. Our Supreme Court laid the doctrine to rest in *Hatcher v. New York C.R. Co.* (1959), 17 Ill. 2d 587, 162 N.E.2d 362. . . .
>
> In the absence of any evidence demonstrating that the passenger did anything other than what an ordinary person would have done at the time, it is the duty of the trial court to direct a verdict for the plaintiff upon this issue, and to eliminate it from jury consideration. Otherwise, the submission of such an issue to the jury is an inference by the trial court that there is a conflict or dispute as to this area which it is then the jury's province to resolve. This could be confusing and cause either the return of an improper verdict or impair an award of the full measure of damages in a liability case.

State Laws on Passenger-Driver Issues

Florida: *Haley v. Commissioner,* 203 F.2d 815 (5th Cir. 1953). A "joint venture" is when a profit is jointly sought by a special combination of two or more persons without any actual partnership. Lack of profit element eliminates joint venture and negligence of driver cannot be attributed to passenger.

Indiana: *Martin v. Roberts,* No. 684 § 249 (6-22-84) 15 pp. On petition to transfer — Court of Appeals of Indiana No. 2-1281 A 418. Merely riding in a vehicle does not constitute incurred risk. Since there was evidence that plaintiff was not able to fully determine the conduct of defendant which would have alerted her to his intoxicated condition or to his otherwise improper driving, and an inference of constructive knowledge is not sufficient to establish an assumption of risk as a matter of law, the issue was one to be decided by the jury as trier of fact.

Massachusetts: *O'Brien v. Janelle,* 321 Mass. 316, 73 N.E.2d 460 (1947). Where an automobile guest has no reason to fear his driver will be incompetent or careless, the guest can go to sleep in the vehicle without negligence.

Wheatley v. Peirce, 354 Mass. 573, 238 N.E.2d 858 (1968). It was a jury issue whether an injured passenger failed to conform to the standard of reasonable care for his own safety when he invited another person to drive his automobile and that driver later drove too fast and got into a crash.

Michigan Law: *Blazo v. Neveau,* 382 Mich. 415, 170 N.W.2d 62 (1969). The negligence, if any, of plaintiff's husband, who was the driver of the car, could not be attributed to plaintiff, who was a passenger in the car.

Boyd v. McKeever, 384 Mich. 501, 185 N.W.2d 344 (1971). To constitute a "joint enterprise" between driver and passenger there must be a community of interest in the use of the vehicle, a common responsibility for its negligent operation, and it must be found that the driver was acting as an agent of the other member of the enterprise.

Vanderah v. Olah, 387 Mich. 643, 199 N.W.2d 449 (1972). The plaintiff was injured in an intersection crash while riding as a passenger in an automobile driven by her husband. She brought suit against the driver and the owner of the other vehicle. Evidence that plaintiff's husband had been intoxicated and that plaintiff had presumptive knowledge of such fact, was relevant to the issue of whether the plaintiff was contributorily negligent for having voluntarily ridden in an automobile driven by a drunken husband.

Flager v. Associated Trade Lines, 52 Mich. App. 280, 216 N.W.2d 922 (1974). A motor scooter being jointly operated by two girls, one operating its brakes and the other its throttle and steering, hit a truck. The scooter could be controlled only by the two girls acting jointly: each was an "operator" of the scooter and negligence by either would bar recovery for one girl's death in the collision.

Kirby v. Larson, 400 Mich. 585, 256 N.W.2d 400 (1977). An automobile passenger's contributory negligence is a fact issue in an injury suit.

In an intersection crash, an automobile passenger, who sought to recover for injuries sustained, had urged her driver to turn and had failed to warn that defendant's vehicle was bearing down on them. Whether the passenger was contributorily negligent was for the jury; the passenger may have been contributorily negligent if jury found that she was able to control the driver by her urgings.

A passenger's failure to warn of a danger he knows of, and which he reasonably believes the driver is unaware of, may be contributory negligence. However, this requires that the driver be negligent, that such negligence be a legally contributing cause of the harm, and that the plaintiff passenger be able to control the driver, i.e., that the driver would heed the warnings, and that exceptional circumstances exist which require the passenger to keep a lookout. Allowance must also be made for the possibility that by interfering under the particular act involved, the passenger will increase the danger.

New York: *Kowalski v. Mohsenin,* 38 A.D.2d 274, 329 N.Y.S.2d 37 (1972). Contributory negligence, if any, of father-driver could not be imputed to infant plaintiff-passenger.

Kalechman v. Drew Auto Rental, Inc., 33 N.Y.2d 397, 308 N.E.2d 886, 353 N.Y.S.2d 414 (1973). Plaintiff passenger may recover for negligent operation of vehicle if evidence proves that he did not contribute through negligence to his injury.

Ohio: *Vonderheide v. Comerford,* 113 Ohio App. 284, 177 N.E.2d 793 (1961). Ohio does not recognize the doctrine of imputed negligence.

Lester v. John R. Jurgensen Co., 400 F.2d 393 (6th Cir. 1968). Under Ohio law, the negligence of a driver of a vehicle can be imputed to a passenger only if it can be shown that the two were engaged in a joint enterprise pursuant to which the passenger had a right to control the acts of the driver in his operation of vehicle.

The negligence of a driver would not be imputed to a passenger merely because both are fellow employees. Nor will the fact that they have a common destination or objective in making the trip, or that the passenger has paid a share of the cost of the trip sustain imputed negligence.

Roberts v. Bohn, 26 Ohio App. 2d 50, 269 N.E.2d 53 (1971), *rev'd, Suchy v. Moore,* 29 Ohio St. 2d 99, 279 N.E.2d 878.

The failure of an occupant of an automobile to use a seat belt is not admissible in action for injuries arising out of an automobile accident.

Pennsylvania: *Riley v. City of Philadelphia,* 333 Pa. 533, 5 A.2d 117 (1939). An automobile guest is not held to the high degree of care required of a driver. The guest can relax. However, an automobile guest is negligent in joining the driver in testing a known or obvious danger, unless the driver is aware of and attempting to avoid the peril. An automobile guest is not negligent in failing to act to discover dangers he does not know of, even though they might be discovered by giving attention to the road.

Balla v. Sladek, 381 Pa. 85, 112 A.2d 156 (1955). Testimony that the plaintiff passenger and defendant driver had been drinking prior to the accident for purpose of showing contributory negligence was properly excluded since the fact alone was not sufficient to show intoxication impairing driver's ability to drive.

Pusateri v. Stanton, 5 Adams L.J. 30 (Pa. Com. Pl. 1963). Even if, at the time of the crash, the driver of the vehicle and the passenger were engaged in some common enterprise or purpose, the negligence of the driver will not be imputed to the passenger unless, at the time of the accident, the passenger had the right of control in whole or in part.

Gorgiadis v. Fuenfstueck, 31 Lehigh L.J. 121 (Pa. 1964). The same contributory negligence which bars recovery to a passenger may also make the passenger liable to another if it is the proximate cause of injuries sustained by a third person.

Tomasek v. Monongahela Ry., 427 Pa. 371, 235 A.2d 359 (1967). Two automobile passengers knew of the existence of a railroad crossing. One passenger even knew of the approximate time a train would traverse the crossing. Both passengers were of the opinion that the driver was not familiar with the crossing, and neither passenger warned the driver of the existence of the crossing. The question of whether the passengers were contributorily negligent in not warning the driver of the presence of the crossing so that he would stop, look, and listen, and in not protesting driver's action in failing to slow down, was for the jury to decide.

Campana v. Bower, 424 Pa. 383, 227 A.2d 887 (1967). A jointly owned auto was being driven by the wife. The husband was a passenger. The vehicle crashed into a guardrail on the highway. The husband-passenger, who knew that his wife had been driving for four hours through darkness and intermittent rain and that the automobile had a defective windshield wiper, was asleep at time of accident. The jury issue was presented as to contributory negligence of the passenger who was killed in the accident.

Weaver v. Clabaugh, 255 Pa. Super. 532, 388 A.2d 1094 (1978). In order to assume risk of harm from driver's conduct the passenger must be subjectively and actually aware of the facts which create danger and must appreciate danger itself and nature, character, and extent which make it unreasonable.

Texas: *Little v. Littlefield,* 311 F.2d 885 (5th Cir. 1962), *amended on denial of rehearing,* 313 F.2d 959 (1963). The jury found that the owner's son, who was driving a car in which the owner was a passenger, was not acting as the owner's agent and there was no joint enterprise. The son's contributory negligence in colliding with another car was therefore not imputable to the owner.

Fuller v. Flanagan, 468 S.W.2d 171 (Tex. App. 1971). Even if a 14-year-old passenger was engaged in a joint enterprise with the driver at the time of the accident, this driver's negligence could not be imputed to a minor.

Hunter v. Carter, 476 S.W.2d 41 (Tex. App. 1972). Where passenger-plaintiff knew that driver was intoxicated, the passenger's contributory fault was a jury issue.

Author's Note — Evidence the passenger knew the driver was drinking should not create a jury issue unless the evidence is that the driver was intoxicated and impaired, and the passenger may [or should] have known about the condition of the driver.

Tipton v. Stuart, 480 S.W.2d 795 (Tex. App. 1972). Generally, a passenger does not have to be paranoid, ready at any moment to seize the wheel. For example, the passenger is not required to keep a lookout and can rely on the vigilance and skill of the driver. However, if, from the manner in which the driver is operating the car, the passenger learns that the driver is likely to be inattentive or careless, the passenger will then have a duty to keep a proper lookout and may even have to seize the wheel. Thus, even paranoids can occasionally be right.

Author's Note — Evidence at trial on this point often becomes a contest about how long before the crash the driver was driving badly, and whether the passenger had any opportunities to leave the vehicle after the driving had begun and before the crash took place.

Galvan v. Sisk, 526 S.W.2d 717 (Tex. App. 1975). The Court would not infer a driver had given up any part of his right to control his own vehicle merely because there was an agreement between the driver and a passenger to share operating costs of the vehicle by the passenger paying for the gas.

Government Employees Ins. Co. v. Edelman, 524 S.W.2d 546 (Tex. App. 1975). Two boys out joyriding were not engaged in a joint venture.

Adama v. Morris, 584 S.W.2d 712 (Tex. App. 1979). Both the driver and his passenger must use reasonable care. That is, the care a reasonably prudent person would exercise under such circumstances. However, as the circumstances of the driver and passenger are different, the conduct required of a passenger to satisfy that duty may be quite different from that required of a driver.

Gutierrez v. Yancey, 650 S.W.2d 169 (Tex. App. 1983). A "joint adventure" arises when parties engage in a joint pursuit of a business performance for profit.

Escamilla v. Garcia, 653 S.W.2d 58 (Tex. App. 1983). Here a front seat passenger was found to be at fault for attempting to intervene and seize the wheel. During the course of a turn the passenger yelled at the driver that they were going to be hit and reached for the driver's arm. This evidence was sufficient to support a jury finding that the collision was proximately caused by both the automobile driver and the passenger, with the passenger being 20 percent negligent.

Author's Note — Had the passenger done nothing as the crash approached, occupants of the other vehicle might have sued the passenger for non-intervening. Passengers can be attacked for doing either too much or too little to interfere with the driver. A passenger's safest course is usually to fall asleep and hope the driver gets him where he wants to go. In addition, passenger and driver can exchange releases before the trial starts.

§ 8-5. The Passenger's Burden of Proof.

Where the passenger is bringing suit against the driver of another vehicle that crossed the center line and struck the vehicle of the passenger, the driver of the other vehicle bears the burden to show he was not negligent. *Calvetti v. Seipp,* 37 Ill. 2d 596, 227 N.E.2d 758 (1967). However, where the plaintiff passenger sues his own driver for negligence, the passenger has knowledge of the defendant's acts prior to the crash, and the plaintiff, therefore, bears the burden to show the defendant driver was negligent. *Crosby v. Disteler,* 38 Ill. App. 3d 1058, 349 N.E.2d 448 (1976).

Massachusetts: *Flynn v. Lewis,* 231 Mass. 550, 121 N.E. 493 (1919). Automobile owner held liable only for gross negligence in operating automobile causing death to daughter's guest.

Bada v. Foley, 302 Mass. 411, 19 N.E.2d 537 (1939). A driver in a following automobile owed duty to people inside the car ahead of him to operate his car in a reasonably careful and prudent manner. Thus, he owed a duty to maintain both a reasonable speed and a reasonable distance. Alas, within the bounds of ordinary care, he had to anticipate that the preceding automobile might be required to stop suddenly.

Missouri: *Wilson v. Tabor,* 656 S.W.2d 299 (Mo. App. 1983). Whether automobile driver was liable under humanitarian negligence doctrine for injuries sustained by passenger when automobile driver made left turn despite passenger's admonition that car door was not shut and passenger spilled out door onto street was for jury.

Ohio: *Bailey v. Brown,* 34 Ohio St. 2d 62, 295 N.E.2d 672 (1973). For there to be "wilful misconduct" within the guest statute, the plaintiff had to show that before the defendant acted, his intent was to perform "misconduct," not merely that defendant intended to take action he thought was innocent, but which in fact caused a crash.

CHAPTER 9

POLICE REPORTS

§ 9-1. Introduction.

The scene of a high speed vehicle crash usually resembles a piece of "hell on earth."

People who witness and/or survive such a crash are initially so shocked, and subsequently so intent on either rescue or escape, that their on-the-spot memories often exclude vital information such as speeds, angles of impact, or points of collision. Afterwards, when plaintiffs and defendants have sorted themselves out, memories are often filtered through substantial levels of self-interest.

In short, the only witness on the scene who will be generally believed by jurors and judges at trial is the police officer. By the time he testifies at deposition or trial, the reporting police officer will have usually "attended" so many other crashes that he will have little, if any, independent recollection of the crash in your case. His testimony then, either as his past recollection recorded or as present recollection refreshed, will hinge on his police report. Thus, police reports are valuable sources of information about the weather, visibility, vehicle speed and road conditions at the time of a specific crash. They are also the single most important tool, in most cases, for the evaluation of transportation facility negligence. These reports are the key to obtaining helpful testimony from immensely persuasive witnesses — the police officers who wrote and will defend their reports. Special statutes and case law decisions determine their availability in most jurisdictions.

§ 9-2. Police Reports and Notice of Dangerous Places.

Police reports of crashes are often an important source of notice to a defendant highway department that something may be wrong on a given transportation facility. Most highway departments, at least in theory, are required to post crash data, or at least serious crash data on what are called "spot maps." The theory is that when enough red pins, or whatever the crash symbol is, accumulate at a specific area, or on a given facility, someone from the department will go out to see what is wrong. These spot maps are obviously items plaintiffs should subpoena early in a transportation facility negligence case.

Police crash reports are also targets for subpoenas. If the jurisdiction attempts, as Illinois does, to create statutory confidentiality at the State level for the reports of other crashes on the facility at issue, the plaintiff's evaluation of the case may well be impaired. The actual reports are full of raw data, such as the number of persons killed and injured and the number of vehicles damaged in each crash that can be compared against statewide averages or nationwide averages on similar facilities. An expert witness can determine from the reports when the defendant had sufficient notice to warrant inspection and improvement of the facility. The state and national averages for fatality crashes, serious injury crashes, and major vehicle damage crashes on similar facilities can often be important to properly interpret a road's prior history. One case, for example, involved a road that did not have a total number of prior crashes exceeding the national average for similar traffic volume roads. If no additional data about the road had been available, the defense could have cited the crash reports as evidence that there was no notice of any unusual danger and hence no evidence of any defect on the road before the plaintiff was injured.

The jurisdiction, fortunately, allowed us to obtain copies of the actual police reports of prior crashes on that road, and an entirely different picture emerged from these reports. The prior crashes on this road were far more serious in extent than, although not exceeding in gross number, the national averages. Thus, the number of serious injuries and the number of vehicles seriously damaged on the road should have alerted the defendant to make necessary improvements long before the plaintiff's crash, a situation we never could have established without access to the actual police reports. The moral of the story is — get the most complete police data your jurisdiction allows. The local department where the crash reports originate generally will have more complete data than the county or stateside police or highway departments. The local police often communicate only crash data summaries to state police and highway departments.

§ 9-3. Dispensing With Police Reports.

Police reports are not always the best source of notice of defects in a transportation facility. Other techniques are available to establish notice, and these must also be employed even where prior crash reports are available.

If the defendant has installed safety devices such as lights or guardrails, those devices must be maintained with due care. *Greene v. City of Chicago,* 73 Ill. 2d 100, 382 N.E.2d 1205 (1978); *Baran v. City of Chicago Heights,* 99 Ill. App. 2d 221, 240 N.E.2d 381 (1968), *aff'd,* 43 Ill. 2d 177, 251 N.E.2d 227 (1969). The mere existence of the safety device suggests that the defendant considers it warranted. If it is allowed to break down or is negligently removed by the defendant, there can be little doubt that the fact finder will hold the defendant to have received adequate notice of its negligence. On the common sense side of the same argument, the defendant will obviously be in a strong position if it can argue that it cannot be held to know every place on its millions of miles of roadway where safety devices have failed before defendant had time to repair. Removing existing safety device is also very risky for a defendant because the very existence of the device constitutes actual notice that some presumably competent engineer felt it was warranted.

Other sources of notice that may circumvent the need for police reports include complaints from motorists, internal recommendations for improvement from defendant's own engineers, and newspaper stories of prior crashes.

§ 9-4. Admissibility of Police Reports.

Illinois: Police reports are generally inadmissible as hearsay. *People v. Olbrot,* 106 Ill. App. 3d 367, 435 N.E.2d 1242 (1982); *Peterson v. Lou Bachrodt Chevrolet Co.,* 61 Ill. App. 3d 898, 378 N.E.2d 618 (1978), *aff'd,* 76 Ill. 2d 353, 392 N.E.2d 1 (1979); *Rodriguez v. City of Chicago,* 21 Ill. App. 3d 623, 316 N.E.2d 88 (1974); *Walls v. Jul,* 118 Ill. App. 2d 242, 254 N.E.2d 173 (1969). However, diagrams or sketches made by the reporting officer in the report are admissible notwithstanding their being part of the report on the ground that they are explanatory; provided, however, that their accuracy is not in question. *Walls, supra,* 254 N.E.2d at 176. If any part of the officer's preparation is based upon information given to him by others, the diagram or sketch will be inadmissible. *Rogall v. Kischer,* 1 Ill. App. 3d 227, 273 N.E.2d 681, 688 (1971). Also, if the diagram is confusing or difficult to understand, it should not be admitted. *Peterson, supra,* 378 N.E.2d at 623. The mere attempt to introduce a report may be reversible error, provided a timely objection is made. *Jacobs v. Holley,* 3 Ill. App. 3d 762, 279 N.E.2d 186, 187 (1972). Pursuant to Illinois Supreme Court Rule 236(b) (Ill. Rev. Stat. ch. 110A ¶ 236(b)), police reports do not qualify under the business records exception to the hearsay rule. The report may contain hearsay statements and conclusions based upon those statements. *Morgan v. Rogers,* 30 Ill. App. 3d 346, 332 N.E.2d 476 (1975). Verbatim testimony read from the reports is also generally improper. *Rigor v. Howard Liquors, Inc.,* 10 Ill. App. 3d 1004, 295 N.E.2d 491 (1973); *Hall v. Checker Taxi Co.,* 109 Ill. App. 2d 445, 248 N.E.2d 721 (1969). The reports may, however, be used to refresh the recollection of the officer when he testifies. *Tuskey v. Callos,* 112 Ill. App. 2d 213, 250 N.E.2d 524 (1969); *Koch v. Pearson,* 219 Ill. App. 468 (1920); see *Taylor v. City of Chicago,* 114 Ill. App. 3d 715, 449 N.E.2d 272 (1983); *Wilkinson v. Mullen,* 27 Ill. App. 3d 804, 327 N.E.2d 433 (1975); *Rigor v. Howard Liquors, Inc., supra; Jacobs v. Holley, supra.*

If the police report refreshes the officer's recollection, his subsequent testimony will be based upon his refreshed recollection, independent of the report, which will not then be admitted into evidence. *Wolf v. City of Chicago,* 78 Ill. App. 2d 337, 223 N.E.2d 231 (1966); *Hoskins v. Zimmerman,* 334 Ill. App. 395, 79 N.E.2d 531 (1948); *D'Oranzo v. Lacny,* 330 Ill. App. 333, 71 N.E.2d 104 (1947). If, however, the report does not refresh the officer's recollection (a situation often caused by the officer's reluctance to testify against the governmental defendant incriminated by the report), the report will have to be qualified as the officer's past recollection recorded before it is admissible by showing (a) that the officer had no independent recollection; (b) that the report fails to refresh his memory; (c) that the facts were recorded at the time of occurrence or soon afterwards; and (d) that the report is accurate and true when made. *Rigor v. Howard Liquors, Inc., supra; Wilsey v. Schlawin,* 35 Ill. App. 3d 892, 342 N.E.2d 417 (1975); see *Strope v. Chicago Transit Auth.,* 71 Ill. App. 3d 987, 398 N.E.2d 1374 (1979).

It is important to recognize that only the part of the report for which past recollection recorded is established is admissible and other parts of the report are still inadmissible and therefore should be obliterated. *Wilkinson v. Mullen, supra.* Thus, in *Wilkinson,* the introduction of portions of a police report containing the factual observations of the officer was allowed under the past recollection recorded doctrine. Conclusions of the officer that are not the product of his personal observations (such as what witnesses told him if he did not see the crash) should be stricken from the report before it is admitted, but, under the *Wilkinson* doctrine, such improper portions of the report will go to the jury if timely objection is not made. It is, however, error to introduce portions of a police report as past recollection recorded without first establishing the foundation that the officer has no independent memory that can be refreshed by the report which he knew was accurate when made. *People v. Harrison,* 384 Ill. 201, 51 N.E.2d 172 (1943); *People v. Watkins,* 98 Ill. App. 3d 889, 424 N.E.2d 701 (1981); *People v. Walls,* 87 Ill. App. 3d 256, 408 N.E.2d 1056 (1980); *People v. Carter,* 72 Ill. App. 3d 871, 391 N.E.2d 427 (1979); *Strope v. Chicago Transit Auth., supra; Lawson v. Belt Ry.,* 34 Ill. App. 3d 7, 339 N.E.2d 381 (1975); *Rigor v. Howard Liquors, Inc., supra; Noumoff v. Rotkvich,* 88 Ill. App. 2d 116, 232 N.E.2d 107, 110 (1967).

In *Hooper v. Mizyad,* 98 Ill. App. 3d 768, 424 N.E.2d 851, (1981), the injured plaintiff called a police officer, who testified that the plaintiff had told him that he had fallen over some grocery bags and hurt his hip. The officer further testified on cross-examination that he had no independent recollection of what the plaintiff had told him and that his recollection was based entirely upon the report of the accident which was prepared by another officer at the scene. The trial court overruled the defendant's objection to this testimony, and the appellate court affirmed the lower court's ruling, stating that the officer testified that his recollection was refreshed by an examination of the report. *Hooper, supra,* 424 N.E.2d at 853-54. Note, however, that if the reporting officer is not present physically or by deposition at trial, the factual observations in the report cannot be admitted.

Police reports may be used to establish any written admissions against the interest of government defendants or by report entries showing government defendants had notice of defects before the crash at issue, provided the reporting officer did not depend upon inadmissible hearsay for such entries in his report. *Wilsey v. Schlawin, supra.*

Great care must be taken in offering police reports as evidence before the jury. The danger, if the report is not admissible, is that the proponent of the report will improperly make it appear to the jury that the opposition, by objecting properly to the report, is keeping the police report from jury consideration, thereby putting the opposition counsel in an unfair position before the jury. Such conduct is highly prejudicial and reversible error, even if no formal objection is made by the opponent. *Morgan v. Rogers, supra. Kelly v. Chicago Transit Auth.,* 69 Ill. App. 2d 316, 217 N.E.2d 560, 564 (1966). It is recommended that a motion in limine be made to limit the examination of the police officer to his own physical observations and not inquire about his conversations with others at the scene or his conclusions as to how the accident happened. This will protect and preserve your right to argue prejudicial error on appeal if opposing counsel acts less than honorably during the trial. See also *Paliokaitis v. Checker Taxi Co.,* 324 Ill. App. 2d 21, 57 N.E.2d 216 (1944); *Smith v. Johnson,* 2 Ill. App. 2d 315, 120 N.E.2d 58 (1954).

These rules concerning the admissibility of materials in police reports are obviously hinged to exclude what would constitute hearsay, as opposed to the presently recollected or previously recorded firsthand knowledge of the reporting officer. This formulation of the evidentiary rules is found in most jurisdictions, as reflected in *McCormick on Evidence,* Ch. 32, Official Written Statements and Certificates 737 (1972).

> Many writings that would otherwise meet the requirement of official written statements consist in part of conclusions of summaries of investigating official or agency. Police reports, for example, routinely contain not only statements based upon the reporting officer's own observations, but conclusions based upon what he was told by others and his own inferential processes. Vigorous application of the requirement of firsthand knowledge had generally resulted in the limitation of the use of these reports to the proof of those things which the reporting official himself observed.

Thus, in the seminal decision of *Johnson v. Lutz,* 253 N.Y. 124, 170 N.E. 517, 518 (1930), the court excluded an accident report which was prepared by a police officer who was not present at the time of the accident, and which report was based on statements made to him by persons present when he arrived. See also *Wells v. State,* 254 Ind. 608, 261 N.E.2d 865 (1970).

If police reports are going to be used to prove the truth of statements therein, most jurisdictions will require authentication of some form from the reporting officer that those statements are known by him to be true.

California: *West's Ann. Vehicle Code § 20013:*

> No police accident report shall be used as evidence in any trial, civil or criminal, arising out of an accident, except that the department shall furnish upon demand of any person who has, or claims to have, made such a report or upon demand of any court, a certificate showing that a specified accident report has or had not been made to the department solely to prove a compliance or failure to comply with the requirement that such a report be made to the department.

Box v. California Date Growers Ass'n, 57 Cal. App. 3d 266, 129 Cal. Rptr. 145 (1976). Traffic accident reports are not admissible in evidence. In this crash case, the trial judge refused to admit either the entire police accident report or the diagram portion thereof into evidence. Sometimes, however, you can get in the back door what you can't get in the front door. *Sherrell v. Kelso,* 116 Cal. App. 3d 22, 172 Cal. Rptr. 667 (1981), held that the statute barring police reports from being used as evidence at trial did not require the exclusion of the contents of the report. The evidentiary bar applied to the report itself.

Florida: *Garvey v. McNulty,* 213 So. 2d 319 (Fla. 1968). It was not error to let the plaintiff ask the investigating officer about the distance between vehicles at various times, even after defendant had introduced statements made by him to the officer regarding such distance.

Michigan: *Willmore v. Hertz Corp.,* 437 F.2d 357 (6th Cir. 1971). The accident report which was jointly prepared by the officer in court and another police officer was not admissible as past recollection recorded, where the officer merely used the report to refresh his recollection. This case points up the difference between present recollection refreshed by the report (in which case the report will not go into evidence) and past recollection recorded (where the report may go into evidence if the jurisdiction allows police reports to be admitted and if the report cannot refresh the reporting officer's present recollection of events).

Moncrief v. City of Detroit, 398 Mich. 181, 247 N.W.2d 783 (1976). A statute prohibiting the use of "red line" police reports in evidence was limited to reports specified by statutes, and had no effect on the general rules of evidence concerning a police officer's personal notes or routine, non red line, reports usually entitled "Motor Vehicle Accident Report," made by the officer from his present sense impressions, and from witness interviews at the scene of an accident. The exclusion of an otherwise admissible routine police report, which is not a "red-line" report, on the basis of this statute would be error. M.C.L.A. §§ 257.622, 257.624. A police report qualifying the reporting officers' past recollections recorded could be admitted. Bear in mind if you want the report to go in as past recollection recorded that it must *not* be able to refresh the officer's recollection in Court.

Kirby v. Larson, 400 Mich. 585, 256 N.W.2d 400 (1977). In a civil case, conduct at a crash cannot be established merely by the issuance of a traffic ticket to one of the parties. The issuance of the ticket is therefore not admissible evidence.

Hewitt v. Grand Trunk W. R.R., 123 Mich. App. 309, 333 N.W.2d 264 (1983). Before a police report can be admitted as past recollection recorded, the proponent of the report must show that the witness had firsthand knowledge of the event; that the written statement was an original memorandum made at or near the time of the event and while the witness had a clear and accurate memory of it; that the witness in court lacks a present recollection of the event; and that the witness can vouch for the accuracy of the written memorandum. This case deals with statements in the report that were hearsay when told to the reporting officer. Here, a police officer's report stated that a witness had told the officer that a victim had jumped in front of a train. The original report entry, the Court held, was hearsay. The report constituted multiple hearsay or "hearsay within hearsay." Thus, including improper evidence in a police report will not cure the original defect in the evidence. Note, however, that if the jurisdiction allows, the reporting officer might be qualified as an expert who normally relies on such evidence pursuant to a variant of Rule 703 of the Federal Rules of Evidence.

Police reports generally do not qualify as business records excepting to the hearsay rule. Here, an accident report filled out by a police officer was not admissible as a business record because the witnesses who were making the statement to the officer were not acting in the regular course of their business while doing so. The analysis in such cases usually hinges on whether either party to the report, the officer or the witness, is recording his own firsthand knowledge in the course of his normal business activity. Here, in a typical result of such analysis, the report was not classified as a business record exception to the hearsay rule because the witness who had the firsthand knowledge was not making the report on a normal business activity, while the reporting officer, who was arguably making the report as part of normal business activity, did not have the requisite firsthand knowledge.

Ohio: Often the admissibility of a report will hinge on whether the contents of the report were known firsthand by the officer who made the report, even if he is not later available as a witness. In *Westinghouse Elec. Corp. v. Dolly Madison Leasing Furn. Corp.,* 42 Ohio St. 2d 122, 326 N.E.2d 651 (1975), the Court construed an Ohio statute making official reports submitted by officers to the state admissible in evidence, even if the report contained hearsay in the facts recorded by public officials who were not present in court as witnesses. The Court further held, however, that the statute would not permit the introduction of reports containing hearsay statements that were merely reported to and not personally known by the reporting officer. Thus, hearsay can sometimes get into evidence, depending on why it's hearsay. A rose by any other name is sometimes even sweeter.

Pennsylvania: *DeVecca v. Ashton,* 45 Berks 257, 67 York 119, 87 Pa. D & C 585 (1954). In an automobile accident case in which both the owner and the only other occupant were killed, fingerprints taken off the steering wheel three days after the accident which did not match the fingerprints of the other occupant are inadmissible as evidence that the owner was driving the car at the time of the accident, where they are not otherwise identified as his or where it appears that the steering wheel might have been touched by any number of persons in the time after the accident.

Johnson v. Peoples Cab Co., 386 Pa. 513, 126 A.2d 720 (1956). Here, a police officer who was not a witness to the crash drew a diagram of how the crash happened. The artist-officer arrived on the scene five or ten minutes after the crash. His drawing attempted to show the point at which the automobiles collided, and noted that one of the vehicles went through a stop sign. The Court barred the drawing as hearsay. Had the officer written out a narrative of the events depicted in his drawing, it would also have been barred as hearsay. Sometimes a picture and a thousand words are equally worthless.

Harvey v. Doliner, 399 Pa. 356, 160 A.2d 562 (1960). In this crash case, the police report contained the reporting officer's opinion (even though he did not witness the crash) that the plaintiff had been drinking at the time of the crash. The report was barred as hearsay because there was no evidence the officer had seen plaintiff, or observed his condition, at the time of the accident, or that the officer had questioned plaintiff about drinking. The report and the officer failed to supply a basis in the officer's observations when he used the report for his opinion on the plaintiff's condition at the time of the crash. Sometimes, however, what you see at the time *can* sustain an opinion about an element or condition in the past. Thus, in a famous old war story, a lawyer cross-examining a witness got the witness to admit he did not see the lawyer's client bite off the plaintiff's ear. "How then," demanded the incautious cross-examiner, "do you know my client bit off Mr. Jones' ear?" The smirking witness answered, "Because I saw your client spit it out."

Texas: *Hinrichs v. Texas & N.O.R.,* 153 S.W.2d 859 (Tex. App. 1941). This case involved the issue of when is a statement a "statement." In *Hinrichs,* a railroad claim agent went to the home of a motorist injured in a grade crossing collision to interview the motorist and his wife concerning the collision. During the interview the agent wrote out a statement which motorist's wife refused to sign. The unsigned paper, of course, contained admissions very helpful to the railroad. When the case came to trial, the agent testified that the plaintiff-driver's wife had made the admissions in the unsigned statement to him. The wife denied having made the admissions to the agent and also denied that the alleged admissions were true. The Court held the railroad could not "bootstrap" the testimony of its agent by introducing in evidence the unsigned statement written by the agent.

§ 9-5. Mapping Techniques With Police Reports.

Police reports of prior crashes may be used to establish the defendant's prior notice of defects in the facility without proving the truth of the statements in the reports. The administrative powers in reviewing the crash reports should react to the number of crash reports on a facility. The significant circumstance about the prior crash reports, for notice purposes, is the fact that the reports were made, rather than proving the truth of the contents of the reports. Therefore, the prior crash reports are notice evidence, rather than hearsay.

The presentation to the jury of the material in the prior crash reports relevant to notice must be carefully handled to exclude objectionable hearsay matters. Indeed, since it will rarely be possible to have all the reporting officers who authored the prior reports available, virtually all of the contents of those reports may be hearsay if the prior crash reports are used to prove the truth of their contents.

Initially, pretrial requests to admit the truth of facts such as are allowed under Illinois Supreme Court Rule 216 should be served upon the opposition to establish those matters in each prior crash report that are relevant to the notice issue, namely the date of the report, the place of the reported crash, the police department authoring the report, the authenticity of an attached copy of the report, and, in some instances, the type of crash reported. Remember, with respect to each of these items, the request to admit should seek to establish the truth that each of these facts was reported. Notice will flow from the fact of the report, not from the truth of the reported facts.

The next procedure to present the authenticated facts in the reports that are relevant to notice issues, if you have sufficient numbers of prior crashes, is to spot map them on a drawing of the facility. Each dot will represent the reported location of a crash. If the spot mapping covers a long time period, a number of annual transparent overlays can be prepared, each showing the reported locations of crashes on the facility for a given year.

These spot maps graphically convey the message that defendants would have received had they been properly attentive, and because they illustrate the subject matter of testimony from the expert who prepared them, they are admissible under *Lawson v. Belt Ry.*, 34 Ill. App. 3d 7, 339

N.E.2d 381, 393 (1975), "for the purpose of portraying a particular situation, explaining certain testimony, or enabling the jury to apply the testimony more intelligently to the facts shown." Such exhibits accompanying expert testimony are admissible even if the dimensions and proportions are not absolutely correct so long as they are not unfairly misleading. *Union Drainage Dist. No. 1 v. Special Drainage Dist.,* 100 Ill. App. 3d 829, 295 N.E.2d 91 (1973).

Of course, if the number of prior crashes is relatively low, spot mapping might not be the most advantageous way to present them to the jury, and alternative procedures to establish prior notices of defects should be considered.

§ 9-6. Admissibility of Evidence of Prior Crashes.

Evidence of prior accidents, whether reported by the police or through other media, may be admitted only if their actual factual details are relevant and they are offered purely to establish notice. Unless both of these factors are present, the prior accidents will be excluded.

Thus, in *Moore v. Jewel Tea Co.,* 116 Ill. App. 2d 109, 253 N.E.2d 636 (1969), *aff'd,* 46 Ill. 2d 288, 263 N.E.2d 103 (1970), the plaintiff consumer brought a strict product liability action against the manufacturer and distributor of a drain cleaner that exploded before it was opened. Three similar explosions of unopened cans of the product were admitted into evidence because this evidence affects the question of actual notice or knowledge to the defendants of the possibility of an explosion. The evidence was competent as tending to show that the common cause of the accidents was a dangerous and unsafe thing. The evidence was admitted even though the prior claims were made after the subject can was manufactured and delivered to defendant Jewel, but before the plaintiff purchased it. The court strongly felt that the matter rested squarely with the sound discretion of the trial court to rule on its admissibility. *Moore, supra,* 253 N.E.2d at 645. *Ray v. Cock Robin, Inc.,* 57 Ill. 2d 19, 310 N.E.2d 9 (1974); *City of Chicago v. Jarvis,* 226 Ill. 614, 80 N.E. 1079 (1907); *Rucker v. Norfolk & W. Ry.,* 64 Ill. App. 3d 770, 381 N.E.2d 715 (1978); *Frisch v. International Harvester Co.,* 33 Ill. App. 3d 507, 338 N.E.2d 90 (1975); *Grant v. Joseph J. Duffy Co.,* 20 Ill. App. 3d 669, 314 N.E.2d 475 (1974); *Matteucci v. High School Dist. No. 208,* 4 Ill. App. 3d 710, 281 N.E.2d 383 (1972); *City of Kankakee v. Phipps,* 135 Ill. App. 585 (1970).

Significantly, because the prior accidents in *Moore* were relevant only on general notice issues, the defendant was not allowed to introduce evidence that consumer misuse or other unforeseeable causes had produced the prior explosions. Thus, the evidence was admitted because the relevance was only directed toward the notice issue and the details of the prior accidents were irrelevant. Furthermore, the court felt that it was significant that the plaintiff had done nothing more than purchase a can of Drano which spontaneously exploded.

In contrast, *Johnson v. Amerco, Inc.,* 87 Ill. App. 3d 827, 409 N.E.2d 299 (1980), involved plaintiffs suing for personal injuries caused when a U-Haul trailer tore loose from their automobile. The plaintiffs offered over 1,000 prior reports of U-Haul accidents on the basis that the prior accidents were relevant to notice. The court ruled that the only way to determine whether the prior crashes should have given notice of the defect causing plaintiff's crash to the defendant would be to examine each prior U-Haul crash to see if it involved identical relevant facts (such as load and coupling details). The mere reporting of prior crashes, without any information as to why they happened, was irrelevant and prejudicial. The *Johnson* court then proceeded to exclude the prior crashes due to the great difficulty, confusion, and delay involved in analyzing large numbers of prior cases. Had the plaintiff originally offered the relevant prior crashes, supporting them with a succinct recital of the identical, relevant facts, the evidence may well have been admitted.

The important point in *Johnson* is that evidence of prior accidents that may have been relevant to notice issues at trial was excluded because (a) the prior accidents were dissimilar to the accident at issue and (b) prior accidents would have swamped the case at bar with proof of the merits of prior accidents. The *Johnson* court distinguished other cases where prior accidents were admitted because "significant and numerous variables were different or unaccounted for in the prior occurrences offered here." *Johnson, supra,* 409 N.E.2d at 316. Additionally, cases such as *Ray v. Cock Robin, Inc., supra,* and *City of Chicago v. Jarvis, supra* were distinguished on the basis that the prior accidents gave notice to the defendant of a dangerous condition at a site under the defendant's exclusive control. *Johnson, supra,* 409 N.E.2d at 316.

Transportation experts may give opinions based upon their review of police reports concerning prior crashes provided such evidence is used to prove notice and not similarity with the case in chief. *Henderson v. Illinois Cent. Gulf R.R.,* 114 Ill. App. 3d 754, 449 N.E.2d 942 (1983); *First Nat'l Bank v. Illinois Cent. Gulf R.R.,* 62 Ill. App. 3d 36, 378 N.E.2d 1329 (1978).

Florida: *Railway Express Agency, Inc. v. Fulmer,* 227 So. 2d 870 (Fla. 1969). Evidence of the occurrence or nonoccurrence of prior accidents in police reports must be substantiated by a showing of similar relevant facts concerning the conditions and equipment at issue.

Ohio: *Rathbun v. Humphrey Co.,* 94 Ohio App. 429, 113 N.E.2d 877 (1953), held that testimony showing the absence of other similar accidents is admissible only if it has rational probative value. Thus, plaintiff confronted with this kind of "negative" evidence that there were no prior crashes can argue it has no probative value unless defendant can also show that the defect causing plaintiff crash also existed during the time period when there were no other crashes.

Coyle v. Beryl's Motor Hotel, 171 N.E.2d 355 (Ohio 1961), held that evidence of prior accidents is relevant to the issue of whether defendant knew or should have known of a dangerous condition of the premises, but such evidence cannot be admitted to show independent acts of negligence.

Stoler v. Penn Cent. Transp. Co., 583 F.2d 896 (6th Cir. 1978). In a grade crossing crash case, it was held error to exclude evidence of prior crashes at the same crossing.

Texas: *McAllen Ky. Fried Chicken No. 1, Inc. v. Leal,* 627 S.W.2d 480 (Tex. App. 1981). Evidence of prior relevant crashes is probative, but not conclusive, on the issue of whether the plaintiff's crash was foreseeable to defendant.

Winkelmann v. Battle Island Ranch, 650 S.W.2d 543 (Tex. App. 1983). Evidence that a person was guilty of negligence [or crime] in the past is generally inadmissible in determining whether that person was guilty of similar negligence [or crimes] on the date in question. Such "prior bad conduct" evidence can also be highly prejudicial. Such evidence may, however, be admitted to show the existence of a dangerous or defective condition; it may also be admitted in rebuttal when an unrelated accident occurred at the same place or through the use of the same instrumentality and under substantially similar conditions.

§ 9-7. Hearing on Admission of Testimony of Reporting Officer — Testimony Stricken.

Several years ago we were able to secure a verdict well in excess of a million dollars based on the negligent design, construction, and maintenance of a curving area of road, known as the "S" curve in an Indiana city. The eye witnesses all agreed that the crash did take place on the "S" curve. Our experts concentrated their testimony on all the defects and road faults the defendants had allowed to remain for too long in that "S" curve.

The defendants then attempted to introduce a police report written and signed by two officers who were not eye witnesses to the crash. The report said the crash did not take place on the "S" curve, but on a different road area over a mile away. We were never able to determine where these officers obtained the misinformation in their report, but at the time of the trial the officer who had gone out to the scene *after* the crash, Officer Fred Myers, had died without giving a deposition. The defendants then, at trial, attempted to introduce the testimony of the other officer who had signed the report, Officer Robert Miller, although Officer Miller was not a witness to the crash, and had not gone out to the scene of the crash on the night of the crash.

Mr. Stephen B. Cohen and Mr. George C. Pontikes of our office demonstrated in the following examination the grave difficulties in the defendant's position.

(JURY EXCUSED)

ROBERT L. MILLER, having been first duly sworn, testified as follows:

DIRECT EXAMINATION BY THE DEFENSE ATTORNEY, MR. HASSETT:

Q. Will you state your name?
A. Robert L. Miller.
Q. Where do you live, Mr. Miller?
A. 825 West 78th Avenue, Merrillville, Indiana.
Q. And what is your occupation or profession?
A. Police officer, City of Gary.
Q. How long have you been so employed?
A. 29 years.
Q. What is your present position with the department?

A. I am a Patrol Sergeant.

Q. What are your duties?

A. I am in charge of a sector, it's an area designated in the City of Gary, which the sector that I am assigned to is the B Sector.

Q. Is that a certain geographical sector?

A. Yes, sir.

Q. And calling your attention to July 27, 1970, were you employed as a police officer with the City of Gary?

A. Yes sir, I was.

Q. What were your duties on or about that date?

A. I was assigned as a detective to the Traffic Division, as an investigating officer.

Q. Did you have occasion to investigate automobile accidents around that time?

A. Yes sir, I done the follow-up work.

Q. Now, officer, do you have any independent recollection of having participated in an investigation of an automobile accident on or about July 27, 1970, in which Robert Casillas and James Edgman were the drivers and were involved in a collision on Cline Avenue in Gary?

A. Not at the scene, but probably the followups.

MR. COHEN: Your Honor, I am going to object to any reference to anything that has to do with the scene of the accident. He was not there, he does not remember anything. He can't know anything because he wasn't there.

MR. HASSETT: Q. Officer Miller, I am going to hand you what's been identified as Exhibit 12, Defendants' Exhibit 12, and ask you if you can identify that.

A. Yes Sir, that is the first copy, I mean first carbon copy off of the original of this accident that occurred on the 27th of July after midnight on Cline Avenue and Gary Avenue overpass.

MR. COHEN: I am going to object, your Honor, to any reference to the location of the accident unless he has an independent knowledge, an independent recollection or he was at the scene.

MR. HASSETT: The purpose of the examination of this witness, your Honor, is to qualify the admission of the Accident Report into evidence as an exhibit in this case.

MR. HASSETT: Would the reporter please read the last question then.

REPORTER: Q. Officer Miller, I am going to hand you what's been identified as Exhibit 12, Defendants' Exhibit 12, and ask you if you can identify that?

A. Yes sir, that is the first copy, I mean first carbon copy off of the original of this accident that occurred on the 27th of July after midnight on Cline Avenue and Gary Avenue overpass.

MR. HASSETT: Q. Does that Exhibit 12 show who the drivers involved in the accident are?

A. Yes sir, they are named.

Q. Who are they?

A. Robert Casillas and a James P. Edgman.

Q. Now, officer, does your name appear on that report?

A. Yes, sir.

Q. Where does it appear?

A. On the back side of the first page.

Q. And were you one of the officers who assisted in the investigation of that accident?

A. I followed up the investigation, yes, sir.

MR. COHEN: We have a continuing objection; go ahead.

MR. HASSETT: Q. Officer, what was your participation in this investigation, what exactly did you do?

A. My job specifically was the followup of all fatal accidents, all severe personal injury accidents, all hit-and-run accidents, and all accidents that involved city property.

Q. And in this case did you conduct a follow-up investigation?

A. Yes sir, at the hospital.

Q. Did you go to the accident scene?

A. No sir, I don't believe I did.

Q. Now, does that report indicate that any other officer participated in the investigation of this accident?

MR. COHEN: Again, your Honor, unless there's a foundation I want the record to show that he has not stated that he's testifying from personal memory or whether this is his memory refreshed, or whether this is any recollection that he has, there's nothing showing that he has any personal knowledge of what anybody else did.

THE COURT: I think that the witness' basis of his testimony in that respect ought to be established, Mr. Hassett.

MR. HASSETT: I'll withdraw that last question.

Q. Officer, are you testifying now of your own independent recollection of the matter, or is your testimony based upon the report itself, the Defendants' Exhibit No. 12?

A. Well, after nine years my recollection is based on the report that I have in front of me.

Q. On the report, and looking at the report now does that indicate that there was another officer involved in the investigation?

A. Yes sir, there was.

Q. And what is the name of that officer as shown on the report?

A. Officer Fred Myers.

Q. Was he the officer who then conducted the on-the-scene investigation?

A. Yes sir, he was.

MR. COHEN: Based on the report, is that what I understand?

MR. HASSETT: Q. Based on the report?

A. Yes, sir.

Q. Did he sign the report?

A. Yes, sir.

Q. Does his signature appear thereon?

A. Yes sir, it does.

Q. Have you knowledge of that officer's signature?

A. Yes sir, I have.

Q. And is that indeed his signature to your knowledge?

A. Yes, sir.

Q. Are Police Accident Reports required to be made out by investigating officers for the Gary Police Department?

A. You mean those officers serving at the scene; yes.

Q. When the officer fills out the report, are they reports such as the one you have before you, Defendants' Exhibit 12?

A. Yes sir, that's what they are.

Q. And then is the officer required then to file that report with the Gary Police Department?

A. Well, on a fatal accident there's at least four copies made, one goes to the State of Indiana, one goes to the Investigating Officer, one goes to the Records Bureau; it is also given a case number so it can be registered on the daily bulletin. It is also given a file number where it is kept in the Traffic Bureau.

Q. And is there a copy that is maintained there in the files of the Gary Police Department?

A. Yes, there should be the original file.

Q. What you have there then is the first carbon copy of that report?

A. Yes sir, it is.

Q. Did you obtain that from the Gary Police Department files?

A. Yes, I did.

Q. And this is the one you have brought with you here today?

A. Yes, sir.

Q. Now, is Officer Myers living or dead?

A. He's deceased.

Q. When did Officer Myers die, if you know?

A. It was either near the end of 1971 or the early part of 1972.

Q. How did he die, if you know?

A. He was killed, shot.

Q. He was shot?

A. Murdered.

Q. Is that report, Defendant's Exhibit 12, a true and accurate representation of what it purports to show to your knowledge?

MR. PONTIKES: Objection to that, your Honor. That he can't possibly know. I have no objection to his testifying it's a true and accurate copy of the report, in fact we will stipulate to that, of the Gary Police Department of whatever. But this man simply can't answer that question under the facts in this case, under this posture, your Honor. He simply can't answer that.

THE COURT: I think that the witness ought to be given the opportunity to answer the question, however.

Do you recall the question, Officer?

MR. HASSETT: Q. Is this Defendant's Exhibit 12, the Police Accident Report you have before you now, is that a true and accurate copy of what it purports to show?

A. Yes, what the officer observed and took at the scene; yes.

MR. PONTIKES: I object to that, he can't answer that. He can say it's a true and correct copy. The point I am making, your Honor, you simply can't ask a man a question he cannot answer. He does not know whether Officer Myers did or did not in fact accurately record. He could say this is an accurate copy of the report that Officer Myers filed, and as to that we have no objection. In fact we will stipulate to that as an accurate copy. But we can't have him testify to that.

THE COURT: His prior testimony is that insofar as the on-the-scene aspect of that —

MR. HASSETT: He did not have any part of that. His investigation was at the hospital.

Q. Is that right; afterward?

A. Yes.

Q. At the time this Accident Report, Defendant's Exhibit 12, was filled out by Officer Myers, was Officer Myers a regular police officer of the Gary Police Department?

A. Yes sir, he was.

Q. Did you know him to be an accurate, reliable, trustworthy person to your knowledge?

A. Yes sir, I do.

MR. HASSETT: Your Honor, Defendant would offer into evidence Defendant's Exhibit 12, the Police Accident Report on the subject accident as evidence in this cause.

MR. COHEN: Hassett did not ask the police officer whether or not he was responsible for filling the 55 mile an hour speed limit, whether or not was part of the report that he completed, therefore, it's obvious that it wasn't, and I think his deposition so points it out. In addition, your Honor, the report is totally based on facts presented or indicated by someone else. He has stated, No. 1, he wasn't there; he has stated, No. 2, he has no personal knowledge of it; and No. 3, there is no way that this can be anything other than hearsay. What they are attempting to do is go to the truth of the matter asserted, and for that reason there is no exception in this case to the hearsay rule. In fact, your Honor, the report for purposes of inclusion of this information can do only one thing, it can only distort rather than confirm the facts. I would like, if permitted, along this line to ask the officer two questions to further my objection.

THE COURT: You may.

VOIR DIRE EXAMINATION

BY MR. COHEN:

Q. Officer Miller, I believe during your deposition you stated that it was normal policy in the Gary Police Department to obtain statements from witnesses; is that correct?

A. Yes, sir.

Q. I also believe that in your deposition you stated that in this case no witness statements were taken from any witnesses at the scene, or they would have been in the jacket; is that correct?

A. Yes, sir.

Q. And I also believe that you stated that because of the death of the two parties and the fact that Mr. Edgman was in severe critical condition when you went to the hospital, you obtained absolutely no statement from anybody involved in the accident; is that correct?

A. That is correct.

Q. So that the follow-up work in this report, this report may have been concerned with, contained absolutely no interviews with witnesses and had no interviews with anybody involved in the accident; is that correct?

A. On my part.

Q. On your part?

A. Yes, sir.

Q. And you found none in the jacket which would have indicated the policy position?

A. There was no notes or nothing that Officer Myers may have left; there was none.

MR. COHEN: Again, your Honor, I renew the objection. I believe that any statement of the facts involved here, the issue of the 55 mile an hour speed limit, if they want to ask him during his testimony whether or not he knew it was posted 55, I have no objection. But to read from the report other than for purposes of notice, we will stipulate that the report may have stated 55 miles an hour for that purpose, the same purpose that we put it in yesterday. But to state where the accident occurred as identifying it with this accident I think would be obviously hearsay under the circumstances.

MR. PONTIKES: I might add, your Honor, that the business record exception of the hearsay rule does not obviate both the issues of the dangers of hearsay in the relevancy question which the Court has to consider. Now, this Court has sat here for two weeks and has heard the issue with regard to where the accident took place, and the Court will recall that both Mr. Madriman and Mr. Gray put the accident at Grand Calumet River structure.

MR. PONTIKES: Yes, and it's quite a bit of distance from Gary Avenue. Now, if you are going to have that report come in which says flatly on it that it happened at the Gary Avenue overpass, you are going to be allowing in effect the testimony of a man who we can't cross-examine, be allowed to testify contrary to what two living witnesses who were subject to vigorous cross-examinations have testified to, I think that will be highly prejudicial to us and will violate the very basis of the hearsay rule. There is nothing else relevant in the report as I'm sure the State will agree to, and the business record exception doesn't extend it that far. It will take care of the problems of authenticity but it will not go to the question of substituting it, that is the report, for live testimony. Now, if it were merely cumulative to somebody else's testimony that it in fact took place at the Gary Avenue overpass, that might render it as a different issue, but it's going to be the sole piece of evidence as I understand it, that the State is going to put into dispute our contention as to where the accident took place. I think that on that basis, you've got all of the problems that the hearsay rule present in its classic form. The man who is going to say contrary to what all the other testimony is in this case as to where the accident took place, and we can't cross-examine him. For that reason we would object.

MR. BLACKMUN (a Defense Attorney): Your Honor, the defendant is offering certain facts in the Police Report pursuant to Rule 804 of the Federal Rules which is a hearsay exception where the declarant is unavailable as a witness. It is our position that since it has been shown that the person who prepared the report is dead and unavailable as a witness, that under subparagraph 5 of that rule, which claims a statement not specifically covered by any of the foregoing exceptions but having equivalent circumstantial guarantees of trustworthiness, if the Court determines that the statement is offered as evidence of a material fact, the statement is more probative on the point for which it is offered than any other evidence which the proponent can procure through reasonable efforts and the general purposes of these rules in the interest of justice be best served by admission of the statement into evidence, however, a statement may not be admitted under this exception unless the proponent of it makes it known to the adverse parties sufficiently in advance of the trial or hearing to provide the adverse party with a fair opportunity to prepare to meet it, intention to offer the statement and the particulars of it, including the name and address of the declarant.

Now, we realize that Madriman and Gray (Ed. Note: the two eyewitnesses to the crash) testified as to where the accident occurred. It is our position that since there was some difference in their testimony and that there is no other evidence which the defendant can procure as to where the accident happened, since Mr. Edgman has no knowledge, that we should be able to introduce that fact from the Police Report as an exception to the hearsay rule.

MR. PONTIKES: Your Honor, the only response I'm going to make to that is, you know, the problem with this report, your Honor, is it's printed.

Now, your Honor, if you look at what they want to introduce, it's a printed form, it says road on which accident occurred, Cline Avenue, at its intersection with Gary Avenue overpass. Now, this isn't even testimony, it's a checking out of the blanks almost. It could have been, to show you this to make my point, your Honor, it could have been anywhere here, and this would be the closest intersection. But the officer is not here for me to state was it here, officer, or was it there, officer. It's impossible. Whereas Mr. Gray and Mr. Madriman were cross-examined at great length on that issue.

MR. KUHLMAN: There is one thing that I thought of that I can add to this, your Honor. In order to make a balancing such as the Federal Rules of Evidence or most rules of evidence have you would have to have, if you decided to allow that to be introduced, it wouldn't be fair to let it go in without some evidence of the fact that the man who wrote it is dead, the man who wrote it was not an eye witness, the man who had authenticated it wasn't there at the scene. The foundation that would have to go in with that report would destroy any relevance it might have in the first place. To let that go in as a purported eye-witness statement would be grossly unfair, because it's not. To let Sergeant Miller authenticate it and purport to be an eye witness would be grossly unfair, because he isn't. To let it go in as purported eye-witness testimony of anybody would be grossly unfair because it's not, in fact it's directly contradictory to the two eye witnesses who have been here. So if you let it in with no foundation or explanation, it grossly distorts the type of evidence that it is, and if your give it a fair foundation you have to destroy its relevancy. Then you deal with the prejudicial value that it has. It's an official Police Report, highly prejudicial to the plaintiff's case with no probative value. If you weigh the probative value against the prejudicial impact, which is one of the Federal Rules have adopted as a test, there's no contest, unless you make it come in as a gross distortion of the type of evidence it purports to be.

MR. HASSETT: We would call the Court's attention respectfully to the time there on the accident, I think that it was phoned in about midnight —

THE COURT: 12:04 —

MR. HASSETT: 12:00 o'clock, and then 12:04 is when the officer got to the scene, I think. So he was there very shortly after the accident happened, and I think that the report contains his personal observation of the various things that are related on it.

MR. COHEN: We don't know what it contains, what he related on it, where he got the information from, or anything else. That's one of the problems.

MR. HASSETT: He's got the names of the two witnesses on it, presumably he got some of it from them.

MR. COHEN: Ha, ha, you see, your Honor, now Mr. Hassett is going basically to the presumptions that would be made, and we already have testimony this morning that it was standard policy to take witness statements and put them into the folder, and there were none, and there was no followup. All of this goes to the ultimate prejudice of this type of testimony being introduced, if it is testimony at that.

THE COURT: It seems to me as I recall the encyclopedia's statements of the risks of hearsay that it's always a greater risk when you are dealing with a Jury, and Courts can be much more liberal when it's a case before a Bench, as presently Judges can somehow know what to exclude

> in their mind and what to consider, filter I guess is the word I am searching for, and here it's that balancing that Courts always have to make. I think somebody suggested its probative value versus prejudice that it might engender, reliability of a particular piece of evidence, the ability to test the reliability of it, and the double hearsay aspect I suppose that even the witness who was on the scene, Myers, now deceased, was a witness after the fact and may have garnered some of his information, may have, from the two witnesses who have already testified in this case, one of whom was clearly an eye witness to the occurrence, and the other who came on the scene very shortly thereafter, and who I expect could be considered disinterested witnesses in their own right as Myers could otherwise be described as well. All of which is by saying I think this Court has before it, and the Jury more importantly, the statements of two witnesses who had every right to and did testify, and had that testimony tested. The Federal Rules are a good effort to liberalize what kind of evidence can come in, and I am philosophically in favor of that notion, but that rule has to be tested on a case to case and evidence to evidence basis, I think with respect to this particular piece of evidence, it has a potential for harm greater than it has potential for benefit. For that reason I'm going to sustain the objection to its admission.

The Court's ruling was sustained by the Appellate Court for the reasons we have discussed in this chapter.

CHAPTER 10

PLEADINGS AND DISCOVERY

§ 10-1. Introduction.

The central interrelationship between pleadings and discovery is that the latter should develop the evidentiary basis to prove the theory of the case laid out in the former. In other words, the legal theories in the pleadings should structure and focus the areas you will concentrate on in discovery. If the Complaint alleges improper sight distances and defective signing on a curve, the plaintiff's discovery should concentrate on signing records, maintenance logs, and prior crashes that could have been caused by improper sight distances and defective signing on the curve at issue.

The discovery itself should start out broad gauge, to find out all possible relevant areas for future discovery. Subsequent waves of discovery can "fine tune" and concentrate on specific issues unearthed by the first, broad spectrum salvos. New facts developed by discovery can also, of course, lead to alterations in the pleadings, which in turn can generate new waves of discovery relevant to the new legal issues and theories raised.

The simple litmus test for all this is that discovery should never be conducted merely to harass, and all forms of discovery should be germain to relevant issues. Whenever you contemplate sending out discovery requests in any form, ask, "Why am I doing this?" If you cannot answer that question, your opponent may drag you before a judge and make your client pay for having the judge ask you that same question. On the other hand, if your questions really are worth asking, make sure you get answers to them.

§ 10-2. Pleadings.

All mighty trees, and weeds, start from small seeds. Chairman Mao said that the longest journey beings with a single step. Similarly, all successful lawsuits begin with a pleading, usually called the complaint, that can set forth the plaintiff's theory of the case at least well enough to avoid a Motion to Strike. In the following sections are reproduced Complaints our office prepared, each of which survived Motions to Strike, and each of which led to a verdict or settlement of over one million dollars.

§ 10-2(A). Complaint for Wrongful Death in a Railroad Grade Crossing Crash.

UNITED STATES DISTRICT COURT
NORTHERN DISTRICT OF ILLINOIS
EASTERN DIVISION

M. CHRISTINE GAMEZ AND GERALDINE BOWIE, as Successor Administrators of the Estate of JESSIE MC KINNION, deceased, and as Administrators of the Estate of GWENDOLYN MC KINNION, deceased and GERALDINE BOWIE as guardian of minors LARRY MC KINNION, DARLA MC KINNION and JENNEL MC KINNION,	)	
Plaintiffs,	)	
v.	)	NO.
THE PENN CENTRAL COMPANY,	)	
Defendants.	)	

COMPLAINT FOR WRONGFUL DEATH

Now comes the Plaintiffs, M. CHRISTINE GAMEZ and GERALDINE BOWIE, as Successor Administrators of the estate of JESSIE MC KINNION, deceased, and as Administrators of the Estate of GWENDOLYN MC KINNION, deceased; by and through their attorneys, STEPHEN B. COHEN, RICHARD S. KUHLMAN, and DAVID R. SCHNEIDER, and complain of the Defendant, the PENN CENTRAL COMPANY, as follows:

COUNT I

1. Plaintiff, M. CHRISTINE GAMEZ is an Indiana resident. Plaintiff GERALDINE BOWIE is an Illinois resident. Both GAMEZ and BOWIE have been appointed by the Superior Court for the County of Lake, State of Indiana, Probate Division, to be the Successor Administrators of the Estate of JESSIE MC KINNION, deceased, and to be the Administrators of the Estate of GWENDOLYN MC KINNION, deceased.

2. At all relevant times enumerated herein, and until their respective deaths, JESSIE MCKINNION AND GWENDOLYN MCKINNION were married to each other and were residents of the State of Indiana.

3. The Defendant, PENN CENTRAL COMPANY is a corporation incorporated, and with its principal place of business in the State of Pennsylvania.

4. The amount in controversy exclusive of interest and costs herein exceeds $10,000.00. The Court has jurisdiction of the subject matter of this lawsuit by reason of 28 U.S.C., Sec. 1332; 28 U.S.C., Sec. 1331, and 45 U.S.C. Sec. 56.

5. The United States District Court for the Northern District of Illinois, Eastern Division, is the proper venue for this action under the provisions of 45 U.S.C., Section 56 because the Defendant is a corporation doing business in the Northern District of Illinois, Eastern Division, with a registered agent located within the Northern District of Illinois who is listed with the Secretary of State of Illinois.

6. At the time of the occurrence hereinafter complained of, and prior and subsequent thereto, the Defendant was a railroad corporation, engaged in business as a common carrier by railroad, and for purposes thereof, owning, operating, possessing and maintaining railroad cars and locomotives and other property throughout the states of Illinois and Indiana and elsewhere.

7. On or about 5:00 p.m. on January 8, 1974, the Defendant did own and operate a certain railroad train that did then cross over, and intersect with County Road 400 East at a railroad crossing hereinafter, referred to as "the railroad crossing", or "the railroad intersection" located at a point just south of the intersection of said County Road 400 East and U.S. Highway 30, located in Porter County, Indiana.

8. At said time, JESSIE MCKINNION, deceased, was within an automobile proceeding over said railroad intersection in a southerly direction on said County Road 400 East. This automobile shall hereinafter be referred to as "the vehicle."

9. At said time and place, Defendant had the duty to ensure trains crossing said railroad crossing observed reasonable care for vehicles upon said crossing.

10. At said time and place, the said railroad train owned and operated by Defendant was negligently operated across said intersection of railroad track with said County Road 400 East in that said train was there and then operating at an excessive and unreasonable speed; personnel on said train were not keeping a proper and reasonable vigilance for vehicular traffic upon said railroad intersection; said train failed to give statutory prescribed, or reasonable warning signals upon

approaching said intersection; statutory prescribed, or reasonable warning devices had not been installed and maintained in a functional condition by said Defendant on the said County Road 400 East before said railroad intersection; and said railroad intersection had not been graded and maintained so as to permit persons in vehicles crossing said railroad intersection to have a proper and reasonable view of oncoming trains.

11. At and prior to the time of the occurrence complained of herein, the said railroad intersection was, and was known by Defendant to be extra hazardous to the public, and particularly to vehicular traffic proceeding over said railroad intersection on County Road 400 East.

12. At said time and place, and due solely, entirely and proximately to the negligence of Defendant cited herein, the occurrence complained of herein took place in that the said railroad train owned and operated by Defendant did there and then negligently, carelessly, and in disregard of the rights and safety of others, collide with great force and violence into the vehicle JESSIE MC KINNION was inside of, thereby directly and proximately causing the death of the said JESSIE MC KINNION.

13. On the date of his death, said JESSIE MC KINNION was 38 years old; was employed as a truck driver with the R.C. Cola Company, located at 47th and California, Chicago, Illinois; earned $250.00 per week and left surviving as natural heirs and next of kin a wife, GWENDOLYN MC KINNION, age 38, and four children: BOBBY MC KINNION, age 18; LARRY MC KINNION, age 15, DARLA MC KINNION, age 13; and JENNEL MC KINNION, age 12. Said wife and children were totally financially dependent upon JESSIE MC KINNION at the time of his death, and anticipated continued support from him thereafter. The said LARRY MC KINNION, DARLA MC KINNION and JENNEL MC KINNION are still minors.

14. On or about January 12, 1974, the estate of JESSIE MC KINNION, as a sole, direct and proximate result of Defendants' said negligence, was required to expend $1,700.00 to pay for said JESSIE MC KINNION's funeral.

15. The Superior Court of Lake County, Indiana issued letters of Administration for the Estate of JESSIE MC KINNION to his surviving widow, GWENDOLYN MC KINNION, on December 27, 1974. The said GWENDOLYN MC KINNION died on February 20, 1975, prior to the filing of this cause, and the Superior Court of Lake County, Indiana subsequently, and by proper process, appointed Plaintiffs M. CHRISTINE GAMEZ and GERALDINE BOWIE to be Successor Administrators of the Estate of JESSIE MC KINNION; and to be Administra-

tors of the Estate of GWENDOLYN MCKINNION; and said court further appointed Plaintiff GERALDINE BOWIE to be the Guardian of LARRY MCKINNION, DARLA MCKINNION and JENNEL MCKINNION, the three minor surviving children of JESSIE MCKINNION and GWENDOLYN MCKINNION.

16. The said negligence of the Defendant solely, directly and proximately caused the death of JESSIE MCKINNION, deceased, by reason of whose death GWENDOLYN MCKINNION, LARRY MCKINNION, DARLA MCKINNION and JENNEL MCKINNION have lost, and will continue to lose, great gains, support, wages, and profits which the said JESSIE MCKINNION would otherwise have earned and have therefore been injured in property and means of support by JESSIE MCKINNION's death.

WHEREFORE, Plaintiffs, M. CHRISTINE GAMEZ and GERALDINE BOWIE, as Successor Administrators of the Estate of JESSIE MCKINNION, deceased, and as Administrators of the Estate of GWENDOLYN MCKINNION, deceased and GERALDINE BOWIE as guardian of minors LARRY MCKINNION, DARLA MCKINNION and JENNEL MCKINNION ask the Court to enter judgment in favor of Plaintiffs and against the Defendant, THE PENN CENTRAL COMPANY, in the amount of $1,000,000.00.

COUNT II

1-9. Plaintiffs hereby reallege and reincorporate Paragraphs 1 through 9 of Count I as, respectively, paragraphs 1 through 9 of Count II.

10. At said time and place the Defendant negligently operated and maintained said railroad crossing in that warning devices required by statute to be affixed upon said railroad crossing and the approaches thereto, and reasonably necessary to protect the public in general, and vehicular traffic in particular, upon said crossing, were not installed and maintained by Defendant in a functional manner upon said railroad intersection and the approaches thereto on said County Road 400 East; and Defendants did there and then further negligently operate and maintain said railroad crossing in that Defendants did not, on or prior to said time, grade and maintain said railroad crossing so as to permit persons in vehicles crossing said railroad intersection to have a proper and reasonable view of oncoming trains.

11-16. Plaintiffs hereby reallege and reincorporate Paragraphs 11 through 16 of Count I as, respectively, Paragraphs 11 through 16 of Count II.

WHEREFORE, Plaintiffs, M. CHRISTINE GAMEZ and GERALDINE BOWIE, as Successor Administrators of the Estate of JESSIE MCKINNION, deceased, and as Administrators of the Estate of GWENDOLYN MCKINNION, deceased and GERALDINE BOWIE as guardian of minors LARRY MCKINNION, DARLA MCKINNION and JENNEL MCKINNION ask the Court to enter judgment in favor of Plaintiffs and against the Defendant, THE PENN CENTRAL COMPANY, in the amount of $1,000,000.00.

COUNT III

1-9. Plaintiffs hereby reallege and reincorporate Paragraphs 1 through 9 of Count I as, respectively, paragraphs 1 through 9 of Count III.

10. At said time and place the said railroad train owned and operated by Defendant, and the personnel of Defendant upon said train, negligently failed and refused to comply with Indiana statutes requiring trains to give prescribed warning signals when approaching public intersections and roadways in that said railroad train did not, beginning not less than 80 rods from said railroad crossing, either sound the whistle on the engine of said train not less than four times until the crossing was reached, or ring the bell attached to said engine continuously from the time of first sounding said whistle until the said train reached, or fully passed, said crossing, nor did said train, due to Defendants further violation of Indiana statutes, stop before said railroad crossing and proceed only after manual protection was provided at the crossing by a member of the train crew or other proper persons.

11-16. Plaintiffs hereby reallege and reincorporate Paragraphs 11 through 16 of Count I as, respectively, Paragraphs 11 through 16 of Count III.

WHEREFORE, Plaintiffs, M. CHRISTINE GAMEZ and GERALDINE BOWIE, as Successor Administrators of the Estate of JESSIE MCKINNION, deceased, and as Administrators of the Estate of GWENDOLYN MCKINNION, deceased and GERALDINE BOWIE as guardian of minors LARRY MCKINNION, DARLA MCKINNION and JENNEL MCKINNION ask the Court to enter judgment in favor of

Plaintiffs and against the Defendant, THE PENN CENTRAL COMPANY, in the amount of $1,000,000.00.

Respectfully Submitted,

STEPHEN B. COHEN

RICHARD S. KUHLMAN

DAVID R. SCHNEIDER,
Attorneys for Plaintiffs

§ 10-2(B). Complaint for Wrongful Death and Personal Injury for Transportation Facility Negligence Causing a Two-Vehicle Crash.

STATE OF INDIANA)
) SS
COUNTY OF LAKE)

IN THE LAKE SUPERIOR COURT
ROOM NUMBER TWO
AT EAST CHICAGO, INDIANA

JAMES P. EDGMAN, in his individual capacity and as Administrator of the Estate of LORENE A. EDGMAN, Deceased, on behalf of himself and said estate,	
Plaintiff,	CAUSE NO. 271 843
vs.	
THE STATE OF INDIANA,	AMENDED COMPLAINT
Defendant.	

Now comes the Plaintiff, JAMES P. EDGMAN, in his individual capacity and as Administrator of the Estate of Lorene A. Edgman, Deceased, on behalf of himself and said estate, by and through his attorneys, Cohen, Cohen, and Bullard, and Foss, Schuman & Drake, and for his complaint against Defendant, the State of Indiana, states as follows:

COUNT I

1. The Cline Avenue "S" curve, hereinafter sometimes referred to for convenience as "the area of public highway," is an area of public highway located within the City of Gary, Indiana. Said area of public highway extends from the Indiana East-West Toll Road overpass on the south to the Gary Avenue exit on the north. Said area of public highway was designed, constructed, and has been maintained to date, by the Defendant, the State of Indiana and its agents, with and through the expenditure of public monies, and it is, and at all relevant times was, the duty of the Defendant to use reasonable care in the design, construction, and maintenance of public roadways such as the "S" curve.

2. The aforesaid area of public highway was negligently construed by the Defendant, the State of Indiana, in that:

A. No lighting facilities were installed along said area of public highway, and as a result the curves in said area of public highway are not apparent to motorists at night or under conditions of poor visibility, which conditions are often created or aggravated by steam and vapours produced by the Vulcan Materials Company, which is located to the east of the north end of said area of public highway, and by the Purex Corporation plant, which is located to the west of the north end of said area of public highway;

B. Said area of public highway was constructed without any painted stripes or other designation of driving lanes or curves;

C. Said area of public highway was constructed without any markers or other designations of its median or outside boundaries;

D. The pavement was improperly applied to said area of public highway, and as a result said pavement quickly became bumpy, uneven and rutted;

E. Motorist approaching the said "S" curve at night would not have adequate visibility or warning of the curve;

F. Motorists who failed to perceive the "S" curves at night would travel into the oncoming lanes of traffic without adequate warning;

G. The said "S" curves were designed and built with improperly short sight distances;

H. The said "S" curves were designed and built with and for improperly high design speeds;

I. The said "S" curves were negligently designed and built with no transition between the uphill approach to said "S" curve and the immediate beginning of said "S" curve; and

J. The said "S" curves were negligently built without a proper median barrier to separate opposing lanes and flows of traffic.

3. The aforesaid area of public highway was, at all relevant times, negligently maintained by the Defendant, the State of Indiana, in that:

A. None of the aforementioned defects in the construction of said area of public highway was corrected prior to the crash at issue by the Defendant, although the Defendant was at all times aware of the existence of each of said construction defects;

B. The Defendant, at all relevant times, failed to apply suitable and adequate cleansing procedures to said area of public highway, and as a result, the surface of said area of public highway was dirty, slippery, and coated with grime;

C. Defendant failed to adequately display speed limit signs along said area of public highway;

D. The speed limit that Defendant allegedly posted along said area of public highway at the time of said crash at issue was too fast for the driving conditions;

E. Proper lighting was not installed along said "S" curve prior to the crash at issue;

F. A proper median barrier was not installed along said "S" curve to separate opposing lanes and flows of traffic prior to the crash at issue;

G. The said "S" curve was not properly cleaned or painted prior to said collision;

H. The Defendant negligently and carelessly ignored both the high rate of serious cross-over collisions on said "S" curve prior to the crash at issue, and the high volume of complaints from citizens and government agents and officials about said "S" curve prior to the crash at issue; and negligently failed to correct the dangers in said "S" curve prior to the crash at issue;

I. The Defendant violated the statutory duty imposed by Indiana Code 9-6-3-1 (47-901) in that said "S" curve was an area of undue hazard for motorists on and prior to the crash at issue, and Defendant failed to enlist proper local or state officials to take timely and reasonable action prior to said crash to overcome or remove said hazard;

J. The Defendant violated the statutory duty imposed by Indiana Code 9-6-3-2 (47-903) in that said "S" curve was a hazard to the travelling public prior to the crash at issue, and failed to take reasonable and timely action prior to the crash at issue to effect such changes in the "S" curve as may be necessary to remove or eliminate the said hazard;

K. The Defendant negligently failed to post signs or notices on the said "S" curve prior to said crash warning motorists that they were:

i) Entering a hazardous area; or
ii) entering an "S" curve; or
iii) entering a horizontal curve.

L. The Defendant negligently constructed and maintained a small curb topped by metal posts in the center of the "S" curve on and prior to the time of said crash, without posting any warning of same for motorists, and said small curb topped by metal posts constituted a dangerous obstacle for motorists on said "S" curve;

M. Defendant negligently failed to meet the statutory duty imposed on it by Indiana Code 36-2905 (8-13-4-5) to illuminate dangerous curves for traffic on highways in the state highway system in that said "S" curve was a dangerous curve for traffic on a highway in the state highway system on and prior to the crash at issue and Defendant did not illuminate said curve prior to said time;

N. The Defendant negligently failed to meet the statutory duties imposed on it by Indiana Code 9-4-2-1 (47-19012) in that the specifications of negligence enumerated above in this Paragraph and each of its sub-paragraphs, constituted a failure by Defendant to conform, prior to said crash at issue, to the standards of the Indiana Manual on Uniform Traffic Control Devices for Streets and Highways;

O. Defendant negligently failed to meet the statutory duties imposed on it by Indiana Code 8-11-4-1 (36-1615) in that, on and prior to said crash at issue, Defendant did not paint the said metal posts on top of the small curb in the center of the "S" curve either white or black and white stripes;

P. Defendant further negligently failed to meet the statutory duties imposed on it by Indiana Code 8-11-4-1 (36-1615) in that, on and subsequent to 1965, neither the Indiana State Highway Commission, or any other agent or agency of the Defendant, prescribed the color or colors to be painted on permanent physical objects on or within the roadway of highways or roads in the state, or in such close proximity to the travelled part of such roadway that the traffic thereon might be endangered thereby or collide therewith;

Q. Defendant further negligently failed to meet the statutory duty imposed on it by Indiana Code 8-13-5-2 (36-107) by failing to maintain said "S" curve with due care and by failing to facilitate and promote the safety of traffic on said "S" curve.

4. As a direct result of the aforementioned negligent construction and negligent maintenance, Defendant has caused and allowed the area of public highway in question to be and remain extremely dangerous and hazardous to motor traffic.

5. Defendant is and has at all relevant times been aware that said area of public highway has been subjected to a heavy volume of motor traffic from the time of its construction to date.

6. Defendant is and has at all relevant times been aware that an extremely and unusually high number of traffic accidents have been occurring upon said area of public highway from the time of its construction to date.

7. On or about 12:05 a.m. on July 27, 1970, Plaintiff, JAMES P. EDGMAN and his wife, LORENE A. EDGMAN, were driving their motor vehicle in a southerly direction over the area of public highway in question. Both JAMES P. EDGMAN and LORENE A. EDGMAN were exercising due and proper care for the safety of their persons and property at said time.

8. At said time and place, and as a direct and proximate result of the Defendant's aforementioned negligent construction and negligent maintenance of said area of public highway, another motor vehicle being driven in a northerly direction over said area of public highway collided with said vehicle being driven in a southerly direction by Plaintiff, JAMES P. EDGMAN, and his wife, LORENE A. EDGMAN. Said collision occurred with great force and violence, causing Plaintiff, JAMES P. EDGMAN, and his wife, LORENE A. EDGMAN, to be hurled with great force against various parts of their automobile.

9. As a direct and proximate result of the Defendant's aforementioned negligent construction and negligent maintenance of said area of public highway Plaintiff, JAMES P. EDGMAN and his wife, LORENE A. EDGMAN, sustained grievous, painful, severe and permanent bodily injuries, both internally and externally, in that LORENE A. EDGMAN was killed in the aforementioned collision and Plaintiff, JAMES P. EDGMAN, as a direct result and consequence of said collision, not only was deprived of the help, company, services, love, affection and consortium of his wife, LORENE A. EDGMAN, but was also himself greatly hurt, bruised and wounded, in that he was rendered unconscious and sustained grievous bodily injuries, which injuries include, but are not limited to, a fractured skull, a severe cranial hemorrhage, a fractured left hip, a fractured left humerus, a fractured left elbow, a loss of a portion of his ability to hear, damage to his nerves and nervous system and his mental faculties were severely injured and shocked; he suffered nausea, vertigo and sleeplessness; he sustained loss of weight and was subjected to great pain; the function and use of all the aforesaid bodily parts and organs were seriously and permanently diminished, impaired, and made painful; he was forced to undergo serious and painful surgery requiring the implant of artificial prosthesis into his

body to replace his naturally given bones; and he became therefrom sick, sore, lame, and disordered and so remained for a long period of time, to-wit: from hitherto, during all of which time he suffered great pain and anguish both in mind and body and will in the future continue to so suffer, and he was by reason of said injuries, hindered and prevented, and permanently will be hindered and prevented, from attending to his usual duties and affairs, and he has thereby lost and will in the future thereby lose, large sums of money, for hospital, medical and surgical services, nursing care and attention in and about endeavoring to become healed and cured of his injuries, and from and after the time of said crash he has been unable to work and earn a living and was thereby forced to discontinue his employment at Inland Steel, causing him to lose the earnings he would have had from said employment, all to his personal damage in the sum of at least $2,500,000.

10. By reason of the Defendant's aforesaid negligence, the Plaintiff's 1969 Ford four-door Country Squire station wagon, was, is and because of the aforementioned collision, demolished completely and beyond repair; and the various parts thereof were destroyed and rendered of no value, to the personal damage to Plaintiff in the sum of Five Thousand Dollars ($5,000.00).

WHEREFORE, Plaintiff, JAMES P. EDGMAN, in his individual capacity, respectfully prays this Court that:

1) The Defendant, the State of Indiana be found liable to JAMES P. EDGMAN, individually, in the amount of at least $2,505,000.00 (Two million five hundred and five thousand Dollars) and that said Defendant be ordered to turn over said sum to JAMES P. EDGMAN;

2) The Plaintiff be given such other and further relief as this Court deems just.

COUNT II

1-8. Plaintiff repeats and realleges Paragraphs 1 through 8 of Count I as, respectively, Paragraphs 1 through 8 of Count II.

9. As a direct result of the collision proximately caused by Defendants aforementioned negligent construction and negligent maintenance of said area of public highway, Plaintiff's decedant, Lorene A. Edgman, was killed.

10. At the time of said collision, and at the time of the death of said Lorene A. Edgman, Plaintiff JAMES P. EDGMAN was the husband of said Lorene A. Edgman and the said JAMES P. EDGMAN and the said Lorene A. Edgman were living together as husband and wife.

11. As a result of the death of Lorene Edgman proximately caused by the Defendant's aforesaid negligence, Plaintiff, JAMES P. EDGMAN has been deprived of the care, guidance, support, love, and affection of the said decedant and has further been deprived the help, company,

services, and consortium of the said decedant and has further been deprived of the financial earnings of said decedant.

12. As a direct and proximate result of the said death of Lorene Edgman caused by the defendant's said negligence, the estate of Lorene Edgman has been forced to undergo expenses for the funeral of said Lorene Edgman, the burial of said Lorene Edgman, and has further lost the earnings of said Lorene Edgman, and said estate has further been forced to undergo costs and expenses of the administration of said estate, *including attorney's fees.*

13. Plaintiff, JAMES P. EDGMAN, is the statutory beneficiary of the estate of Lorene Edgman under the Indiana Wrongful Death Act, Indiana Code 34-1-1-2 (2-404) and is also administrator of said estate.

WHEREFORE, Plaintiff, JAMES P. EDGMAN, in his capacity as administrator of the estate of Lorene Edgman, respectfully prays this Court that:

1) The Defendant, State of Indiana, be found liable in damages for wrongful death to the estate of Lorene A. Edgman in the amount of $2,500,000.00 (Two Million Five Hundred Thousand Dollars);

2) That Plaintiff be given such other and further relief as this Court determines just.

§ 10-2(C). Complaint for Wrongful Death Alleging Transportation Facility Negligence Causing a One-Vehicle Crash.

STATE OF ILLINOIS)
) SS
COUNTY OF COOK)

IN THE CIRCUIT COURT OF COOK COUNTY, ILLINOIS
COUNTY DEPARTMENT, LAW DIVISION

THERESA LUING, individually, and as Special Administrator of the Estate of Robert D. Luing, deceased,	)	
Plaintiff,	)	
vs.	)	NO. 81 L 19892
COOK COUNTY, ILLINOIS and THE VILLAGE OF BARRINGTON HILLS, ILLINOIS,	)	
Defendants.	)	

FOURTH AMENDED COMPLAINT

NOW COMES the Plaintiff, Theresa Luing, individually, and as Special Administrator of the Estate of Robert D. Luing, deceased, by and through her attorneys, Foss, Schuman & Drake/Cohen and Bullard, and William Jakofsky, and alleges as follows:

COUNT I

1. On or about 10:58 p.m. on August 26, 1980, Robert D. Luing, (hereinafter referred to as "the Decedent"), was riding lawfully in a Harley Davidson Motorcycle in an eastbound direction on a certain roadway most readily identifiable as Penny Road (hereinafter referred to as "the road") at a location (hereinafter referred to as "the location on Penny Road") approximately three-tenths of a mile west of Old Sutton Road in the County of Cook, State of Illinois. This location on Penny Road, and all of Penny Road between Old Sutton Road and Healy Road was at said time located within the Defendant Village of Barrington Hills, and traffic on said road and said road location was policed and regulated by said Defendant Village of Barrington Hills. This said road and road location was also at said time within the signing, marking and maintenance jurisdiction of Defendant Cook County, Illinois.

2. At said time and place, (hereinafter respectively referred to as "the time and place of injury"), the decedent's motorcycle ran off an unlit curve in the roadway and came into violent collision with a tree in the adjacent area south of said roadway curve. This curve shall henceforth be referred to as "the curve."

3. The said curve in said roadway that was the place of injury was designed, constructed, and was at the time of injury under the maintenance jurisdiction of Defendant Cook County, Illinois.

4. Defendant Cook County had, on and prior to the time of injury, a duty to design, construct, and maintain the said roadway curve that was the place of injury and adjacent area south of said curve with due care.

5. Prior to and at the time of injury, the roadway curve and adjacent area to the south of said curve was negligently designed, constructed, and maintained by Defendant Cook County in that:

A. Said curve required lighting, but was illuminated by no street lights;

B. Said curve was too sharp, narrow, and abrupt for motorists to adjust the operation of their vehicles;
C. The banking and superelevation of said curve was improper in that the right edge of the road was higher than the left;
D. Delineators and reflectors were warranted and required along the outer edge of said curve, but had not been posted;
E. No clear recovery area had been provided for vehicles, such as decedent's, going off said curve;
F. Warning signs of said curve were warranted and required for eastbound traffic, but Defendant had failed to provide any such signs;
G. The posted speed on mid curve was too high;
H. Standards and procedures warranted by the Illinois Uniform Manual on Traffic Control Devices for both setting speed limits and authorizing curve warning signs were not followed, so that at the time of said crash the said curve and the said road of roadway adjacent to said curve to the south had not received from said Defendant warranted speed limits, warranted speed limit signs, warranted curve warning signs, warranted lights, warranted slopes, and warranted clear zones;
I. The road shoulders along said curve were too steep and narrow;
J. Illinois Revised Statutes, Chapter 95-1/2, Section 11-301, providing that,

"The Department shall adopt a State manual and specifications for a uniform system of traffic-control devices consistent with this Chapter for use upon highways within this State. The manual shall specify insofar as practicable the minimum warrants justifying the use of the various traffic control devices. Such uniform system shall correlate with and, where not inconsistent with Illinois highway conditions, conform to the system set forth in the most recent edition of the national manual on Uniform Traffic Control Devices for Streets and Highways."

And,

Illinois Revised Statutes, Chapter 95-1/2, Section 11-304, providing that,

"Local authorities and road district highway commissioners in their respective maintenance jurisdiction shall place and maintain such traffic-control devices upon highways under their maintenance jurisdiction as are required to indicate and carry out the provisions of this Chapter, and local traffic ordinances or to regulate, warn, or guide traffic. All such traffic control devices shall conform to the State Manual and Specifications and shall be justified by traffic warrants stated in the Manual. Placement of traffic-control devices on township or road district roads also shall be subject to the written approval of the County Superintendent of Highways."

And,

Illinois Revised Statutes, Chapter 85, Section 3-104(b) providing that,

"Neither a local public entity nor a public employee is liable under this Act for an injury caused by the failure to provide traffic warning signals, signs, markings or other devices unless such a signal, sign, marking or device was necessary to warn of a condition which endangered the safe movement of traffic, and which would not be reasonably apparent to or anticipated by a person in the exercise of due care."

Were all violated by the following violations of the Illinois Manual on Uniform Traffic Control Devices, which also created dangers to the safe movement of traffic at said road location which would not be reasonably apparent to or anticipated by a person in the exercise of due care:

i. Warranted curve warning signs and advisory speed signs required for east bound traffic approaching the curve were not posted;
ii. Required lighting at said curve and said road location had not been provided;
iii. Said curve was too sharp, narrow, and abrupt for motorists to adjust the operation of their vehicles, and said curve had a negative superelevation;
iv. The banking and superelevation of said curve was improper in that the right edge of the road was higher than the left;
v. Delineators and reflectors were warranted and required along the outer edge of said curve, but had not been posted;
vi. No clear recovery area had been provided for vehicles, such as decedent, going off said curve;
vii. Warning signs of said curve were warranted and required for eastbound traffic, but Defendant had failed to provide any such signs;
viii. The posted speed on said curve was too high;
ix. Standards and procedures warranted by the Illinois Uniform Manual on Traffic Control Devices for both setting speed limits and authorizing curve warning signs were not followed, so that at the time of said crash the said curve and the said road of roadway adjacent to said curve to the south has not received from said Defendant warranted speed limits, warranted speed

limit signs, warranted curve warning signs, warranted lights, warranted slopes, and warranted clear zones.

K. Defendant Cook County, on and prior to the time and place of injury, had negligently failed to adequately police said road area, had negligently failed to request, obtain or assess traffic crash data on the subject Penny Road area between Old Sutton Road and Healy Road from Defendant Barrington Hills, and had negligently failed to implement any program to locate or correct dangerous areas, including the curve at issue, on said Penny Road that said crash data available from Defendant Barrington Hills revealed.

6. At the time of injury and for a considerable time prior thereto, the said Defendant Cook County knew or should have known that said roadway, as designed, constructed and maintained by said Defendant Cook County was not reasonably fit for travel.

7. The dangerous condition of the roadway as above described at said time and place of injury endangered the safe movement of traffic along and upon the roadway and was not reasonably apparent to and could not reasonably be anticipated by a person in the exercise of due care; and the existence of adequate turn and curve warning signs, proper speed limits, reflectors, proper banking, lighting shoulders, clear zones, and other devices was necessary to warn persons traveling along the roadway of such conditions. All said necessary warning devices were absent from said road at the time of injury.

8. As a direct and proximate result of the aforesaid condition of the roadway and the adjacent area to the south and of Defendant Cook County's negligence, the vehicle in which the Decedent was riding at the time of injury was caused to run off the roadway and strike the said tree with great force and violence, as aforesaid, and the Decedent thereby sustained grave and mortal injuries to his head, brain, spine, neck, lungs, and chest, and on or about August 26, 1980, the Decedent died from said injuries.

9. As a direct and proximate result of the foregoing, the Plaintiff, Theresa Luing, wife of Decedent, and the minor children of Decedent, Ashley Luing and Leslie Luing, all of whom were being supported by the Decedent prior to the time of the injury, were deprived of the Decedent's financial support; the minor Plaintiffs, all of whom lived with the Decedent prior to the time of the injury, were deprived of the care, guidance, support, love, and affection of the Decedent; and the Plaintiff, Theresa Luing, the wife of the Decedent, was deprived of the help, company, love, affection and consortium of the Decedent.

10. The said Defendant was given and received timely notice of the claims in this suit as required by the statute in such cases made and provided.

WHEREFORE, the Plaintiff, Theresa Luing, individually, and as Special Administrator of the Estate of Robert D. Luing, deceased, prays that the Defendant, Cook County, be found liable to the Plaintiff for the death of the Decedent and that the said Defendant be ordered to pay the Plaintiff damages in the amount of $5,000,000.00.

COUNT II

1. - 7. Plaintiff repeats and realleges Paragraphs 1. through 7. of Count I as, respectively, Paragraphs 1. through 7. of Count II.

8. As a direct and proximate result of the aforesaid condition of the roadway and the adjacent area to the south and of Defendant Cook County's negligence, the vehicle in which the Decedent was riding at the time of injury was caused to run off the roadway and strike the said tree with great force and violence. Decedent thereby sustained grave and mortal injuries to his head, brain, spine, neck, lungs and chest, of which he endured excruciating agony, pain, soreness, and swelling. Subsequently, on or about August 26, 1980, the Decedent died from said injuries.

9. - 10. Plaintiff repeats and realleges Paragraphs 9. and 10. of Count I of this Complaint as, respectively, Paragraphs 9. and 10. of Count II of this Complaint.

WHEREFORE, the Plaintiff, Theresa Luing, individually, and as Special Administrator of the Estate of Robert D. Luing, prays that the Defendant Cook County, be found liable to the Plaintiff for the injuries to and death of the Decedent and that the Defendant be ordered to pay the Plaintiff damages in the amount of $5,000,000.00.

COUNT III

1. - 7. Plaintiff repeats and realleges Paragraphs 1. through 7. of Count II as, respectively, Paragraphs 1. through 7. of Count III.

8. As a direct and proximate result of the aforesaid condition of the roadway and the adjacent area to the south and of Defendant Cook County's negligence, the vehicle in which the Decedent was riding at the time of injury was caused to run off the roadway and strike the said tree with great force and violence, and on or about August 26, 1980, the Decedent died from the injuries sustained in this crash.

9. Plaintiff Theresa Luing, individually, was at the time of said injury and death of decedent Robert Luing, the lawful wedded wife of said decedent Robert Luing and was living, consorting, and cohabiting with said decedent.

10. As the direct and proximate consequence of the Defendants said wrongful and negligent acts and conduct, individual Plaintiff Theresa Luing's husband, Robert Luing, was killed, as enumerated herein. Plaintiff has suffered the loss of the services of her husband, which had been prior to said husband's death of great value to Plaintiff, and has been deprived of the affection, society, companionship and consortium of her husband due to Defendants' negligence. Plaintiff has been and will continue to be hindered and prevented from transacting and attending to her usual business and affairs, and has been caused to lay out and expend large sums of money in and about having the services performed for her which had previously been performed by her husband, and will be compelled permanently in the future to expend large sums of money for the services which her husband could and would have performed for her, and has been and will continue to be otherwise greatly injured, inconvenienced and harassed by means of the wrongful and unlawful conduct of Defendant.

11. The said Defendant was given timely notice of the claims in this suit as required by the Statute in such cases made and provided.

WHEREFORE, the Plaintiff, Theresa Luing, individually, and as Special Administrator of the Estate of Robert D. Luing, deceased, prays that the Defendant, the County of Cook, be found liable to the Plaintiff for the death of the Decedent and that the Defendant Cook County be ordered to pay the Plaintiff damages in the amount of $5,000,000.00.

COUNT IV

1. - 2. Plaintiff repeats and realleges Paragraphs 1. and 2. of Count III as, respectively, Paragraphs 1. and 2. of Count IV.

3. At the time of the injury and for a considerable time prior thereto, Defendant Village of Barrington Hills knew or should have known that the portion of Penny Road, including the subject curve, within the Village of Barrington Hills, as designed, constructed and maintained by Defendant Cook County, was not reasonably safe for travel. Defendant Village of Barrington Hills was clearly put on notice of the unsafe condition of said roadway as Defendant Village of Barrington Hills had on file police reports of crashes that occurred at said road location. These police reports were of such quantity as to indicate dangerously high crash and injury rates.

4. At said time and place, Defendant Village of Barrington Hills had the duty to warn motorists of dangerous conditions on Penny Road, including the subject curve, that were within said Village of Barrington Hills. At and prior to said time, Defendant Village of Barrington Hills

had negligently and carelessly failed to meet this duty by failing to provide effective public warning as warranted by the high crash and injury rates on said road location.

5. Plaintiff repeats and realleges Paragraph 7. of Count I as Paragraph 5. of Count IV.

6. As a direct and proximate result of the aforesaid condition of the roadway and the adjacent area to the south and of Defendant Village of Barrington Hills' negligence, the vehicle in which the Decedent was riding at the time of injury was caused to run off the roadway and strike the said tree with great force and violence, as aforesaid, and the Decedent thereby sustained grave and mortal injuries to his head, brain, spine, neck, lungs and chest, and on or about August 26, 1980, the Decedent died from said injuries.

7. - 8. Plaintiff hereby repeats and realleges Paragraphs 9. and 10. of Count I of this Complaint, respectively, as Paragraphs 7. and 8. of Count IV of this Complaint.

WHEREFORE, the Plaintiff Theresa Luing, individually, and as Special Administrator of the Estate of Robert D. Luing, deceased, prays that the Defendant Village of Barrington Hills be ordered to pay the Plaintiff damages in the amount of $5,000,000.00.

COUNT V

1. - 7. Plaintiff repeats and realleges Paragraphs 1. through 7. of Count IV as, respectively, Paragraphs 1. through 7. of Count V of this Complaint.

8. As a direct and proximate result of the aforesaid condition of the roadway and the adjacent area to the south and of Defendant Village of Barrington Hills' negligence, the vehicle in which the Decedent was riding at the time of injury was caused to run off the roadway and strike the said tree with great force and violence. Decedent thereby sustained grave and mortal injuries to his head, brain, spine, neck, lungs and chest, of which he endured excruciating agony, pain, soreness, and swelling. Subsequently, on or about August 26, 1980, the Decedent died from said injuries.

9. - 10. Plaintiff repeats and realleges Paragraphs 9. and 10. of Count II as Paragraphs 9. and 10. of Count V of this Complaint.

WHEREFORE, the Plaintiff, Theresa Luing, individually, and as Special Administrator of the Estate of Robert D. Luing, prays that the Defendant Village of Barrington Hills be found liable to the Plaintiff for the injuries to and death of the Decedent and that the Defendant be ordered to pay the Plaintiff damages in the amount of $5,000,000.00.

COUNT VI

1. - 8. Plaintiff repeats and realleges Paragraphs 1. through 8. of Count V as, respectively, Paragraphs 1. through 8. of Count VI of this Complaint.

9. - 11. Plaintiff hereby repeats and realleges Paragraphs 9. through 11. of Count III, as respectively, Paragraphs 9. through 11. of Count VI of this Complaint.

WHEREFORE, the Plaintiff, Theresa Luing, individually, and as Special Administrator of the Estate of Robert D. Luing, deceased, prays that the Defendant Village of Barrington Hills, be found liable to the Plaintiff for the injuries to and death of the Decedent and that the said Defendant be ordered to pay the Plaintiff damages in the amount of $5,000,000.00.

Respectfully submitted,

By: ______________________

Attorney for Theresa Luing,
individually and as next friend,
guardian, and representative of
the minor children, Ashley Luing
and Leslie Luing.

FOSS, SCHUMAN & DRAKE
Attorneys for Plaintiffs
11 South LaSalle Street
Chicago, IL 60603
312/782-2610

§ 10-3. Discovery.

The following discovery instruments illustrate the transition from broad and general to narrow and specific questions. The more you know, the better your inquiries should become, which is why the ancient Greeks used to say that in order to ask an intelligent question you usually had to already know at least half the answer.

§ 10-3(A). Broad Spectrum Discovery.

The first phase of discovery should reach out into lots of the million and one possible relevant nooks and crannies in a transportation facility negligence case. The initial answers will give you most of the basic information you need. Remember that the Plaintiffs' first wave of discovery must *always* include a Notice to Produce the Final Design Plans and the "As Built" plans showing what the transportation facilities geometrics were at the time of the crash.

§ 10-3(A)(1). Broad Spectrum Interrogatories to a Highway Department.

STATE OF INDIANA)
) SS
COUNTY OF LAKE)

IN THE LAKE SUPERIOR COURT
ROOM NUMBER TWO
EAST CHICAGO, INDIANA

JAMES P. EDGMAN, et al.,)
)
Plaintiffs,)
)
) CAUSE NO. 271 843
vs.)
)
THE STATE OF INDIANA,)
)
Defendant.)

INTERROGATORIES TO DEFENDANT

Now comes the Plaintiff, JAMES P. EDGMAN, et al., by and through his attorneys, Cohen, Cohen & Bullard and Foss, Schuman & Drake, and propounds the following written interrogatories to be answered in writing and under oath within 30 days by the Defendant:

1. At the time of the crash in question, what was the functional classification of the area of Cline Avenue between the Toll Road and the Gary Avenue Overpass:

   a) was it a freeway?
   b) was it an expressway?
   c) was it an arterial highway?
   d) was it a collector highway?
   e) was it a local road?

f) If none of the above, please indicate the functional classification.

2. If said area of Cline Avenue was an expressway, did freeway design standards apply to it?

3. At the time of the crash in question, was said area of Cline Avenue an urban road or a rural road?

4. Please specify any documentation regarding the classification of said area of Cline Avenue that was in existence prior to the time of the crash in question, specifying the present location if known of any documentation, the authors of said documentation, and the dates of said documentation.

5. What was the state-wide accident rate for locations of a similar classification to said area of Cline Avenue in the year 1970? Please indicate the source of this answer and please specify whether this accident rate is measured in total accidents per million vehicle miles, injuries per million vehicles miles, fatalities per million vehicle miles, or some other measurement in which case please indicate the measurement standard used for the state-wide accident rate.

6. What was the state-wide accident rate for locations of a similar classification to said area of Cline Avenue in the year 1969? Please indicate the source of this answer and please specify whether this accident rate is measured in total accidents per million vehicle miles, injuries per million vehicle miles, fatalities per million vehicle miles, or some other measurement in which case please indicate the measurement standard used for the state-wide accident rate.

7. What was the state-wide accident rate for locations of a similar classification to said area of Cline Avenue in the year 1968? Please indicate the source of this answer and please specify whether this accident rate is measured in total accidents per million vehicle miles, injuries per million vehicle miles, fatalities per million vehicle miles, or some other measurement in which case please indicate the measurement standard used for the state-wide accident rate.

8. What was the state-wide accident rate for locations of a similar classification to said area of Cline Avenue in the year 1967? Please indicate the source of this answer and please specify whether this accident rate is measured in total accidents per million vehicle miles, injuries per million vehicle miles, fatalities per million vehicle miles, or some other measurement in which case please indicate the measurement standard used for the state-wide accident rate.

9. What was the state-wide accident rate for locations of a similar classification to said area of Cline Avenue in the year 1966? Please indicate the source of this answer and please specify whether this

accident rate is measured in total accidents per million vehicle miles, injuries per million vehicle miles, fatalities per million vehicle miles, or some other measurement in which case please indicate the measurement standard used for the state-wide accident rate.

10. What was the state-wide accident rate for locations of a similar classification to said area of Cline Avenue in the year 1971? Please indicate the source of this answer and please specify whether this accident rate is measured in total accidents per million vehicle miles, injuries per million vehicle miles, fatalities per million vehicle miles, or some other measurement in which case please indicate the measurement standard used for the state-wide accident rate.

11. What was the state-wide accident rate for locations of a similar classification to said area of Cline Avenue in the year 1972? Please indicate the source of this answer and please specify whether this accident rate is measured in total accidents per million vehicle miles, injuries per million vehicle miles, fatalities per million vehicle miles, or some other measurement in which case please indicate the measurement standard used for the state-wide accident rate.

12. What was the state-wide accident rate for locations of a similar classification to said area of Cline Avenue in the year 1973? Please indicate the source of this answer and please specify whether this accident rate is measured in total accidents per million vehicle miles, injuries per million vehicle miles, fatalities per million vehicle miles, or some other measurement in which case please indicate the measurement standard used for the state-wide accident rate.

13. Would accident rates on roads of a similar classification to said area of Cline Avenue compiled from other states be relevant for evaluation of the accident rate on said area of Cline Avenue assuming identical time periods and measurement where used?

14. If your answer to the above interrogatory was in the negative, please indicate the reasons for your answer.

15. During each of the years from 1966 through 1970, please specify what criteria were used by the Indiana Highway Commission to identify hazardous roadway locations in the State of Indiana.

16. During each of the years from 1966 through 1970, did the Indiana Highway Commission consider the accident rates on highway locations relevant to the identification of hazardous road locations?

17. For each of the years from 1966 through 1970, what criteria were used to identify roadway locations that needed safety improvements?

18. For each of said years, what measurements or criteria were used by the State of Indiana to determine what priority should be given to highway locations requiring safety improvements?

19. How much money was spent on highway safety improvements in the State of Indiana during each year from 1966 through 1970?

20. Please indicate where the money spent on highway safety improvements in the State of Indiana during each year from 1966 through 1970 came from, i.e., whether the Federal Government, the State of Indiana, both, or additional sources.

21. How much money did the Federal Government make available to the State of Indiana for highway safety improvements during each year from 1966 through 1970?

22. What highway safety improvements projects were actually undertaken in the State of Indiana on Indiana State roads during each year from 1967-1970? With respect to each project please indicate whether the State of Indiana or the Federal Government or both funded said project, how much money was spent on said project, what were the reasons for undertaking said project, how many accidents per year had taken place at the location of each said project, how many injuries had occurred per year at each location, how many fatalities had occurred each year at each said location, how much property damage occurred each year at each said location, how many vehicle miles were measured each year at each said location, average daily traffic measurements for each said year at each said location, the nature of the improvements at each said location, and the source of the money for each said improvement if said funds were not 100 percent provided by the Federal Government.

23. How much must the accident rate and/or the injury rate and/or the fatality rate on a section of roadway exceed the state average for that section of roadway to be considered "hazardous" or "dangerous" during each year from 1966 through 1970?

24. Are the police accident reports supplied to both parties by the Indiana State Police in connection with this case all of the Cline Avenue police accident reports known to be in existence at this time?

25. Do the police accident reports provided by the Indiana State Police in connection with this case list as fatalities only persons brought into hospitals dead on arrival from the accident location, or do said police reports also list as fatalities persons who die of injuries received after arrival at the hospital?

26. Did the State of Indiana's policy on the installation of highway lights change from 1966 through 1974? If any said change occurred, please indicate the date of said change and the nature of said change.

27. How many cities border the east side of Cline Avenue from the Toll Road through Gary Avenue?

28. How many cities border the west side of Cline Avenue from the Toll Road through Gary Avenue?

29. Did any city bordering Cline Avenue from the Toll Road through Gary Avenue on either the east or west side at any time prior to July, 1970 ever request the installation of lights on the section of Cline Avenue said city borders?

30. How many highway safety improvement projects costing $30,000 or less were effectuated in the State of Indiana during each year between 1967 to and including 1970?

31. With respect to each said project or at least five said projects each year, please specify:

a. whether the State of Indiana or the Federal Government or both funded said project;
b. how much money was spent on said project;
c. what were the reasons for undertaking said project;
d. how many accidents per year had taken place at the location of each said project;
e. how many injuries had occurred per year at each location;
f. how many fatalities had occurred each year at each said location;
g. how much property damage occurred each year at each said location;
h. how many vehicle miles were measured each year at each said location;
i. average daily traffic measurements for each said year at each said location;
j. the nature of the improvements at each said location;
k. the source of the money for each said improvement if said funds were not 100 percent provided by the Federal Government.

(Signed) RICHARD S. KUHLMAN

COHEN, COHEN & BULLARD
3609 Main Street
East Chicago, IN 46312
Tel: 219/EX7-0903

FOSS, SCHUMAN & DRAKE
11 S. LaSalle Street
Chicago, Il 60603
Tel: 312/782-2610

§ 10-3(A)(2). Broad Spectrum Supplemental Interrogatories to a Highway Department.

STATE OF INDIANA)) SS COUNTY OF LAKE)	IN THE LAKE SUPERIOR COURT CAUSE NO. 271-843

JAMES P. EDGMAN, in his individual capacity and as Administrator of the Estate of LORENE A. EDGMAN, on behalf of himself and said Estate and all other members of a class consisting of sensatives of those persons, who have sustained serious or fatal bodily injuries as a result of driving or being driven upon the negligently constructed and maintained area of public highway located in the City of Gary, Indiana, known as the Cline Avenue S-Curve stretching from the Indiana East-West Toll Road overpass on the South to the Gary Avenue Exit on the North,

Plaintiffs,

v.

STATE OF INDIANA,

Defendant.

SUPPLEMENTAL INTERROGATORIES

Now come the Plaintiffs, JAMES P. EDGMAN, et al., by COHEN, COHEN & BULLARD and FOSS, SCHUMAN & DRAKE, their attorneys, and respectfully propound the following Supplemental Interrogatories for the Defendant to answer within Thirty (30) days of receipt thereof:

1. Was federal money used in construction of the Cline Avenue S-Curve?
2. When was the Cline Avenue S-Curve designed?
3. When was the Cline Avenue S-Curve opened to traffic?

4. Where any State or Federal Highway Design Standards adopted in the design and construction of the S-Curve?

5. If the answer to #4 was affirmative, please specifically identify each such Highway Design Standard. In response to this Interrogatory, it will suffice to list the titles and effective dates of any published works or literature generally available, adopted at such a standard (e.g., The A.A.S.H.O. Bluebook 1965). For non published or non generally available standards, please specify the effective date, general title, author, nature and the place where such standards may be presently obtained. If you will do so without a Notice to Produce, please attach a copy of each such non published or non generally available Highway Design Standard.

6. In the event of conflicts between any of the aforementioned Highway Design Standards on the Cline Avenue S-Curve, were there any rules or priorities as to which standards would prevail? If so, please designate each said rule or priority.

7. Were waivers of any of the aforementioned Highway Design Standards applied for or authorized for the designed and/or construction of the Cline Avenue S-Curve? If so, please designate:

(a) The date of each such waiver;
(b) The person authorizing each such waiver;
(c) The standard waived in each such waiver and the criteria used to replace it;
(d) The reason for each such waiver.

8. The old Cline Avenue was originally straight in the area where the S-Curve now exists. Why was the S-Curve designed and constructed? Why was the Cline Avenue S-Curve designed as a curve rather than straight?

9. Is the State of Indiana now in possession of any land acquisition records concerning the construction of the S-Curve? If so, will they be made available without a Notice to Produce? If not, please state who has such records and where such records can be found.

10. Has the State of Indiana done any comparisons of the incidence of traffic accidents on the S-Curve of Cline Avenue and the incidence of traffic accidents on other areas of public highway in the State of Indiana? If so, please designate:

(a) The date of each such comparison;
(b) The persons or departments making such comparisons;
(c) With respect to each such comparison, how did the number and severity of accidents on the Cline Avenue S-Curve compare with accidents on the other areas of highway studied? Please state the results and conclusions of all such studies or comparisons.

11. Has the State of Indiana adopted any system to designate hazardous locations on public highways? If so, please designate:

(a) The criteria used in said systems;

(b) Has the Cline Avenue S-Curve ever been analyzed under said system and, if so, with what results?

12. In response to Plaintiffs Interrogatory No. 19, the State of Indiana answered that the guardrail contract on the Cline Avenue S-Curve was awarded in June, 1970, and completed in December, 1970, and the median concrete barrier wall contract was awarded July 20, 1972, and completed in July, 1973. With respect to said answer, please designate:

(a) Was the guardrail completed in December, 1970, located between the north and south bound traffic on the Cline Avenue S-Curve or did it have some other location, and if so, what was the other location?

(b) What was the height of the guardrail completed in December 1970?

(c) Why was the guardrail completed in December, 1970, not included in the original design or construction of the Cline Avenue S-Curve?

(d) Why was it necessary to install the guardrail completed in 1970 along the Cline Avenue S-Curve?

(e) Why was the median concrete barrier wall completed in July, 1973, not included in the original design or construction of the Cline Avenue S-Curve?

(f) Why was it necessary to install the median concrete barrier wall completed in July, 1973, along the Cline Avenue S-Curve?

(g) Had any studies of the incidence of traffic accidents on the Cline Avenue S-Curve been completed by or for the State of Indiana on or prior to the dates when the guardrail or median concrete barrier wall cited in Defendants Interrogatory Answer No. 19 were authorized?

(h) Did the incidence of traffic accidents on the Cline Avenue S-Curve influence the decision to authorize the guardrail and median concrete barrier wall cited in Defendants' Answer to Plaintiffs' Interrogatory No. 19?

(i) Did any factors not previously mentioned in Answers to these Supplemental Interrogatories influence the decision to authorize the guardrail and medians concrete barrier wall cited in Defendants' Answer to Plaintiffs' Interrogatory No. 19? If so, please specify each such factor.

13. At the time of the collision in question on July 27, 1970:

(a) Was there any barrier between the northbound traffic lanes and the southbound traffic lanes along the Cline Avenue S-Curve at the place where the collision occurred?

(b) If the answer to Interrogatory No. 13(a) above was affirmative, please designate:

1. The height of the barrier;
2. The material composing the barrier;
3. The length of the barrier, including the point where said barrier began and ended;
4. The design of the barrier.

14. On July 27, 1970:

(a) How far North of the Cline Avenue S-Curve was the nearest speed limit sign for Southbound traffic, and what was the posted speed on that sign?

(b) How far South of the Cline Avenue S-Curve was the nearest speed limit sign for Northbound traffic, and what was the posted speed on that sign?

(c) Where there any speed limit signs on the S-Curve itself, and if so, please give the specific location of each such sign, state where each such sign was posted for north or southbound traffic, and what was the posted speed limit on such signs?

15. Was there, on or prior to July 27, 1970, any warning sign or designations on either the northern or southern approaches to the Cline Avenue S-Curve indicating:

(a) The presence of a curve or a reverse curve?
(b) The presence of a change of grade?
(c) The presence of a hill?
(d) The presence of a dip?
(e) The pavement is slippery when wet?
(f) That motorists should reduce speed when traversing the S-Curve?
(g) That motorists should exercise caution in traversing the S-Curve?
(h) That the S-Curve was in any other way dangerous, and if so, in what was such danger was so designated?

16. If the Answer to Interrogatory No. 15 was in any way affirmative, please specifically designate:

(a) The exact location, including the distance north or south of the S-Curve, of each such sign or designation;
(b) The wording of, or the symbol on, each such sign or designation.

17. What is the location of the "Highway Avenue" referred to in Defendants' Answer to Plaintiffs' Interrogatory No. 44?

18. Have any changes or alterations been made in the design of the Cline Avenue S-Curve or any portion thereof since the S-Curve was first opened to traffic? If so,

(a) What changes or alterations in design were made?
(b) Where were those changes made?
(c) When were they made?
(d) With respect to each such change, please state why it was made.
(e) Was the Cline Avenue S-Curve altered in accordance with those changes?

19. Was the area of public highway known as the Cline Avenue S-Curve designed under the authority of the State of Indiana?

20. If the answer to the above Interrogatory was in the negative, please designate:

(a) Under the authority of what governmental body or agency was the Cline Avenue S-Curve designed?
(b) Give the name and address of the person or entity who designed the Cline Avenue S-Curve.
(c) When was the Cline Avenue S-Curve designed?

21. At the time of the collision in issue on July 27, 1970:

(a) Was the Cline Avenue S-Curve unstriped?
(b) Were the driving lanes on the Cline Avenue S-Curve unstriped?
(c) Were the driving lanes on the Cline Avenue S-Curve distinguishable?
(d) Were there median boundaries of the Cline Avenue S-Curve, and if so, how were they marked?
(e) Were the outside boundaries of the Cline Avenue S-Curve marked, and if so, how were they marked?
(f) Was the pavement of the Cline Avenue S-Curve bumpy and/or uneven and/or rutted?
(g) Was the surface of the Cline Avenue S-Curve dirty?
(h) Were the shoulders of the Cline Avenue S-Curve heaped with road grime?

22. What was the reason for the structure over the Calumet River on the S-Curve being low?

(a) Was the Calumet River a navigable stream when the S-Curve was constructed?
(b) Was the present bridge over the Calumet River on the S-Curve constructed in conformance with Army Corps of Engineering Standards?
(c) If the answer to the above Interrogatory (b) was in the negative, please specify who waived said requirements, when said requirements were waived, whether there are any written records of such waiver, and if so, where are said written records presently located and who has custody of said records?

(d) If the answer to Interrogatory (b) was that Army Corps of Engineering standards were waived in constructing the said bridge, why were said standards waived?

(e) Why was the bridge on the S-Curve over the Calumet River not constructed level with the Toll Road and Gary Avenue Bridges?

23. Why were vertical curves introduced into the design of the S-Curve?

24. When were vertical curves introduced into the design of the S-Curve?

25. Who approved the design of the S-Curve incorporating vertical curves?

26. When was the last date prior to July 27, 1970, when the lanes were painted on the S-Curve?

27. Are you presently in possession of the field reports from the maintenance crews who painted the lanes on the S-Curve on the dates specified in answer to the above Interrogatory? If so, will you produce said field reports without a subpoena? If not, where are said field reports located and who has custody of them?

28. On the date of the Edgman collision, July 27, 1970, were any traffic information signs located north or south of the S-Curve to inform motorists that:

(a) They were approaching a curve?

(b) They were approaching a reverse curve?

(c) They were approaching a dip?

(d) They were approaching a hill?

(e) What the speed limit was?

(f) Any other information?

29. At what stations were each sign indicated in the answer to the above Interrogatory posted? Please specify which sign was posted at which station.

30. When is the last date prior to the Edgman collision, July 27, 1970, when:

(a) The S-Curve was swept?

(b) The debris was picked up and removed from the S-Curve?

(c) The rails along the S-Curve were repaired?

(d) The concrete on the S-Curve was patched?

31. With respect to each answer in the above Interrogatory please specify whether the field reports from the maintenance crews that did said work are available, and if so, whether you will produce them without a subpoena, and if you will not so produce them, then please indicate where said field reports are presently located and who has care and custody of them.

32. Were Federal funds used in the initial design of the Cline Avenue S-Curve?

33. Were Federal funds used in the initial construction of the Cline Avenue S-Curve?

34. Were Federal funds used in any subsequent improvements to, changes in, or additional construction of the Cline Avenue S-Curve? If the answer to this Interrogatory is in the affirmative, please specify the date and reason for each said Federal expenditure.

35. At the time of the Edgman collision on July 27, 1970, did any of the guardrails or guard structures, median structures or posts along the northern boundary of the S-Curve or the southern boundary of the S-Curve or in the center of the S-Curve have reflectorized paint, or reflectorized buttons or lights? If the answer to this Interrogatory is in the affirmative in any way, please specify:

(a) The exact location of each indicated area bearing reflectorized paint and/or lights and/or reflectorized buttons.
(b) The type of illumination device bore by each structure so indicated.

36. At the time of the Edgman collision on July 27, 1970, were there any lights, signs, flairs or other warning devices placed north or south of the S-Curve to warn motorists of the presence of the median structures between the north and south bound lanes? If the answer to this Interrogatory is in the affirmative, please specify:

(a) The station where each said sign or warning device was located.
(b) The type of sign or warning device at each such station.
(c) The date when each such sign or warning device was installed.

37. Was any repair work done on the Cline Avenue S-Curve, or any median structures thereon, or any guardrails thereon or any other part thereof during the period of Ninety (90) days prior to the Edgman collision?

38. If the answer to the above Interrogatory was in the affirmative, please indicate:

(a) The type of repairs made;
(b) The date or dates when such repairs were made;
(c) The precise location on the S-Curve where such repairs were made;
(d) Whether there are written records existent of such repairs, and if so, the person or entity now having charge, care, custody, or control, of said records and whether you will produce said records without a written Notice to Produce.

39. Were any warning flairs, lights or other illuminated warning devices operating at any point along the Cline Avenue S-Curve at the time of the Edgman collision?

40. If the answer to the above Interrogatory was in the affirmative, please describe the nature, size, and location of each such warning flair or light and the date and time when such warning flairs or lights were subsequently removed after the Edgman collision.

41. Has any claim for damages been made against the State of Indiana by anyone other than this Plaintiff or persons you previously listed in Interrogatory Answers for injuries received on the Cline Avenue S-Curve during the period of time from and after the Edgman collision?

42. If the answer to the above Interrogatory was in the affirmative, for each claim please state:

(a) The date of the claim;
(b) The name and address of the claimant;
(c) A description of any disposition made of the claim and the amount of any settlement or damage verdict.

43. In your answer to Plaintiff's Interrogatory No. 44 you stated that 55 m.p.h. speed limit signs were installed at or near the the Cline Avenue S-Curve on June 30, 1970, and that the location of such signs was "as prescribed in the Indiana Manual on Uniform Traffic Control Devices from 1500' North of Highway Avenue U.S 12." With respect to this answer, please indicate:

(a) The precise location along both the north and south bound lanes of the S-Curve where such signs were installed on June 30, 1970;
(b) The number of such speed limit signs installed on June 30, 1970;
(c) The size and color of each such sign;
(d) Whether the paint on each such sign was reflectorized;
(e) Whether there are written records existent reflecting the installation of said signs, and if so, the persons or entities having care, custody or control of said records.

44. For each person known to you, your agents, employees, or attorneys, or any other agents or servants of the State of Indiana or any subdivision thereof, who witnessed this collision or were in the vicinity thereof, at the time of, or within 30 minutes after said collision, please state:

(a) The name and last address of each said person;
(b) The last known place of employment of each such person;
(c) The telephone number of each such person;
(d) Whether each such person was a witness to the collision or not.

45. For each person known to you, your agents, or any other employees or attorneys of the State of Indiana or any subdivision thereof, who possess or claim to possess knowledge of any fact or record relevant to this collision who have not been previously listed with response to the above Interrogatory, please state:

(a) The name and address of each such person;
(b) The place of employment of each such person;
(c) The telephone number of each such person;
(d) Whether each such person was a witness to the collision or not.

46. Describe each paper, photograph, document or physical object of any nature which you intend to offer or use or which might be offered or used as evidence at the trial.

47. Have any persons made any statements, written or otherwise, while being interviewed or questioned by agents or servants of the State of Indiana in connection with this collision?

48. If the answer to the above Interrogatory was in the affirmative, please indicate:

(a) The name, address, place of employment and relationship to the State of Indiana, if any, of the maker of each statement;
(b) The date of each said statement;
(c) The maker's telephone number;
(d) Whether each said statement was written or oral, and if written, whether signed or unsigned;
(e) The name and address of the person having the present custody and control of such statements if written or recorded.

49. State the name, present residence address and areas of expertise of every person who has been consulted or employed by the State of Indiana or anyone acting on its behalf as an expert witness or consulting expert or potential expert witness in any way regarding this collision, the Plaintiff's injuries, damages and/or any other issues pertaining to this lawsuit, and as to each such person, state the date as best you can when such person was first consulted and employed, whether each such person has submitted a written report, diagnosis, opinion or evaluation, and if so, the name and address of person or entity having custody and control of said writings. Please further indicate whether you will make said writings available without a written Notice to Produce.

50. Please list the expert witnesses which the Defendant intends to use in the trial of this lawsuit.

51. Please list the witnesses which the Defendant intends to use in the trial of this lawsuit.

Respectfully submitted,

JAMES P. EDGMAN, et al.,
Plaintiff

By: ______________________________
RICHARD S. KUHLMAN, one
of the Attorneys for Plaintiff

COHEN, COHEN & BULLARD
3609 Main Street
East Chicago, IN 46312
(219) EX7-0903

FOSS, SCHUMAN & DRAKE
11 South LaSalle Street
Chicago, Illinois 60603
(312) 782-2610

§ 10-3(A)(3). Broad Spectrum Request to a Highway Department to Produce Documents.

In the Lake Superior Court
East Chicago, Indiana

JAMES P. EDGMAN, in his individual capacity and as Administrator of the Estate of LORENE A. EDGMAN on behalf of himself and said Estate and other members of a class consisting of all those persons, or the legal representatives of those persons, who have sustained serious or fatal bodily injuries as a result of driving or being driven upon the negligently constructed and maintained area of public highway located in the City of Gary, Indiana known as the Cline Avenue S-Curve stretching from the Indiana East-West Toll-Road overpass on the south to the Gary Avenue Exit on the north,	)	
Plaintiff,	)	
vs	)	NO. 271843
THE STATE OF INDIANA,	)	
Defendant.	)	

REQUEST TO PRODUCE

To: Offices of Attorney General
Theodore L. Sendak,
Attorney General
State of Indiana
219 State House
Indianapolis, Indiana 46204

Attorney for Defendant
The State of Indiana:

Plaintiff, by and through his attorneys in this matter, pursuant to Indiana Trial Rule 34, requests that Defendant produce the following documents for inspection and to be copied and be reproduced by Plaintiff by his attorneys no later than 30 days after the service of this Request to Produce, at the hour of 9:00 a.m. in the offices of Foss, Schuman & Drake, 11 South LaSalle Street, Chicago, Illinois. Said documents are as follows:

1. All personnel records showing the full names and present address (or if unknown, the last known addresses) of all persons not deceased holding or who have held the positions of Chief Highway Engineer and the Chief Engineers in charge of Design, Traffic, Maintenance, and Bridge and Structure for the State of Indiana for the period of 1955 through the date of this Request to Produce inclusive.
2. All personnel records showing the full names and present (or last known) addresses of all persons in charge of highway construction and maintenance in the LaPorte District for the period specified in Paragraph 1 herein.
3. All personnel records showing the names and present (or last known) addresses of all sub-district supervisory personnel involved in maintenance and/or construction in the LaPorte District for the period specified in Paragraph 1 herein.
4. All records showing the names and present (or last known) addresses of all Chairmen and Board Members of the Highway Commission of the state of Indiana for the period specified in Paragraph 1 herein.
5. The log of the Project Engineer on the original construction job of the Cline Avenue S-curve.
6. The logs of all Project Engineers on any subsequent construction jobs on said highway.
7. Contract No. R-66348.
8. Any and all "as built" drawings for said Cline Avenue S-curve.
9. All cross sections from stations numbers 215 through 250, inclusive, in the original contract documents for said Cline Avenue S-curve, and in any subsequent contract documents for said highway.

10. Any "as built" survey for said highway.

11. Any and all contract documents (including, but not limited to, drawings) regarding the amount and location of any median guardrails on said highway, and reflecting when such rails were installed.

12. All maintenance department records reflecting when the quardrails on said highway were painted, from 1960 to the date of this Request to Produce.

13. All accident records regarding said highway from 1960 to the date of this Request to Produce.

Plaintiff further requests that Defendant permit access to said highway for the purpose of inspection and measuring, surveying, photographing, testing, or sampling the right of way upon which said highway is located or any structure located thereon.

The above described documents, records, and real estate are relevant to the subject matter of the above-captioned action.

Dated this __________ day of ________________, 1976.

FOSS, SCHUMAN & DRAKE
Attorneys for Plaintiff

By: ______________________________

§ 10-3(B). Narrow Spectrum Follow-Up Discovery.

The following state discovery later closes in on and seeks to "fine tune" issues raised in earlier, broader discovery.

§ 10-3(B)(1). Follow-Up Interrogatory and Answer Concerning Color of Median Posts.

STATE OF INDIANA)) SS: COUNTY OF LAKE)	IN THE LAKE SUPERIOR COURT ROOM NUMBER TWO AT EAST CHICAGO, INDIANA

JAMES P. EDGMAN, in his)
individual capacity and as)
Administrator of the Estate of)
LORENE A. EDGMAN, deceased,)
on behalf of himself and said)
estate,)

Plaintiff,	)
vs.	)
THE STATE OF INDIANA,	)
Defendant.	)

ANSWER TO PLAINTIFF'S INTERROGATORY CONCERNING THE COLOR OF THE MEDIAN POSTS INTO WHICH THE CASILLAS VEHICLE PASSED BEFORE ENTERING THE OPPOSING LANES OF TRAFFIC

Defendant, State of Indiana, by THEODORE L. SENDAK, Attorney General of Indiana, by Robert F. Hassett, Deputy Attorney General, and submits its Answer to plaintiff's interrogatory concerning the color of the median posts into which the Casillas vehicle passed before entering the opposing lanes of traffic:

INTERROGATORY No. 1: Paragraph 212 of the Request to Admit Truth of Facts and Genuineness of Documents called upon Defendant to admit that the metal median posts that Casillas vehicle passed through before entering the opposing lanes of traffic were not painted any color. If you denied that fact, what color were those median posts at the time of the collision when the Casillas vehicle passed through them?

ANSWER: To the defendant's knowledge the Casillas vehicle did not pass through any median post.

Respectfully submitted,

THEODORE L. SENDAK
Attorney General of Indiana

By: ______________________

Robert F. Hassett
Deputy Attorney General
Attorneys for defendant.

§ 10-3(B)(2). Follow-Up Request to Produce Documents.

STATE OF INDIANA)		IN THE LAKE SUPERIOR COURT
) SS:		
COUNTY OF LAKE)		CAUSE NO. 271-843

JAMES P. EDGMAN, in his individual capacity and as Administrator of the Estate of LORENE EDGMAN,	)
Plaintiff,	)
vs.	)
STATE OF INDIANA,	)
Defendant.	)

REQUEST FOR THE PRODUCTION AND INSPECTION OF DOCUMENTS

Now comes the Plaintiff, JAMES P. EDGMAN, by and through his attorneys, COHEN, COHEN & BULLARD and FOSS, SCHUMAN & DRAKE, and, pursuant to Rule 34 of the Indiana Rules of Trial Procedure, Requests the Defendant, THE STATE OF INDIANA, to permit Plaintiff to inspect and copy the following documents on November 30, 1978, at the hour of 8:00 A.M., said inspection to take place at the office of Jack N. Smitherman, Secretary to the Highway Commission, Room 1101, State Office Building, 110 North Senate Avenue, Indianapolis, Indiana 46204, which is the situs indicated in Defendant's Answers to Supplemental Interrogatories for the following requested documents:

A. The Highway Design Standards indicated in Defendant's Answers to Supplementary Interrogatory #5, namely:

A.A.S.H.O. - A Policy on Geometric Design of Rural Highways, 1954;
A.A.S.H.O. - A Policy on Arterial Highways in Urban Areas, 1957;

Standard Divided Lane (Interstate)	Rev. 5/15/64
Standard Cross Section, E-11-IR	Rev. 4/17/64
Standard Cross Section, E-11-JR	Rev. 8/11/61
Standard 10 Inch Ramp Sections	Rev. 4/23/59
Standard Pavement Joints, Sheet A	Rev. 5/11/63
Miscellaneous Standards, Sheet "MA"	Rev. 2/01/64
Miscellaneous Standards, Sheet "MB"	Rev. 2/01/64
Miscellaneous Standards, Sheet "MC"	Rev. 4/01/59
Miscellaneous Standards, Sheet "MC1"	Rev. 7/06/60
Miscellaneous Standards, Sheet "MD"	Rev. 5/26/59
Miscellaneous Standards, Sheet "MD1"	Rev. 3/06/59
Miscellaneous Standards, Sheet "ME"	Rev. 9/01/64
Miscellaneous Standards, Sheet "MH"	Rev. 2/01/64

Miscellaneous Standards, Sheet "MI"	Rev. 2/01/64
Miscellaneous Standards, Sheet "MJ"	Rev. 2/01/64
Miscellaneous Standards, Sheet "MN"	Rev. 4/11/61
Miscellaneous Standards, Sheet "MP"	Rev. 11/20/63
Miscellaneous Standards, Sheet "MR"	Rev. 4/17/64
Miscellaneous Standards, Sheet "S"	Rev. 8/06/54
Miscellaneous Standards, Sheet "MT-1"	Adopted March 1963
Miscellaneous Standards, Sheet "MU"	Rev. 2/01/64
Miscellaneous Standards, Sheet "MV"	Rev. 2/01/64
Miscellaneous Standards, Sheet "MV-1"	Rev. 2/01/64
Miscellaneous Standards, Sheet "MV-2"	Rev. 2/01/64
Miscellaneous Standards, Sheet "ME-1"	Rev. 2/01/64
Miscellaneous Standards, Sheet "MJ-1"	Adopted Fed. 1961
Miscellaneous Standards, Sheet "MP-1"	Rev. 11/20/63
Standard Headwalls, May 1949	Rev. 6/16/50
Standard Reinforced Concrete Box Culvert, 45 Skew	Rev. 1/30/47
Standard Structure Connections for Extension	Adopted March 1934
Beam Guard Rail "GR-1"	Rev. 5/25/61
Typical Beam Guard Rail Details, Sheet "GR-A"	Rev. 5/25/61
Bridge Standard Sheet "M-5"	Rev. 10/4/61
Standard for Superelevation	Adopted January 1961

(Standards are as listed in plans for this project)

B. The land acquisition records concerning the construction of the Cline Avenue S-curve referred to in Defendant's Answer to Plaintiff's Supplemental Interrogatory No. 5.

C. The written records concerning the installation of speed limit signs on the Cline Avenue S-curve referred to in Defendant's Answers to Plaintiff's Supplemental Interrogatory No. 43.

Respectfully submitted,

Plaintiffs, JAMES EDGMAN, et al.,
by and through his attorneys,
COHEN, COHEN & BULLARD and
FOSS, SCHUMAN & DRAKE

By: ______________________

FOSS, SCHUMAN & DRAKE
11 South LaSalle Street
Suite 600
Chicago, Illinois 60603
312/782-2610

COHEN, COHEN & BULLARD
3609 Main Street
East Chicago, Indiana 46312
219/EX7-0903

§ 10-3(B)(3). Motion to Compel Disclosure of Experts Before Trial.

Many jurisdictions do not require the disclosure of experts before trial unless an appropriate motion is made. It is almost always appropriate to file such a motion so that you can prepare for, and take the experts pre-trial deposition from which you will, hopefully, be able to build your cross-examination of the expert. One form for such a Motion follows.

STATE OF INDIANA)) SS: COUNTY OF LAKE)	IN THE LAKE SUPERIOR COURT CAUSE NO. 271-843

JAMES P. EDGMAN, in his individual capacity and as Administrator of the Estate of LORENE EDGMAN,)
)
Plaintiff,)
)
vs.)
)
STATE OF INDIANA,)
)
Defendant.)

MOTION TO COMPEL DEFENDANT TO DISCLOSURE ITS EXPERT WITNESSES BEFORE TRIAL

Now comes the Plaintiff, JAMES P. EDGMAN, by and through his attorneys, FOSS, SCHUMAN & DRAKE, and COHEN, COHEN & BULLARD, and in support of this Motion states as follows:

1. Plaintiff's Supplemental Interrogatory No. 50 requested Defendant to list the expert witnesses it intends to use at trial. Defendant answered it had not yet determined "such matter".

2. Plaintiff's Supplemental Interrogatory No. 49 requested Defendant to state each "expert witness or consulting expert or potential expert witness" consulted by Defendant on this case. Defendant answered "No expert witnesses other than employees of the Indiana State Highway Commission have been consulted".

3. Plaintiff is obviously entitled to learn the identity of the Defendant's expert witnesses sufficiently in advance of the trial to institute adequate discovery procedures. In addition, the fact that a defense expert may work for Defendant, in the Highway Commission or any other capacity, is not an acceptable reason for Defendant to withhold said expert's identity.

WHEREFORE, Plaintiff prays the Court to enter an Order directing Defendant:

1. To disclose the experts it has consulted on this case, as requested in Plaintiff's Supplemental Interrogatory No. 49;

2. To promptly disclose, before trial, the experts, if any Defendant decides to use as witnesses at trial, so that Plaintiffs may institute appropriate pre-trial discovery.

3. Plaintiffs further pray that Defendant be barred from using at trial any expert witness not so disclosed before trial.

Respectfully submitted,

Plaintiffs, JAMES P. EDGMAN, et al.,
by and through his attorneys
COHEN, COHEN & BULLARD and
FOSS, SCHUMAN & DRAKE

By: ______________________________

FOSS, SCHUMAN & DRAKE
11 South LaSalle Street
Suite 600
Chicago, Illinois 60603
312/782-2610

COHEN, COHEN & BULLARD
3609 Main Street
East Chicago, Indiana 46312
219/EX7-0903

CHAPTER 11

RAILROAD CROSSING CRASHES

§ 11-1. Introduction.

Transportation facility negligence situations in railroad crashes warrant separate treatment because, while all the factors mentioned in other chapters apply to such cases, there are special rules that apply mainly to railroad crashes.

§ 11-2. Applicable Rules, Statutes, and Ordinances.

The first, and perhaps most important, step involved in railroad crash litigation is to unearth all the federal, state, local, and industrial rules involved in your case. Every level of government, trade and industry in this country has been regulating railroads since the mid-nineteenth century, and every distinct rule you unearth could, if violated by the railroad, provide a jury with the basis for a verdict against the railroad. Defects in the coupling of cars, for example, could fall under local ordinances, statutes, strict construction or products liability precedents, Uniform Commercial Code implied warranty theories, negligence theories, municipal safety ordinances, Interstate Commerce Commission regulations, and the Federal Safety Appliances Act of 1893, 45 U.S.C. § 1 *et seq. See Boyer v. Atchison, Topeka & Santa Fe Ry.*, 38 Ill. 2d 31, 230 N.E.2d 173 (1967). Similarly, each city, town, village, and state has some type of rule on how engines approaching crossings within its jurisdiction are supposed to sound their horns, toot their whistles, ring their bells, and shine their lights. Remember, railroads were legislatively regulated long before the automobile was invented.

California Statutes Concerning Railroads: *Hogue v. Southern Pac. Co.*, 1 Cal. 3d 253, 460 P.2d 965, 81 Cal. Rptr. 765 (1969). Statutes concerning railroad crossing signals are only a minimum standard of care a railroad must meet. The railroad will not necessarily avoid negligence even if it may have literally complied with safety statutes or procedures.

Florida Statutes Concerning Railroads: *Atlantic Coast Line R.R. v. Ponds*, 156 So. 2d 781 (Fla. App. 1963). In evaluating whether the negligence of a motorist or the negligence of a railroad caused a crash, the railroad presented evidence showing due care, and the widow of the truck driver had to prove her case against the railroad, as in any other case and she had the burden of showing the railroad's negligence proximately caused the crash.

St. Louis-San Francisco Ry. v. White, 369 So. 2d 1007 (Fla. App. 1979). The statute requiring crossbucks at grade crossings was enacted to protect motorists from collisions with trains by requiring crossbucks to warn of the presence and location of the tracks. A violation of such statute is negligence per se.

Indiana Statutes Concerning Railroads: In Indiana, motorists approaching railroad crossings are entitled by law to assume that the railroad has used due care in maintaining the crossing and has obeyed all applicable statutes, ordinances, and regulations governing warning signs at, and train operations over, the crossing. *Chicago, S.S. & S.B.R. Co. v. Luca,* 91 Ind. App. 521, 170 N.E. 564 (1930); *Southern Ind. Ry. v. Drennen,* 44 Ind. App. 14, 88 N.E. 724 (1909); *Lake Erie & W.R.R. v. McFarren,* 188 Ind. 113, 122 N.E. 330 (1919); *Cleveland C., C. & St. Ry. v. Sammons,* 68 Ind. App. 657 (1918).

Based on these concepts, the Indiana Court in *New York Cent. Ry. v. Powell,* 42 N.E.2d 384, 387 (Ind. App. 1942), while upholding a jury verdict against a defendant railroad whose train struck plaintiff's car at a negligently maintained crossing after the train had given the statutory warning signals of its approach, held: "[W]e cannot say that, even though signals of the approach of the train were given by bell and whistle, the negligent maintenance of the right of way was not the dominant factor in the failure of appellee's decedent to hear or observe such signals."

Indiana law imposes the clear duty upon railroads to install and maintain the warning signs and devices required under Ind. Code § 8-6-6-1 (1976), and violation of that statute is negligence *per se. Wroblewski v. Grand Trunk W. Ry.,* 276 N.E.2d 567 (Ind. App. 1971).

A railroad's negligence can be predicated, without more, upon its failure to erect and maintain safeguards at a public highway crossing that are required by statute, the public service commission, or other duly constituted authority. *Indianapolis Union Ry. v. Walker,* 318 N.E.2d 578 (Ind. App. 1974); *Wroblewski v. Grand Trunk W. Ry.,* 276 N.E.2d 567 (Ind. App. 1971).

The railroad is chargeable with defects in its warning signs at the crossing that it had actual notice of and is also chargeable with knowledge of those defects which it could have learned of with ordinary care. *Henry v. Hack,* 53 Ind. App. 47, 100 N.E. 116 (1912).

The Indiana Manual on Uniform Traffic Control Devices for Streets and Highways, Signs, Markings and Traffic Signals requires railroads to post notice of the existence of two or more parallel tracks within 100 feet of each other at a crossing.

Indiana Code § 8-6-2-1 provides as follows:

> Uniform danger signs. In addition to the highway crossing signs which steam and interurban railroad companies are now required by law to install and maintain at grade crossings on public highways in this state, additional uniform danger signals shall likewise be installed and maintained at all such grade crossings in the manner hereinafter prescribed in this act. [Acts 1921, ch. 232, § 1, p. 678.]

Indiana Code § 8-6-2-2 states:

> Installation of signs. All such additional danger signs shall be uniform, in appearance, character, size, material, color and lettering throughout the state, shall be installed at each grade crossing in this state at a distance of three hundred (300) feet in either direction from the point of intersection of the highway and the stream or interurban railroad, and on the right hand of persons approaching such railroad crossing, shall be securely set in concrete, within the highway, and as near to the edge of the traveled part thereof as may be safest and most convenient to the traveling public, and shall be erected at such height above the surface of the highway as to be seen to the best advantage by the reflection of the ordinary lights used on automobiles approaching the crossing. [Acts 1921, ch. 232, § 2, p. 678.]

Michigan Statutes Concerning Railroads: *Furness v. Michigan Pub. Serv. Comm.,* 100 Mich. App. 365, 299 N.W.2d 35 (1980). The duty to make grade crossings safe rests with the governmental entity with jurisdiction over the intersecting highways. The Public Service Commission's duty to determine whether to order railroads to provide flashing lights and gong signals is discretionary and cannot provide a basis for liability.

Beasley v. Grand Trunk W. Ry., 90 Mich. App. 576, 282 N.W.2d 401 (1979). A railroad's statutory duty to provide certain precautions at railroad crossings attaches only at intersections involving public highways. (Mich. Comp. Laws Ann. §§ 466.1 *et seq.,* 469.1 *et seq.*

§ 11-3. Relation of Crossing Negligence to Train Speed and Visibility.

Unless the railroad has failed to comply with legislation mandating certain signing, warning, or operational procedures (such as Ind. Code Ann. § 8-6-6-1 [55-2001] (mandating a posted notice of the fact of two separate tracks crossing a road) or Ill. Rev. Stat., ch. 114 ¶ 70 (preventing non-disabled trains from blocking grade crossings for more than ten minutes)), the crossing issue will not, in most instances, be open to first glance statutory condemnation for prima facie negligent design, maintenance or operation. Because most passively protected grade crossings were designed and built at a time when standards were low, it is difficult to find one such crossing markedly worse than the rest. The situation is further complicated by the fact that standards and technology for passively protected crossings have not improved very much over the years, the trend in both law and technology being to electrify passively protected crossings where appropriate.

It has also been very difficult to establish that a passively protected crossing warranted electrification.

Such extraordinary precautions are justified only if the crossing is "extra-hazardous." *First National Bank of Normal v. Illinois Central Gulf R.R.*, 62 Ill. App. 3d 36, 378 N.E.2d 1329 (1978). In determining whether the crossing is sufficiently extra-hazardous to warrant electrification, the court will consider physical obstructions to vision, the volume and speed of vehicular and train traffic over the crossing, the warning facilities at the crossing, the angle and character of the intersecting highway, the width of the crossing, and relevant sight distances. *Baker v. Norfolk & Western Ry.*, 120 Ill. App. 2d 296, 256 N.E.2d 887 (1970).

Very few crossings qualify for electrification under this test, perhaps because many railroads are bankrupt and cannot afford to electrify their stations, let alone their crossings. As a consequence, plaintiffs attacking the design or maintenance of a passively protected crossing will face the dual hurdles that the crossing, however bad, will probably not qualify for electrification and the need to demonstrate that one particular passively protected crossing has fallen significantly below the standards for passively protected crossings.

Consequently, because the crossing usually cannot be condemned by itself in absolute terms, its design and maintenance must be condemned under relevant standards for being insufficient as to visibility, warnings given, and the speed maintained by trains as they approach the crossing. The attack on a crossing facility, then, will rely centered on the facility itself. Rather, it will contend that the defendant maintained an excessive train speed in light of all the existing relevant conditions including the geometrics and sighting at the crossing. *Chicago & Eastern R.R. v. Mochell,* 193 Ill. 208, 61 N.E. 1028 (1901). As the court stated this basic formulation in *Baker v. Fisher,* 153 Ind. App. 581, 288 N.E.2d 263 (1972):

> [Train] speed may constitute negligence in the light of all the surrounding circumstances.
>
> A motorist has the right to assume, that if a train is approaching, the railroad will exercise due care and to act upon such assumption.
>
> . . . .
>
> [T]here is more than mere speed involved from which negligence might have been inferred by the trier of fact as to [the defendant]. Such existing conditions and surrounding circumstances [include] . . . [that] the train was operating at a speed of 75 m.p.h. and approaching the big curve immediately to the west of the crossing in question and as it passed through the curve heading towards the crossing in question . . . [and] the curve is a sharp right-hand curve and a train traveling in an easterly direction approaching the crossing does not come out of the curve until it is approximately 1,000 feet west of the crossing. 288 N.E.2d at 265-67 (emphasis added).

An attack on train speed as excessive under existing visibility and weather conditions for the crossing at issue may well require one expert witness to analyze the crossing and a second expert witness to establish the train speed. Excerpted portions of the trial testimony of Dr. Gary Long, analyzing a crossing as inadequate under existing conditions to justify certain train speeds, are attached to this chapter at § 11-5(A) as an Appendix. Portions of the testimony of Professor Robert MacRae, a train operations specialist, establishing train speed are attached at § 11-5(B) as an Appendix.

§ 11-3(A). Safe Crossing Rules.

California: *Seimon v. Southern Pac. Transp.,* 67 Cal. App. 3d 600, 136 Cal. Rptr. 787 (1977). In this case the railroad had notice that the crossing where the crash had occurred had approximately three train movements per day in each direction, had about 2,000 vehicles per day, was blind on both sides when approached from the south, had a significant number of tractor trailer crossings, had no visual warnings of oncoming trains, intersected at a 59 degree angle, had a confusing street pattern, and had prior crashes, sufficiently supported a finding that the railroad had acted in conscious disregard of motorists' safety in not posting needed warnings. Thus, the defendants negligently perpetuated crossing defects invoked a duty to post warnings of those defects, and the failure to meet that duty constituted additional negligence.

Jackson v. Atchison, T. & S.F. Ry., 172 Cal. App. 2d 184, 343 P.2d 337 (1959). Where railroad crossing had been extremely rough, with holes extending in depth to ties, for three years immediately preceding collision between train and truck which had stalled when hit a big bump, applied brakes, and motor died, and railroad had knowledge of that condition for six months before collision, railroad was negligent in manner in which it maintained crossings.

Florida: *Department of Transp. v. Webb,* 438 So. 2d 789 (Fla. 1983). Case properly went to jury on plaintiff's theory of defendant's negligent failure to maintain railroad crossings, including defendant's failure to warn motorists of known dangerous conditions.

Transit Cas. Co. v. Puchalski, 382 So. 2d 359 (Fla. App. 1980). A common carrier is expected to use the highest degree of care consistent with practical operation of its vehicle.

Illinois: Railroads must maintain crossings in a reasonably safe condition. *Illinois Cent. R.R. v. Stewart,* 230 Ill. 204, 82 N.E. 590 (1907).

A railroad must maintain its crossings so that the public has a reasonable view, free from encumbrances, of approaching trains. *Chicago & Alton R.R. v. Adler,* 28 Ill. App. 102 (1888), *aff'd,* 129 Ill. 335, 21 N.E. 846 (1889).

Railroads must use due care to avoid injuring persons at public crossings. *Illinois Cent. R.R. v. Scheffner,* 106 Ill. App. 344 (1903), *aff'd,* 209 Ill. 9, 70 N.E. 619 (1904); *Chicago & Alton R.R. v. Dillon,* 17 Ill. App. 355 (1885).

Railroads are charged with knowledge of the dangers at their crossings. *Paulison v. Chicago, Milwaukee, St. Paul & Pac. R.R.,* 74 Ill. App. 3d 282, 392 N.E.2d 960 (1979); *St. Louis, Vandalia & Terre Haute R.R. v. Faitz,* 23 Ill. 498 (1887).

The nature of the crossing protection provided is dependent upon the circumstances existing at the particular crossing, at the particular time of the approach of the vehicle. These factors include population and traffic in the area, physical obstruction of view, and the effect which confusion incident to railroad or other business in the area would have had on the sight or hearing of ordinary signals. The fact that a statute may provide one precaution does not relieve the railroad from adopting such others as public safety or common prudence may dictate. That the Illinois Commerce Commission has not ordered a certain warning or signalling device at a crossing does not thereby relieve a railroad of negligence in not providing such device. *Merchants Nat'l Bank of Aurora v. Elgin, Joliet & Eastern Ry.,* 121 Ill. App. 2d 445, 257 N.E.2d 216 (1970), *aff'd,* 49 Ill. 2d 118, 273 N.E.2d 809 (1971); *Paulison, supra.*

A defendant railroad owes a duty to maintain a crossing and approach thereto in a reasonably safe condition. Whether a railroad's failure to remove ice and snow or spread abrasive material is negligence which contributed to defendant's failure to make the crossing reasonably safe for the traveling public, is for the jury. *Kelleher v. Toledo, Peoria & Western R.R.,* 129 Ill. App. 2d 110, 262 N.E.2d 744 (1970).

There is no duty on the part of one railroad to protect the crossing of another railroad against approaching trains owned and operated by a third railroad. *Hamilton v. Peoria & Pekin Union Ry.,* 29 Ill. App. 3d 182, 329 N.E.2d 842 (1975). The duty of the railroad to sound a bell, whistle or horn for a quarter of a mile before only applies to a public highway or street, and not a private road. *Daniel v. Elgin, Joliet & Eastern Ry.,* 58 Ill. App. 2d 414, 208 N.E.2d 311 (1965).

There is a common law duty devolving upon railroads to exercise such care and use such precautions as will enable the traveler on the highway to ascertain, in the nighttime, the approach of a train over a street crossing. Special conditions creating special hazards at crossings require watchmen, gates or other warnings to travelers. *Wagner v. Toledo, Peoria & Western R.R.,* 352 Ill. 85, 185 N.E. 236 (1933).

A railroad has a duty to maintain a crossing in a safe condition (Ill.Rev.Stat., ch. 114, ¶ 62) to ring a bell when approaching a crossing (Ill.Rev.Stat., ch. 114, ¶ 59) and to use a headlight on its locomotives (Ill.Rev.Stat., ch. 114, ¶ 187). A railroad also has a duty to maintain a crossing in a safe condition (Interstate Commerce Commission General Order Number 138, Rule 206), to maintain signs in a state of efficiency (Interstate Commerce Commission General Order Number 138, Rule 208), and to operate an automatic flashing light signal for not less than 20 seconds before the train reaches the crossing, to give warning of a train's passage (Interstate Commerce Commission General Order Number 138, Rules 342 and 344). *See Barthel v. Illinois Central Gulf R.R.,* 74 Ill. 2d 213, 384 N.E.2d 323 (1978). Despite the violation of the Commerce Commission Rule or statute, contributory negligence is still consideration and the ICC rules do not provide for strict liability. *See Barthel, supra.* Rule 205 of the Illinois Commerce Commission provides that: "Every railroad company shall keep its right-of-way reasonably clear of brush, shrubbery, trees, weeds, crops and other unnecessary obstructions for a distance of at least 500 feet each way from every grade crossing where such things materially would obstruct the view of approaching trains and travelers on the highway." Rule 205 applies to the continued presence of freight cars on a siding, and is relevant to the determination of whether the railroad failed to keep its right-of-way "reasonably clear" of "unnecessary obstructions." (*Rucker v. Wabash R.R.,* 418 F.2d 146 (1969). In *Rucker* the United States Court of Appeals held it was error to exclude testimony tending to show how long the box cars in question had been standing on a side track.

Indiana: Railroads must maintain reasonably safe crossings. *New York Cent. R.R. v. Wyatt,* 135 Ind. App. 205, 184 N.E.2d 657 (1962).

Railroads must use reasonable care to avoid injuring people at public crossings. *Pennsylvania R.R. v. Mink,* 138 Ind. App. 311, 212 N.E.2d 784 (1966); *Minninger v. New York Cent. R.R.,* 123 Ind. App. 338, 109 N.E.2d 104 (1952).

A railroad's duty of care is higher in places where harm is more likely to ensue if the railroad is negligent, and track road intersections are such places. *Indianapolis Union Ry. v. Boettcher,* 131 Ind. 82, 28 N.E. 551 (1891); *Illinois Cent. R.R. v. Chicago T. & T. Co.,* 79 Ill. App. 623 (1899).

Indiana law implies an invitation from a railroad to the public to use a public railroad crossing and where a railroad invites people to use its crossing, it must exercise ordinary care to maintain the crossing and to operate trains over it. *New York Cent. R.R. v. Wyatt,* 135 Ind. App. 205, 184 N.E.2d 657 (1962); *Lake Erie & W.R.R. v. Fleming,* 183 Ind. 511, 109 N.E. 753 (1915); and *McGunegill v. Chesapeake & O. Ry.,* 199 F.2d 302 (7th Cir. 1952).

Massachusetts: *Longley v. City of Worcester,* 304 Mass. 580, 24 N.E.2d 533 (1939). Where a railroad crosses a public road at grade, the railroad is required to guard its rails in such a way that motorists can safely and easily pass across the track.

Quinby v. Boston & M.R.R., 318 Mass. 438, 61 N.E.2d 853 (1945). Evidence that gates were lowered and trapped an automobile after the automobile had stopped and stalled to avoid hitting gates at the other end of the crossing, so that the car could not be removed when the gate was raised in time to avoid being struck by locomotive, warranted a special finding that the gate tender was negligent.

Michigan: *Johnson v. Grand Trunk W.R.R.,* 58 Mich. App. 708, 228 N.W.2d 795 (1975). The statutory requirements respecting installation of signs and signals at railroad crossings have not abrogated a railroad's common-law duty to maintain such crossings with reasonable care.

Martin v. Ann Arbor R.R., 76 Mich. App. 41, 255 N.W.2d 763 (1977). In this crossing crash case, the plaintiff's evidence of negligent placement of speed limit and warning signs, the absence of flashing light warning devices and visual obstruction of tracks, and evidence of prior accidents, was sufficient proof of negligence to get the case to the jury.

Johnson v. Billot, 109 Mich. App. 578, 311 N.W.2d 808 (1981). Violation of duties imposed by administrative rules, regulations or safety codes is evidence of negligence, and a trial judge may instruct jury to consider typical industry practices. It would be reversible error not to instruct jury concerning applicable rules and regulations promulgated by an administrative agency.

Ebel v. Board of County R. Comm'rs, 386 Mich. 598, 194 N.W.2d 365 (1972). A railroad may have to post warnings at crossings beyond what is required by statute in order to meet the duty of due care. The test is not whether conditions were unusually dangerous but whether what was done under the circumstances met test of ordinarily prudent man under the same or similar circumstances.

Ohio: Severe visibility restrictions at crossings where defendants' train hit plaintiff's car precluded a finding that plaintiff was contributorily negligent as a matter of law. *Tollover v. Consol. Rail Corp.,* 11 Ohio 3d 56 (1984).

Neighbarger v. Central Ohio Transit Auth., 9 Ohio App. 3d 83, 458 N.E.2d 388 (1982). A common carrier owes to its passengers the highest degree of care consistent with practical operation of the system.

Strohm v. Baltimore & O.R.R., 32 Ohio App. 2d 333, 291 N.E.2d 783 (1972). In this truck-train crash case, evidence on the deceptive nature of how approaching lights would appear created jury issues.

Pennsylvania: *Buchecker v. Reading Co.,* 271 Pa. Super. 35, 412 A.2d 147 (1979). The failure to provide a specific safety device at a specific grade crossing would not be negligence per se, but on an individual case basis, the failure to provide a needed sign at a crossing could well constitute negligence.

Marinelli v. Montour R.R., 278 Pa. Super. 403, 420 A.2d 603 (1980). A railroad company must maintain public crossings that are safe for travelers upon the highways.

When a railroad bridge is built over a public highway, the railroad's duty to maintain a safe crossing includes the duty to build its bridge with reasonable clearance for ordinary vehicles; if a railroad breaches that duty by maintaining a bridge that is unreasonably low, the railroad will be negligent.

Dollison v. Baltimore & O.R.R., 446 Pa. 96, 284 A.2d 704 (1971). A railroad's private operating rules may be prejudicial to the railroad when those rules establish a standard of care greater than, or more inflexible than, law requires. However, there is no error admitting such rules into evidence no more than set standards that are no greater than that imposed by law. This case ignores a defendant's right to set, and a plaintiff's right to invoke, safety standards above the legal minimums.

Texas: *Kansas City S. Ry. v. Leatherwood,* 519 S.W.2d 533 (Tex. App. 1975). A statute requiring a railroad to keep its crossings in proper condition for use of the traveling public controlled a grade crossing crash case.

Lewis v. Thompson, 244 S.W.2d 286 (Tex. App. 1951). In an auto-train crash case, a jury issue existed on the issue of whether the motorist was guilty of contributory negligence that was a proximate cause of the collision. The court erred in directing verdict for the railroad, even though the motorist admitted he did not look to see if the train was approaching and did not see the train before it hit him. There was evidence that a signal device was not clearly visible and did not give warning of an immediately approaching train. There was no crossing gate or flagmen present and there was no signal sounded, or any evidence that the approaching train was plainly visible.

Texas & N.O.R.R. v. Broadway, 345 S.W.2d 814 (Tex. App. 1961). Whether motorists whose vehicles were hit by a freight train at a crossing were contributorily negligent in failing to observe the approaching train through grass and weeds blocking or obscuring the view was a jury issue.

Holeman v. Greyhound Corp., 396 S.W.2d 507 (Tex. App. 1965). Under Texas law, public transportation companies do not guarantee the safety of their passengers, but they must use the foresight of dangers and the prudence in guarding against those dangers that would be used by very cautious, prudent, and competent persons under similar circumstances.

§ 11-3(B). Train Operation Rules.

California: *Herrera v. Southern Pac. Co.,* 155 Cal. App. 2d 781, 318 P.2d 784 (1958). A train crew cannot assume that an urban grade crossing will be clear. The crew must keep a reasonable lookout for the presence of intersecting traffic. Even the installation of automatic crossing signals will not relieve the train crew of their duty to maintain reasonable lookout as the train approaches the crossing.

Downey v. Santa Fe Transp. Co., 286 P.2d 40, 134 Cal. App. 2d 720 (1955). Persons in charge of train switching operations owed a duty to give reasonable warnings that an engine was going over a highway at a spur track crossing.

Essick v. Union Pac. R.R., 182 Cal. App. 2d 456, 6 Cal. Rptr. 208 (1960). The trains crew's duty to exercise due care to discover people on the right-of-way logically includes the duty to "look out" for people, and the latter duty need not be specifically charged.

Rice v. Southern Pac. Co., 55 Cal. Rptr. 840, 247 Cal. App. 2d 701 (1967). A railroad's common-law duty at its crossing is the same duty borne by all others: the railroad must use the care which could be exercised by a reasonably prudent man under the same or similar circumstances; when a railroad acts in the usual or customary manner in which trains are operated under such circumstances, the railroad is not negligent. However, the railroad must use care reasonably sufficient to give notice and warning of the movement of its trains and cars.

Greene v. Atchison T. & Santa Fe Ry., 120 Cal. App. 2d 135, 260 F.2d 834 (1953). It is usually presumed that an engineer of a moving train sees what is in the range of his vision ahead of his train.

Florida: *Massey v. Seaboard Air Line R.R.,* 132 So. 2d 469 (Fla. App. 1961), *cert. denied,* 142 So. 2d 296 (1962). There is a limited presumption of a railroad company's negligence when damages are caused by its running of locomotives or cars.

Jones v. Atlantic Coast Line R.R., 117 So. 2d 234 (Fla. App. 1960). In a train-car crash case, the plaintiff alleged the train was proceeding at a negligently high speed. The counter refusal to admit proferred testimony of an officer concerning tests be made of the speed that railroad company's trains reach from a standing start was not error.

Florida E. Coast Ry. v. Soper, 146 So. 2d 605 (Fla. App. 1962). A railroad could be held negligent for its operation of a train over a grade crossing, even though a "crossbuck" warning sign was located at the crossing complying with statute, and even though train approached with its whistle blowing, bell ringing, and oscillating headlight in operation. All relevant factors at the time of the crash, including visibility and speed, may constitute negligence.

Illinois: Trains must maintain reasonable speed and warning signals must increase when approaching crossings in reduced visibility. *Petricek v. Elgin, Joliet & E. Ry.,* 21 Ill. App. 2d 60, 157 N.E.2d 421 (1959); *Wagner v. Toledo, Peoria & W. R.R.,* 352 Ill. 85, 185 N.E. 236 (1933).

Indiana: Train speed should be reduced, and warning signals should increase, under reduced visibility conditions. *Lake Erie & W.R. Co. v. Fleming,* 183 Ind. 511, 109 N.E. 753 (1915); *M. Gunegill v. Chesapeake & O. Ry.,* 199 F.2d 302 (7th Cir. 1952); *Cleveland, Cincinnati, Chicago & St. Louis Ry. v. Gillespie,* 96 Ind. App. 535, 173 N.E. 708 (1930).

Railroads under Indiana law must, as part of their duty to operate trains with reasonable care, operate those trains at speeds that are not excessive in light of weather, visibility, and all other relevant conditions including warning signs at, and condition of, the crossing. *New York Central R.R. v. Wyatt,* 135 Ind. App. 205, 184 N.E.2d 657 (1962); *New York Central R.R. v. Milhiser,* 231 Ind. 180, 106 N.E.2d 453 (1952); *Minninger v. New York Central R.R.,* 123 Ind. App. 338, 109 N.E.2d 104 (1952); *Elgin J. &*

E. R.R. v. Scherer, 98 N.E.2d 369 (1951); and *Baker v. Fisher,* 288 N.E.2d 263 (1972).

It is the duty under Indiana law of persons operating a train to exercise ordinary care in looking ahead to discover persons or objects on the tracks at highway crossings, and to exercise similar care to avoid collisions. *Chesapeake & Ohio Ry. v. Pace,* 132 Ind. App. 321, 175 N.E.2d 895 at 909 (1961); and *Pittsburgh, Cincinnati, Chicago & St. Louis Ry. v. Pence,* 185 Ind. 495, 502, 113 N.E. 7 at 9 (1916).

It is the duty under Indiana law of the employees of a railroad company to exercise ordinary care in the operation of its trains, and failure to do so constitutes negligence. *Cleveland, C. & St. Louis R.R. v. Gillespie,* 173 N.E. 708 at 712 (Ind. App. 1930).

Under Indiana law a railroad is under a duty to use reasonable care to avoid injury to a traveller on a highway or road crossing its tracks, and it must operate its trains on and over such crossings with reasonable care and due regard for the use of the crossing by others. *Pennsylvania R.R. v. Mink,* 138 Ind. App. 311, 212 N.E.2d 784 (1966); *New York Central R.R. v. Wyatt,* 135 Ind. App. 205, 184 N.E.2d 657, at 670 (1962).

Massachusetts: *Fitzgerald v. Boston & Me. R.R.,* 328 Mass. 297, 103 N.E.2d 245 (1952). A railroad must operate its locomotives and trains with due care so as not to injure persons or property which are rightfully on a grade crossing.

Hunt v. Boston & M.R. Co., 250 Mass. 434, 146 N.E. 30 (1925). If a crash could be avoided using due care then the railroad had a duty not to damage an automobile stalled on its crossing.

Capithorn v. Boston & Me. R.R., 301 Mass. 510, 17 N.E.2d 713 (1938). In absence of statutes to the contrary, a train has the right of way in passing over a grade crossing against a motorist, but both parties are charged with the natural duty of keeping a careful lookout for danger.

Under common law, the care to be exercised at a grade crossing by train crews and motorists is such as a prudent man would exercise under the facts.

Hoban v. Trustees of New York, New Haven & Hartford R.R., 326 Mass. 566, 95 N.E.2d 651 (1951). Evidence of negligence is when a violation of law prohibiting locomotive from standing on public way without lights during a period from one half hour after sunset to one half hour before sunrise.

Michigan: *Bauman v. Grand Trunk W.R.R.,* 376 Mich. 675, 138 N.W.2d 285 (1965). The common-law duty of a railroad to use ordinary care and prudence reasonable under the circumstances should be applied without encumbrance by analysis — crippling semantics of "special conditions," or "unusual conditions," or "special circumstances."

Beasley v. Grand Trunk W.R.R., 90 Mich. App. 576, 282 N.W.2d 401 (1979). Railroad was relieved of its statutory duties toward general public insofar as taking precautionary measures. However, jury issues were presented as to whether railroad breached its common-law duties by allegedly failing to maintain clear view for motorists. Mich. Comp. Laws Ann. §§ 466.1 *et seq.,* 469.1 *et seq.*

Ohio: *Hensler v. Baltimore & O.R.R.,* 39 Ohio App. 2d 146, 316 N.E.2d 911 (1973). Witnesses who were in a position to hear a warning whistle, and their testimony that they heard no whistle was of probative value and issue before the jury, where the weight and credibility of such testimony would then be tested on the issue of failure to sound a whistle.

Strahm v. B. & O.R.R., 32 Ohio App. 2d 333, 291 N.E.2d 83 (1972). A railroad safety rule requiring speeds under 25 miles per hour at the point of collision was applicable in deciding whether a railroad was negligent. The Court rejected the railroad's claim that the rule only applied to the protection of railroad personnel concerned with hitting trucks filled with inflammable liquids.

The speed at which a train is operated does not become negligence per se. However, the operation of a train at an unreasonable rate of speed for the conditions may constitute negligence.

A road crossing railroad tracks at the scene of a crash was heavily traveled. The crossing was in a developed area. Visibility was obstructed, and lights from a highway nearby could create ambiguities as to the approach of a train. Under these factors, a railroad, in order to experience due care, had to operate trains over the crossing at reduced speeds.

Pennsylvania: *Fallon v. Pennsylvania Cent. Transp. Co.,* 444 Pa. 148, 279 A.2d 169 (1971). In a train-car crash case, the testimony of plaintiff and another witness that they did not hear any warning signal when each was prepared to cross the tracks created issues for the jury about whether a warning signal was given. The railroad offered "affirmative" testimony by three railroad employees that a whistle was blown, but this evidence could not preclude submitting the case to the jury.

Haller v. Pennsylvania R.R., 306 Pa. 98, 159 A. 10 (1932). A railroad must so regulate its trains as to enable driver to cross tracks safely if he has properly stopped, looked, and listened.

An engineer, if he knew about the bewilderment of a motorist who stopped on tracks, should have reduced speed and stopped, if possible.

Figard v. Pennsylvania R.R., 361 Pa. 380, 65 A.2d 411 (1949). Operators of train approaching a permissive crossing had duty to keep looking ahead to see if track was clear at crossing, even though they blew whistle or rang bell, and to make every reasonable effort to stop train before striking minor who was of such tender age that minor would probably pay no attention to a blown whistle or rung bell.

Geelan v. Pennsylvania R.R., 400 Pa. 240, 161 A.2d 595 (1960). In order for the engineer of a train that killed a motorist at a grade crossing to be guilty of wanton misconduct, the engineer must have actual knowledge of the motorist's peril for a sufficient length of time before the crash to give him a reasonable opportunity to stop the train and avoid the accident. Such actual knowledge on the part of the engineer may be deduced from the facts.

Texas: *Texas & New Orleans R.R. v. Adams,* 368 S.W.2d 902 (Tex. Civ. App. 1963). In action for damage to a truck there was a jury issue whether warning signal was given by engineer as train approached crossing.

Texas & Pac. Ry. v. Hoyle, 421 S.W.2d 442 (Tex. Civ. App. 1967). Train operators approaching busy crossing must keep a proper lookout reasonable under the circumstances.

Missouri Pac. R.R. v. Shaw, 620 S.W.2d 161 (Tex. Civ. App. 1981). A train must be operated with the care and caution of a reasonably prudent person to avoid a collision even though a train may have the right-of-way at a railroad crossing.

Southern Pac. Transp. Co. v. Peralez, 546 S.W.2d 88 (Tex. Civ. App. 1976). The engineer and other trainmen must operate a train with ordinary care.

§ 11-3(C). Extra-Hazardous Situations.

California: *Bains v. Western Pac. R.R.,* 56 Cal. App. 3d 902, 128 Cal. Rptr. 778 (1976). The existence of an extra-hazardous crossing was shown by evidence that crossing gates (which it was cited reduce accidents by 90 percent) were not installed; that only 16 trains per day traveled over the rural railroad crossing at issue; that the train was traveling in excess of the speed limit and failed to apply emergency brakes until collision was imminent; and that better braking system should have been employed on train.

Illinois: *Paulison v. Chicago, Milwaukee, St. Paul & Pac. R.R.,* 74 Ill. App. 3d 282, 392 N.E.2d 960 (1979), held that there may be a duty upon a defendant railroad to install automatic gates, notwithstanding the fact that they were not required under the state standards. The testimony that there are advantages in automatic gates over flashing lights alone is sufficient to support a prima facie case to allow a jury to determine whether the crossing was safe. The fact that a statute may provide one precaution does not relieve the company from adopting such others as public safety or common prudence may dictate. Whether the railroads have a duty to provide automatic gates over flashing lights alone, although not required by state law, is a question of fact for the jury.

The case of *Baker v. Norfolk & W. Ry.,* 120 Ill. App. 2d 296, 256 N.E.2d 887 (1970), held that the jury's determination that a crossing is extra-hazardous is implicit in its finding that the defendant did not act in a reasonably careful manner in failing to provide flares, lights, bells or gates, considering the condition existing at that crossing, as shown by the evidence. In *Baker,* no statute or regulation of the Illinois Commerce Commission required additional protection at the crossing. However, independent of statute or regulation, there is a common law duty on railroads to protect crossings with adequate safety devices other than the usual crossbuck sign where special or unusual conditions cause such crossings to be "extra-hazardous," and warrant additional protection. Factors which have been considered in determining whether a particular crossing is extra-hazardous include physical obstructions to vision (whether moveable or immovable), volume and speed of vehicular traffic, volume and speed of train traffic, the railroad's facilities present at the crossings (the track arrangements), the intersecting driveways and roadways, and the character of the highway and width of crossing. *See also Merchants Nat'l Bank v. Elgin, Joliet E. Ry.*, 121 Ill. App. 2d 445, 257 N.E.2d 216 (1970), *aff'd,* 49 Ill. 2d 118, 273 N.E.2d 809 (1971); *Tonarelli v. Gibbons,* 121 Ill. App. 3d 1042, 460 N.E.2d 464 (1984).

Indiana: Under Indiana law a railroad crossing may be extra-hazardous for motorists either because of its permanent features or because of temporary circumstances, such as weather and visibility affecting the crossings used at a particular time. *Central Ind. Ry. v. Anderson Banking Co.,* 252 Ind. 270, 247 N.E.2d 208 (1969); *Indianapolis Union Ry. v. Walker,* 162 Ind. App. 166, 318 N.E.2d 578 (1974).

Massachusetts: *Boucher v. New York, N.H. & H.R. Co.,* 196 Mass. 355, 82 N.E. 15 (1907). Evidence of how many tracks a crossing had, and how many trains used the crossing, warranted a finding that it was a dangerous crossing, at which gates should have been erected.

Michigan: *Ellis v. Grand Trunk W. Ry.,* 109 Mich. App. 394, 311 N.W.2d 364 (1981). Trial court erred in excluding a report and an order recommending installation of flashing light signals at railroad crossing. This report would have been helpful in assisting jury in determining whether crossing was dangerous. Author of such report was available for cross-examination.

Ohio: *Stoler v. Penn. Cent. Transp. Co.,* 583 F.2d 896 (6th Cir. 1978). If conditions at a crossing are sufficiently dangerous a railroad may be required under Ohio law to take additional precautions beyond those imposed by statute.

Matkovich v. Penn. Cent. Transp. Co., 69 Ohio 2d 210, 431 N.E.2d 652 (1982). A railroad had a duty to exercise due care to protect public safety of motorist requiring additional warning of the presence of trains at certain crossings because the accident at the crossing occurred on a dark night. In view of the speed of the train and the normal rate of speed of today's motor vehicles, plaintiff may not have had enough time to stop and avoid collision after it became evident to him that the train was blocking the road ahead.

Texas: *Missouri-Kansas-Texas R.R. v. May,* 600 S.W.2d 755 (Tex. 1980). In a train-car crash evidence of earlier accidents which occurred under reasonably similar but not necessarily identical circumstances was admissible to support motorist's contention that crossing was extra-hazardous, and trial court's exclusion of the similar accidents was reversible error.

Missouri-Kansas-Texas R.R. v. Hamilton, 314 S.W.2d 114 (Tex. Civ. App. 1958). In a train-car crash case, testimony of prior written and oral notice to the railroad of the condition of the crossing was admissible.

Texas & New Orleans Ry. v. Hart, 356 S.W.2d 901 (Tex. 1961). If you put in a safety feature you must maintain it. Railroad which has elected to warn motorists at extra-hazardous crossing by electric flashing light device has responsibility of seeing that device operates.

Southern Pac. Transp. Co. v. Peralez, 546 S.W.2d 88 (Tex. Civ. App. 1976). A railroad crossing is extra-hazardous when the crossing is so dangerous that a prudent person could not use the crossing in safety unless the railroad employed a flagman or other means to signal the approach of a train. When a crossing is extra-hazardous it is the responsibility of the railroad to employ the necessary extraordinary means of warning.

Osuna v. Southern Pac. R.R., 641 S.W.2d 229 (Tex. 1982). The duty to maintain safety devices that might not have been required is triggered once the devices are installed, even though signal was not legally required.

Panhandle & Santa Fe Ry. v. Sutton, 125 Tex. 401, 81 S.W.2d 1005 (1933). Pedestrian might have been licensee, to whom railroad owed a duty to exercise due care to avoid injuring him, if crossing was not a public crossing.

§ 11-3(D). Train Speed.

California: *Deshotel v. Atchison, T. & S.F. Ry.*, 126 Cal. App. 2d 303, 272 P.2d 71 (1954). Negligence in respect to a warning device could be one of the proximate causes of an accident since the warning device was insufficient to alert a driver of the crossing and whether the railroad was negligent was not to be judged by speed of train alone.

Florida: *Tynan v. Seaboard Coast Line R.R.*, 254 So. 2d 209 (Fla. 1971). Fact questions as to negligence of railroad, proximate cause, and plaintiff's negligence, were presented in an accident case including evidence of excessive speed of train.

Florida E. Coast Ry. v. Soper, 146 So. 2d 605 (Fla. App. 1962). A train can be going too fast for circumstances, even if that speed is within allowable limits. This may be considered along with other factors in determining whether reasonable care and caution had been exercised by the railroad in approaching a grade crossing.

Illinois: Speed is not negligence, per se, but may become negligence under certain circumstances. *Merchants Nat'l Bank v. Elgin, Joliet & Eastern Ry.*, 121 Ill. App. 2d 445, 257 N.E.2d 216 (1970), *aff'd*, 49 Ill. 2d 118, 273 N.E.2d 809 (1971). When the only evidence of negligence or violation of duty by a railroad is that the train was entering the siding at twice its usual rate of speed, and there is no testimony to establish what the usual rate of speed was, a directed verdict is appropriate. To do otherwise would be allowing a jury to speculate about the speed which would be improper. The jury cannot be allowed to predicate a verdict on mere conjecture or surmise. The plaintiff has the burden to establish evidence to prove its allegation that defendant caused its railroad cars to move at a dangerous and unsafe rate of speed. It is proper to have witnesses characterize a vehicle as moving "fast" or "very fast," but to allow testimony that the train was going twice as fast as usual with no evidence as to what the usual speed was, is not sufficient to allow the case to go to the jury. *Publication Corp. v. Chicago River & Indiana R.R.,* 49 Ill. App. 3d 508, 364 N.E.2d 523 (1977).

In *Nice v. Illinois Cent. R.R.,* 303 Ill. App. 292, 25 N.E.2d 104 (1940), it was held that it was not negligence, per se, for the railroad to operate a train at 90 miles per hour through an unincorporated village of 300. However, the railroad was negligent in operating its train at 35 miles per hour through a main crossing in a town of 1,600 people, in view of the fact that there was no adequate warning given, especially since the gates were not working. *Smith v. Illinois Cent. R.R.,* 343 Ill. App. 593, 99 N.E.2d 717 (1951). In addition, the railroad was negligent in driving its train at 80 miles per hour through an unguarded crossing when the view down the tracks was obstructed. *Bunton v. Illinois Cent. R.R.,* 15 Ill. App. 2d 311, 146 N.E.2d 205 (1957).

The law does not establish a speed limit at which the defendant shall operate its trains, but the speed must be consistent with the exercise of ordinary care on the part of the defendant. In cases where the plaintiff is a passenger on the defendant train, the railroad has the duty of the highest degree of care that could have been used in the practical operation of its business as a common carrier in the operating speed of its trains. I.P.I. — Civil No. 73.02.

Massachusetts: *Peterson v. Boston & Me. R.R.,* 310 Mass. 45, 36 N.E.2d 701 (1941). The fact a train that hit a car may have been travelling above the railroad's own posted speed did not constitute negligence in favor of passengers in the car, since it could not be assumed that the rule was established for protection of the public at grade crossing. Note: It is hoped this dreadful old case will no longer be followed anywhere.

Pennsylvania: *Muehlhof v. Reading Co.,* 309 Pa. 17, 162 A. 827 (1932). The distance a train traveled after a collision at a crossing was relevant in determining the train's speed.

§ 11-3(E). Maintenance.

California: A railroad is not necessarily free from negligence just because it obeyed safety statutes in maintaining its crossing. Circumstances may demand a higher standard of care; for example, if the particular circumstances of a crossing call for installation of automatic protection or the upgrading of existing automatic protection, the railroad may be guilty of negligence in failing to provide such protection. *Romo v. Southern Pac. Transp. Co.,* 71 Cal. App. 3d 909, 139 Cal. Rptr. 787 (1977).

Florida: *Seaboard Coast Line R.R. v. Scudder,* 215 So. 2d 760 (Fla. App. 1968). Contributory negligence of a motorist involved in a collision with a train was for jury because crossing had obstructed motorist's visibility.

Florida E. Coast Ry. v. Schweida, 151 So. 2d 655 (Fla. App. 1963). Greater degree of care is required at more often used railroad crossing.

St. Louis-San Francisco Ry. v. Burlison, 262 So. 2d 280 (Fla. App. 1972). In a train-vehicle crash case, evidence was sufficient that the railroad was negligent because it had not observed signalization procedures conforming to recommended practices for railroad highway grade crossing protection adopted by the American Association of Railroads.

Reinhart v. Seaboard Coast Line R.R., 422 So. 2d 41 (Fla. App. 1982). Evidence of prior incidents in which front wheels of bicycle had become wedged in between railroad track and pavement, was relevant crash case to show that a hazardous condition existed and that railroad had notice of the condition.

Lawrence v. Florida E. Coast Ry., 346 So. 2d 1012 (Fla. 1977). In a train-car crash, the trial court exercised its discretion in allowing evidence for showing notice of defective system and not for the showing that crossing was dangerous.

Illinois: ICC Rule 206 provides that "at every grade crossing where the duty of constructing or maintaining either the crossing proper or its approaches (or any part thereof) is, by statute, by order of the Commission or in any lawful manner, placed upon a railroad company, it shall be the duty of the railroad company to construct and maintain the crossing and approaches so that at all times they will be safe as to persons and property." It is the duty of the railroad to exercise ordinary care in the operation and maintenance of its right-of-way so that the crossing or approaches will be safe as to persons and property. In addition, Ill. Rev. Stat., ch. 114, ¶ 62, provides that the railroad, at all of its crossings of highways and streets in the State of Illinois, shall construct and maintain its crossings and the approaches within their right-of-way so that at all times they are safe as to persons and property. The railroad had a duty to maintain its crossings and the approaches within its right-of-way in a reasonably safe condition. *McElligott v. Illinois Cent. R.R.*, 27 Ill. 2d 459, 227 N.E.2d 764 (1967).

A railroad does not have a duty with respect to areas which it does not own or maintain. It is the duty of each owner to maintain the crossing in a reasonably safe condition. It is not reasonable to impose a duty on a railroad which owned neither the train nor the track involved in the collision, and was not a party to any agreement to maintain the crossing. *Hamilton v. Peoria & Pekin Union Ry.*, 29 Ill. App. 3d 182, 329 N.E.2d 842

(1975). The duties of a lessor-owner of a railroad (fending) and the lessee operator of a train to an injured party, although different, when breached will result in a joint and several liability. *American Nat'l Bank & Trust Co. v. Pennsylvania R.R.*, 35 Ill. 2d 145, 219 N.E.2d 529 (1966).

Michigan: *O'Loughlin v. Detroit & Mackinac Ry.*, 22 Mich. App. 146, 177 N.W.2d 430 (1970). The electric signal at highway intersection was not functioning during a period preceding train-car crash. The finding that railroad knew or should have known of condition of signal was supported by relevant evidence.

Pennsylvania: *Geelen v. Pennsylvania R.R.*, 400 Pa. 240, 161 A.2d 595 (1960). Motorist's failure to stop before entering railroad crossing since train was around bend and out of sight did not constitute contributory negligence and did not bar recovery for crash which happened when the wheel of his automobile fell in hole obscured by snow.

Buchecker v. Reading Co., 271 Pa. Super. 35, 412 A.2d 147 (1979). Where it was impossible to safely look down railroad's tracks, motorist's failure to stop did not bar recovery; furthermore, evidence that no motorist ever stopped in absence of flashing red light, that signal was not operating at the time, that signals were so placed that light of rising sun affected visibility of signals, that railroad had placed sign on a pole stated "Stop on Red Signal," and that sound warning was unreliable, precluded conclusion that motorist was as a matter of law guilty of contributory negligence.

§ 11-3(F). Operation and Equipment.

Illinois: Every railroad has a duty to cause a bell and whistle or horn to be placed and kept on each locomotive, and shall cause the same to be rung and sounded by the engineer or fireman at a distance of at least 80 rods (one-quarter mile) from the place where the railroad crosses or intersects any other highway, and shall be kept ringing or sounding until the highway is reached. Except at the crossings where the Illinois Commerce Commission shall, by general or specific order direct, the railroad may be excused from giving warning provided by the statute. See I.P.I. — Civil No. 73.03; also Ill. Rev. Stat. ch. 114, ¶ 59; and *General Wholesale Co. v. Illinois Cent. R.R.,* 26 Ill. App. 2d 165, 167 N.E.2d 272 (1960).

It is unlawful for a railroad corporation to permit any train, railroad car or engine to obstruct public travel at a railroad-highway grade crossing for a period in excess of ten minutes, except where such train, railroad car or engine cannot be moved by reason of circumstances over which the railroad corporation has no control. Ill. Rev. Stat., ch. 114, ¶ 70; *Rice v. Gulf, Mobile & Ohio R.R.,* 84 Ill. App. 2d 163, 228 N.E.2d 162 (1967). This law applies not only to standing trains, but moving trains as well. *People v. Indiana Harbor Belt R.R.,* 102 Ill. App. 3d 811, 430 N.E.2d 104, 58 Ill. Dec. 162 (1981). A City of Chicago ordinance provides that no train shall prevent the use of any street for purposes of travel, for a period longer than five minutes. Chapter 188-49.

§ 11-3(G). Rights of Travelers at Crossings.

California: *Grimes v. Southern Pac. R.R.,* 243 Cal. App. 2d 304, 52 Cal. Rptr. 60 (1966). Motorist was within disputable presumption that he was exercising due care for his safety. His heirs were entitled to benefit of the presumption until evidence was sufficient to disperse it.

Klein v. Southern Pac. Co., 203 Cal. App. 2d 72, 21 Cal. Rptr. 233 (1962). Automobile passengers were entitled to presumption of due care when they presented no testimony which was irreconcilable with the presumption. There was no corresponding presumption in favor of railroad and its employees who testified or to their acts and conduct immediately preceding and at time of accident. It was prejudicial error to instruct that they were entitled to a presumption of due care.

Larsen v. Atchison, Topeka & Santa Fe Ry., 176 Cal. App. 2d 21, 1 Cal. Rptr. 36 (1960). In a train-car crash case, the burden was on the railroad to establish by preponderance of evidence that motorist was negligent and that such negligence was a proximate cause of accident.

Indiana: Under Indiana law the rights of a traveler on a highway crossed by a railroad are not subordinate to or superior to those of the railroad, but equal; each has a right to pass and each is bound to use ordinary care and diligence to avoid injury to the other. Travelers on the highway may act upon the presumption that the employees of a railroad will act in accordance with the legal rights and duties of the traveler and the railroad. *Chesapeake & Ohio Ry. v. Pace*, 132 Ind. App. 321, 175 N.E.2d 895, 903 (1961).

Under Indiana law motorists approaching a railroad crossing are entitled to assume that the railroad has used due care in maintaining the crossing and has obeyed all applicable statutes, ordinances, and regulations concerning warning signs at the crossing and train operations over the crossings. *Chicago S.S. & S.B. R.R. v. Luca*, 91 Ind. 521, 170 N.E. 564 (1930); *Southern Indiana R.R. v. Drennen*, 44 Ind. App. 14, 811 N.E. 724 (1909); and *Lake Erie & W.R. Co. v. McFarren*, 188 Ind. 113, 122 N.E. 330 (1919).

Massachusetts: *Borden v. New York, N.H. & H.R. Co.*, 158 N.E.2d 464 (1959). In train-vehicle crash case, the burden was on the railroad to show motorist's lack of care under common-law counts and also under the statutory counts.

Rich v. Burton & Me. R.R., 327 Mass. 479, 99 N.E.2d 465 (1951). A person approaching a railroad crossing must look and listen in such a manner as will enable him to see or hear an approaching train. There is no requirement that he stop, look, and listen. Circumstances may excuse him from looking and listening.

Nickerson v. Boston & Me. R.R., 342 Mass. 346, 173 N.E.2d 248 (1961). Motorist in crossing railroad tracks in which train may come from both directions must take some risk, since he cannot look in both directions at once.

Michigan: *O'Loughlin v. Detroit & Mackinac Ry.,* 22 Mich. App. 146, 177 N.W.2d 430 (1970). Motorist on highway who knew of electric flashing signal at railroad crossing could rely on signal.

Pennsylvania: *Evans v. Reading Co.,* 242 Pa. Super. 209, 363 A.2d 1234 (1976). Plaintiff's witnesses testified that foliage surrounding railroad tracks prevented motorists from seeing approaching train and they heard no whistles or bells and saw no lights at crossing where the train hit their truck. This "negative" testimony was entitled to the same strength as "positive" testimony of defendant's witnesses that flashing lights were working prior to accident and that engineer sounded train's whistle and bells until crash.

Texas: *Missouri, Kan. & Tex. R.R. v. Young,* 127 S.W.2d 489 (Tex. Civ. App. 1939). A pedestrian crossing railroad tracks had the right to rely on the railroad's following laws regarding train speed and bell ringing.

Texas & New Orleans R.R. v. Adams, 368 S.W.2d 902 (Tex. Civ. App. 1963). There was no obligation for the driver of a truck to stop, get out of his truck and call up to railroad tracks before crossing tracks.

Lilley v. Southern Pac. Transp. Co., 584 S.W.2d 720 (Tex. Civ. App. 1979). The fact to be considered in determining whether the motorist maintained proper lookout is that the motorist was familiar with the tracks.

§ 11-3(H). Travelers' Response to Onrushing Trains.

In determining whether the last clear chance doctrine is applicable in collision case involving automobile and train, the nature reflex time in communicating an emergency stop and the time for effective brake action must be considered, together with the speed and ability to stop the train in a given distance.

§ 11-4. Legal Standards for Railroad Crash Cases.

§ 11-4(A). Some Rules for Plaintiffs.

1. Railroads must maintain crossings in reasonably safe conditions. *Illinois Central R.R. v. Stewart,* 230 Ill. 204, 82 N.E. 590 (1907); Indiana Accord, *New York Central R.R. v. Wyatt,* 135 Ind. App. 205, 184 N.E.2d 657 (1962).

2. A railroad must maintain its crossings so that the public has a reasonable view, free from encumbrances, of approaching trains. *Chicago & Alton R.R. v. Adler,* 28 Ill. App. 102 (1888), *aff'd,* 129 Ill. 335, 21 N.E. 846 (1889).

3. Railroads have the duty to use all reasonable precautions to avoid injuring persons at public crossings. *Illinois Central R.R. v. Scheffner,* 106 Ill. App. 344 (1903), *aff'd,* 209 Ill. 9, 70 N.E. 619 (1904); *Chicago & Alton R.R. v. Dillon,* 17 Ill. App. 355 (1885). Indiana Accord, *Pennsylvania R.R. v. Mink,* 138 Ind. App. 311, 212 N.E.2d 784 (1966); *Minninger v. New York Central R.R.,* 123 Ind. App. 338, 109 N.E.2d 104 (1952).

4. Railroads are charged with knowledge of the extent of danger at their crossings. *Paulison v. Chicago, Milwaukee, St. Paul & Pacific R.R.,* 74 Ill. App. 3d 282, 392 N.E.2d 960, 30 Ill.Dec. 195 (1979); *St. Louis Vandalia & Terre Haute R.R. v. Faitz,* 23 Ill. App. 498 (1887).

5. A train crew must give appropriate increased warnings when trains are standing across grade crossings under

reduced visibility conditions. *Petricek v. Elgin, Joliet & Eastern Ry.,* 21 Ill. App. 2d 60, 157 N.E.2d 421 (1959). This is closely related to the rule that railroads must use reasonable care, under the given visibility conditions, to warn travelers that a train is approaching the crossing. *Wagner v. Toledo, Peoria & Western R.R.,* 352 Ill. 85, 185 N.E. 236 (1933). Indiana Accord, *New York Central R.R. v. Wyatt, supra; Lake Erie & W. R. Co. v. Fleming,* 183 Ind. 511, 109 N.E. 753 (1915); *McGunegill v. Chesapeake & O. Ry.,* 199 F.2d 302 (7th Cir. 1952); *Cleveland, Cincinnati, Chicago & St. Louis Ry. v. Gillespie,* 96 Ind. App. 535, 173 N.E. 708 (1930). Under these rules, obviously, the train crew must use greater care when visibility is reduced and when the crossing is passively protected.

§ 11-4(B). Some Rules for Defendants.

1. A train has the right of way over travelers at a grade crossing. *Robertson v. New York Central R.R.,* 388 Ill. 580, 58 N.E.2d 527 (1945).

2. Trains approaching a crossing may assume vehicles will yield the right of way to the train, at least until it becomes reasonably clear the vehicle will not yield. Ill. Rev. Stat., ch. 114, ¶ 59; I.P.I. No. 73.01; *Rakers v. Southern Ry.,* 8 Ill. App. 3d 877, 290 N.E.2d 421 (1972). This rule is immensely valuable to defendants because trains operating even at low speeds often require a longer distance to stop than the length of track from the point where the train crew can first see an approaching vehicle as the train rounds a curve to the point of impact at the grade crossing.

3. A railroad owes trespassers on the right of way only the duty to refrain from wilful and wanton conduct. *Spring v. Toledo, Peoria & Western R.R.,* 44 Ill. App. 3d 3, 357 N.E.2d 1330 (1976), *aff'd,* 69 Ill. 2d 290, 371 N.E.2d 621 (1977).

§ 11-4(C). Balanced Rules for Plaintiffs and Defendants.

1. Train crews and vehicle drivers simultaneously approaching grade crossings have reciprocal duties to exercise reasonable care. *Humbert v. Lowden,* 323 Ill. App. 557, 56 N.E.2d 323 (1944).

2. A railroad's duty of care at a crossing is commensurate with the danger involved. *W. C. Norris Manufacturing v. Baltimore & Ohio R.R.,* 333 Ill. App. 247, 77 N.E.2d 434 (1948). The danger involved will be decided, retroactively, of course, on a case-by-case basis, considering the visibility, the train speed, the population around the crossing, the traffic flow over the crossing, physical obstructions to view at the crossing, and confusion improved crossing signals would cause the local population. *Merchants National Bank of Aurora v. Elgin, Joliet & Eastern Ry.,* 121 Ill. App. 2d 445, 257 N.E.2d 216 (1970), *aff'd,* 49 Ill. 2d 118, 273 N.E.2d 809 (1971).

3. A crossing must be "extra-hazardous" to warrant extraordinary protective measures by the railroad. *First National Bank of Normal v. Illinois Central Gulf R.R.,* 62 Ill. App. 3d 36, 378 N.E.2d 1329 (1978). The extra-hazardous situation, however, need not be permanent, and can be something, such as a train across the crossing, existing only at the time of the crash. *Reiser v. Illinois Central R.R.,* 132 Ill. App. 2d 941, 270 N.E.2d 856 (1971). Unless visibility is reduced, however, a train moving or standing at a crossing generally constitutes adequate notice, without additional warning signals, of its presence to motorists. *Bachman v. Illinois Central R.R.,* 132 Ill. App. 2d 277, 268 N.E.2d 42 (1971).

4. Railroads are chargeable with notice of all the perilous circumstances of their crossings. *St. Louis, V. & T.H.R. Co. v. Faitz,* 28 Ill. App. 498 (1887). All railroad crossings, however, are dangerous and motorists approaching such

crossings must diligently use all their senses and exercise great care commensurate with the known danger. *National Bank of Bloomington v. Norfolk & Western Ry.*, 73 Ill. 2d 160, 383 N.E.2d 919 (1978). The motorist's duty to stop, look and listen may, in turn, be mitigated or exercised by obstructions to vision or distracting circumstances. *McEvers v. Missouri Pacific R.R.*, 528 F.2d 220 (7th Cir. 1975). The motorist's duty approaching a crossing does not, in addition, impose a general obligation for either continuous lookout or a complete stop. *National Bank of Bloomington v. Norfolk & Western Ry., supra.* The motorist must, on the other hand, approach the crossing with even greater care if he is aware in advance of obscured visibility or other dangers at a known crossing. *Moudy v. New York, Chicago & St. Louis R.R.*, 385 Ill. 446, 53 N.E.2d 406 (1944); *Jellen v. New York, Chicago & St. Louis R.R.*, 53 Ill. App. 2d 44, 202 N.E.2d 665 (1964).

5. Where the railroad maintains an electrified crossing, the fact that the gates are up constitutes an invitation and assurance of safety to approaching motorists. *Surdyk v. Indiana Harbor Belt R.R.*, 148 F.2d 795 (7th Cir. 1945). However, a motorist who should have seen a train approaching such a defective electrified crossing will be guilty of contributory negligence if he does not stop. *Groesch v. Gulf, Mobile & Ohio R.R.*, 241 F.2d 698 (7th Cir. 1957).

6. Motorists may reasonably assume trains will give all required signals as they approach crossings. *Davenport, Rock Island & Northwestern Ry. v. DeYaeger*, 112 Ill. App. 537 (1904). However, if the motorist should have seen the approaching train, the train signals generally become irrelevant. *Robertson v. New York Central R.R.*, 321 Ill. App. 313, 53 N.E.2d 144 (1943), *rev'd on other grounds,* 388 Ill. 580, 58 N.E.2d 527 (1944).

§ 11-5. Appendices.

§ 11-5(A). Sample Direct Examination of Plaintiff's Expert, Dr. Gary Long — Adequacy of Grade Crossing Site.

Q. Dr. Long, when we were last in court last week, you were just testifying that there is a standard in the transportation engineering profession that a motorist at an electrically protected crossing will be given 20 seconds warning time, is that correct?

A. That is correct.

Q. And you had shown the court and jury the authoritative literature on that proposition.

A. I did.

Q. Let me ask you this, then: Is this County Road 400 East crossing actively or passively protected?

A. It is passively protected.

Q. Do passively protected crossings require more or less warning time than actively protected crossings?

A. They require more.

Q. Why is that?

A. Because on an active crossing the automatic signal mechanism does must of the decision work for the driver. It simply tells him that a train is coming. But at a passive crossing the driver is left to his own resources to detect a train, gauge its speed, and determine whether he can safely cross the crossing.

Q. Last week you told us that a motorist at this County Road 400 East crossing who could see a train approaching him at 70 miles an hour — but which was 300 feet away — would have 2.92 seconds of warning time.

Now would you consider that to be adequate warning time for a driver to react to an approaching train?

A. Certainly not.

Q. You told us a motorist at this crossing who could see a train approaching him at 70 miles an hour when it was 400 feet away would have 3.9 seconds of warning. Would you consider that adequate warning time for a driver to react to an approaching train?

A. Certainly not.

Q. If the motorist could see the train approaching at 70 miles an hour when it was 500 feet away, you testified he would have 4.87 seconds of warning. Would you consider that to be adequate reaction time for a motorist to respond to an approaching train?

A. Certainly not.

Q. Now, Dr. Long, you have testified that the PIEV reaction time for perceiving and thinking and feeling and acting is 3 to 4 seconds. Why is the standard for motorist warning time at a passive crossing greater than 20 seconds?

A. Because is addition to perceiving the problem, to thinking about it, the emotion time and volition time, the motorist still has to, after he makes his decision, cross the crossing, and that is the reason that the manuals say that 20 seconds is the absolute minimum and only if the tracks are no more than 35 feet apart because if they are more than 35 feet apart, then the vehicle is going to take extra time to go across a further distance.

Q. Would you consider this crossing to have been adequately protected on the date of the collision here if trains were operating over that crossing at that time at speeds of 70 miles per hour under conditions where motorists at the crossing could have visibility of 3 to 5 hundred feet?

A. No.

Q. Why not?

A. Well, the motorist only — if the train was operating at 70 miles an hour and the motorist was only 3 to 5 hundred feet away from the track, the motorist would only have between 2 and 5 seconds warning time which is far less than the 20 seconds at the standard is in order to provide this ample time to see and react and travel across the crossing.

Q. If trains are going to operate over this crossing at a speed of 70 miles an hour under such visibility conditions, do you have any opinion as to whether the crossing should be actively or passively protected?

A. I do.

Q. What is that opinion?

A. It certainly should be actively protected.

Q. Are there any standards or concepts in the profession of transportation engineering for how drivers react when confronted with sudden emergency situations such as trains coming at them with short visibility distances?

A. Yes.

Q. Is there any authoritative literature on this subject?

A. Yes, there is.

Q. Are you familiar with the work "Driver Reaction Time in Traffic" by G. M. McKay of the University of Birmingham in the December — January/1967 — 1968 volume of New Zealand Road Safety?

A. I am.

Q. Have you read it?

A. I have.

Q. I show you a copy of that article and I ask you if that is the article that you, in fact, read.

A. That is.

Q. Would you agree or disagree with this language on page 18 of that work —

By the way, do you consider that work to be competent?

A. I do.

Q. Would you agree or disagree with this passage from page 18 of that work:

> In cases of extreme emotional stress a pathological situation may arise in which the normal response to traffic may be suspended.

Would you agree or disagree with that statement?

A. I concur with that.

Q. Are your familiar with the work "Preliminary Investigation into a Physiological Assessment of Driving Stress" by Dr. T. J. Hunt published by the Division of Human Physiology, Institute for Medical Research, Medical Research Council, London, England, July of 1968?

A. I am.

Q. Have you read that?

A. I have.

Q. I show you a copy of that work and I ask you if this is, in fact, the work that you read.

A. It is.

Q. Would you consider that work to be competent?

A. Yes.

Q. Would you agree or disagree with this statement from page 36 of that work:

> Records of journeys show that as a result of exposure to fear, a driver may continue in a state of apprehension and/or uncertainty for a minute or even longer following the actual incident which initiated the danger. Incorrect decision making may therefore continue for some time after the unexpected incident, and any accident or error in driving occurring during that period may be occasioned by the continuing effects of startle, rather than as a direct result of the incident itself.

A. I believe that would be true.

Q. Are you familiar with the report "Psychology and Behavior of Drivers in the Causation of Accidents" by E. C. Poulton, Assistant Director of the Medical Research Council, Applied Psychology Research Unit, Cambridge, England, published in Volume 14, No. 4, International Road Safety and Traffic Review?

A. Yes, sir.

Q. Have you read it?

A. I have.

Q. I show you a copy of that article and ask you if this is the article that you read.

A. It is.

Q. Would you agree or disagree with this statement from page 16 of that work:

> One of the most interesting pieces of experimental research carried out at the British Road Research Laboratory concerns overtaking on a two-lane road. The driver was following a car, and there was a car ahead coming in the opposite direction. At a given signal he had to decide whether or not to overtake. Decision times ranged from an average of about 1.0 second when the driver had four seconds to spare after overtaking, to about 2.0 seconds when the driver had no time to spare. Thus the decision times reflected the difficulty of the decisions. When the driver should have started to overtake at once if he was to do so at all, because he had little or no time to spare, his manoeuvre was delayed owing to the difficulty of deciding whether or not to overtake. Clearly drivers should not need to find themselves in such a difficult and dangerous situation.

Would you agree or disagree with that statement?

A. I agree.

Q. Now, Dr. Long, how effective are train whistles in warning motorists of approaching trains?

A. They are not very effective.

Q. Why not?

A. Sound is — the human sense is not particularly acute to sound and so although the human ear can hear it, frequently it can't decide precisely what direction the sound is coming from. Moreover, there are problems with sound in that its intensity decreases with the square of the distance. So as you move twice as far from an object, the sound is only one-fourth as great.

So as trains are further and further away, the intensity of the sound is very low. The automobile tends to insulate the sound in the wintertime which is when this accident occurred. There is every reason to suspect that the windows probably would be rolled up, there would be internal car noises from the heater fan, that sort of thing, possibly a radio playing, so there is other localized sound which might tend to disguise the sound of the train. As a consequence there has been quite a bit of research involved in just how effective train whistles are, particularly because they are a nuisance and so many citizens and residents complain about them and try to see if the railroad couldn't stop using them at no cost to safety of this research has found virtually the same thing and that is that sound is not an adequate means, a train whistle is not an adequate means to advise motorists of the coming of the train, particularly because motorists don't have to have hearing, they can be deaf and still be issued a driver's license.

Q. Dr. Long, let me ask you this: If a train were approaching this County Road 400 East crossing from the west and a car were approaching on County Road 400 East from the north and the train crew could first see the car when the car was halfway between U.S. 30 and the crossing and the train was 300 feet from the crossing when the train crew could first see the car and the distance between U.S. 30 and the crossing were 93 feet and the car was doing 20 miles an hour when first seen by the train and the car never stopped or slowed down and the train and the car collided on the southernmost track of the crossing, do you have an opinion based upon a reasonable degree of scientific and engineering certainty as to how fast the train was going when the train crew first saw the car?

A. I do.

Q. What is that opinion?

A. If you will permit me to refer to my notes, when I calculated that, the train would have to be doing 120 miles an hour.

Q. Did you calculate that yourself?

A. I did.

Q. If a train were approaching this crossing from the west and a car were approaching on County Road 400 East from the north and the train crew could first see the car when the car was half way between U.S. 30 and the crossing and the train was 400 feet from the crossing when the train crew first saw the car and the distance between U.S. 30 and the crossing was 93 feet and the car was doing 20 miles an hour when first seen by the train and the car then stopped or slowed down and the train and the car collided on the southernmost track, do you have an opinion based upon a reasonable degree of scientific and engineering certainty as to how fast the train was going when the train crew first saw the car?

A. I have.

Q. What is that opinion?

A. 160 miles an hour.

Q. Did you calculate that yourself?

A. I did.

Q. If a train were approaching this crossing from the west and a car were approaching on County Road 400 East from the north and the train crew could first see the car when the car was half way between U.S. 30 and the crossing and the train was 500 feet from the crossing when the train crew first saw the car and the distance between U.S. 30 and the crossing was 93 feet and the car was doing 20 miles an hour when first seen by the train and the car then stopped or slowed down and the train and the car collided on the southernmost track, do you have an opinion based upon a reasonable degree of scientific and engineering certainty as to how fast the train was going when the train crew first saw the car?

A. I have.

Q. And what is that opinion?

A. It would to have been going 200 miles an hour.

Q. Did you calculate that yourself?

A. I did.

Q. If a train were approaching this crossing from the west and a car were approaching on County Road 400 East from the north and the train crew could first see the car when the car was half way between U.S. 30 and the crossing and the train was 300 feet from the crossing when the train crew first saw the car and the distance between U.S. 30 and the crossing were 93 feet and the car was doing 25 miles an hour when first seen by the train and the car never stopped or slowed down and the train and the car collided on the southernmost track, do you have an opinion based upon a reasonable degree of scientific and engineering certainty as to how fast the train was going when the train crew first saw the car?

A. I have.

Q. What is that opinion?

A. It would have been doing 150 miles an hour.

Q. Did you calculate that yourself?

A. I did.

Q. If a train were approaching this crossing from the west and a car were approaching on County Road 400 East from the north and the train crew could first see the car when the car was half way between U.S. 30 and the crossing and the train was 400 feet from the crossing when the train crew first saw the car and the distance between U.S. 30 and the crossing were 93 feet and the car was doing 25 miles an hour when first seen by the train and the car never stopped or slowed down and the train and the car collided on the southernmost track, do you have an opinion based upon a reasonable degree of scientific and engineering certainty as to how fast the train was going when the train crew first saw the car?

A. I have.

Q. What is that opinion?

A. The train would have to be going 200 miles an hour.

Q. If a train were approaching this crossing from the west and a car were approaching on County Road 400 East from the north and the train crew could first see the car when the car was half way between U.S. 30

and the crossing and the train was 500 feet from the crossing when the train crew first saw the car and the distance between U.S. 30 and the crossing were 93 feet and the car was doing 25 miles an hour when first seen by the train and the car never stopped or slowed down and the train and the car collided on the southernmost track, do you have an opinion based upon a reasonable degree of scientific and engineering certainty as to how fast the train was going when the train crew first saw the car?

A. I have.

Q. What is that opinion?

A. The train would have to be going 250 miles an hour.

Q. If a train were approaching this crossing from the west and a car were approaching on County Road 400 East from the north and the train crew could first see the car when the train was 300 feet from the crossing and the car was midway between U.S. 30 and the tracks when first seen by the train crew and the distance between U.S. 30 and the crossing were 93 feet and the car was doing 20 miles an hour when first seen by the train crew and the car never stopped or slowed down and the train was doing only 69 or 70 miles an hour when the train crew first saw the car, do you have an opinion based upon a reasonable degree of scientific and engineering certainty as to whether this train and that car would have collided at all?

A. I have.

Q. What is that opinion?

A. They would not have collided.

Q. What is the reason for that opinion?

A. The car would cross the tracks long before the train ever got there.

Q. If a train were approaching this crossing from the west and a car were approaching on County Road 400 East from the north and the train could first see the car when the train was 400 feet from the crossing and the car was midway between U.S. 30 and the tracks when first seen by the crew and the distance between U.S. 30 and the crossing were 93 feet and the car was doing 20 miles an hour when first seen by the train and the car never stopped or slowed down and the train was doing only 69 or 70 miles an hour when the train crew first saw the car, do you have an opinion based upon a reasonable degree of scientific and engineering certainty as to whether this train and that car would have collided at all?

A. I have.

Q. What is that opinion?

A. The would not have collided.

Q. And what is the reason for your opinion?

A. Again, the car would cross the tracks long before the train reached the crossing.

Q. If a train were approaching this crossing from the west and a car were approaching on County Road 400 East from the north and the train crew could first see the car when the train was 500 feet from the crossing and the car was midway between U.S. 30 and the tracks when first seen by the train crew and the distance between U.S. 30 and the crossing were 93 feet and the car was doing 20 miles an hour when first seen by the train and the car never stopped or slowed down and the train was doing only 69 or 70 miles an hour when the train crew could first see the car, do you have an opinion based upon a reasonable degree of scientific and engineering certainty as to whether this train and that car would have collided at all?

A. I have.

Q. What is that opinion?

A. They would not have collided.

Q. What is the reason for your opinion?

A. Again, the car would have crossed the tracks before the train reached the crossing.

Q. If a train were approaching this crossing from the west and a car approaching on County Road 400 East from the north and the train crew could first see the car when the train was 300 feet from the crossing and the car was midway between U.S. 30 and the tracks when first seen by the train crew and the distance between U.S. 30 and the crossing were 93 feet and the car was doing 25 miles an hour when first seen by the train and the car never stopped or slowed down and the train was doing only 69 or 70 miles an hour when the train crew first saw the car, do you have an opinion based upon a reasonable degree of scientific and engineering certainty as to whether this train and that car would have collided at all?

A. I have.

Q. What is that opinion?

A. They would not have collided.

Q. What is the reason for that opinion?

A. Again, the car would have crossed the tracks before the train reached the crossing.

Q. If a train were approaching this crossing from the west and a car were approaching on County Road 400 East from the north and the train crew could first see the car when the train was 400 feet from the crossing and the car was midway between U.S. 30 and the tracks when first seen by the train crew and the distance between U.S. 30 and the crossing were 93 feet and the car was doing 25 miles an hour when first seen by the train and the car never stopped or slowed down and the train was doing only 69 or 70 miles an hour when the train crew first saw the car, do you have an opinion based upon a reasonable degree of scientific and engineering certainty as to whether this train and that car would have collided at all?

A. I have.

Q. What is that opinion?

A. They would not have collided.

Q. What is the reason for that opinion?

A. The same reason, the car would have crossed the tracks long before the train reached the crossing.

Q. If a train were approaching this crossing from the west and a car were approaching on County Road 400 East from the north and the train crew could first see the car when the train was 500 feet from the crossing and the car was midway between U.S. 30 and the tracks when first seen by the train crew and the distance between U.S. 30 and the crossing were 93 feet and the car was doing 25 miles an hour when first seen by the train and the car never stopped or slowed down and the train was going only 69 or 70 miles an hour when the train crew first saw the car, do you have an opinion based upon a reasonable degree of scientific and engineering certainty as to whether this train and that car would have collided at all?

A. I have.

Q. And what is that opinion?

A. They would not have collided.

Q. What is the reason for your opinion?

A. Again, the car would have cleared the tracks before the train reached the crossing.

Q. Dr. Long, if all of the factors to which you have just testified are taken into account, would this collision have taken place if the speed of the train was 70 miles an hour or less?

A. No.

Q. Why not?

A. The car would have crossed the tracks before the train reached the crossing.

Q. Should trains operate at maximum speeds no matter how poor the visibility conditions are?

A. Certainly not.

Q. Why not?

A. Because a driver cannot make a proper decision whether it is safe to cross the tracks.

Q. Is this County Road 400 East crossing adequately protected for trains to operate at over speeds of 70 miles an hour under good visibility conditions?

A. No.

Q. Was this always your opinion?

A. No.

Q. What changed your opinion?

A. Mr. Alroth took some more measurements out in the field and he found as you move further away from the tracks up in the vicinity of the advance warning sign, the visibility is only 1,210 feet and with the train travelling at 20 miles an hour, this would give the driver less than 12 seconds of advance warning time which certainly is less than 20 and insufficient for a driver to be able to cross the track safely.

Q. How fast would that train be travelling?

A. At 70 miles an hour.

Q. Are you familiar with the study "Drivers' Brake Reaction Time" by Johanson and Rumar?

A. I am.

Q. Have you read it?

A. I have.

Q. Are you familiar with it?

A. I am.

Q. Do you consider the .9 of a second median driver reaction time found in the experiment reported in that study to be appropriate and normal reaction time for drivers in emergency situations as passively protected railroad crossings under reduced visibility conditions?

A. No.

Q. Why not?

A. Well, just from a purely intuitive point of view, less than one second is very little time to make a decision to perceive a train, think about it, decide what action to take and to take this action. But, moreover, when you look at the basis for that article, that is a median reaction time which implies that if you use that, half the population can't react in that amount of time which means that half of the population would be subjected to a potentially disastrous situation in attempting to get across the tracks with only .9 of a second.

Furthermore, if you examine the article a little more closely, they retested some drivers over and over again. So drivers were certainly alerted to the stimuli and they had a prepared or alerted response.

Furthermore, they threw away the first observations of each one of the drivers that they tested over and over again because they decided that those drivers' responses were too slow due to thinking.

So it is certainly a biased article.

Moreover, there is the additional problem that the stimuli which they were reacting to were simple, it was merely when a horn came on they were to step on the brakes and that is certainly not the case of a driver making a decision at a railroad crossing.

Q. One last question, Dr. Long: This scale drawing of the crossing that has been introduced into evidence, how long an area east of the crossing does it show?

A. One mile.

Q. This entirely scale drawing, if unrolled by the jury, would stretch how long?

A. In just the direction east of the railroad crossing, you mean?

Q. Just the area of the track east of the crossing, about how long would that be?

A. It would be about 45 feet.

§ 11-5(B). Sample Direct Examination of Plaintiff's Expert, Professor Robert MacRae — Qualifications of Witness to Calculate Train Speeds.

Q. Now you have been retained in this case as an expert witness by the plaintiffs for that very purpose, correct?

A. That is correct.

Q. And you are being compensated for your time and expenses?

A. That's correct.

Q. And we have discussed this case before?

A. We have.

Q. And we have discussed the questions that I am going to ask you before?

A. Yes.

Q. Are there any scientific laws or principles by means of which a person trained in physics and engineering can calculate how fast the train was going before it applied its brakes, if he did not actually see the train moving?

A. Yes.

Q. Have you, yourself, ever made such a calculation?

A. I have.

Q. Approximately how many times have you made such a calculation?

A. Oh, at least several hundred times.

Q. Under what circumstances have you made such a calculation?

A. These calculations arise in my teaching, both at the lower level and the advanced undergraduate level for engineering students and also as a part of my work, recently assumed, as a consultant in cases of this nature.

Q. And you have trained other people in how to make such calculations?

A. I have.

Q. What kind of people have you trained in how to make such calculations?

A. Principally engineers and physicists.

Q. How long have you been training people in how to make such calculations?

A. Seventeen years.

Q. Approximately how many people have you trained to make such calculations?

A. Several hundred.

Q. What are the factors that a person trained in physics and engineering considers in calculating how fast an object was moving if he did not see it moving?

A. I want to refer to some notes here so I will be sure not to leave out any considerations.

I would like to know the number of cars and the number of engines on the train, whether these are passenger cars or freight cars and the weights, if available, of the cars in the total train.

I would like to know the condition of the track and the condition of the road bed.

I would also like to know if the brakes were in good working order. My calculations are limited to situations where emergency braking was performed.

In addition, I would need to know, or like to know at least, the stopping distance of the train.

Q. Are there any authoritative sources of literature that a person trained in physics and engineering would consult in order to become familiar enough with train operations to calculate the speed at which a train was going before its emergency brakes were applied?

A. Yes.

Q. And what are these?

A. One of these is a book entitled, "The Management of Train Operation and Training Handling," published by the Air Brake Association.

Q. Have you read that?

A. I have.
Q. Are you familiar with it?
A. I am familiar with it.
Q. Do you consider it competent?
A. I consider it competent.
Q. All right. Go ahead.
A. The second text is entitled, "The Engineering and Design of Railway Brake Systems," also published by the Air Brake Association.
Q. Have you read that?
A. I have read that.
Q. Are you familiar with it?
A. I am familiar with it.
Q. Do you consider it competent?
A. I consider it competent.
Q. Do you belong to the Air Brake Association personally?
A. Yes, I do belong to the Air Brake Association.

The next reference I have just a photocopy of and the title of this is, "Introduction to Railway Braking," by H.R. Broadbent.

Q. Have you read that?
A. I have read that.
Q. Are you familiar with it?
A. I am.
Q. Do you consider it competent?
A. I consider that competent.

The next reference, also a photocopy, is entitled, "Mastering Momentum," by Silcox.

Q. Have you read that?
A. I have read it.
Q. Are you familiar with it?
A. I am familiar with it.
Q. Do you consider it competent?
A. Yes.
Q. Are the principles and facts about railroad trains in those texts that would allow a person trained in physics and engineering to compute the speed of a railroad train?
A. Yes.
Q. What principles and facts about railroad trains are you referring to?
A. I am referring to the performance of the brakes, basically, and the sequencing of the brakes and the way in which this braking force is applied eventually to the wheel, rail contact.

Q. Are you familiar with the agreed facts in this case about the train that killed Jessie McKinnion?

A. Yes, I am.

Q. What is friction or frictional force?

A. Frictional force is the force that exists between two objects that are trying to move relative to one another. For instance, if I place my hand on a surface and move it sideways, I would feel some reluctance for my hand to move. That would be due to friction.

Q. What is wheel rail friction?

A. Wheel rail friction is a friction that exists between the wheel of the train, in this case, and the rail.

Q. Is wheel rail friction related to the ability of the train to stop?

A. Yes, it is.

Q. How so?

A. The ability of a train to stop depends on the ability to use up or dissipate the energy of the train. Most of this is accomplished by having the wheels grip the rails and slow down.

The wheels are slowed by the brake shoes and then ultimately the contact of the wheel with the rail determines the rate at which the train can slow down.

In summary, then, the ability of the wheel to grip the rail determines to a large extent the speed at which the train can be stopped.

Q. What is meant by a coefficient of friction?

A. Coefficient friction is the relationship between the weight of a body and the frictional force it experiences as you try to move it horizontally.

Q. How do you determine the coefficient of friction?

A. Well, if I were to determine the coefficient of friction of a body on a surface like a piece of wood, I would place the body on the surface, knowing the weight of the body, and then exert a pull horizontally, measure how much the pull would be and then I would define the coefficient of friction as the pull divided by the weight of the body. This is a number that is somewhere between zero and one. One is the maximum value of a coefficient.

Q. Does the presence of water on the rail change the coefficient of friction between the rail and the wheel?

A. Yes.

Q. Is the coefficient of friction affected by the grade or slope of the ground over which a train is moving?

A. No.

Q. Can you determine the speed of a train prior to the application of the emergency brakes if you know the stopping distance and other factors?

A. I can.

Q. And I think you previously mentioned some of those factors.

What types of braking systems are currently used in passenger trains in the United States?

A. All trains use air braking systems. This is called a pneumatic system.

In some passenger trains this pneumatic system is augmented somewhat with an electrical signal that speeds the application of the pneumatic or air brakes but basically all the braking is actually done by air pressure.

Q. How long have these been the generally used passenger train brakes in this country?

A. For many, many years, certainly since the turn of the century.

Q. How do these different brake systems differ in emergency usage?

A. There is no difference once the brake signal gets to the brake shoe which rubs on the train wheel.

In the case of the electro-pneumatic system, the speed of travel of the signal that says it is time to go into emergency action, is a little more rapid.

In a normal pneumatic system the information that an emergency has occurred or an emergency action needs to be taken, travels at the speed at which the pressure in the brake line can be vented to the atmosphere. This is approximately 900 feet per second. In the case of electromagnetic braking, the information is sent to each car essentially simultaneously rather than having to travel by pressure reduction in the brake line.

Q. With either type of braking system, once the emergency brakes of a train are turned on, what happens in the braking system of the train?

A. The pressure in the brake line is immediately vented to the atmosphere, meaning the pressure goes to zero. That simultaneously starts an action in each car which results in the application of maximum braking on each car.

Q. Can the emergency brakes just be turned off after they are turned on under either of those braking systems?

A. No.

Q. Why not?

A. The process is irreversible because the only way you can remove the brakes is to, in effect, pump the pressure line back up. The brakes, in a sense, are normally on and you put pressure in the brake lines to hold them off so you can drive the train. Once you vent all of the pressure in the line, then the brakes cannot be removed from the train until you have pumped up that line again and that comes from a compressor in the engine only.

Q. What is the maximum usable braking force?

A. That is a term I invented to represent the maximum amount of braking you could get when the limitation to braking is one determined by the friction that the wheels can make with the rails. In other words, if you have a greasy rail and very bad conditions and you cannot get much of a grip, it would not take very long for the brake pressure to build to a sufficient value to make the wheels slide.

Contrastingly, if the braking conditions were ideal, dry rail, maybe sand on it, then the brake pressure could build for a considerable length of time before maximum braking occurred. In other words, you can brake to a much greater extent if you have ideal friction conditions existing than if you have, say, an oily rail with poor conditions existing.

Q. How long does it take for a passenger train to obtain maximum usable braking force after the emergency brakes are turned on?

A. That depends on the frictional value of the rail/wheel interaction. In the case we are considering here, about two to three seconds after the emergency brake handle is applied, almost maximum braking is available at all cars in the train.

Q. Are there any particular scientific or mathematical formulas or equations by means of which a person trained in physics and engineering can use the factors that you have just described to calculate what the speed of a railroad train was at a given time before its brakes were applied?

A. Yes.

Q. Are you familiar with those forms of equations?

A. I am.

Q. Have you worked with them?

A. I have.

Q. Have you taught them to others?

A. I have.

Q. What are those formulas or equations?

A. I have a formula written on the easel.

BY THE WITNESS:

A. The symbol D stands for the distance that the train travels while the braking takes place. This is from the time that the emergency signal is first applied by the engineer until the time the train is brought to a stop or at least to some lower speed.

The S — look just at the symbol for a moment — represents the final speed — in most cases the zero speed and S original means the speed it was traveling when we initiated the braking situation.

The two superscripts mean that these quantities are square.

If you have forgotten a little bit about your mathematics, a square quantity means a quantity multiplied by itself. So if this number happened to be 10, then 10 square would be 100.

The A symbol represents the rate at which we can accomplish a slowdown, how many miles per hour, per second, can we lose, for instance, that would be one way.

The 2 is a constant that is derived in the equation and has no particular significance other than it has to be there for the mathematics.

MR. KUHLMAN: Thank you.

. . . .

BY MR. KUHLMAN:

Q. Professor MacRae, have you ever qualified and testified in a court of law as an expert witness on the subject of calculating train speed?

A. I have.

Q. When was that?

A. In 1975 in the Circuit Court of Calhoun County, Alabama.

Q. What was the name of that case?

A. The name of the case was J.D. Smith versus Southern Railway Company, Case No. 10828.

Q. Did you undertake any analysis in that case?

A. I did.

Q. What did you analyze?

A. I calculated the speed of the train based on the distance required for it to stop.

Q. Did you testify about that in court?

A. I did.

Q. Were there any other instances when you qualified and testified in a court of law as an expert witness on the subject of calculating how fast an object has been moving before it applied its brakes?

A. Yes.

Q. When was that?

A. In 1971 I reconstructed an automobile accident in which a collision took place at right angles and there were no witnesses and no police report and I determined what the speeds of the two cars were, based on the way they left the collision point.

Q. What court was that in?

A. This was also in the Circuit Court of Calhoun County, Alabama. And the case number was 9058.

Q. Have you visited the scene of the County Road 400 East crossing?

A. I have.

Q. How was the weather when you were there?

A. Clear with good visibility.

Q. Did you observe the tracks to the east of the crossing?

A. I did.

Q. For how long a period did you observe them, how long an area of track?

A. I observed the track at varying points for about five miles.

Q. Was the track straight or curved?

A. It was straight.

Q. Was there any significant grade or elevation in those tracks east of the crossing?

A. A very, very slight grade, almost imperceptible.

Q. Did you observe the kind of rails that were on the southernmost track when you visited the crossing?

A. I did.

Q. What kind of rails were there?

A. There were continuously welded rails rather than joint rails — jointed rails.

Q. Were those the kind of rails that existed on the southernmost track at the time of the collision?

A. Yes.

Q. How do you know?

A. I observed photographs taken at the time of the accident and I was able to determine that there were no joints in the rails at that time.

Q. What other kinds of rails besides these continuous welded rails are there?

A. The jointed rails.

Q. What difference would there be between the two different kinds of rails in the ability of a train to stop?

A. Well, the jointed rails require the wheel to take a little bounce every time it goes over a joint. If you have ridden the trains you know the clickety-clickety-click that you hear. This results in a slight lift in the wheel which means it doesn't get quite as much of a bite into the rail. Thereby, it would not be able to stop quite as rapidly if the occasion arose on a jointed rail as it would on a smooth, continuous welded rail. There are no joints at all in that kind of a rail.

Q. From your professional work and study in the area of physics and railroad train brake systems and operations, tell the court if the speed at which a railroad train was moving at a time in the past, before its emergency brakes were applied, can be calculated with a reasonable degree of scientific and mathematical certainty assuming that sufficient facts are developed and investigated?

A. Yes.

Q. Can it?

A. It can be calculated.

Q. I want to ask you a question involving certain factual assumptions that we have previously discussed.

I want you to assume hypothetically these circumstances:

A railroad passenger train consisting of four diesel locomotive units and 14 cars was approaching the County Road 400 East intersection from the west; each locomotive unit, with tender and fuel, weighed approximately 336,000 pounds, the 14 cars in the train weighed approximately 1,840,160 pounds. Each car had two wheel trucks and each wheel truck had four wheels.

Assume further that this train approached the intersection from the west at approximately 5:00 p.m. on an afternoon when it was snowing and the wind was blowing out of the east and that the railroad tracks over which it traveled were in good condition, with the descending grade beginning near the crossing and extending westward at .16 degree variation.

Assume further that brakes on the train were to be applied by the train engineer using a lever, that all the train cars had power brakes applied by the engineer and that emergency brakes were applied by an emergency brake handle lever, that each car of the train did not have a sanding application or applicator and that the braking system of the train was in good working order.

Assume further that the rail surface was wet, contaminated with dirt and oil and that the tracks to the east of the crossing are generally straight and without any pronounced grade or elevation for a distance of at least one mile.

Assume further that this train made a full and sudden application of its emergency brakes at a point between the crossing and 500 feet west of the crossing.

Assume further that the train then proceeded to strike a 1962 Chevrolet at the intersection and that this train, carrying this vehicle on its lead locomotive unit, then proceeded one mile east of the crossing before coming to a stop.

Now, assuming all those factors, do you have an opinion, based upon a reasonable degree of engineering and mathematical certainty regarding whether this railroad train was traveling at more or less than 70 miles an hour immediately before it applied its emergency brakes?

A. I have an opinion.

Q. What is that opinion?

A. My opinion is that the speed of the locomotive prior to the impact was in excess of 70 miles an hour.

Q. And what is the reason for that opinion?

A. I calculated that under the conditions indicated, a wet rail with moderate oil contamination but in good mechanical condition would require a distance of 1980 feet to come to a complete stop from a speed of 70 miles an hour.

Q. How many feet are there in a mile?

A. 5,280.

Q. Assuming all those factors again in the hypothetical question I asked you, do you have any opinion, based upon a reasonable degree of engineering and scientific certainty, regarding whether this railroad train was traveling at more or less than 80 miles an hour immediately before it applied its emergency brakes?

A. It is my opinion that it was exceeding 80 miles an hour.

Q. Why is that?

A. Because my calculation for the stopping distance required for 80 miles an hour is 2,540 feet, which is less than the stated stopping distance.

Q. Now again assuming all those factors in the hypothetical question, do you have any opinion, based on a reasonable degree of engineering and scientific certainty, regarding whether this railroad train was traveling at more or less than 90 miles an hour immediately before it applied its emergency brakes?

A. Yes.

Q. And what is that opinion?

A. It is my opinion that the train was exceeding 90 miles an hour.

Q. Why is that?

A. Because I calculated that the stopping distance from 90 miles an hour should be 3,210 feet, which is less than 5,280 feet per mile.

Q. What assumptions, if any, were you making in each of the calculations that I have asked you for an opinion?

A. The assumptions I made in the calculations were that the rails were jointed rails and were in good condition, that the rails possibly had moderate oil contamination and that there was possibly the presence of water because of the weather conditions then.

I also assumed only minimum performing ability from the brake shoes. This is the shoe that rubs against the wheel to bring the wheel speed down.

I assumed that the stopping ability of the train was primarily limited by the ability of the train wheel to grip the rail rather than in the ability of the brake system within the train to reach some very large value of pressure.

Q. Now were all of these assumptions that you have made actually substantiated by the available evidence?

A. No, they were not.

Q. Which assumptions were not substantiated by the available evidence?

A. I had assumed jointed rails in good mechanical condition. When I observed the intersection, I found that the rails were continuously welded rails, which would give a slightly higher ability for the wheel to bite into the rail and produce a stop.

I also found that the rails were probably dry after I observed the weather report from a nearby station, I think it was about five miles away, indicating that in spite of the fact that there were snow flurries that day, the maximum temperature was 16 degrees Fahrenheit, which means there would be no chance for the snow to melt. So all we would have on the track would be some light blowing snow which would be dry. Therefore, it turns out, my guess is that the rail was dry at the time.

I also did not see any indication at the present time of significant oil contamination.

Q. Once again assuming all those facts about the train and the rails that I asked you about in the hypothetical question, do you have an opinion as to how far over 90 miles an hour that train was going immediately before it applied its brakes?

A. I do not wish to make a statement on that.

Q. Why not?

A. Because the calculations involve variables that are getting reasonably large. I feel confident in the numbers up to 90 miles an hour, but things like air friction with the train, local variations in the quality of the rail, make me not so confident of results above 90. I would prefer to leave my evaluation at just the train was doing in excess of 90.

Q. You spoke about variables. Are there any variables with respect to the train speeds that you calculated for varying stopping distances here?

A. The numbers I have written to correspond to a given speed are what I consider the best numbers. But in any calculations there is a certain amount of uncertainty in it because I am assuming certain conditions in terms of performance of the train.

In the case of the 70-mile calculation, I would assume that 1,980 feet is the best stopping distance I can calculate for a speed of 70 miles an hour plus or minus three. In other words, if the train were doing anywhere between 67 and 73, 1,980 feet is the number that I would say is the best number for the stopping distance.

Q. What is the margin of uncertainty for the stopping distance you calculated for a speed of 80 miles an hour?

A. The margin goes up as the speed goes up.

My margin at 80 miles an hour is plus or minus four miles an hour, meaning that if the train speed were anywhere between 76 and 84 miles an hour, my calculations would indicate 2,540 feet as an appropriate distance for a stop under the conditions indicated.

Q. And what is the margin of uncertainty for the stopping distance calculated at a train speed of 90 miles an hour?

A. The uncertainty there is plus or minus five miles an hour. So I would say that if the train speed was between 85 and 95, the best calculated speed stopping distance would be 3,210 feet.

Q. Assuming all of the facts in the hypothetical question I asked you, if this train had applied its emergency brakes 1650 feet west of the crossing and if it had been traveling at only 69 or 70 miles an hour before it applied its emergency brakes, how far east of the crossing would that train have come to rest?

A. If the brakes were applied at 1,650 feet west of the crossing and I calculate 1,980 as the stopping distance, that would mean the train would come to a stop 300 or 400 feet east of the crossing, after passing the crossing.

Q. Assuming all the factors in the hypothetical, if the emergency brakes on that train had been applied at a distance of 1650 feet west of the crossing, would the train have been slowed to any appreciable extent by the time it reached the crossing?

A. It would have.

Q. Can you calculate how much that train would have been slowed down by the time it reached the crossing if it had been traveling 70 miles an hour when it applied its emergency brakes 1650 feet west of the crossing?

A. Yes.

Q. How much would it have been slowed?

A. I estimate that the train speed would have been reduced from 70 to about 40 miles an hour by the time he got to the crossing.

Q. Would that slowing down have increased the time for the train to reach the crossing from a distance of 1650 feet west of it?

A. It would.

Q. And how much would that slowing down have increased the train time?

A. Approximately 5 seconds.

Q. Can you calculate how much the train would have been slowed down by the time it reached the crossing if it had been going 80 miles an hour when it applied its emergency brakes at 1650 feet west of the crossing?

A. Yes. The speed would have dropped to about 50 miles an hour by the time the crossing was reached.

Q. Would that slowing down have increased the time for the train to reach the crossing a distance of 1650 feet?

A. Yes, but less about three seconds.

Q. Can you calculate how much the train would have been slowed down by the time it reached the crossing if it had been going 90 miles an hour when it applied its emergency brakes 1650 feet west of the crossing?

A. Yes.

Q. How much?

A. I estimate the speed would have been between 60 and 65 miles an hour at the time it reached the crossing.

Q. Would that slowing down have increased the time for the train to reach the crossing?

A. Yes, but only two seconds in this case.

Q. Assuming all the factors in that hypothetical question, if this train had applied its emergency brakes 500 feet west of the crossing and if it had been traveling at 69 or 70 miles an hour before it applied the brakes, how far east of the crossing would it have come to rest?

A. Approximately 1500 feet east of the crossing.

Q. Assuming all the factors in the hypothetical question, if this train had applied its emergency brakes 400 feet west of the crossing and if it had been traveling at 69 or 70 miles an hour before it applied the brakes, how far east of the crossing would it have come to rest?

A. About 1600 feet.

Q. Assuming all the factors in the hypothetical question, if this train had applied its emergency brakes 300 feet west of the crossing and if it had been traveling at 69 or 70 miles an hour before it applied the brakes, how far east of the crossing would it have come to rest?

A. About 1700 feet.

Q. Now assuming all the factors in the hypothetical, if the train applied its emergency brakes at the spot where the tracks intersect County Road 400 East, at the spot where it hit the McKinnion car and if the train had been traveling 69 or 70 miles an hour before it applied those brakes, how far east of the crossing would that train come to rest?

A. Approximately 1,980 feet.

Q. Does it make any difference in relation to those calculations you have made, which of the two different types of passenger train braking systems that you mentioned earlier this train actually had?

A. I have assumed minimum performance, which means that I really calculated it on the basis of pure pneumatic, without any kind of augmenting effect from the electromagnetic system.

Q. So would it make any difference —

A. It would make no difference.

Q. What is emergency brake sequencing?

A. Emergency brake sequencing is the series of actions that take place from the time that the engineer or some other train member activates the emergency brake system, to the time that the pressure drops in the line, the pressure drop is transmitted to the brake cylinders, the brake cylinders push the brake shoes against the wheels, the wheels grip the rails and the train finally comes to a stop.

Q. Does it make any difference in relation to these calculations you have made what the brake sequencing of this train was?

A. There is essentially only one general form of brake sequencing and I have assumed that in my calculations.

Q. So would it make a difference?

A. No, sir.

Q. What are brake shoes?

A. Brake shoes are curved pieces of metal or coated metal that press against the wheels to reduce the speed of the train. They are very similar to the shoes that you would use inside the wheel of an automobile.

Q. Does it make any difference in relation to these calculations you have made what kind of brake shoes were on that train?

A. I have assumed the minimum performance of brake shoes that are currently available.

Q. So it doesn't make any difference?

A. It would not make any difference what kind of brake shoes they were.

Q. The wind and the speed direction are relevant considerations in your calculations?

A. You mean the speed of the wind, the direction?

Q. The speed of the wind, and its direction.

A. I assumed they would be very small compared to the speed of the train. It would not substantially affect the behavior of the train.

Q. Is the weight of the car being carried a relevant consideration in your calculations?

A. No.

Q. Why not?

A. Because it is so very small compared to the weight of the locomotive.

Q. Did you visit the scene of the collision before making these calculations?

A. I did not.

Q. Was it necessary to visit the scene to make those calculations?

A. No.

Q. Have you consulted any documents in making or confirming these calculations?

A. I have some track profiles provided by the railroad company which show a layout of the tracks, the curvature in the vicinity and also the grade. This is all the information I need in addition to what I have already stated in order to make the calculation.

Q. Have you inspected the scene since you made the calculation?

A. I have.

MR. KUHLMAN: Thank you, Professor.

CHAPTER 12

THE JURY AND HIGH TECHNOLOGY LITIGATION

§ 12-1. High Technology Litigation.

Transportation facility negligence cases involve engineering, physics, higher mathematics, and many other technical skills. As such, they fall into the rapidly growing area of litigation involving complex technology that also includes, but certainly is not limited to: medical malpractice, patent law, anti-trust law, economic regulation, and the structuring of administrative rules and laws for "emerging" technologies such as nuclear energy and chemicals. These areas of litigation cut across many traditional legal distinctions. Some of them are in the personal injury or tort field and some are not. What these litigation areas have in common, however, is sufficient to justify grouping them together as one of the great emerging fields of the law. This is because most high technology cases share the problem of how to communicate complicated, difficult facts to a fact finder with relatively little technical background in the relevant technologies. Thus, a patent lawyer who must convey the essence of a lawsuit hinging on whether particular micro chip circuitry constitutes "New Art" to a judge who used to be an alderman and can't work his twelve-year-old son's home computer, shares the same basic legal problem facing a personal injury attorney who must convey the engineering concepts in a transportation facility negligence case to a jury of housewives and retired plumbers. This problem extends far beyond the boundaries of the courtroom, or of the legal system as a whole. Simply put, the basis of the problem is that our entire democracy rests on the assumption that the common citizen can understand and decide the critical issues entrusted to him, from popular elections for political office to trial by jury. This foundation is rapidly eroding because technology is becoming more complex and diffuse, confronting the average citizen in an alarmingly wide area of activity with facts so difficult that he cannot understand them. When this happens, of course, the decisions supposedly resting on a mastery of these facts become travesties of the democratic process. If and when this problem becomes sufficiently widespread it must be fatal to our form of government, for no democracy can survive when its average citizens (represented in law by the "reasonable man") cannot understand the facts essential for a meaningful exercise of their rights.

In the field of litigation, high technology cases require the attorney to bring this essential factual understanding to a previously ignorant (but not stupid) fact finder through meaningful communication. This process may sometimes require finding a simple way to explain something technical and complex. In other instances, it may require the litigator to find a nontechnical alternative explanation to technical arguments advanced by the opposition. In any event, litigators in the high technology fields must communicate technical facts to human beings (a category that usually even includes judges), and therefore it is relevant to know how people, now and in the past, have felt about technology.

This chapter is addressed to these factors central to meaningful communication of complex technology to a lay fact finder (and as technology continues to grow more complex virtually everyone stands before it as an awed layman). High technology cases will invariably be decided on the issue of which side does a better job at such communication. If neither side can perform this function meaningfully (either due to lack of skill by the attorneys or factual issues that become impossibly complex), then a jury trial would become as much of a sham as a popular election decided by an ignorant electorate on the basis of which candidate had the prettiest smile (or legs).

Attorneys bear a particular responsibility to understand and master these issues, for it is certain that technology will continue to grow more complex and diffuse throughout society. Every area of the law will require the practicing attorney to know and meaningfully communicate technology to laymen. If our profession cannot meet this responsibility, our practices, and certainly our litigation, will become a series of high-priced popularity contests, and history shows us that no democracy has ever been able to survive without a meaningful legal system.

§ 12-2. Technology Is Altering Jurors.

For decades, if not generations, attorneys have been guided in jury selection by concepts based upon racial stereotyping and the social demographics that existed before the First World War. Thus, jurors popularly believed to favor the plaintiff in a civil case and the defendant in a criminal case were drawn from the waves of immigration that reached this country in the late nineteenth and early twentieth century from central and southern Europe, who were consequently still on the lower levels of the social power structure: (Italians, Greeks, Slavs, Spaniards),[1] together with other racial types historically excluded from many, or any, of the levers of power (Jews and Blacks). Conversely, the defendant in a civil case and the prosecution in a criminal case were considered better served by jurors from earlier, better established waves of immigration from Northern Europe (English, German, Scandinavian).[2] The rationale behind this incipient racism seems to have been that outsiders will identify with outsiders and underdogs. Whatever merit these classifications may have had has been largely outmoded by the technological expansion that has produced general improvement of social and economic conditions among most areas of the population in recent decades, a phenomenon evidenced among other things by the fact that the children and grandchildren of the relatively impoverished city dwelling immigrants who sustained the New Deal are now living in the suburbs, investing in mutual funds, stuffing their parents and grandparents into nursing homes, and voting for Ronald Reagan.

The prospective juror must, in short, be reviewed on an individual basis, particularly in high technology or complex cases, such as transportation facility negligence cases usually are, because the appropriateness of a juror to sit in judgment on such cases is uniquely dependent upon such

1. *Goldstein, Trial Technique,* § 9.29 (2d ed.).
2. *Id.* at § 9.31.

individual traits as intelligence, education, and perception.[3]

§ 12-3. Technology Is a Legal and Social Acid.

Technology, of course, has not been the only significant cause of corrosive legal or social change; but significant new technology has always produced significant, corrosive legal and social change. Gunpowder ended the Age of Chivalry, rendering feudal law an anachronism (outside of Law School Real Property Classes and Bar Exams). The printing press brought books, and particularly the Bible, into the mass market, allowing laymen to read and interpret scripture, a development that was the foundation for the Reformation and a century of devastating religious warfare throughout Europe. The development of ships and navigational devices reliable enough for Trans Oceanic voyages were essential predecessors to the discovery of the New World and the establishment of the United States. The negligence theory was created to give the fledgling entrepreneurs who built the factories and railroads launching the Industrial Revolution a defense against the catastrophic damages that earlier strict liability laws would have imposed on them when their new machines started killing people. The list of examples is almost endless: technological change quickly eats away at existing

3. It should not be overlooked that attorneys representing positions with dubious merits in complex and high technology litigation may be well-advised to avoid intelligent, educated, and perceptive jurors. In criminal defense work, similarly, attorneys often seek jurors of low intelligence on the theory that if such jurors do not understand the evidence they are more likely to find that the prosecution has not established the defendant's guilt beyond a reasonable doubt. Indeed, down through the years, democratic societies have enshrined the jury system as a microcosm of their most sterling virtues without consciously realizing how often an individual should be insulted to be accepted to serve on such a panel.

legal and social structures, producing massive changes in most other aspects of life, which is why most major human societies before the European Industrial Revolution treated technology like an acid — something to be avoided or at best, something to be used in strictly limited amounts for the solution of specific, limited problems.

High technology litigation today is so complex, and evolving so rapidly, because our society has been the first one to base itself upon unlimited technological progress, and the constant social, economic, and legal changes flowing from this onrushing technology. As the complexity of technology escalates, the laws and rules governing the use of that technology have proven increasingly incapable of functioning.[4]

---

4. Governmental action has often exacerbated the problem of controlling technology through ignorance. For example, the older now-abandoned toxic dump sites are most dangerous to the environment due to packaging deterioration, yet the Resource Conservation and Recovery Act of 1976, the main legislative response to the problem, does not deal with abandoned sites at all. M. Brown, *Laying Waste: The Poisoning of America by Toxic Chemicals,* note 43, at 311-12 (1979). Other areas of difficulty can best be attributed to governmental-bureaucratic ineptitude. Thus, our nuclear energy program is supposedly controlled by several overlapping, uncoordinated, independent regulatory agencies, a situation which "assure(s) a regulatory situation in which it is virtually impossible to predict the final decisions that will be rendered or when they will be made." Golay, *How Prometheus Came To Be Bound: Nuclear Regulation in America,* Technology Rev. 30 (June/July 1980). Similarly, although § 3001 of the Resource Conservation and Recovery Act of 1976 called for laboratory tests to determine what toxic substances should be proscribed, the various drafting committees fought unending battles, and wasted unreasonable amounts of time, over how the tests should be structured. *Laying Waste, supra* note 43, at 312. As one expert observed:

> Had a malevolent deity set out to test our system for overseeing technological decisions, he would have enabled the creation of a technology with overwhelming military importance, distanced its underlying physical laws from ordinary experience, given it attrac-

The litigation, and litigation problems, generated by technology advancing beyond the limits, and capabilities, of the law will be further exacerbated by the increasingly rapid rate at which advances are occurring in the pervasiveness[5] and productivity[6] of modern technology. Neither

---

tive commercial applications, and designed those applications to endanger public health. Moreover, he would have national security problems arise when the legitimacy of administrative government had been settled, and after economic, military and social crises had encouraged unquestioning faith in the efficiency and dispassion of governmental experts. Under these circumstances he could have been confident of an extraordinarily deferential judiciary and could have expected technological enthusiasm to overshadow the constraints of legislative oversight and safety regulations. . . . The data [from nuclear power] cannot be ignored, for they suggest there are inherent weaknesses that prevent existing institutions from adequately controlling the risks that flow from technological decisions. Yellin, "High Technology and the Courts: Nuclear Power and the Need for Institutional Reform." 94 Harv. L. Rev. 489, note 28, at 490 (1980).

5. Between 1920 and 1940, in the United States alone, the number of industrial research laboratories increased from 300 to over 2,000. They produced or discovered, among other things: cellophane, synthetic rubber, nylon, plywood, plexiglass, lucite, vinylite, the photoelectric cell, television, commercial radio, the sodium lamp, polaroid lamps, the portable radio telephone, the coaxial cable, the electric organ, dry ice, frozen foods, synthetic vitamins A, B, and K, anticoagulant drugs (Heparin), sulfa drugs, typhus vaccine, commercial dessuated blood plasma, the artificial lung, insulin shock treatment, the electroencephalogram, the astronomical Red Shift, the electron microscope, Deuterium, and the atom smasher. D. Wecter, *The Age of the Great Depression* 279-90 (1948). Most of these items produced their own consumer demand: like any other narcotic, the ingestion of technology creates an addiction for more. Thus, the mass market for the products of science and industry created by these 1920-1940 products stimulated the even more pervasive contemporary technology of computers, transistors, commercial television, and nuclear energy.

6. Between 1850 and 1900 the population and agricultural productivity of the United States tripled, while industrial output increased 11 times, making this country the greatest manufacturing nation in the world by 1898. H. Faulkner, *The Quest for Social Justice* 28 (1971). By 1929, technical and industrial productivity had far outstripped the

modern law nor modern science can cope with this flood of technology.[7] Lawyers engaged in the evolving field of high

---

purchasing power of the consumer; the resulting disparity was one of the major causes of the Great Depression. *Wecter, supra* note 42, at 9. World War II caused the greatest production boom in American history — the 1940 gross national product of one hundred billion dollars actually doubled to over two hundred billion by 1945. *The Great Republic — A History of the American People* 1101, 1103 (Bailyn ed. 1977).

Today, the gross national product exceeds one trillion dollars and, in the wake of this unique productivity, we have drastically reduced our fossil fuel reserves, seriously damaged our environment, and polluted ourselves. For example, in the past 15 years American production of organic solvents increased 700%, while plastic production rose 2,000% and synthetic fiber production rose 4,000%. M. Brown, *Laying Waste: The Poisoning of America By Toxic Chemicals* 225 (1979) [hereinafter cited as *Laying Waste*]. Our overall organic chemical production has increased 10% each year since 1954, and we are now creating and marketing over 1,000% new chemicals every year. *Id.* at 293. As a byproduct of this productivity, however, our production of toxic wastes has increased from 10 million tons in 1970 to 35 million tons in 1979, and production of 400 million tons in 1984. We have no effective procedure to dispose of these wastes. *Id.* at 293-94.

7. Some 57 million tons of hazardous industrial waste are produced annually. More than 90% of that waste is disposed of improperly. *See* S. Rep. No. 848, 96th Cong., 2d Sess. 3 (1980) (citing Environmental Protection Agency estimate). A critic of public and private handling of toxic chemicals reports a chilling governmental study conducted on behalf of the State of New York. The study sought to determine the cost of toxic waste pollution by putting a monetary value on human life. *Laying Waste, supra* note 412, at 324-27. The researchers "took into consideration such factors as an individual's income, his productivity, and what it would cost to treat his ailment in order to determine whether the state's monies would be wisely invested in reducing the possibility of cancer." *Id.* at 325. The report noted that "it was unlikely that one or two dozen extra deaths from toxic exposure in the entire state would cause public concern." *Id.*

On September 11, 1980, the Surgeon General of the United States reported that industrial pollution and dumping has now reached such proportions that "virtually the entire population of the nation, and indeed the world, carries some burden of one or several . . . [toxic chemicals]." *Time,* Sept. 22, 1980, at 58.

technology litigation, including transportation facility negligence litigation, will be increasingly called upon to fit new facts into the patterns of old law, or to accomplish the even more difficult task of persuading courts and legislatures to create new legal patterns.[8]

The flood of new technology, including highway engineering and safety technology, is only part of the problem. Another major factor generating the "boom market" in high technology litigation involves consideration of the

8. Increasing complexity in technology and social organization has always produced a corresponding increase in the complexity of laws and litigation because "[t]here . . . can be no law before a condition arises to which it can be applied. A rule of law . . . cannot exist where the relations on which it is founded do not exist." J. Zane, *The Story of Law* 48-49 (1927). Thus, the creation of mass production facilities and the interstate railroad network after the Civil War destroyed the ability of the individual states to exercise meaningful legal control over these technologies, as evidenced in Wabash, St. Louis & Pac. Ry. v. Illinois, 118 U.S. 557, 7 S.Ct. 4, 30 L.Ed. 244 (1886). These developments forced the federal government to create legal machinery to meet the new problems through the Interstate Commerce Commission Act of Feb. 4, 1887, ch. 104, 24 Stat. 379; the Sherman Act of July 2, 1890, ch. 647, § 1, 26 Stat. 209; the Federal Food & Drug Act of June 30, 1906, 21 U.S.C. §§ 1-15 (1934); and the myriad other governmental regulations which, at least in the aggregate, many people complain of today. *See* L. Friedman, *A History of American Law* 384-409 (1973). Consequently, "it was of no use to talk of 'state rights' when the economy was ignoring state boundaries and could be regulated only by some central authority." W. Durant & A. Durant, *The Lessons of History* 68 (1968) [hereinafter cited as *Durant*].

Furthermore, a condition must be known before it can be the subject of legislation and jurisprudence. Thus, the five corporations that virtually control the international grain trade and all of its attendant technology from farm to final market have largely escaped regulation because they keep a low profile and few lawmakers or potential litigants know of their existence. Two of these corporations, Cargill Inc. and Continental Grain Co., are the two largest privately held corporations in the United States. Cargill has annual sales exceeding those of Sears, Roebuck & Co. C. Morgan, *Merchants of Grain,* 28-30 (1980).

legal institutions receiving this technological inundation. The somewhat surprising fact is that most of the legal concepts central to life in the United States today originated before the development of the Industrial Revolution, in earlier times unaware of the corrosive changes modern technology would cause.[9]

§ 12-3(A). Effect of Technology on the Right to Trial by Jury.

The right to trial by a jury of laymen, for instance, originated with the early Hebrews,[10] Romans,[11] Germans,[12] Scandinavians,[13] and Greeks.[14] The American colonists valued this right so highly that one of the primary popular grievances against England at the time our incipient and pre-industrial[15] nation revolted from England was the

9. "Many of the formative conditions [of American democracy] have disappeared . . . [t]hrough the impersonal fatality of economic development. . . . Every advance in the complexity of the economy puts an added premium upon superior ability, and intensified the concentration of wealth, responsibility, and political power." *Durant, supra* note 4, at 77.

10. *Exodus* 22:10, 22:11.

11. I.F. Busch, *Law and Tactics in Jury Trials,* note 18, at p. 1.

12. W. Forsyth, *History of Trial by Jury,* at ch. III (1875).

13. *Id.*

14. 2 P. Vinogradoff, *Outlines of Historical Jurisprudence* 77 (1920); W. Fowler, *The City State of the Greeks and Romans* 136 (1895).

15. The present supermechanized economy of the United States, with an annual gross national product exceeding a trillion dollars, is governed at least in theory through the legal framework of a Constitution produced by a society in which only 1/20 of the population lived in urban or semiurban communities. E. Green, *The Revolutionary Generation* 2 (1943). Only seven business corporations had been chartered in the United States before 1781, and only three banks were incorporated before 1789. *Id.* at 355. Thomas Jefferson expressed the widespread distrust of industry: "[A]rtificers [are] the instruments by which the liberties of a country are generally overturned." *Id.* at 356-57. There was

English restriction on the colonial right to jury trials.[16] One of the "repeated injuries and usurpations of the English King" cited in the Declaration of Independence was that George III "deprived us in many cases of the benefit of trial by jury."[17] By 1776, "the jury system was an established colonial institution in both civil and criminal cases, and was esteemed a valuable right."[18]

After the Revolution, one of the strongest popular arguments against the Articles of Confederation and in favor of the proposed Constitution was the need for a national government strong enough to prohibit the states from abolishing or abridging civil trial by jury.[19] The fact that the Constitution itself failed to recognize the right to civil jury trial in the proposed federal court system[20] raised objections to the Constitution itself which were "pressed with an urgency and zeal which were well nigh preventing its ratification."[21]

---

no large scale industrial production at all in 1787. R. Brown, *Charles Beard & The Constitution — A Critical Analysis of an Economic Interpretation of the Constitution* 53 (1956) [hereinafter cited as *Brown*]. There was no industrial working class. Almost everyone owned property; over 90% of the nation's wealth was in real estate. *Id.* at 49-50.

16. Parklane Hosiery Co. v. Shore, 439 U.S. 322, 340 (1979).

17. I.F. Busch, *Law and Tactics in Jury Trials,* note 18 at p. 14 (1959).

18. *Id.*

19. Both the First Continental Congress in the 1774 Declaration of Rights, 1 J. of Cong. 28, and the Judiciary Act of 1789, 1 Stat. 73, 77, attempted to establish the right to civil jury trial in federal courts. Before the adoption of the Constitution, the legislatures of at least five states had attempted to abolish or substantially abridge the right to a jury trial supposedly established in their own state constitutions. The Constitutional Convention of 1787 specially considered, and condemned, all five of these attempts. C. Warren, *Congress, The Constitution and the Supreme Court* 43-44 (1925); Busch, *supra* note 18, at 15.

20. The original draft of the Constitution protected only the right to jury trial in "all crimes except in cases in impeachment." Busch, *supra* note 18, at 15-16.

21. 2 J. Story, *Commentaries on the Constitution* § 1757 (1970). *See*

To meet these objections, which endangered the entire Constitution, the seventh amendment was drafted to "[c]onstitutionally preserve the right of trial by jury as it existed under the English common law when the Amendment was adopted."[22]

Simply put, then, the right to trial by jury is one of the basic legal structures underlying our democracy. The reasons for this were noted as long ago as 1835 by Alexis de Tocqueville, the noted French observer of the United States as it entered the industrial era:

> (t)he institution of the jury may be aristocratic or democratic, according to the class from which the jurors are taken; but it always preserves its republican character, in that it places the real direction of society in the hands of the governed . . . and not in that of the government.[23]

The increasing complexity of technology and high technology litigation has, however, undermined this hallowed bulwark of the Republic by generating a legal dispute concerning the right of a federal trial court to limit the right to a trial by jury in an otherwise appropriate civil case because the issues involved are assumed to be too technical and complex for the common citizen to compre-

---

also The Federalist, No. 83, at 146 (1901), in which Alexander Hamilton, who may have been the most elitist founding father, anticipated Chief Justice Burger as follows:

> The circumstances that constitute cases proper for courts of equity are in many instances so nice and intricate, that they are incompatible with the genius of trials by jury. They require often such long, deliberate, and critical investigation as would be impracticable to men called from their occupations, and obliged to decide before they were permitted to return to them.

22. Baltimore & C. Line v. Redman, 295 U.S. 654, 657 (1935); Parsons v. Bedford, 28 U.S. (3 Pet.) 433, 436-48 (1830).

23. 1 Alexis de Tocqueville, *Democracy in America* 282 (1972).

hend. The controversy reached major proportions in *Ross v. Bernhard,*[24] where the United States Supreme Court, reacting to the increasing complexity of litigation, suggested that the "legal" nature of an issue, upon which the right to a jury trial traditionally depended,[25] should be

24. 396 U.S. 531 (1970).

25. The jury trial was a creature of law and unknown to the courts of chancery, which is the reason that equity does not presently provide for jury trials on matters within its jurisdiction. It should be noted that, although the major thrust of English and American history has been to enhance the scope and stature of jury trials, there also has been a consistent countervailing effort to preclude jury review of matters considered too complex for laymen. Thus, Blackstone endorsed the use of special juries in cases "of too great nicety for the discussion of ordinary freeholders." 3 W. Blackstone, Commentaries 357. In 1603, English law recognized at least some instances in which judges were "better able to judge [account books] than a jury of ploughmen." Clench v. Tomley, 21 Eng. Rep. 13 (1603). Complexity of issues was also recognized as a basis for consigning a case to equity rather than law in O'Connor v. Spaight, 1 Schoale & Lefroy's Reports 305, 309 (1804) (decided by the Lord Chancellor of Ireland). English Chancellors had occasionally claimed a limited right to "interfere" in legal actions where the remedy of law had become "difficult." See Benson v. Baldwin, 26 Eng. Rep. 377 (1739). Certain relatively obscure American cases had concurred, citing the "complexity of accounts" as grounds for equitable jurisdiction. *See, e.g.,* Kirby v. Lake Shore & Mich. S.R.R., 120 U.S. 130, 134, 76 S.Ct. 430, 30 L.Ed. 569 (1887) (complicated nature of accounts sufficient to justify intervention of equity); Fowle v. Lawrason's Ex'r, 30 U.S. (5 Pet.) 494, 503 (1831) (great complexity ought to exist in the accounts). *See also* Bernstein v. Universal Pictures, Inc., 79 F.R.D. 59, 70 (S.D.N.Y. 1978) (complexity of issues beyond abilities of jury); In re Boise Cascade Sec. Litig., 420 F. Supp. 99, 103 (W.D. Wash. 1976) (complex accounting issues beyond abilities of jury). The major current of jurisprudence has, however, traditionally rejected "mere complication of facts" as a basis for equitable jurisdiction. Curriden v. Middleton, 232 U.S. 633, 636, 34 S.Ct. 458, 58 L.Ed. 765 (1914). *See also* Beacon Theatres, Inc. v. Westover, 359 U.S. 500 (1959) (only under the most "imperative circumstances" can the right to a jury trial of legal issues be lost through a prior judicial determination of equitable issues in the same

determined by, among other things, "the practical abilities and limitations of juries."[26] Subsequently, the Ninth Circuit declined to apply this standard, refusing "to read a complexity exception into the Seventh Amendment."[27] The Third Circuit, on the other hand, has held that requiring jurors to decide issues too complex for their understanding would itself violate due process rights.[28]

In a 1979 address to the state chief justices, Chief Justice Burger fanned the dispute by saying that there should be a complete reexamination of the validity of jury trials in complex cases.[29] Theodore I. Koskoff, President of the Association of Trial Lawyers of America, responded that the Chief Justice has "a patronizing attitude demonstrat-

---

case); United States v. Bitter Root Dev. Co., 200 U.S. 451, 6 S.Ct. 318, 50 L.Ed. 550 (1906) (action for unliquidated damages does not necessarily confer equity jurisdiction).

26. Ross v. Bernhard, 396 U.S. 531, 538 n. 10 (1970).

27. In re United States Fin. Sec. Litig., 609 F.2d 411, 431 (9th Cir. 1979).

28. In re Japanese Elec. Prods. Antitrust Litig., 631 F.2d 1069, 1084 (3d Cir. 1980). The court commented as follows on both the revolutionary content of footnote 10 in Ross v. Bernhard, and the propriety of using footnotes to enunciate major changes in the law:

> [The footnote] plainly recognizes the significance . . . of the possibility that a suit may be too complex for a jury. . . . [It] strongly suggests that jury trial might not be guaranteed in extraordinarily complex cases. . . . We . . . find it unlikely that the Supreme Court would have announced an important new application of the seventh amendment in so cursory a fashion. Yet, at the very least, the Court has left open the possibility that the "practical abilities and limitations of juries" may limit the range of suits subject to the seventh amendment decisions as not precluding such a ruling.

Id. at 1079-80. *Cf.* United States v. Hunt, 265 F. Supp. 178 (W.D. Tex. 1967) (illustrating selection of jury in criminal context — violation of due process to allow defendant to be deprived of life, liberty or property by jurors who did not understand and comprehend evidence).

29. 48 U.S.L.W. 2118-19 (Aug. 14, 1979).

ing little faith in the jury system and not borne out by those who are experienced in the trial of complicated cases."[30]

In a second level of attack on jury trials in federal civil cases, the Judicial Conference of the United States, presided by Chief Justice Burger, is studying curtailment or elimination of jury trials in complex cases by court rule.[31] While these federal proceedings would not be directly binding on state courts,[32] there clearly would be great pressure on state courts to follow if the Supreme Court subjects all federal courts to jury trial limitations. The fourteenth amendment does not require the states to provide civil jury trials in all cases.[33] Thus, each state has the legal right to modify or limit civil jury trials.[34] However, each state constitution now protects jury trials through provisions similar to the seventh amendment. State courts customarily follow Supreme Court interpreta-

---

30. Speech before the Sixth Circuit Meeting of the American Trial Lawyers' Assoc., reported at 48 U.S.L.W. 2218 (Sept. 25, 1979).

31. 66 A.B.A.J. 953-54 (1980).

32. The seventh amendment jury trial requirement applies only to federal courts and is not made applicable to the states via the fourteenth amendment. Fay v. New York, 332 U.S. 261 (1947). The seventh amendment, however, will apply to the enforcement in state courts of rights created by federal statute. Dice v. Akron, C. & Y.R.R., 342 U.S. 359 (1952); Bailey v. Central Vt. Ry., 319 U.S. 350 (1943).

33. New York Cent. R.R. v. White, 243 U.S. 188, 37 S.Ct. 247, 61 L.Ed. 667 (1917) (state's denial of jury trial not violative of due process clause of fourteenth amendment); Walker v. Sauvinet, 92 U.S. 90 (1875) (trial by jury in state court civil proceeding not a privilege or immunity of federal citizenship which states are forbidden to abridge). *Cf.* Snyder v. Massachusetts, 291 U.S. 97 (1934) (illustrating rule in criminal context).

34. Iowa Cent. Ry. v. Iowa, 160 U.S. 389, 16 S.Ct. 344, 40 L.Ed. 467 (1896) (fourteenth amendment does not control power of state to determine process of asserting legal rights or enforcing legal obligations, so long as methods adopted afford due process). *Cf.* Palko v. Connecticut, 302 U.S. 319 (1937) (illustrating rule in criminal context).

tion of federal constitutional provisions that are analogous to state constitutional provisions.[35] Therefore, if the Supreme Court creates a complexity exception to the seventh amendment, state courts are likely to do the same with similar state constitutional provisions.

§ 12-3(B). Effect of Technology on the Free Market Theory of Economic Competition.

The basic economic concepts of free market competition between large numbers of small productive units underlying the economic regulation and anti-trust laws of the United States since its inception predate, and have been largely outmoded by, the Industrial Revolution and its resultant technology. These concepts stem from such works as *The Wealth of Nations,* published by Adam Smith in 1776, or the writings of David Ricardo, such as *The Principles of Political Economy,* dating from the late eighteenth century. When these books were written, modern technology did not exist, but they continue to dictate the economic structure of American law, which is biased in favor of free competition and against the concentration of productive units that every industrialized state has followed in order to achieve economies of scale (which means one big factory can usually produce 1,000 widgets more cheaply than the total cost for 10 smaller factories to produce 100 widgets apiece during the same time span).[36]

---

35. *See, e.g.,* People v. Jackson, 22 Ill. 2d 382, 176 N.E.2d 803 (1961) (Illinois Supreme Court will follow decisions of United States Supreme Court on identical state and federal constitutional problems). *See generally* I.F. Busch, *Law and Tactics in Jury Trials* § 21 (1959) [hereinafter cited as *Busch*].

36. "The heart of our national economic policy long has been faith in the value of competition." Standard Oil Co. v. Federal Trade Comm'n, 340 U.S. 231, 248 (1951), quoted in National Soc'y of Professional Eng'rs v. United States, 435 U.S. 679, 695 (1978). "The basic purpose [of the Sherman Act in 1890 and the Clayton Act in 1914] . . . was to prevent

The virtually unlimited productive capacities of industrial technology struck these economic and legal theories with the devastating impact of a nuclear weapon. Revolutionary increases in production after the Civil War produced tremendous displacement of labor, which in turn caused periodic unemployment. The new volume of goods and services also caused a fall in prices that ruined many businesses. To deal with the industrial instability and murderous competition created by the new production capacities of industry, corporations began forming pooling agreements and holding companies dedicated to the proposition that combination and control of competition were necessary and inevitable steps in industrial evolution. Ida Tarbell, a historian of the Standard Oil Company, described this process:

> Through the use of machinery the manufacturer had learned how to double, treble or even more greatly multiply his output. He had been taking full advantage of every new labor saving device with little or no regard to its effect on either markets or labor. . . . A fifty percent displacement of labor was not unusual. Production outstripped consumption alarmingly in some instances. . . . Under the pressure of a wanton production the weaker producer went to the wall, thus still further curtailing purchasing power.

---

economic concentration in the American economy by keeping a large number of small competitors in business." United States v. Von's Grocery Co., 384 U.S. 270, 275 (1966). A state court decision around the turn of the last century gave a somewhat more detailed explanation of this rationale as the reason for dissolving the local appendages of the Standard Oil Company:

> A society in which a few men are the employers and a great body are merely employees or servants is not the most desirable in a republic; and it should be as much the policy of the laws to multiply the number engaged in independent pursuits, or in the profits of production, as to cheapen the price to the consumer. Tarbell & Repley, ed. *Trusts, Pools and Corporations,* 249. *See also* State v. Nebraska Distilling Co., 29 Neb. 700 (1890).

> Overproduction sooner or later forced prices too low for profits, causing bankruptcy of the weak, temporary losses for the strong, short or long periods of unemployment and general business instability. In every considerable industry attempts were made to correct this instability.[37]

The actual development of industrial economics based on modern technology, then, has produced an anti-competitive concentration of productive units totally contrary to the underlying economic and legal concepts of this country. John Kenneth Galbraith noted how technology forced concentration of productivity to gain economics of scale, thereby producing corporate[38] producers large enough to dictate terms to our supposedly free market economy:

> It is held that nothing must interfere with the independent operation of the market mechanism to which the corporation is subject. The reality in the case of the mature corporation . . . is that prices are substantially controlled by the firm and it goes on to exercise influence on the amounts that are purchased and sold at these prices. The imperatives of technology

---

37. Ida Tarbell, *The Nationalizing of Business,* 68-69, 88 (1971 ed.).

38. Corporations, as a legal personality, were recognized as early as the Code of Hammurabi and existed in Ancient Rome (the Roman Republic was a corporation), feudal Europe, and 14th century England. H. Henn, *Handbook of the Law of Corporations,* at 10-12 (1961). It was only after the Industrial Revolution created modern technology and, in America, entrusted this technology to corporations, that the modern corporate concentration discussed here began.

> "Industrialization," a scholar of the period noted, "was accompanied by a pronounced movement toward concentration of ownership." Faulkner, *The Quest for Social Justice* 28 [1971 ed.]. By 1914, corporations with annual cash flow exceeding $100,000 were only 1/8 the total of all corporations, but they employed 3/4 of all wage earners and produced 4/5 of the nation's products. Moreover, even by this relatively early date, nearly 1/2 of the nation's products were being produced by the 1.4% of corporations with an annual output exceeding one million dollars. *Id.* at 29.

> and capital use do not allow the corporation to be subordinate to the market.[39]

This increasing concentration of the national productive capacity thrust by modern technology into a rapidly decreasing number of rapidly swelling corporations carries ominous implications for many aspects of our national legal and political affairs. In 1961, the upper 0.2 percent of American corporations owned 65 percent of all corporate assets (including research and production facilities). By 1968 the 500 largest corporations (out of a total of 4,797,000 corporations) were generating 42 percent of the entire gross national product.[40] By 1970, the 200 largest corporations owned two-thirds of American manufacturing assets.[41]

Concentration at this rate of the ability to generate (and thereby to control at the source) the flood of new technology into the hands of a shrinking number of profit oriented

---

39. J. Galbraith, *The New Industrial State* 170 (1967). The increased cost efficiency of larger, more competitive productive units has been well documented. *See* Peltzman, "The Gains and Losses From Industrial Concentration," 22 *Journal of Law & Economics* 97; Bond & Greenberg, "Industry Structure, Market Rivalry, and Public Policy," 19 *Journal of Law & Economics* 201 (April, 1976). The Presidential Task Force on Anti-Trust Policy acknowledges this corporate concentration, and its anti-competitive market power:

> It is the persistence of high profits over extended time periods and over whole industries rather than in individual firms that suggests artificial restraints on output and the absence of fully effective competition. The correlation of evidence of this kind with the existence of very high levels of concentration appears to be significant. (U.S. President's Task Force on Antitrust Policy (1969) (Reprinted in 115 Cong. Rec. § 13890, § 13892 (5/27/69).)

40. F. Lundberg, *The Rich and the Super Rich* 249 (1968).

41. T. Christoffel, *Up Against the American Myth* 9-10 (1970). In 1969 the five largest industrial corporations owned 11% of all manufacturing assets, and the 87 corporations with assets over one billion dollars owned 46% of all manufacturing assets. Galbraith, note 39, at 87.

corporations will generate a great deal of complex litigation in the economic and Anti-Trust areas as our legal framework becomes increasingly irrelevant to industrial reality. A noted legal scholar described this technological concentration undermining pre-industrial legal and economic theory as follows: "Antitrust, indeed, is founded on a populist tradition, quite at odds with the scientific rationality that informs economic theory, [and] on a nostalgia for that mythical past when social, governmental and economic organization was simpler, more comprehensible."[42]

---

42. Sullivan, *Handbook of the Law of Antitrust* 11 (1977). This work also points out how the characteristic American form of industrial concentration, oligopoly, operates in a monopolistic fashion and contrary to free market forces.

> Firms in an oliogopolistic industry will recognize that it would be in their interests to make price and output decisions concertedly, thereby achieving jointly a control over price and output similar to that which a monopolist exercises; they are not likely to see the problems of coordination as being unmanageable.
>
> If they do engage in such concerted conduct by joining together (in what is usually termed a "cartel") to set prices at a level which tends to maximize industry profits and to allocate production on an agreed basis, performance will be more like that in a monopolistic industry than in a competitive one. And if an oligopolistic structure is tight enough, something similar to concerted conduct to fix price and to divide output may occur, as Harvard school theory supposes, even without any agreement, express or implied.
>
> Suppose, for example, there were only three firms in an industry, one with half of the market, the others with one-fourth each. Suppose that in such an industry prices were at a competitive level and that there then occurred a change in demand and supply conditions of a kind which in a competitive market would have prompted a price reduction. Each firm would be aware that if it reduced price toward the new competitive level, the other firms would do the same; the result of any reduction would be to share the business in the same proportion but at a lower return for each. On these assumptions the three firms may each forebear to reduce prices. Thus, prices may settle at a level which under comparable conditions would be established by a monopolist. Consequently, the industry profits which the firms share will be maximized. If so, noncollusive but interdependent market responses will have resulted in prices and profits which are higher and output which is lower than under competition —just as in the case of a monopoly or

This divorce between economic reality and the law will also produce high technology litigation in the areas, at least, of personal injury and public welfare. These developments are perhaps inevitable consequences of allocating such massive productive capacity to entities legally required to operate primarily from a profit motive.[43] There is substantial evidence that profit oriented corporate behavior has often exacerbated the problems of controlling technology. Thus, in response to the Resource Conservation and Recovery Act of 1976, which sets 1981 as the target year to eliminate illegal dumping of toxic substances, many corporations massively increased the amount of toxic dumping to beat the deadline.[44] The oil

---

of a cartel. Concentrated structure, by stimulating interdependent market conduct, will have resulted in poor market performance.

Theoretical studies suggest that this often occurs, that many oligopolistic markets tend to perform more like monopolies than like competitive markets, that firms do work out some kind of a mechanism (leave for the moment whether it is cartelization or something else) but pricing in ways which maximize not individual returns, but returns to the industry. *Id.* at 26-27; 338.

For additional documentation on the monopolistic behavior of technologically concentrated oligopolies, *see e.g.,* K. Boulding, Economic Analysis 582ff (1948); Stigler, "A Theory of Oligopoly," 72 J. Pol. Econ. 44 (1964); Markham, "The Nature and Significance of Price Leadership," 41 Am. Econ. Rev. 891 (1951); Stigler, "The Kinky Oligopoly Demand Curve and Rigid Prices," 55 J. Pol. Econ. (1949). A. Phillips, *Market Structure, Organization and Performance,* chs. 2 & 3 (1962); K. Boulding, *A Reconstruction of Economics* (1950); W. Baumol, *Business Behavior, Value and Growth* (1959).

For general discussion, *see* J. Bain, *Industrial Organization* 112-23, 273-87, 315-20 (1959); F. Schere, *Industrial Market Structure and Economic Performance* (1970).

43. The officers and directors and employees of a noncharitable corporation are generally mandated by law to maximize the profit of the corporation and usually bear a fiduciary duty to refrain from actions that would impair that profit. H.G. Henn, *Handbook of the Law of Corporations* 17 (1961).

44. *Laying Waste, supra* note 6 at 312.

companies did not voluntarily put their tremendous revenues from the sale of high-priced gasoline into efforts to expand American energy resources. In the words of a president of Standard Oil of Indiana, this policy was justified because oil companies "are not in the energy business. [They] are in the business of trying to use the assets entrusted to [them] by [their] shareholders to give them the best return on the money they've invested in the company."[45] A large auto company marketed a new vehicle with a rear fuel tank that could burst into flames on impact and, in efforts to maximize profits, sold 1,513,339 such vehicles with knowledge of this danger from crash tests conducted before the car went on the market.[46]

Clearly, technology is restructuring or evading our economic and legal institutions to satisfy its own imperatives. High technology litigation will be on the cutting edge of these changes for years to come.

§ 12-3(C). Effect of Technology on Negligence Law.

As noted earlier, industrial technology restructured the law of personal fault to allow industrial development. Before the industrial revolution, negligence as a distinct cause of action for individual injury and damage really did not exist, and such matters were generally treated under the strict liability formula that concentrated on the plaintiff's injuries rather than the defendant's fault. The negligence cause of action, premised on the defendant's fault, emerged around 1825.[47]

It was not by chance that this development (of the negligence theory) coincided with the industrial revolution. It was but another manifestation of the individualism

45. B. Commoner, *The Politics of Energy* 72 (1979).

46. L. Strobel, *Reckless Homicide* 80-89 (1980).

47. 2 F. Harper & F. James, *The Law of Torts* 122 (1956); W. Prosser, *The Law of Torts* 139-40 (4th ed. 1971).

which underlies laissez-faire as a political philosophy. . . . A fleet of trucks cannot be operated, a railroad run, or a skyscraper built without the certainty that the enterprise will take some toll in human life and limb. It is the very gist of the fault principle to privilege the entrepreneur to take this toll, so long as the activity is lawful and carried on with reasonable care.[48]

§ 12-3(D). Effect of Technology on Popular Elections.

Perhaps free men have clung so tenaciously to the right to trial by jury (see § 12-2(A)) because it represents, in microcosm, the same democratic control of issues and events by the lay citizen, through his vote, that is enacted on a larger stage in a popular election for public office. Certainly, the essential similarities between the citizen's "vote" on a jury and in an election are striking. This being said, however, it must be added that if increasing technical complexity can prevent a juror from understanding the essential facts and issues in a trial, the same complexity may reduce the right to elect political representatives to a popularity contest.

This fear of rule by ignorant rabble was what gave democracy a bad name between the demise of the Roman Republic (when citizens turned in disgust from the anarchy and civil wars of the Republican era and supported Augustus in establishing the Empire),[49] and the emergence

---

48. Harper & James, *supra,* at 752. *See also* Winfield, "The History of Negligence in the Law of Torts," 42 L. Q. Rev. 184, 195 (1926).

49. Will Durant notes the demise of meaningful elections in Rome after decades of anarchy and war had turned the electorate into ignorant rabble unable to decide their own affairs:

> The people of Rome seem to have thought for a while that the "restoration" was real, and that they were receiving back the Republic in return for an adjective. Did not the Senate and the assemblies still make the laws, still elect the magistrates? It was so;

of the mass electorate in Western Society after the Industrial Revolution.[50] The danger signals of a return to this degraded state of affairs can be seen in the televised debates between candidates, which often become no more than a contest between two equally incomprehensible streams of numbing statistics. If the issues are really as complex as these debates often suggest, the lay voter, just like the lay juror sitting on a high technology lawsuit, may well have his vote reduced to an exercise in ignorance or irrelevance.[51]

> Augustus or his agents merely "proposed" the laws and "nominated" the more important candidates. As imperator and consul he ruled the army and the Treasury and administered the laws; and by his tribunician privileges he controlled all other activities of the government. His powers were not much greater than those of Pericles or Pompey, or any energetic American president; the difference lay in their permanence. In 23 he resigned the consulate, but received from the Senate a "proconsular authority" that gave him control of all officials in all provinces. Again no one objected; on the contrary, when a scarcity of grain threatened, the people besieged the Senate with demands that Augustus be made dictator. They had fared so ill under the Senatorial oligarchy that they were inclined toward a dictatorship, which would presumably cultivate their favor as a foil to the power of wealth. Augustus refused; but he took charge of the annona, or food supply, quickly ended the shortage, and earned such gratitude that Rome looked on with complacency as he remolded its institutions in his image. Will Durant, *Caesar and Christ* 214 (1944).

50. Beginning in England around 1830 and thereafter sweeping over most of western Europe during the ensuing fifty years, ruling aristocracies were defeated and supplanted by bourgeois power that created modern industry, giving an economic function and subsequent political power, to the working classes. E.J. Hobsbawm, *The Age of Revolution 1789-1848,* at 137-62 (1962).

51. Jack Germond and Jules Witcover documented how technology has made presidential elections increasingly irrelevant to the real issues between the candidates:

> But the most important change over those two decades since 1960 was that television had assumed a dominant, central position in the very life of the country. Along with such innovations as fast-food restaurants, the national networks had become a homogenizing force in American society. Whether voters lived in Sarasota or

§ 12-4. The Nontechnical Persuasive Option.

Attorneys litigating, and therefore communicating, in high technology fields must have some understanding of how people, past and present, have felt about technology in order to structure their evidence and arguments in the most persuasive possible form.

§ 12-4(A). People are Afraid of Technology.

There is, obviously, no secret about the corrosive nature of technology discussed in earlier sections. Technology is strong stuff and people are afraid of it. Technology eats through the laws and social institutions like an acid, and there is a general popular perception that, in many areas, it is out of control. The near nuclear disaster of Three Mile Island, the chemical disaster of Love Canal, the acid rain killing all life forms in many lakes and forests of New England, the gassing and mass death in Bhopal, India, all these are only relatively recent examples of technology run amok. Going back a few decades, DDT insecticide was used widely on all types of food items until, in 1951, it was learned that the substance could enter the fatty tissues of warm blooded animals and cause various diseases, includ-

Butte, in Bangor or San Diego, they were all fed the staples of their diet of political news from the same sources — Walter Cronkite and John Chancellor and Frank Reynolds. Newspapers might provide greater detail and more analysis and commentary, but the raw material for most Americans was what they heard and saw on the evening news broadcasts.

Thus the aim of the new political technology was to control the images on those millions of television screens every night — to present the candidates not necessarily as they really were but as they would prefer to be seen. Advertising was tailored to touch the popular nerves the pollsters had identified. And in exploiting what the politicians called "the free media" — meaning television news coverage — the imperative was to create, each day of the campaign, a "visual" that would express the things that concerned most voters. Jack Germond & Jules Witcover, *Blue Smoke and Mirrors,* at XV (1981).

ing rickets. Going back even further, the new iron plows and oxen yokes that allowed feudal Europe to open forest and waste land to agriculture also produced unexpected and severe deforestation, floods, and erosion.[52] In truth, it can safely be said, based upon thousands of years of experience, that it is impossible to foresee all the consequences of a technical action, and every technical advance brings negative reverse side effects. Rene DuBois, the noted French student of technology, has said of this contemporary reaction to technology:

> Technology now evolves as if it had escaped from human control and acquired a life of its own. It has emerged as a highly integrated social structure involving scientific, managerial, economic, and political forces interrelated in such a complex manner that men are no longer able to understand it or give it direction. . . . A new form of panic is being generated among the general public by the thought that the human mind cannot possibly apprehend the complexity of the interrelationships between the social structure and scientific technology.[53]

Simply put, the genie is out of the bottle, and everybody is afraid of it because we don't know what it is doing and we can't put it back in.

§ 12-4(B). People Have Always Been Afraid of Technology.

One must always be careful in drawing comparisons between different societies in different eras, but an attorney seeking to evaluate how his prospective jurors today will react to complex evidence in a high technology case should be aware of the fact that people in most major earlier human societies have feared and disliked technol-

52. J. de Castro, *The Geography of Hunger.*

53. R. DuBois, *A God Within* 204-05, 208 (1972).

ogy at least as much, if not more, than people do today in our society. This knowledge is relevant because the attitude toward technology may constitute one of those constant human threads (like the desire to enjoy eating, dressing, and having babies) uniting people in all societies. Certainly, in order to dismiss the attitudes of these other societies to technology as irrelevant, one would have to conclude it was a mere coincidence that all of these earlier peoples agreed with each other, and with people today, on that issue. No basis, to my knowledge, exists for such a rash conclusion.

§ 12-4(B)(1). Ancient Egypt.

Ancient Egypt developed technology to solve the specific problems of harnessing the Nile River: how to channel the floods between June and October; how to preserve the flood run-offs during the dry season after October; how to prevent the desert ("Red Land") from taking over the fertile land ("Black Land"), and how to develop the necessary language and mathematical skills to do these things on a repeated basis.[54] All of the skills and technologies necessary to do these things were developed by 3,000 B.C., before the Age of the Pyramids, after which society stagnated without further technological progress[55] for over 4,000 years.[56] Indeed, most of the technological progress took place in this society before the age of the Pharaohs, when the more technically advanced South conquered the less technically advanced North and unified the state.[57] The power elite of the emergent state[58] avoided further

54. J.E. White, *Ancient Egypt* 2-4 (1970).

55. *Id.* at 144-45.

56. Arnold Toynbee, *A Study of History* 30 (1947).

57. M. Hoffman, *Egypt Before the Pharaohs* 211-12 (1979).

58. *Id.* at 259.

technological progress for the remaining three-quarters of this society's existence in order to avoid change.[59] Egypt let the genie do what had to be done, and put it back in the bottle.

§ 12-4(B)(2). Ancient Greece and Rome.

J. G. Landels, a student of ancient engineering, noted a fact about the ancient Greek attitude toward change that was directly in line with the attitudes of ancient Egypt:

> It is possible to see, in almost every branch of Greek literature, a particular trait of the Greek mind which had important effects in scientific thought. It was a liking for stability, rest and permanence, and a corresponding dislike, almost a mistrust, of change, movement and what they called *genesis* and *phthora,* "coming to be" and "passing away."[60]

Because of this desire to avoid change, the Romans and Greeks kept their science an abstract philosophy, rejecting wherever possible practical inventions that would alter existing conditions.[61] The aim of classic science was to know, not to do.[62] This popular fear of change, and practical technology that would cause it, prevented the classic world from such simple technical "advances" as converting the existing complex weather vanes into windmills,[63] and even the water mill, the greatest source of concentrated energy in that society, was resisted and rejected as a "newfangled contraption" by the general population for six hundred years.[64] Roman inventors devised ox powered mechanical reapers, similar to those used in Europe until the nine-

---

59. *Id.* at 304, 319.

60. J.G. Landels, *Engineering in the Ancient World* 186 (1978).

61. *Id.* at 186-87.

62. M.I. Finley, *Economy and Society in Ancient Greece* 180 (1981).

63. *Id.* at 183.

64. *Id.* at 183-84.

teenth century, but these devices were totally rejected and ignored.[65]

The perfect symbol for Classic society, and what it thought about our technical genie, is Archimedes, who destroyed each of his inventions after they had demonstrated the theory he was attempting to establish, in order to ensure that nothing would thereafter exist to cause unwanted change.

§ 12-4(B)(3). Ancient China.

Ancient China went through periods when technology and the commercial classes necessary to develop it (as occurred during Europe's Industrial Revolution) were favored by the Emperors.[66] During such eras, China developed the world's most progressive technology. China could cast iron by 513 B.C., a feat Europe could not duplicate until the Middle Ages,[67] and Chinese mills were producing steel by 200 B.C., a product Europe would not be able to match for almost a thousand years.[68] By the first century

---

65. *Id.* at 177.

66. Han Dynasty support of trade and commerce around 200 B.C., for example, stimulated new technology in metals, salt, silks, and lacquers.

> Around 800 A.D., Imperial approval was extended to the merchants and commercial classes under the T'ang Dynasty, and a dramatic upsurge in technology and its necessary financial infrastructure, including the creation of Bills of Exchange and negotiable banknotes, ensued. A similar development occurred around 1520 A.D., when official favor of the Mings shifted from the landed gentry to commerce and industry, stimulating the creation of new technology in cotton mills, iron, steel, silk, cotton, porcelain, and paper. By the end of the 16th century, over 50,000 workers were employed in 30 large paper factories in Kiangse province alone. Jacques Gernet, *A History of Chinese Civilization* 264 (1972).

67. *Id.* at 69.

68. *Id.* at 140.

A.D., Chinese technology had produced the world's first seismograph,[69] the first equatorial circle,[70] and the first true paper,[71] a substance that would not reach Europe until the thirteenth century.[72]

By 1024 A.D., China had developed the financial infrastructure (paper money, loans on security, banking, stock companies, auction sales),[73] that would finance the Industrial Revolution and the birth of modern technology in Europe seven centuries later.

With all these technical advantages, and more, the apparent miracle is that the Industrial Revolution and subsequent world domination did not take place in China. The reasons for this failure are many, but one of the most important is that Chinese society, and the Chinese people, did not trust or desire trade or technology,[74] with the result that technological development ceased when the Emperors stopped pushing for it, and new creations by Chinese inventors were ignored by the Chinese people, even if those inventions were potent enough to revolutionize other societies.

The history of three Chinese inventions clearly demonstrates the popular disdain for revolutionary technology in Chinese society.

Printing with movable type, perhaps the most important of all Chinese inventions, was discovered there in the ninth century, some five hundred years before the concept reached Europe.[75] Chinese society strongly rejected the

---

69. *Id.* at 162. Developed in 132 A.D.

70. *Id.* at 162. Developed in 52 B.C.

71. *Id.* at 288. Developed in 100 A.D.

72. *Id.*

73. *Id.* at 231-32, 265.

74. William McNeill, *The Rise of the West,* 468-69 (1963); Gernet, note 66, at 144; Spengler, *Decline of the West,* Vol. II, at 501 (1980 ed.).

75. F. Braudel, *The Structures of Everyday Life* 399 (1979).

new printing processes, based on wood block type, for centuries,[76] and the invention had made little impact on China when it reached Europe, spread like wildfire[77] and revolutionized every aspect of life.[78]

The second epochal invention, gunpowder, was created in China around 904 A.D., almost four hundred years before it reached Europe.[79] Due to the resistance of Chinese society to the new technology, firearms were not developed to harness the new explosive until the eleventh or twelfth centuries.[80] Overall, this substance, which brought about drastic changes in the military and social balances of Europe,[81] was largely rejected and ignored by its Chinese creators.[82]

The final Chinese inventions, the compass and deep sea navigation and shipbuilding techniques, also preceded

---

76. Gernet, note 66, at 333; McNeill, note 74, at 530-31.

77. "The first European printing press appeared in Paris in 1470. Subsequently, presses were reported in Lyon in 1473, Poitiers in 1479, Naples in 1471, Louvian in 1473, and Cracow in 1474. In 1480, some 110 European towns had presses. By 1500, this number had grown to 236 towns. In 1500, Europe had 70 million people and 20 million printed books. During the 16th century, the European population increased 500%, rising to 100 million, but fell behind the book population, which grew to 200 million." Braudel, note 75, at 399-400.

78. As Eric Hoffer pointed out in *The True Believer,* "the European Church was probably more corrupt in the tenth century than in the time of Luther, but there was no tenth century Reformation because at that time so few people outside the Church could read that there would have been no basis for Luther's demand that laymen be allowed to read and interpret scripture."

79. Gernet, note 66, at 311, reports gunpowder in Europe around 1285 A.D.

80. McNeill, note 74, at 385.

81. "Firearms were rapidly developed by all European states and, wherever adopted, they allowed a peasant with a musket to defeat an aristocrat in armor on a horse, thus destroying the armored knights supporting the feudal system." Gernet, note 66, at 311-12.

82. *Id. See also* McNeill, note 74, at 530-31.

similar developments in Europe. China was able to launch deep oceanic penetrations in the eleventh century,[83] several hundred years before Spain and Portugal began exploring the world for Europe.[84] These Chinese expeditions, launched by the Imperial Government, were carried out by the world's first ships with watertight compartments. The Sung and Ming age deep sea junk was clearly superior to European ships of the age, carrying 12 large sails and over 1,000 men on four decks.[85] These eleventh century Chinese Mayflowers sailed with compasses that Europe would not have for another two centuries[86] to Indochina, Malaya, Java, Sumatra, India, Arabia, and to the horn of Africa.[87]

And then, around 1433 A.D., after several centuries of maritime expansion, with all this technology geared up to conquer the water routes of the world, the Emperors withdrew support from deep sea ventures and the rest of Chinese society ignored them.[88] But for this failure of will, Chinese navigators and ships could easily have sailed westward and met, or beaten, the Spaniards and Portuguese as they sailed east around the Cape of Good Hope or

---

83. Gernet, note 66, at 326.

84. "European trans oceanic expansion began when Portuguese fleets commenced voyages down the West African coast in 1419." G. Scammell, *The World Encompassed,* at 227 (1981).

85. *Id.* at 328, 398.

86. *Id.* at 328.

87. *Id.* at 400-02.

88. Braudel, note 75, at 407.

Cape Agulhas, the southern gateway between the Indian and Atlantic Oceans.[89]

The conclusion from all of this evidence is somewhat humbling for members of western society: China clearly preceded Europe to a technological base from which Industrial Revolutions, worldwide seafaring expansions, and global dominion could have been launched. China failed to develop along these lines, in large part, because every time the Emperors became busy with other things, the people and society rejected and ignored their existing technology.

It is, obviously, highly unlikely that attorneys engaged in modern, technical litigation will be confronted with jurors from Ancient Egypt, the Rome of Caesar, or medieval China. It is, however, equally clear that the people of most of the great technical societies preceding our own had serious reservations about technology that are mirrored in the feelings of many people, and jurors, today (see § 12-4(A)), *supra,* and Dubos, Note 53, at 204-05). This unease and dislike for our machine creations is reflected all around us (for example, Hal, the computer that goes insane in the movie *2001 — A Space Odyssey;* and the admonition Obi-Wan gives Luke Skywalker in *Star Wars* to ignore his computer and robots and "go with the force").

This common thread linking people in all ages against the unlimited adoption of technology that has become a commercial imperative of our age would be difficult to attribute to mere coincidence. Certainly, if a gambler in Las Vegas playing with dice supplied by the house just

89. *Id.* "An example of the potency of Chinese seafaring technology came in 1521 A.D., when Portuguese fleets, equipped with state of the art European vessels and equipment, were defeated by Chinese fleets in an engagement at the mouth of the Pearl River." Scammell, note 84, at 239. A principal reason for European oceanic expansion eclipsing that of China was Chinese rejection of technology at least equal to that of Europe.

happened to roll snake eyes on every first throw, he would be reluctant to accept the "just coincidence" explanation from the croupier. Indeed, the odds are excellent, particularly in light of the psychological research reviewed in the next chapter, that the complexity, upheaval and increasing impersonality generated by technology as it permeates a society offends basic elements in human nature. Attorneys attempting to persuade juries in cases dealing with technology must be aware of this because the medium of all successful communication, however technical the message, must be as simple and nontechnical as possible.

§ 12-4(C). Avoid Technology Wherever Possible in Technical Litigation.

From the preceding analysis of past reactions to technology, and from the psychological research on persuasive techniques discussed here and in the next chapter, the conclusion is surprisingly obvious that attorneys engaged in litigation, however technical, should be as simple, clear, and nontechnical as possible in every facet of the case.

§ 12-4(C)(1). Communicate Simply and Clearly.

Initially, of course, this concept applies to the way facts and arguments are communicated to the jury. It is virtually impossible to persuade jurors (or anyone) to accept something they do not understand, and the probable result of communicating in big words nobody comprehends is that the jury will resent you for doing it. Recent psychological research on the need for clear, persuasive communication of complex technical data to a jury concluded:

> The word is the attorney's paramount tool. But it must be realized that the meaning of words exists in our heads, not in the words themselves. And all communication depends on people's perception of words. Since words play such an important part in the

> juror's understanding, the attorney should logically choose language which carries the most common meaning to all people. So, the wise attorney in addressing the jury should keep his message simple, avoid multisyllable words, avoid vague legal [or technical] jargon, and avoid rambling.[90]

This concept must be followed by the attorney himself and by witnesses as well, particularly the "expert." Technical terms must be defined when used, the verbiage must always be as simple as possible, and the ideas being communicated must be clear to a layman. If these ideas do not get through to the laymen, the point of the entire procedure is lost, and you will sustain a net loss in jury resentment of your failure to give them the communication they expect.

§ 12-4(C)(2). Put Emphasis on the Nontechnical — Occam's Razor.

At the beginning of the fifteenth century, William of Occam laid down a rule of philosophy and logic that goes a long way toward explaining why attorneys faced with technical and nontechnical options (or explanations) should strive to emphasize the latter before the jury. William's rule, known as Occam's Razor, states that whenever there are several possible causes, or explanations, the simplest is usually the most likely. Modern psychology would add that the simplest option is also usually the most persuasive, particularly to laymen.

The application of Occam's Razor to high technology litigation is based on the fact that technology is rarely simple. When an event may have both a technical and a nontechnical explanation, a jury is most likely to under-

90. Professor A.W. Laird, "Persuasion: A Tool of Courtroom Communication," *Psychology: A Quarterly Journal of Human Behavior* Vol. 19 (213), at 51 (1982).

stand, believe, and be comfortable with the option that has as little as possible to do with technology.

My friend Theodore Postel, an excellent Chicago trial attorney, tells of an experience early in his career where this jury tendency to put emphasis on the nontechnical was made very clear. The plaintiff was claiming a work-related injury under a predecessor of the Illinois Workman's Compensation Statute. The specific charge was that a particular poisonous insect had bitten the plaintiff on the defendant employer's premises while he was at work. The defendant countered this evidence with long-winded testimony from an expert on poisonous insects, who contended in great detail and with lots of big words, that insects such as the plaintiff described were normally found only in South America and had never been reported within a thousand miles of Chicago. In rebuttal, the plaintiff put a nine-year-old Chicago bug collector on the stand. The boy claimed to have found a bug identical to the one the plaintiff described in an empty lot around his house. The defendant's case was lost when the boy pulled out a bottle containing the bug at issue.

A useful corollary of this idea is that, wherever possible, technical matters should be demonstrated, and communicated to the jury in nontechnical ways. Whenever I have an engineer describe the engineering defects in a road area or machine, I try to have the witness simultaneously demonstrate his points to the jury on a simple drawing or model. Medical experts discussing anatomy and psychology should be similarly equipped with something nontechnical, or at least nonverbal, that the jury can look at while the witness is talking. There are really two reasons for this. In the first place, pictures are easier for most people to understand than words (which is why one of the former is usually worth a thousand of the latter). Beyond this, recent medical and psychological research has found that jurors tend to believe real or demonstrative evidence more than they believe mere testimony.[91] People simply tend to believe their eyes more than their ears, and they certainly believe what both senses tell them more than what they learn from one sense alone. The phenomenon is related, but not limited, to receiving greater *understanding* of what we both see and hear than of what we only hear. In fact, at the end of a trial most jurors do not remember where in the proceedings they learned the facts they believe to be decisive.[92] Therefore, what you *show* jurors to back up technical testimony from your experts may be the most helpful way to make sure the jurors understand and believe the experts, even though what the experts say is really evidence, and the simple illustrative drawings and pictures the expert points to as he goes along are not really evidence at all.

§ 12-4(C)(3). Do Not Ignore Technology — You Can't Beat Something With Nothing.

None of the concepts advocated in this chapter are intended to minimize the devastating effect that technical evidence and testimony can have, particularly where it is not contested with equally plausible alternatives. As a great philosopher, who I think was Casey Stengel, once said: "You can't beat something with nothing." There is every reason to emphasize and use technical evidence where it is your best method of proof. The only time it is justifiable to attempt a refutation of technical evidence without offering an equally plausible nontechnical alternative, or countering with your own technical points, is where

---

91. Laird, note 90, at 54.

92. D. Mack, L. Wrightsman, T. Pyszczynski & J. Greenberg, "Opening Statements in a Jury Trial: The Effect of Promising More Than the Evidence Can Show," *Journal of Applied Social Psychology* 11, 5, at 442 (1981).

there is no equally plausible nontechnical alternative or countervailing technical points. This seems to have been the dilemma confronting the defense in the widely publicized murder trial of Dr. Jeffrey MacDonald, who had no satisfactory explanation for, or alternative to, the technical evidence he had murdered his wife and daughters, based on analysis of stab wounds, torn garments, and testing of blood stains. The core of the case against MacDonald, devastating because it could not be explained away nontechnically, nor countered with other technology, was delivered thusly:

> During the fourth week of trial, the jurors did hear from Paul Stombaugh of the FBI laboratory. He was a fifty-two-year-old former football player from Furman College who had spent twenty-five years in the FBI before his retirement in 1976. For the last sixteen of those years he had worked in the FBI laboratory in Washington and had testified as an expert in hair, fiber, bloodstain, and fabric analysis in more than 300 criminal cases in forty-eight of the fifty states, and had appeared as an expert witness before the Warren Commission's investigation into the assassination of John F. Kennedy.
>
> His testimony was considered by many observers to be the most damaging to MacDonald of any given at the trial. It was through Stombaugh that the prosecution first informed the jurors of the following:
>
> ——that the cuts made in the pajamas worn by Colette, Kimberly, and Kristen MacDonald had been made by the sharp, straight Old Hickory knife and not the dull, bent Geneva Forge knife;
>
> ——that the cuts in Jeffrey MacDonald's torn blue pajama top had been made by the Geneva Forge knife;
>
> ——that no cut in the pajama top corresponded to the location of the chest wound which had caused the puncture of Jeffrey MacDonald's right lung;
>
> ——that the pajama top had been torn down the left front seam and down the left sleeve in a manner which

indicated that someone standing in front of Jeffrey MacDonald had ripped it as he spun away, and not — as he had told investigators — that it had either been torn over his back as he had fought with intruders or that he had torn it from his wrists himself as he had entered the master bedroom;

——that the top had been stained by Colette MacDonald's blood in at least four locations *before* it had been torn;

——that the forty-eight puncture holes in the pajama top were perfectly round with no tearing around the edges, indicating that they had been made while the top was stationary, and not while MacDonald was using it as a shield to fend off an icepick-wielding intruder;

——that bloodstains on the Hilton bath mat corresponded with the shape and dimensions of the Old Hickory knife and the ice pick, indicating that someone had either rested them or attempted to wipe them on the bath mat before discarding them out the back door;

——that bloodstains on the sheet found on the master bedroom floor matched impressions made by the bloody sleeves and cuffs of both Jeffrey's and Colette's pajamas, indicating that persons wearing those garments had come into direct contact with the sheet while the garments were still wet with blood;

——that the sheet also contained bloody handprints and, in blood, the outline of a bare human shoulder;

——that "when the pajama top was folded as near as possible to the way it was folded on top of the body at the time the photographs were taken," twenty-one holes were discernible in the top layer of the garment, and that these fell into a grouping — sixteen on the left side and five on the right — which was consistent with the grouping of sixteen ice pick holes on the left and five on the right side of Colette MacDonald's chest; and further, that the remaining holes in the garment could be aligned with those twenty-one in a manner

> which indicated that it would have been possible for someone to have made all forty-eight with twenty-one thrusts of an ice pick — the same thrusts that had made the ice pick holes in Colette's chest.[93]

Few juries would be willing to disregard that much technical evidence simply because a defendant, however likeable and sympathetic, denied the conclusion of the pertinent evidence. The MacDonald jury might, however, have felt differently about the merits of that case if a plausible nontechnical explanation, accounting for at least some of the most important prosecution points, had been presented to them. It was not enough in the MacDonald case, and rarely suffices in any other case, to rely on cross-examination of the hostile experts as a means of neutralizing the technical evidence they offer.

---

93. Joe McGinnis, *Fatal Vision,* at 501-02 (Signet 1983).

CHAPTER 13

THE HINGE OF FATE — OPENING STATEMENT

§ 13-1. Formation of the Jurors' Viewpoints.

It is obvious under the Rule of Primacy (see § 14-1), requiring important facts and data to be presented as soon as possible to the jury, that the Opening Statement will be a crucial point in the trial. In most situations, even if attorneys are allowed to participate in *voir dire,* but particularly if they are not, the opening statement will be the first point in the trial where the jury receives a coherent picture of your facts and case theories. This is, perhaps, the most important application of the Rule of Primacy in all of litigation, for repeated studies have confirmed that a substantial majority of jurors have formed the opinions they will hold at the end of the case by the conclusion of the opening statements.[1]

---

1. McElhaney, "Opening Statements," in *Trial Notebook* at 37, and James Jeans, in *Trial Advocacy* (1975), report that 80% of jurors have reached what will be their final decision at the end of opening statements. Earlier studies at the University of Chicago by Professor Calvin are in accord.

Medical and psychological research on mock juries exposed to opening trial statements have found that during these openings the jurors usually form the orientation and viewpoint from which they will interpret evidence and argument during the rest of the trial. The result of this process is that by the end of opening statements, before one piece of evidence or testimony has been introduced, most jurors have become partisans of one side or the other,[2] for reasons essentially unrelated to the actual evidence, which they have not yet heard.[3] Moreover, once these viewpoints

---

2. Opening statements predisposed jurors to favor one side or the other very early in the trial, and jurors tended to maintain this predisposition throughout the course of the trial. From a psychological perspective, opening statements may serve to create thematic frameworks or schemata that guide jurors in their processing and interpretation of the actual testimony and evidence that are presented later in the trial. [This framework is] any subset of existing knowledge, based on prior experience and relevant to a limited domain, which people use as a framework to guide their observation, organization, and retrieval from memory of perceived events.

T. Pyszczynski & L. Wrightsman, "The Effects of Opening Statements on Mock Juror's Verdicts in a Simulated Criminal Trial", *Journal of Applied Social Psychology,* at 301-02 (1981).

3. This pre-evidentiary viewpoints' ability to determine how subsequent logical processes will interpret data and information, has been repeatedly documented.

> In one experiment, two groups of subjects studying psychology listened to tapes of an interview between two people. One group of students was told the conversation was a psychiatric intake interview, the other group of students was given no such information. When the two groups of students were asked to analyze the interview, the group believing the conversation was a psychiatric intake process found the interviewee's comments to be crawling with clinical pathology. The other group of students found the interviewee to be essentially normal. Pyszczynski, note 2, at 303.

The groups viewed the interview through the different frameworks from which the two groups started. "The frameworks and viewpoints," they concluded, "affect not only the encoding and retrieval of informa-

are formed they are quite tenacious, and difficult to alter.[4]

§ 13-2. When the Juror's Viewpoint Is Formed.

Studies show that most jurors will form an emotional viewpoint, or predisposition, favoring the side that first presents an informative, emotion-stimulating, and extensive opening statement.[5] In compiling statistics on mock criminal trials in controlled situations, the researchers found that most jurors were disposed toward the prosecution at the end of the opening statement and at the end of the trial when the prosecution, which presents the first opening statement, made a detailed presentation.[6] The studies also found that most jurors were disposed towards the Defendant at the end of the opening statement and at the end of the trial, only where the prosecution had made only a cursory opening statement.[7] The jurors' opinions swung wildly during the trial, only where both sides made weak openings.[8] The studies concluded:

> Thus it appears that the first strong persuasive communication jurors received served to create thematic frameworks that were important determinants of their final verdict. . . . An explanation for the obtained predisposing effects of opening statements is that the opening statements served to create thematic frameworks which jurors used in interpreting the evidence in the trial.[9]

---

tion from memory, but also the interpretation that is placed on that information." *Id.* this research confirms 1940 experiments by Weld and Danzig. *Id.*

4. McElhaney, note 1, at 37.

5. Pyszczynski, note 2, at 308-09.

6. *Id.* at 308-10.

7. *Id.*

8. *Id.* at 310.

9. *Id.* at 309-10.

§ 13-3. The Opening of the Opening — Front End Load.

The first part of any presentation in court, including the opening statements, will be the most important, because the fact finders will then be the most open and receptive.[10] The first few minutes of the opening statement have been found to be crucial to the success or failure of the entire opening, for it is during these first few minutes that the jurors make the subconscious decision whether to form the impressions and viewpoints in your favor through which they will interpret subsequent evidence and argument.[11] What is said in the first stages of the opening statement will also be remembered longest by the jurors.[12] It is therefore incumbent upon attorneys making opening statements to deliver a short theme, overview, or synopsis of their case's core in the initial few minutes of the opening.[13]

§ 13-4. Don't Drown the Jury in Ants — Provide Themes for Liability and Damages.

One lazy summer afternoon, I took a walk in the woods. In the course of my wanderings I came upon an ant hill, covered with millions of tiny creatures intent on business important to themselves and utterly unknown to me. Each ant knew, without even thinking (presumably), what he or she or it was doing, but I would never know what any of them were engaged in. To the ants (and to experts on ants) the scene may well have been perfectly organized and clear. To me, it was chaos — a perfect mess.

---

10. McElhaney, note 1, at 38.

11. *Id.*

12. *Id.*

13. *Id.*; James Jeans, *Trial Advocacy,* § 8.6 (1975); David Baurn, "The Plaintiff's Approach in Opening Statement," *The Lawyer's Speak,* at 18.

Ever since that walk in the woods, the picture of that ant hill has struck me as a fairly apt analogy for the dangers attorneys confront in presenting their essential facts to a jury in the opening (and closing) statements. If you view each fact as an ant, the confusion I felt watching the ant hill may convey the problems jurors may have with your facts if they are not properly organized and presented. Even if the significance and interrelationship of your facts is obvious to you, those strands of meaning may be as murky to your fact finder as the goals of all those ants were to me.

Research has found that one important method in letting the jurors see the meaning of your facts is to present unifying themes essential to your theories on liability and damages early in the opening statement.[14] These themes should precede your narration of what the facts will be, both to help the jurors follow the significance of those facts, and to prod the jurors into forming viewpoint frameworks to interpret those facts. Even if the jurors do not recall all the evidence supporting these themes, they are probably going to remember the themes themselves, and the themes may well precipitate their final decisions unless the jurors get what my friend Sheldon Gardner calls "a sense of feeling" that your facts have not established your themes.

Thus, on liability themes early in the opening, a female plaintiff's decedent should be projected thematically as a homemaker who was the foundation of her family; a male plaintiff's decedent becomes the breadwinner and father who held his family together; and the defendant's negligence becomes the failure to spend very small sums that could have prevented the plaintiff's injuries. The themes on damages, similarly, must project not only compensation, but the need for present and future medical care, treat-

14. McElhaney, note 1, at 38; James Jeans, *Trial Advocacy,* § 8.4 (1975).

ment, and equipment in order to allow plaintiff the fullest possible relief from his injuries. Dollar figures on damages really should not be delivered in the opening (specific numbers are safer in the closing statement, after all the evidence is in and the jury is more psychologically prepared to think in terms of specific dollars),[15] but the underlying conditions justifying these damages (catastrophic injuries; astronomical medical needs and bills) can and should be projected in the opening statement to aid the jurors in forming their analytical frameworks for the rest of the trial.

§ 13-5. Building Your Cause.

Many attorneys find it difficult to ask a jury to award damages for an individual plaintiff without almost apologizing for the request. It is much easier, and a stronger argument, to present the plaintiff as part of a large group placed in similar jeopardy by the defendant's negligent or improper conduct. For one point, the plaintiff's attorney is thus in a stronger psychological position, for he is now in effect seeking social justice for a group, not mercy or charity for an individual. For another point, the jury is put in a posture more conducive to a large award, for the defendant has been guilty of a much more socially significant wrong. For a third point, the defendant will have greater difficulty in establishing such affirmative defense as contributory fault or assumed risk, for it is more unlikely that a whole group (of the plaintiff's peers) would have been guilty of such fault than it is that the plaintiff alone would be guilty. Finally, a presentation on this group basis enhances the plaintiff's prospects for a punitive award, if such damages are appropriate.

---

15. McElhaney, note 1, at 41.

Clarence Darrow was one of the greatest masters of this "larger than life" projection of the relevant issues. In the *Kidd* case, for instance, where Darrow defended a labor official charged with organizing a strike in violation of the criminal conspiracy laws, Darrow projected the issues at bar to the jury as follows:

> Gentlemen, here is Thomas I. Kidd. It is a matter of the smallest consequence to him or to me what you do; and I say it as sincerely as I ever spoke a word. . . . I do not appeal for him. That cause is too narrow for me, much as I love him and long as I have worked by his side. I appeal to you, gentlemen, not for Thomas I. Kidd, but I appeal to you for the long line — the long, long line reaching back through the ages, and forward to the years to come — the long line of despoiled and down-trodden people of the earth.[16]

§ 13-6. The Innoculation of the Jury — Anticipate and Deflect the Opponent's Most Virulent Germs.

Psychologists have recently conducted research on the issue of whether it is a better trial tactic to rebut, or to ignore, the anticipated strong points the opposition will make against you. The researchers found that, "[t]he most effective way to innoculate existing opinions against subsequent persuasive communication is by preexposure to opposing argument in a refuted, thus weakened form."[17] This description, strikingly similar to the procedures for protective innoculation, mandates exposing the jury to your problem areas, and your solutions to those problems, in the opening statement.

---

16. Kevin Tierney, *Darrow — A Biography,* at 156 (1979).

17. Professor A.W. Laird, "Persuasion: A Tool of Courtroom Communication," *Psychology: A Quarterly Journal of Human Behavior,* Vol. 19 (213) at 52 (1982).

§ 13-7. Do Not Exaggerate Opening Statement.

Attorneys sometimes make claims in their opening statements that they cannot, or at least do not, prove. This is sometimes caused by good faith errors in evidentiary conclusions by either the lawyers themselves, or by judges ruling on evidentiary matters. In other instances, the opening statement may deliberately include claims that the evidence will not establish because the attorney making the opening is a high stakes gambler well versed in current psychological research.

Without going into the obvious ethical problems involved in promising what you know your case cannot deliver, it must be noted that current studies strongly indicate that you will get away with such tactics unless your opponent is sharp enough to point out to the jury what you have done. The studies found that, at the end of the case, the jurors do not distinguish between facts they were given in the evidence and facts they were promised in the opening statement but not given through evidence. Thus, unless the opposition closing argument can point out to the jurors that your opening statement made unsubstantiated claims, the odds are that the jury, in final deliberations, will act as if, everything you claimed in the opening had actually been supported by evidence.[18] The risk, of course, is that you may lose all credibility, and will certainly lose some credibility, with the jurors if your opponent is alert enough to remind the jury that you have not substantiated important claims in your opening.[19]

The phenomenon of jurors merging the opening statement and the evidence is, however, so strong that the researchers concluded by urging attorneys to:

---

18. D. Mack, L. Wrightsman, T. Pyszczynski, & J. Greenberg, "Opening Statements in a Jury Trial: The Effect of Promising More Than The Evidence Can Show." *Journal of Applied Social Psychology*, 434-44 (1981).

19. *Id.* at 435-36.

> [m]ake the strongest, most extensive opening (that is) plausible. By so doing, the attorney may provide a favorable framework that jurors will use to interpret later evidence. Even if the evidence provided later in the trial does not fully substantiate all his/her claims, the present results suggest that the final verdicts will not be less favorable than if such strong claims had not been made.[20]

In short, when you are making your opening statement, don't promise what you know you cannot deliver, but resolve all the doubts in favor of yourself. And when your opponent is delivering an opening statement, listen carefully to what is said, because every unfulfilled promise you do not catch will be taken as evidence by the jury.

§ 13-8. Sample Opening Statement.

The following opening statement was intended to orient the jury to the plaintiff's position in the transportation facility negligence case of *Edgman v. State of Indiana.* The case involved the negligent design, construction, and maintenance of a defective road area on Cline Avenue in Hammond, Indiana, that was known as "the S curve," or "the killer curve." In order to clarify the technical engineering points, the presentation was supported by charts, drawings, and photographs of the S curve, which ran for about 1/2 mile. At the conclusion of the case, the jury awarded 1.8 million dollars. After the Appellate Court sustained the verdict, the defendant paid the award together with interest. Hopefully, the opening statement had played a part in this outcome.

---

20. *Id.* at 443.

MR. KUHLMAN MAKES OPENING STATEMENT ON BEHALF OF PLAINTIFF AS FOLLOWS:

MR. KUHLMAN: May It Please The Court, Ladies and Gentlemen of the Jury and Counsel: Good morning.

This is the first time that I have had a chance to talk to you. My name is Richard Kuhlman; I'm one of the lawyers for the plaintiff in this case. I would like to introduce to you some of the other lawyers and people involved in bringing this case to Court for you to hear.

This is Mr. Cecil Cohen, of Cohen, Cohen and Bullard; Mr. Cohen is now celebrating his 80th year. Mr. Pontikes and Mr. Stephen Cohen you have already met. This is Mr. Cary Barr and Mr. Gerald Ortman,[21] you are going to see them during the course of this trial bringing you documents and bringing in witnesses. There are a lot of people coming here from all over the country to tell you the story of the Cline Avenue S-Curve. And most importantly of all, this is Jim Edgman; this is the man who had his health ruined and his wife killed at midnight on July 27, 1970. The evidence will show layers and layers and layers of negligence that the State of Indiana was guilty of on that night, and for years prior to that night with respect to that road.[22]

Now, Mr. Edgman is bringing this lawsuit; he is the plaintiff. The defendant being sued is the State of Indiana. The State is being sued, as the Judge just told you, for negligently building, maintaining, and designing the area of Cline Avenue between the Toll Road in the south and Gary Avenue in the north, an area of road that was known around 1970 as the Cline Avenue S-Curve. And the evidence will show that the negligence of the State with all those layers and layers of negligence was a substantial contributing factor to the crash that occurred on that midnight on July 27, 1970.

In this crash, Jim Edgman sustained terrible injuries and his wife Lorene Edgman, was killed; and the other driver, Robert Casillas, was killed. And His Honor has told you in great detail all these allegations legally of negligence and what they mean, and all the things that weren't on that road that night that should have been there.

Now, an Opening Statement, the purpose of a lawyer getting up and talking to you is to tell you not only what the evidence will be, but also

---

21. Introduce everyone at your table quickly and get it over with.

22. This sets a theme, the Defendant did everything possible wrong. Even if your evidence does not prove everything you anticipate, if you promise and deliver enough "layers of negligence" against the Defendant nobody will notice, or care, what you left out.

what the evidence is and how it all fits together. Evidence is going to come in in this case in many different ways. There are going to be witnesses who will tell you things; there are going to be documents and letters, and there are going to be reports of crashes, and there are going to be people with blueprints, and there are going to be authoritative literature, and there are going to be books, and there are going to be engineers, because to tell you what's wrong with the road and to go back to September of 1966 you need things like this. And when you are dealing with this many witnesses and this many documents, and you are dealing with doctors, and you are dealing with surgeons, and you're dealing with orthopedic surgeons, and you are dealing with people who are eminent in fields of engineering, transportation engineering, you have to take people when they are available. There are people now coming into this courtroom on airplanes and in cars; they are coming in from all over the state and all over the country, and we have to put them on when they are available. So you may see a document coming in from the beginning of the case followed by a witness from the middle, followed by a witness from the beginning, followed by a witness from the end, and I am telling you the Opening Statement now to let you know how all these pieces fit together. It's like the table of contents of a book, because unfortunately we won't be able to see all the pages actually come in in the same order that a book would be presented to you. I can give you the table of contents now, but you are going to get Page 1 and then Page 3 and then Page 2, and then Page 6. It's a simple case, understand that. If you can follow the different pieces and the different categories that they fit into, this case is simple.

Now, this is a negligence case. Negligence is a very simple thing. It just means the failure to use reasonable care.

Now, the evidence will show you that here the state negligently designed and maintained the Cline Avenue S-Curve from September of 1966 up to and including midnight of July 27, 1970. And if we tell you that the State failed to use reasonable care, then it is our burden to show you what reasonable care was. We have to show you the standards that competent people in the business of building and designing highways and striping them and putting driver lanes on them, and putting warning signs and speed signs on them followed, because there were rules in this business, there were rules that were established throughout the country.

Now, in the United States from 1966 through midnight of July 27, 1970, there was an association of road design engineers, called the American Association of State Highway Officials that's called AASHO. They published the authoritative standards that road designers and road builders were to follow in building the roads and in designing their roads. And the books and the standards that AASHO published in this case which were violated repeatedly by the defendant were the 1954 Blue Book, the 1957 Red Book, the 1965 Blue Book, and the 1967 Yellow Book; and the witnesses who come on the stand will tell you what all these books said and how the State violated these standards. In addition, in 1968 the State of Indiana published a manual that was called the 1968 Indiana Manual on Uniform Traffic Control Devices. Now, the AASHO standards applied throughout the United States. The Indiana Manual applied to the State of Indiana, and the evidence will show you that that Manual is the guide that engineers and traffic designers and traffic safety people in this State were supposed to follow with State roads. It set the rules for the driver lane lines that had to be on the outside of roads, it set the rules for the lanes of driver lanes and skip lines that have to be in the middle of the road so that a driver could follow what lane he was in. It set the standards for establishing that that little curb in the middle of the Cline Avenue S-Curve that you will hear about should have been painted, and it set the standards that established that the pavement in front of that little median curb in the middle of the S-Curve, that little 6 to 10-inch curb you are going to hear about, that should have been painted. And the evidence will show you that none of these things were painted in either the north lane or the south lanc of the Cline Avenue S-Curve on midnight of July 27, 1970. And those things were not required by the Uniform 1965 Manual for art work. The evidence will show you that those things were supposed to be on the roadway to guide motorists around that curve, and that curb, c-u-r-b, should have been painted so that people wouldn't hit it and fly into the opposing lane of traffic; that none of those things were present.

Now, these books and other traffic engineering standards that you will learn about established concepts that are just common sense. All you need to follow this case is just common sense. Now, the rules that were supposed to be followed were supposed to put median barriers on State roads, median barriers down the middle of the road on that little median 6 to 10-inch curb, and they are supposed to be there to protect people traveling on State roads.

These concepts and rules that you will learn about are the standards of what should have been done for the Cline Avenue S-Curve, and that's why they are the standards of reasonable care. They are the standards against which you should measure the actions of the State of Indiana in this case from 1966, September, to midnight on July 27, 1970. Under these standards of reasonable care established by these National authorities and by these Indiana authorities, the first and foremost rule of reasonable care for people in charge of making and protecting roads is that nothing is of greater importance and nothing is of equal importance to the safety of the motorist on the road. And safety should come first.

The second point the evidence will show is that if the State had either a 55-mile an hour speed limit posted for traffic on that road, or no speed limit posted on that road, then the Cline Avenue S-Curve on the night of July 27, 1970, was not marked with reasonable care to properly regulate northbound traffic on that road from the Toll Road north to the Grand Calumet River.

Design speed is a speed that is the highest theoretical speed of traffic the road can take. That's what the evidence in this case will show. That is because design speed should be the very, very, very highest theoretical speed a motorist can go and still have sufficient visibility over the curves in the road to let him see far enough ahead to stop before he hits something. That's design speed. When they make a blueprint of a road that says design speed 50, design speed 70, design speed 80, whatever it is, and when that thing goes down the pike to other engineers they will get it and they say, well, whatever else happens that road can handle speeds up to that design speed. It's designed to handle traffic going that fast or slower.

Now, as common sense will tell you, the faster the speed you are going, the farther ahead the motorist must be able to see on the road if he is going to be able to stop before he hits something. So the faster your design speed, the farther ahead you have to be able to see. Every motorist, the evidence will show, should be able to see far enough ahead on a road to be able to stop at the design speed or lesser speed before hitting something in the road, and that's called the minimum stopping sight distance. And everyone of those AASHO National authorities from 1954 on, that I told you about, say minimum stopping sight distance is required on a road and minimum means what you and I know in common sense it means. Minimum is the least allowable amount; minimum is not desirable. Minimum, the evidence will show you, means the least it can be. Minimum stopping distance on the Cline Avenue S-Curve should have been present; every road must have minimum stopping sight distance.

The AASHO Blue Books and the AASHO Red Books have tables, charts, that you can look up how long a curve must be to give minimum stopping sight distance at a given speed. And under the AASHO Standards, the minimum in minimum stopping sight distance means the shortest allowable. Now, the actual posted speed the evidence will show that is put on signs, the actual speed limit signs on a road, should never be the design speed. They should never be the very, very highest theoretical speed a motorist can go and still have safety. And the reason for that is that people overdrive speed limit signs. If the road that you drove on here today had a speed limit sign of 30 miles an hour, there were a lot of people on that road driving over 30; there were some driving under. If the road you drive on today when you go home has a posted speed of 20, there's going to be people doing less and there's going to be people doing more. But if you put a posted speed out there that is the very, very, very highest theoretical mile power that a man can go safely and still stop, and still have minimum stopping sight distance, then everybody who goes over that minimum stopping sight distance, everybody who goes over that posted speed is going to have no minimum stopping sight distance, he won't be able to stop. So there has to be a gap between the design speed, the highest theoretical speed you can have, and the posted speed. You can't put a speed sign at the very top of the throat.

Finally, a road should never under these authorities be designed or posted with speed signs in such a negligent manner that it is unsafe and it fails to give minimum stopping sight distance at both the design speed and the posted speed. But that is exactly what the evidence will show did happen in this case if there was a posted speed limit of 55 miles an hour on the Cline Avenue S-Curve between the Toll Road and Gary Avenue on midnight, July 27, 1970. If they posted 55 for traffic on that road, it was unsafe for the design speed they had on that road, which was 70 miles an hour, and it was unsafe at 55 miles an hour; and if they had no posted speed on the road, it was even worse.

Now, the State road in question in this case on which the evidence will show you that the State was violating these standards and other standards, in September, 1966, until the time of this crash, is Cline Avenue, between the Toll Road in the south and Gary Avenue in the north.

Now, let me tell you some of the things about these things which are not evidence but which will be evidence. It's very hard to describe a road, so we need some diagrams and pictures to show.

This is an aerial photograph of Cline Avenue as it goes over the Toll Road in the south; this is the Toll Road. This is the first curve; and we'll talk about the curves in a minute.

This is the Grand Calumet River, right in the middle; and this is the Grand Calumet River bridge which is a fine line, which you can't quite see in this aerial photo. The road then goes into a second curve and proceeds north to Gary Avenue; this is Gary Avenue up here.

Now, from this aerial photo and from the blueprints and from the charts that were used in the construction of this road, this photo is not evidence yet either, but it will be, competent engineers and surveyors have prepared this schematic scale drawing which will also be in evidence. Now, can everybody see this?

Now, this is a scale drawing of the Cline Avenue S-Curve. It shows you the road in two ways. The diagram on top is the view from the air; this is what you would see if you were flying over the Cline Avenue S-Curve. It's very similar to that aerial photograph which is one of the things that it was prepared from.

The drawing on the bottom is what you would see if you were standing on the ground some distance away from this road to the east, I guess, and you were looking at it just to see how the road went. To explain to you how the road is again, this is south; this is north; this is east over here; and that's west towards the ceiling. Now, the two drawings are exactly in scale to one another, so that what you see at one point on the profile is exactly what you would see corresponding to the upper view if you were flying over it in an airplane.

This is the Toll Road bridge over here in the south from the side, and this is the Toll Road bridge viewed from above.

This is the Grand Calumet River bridge viewed from the side; this is the Grand Calumet River bridge view from above; this is the Gary Avenue bridge to the north viewed from the side; this is the Gary Avenue bridge from on top viewed from above.

It is about a quarter of a mile from the Toll Road to the north end of the River Bridge, and it's about another quarter of a mile from the north end of the River Bridge to the Gary Avenue north end, north end of the Gary Avenue bridge.

Now, there are curves marked on this diagram, and it's simple to understand what the curves are and what they do.

There are two kinds of curves in a road, they are called vertical curves and horizontal curves. Vertical means up and down. A vertical curve can go up or it can go down. If it goes up they call it a crest curve, it's going up like a crest on a hill. If it goes down it's called a sag curve going down. A horizontal curve goes horizontally from side to side. A horizontal curve can go to the left or can go to the right, although I just did it backwards; to the right or to the left — this stuff isn't easy.[23]

As you come over the Toll Road bridge from the north, it will come to a vertical Curve No. 1, that's called a crest curve that's going up — can everybody see it, vertical Curve No. 1?

---

23. It's not a bad idea to make such a mistake in trying to explain technical points to the jury — the jurors will be having even more difficulty understanding you, and your error will help them to identify with you.

As a motorist approaches the Toll Road from the south going north, he comes over vertical Curve No. 1. Now, the evidence will show you that on midnight of July 27, 1970, a motorist coming over this vertical Curve No. 1 would not have minimum stopping sight distance at either the design speed of this road which is 70 miles an hour, or at the allegedly posted speed of 55 miles an hour. So that was an unsafe curve for either of those speeds.

Proceeding over the Toll Road the motorist would come to a second crest vertical curve, that's another curve that goes up and down; a crest vertical curve. The evidence will show you that the northern end of that second crest vertical curve, what we call Crest Curve 2, was chopped off by the project that built the Cline Avenue S-Curve, and they put a sag curve right in the northern end of it, so the road went like that; you went from the crest curve into the sag curve like that. And the evidence will show you that on midnight of July 27, 1970, on this combination of the second crest vertical curve and the sag curve, a motorist would not have minimum stopping sight distance at either 70 miles an hour or at the allegedly posted speed of 55 miles an hour. And there will be a lot of evidence that there wasn't any posted speed, and that traffic shot through here at speeds much faster than 55 miles an hour. But the evidence will be that if they posted 55, it was an unsafe speed.

After a motorist comes out of vertical Crest Curve 1 and vertical Crest Curve 2 and the sag curve, he goes into the first horizontal curve. That's a curve that's turning horizontally. He goes right into that. In fact, the first horizontal curve here begins in the sag curve, so that this road at the same time is going down into the sag curve, it's turning into the horizontal curve, and it's tipping as the horizontal road tips. So the motorist at night on this road, which didn't give him minimum stopping sight distance at 55, let alone anything higher, went down into the sag, spun horizontally and tipped at the same time. And under the standards for horizontal curves that the State itself used in the construction of this road, that horizontal curve wasn't long enough. And the combination of all of these things could disorient a driver; and this too short, defectively short horizontal curve ended at the south end of the Calumet River bridge.

Now, if you look at this from the side you will see that the Calumet River bridge is in a valley. You come over this crest curve here at the Toll Road if you are going north, or you come over this crest curve here at Gary Avenue if you are going south, and either way you go down into the valley. And on midnight of July 27, 1970, there was a moon out but it was dark in that valley at the Grand Calumet River bridge. And the evidence will show you that Robert Casillas hit around that Calumet River bridge in that valley.

Now, the evidence is going to show you that Cline Avenue from the Toll Road north to Gary Avenue, and as I refer to these things can you all see what they are — this is Gary Avenue, that's the Toll Road, that's the Toll Road and this is Gary Avenue — I'm sorry that's the Toll Road, this is the river, and this is Gary Avenue. The evidence will show you that Cline Avenue in this area was being designed in the early 1960's as a four lane curving road, with two lanes of traffic going north and with two lanes of traffic going south, and a little 6 to 10-inch curb in the middle of the road. The middle of the road is called a median. So the little curb in the middle of the road is called the median curb.

This area of roadway had a design speed of 70, so 70 was the very highest theoretical speed that the road was supposed to be able to handle safely, and the top speed that would give the motorist minimum stopping sight distance. But northbound motorists on this road coming over the Toll Road and going toward the river wouldn't have that minimum stopping sight distance at either 70 or at 55. And it would be negligent to post a speed of either 70 or 55 on that road. Also, the road was set up in such a way that northbound drivers at night coming over the Toll Road had to go through a series of vertical curves before they came to the horizontal curve, and that would be negligent if you posted it at 55 or 70.

The design rule is simple, horizontal curves which are flat and turn to one side or the other ought to come before up and down curves, so that you can see the up and down curves. You are going along flat and you see an up and down curve coming and you are ready for it. If you do it the other way, you are going up and down, and up and down, and you can't see the horizontal curves that are on the other side of the vertical curves. So the rule of design is that horizontal curves ought to lead or come in front of, ought to come after vertical curves. But this reversed the process. You've got a vertical curve here, the highest, the horizontal curve here, this is up and down here, and when you are going up and down here, you can't see the horizontal curve here. If you are coming the other way, it's the same thing, you are going up and down at Gary Avenue, and that's hiding the horizontal curve over here. So they reversed the process. They reversed it and they put the vertical curves in front of the horizontal curves so that either way a motorist is coming into that valley at the Grand Calumet River he would be hitting the up and down vertical curves before he came to the horizontal curves.

Now, in July of 1970, at midnight, this road had no lights; that's another thing the evidence will show. And in that valley of the Grand Calumet River at midnight it was dark. And these crest curves and the sag curve at the Toll Road, those two up and down curves and then the curve that it dips down into reduced the northbound motorists' visibility coming over the Toll Road, especially at night, so that he wouldn't have his minimum stopping sight distance at 70 or 55. So it would be negligent to post 55 on that road or any higher speed.

Back in the early 1960's, in 1962, before the road was built, before the road opened to traffic, the designers of this road, Consoer, Townsend and Associates, and other road designers and engineers were hired by the State to design the road, they are the people who designed the road, they looked at this design and they looked at the fact that this road was going to handle heavy traffic flow, and they looked at the fact that there weren't going to be any lights on it, and the fact that this little curb in the middle, the 6 to 10-inch median curb, was going to be the only thing that stood between two lanes of heavy curving traffic going north and two lanes of heavy curving traffic going south. And Consoer, Townsend, and other reputable traffic engineers, in 1962, recommended to the State of Indiana that median barriers be built in the middle of this road on that little curb between Gary Avenue bridge and the Toll Road bridge, if not further. They said put median barriers there so they won't have cross-over crashes. And the State ignored them.

This first horizontal curve the evidence will also show you is a sharp curve. Under the standards for horizontal curves that the State used in building this road, a horizontal curve that was sharper than 2 degrees 30 minutes should only be used under very unusual circumstances. That's the language that the blueprints used; that's the State's own standards. That's a 3-degree 30-minute curve horizontally here, and that's a 3-degree 30-minute curve horizontally here. By the State's own standards these two horizontal curves could only be used under very unusual circumstances and this one isn't long enough either.

Under competent design and engineering standards that competent road designers and engineers were using, that type of a design on that type of traffic flow, with that kind of a narrow median curve required median barriers before that road opened. Consoer, Townsend was right. And the other engineers who recommended median barriers on that road before it opened were right.

About September 26, 1966, the State opened the new four-lane Cline Avenue and negligently ignored those recommendations and failed to have median barriers on the center curb between the Toll Road and Gary Avenue, and the crashes started. In the three months of 1966 that this road was opened, that's October, November, and December, most of the crashes involved local area drivers. Almost all the crashes involved local area drivers. Most involved local area drivers crossing the median curb into the opposing lane of traffic, and most of them took place in the quarter mile distance from the Toll Road bridge there in the south to the Grand Calumet River, and lots of these crashes involved injuries.

Under competent engineering rules and standards then in effect, the evidence will show you that the State should have been particularly sensitive to cross median crashes on that road when they opened it, because of the geometrics, the heavy traffic flow, the low median curb, and the recommendations of their own designers that they ignored.

So the 1966 crashes on Cline Avenue from the Toll Road to Gary with such a heavy percentage of local drivers crossing the median into opposing lanes of traffic should have been the final proof, if final proof was needed that late, that a median barrier should go into Cline Avenue from the Toll Road to Gary, but the State ignored them.

In 1967 the crashes continued on Cline Avenue between the Toll Road and Gary, and they were still involving almost all local drivers. They still had an unacceptably high percentage of people crossing over the median into the opposing lane of traffic, and they still involved a lot of injuries.

So in 1967, the Indiana Highway Commission sent people out to look at this road. They inspected it, they measured, they did presumably what competent engineers are supposed to do, and they made a recommendation. The Indiana Highway Commission's own people in 1967, their own engineers said, we recommend a median barrier on Cline Avenue in this area, other areas, put a median barrier in the middle of the road. And the State ignored that.

Also in 1967, the American Association of State Highway Officials made a survey of what was going on on highways throughout the United States. It was a state of the art survey, what's going on on highways, what are the dangers, what are the things that we ought to be doing to correct. Remember, this is the most authoritative design of road design and transportation engineering group in the United States. The state itself, the evidence will show, has listed their books as standards that they supposedly followed in building this road. Well, in 1967 the AASHO Yellow Book came out, and it said, we must make a crash program throughout this country to make the roadsides safe and to prevent people from crossing over the median. We must make a crash program everywhere to make the roadside safe. And the State ignored the AASHO Yellow Book, and it ignored the crashes that were happening in 1967 with local people crossing over, and it ignored the recommendation of its own engineers who in 1967 went out there and looked at the road; and it ignored the recommendations that Consoer, Townsend and other engineers had made back in 1962, and it continued to have no median barrier on that road.

In 1968 and in 1969, and up to June of 1970, when they let the contract for median barriers, the crashes continued. And the complaints started coming in. State Troopers wrote to them saying you need a median barrier on the road. Industrialists wrote to them, drivers, citizens wrote to them, put a median barrier on the Cline Avenue S-Curve and they were all ignored.

On the night of July 27, 1970, around midnight, Jim Edgman picked up his wife from work at Inland Steel where she had a good job as a chemist. Jim had a good job at Inland, too. He worked as an ironworker. And he started driving her home going south into the Cline Avenue S-Curve. When he entered the area from Gary Avenue to the Toll Road going south, the pavement had not even been painted in either the north or the southbound lane. And to engineers and traffic officials in this State at that time, under the 1968 Indiana Manual on Uniform Traffic Control Devices, it was mandatory that pavement on State roads like this State road be painted, so that neither Casillas going north or the Edgmans going south had the guidance of outer edgeline striping on the outside of the road, skip lines down the middle of the road to tell a driver what lane he was in, the combination of the two to tell the driver whether the road was curving or going up or down, they had no painting on the median curb in the middle to let them know where they were going to hit it, or if they were going to hit it, and they had no painting on the pavement in front of that median curb on the left side of the road to tell them they were close to an obstacle, and under the Uniform Manual all those things should have been done.

And on Cline Avenue between the Toll Road and Gary Avenue that night, at midnight, there weren't any warning signs, there weren't any turn signs, there weren't any curve signs, there weren't any danger signs, there weren't any dip signs, there weren't any watch-out signs, there weren't any look-out signs, there weren't any speed limit signs, there weren't any lights, and there weren't any median barriers.

As the Edgmans were entering this area of Cline Avenue from the east in their station wagon close to midnight on that night, Robert Casillas was driving north over that Toll Road bridge in a Pontiac, and at this time there was either no posted speed on the road or there was speed of 55 miles an hour posted on the road. The drivers on that road didn't know of any speed limit sign. They didn't know it was the 55-mile an hour speed limit road, they didn't know of any posted speed on that road at all, and traffic was averaging a lot faster than 55 miles an hour on the Cline. It was dangerous to go slower than the average speed of traffic on the Cline. It was called the speedway.

Around midnight on July 27, 1970, Robert Casillas traveled north over the Toll Road, over these road conditions. He traveled right here, over Crest Curve 1 where he wouldn't have his minimum stopping sight distance at 55 if they posted it; he traveled over Crest Curve 2 and Crest Curve 3, the sag curve, where he wouldn't have his minimum stopping sight distance at that speed if they had posted it; and right about here, Grand Calumet River bridge, Robert Casillas joined that long list of local drivers who had been crossing over into the opposing lanes of traffic since September of 1966, and he hit the Edgman car at the river bridge in the outer lane of southbound traffic.

The evidence will show you that the negligence of the State and all these things was a substantial contributing factor and the proximate cause of this crash for two basic giant categories of reasons. The guidance systems that should have been on that road that night, the lights, the striping, the delineators, the reflectors that should have been along the outer edge of the road which weren't there, the painting on the curb, the warning signs, turn signs, the curve signs, they all weren't there. And those were things that should have been there to get Casillas around that curve. But the second reason is that even if Casillas was going out there to kill himself, if Casillas was a Kamikaze who wanted to die, the median barrier should have been in the center of that road to protect the Edgmans who were going within reasonable and lawful traffic speeds as they proceeded here south, just a man picking up his wife from work and taking her home. So that even if Casillas couldn't have gotten around that curve with all the warnings and all the speed signs and all the painted edgelines and all the guidance systems in the world, he shouldn't have been able to get through to kill Lorene Edgman and ruin Jim Edgman's life. And that's what the evidence will show. And that's why the evidence will show you that the negligence of the State of Indiana was not only a substantial contributing factor to this crash, but *the* substantial contributing factor to this crash.

Finally, this case is going to involve damages. The State of Indiana was negligent. Its negligence was the proximate cause of the crash and the State is responsible for the damages that its negligence caused the Edgmans. These damages will come in several different categories.

Both Mr. and Mrs. Edgman had good jobs at Inland Steel. Mrs. Edgman was killed in the crash. Jim Edgman was injured so badly in this crash he was never able to work again. Expert testimony of economists and experts who established that out-of-pocket earnings, wages, and benefits that the Edgmans have lost together here were over $900,000.00.

Secondly, Mr. Edgman has been in constant pain since this crash. The crash caused him permanent disability from a displaced fracture of the left elbow, he can only raise it about half way. His left patella, that's your knee cap, was fractured. The crash fractured the bones in his left hip joint. Due to this he had to have a serious operation on June 13, 1974, to receive an entire surgical hip replacement, putting in an artificial hip. This operation has failed. He now needs a second and even more serious operation. They have to open him up now, take out the artificial hip that did not take, and put in a new artificial hip. These operations and other damages from the crash have permanently and significantly shortened his left leg, so he walks with a permanent limp. The crash seriously injured his head. He sustained a severe basic fracture of the skull. He also suffered in this crash a vertical linear fracture in the temporal bone near the left ear, that's around here. He was disoriented for several weeks after this crash. He suffered a severe loss of hearing; he has tinnitus, and that's a permanent ringing in your ear, like a bell in your ear. And there is evidence of brain damage. All these injuries have caused him terrible pain and agony, and even now whenever the weather changes Jim Edgman has terrible pain over the whole left side of his body originating from the area of the left hip. He has suffered very substantial medical bills for these injuries; you will hear about those.

Finally, Jim Edgman lost a good wife. He can recover, the evidence will show you what it cost to bury her, and he can recover what you think her value was to him.

The evidence will show you that the State was negligent. The evidence will show you that the negligence of the State was a substantial and *the* substantial contributing factor to this crash. The evidence will show you Casillas should have had help around that curve from the State, and even if he was going to kill himself, the Edgmans should have been protected from all those engineers and all those safety features on the Cline Avenue S-Curve from 1966 on.

Finally, the evidence is going to show you Jim Edgman is entitled to damages of well over 1 million dollars.[24]

---

24. It is well advised not to request a specific amount of damages in the opening, but if you are going after a substantial award both *voir dire* and opening statement should seek to establish that the jurors know the ballpark you are playing in.

CHAPTER 14

THE PROCEDURES OF PERSUASION

§ 14-1. Primacy — The Fast Break.

The healthy human mind, like the rest of the body, follows certain more or less predictable procedures in its operation. Litigation in all forms consists of competitive efforts to persuade people to accept various concepts of fact, (as being true) and law, (as being applicable). It follows, then, that litigation tactics based on a recognition of how the human mind works will have a better chance of implanting ideas into those minds than tactics that do not. Simply put, attorneys with no idea of how a mind works minimize their chances of changing it. The following psychological processes, supported by research and experimentation, should be noted, for they will be relevant to a host of trial situations not covered in this, or any other book. Subsequent sections, while in no way intended as an exhaustive litany of trial tactics, will suggest litigation applications for these psychological procedures. Certainly, any attempt to persuade will increase its prospects of success if it moves with, not against, the normal workings of the jurors' mental and emotional deliberations.

The psychological concept of primacy is that people are most likely to remember and believe what they hear first, and less likely to remember or believe what they hear later. Psychological experimentation has found that this rule applies to litigation situations, particularly where the facts are complex, technical, and unfamiliar to the fact finder.[1]

§ 14-1(A). The Front End Load — Important Facts and Arguments.

In the opening and closing statements, direct examination and cross-examination, the jury will be most likely to remember and believe what it hears first. The important facts and arguments upon which your position hinges should be placed in this opening sequence.[2]

§ 14-1(A)(1). Strong Witnesses and Testimony Should Precede Weaker Witnesses and Testimony.

In recent experiments to determine the impact that a witness' place in the trial "batting order" had on jurors, the experimenters were confounded when their expectation that strong witnesses would be most effective at the end of the order proved invalid. The actual results led the researchers to conclude: "The greatest number of desired

---

1. Professor A.W. Laird, "Persuasion: A Tool of Courtroom Communication," *Psychology: A Quarterly Journal of Human Behavior,* Vol. 19 (213) at 53 (1982).

2. Y. Schul & E. Burnstein, "The Informational Basis of Social Judgments: Memory for Informative and Uninformative Arguments," *Journal of Experimental Social Psychology,* Vol. 19, at 422-23 (1983).

verdicts by simulated jurors occurred when the strongest witnesses [of the proponent] came first,"[3] and "[i]n a trial lasting a number of days or more, jurors may pay greatest attention to witnesses going first, while at the same time paying more attention to the evidence witnesses give at the start of their testimony."[4]

§ 14-1(A)(2). In Cross-Examination, the Strongest Points Must Be Made Quickly.

At the start of cross-examination, particularly of a hostile expert, bear in mind that your target witness begins the contest in the strongest possible position — the end of a direct examination based on questions he (or she) and your opposing counsel have had years to work on. During this direct exam, your target witness, aided by your opponent, has done everything he could think of to present his testimony as competent, unbiased, honest, thorough, fair, reasonable, and (just by coincidence) thoroughly devastating to the side not paying him — which is you. The jury will continue to hold all those evaluations of your target witness stemming from the direct examination unless and until you "break the spell." If you intend to do this, you had best do it quickly, both because under the Rule of Primacy the jury will pay most attention to the start of your cross, and also because a lot of your telling points will be lost and wasted if you wait so long to make them that the jury's favorable impressions of the witness created in direct exam and not shaken in the start of your cross have solidified and become permanent.

If you can shake the witness the jury *expects* you to do it quickly. They will pay attention to the start of your cross

---

3. D. Pennington, "Witnesses and Their Testimony: Effects of Ordering on Jury Verdicts," *Journal of Applied Social Psychology,* Vol. 12, No. 4, at 318 (1982).

4. *Id.* at 331.

examination to see if you can do that. If you do not make points at the start they will give up on you and ignore the same points when you make them later on in your cross exam. Professor Laird explained this concept thusly:

> The cardinal rule in cross examination is to make your most important point right away. By striking at the outset and eroding the witness' credibility, you stand a much better chance of getting the jury to go along with you in those areas of your attack where you are weaker.[5]

§ 14-1(B). Important Facts and Arguments Maximize Information and Thematic Relatedness to Other Relevant Facts and Arguments.

"The memory for an argument will increase with its informativeness and with its thematic relatedness to other arguments. . . . By dint of their closer association with the decisions they occupy a more central position in the representations of an opinion than uninformative ones. This implies that an informative argument should be accessed and reported prior to an uninformative argument. . . ." "If arguments are thematically related, they will be linked by a denser network of associations than if they are unrelated."[6]

§ 14-2. Emotionally Charged Information Is Remembered More Easily, and Is More Persuasive Than Duller, Technical Material.

Under the concept of primacy (see § 14-1), emotionally charged material will be more important in the fact

---

5. Laird, note 1, at 54.

6. Yaacov Schul & Eugene Burnstein, "The Informational Basis of Social Judgments: Memory for Informative and Uninformative Arguments," *Journal of Experimental Social Psychology*, Vol. 19, at 422-33 (1983).

finders' deliberations, and should therefore precede duller, technical information in opening statement (telling what the evidence will be), direct testimony (presenting the evidence), and in final argument (reminding the juror what the evidence was). The researchers establishing this primacy of emotion over "duller" technical data concluded that:

> Information of high emotional interest is more easily recalled from memory at a later time and is given more weight when making judgments than information which is less vivid. . . . When highly vivid or emotionally laden testimony appears first, or with rape trial material, it might serve to encourage people to pay less attention to later information or to discount it.[7]

Professor A.W. Laird, Professor Emeritus of Psychology of Western Kentucky University, reported similar findings:

> No matter how well he is grounded in the particular facts of his case, no matter how much he has studied and researched the law, the trial lawyer cannot do an effective job unless he understands something about the human reaction of the judge and jury. Cicero emphasized this point in his statement that, men make a decision of tenor through feeling rather than through fact or law. They are moved by emotion. The only way to refute feeling is by feeling. . . . The use of highly emotional words and intense arguments tends to be more effective than the rational approach in persuasion.[8]

---

7. D. Pennington, "Witnesses and Their Testimony: Effects of Ordering on Jury Verdicts," *Journal of Applied Social Psychology,* Vol. 12, No. 4, at 332 (1982).

8. Professor A.W. Laird, "Persuasion: A Tool of Courtroom Communication," *Psychology: A Quarterly Journal of Human Behavior,* Vol. 19 (213), at 50-51 (1952).

One obvious litigation application for this priority given to emotion over logic or data is to put emotion-triggering facts (injuries, outrageous negligence or contributory fault) up front in the prime sections of the opening statement and, again, in the closing statement. First, get the emotion of the jurors to tell them that you *ought* to win, then let the logic of the jurors figure out how and why you, in fact, deserve to win. The late Bertrand Russell described this process fairly well when he stated that emotion tells you what to do, and logic gives you an excuse to do it.[9]

§ 14-3. The Form of a Question Can Influence the Answer.

Dr. Elizabeth F. Loftus, Research Psychologist at the University of Washington, conducted extensive research on how different forms of questions influenced the answers given by eyewitnesses to events. She reported: "I have found that the questions asked about an event influence the way a witness remembers what he saw. Changing even one word in a single question can systematically alter an eyewitness account."[10] Dr. Loftus reports, for example, that the witness can be psychologically oriented, in a crash case, to the plaintiff's perspective by questions using the term "crash," and to the Defendant's perspective by using the term "accident."

---

9. Professor Laird documented how this concept works in litigation:

> In commentary on the Plaintiff's injury in summation, wherever possible, try to get the jury indignant about the wrong done to your client. If the jurors are indignant, if they feel that an injustice has been done to this poor soul, then they will go out of their way to bring in not only a verdict, but a very adequate one. Laird, *supra* note 1 at 55.

10. Dr. Elizabeth F. Loftus, Research Psychologist at University of Washington, "Reconstructing Memory: The Incredible Eyewitness," *Psychology Today,* Vol. 8, No. 1, at 116 (1974).

Similarly, when seeking to have the witness verify that a disputed fact really existed, the witness may be motivated somewhat toward the desired answer by a question assuming that fact's existence. For example, if the issue is of whether *A* and *B* had a fight at noon, the question "Did you see *the* fight?" has a better chance of an affirmative answer, Dr. Loftus reports, than the non-assuming question "Did you see *a* fight?" Bear in mind that we are speaking of questions here in client interviews before trial, which can be as leading as desired.

Again, in a "crash" or "accident" case distances are obviously often crucial. Dr. Loftus reports that the witness will often *increase* amounts if asked questions suggesting bigness ("How big?" or "How far?"), while the answer often reduces amounts for questions suggesting smallness ("How close?" or "How small?")

§ 14-4. The Identification Rule — People Favor Parties, Issues, and Things They Can Identify With.

From the beginning of human history, for reasons preexisting our ability to contemplate or question them, we humans have felt instinctive hostility toward people and things unlike ourselves. Conversely, we have usually concluded that people and things we can identify with must be reasonably acceptable.

The obvious application of these factors to litigation is that every effort must be made to present your client and your position on crucial issues to the jury in a context maximizing the odds of the jury identifying with and accepting them. Professor A.W. Laird reported this conclusion thusly:

> The final deliberations have a tendency to depend almost exclusively on the memory of the jury, and the following "laws of memory" should be noted. Juries

> will probably remember: (1) that which has meaning to them; (2) that which is familiar to them, or at least that which in some way can be associated with something they already know or can easily learn; (3) those items of evidence they can fit into an overall picture; and (4) that which is repeated.[11]

One important application of this concept is that, to the extent possible, your client and important witnesses must *look* acceptable to the jurors. Research has clearly shown that jurors have great difficulty believing information, even if self-evidently true, from witnesses who appear, by dress or behavior, to be "different" or odd. Professor Laird reports:

> Witnesses' credibility can be directly related to objectively irrelevant factors. People do not necessarily make use of their ability to understand the objective character of a presentation. . . . Sloppy or bizarre dress greatly decrease credibility unless the audience is of a similar propensity. Though persuasion should depend on what a speaker says and not what people think of his character before he begins, it simply does not in many instances.[12]

§ 14-5. Real Evidence or Demonstrations Have More Persuasive Power Than Testimony.[13]

A juror will probably not be persuaded by something he cannot remember: memory is one of the key attributes of persuasion.[14] The chances of a juror recalling and being persuaded by a demonstration or illustrating testimony far exceed the chances that the testimony by itself will be recalled, particularly if the testimony is technical or otherwise dull.

---

11. Laird, *supra* note 1, at 52.

12. *Id.* at 51.

13. *Id.* at 54.

14. Schul & Burnstein, *supra* note 2, at 422-33; Laird, *supra* note 1, at 52.

The crucial points in testimony, particularly technical testimony, should be illustrated or demonstrated whenever possible. In a recent death case trial, for instance, I put on the stand an engineer to testify at great length about how robbers were able to break into the defendant's motel and kill my plaintiff's decedent due to the defective nature of defendant's door, lock, and the lack of needed alarms. At the conclusion of this engineering testimony, to make sure the points were understood by the jury, I had the engineer show the jurors a toy door attached to batteries of blinking lights, loud buzzers, and various whirring alarms that *could* have been put on the real door by defendant. The witness *showed* the jury, on this toy, what his technical testimony had been saying, and every time he finished a major theme he set off something loud or very bright in the toy. I could tell, watching the jury, that the model was what they understood (the expression of jurors listening to engineers and medical experts is usually closely akin to that of small dead rodents in a Taxidermist's window), and when they eventually returned a verdict in excess of a million dollars many of them referred to "the buzzing whatchamacallit" as a vital piece of evidence, even though technically it was a demonstrative aid and not evidence at all.

§ 14-6. Conclusion — The Building Blocks.

No book, including this one, can anticipate or prescribe solutions to all the problems that will require persuasive techniques during a trial. The research data in this chapter, and in Chapter 12, can be applied to a large number of situations, like building blocks in various combinations to erect different kinds of structures needed for varying reasons. Knowledge of the central themes of this research, such as the Primacy Factor, the Front End Load, and the Identification Rule, should be used as a guide to the particular trial persuasion tactics needed for litigation situations as they arise.

CHAPTER 15

CROSS-EXAMINATION

§ 15-1. The Indirect Approach.

Here's a question for trivia lovers: what do Pickett's charge at the Battle of Gettysburg, the advance of Napoleon's Old Guard at the Battle of Waterloo, and almost every battle in the First World War have in common with most miserably unsuccessful cross-examinations? The answer, of course, is that each of the preceding involved a direct frontal attack on a pre-warned, entrenched, sullen opponent who was able either to defeat the attack or make it pay an exorbitant price to achieve its objective.

With few exceptions (such as the Civil War charge of the Army of the Cumberland up and over Confederate defenses on Missionary Ridge outside of Chattanooga), almost all direct frontal attacks against a prepared opponent who could anticipate the place of attack have failed. Similarly, almost all cross-examiners who directly confront a hostile witness with anticipated questions and issues achieve no real gain, and generate only the heated exchange of successive salvos of "Yes, you did!" and "No, I did not!" If you approach a hostile witness with questions obviously intended to make him look like a liar or a fool, the odds are excellent the witness will do his best to give you answers fitting neither category. Nobody can be expected to participate voluntarily in his own tar and feathering.

Most truly successful offensive operations, whether military, legal, or otherwise dependent upon psychology, have depended upon the *indirect* approach to *clear* objectives. Julius Caesar, for example, never lost a battle and never approached an enemy straight on. Clarence Darrow, never, to my knowledge, based cross-examination on a direct demand that the witness just admit he was a knave or a fool.

The concept is simple: your opponents and their witnesses are (at least) as smart as you are, and they know the points you will attack in your cross-examination because they would attack the same points if they had your side of the case. It therefore follows that your opponents and their witnesses are prepared to defend those areas; and their defenses will be triggered as soon as they realize what you are after. Under such circumstances, a direct attack would only be prudent where you are reasonably certain that your opponent has no defenses to worry about. This, of course, is primarily an issue of intelligence gathering: discovery processes, particularly advance depositions, are the main sources for successful cross-examination at trial, for they tell you what the answers to your questions will be. If possible, try never to ask a "live" question on cross-examination before the jury to which you do not already have a "pin" on what the witness should answer, based on interrogatories, depositions, or other sources.

There will, nevertheless, be many instances when you will be required to engage in "first impression" cross-examination, without the benefit of a prior deposition of the witness. One crucial area where this situation will exist is in the deposition itself, where you make initial pre-trial contact with the witness and seek to establish your "pins" for the trial cross-examination. In addition, for many reasons (all of which are unfortunate) we all often find ourselves, in both criminal and civil cases, required to cross-examine witnesses we have never met before "cold" in front of a jury (and judge).

Certain cross-examination targets, particularly in the area of qualifications, can and must be approached directly. As the song from "La Cage Aux Folles" indicates, we are what we are, and the only way to find out if the witness is a Registered Engineer or a Board Certified Physician is to ask him. Attempting an indirect approach on issues like this would be futile and ludicrous.

And now we are left with the remaining 99.99% of first impression cross-examination situations, where you do not know what the answers will be in advance, the witness has an opportunity to avoid your hook, and your chances of success depend largely on how close you can get to your target without alerting the target defenses or looking like a fool to the jury. Just think of it all as one big air raid from which you may or may not return.

The indirect approach indicated for such situations simply calls for following these precepts in cross-examination:

(1) Never begin indirect approach cross-examination with questions that will suggest what you are after to the witness;

(2) Between the start of your cross-examination and the moment you close in for the kill, try to ask questions that drive the witness in the direction you want without overtly calling his attention to what that direction is; short, "bit by bit" questions are fine here;

(3) When you are ready to close in for the kill, do it quickly — Do not draw it out. The more questions you ask in this "end game," or the longer those questions are, the more chance your target has to escape. Remember, whatever can go wrong probably will: the fewer answers you ask for, the fewer chances the witness has to give you something you don't want.

(4) Keep the entire cross as short as possible.

Jerome Lawrence and Robert E. Lee provided an excellent display of indirect approach cross-examination in the climactic moment of their famous play, "Inherit The Wind," when the Clarence Darrow character (Henry Drummond) calls the William Jennings Bryan character (Matthew Harrison Brady) to the stand to be cross-examined as an expert on the Bible. The objective of the cross-examination, of course, was to establish that every word in the Bible need not be taken precisely and literally as written, thereby allowing possible validity to Darwin's theory of evolution, as taught in Hillsboro, Tennessee, in public schools by the Paul Scopes character, Bertram Cates.

Drummond first tries the direct attack:

Q. Now tell me. Do you feel that every word that's written in the Bible should be taken literally?[1]

Brady, being handed the tar and feathers, understandably refuses to apply them to himself:

A. Everything in the Bible should be accepted exactly as it is given there.[2]

---

1. Jerome Lawrence & Robert E. Lee, *Inherit the Wind* at 78 (Bantam, 1981).

2. *Id.*

After a few more direct attacks do no better, Drummond switches to the indirect approach:

Q. I recollect a story about Joshua, making the sun stand still. Now as an expert you tell me that's true. Right?[3]

Brady, who has already literally accepted the story of how the whale swallowed Jonah "nods blandly," seeing this as no more than another example of God's ability to do whatever he wishes.

Drummond then moves in.

Q. That's a pretty neat trick. You suppose Houdini could do it?[4]

Brady, still possibly not seeing the avenue of attack, sticks to his guns.

A. I do not question or scoff at the miracles of the Lord — as do ye of little faith.[5]

Drummond, with a little theatrical license, then moves in for the kill:

Q. Have you ever pondered just what would naturally happen to the earth if the sun stood still. . . . If they say that the sun stood still, they must've had a notion that the sun moves around the earth. Think that's the way of things? Or don't you believe the earth moves around the sun?[6]

All along in this sequence of cross-examination, the target (Brady) has been conditioned to defend the position that the Bible can be taken literally, whatever it says, because God can suspend any natural laws. A whale can swallow Jonah and allow him to emerge unharmed. The stars and planets can be stopped in their normal and natural courses. But at the end of the sequence, Drummond pinned Brady on a passage revealing the authors did not know what the natural laws really were. God might, for whatever celestial reasons, stop the earth as it revolved around the sun, but he could not stop the sun from revolving around the earth without re-writing and changing all natural law because, so far as we know, the sun does not now and never has revolved around the earth.

Brady, the target, has now been shaken, but can still fall back on God's ability to change, as well as suspend, natural laws. He therefore responds:

A. I have faith in the Bible.[7]

After a few inconsequential skirmishes, Drummond feels strong enough to try another direct attack:

Q. Listen to this: Genesis 4-16, "And Cain went out from the presence of the Lord, and dwelt in the land of Nod, on the East of Eden. *And Cain knew his wife*!" Where the hell did *she* come from?[8]

A. Who?

---

3. *Id.*

4. *Id.*

5. *Id.* at 79.

6. *Id.*

7. *Id.* at 79.

8. *Id.*

Q. Mrs. Cain. Cain's wife. If "In the beginning" there were only Adam and Eve, and Cain and Abel, where did this extra woman come from? Ever figure that out?

A. No sir. I will leave the agnostics to hunt for her.

Q. Never bothered you?

A. Never bothered me.

Q. Never tried to find out?

A. No. . . . The Bible satisfies me, it is enough.

Another frontal attack shot flat. After several pages of theatrics irrelevant for our purposes, Drummond tries another indirect approach:

Q. Look, Mr. Brady, these are the fossil remains of a pre-historic marine creature, which was found in this very country — and which lived here millions of years ago, when these very mountain ranges were submerged in water.[9]

A. I know. The Bible gives a fine account of the flood. But [you] are a little mixed up on his dates. That rock is not more than six thousand years old.

Q. How do you know?

A. A fine Biblical scholar, Bishop Usher, has determined for us the exact date and hour of its creation. It occurred in the year 4004 B.C.

Q. That's Bishop Usher's opinion.

A. It is not an opinion — It is literal fact, which the good Bishop arrived at through careful computation of the ages of the prophets as set down in the Old Testament. In fact, he determined that the Lord began the Creation on the 23rd of October in the year 4004 B.C. at 9:00 a.m.

Q. The first day. Was it a twenty-four hour day?

A. The Bible says it was a day.

Drummond then moves in for the kill.

Q. There wasn't any sun. How do you know how long it was?

A. The Bible says it was a day.

Q. A normal day, a literal day, a twenty-four-hour day?

A. I do not know.

The defenses having been cracked, Drummond soon pushes through for a little final looting and pillaging:

Q. Isn't it possible that first day was twenty-five hours long? There was no way to measure it, no way to tell! *Could* it have been twenty-five hours?

A. It is . . . possible.

Q. Oh. You interpret that the first day recorded in the Book of Genesis could be of indeterminate length?

A. I mean to state that the day referred to is not necessarily a twenty-four-hour day.

Q. It could have been thirty hours! Or a month! Or a year! Or a hundred years! Or ten million years![10]

---

9. *Id.* at 85.

10. *Id.* at 86.

Thus, in a series of short, indirect attacks where the opening questions did not suggest the tactical objective, Drummond backed Brady into conceding the overall strategic objective, that every word in the Bible might not be literally true. The passage is a good example of indirect approach cross-examination, admittedly with a captive target witness; it also brings out some other relevant points. For one thing, this questioning holds interest. Indeed, for the authors that was *the* main consideration: they were writing dialogue to hold a paying audience, not to illustrate indirect approach cross-examination. It is, however, obvious that the interest of a jury can be held where the interest of a theater audience was held, and indirect approach cross can hold both for the same reason the target witness has such difficulty defending against it: nobody knows where things are going.

§ 15-2. Take Them Out Quickly.

As earlier chapters have indicated, the psychological doctrine of primacy establishes that the first impressions a juror has of a proceeding will most likely be that juror's final impressions as well.[11] In cross-examination, this means that the jurors expect you to quickly do your best to neutralize the witness you are cross-examining, and the impressions you make early on in the examination will form a large part of the jurors' evaluation of how well you did. This is not to deny the need to finish the cross-examination (or any proceeding before the jury) on a strong

---

11. W. Lundquist, "Advocacy in Opening Statements," 8 *Litigation* No. 3, at 23 (Spring 1982); D. Baum, "The Plaintiff's Approach to Opening Statement," *Persuasion: The Key to Success in Trial,* G. Holmer, ed. (1978).

note. A jury will have maximum attention at the beginning and at the end of a communication,[12] and common sense dictates the need for a strong finish. The beginning of a cross-examination is, however, even more important than the end, because if the jurors conclude from the early portion of the cross that you have not seriously damaged the witness, they are likely to conclude you can do no better (or you would have done so) and tune out the rest of what you have to say. Professor A.W. Laird, Emeritus Professor of Psychology at Western Kentucky University concluded that:

> Before an advocate rises to cross-examine a witness, he must ask whether the witness has testified to anything that is material against him: whether the testimony has injured his side of the case; and ultimately whether one should cross-examine the witness at all. When a witness does testify to material facts which injure an advocate's position, it becomes the advocate's duty to break the force of it. How well the cross-examiner achieves the elusive commodity of truth will depend upon his psychological understanding of the witness. Kramer says that the cardinal rule in cross-examination is to make your most important point right away. By striking at the outset and eroding the witness' credibility, you stand a much better chance of getting the jury to go along with you in those areas of your attack where you are weaker.[13]

If these findings are correct, they strongly argue for abolishing the old "hide in the weeds" style of cross-examination lawyers have been following since the days of Clarence Darrow and Earl Rogers. In this procedure, the witness (and the jurors) are lulled into a false sense of security through a long, deadly dull series of innocuous

12. A.W. Laird, "Persuasion: A Tool of Courtroom Communication," *Psychology: A Quarterly Journal of Human Behavior,* Vol. 19 (213), at 50-57 (1982).

13. *Id.* at 45.

questions, setting up the witness for admissions. The basic concept of diverting the attention of the witness from the objectives of the examiner is, of course, fine, (see § 15-1). However, a short, indirect approach to the goal is a much better way to do this than a long, dull lead in that may lead the jurors to dismiss the entire subsequent examination, including the "good stuff" hoarded at the end, as a boring failure.

§ 15-3. Target Areas.

Cross-examination of most witnesses, experts, and non-experts, can be organized around at least some of the suggested headings, which constitute a collection of classic attack paths used to "take a witness out." Specific questions appropriate for a particular case should, of course, be organized under each relevant topic heading.

§ 15-3(A). The Witness Cannot Be Believed Due to Prejudice.

1. Is the witness a social friend or employee of the opposing party?
2. Is the witness a social friend or employee of crucial opposition witnesses?
3. Has the witness testified or been retained by the opposing party before?
4. Has the witness testified or been retained by the opposing lawyer before?
5. How much is the witness being paid?
6. How much has the opposing party or opposing lawyers paid the witness on other cases?
7. Has the witness previously accepted retainers from both plaintiffs and defendants, or is the witness a "hired gun" working only one side of the street?
8. Does the witness have any financial interest in the litigation, either through an ownership interest in a party, or an incentive fee as an expert?

§ 15-3(B). The Witness Cannot Be Believed Due to Lack of Qualifications.

1. *If a physician:*
   (a) Board Certified in relevant areas?
   (b) Experience on training in relevant areas?
   (c) Access to relevant records?
   (d) Sufficient examination of persons and records?
   (e) Hospital and teaching positions?
   (f) Writings in relevant areas?
   (g) Prior lawsuits against him or her?
   (h) Familiarity with relevant standards?
2. *If an engineer:*
   (a) Registered?
   (b) Positions held and qualifications?
   (c) Experience and training in relevant areas?
   (d) Teaching positions?
   (e) Writings in relevant areas?
   (f) Practical engineering work done?
      (i) When?
      (ii) Where?
      (iii) What was built?
   (g) Familiarity with relevant standards?

§ 15-3(C). The Witness Cannot Be Believed Because He Did Not Know Relevant Facts When He Formed His Opinions.

An expert opinion is like a newborn infant: it better have everything it needs when it starts out because it is very hard to add anything later on. You therefore want to pin the witness down on when he formed his opinions, when he put them in writing or on tape, when he communicated them to anyone else, and what he knew about the relevant facts and documents at each of those times.

§ 15-3(D). The Witness Cannot Be Believed Because He Is Wrong on the Merits.

If the witness, even an expert operating in his field of expertise, is wrong on the merits, first pin him down on what his opinions are (if he is an expert) or what his testimony is (if he is an occurrence witness). Then cross-examine him with whatever evidence or expert literature you may have that refutes what he says. In your cross, try to develop ways in which the target witness is less reliable or less qualified than your witnesses. Then bring in your own witnesses at trial to refute him.

§ 15-3(E). The Witness Cannot Be Believed Now Because He Is Tied to an Earlier Adoption of Something to the Contrary.

No witness ever comes to the witness stand without leaving a long trail of interaction with other people. Experts have often taught from books, and written papers, that you can obtain to examine for contrary positions. Non-expert witnesses may have expressed contrary opinions to what they say in your case before other juries, to friends, or to co-workers. An ounce of digging in these areas can produce tons of pay dirt.

§ 15-3(F). The Witness Cannot Be Believed Because He Said Something Incredible, and You Can Disregard Everything Else He Said.

Most jurisdictions provide a "weak link" instruction in some form, which tells the jury that if they find something a witness said, particularly an expert, to be incredible, they may disregard everything else the witness said. In cross-examination you should obviously stress efforts to produce such incredible statements. Once you get them, move immediately to something else. Do not guild the lily, and give the witness a chance to rehabilitate himself. Remember, the closed mouth gathers no toes.

§ 15-4. Whether to Cross-Examine.

If you do not have effective cross-examination fitting into one of these categories, seriously consider not cross-examining at all. Here are some guidelines:

A. It is not necessary to cross-examine every witness. If the witness is not important or has not hurt you, it is generally a wise idea not to cross.

B. If the witness can be believed and is correct, but you rely on other facts or arguments to establish that the witness' testimony is not relevant to your case, engage in little or no cross.

C. If the witness has made statements damaging to your opponent on direct examination, do not go into those areas on cross-examination. Save them for closing argument. Do not guild the lily. This rule may preclude cross-examination in the relevant area of direct testimony. If that happens waive all cross, don't waste time fighting over insignificant things.

§ 15-5. Additional Points.

§ 15-5(A). Do Not Guild the Lily.

Do not elaborate or explain on cross-examination. Secure your points, move on, and explain their significance in opening and closing: Never guild the lily. Do not compare the purpose of cross-examination, which is to make your points, with the purpose of the closing arguments, which is to tell the jury what those points mean.

§ 15-5(B). Use Honey, Not Vinegar.

Be as friendly as possible during cross-examination. This will lower the defenses of the witnesses. You will catch more flies with honey than with vinegar, especially if the witness (fly) does not realize your innocent-seeming questions (honey) are designed to lay a foundation from which, in closing argument, you can persuade the jury that he is a liar, fool, and horse thief. The offer of food and soft drinks to opposing witnesses and lawyers at a deposition, for example, often produces a most salutory softening effect quite helpful for indirect approach questioning.

§ 15-5(C). Break the Expert on His Weakest Link — Facts.

In order to attack the opinions of a hostile expert in your closing argument, remember that an opinion is usually no stronger than the factual base supporting it. Depositions and cross-examinations of the hostile expert should therefore concentrate more on what the hostile expert does not know than on what his opinions are. If the hostile expert has not done his homework, you may find he lacks essential information that undermines the weight of his opinion, and that is invariably a more productive area to explore than the expert's opinions. (After all, if his opinions did not favor the other side, why would they have listed him as their expert?)

Sometimes, particularly where your opponent's cross-examination of several witnesses falls into a routine pattern, you can structure your direct examination in such a way as to highlight, and undermine, the anticipated cross-examination.

In the following section, that is what happened. We were presenting a transportation negligence case and one of the important witness groups for such a case is "road witness," drivers familiar with what it was like to drive the road in question at the time in question. We had previously presented several road witnesses, each of whom testified how dangerous it was to drive the area in question, the

Cline Avenue "S" curve, at night, at and prior to the time of the crash. The cross-examination by the defense of each such witness had started by pointing out that the witness had not been involved directly in a crash of his own, thereby trying to make the points with the jury that our Plaintiff driver must have somehow been less skillful than any of the road witness drivers.

With that pattern in mind, my partner, George Pontikes, presented a road witness named Crosby Eugene Harris. Mr. Harris had been involved in a crash under strikingly similar circumstances on the very roadway at issue. Relying upon the pattern of cross-examination the defense had followed, we gambled that if we did not bring out the prior crash on direct, the defense would do our work for us and bring out with even more emphasis everything we wanted in the course of their cross. This is what followed:

CROSBY EUGENE HARRIS, having been first duly sworn, testified as follows:

DIRECT EXAMINATION
BY MR. PONTIKES:

Q. Mr. Harris, would you state your name, please?

A. Crosby Eugene Harris.

Q. And where do you reside?

A. Gary, Indiana; 823 King Street.

Q. What is your occupation, sir?

A. I am a labor-pusher at Inland Steel.

Q. Are you familiar with the Cline Avenue roadway?

A. Yes.

Q. Have you traveled that roadway?

A. At least six times a week.

Q. How long have you been traveling that roadway for that number of times each week?

A. Ever since it was built. I go back and forth, I use that going back and forth to work.

Q. And to the best of your recollection when was the roadway built?

A. Have to be about '65 or '64, something like that.

Q. And did you have occasion from that time through July 27, 1970, to travel on the Cline Avenue roadway?

A. Yes.

Q. Specifically did you travel on the Cline Avenue roadway in July of 1970?

A. Yes.

Q. Did you travel both during the daytime and in the evening?

A. Both.

Q. Now, during July, 1970, how often would you be traveling Cline Avenue roadway?

A. Could you state that question again, please?

Q. During July, 1970, how often were you traveling on the Cline Avenue roadway?

A. Oh, the same time, six times a week every day.

Q. And were you traveling both during the day and in the evening during that time?

A. Yes.

Q. Are you familiar with the area of Cline Avenue roadway known as the S-Curve?

A. Yes.

Q. Were you traveling over that area during the month of July, 1970?

A. Yes.

Q. Now, calling your attention to that specific area of Cline Avenue roadway, in July, 1970, were there any lights on that roadway?

A. No, there were no lights.

Q. Was there any paint on the center curb?

A. When you speak of the center curb, are you speaking of the median?

Q. The center median, correct?

A. The center median, correct?

No.

Q. Were there any delineators on either side of the roadway?

A. Again what do you mean when you say delineators?

Q. Delineators, I mean any kinds of marks or indications to set off the road?

A. No.

Q. Were there on the S-Curve in the month of July, 1970, any warning signs?

A. There were no warning signs.

Q. Now, during that same month, July, 1970, did you see any posted speed signs showing the speed limit?

A. None.

Q. Were you aware of what the speed limit was in the State of Indiana for roadways in July, 1970?

A. 70 miles an hour.

Q. And was there a barrier on the median in the S-Curve on Cline Avenue during July, 1970?

A. Are you speaking of the concrete?

Q. I'm speaking of the concrete.

A. No.

Q. Now, Mr. Harris, as a result of these conditions was your ability to drive safely on the S-Curve northbound and southbound affected? Was your ability to drive northbound and southbound on Cline Avenue affected?

DEFENSE LAWYER: I object to that question, your Honor, as not being relevant to this case. This man was not in the car that Robert Casillas was driving that night, and what his own reaction is while driving or was at the time, back at the time of his time frame of his accident would not be relevant to this cause.

THE COURT: The objection is overruled.

Mr. Harris, do you recall the question?

A. Could you state it again?

MR. PONTIKES: Q. As a result of the condition you just told us about —

A. Okay —

Q. Were you able to safely drive northbound or southbound on the S-Curve on Cline Avenue?

A. No, I wasn't.

CROSS EXAMINATION FOR THE DEFENSE

Q. Mr. Harris, by stating you weren't able to safely drive, does that mean you had an accident out there?

A. Yes, I had an accident there.

Q. In the S-Curve?

A. In the S-Curve.

Q. What happened in that S-Curve?

A. Well, I was going north, I was going to work.

Q. Let me ask you this: Did that involve a car crossing the center from one lane and hitting somebody going the opposite way?

A. Yes, the car, there was a car going south and I was going north, and he went over the median, came toward me and went back on his side, and he sideswiped another car. Then when I seen him, I put on my brakes and I stopped and I was in the inside lane and I stopped to keep from hitting him. But he had crossed over the median back over to his side, and about, I'll say about so many seconds another car came over the hill into the S. I was down in the S where you make a curve like a valley like, and the guy came and hit me in the back.

Q. So that this involved a situation where you were rear ended?

A. Right.

Q. What date did that accident happen?

A. Had to be the year of 1968.

Q. Did that accident happen — what time of the day did that happen?

A. It happened around about 1 — about 15 after 1:00. When I say around that time, at the time I was working at Youngstown Sheet and Tube and I was working at 3 to 11, and I had to be at work about 1, about a quarter to 2 at the time. So it had to be around 1:15 or 1:30 when it happened.

Q. In the afternoon?

A. Yes.

Q. You weren't present, were you, when Mr. Casillas had his accident, the accident you are testifying about here today?

A. No.

Q. You didn't see what the car did at that time, did you?

A. No.

Q. You have no idea what caused the accident there, do you?

A. I don't know anything about it.

No further questions.

Exhibit

Sample of Cross-Examination

[A] FACTS.

At a passively protected railroad grade crossing, a train hit a car with two occupants during a snowstorm, killing the occupants of the car. The train crew had testified that they could not see the car as the train rounded a curve, until seconds before the crash, at which time there was nothing they could do to avoid the crash. The expert had testified on direct examination that the railroad had used reasonable care, and the people in the car should have seen the approaching train long enough before the crash to safely get out of the way. In fact, the expert had testified that the occupants of the car should have seen and reacted to the train in 9/10 of a second.

The defense engineer had given long and impressive testimony for several hours, and many of the jurors were smiling at him in a distressingly friendly way when I began the cross-examination. I therefore needed a sharp, punchy opening that would immediately put doubts into the jurors' minds about what he had told them. The two best subjects to use for such an opening are qualifications and bias of the expert.

[B] I began with holes in the expert's qualifications:

BY MR. KUHLMAN:

Q. Do you have a Ph.D. degree?

A. No, I do not.

Q. Do you have a master's degree?

A. No, I do not.

Q. Are you a tenure professor at any university?

A. No, I am not.

Q. Have you ever been?

A. No.

Q. Did you ever take any graduate courses in physics?

A. Not graduate, no.

Q. Did you ever teach physics?

A. No.

Q. Are you a member of the Transportation Research Board?

A. No, I am not a member.

Q. Are you a member of the Transportation Research Forum?

A. No.

Q. Have you ever been personally employed by any federal or state government agency to work on analysis of car-train collisions?

A. No.

Q. Does your engineering certificate in the State of Illinois say anything about any specialization that you have in analysis of car-train collisions?

A. No specialization, no.

[C] Having attempted to raise doubts about the expert's background, I then attacked various calculations the expert had made for the defense by pointing out the unfair assumptions in those questions, which was that the car occupants should have been able to see the approaching train in time to avoid the crash in good weather with clear visibility. Under the evidence the jury had already heard, this crash took place in a snowstorm.

Q. All those calculations you just reeled off there for the railroad lawyer of how far away a motorist would see an approaching train, they assumed good visibility, didn't they?

A. Yes. They would assume that the train could be seen that far.

Q. So let me ask you a question: Could conditions such as snow falling from the sky, snow blowing in the air, fog, and reduced sunlight affect and reduce visibility?

A. They could reduce visibility.

Q. Can these factors reduce the visibility of a motorist at a railroad crossing?

A. They can.

Q. Or the visibility of a train crew as they are in a train that approaches a railroad crossing?

A. Yes.

Q. Let me ask you this question: Do you believe that trains operating over tracks intersected by public roads should reduce their speed below the maximum speed limit for such trains if weather and visibility conditions are sufficiently severe, or do you believe the train should operate under their maximum speed limit no matter how bad the weather and visibility conditions are?

DEFENSE LAWYER: Objection as beyond the scope.

MR. KUHLMAN: Are you stipulating he is not qualified to answer?

THE COURT: Just a minute.

What is the objection?

DEFENSE LAWYER: I didn't hire him to get into that subject.

MR. KUHLMAN: If he stipulates he is not qualified, I will withdraw the question.

THE COURT: Proceed.

[D] I then went into other areas of bias the expert might have had for putting unwarranted, pro-defense factual assumptions into his calculations on direct examination:

Q. Have you worked previously on collision cases for the railroad lawyers in this case?

A. Yes, I have.

Q. Have you previously worked on train collision cases for The Penn Central Railroad and Amtrak?

A. Yes, I have.

Q. Are you currently working on pending cases for the railroad lawyers in this case, Penn Central or Amtrak?

A. I believe so, yes.

Q. How much is the railroad paying you in this case?

A. Well, our fees are based on an hourly time charge.

Q. How much have your charged so far?

A. I can't recall it specifically on this particular case.

Q. Have you submitted your bills yet?

A. No.

Q. Have you submitted any bills on this case yet?

A. Not this particular case, no.

Q. Do you charge for your time right here in court now?
A. Yes, I would be.
Q. Do you charge as much for your time in court as your time out of court?
A. Yes. Our fees are standard.
Q. How many times have you submitted a professional resume to a railroad?
A. To a railroad?
Q. To a railroad.
A. Oh, I am not — I can't recall exactly. I would just have to give a very rough estimate of 15 or 20. I am really not sure of that.
Q. Have you submitted previous resumes to Penn Central or Amtrak?
A. I probably did, yes.

[E] Mae West was not necessarily correct: Sometimes too much of even a great thing can be boring. With that in mind, I then moved off the bias issues and brought up affirmative expert literature the witness had ignored on direct examination which called for safety measures the railroad had not installed at the crossing in question prior to the crash.

Q. Are you familiar with the work of "Policy on Geometric Design of Rural Highways" published in 1965 by the American Association of State Highway Officials?
A. Yes, I am.
Q. Do you consider that competent?
A. Yes, I do.
Q. Do you consider it authoritative?
A. Yes.
Q. Do you agree with this statement from page 384 of that work:

> Regardless of the type of control, the roadway gradient should be flat at and adjacent to the railroad crossing to permit vehicles to stop when necessary and then proceed across without difficulty.

[F] I then moved into the expert's direct testimony on reaction times, which I knew (but the jury did not) were based upon non-stress testing and did not allow for the slowed or paralyzed reactions the people in the car might have had if a hurtling train suddenly shot out of a wall of falling snow only a few feet away from their car:

Q. You testified as to human reaction time for normal drivers — I think that is what you just said — .9 of a second in emergency situations? Those calculations that you made as to driver reaction time, they incorporated a reaction time of .9 of a second for normal drivers?
A. That is right.
Q. Reaction time is not a constant unchanging thing, is it?

A. That is right.

Q. It takes different amounts of time for motorists to react to different situations, doesn't it?

A. It would depend primarily on the motorist and, of course, the conditions and the situation.

Q. Like visibility and things like that, right?

A. Well, the visibility would be a function of how far it could be perceived.

Q. A motorist must be able to see a problem such as an approaching train before he can react to it, right?

A. That is right.

Q. And weather conditions impairing visibility such as falling or blowing snow or fog, and reduced sunlight, they will reduce a motorist's ability to see and recognize a problem such as an oncoming train?

A. They could.

Q. And if a motorist saw a light approach in the middle of a heavy snowfall with snow blowing in the air and falling from the sky and reduced visibility, and the motorist had to determine what that light was, could those weather conditions impair his ability to recognize what the light was?

THE WITNESS: Without any other information, it could affect the person's response to seeing a light but you have to have other information in terms of what you know that person is driving and with what conditions.

MR. KUHLMAN: Are you saying you cannot answer the question?

THE WITNESS: I am saying there needs to be more information than just seeing a light.

BY MR. KUHLMAN:

Q. Did you ever feel that that question had enough information to be answerable?

A. I am not sure if I follow that.

Q. Well, at your deposition were you asked this question and did you give this answer at the bottom of page 82:

> Q. If you saw a light approaching you in the middle of a heavy snowfall with snow blowing in the air and snow falling from the sky and reduced visibility and you had to determine what the light was from, might those weather conditions impair your ability to recognize what the light was from?
> A. I would have to say in most — well, I would have to put that in context of where the motorist is at the time.
> Q. Well, a person under any situation.
> A. Under any situation?
> Q. Isn't it possible?

A. Ask the question again. Restate it.
MR. KUHLMAN: Read it back.
(Whereupon the record was read as requested.)
BY THE WITNESS:
A. Without any other orientation than that, I would say they could.

Now were you asked those questions and did you give that answer at your deposition?

A. I gave those answers.

Q. Is it not a fact, that those conditions would affect the motorist's ability to judge how fast the light was approaching as well, isn't that true?

A. Pardon?

Q. Isn't it a fact that those weather conditions we have just discussed, heavy snow, reduced light, snow blowing and falling in the air, they could also reduce the motorist's ability to tell how fast the light was approaching, isn't that true?

A. To some extent they could.

Q. Is it not a fact that the longer it takes a motorist to recognize what an object is after he has seen it, the longer it will take him to react to it after he has first seen it?

A. Again I would have to go back to the circumstances, and if the motorist is aware, for example, that he is approaching a railroad crossing and seeing a light where, you know, a track would be located.

Q. Wait a minute. I don't think it is that esoteric. Let me ask you this question: If a man is driving a car and he is drunk and he can't see straight and he sees a blurr out in front of the road and he doesn't know what it is and it takes a while to recognize what it is — okay?

A. Yes.

Q. Now he can't respond to that until he realizes what it is, is that right?

A. That is right.

Q. That is all I am asking.

The further you have to turn your head or eyes from the direct line of sight to see something, isn't it true that that affects how long it takes you to perceive and react to it?

A. Here again, if you have to turn your head away from a normal frontal view any significant angle, it would take some time to turn your head if you are looking —

Q. Turn it to the left or turn it to the right, sometimes turn it to the left and look and sometimes turn it to the right and look and, sometimes look and not know what you are seeing, that can all happen to a motorist, can't it?

A. Yes, it can.

Q. It sure can.

Isn't it a fact that a motorist might not be able to see a train approaching him as far away under poor weather and visibility conditions as he can under the perfect kind of weather and visibility conditions you were assuming in your answer to the railroad's questions?

A. Yes, it can.

Q. If the train were coming towards such a motorist at, say, 50 miles an hour, then he would have less time to react to it if he could first perceive it at 100 feet than if he could first perceive it at 1,000 feet?

A. So I understand that, if—

Q. If the train were coming toward a motorist at 50 miles an hour and the motorist could first perceive it at 100 feet he would have less time to react to it than if he first perceived it at 1,000 feet.

A. Yes.

Q. Sure. Isn't it a fact that the further away the motorist can see and perceive the train coming to him at a crossing, the more time the motorist will have to react to the train?

A. Yes.

Q. Sure. And the closer the train is when the motorist can first see it, then the less time the motorist will have to react to the train.

A. That is true.

Q. Sure. And isn't there a relationship between the speed at which a train approaches a crossing and how far down the track the motorist must be able to first see the train in order to safely cross the track?

A. Well, it can be determined by a function of the train speed and the vehicle speed.

Q. I don't think it is that complicated, is it? Isn't it just the fact that the faster a train is going, the further away the motorist must first be able to see it to get out of its way?

A. Basically in simple terms, yes.

Q. Sure.

All right.

[G] It can be painfully dull to cross-examine an expert by citing an endless barrage of expert literature. As title follows title, you can literally see the juror's eyes glaze over. I therefore broke up the expert literature on this cross-examination, interspersing it between other sections. I now brought up literature geared to reaction times being effected by sight distance and the fact that this crash had occurred on a crossing with two sets of tracks crossing the road. The car had succeeded in safely getting over the first set of tracks and the railroad had failed to post a required sign warning of the second set of tracks, which the car was going over when the train hit it:

Q. Now are you familiar with the "National Cooperative Highway Research Program Report No. 50"?

A. Yes.

Q. Do you consider that authoritative?

A. Yes, I do.

Q. Do you agree with this from page 25 of that work:

> The driver must be able to see a sufficient distance along the tracks to allow him to judge if it is safe to proceed. This is the third sight distance which the driver finds important to safe navigation of the crossing. Required sight distance No. 3 is dependent on the train's speed.

Do you agree with that?

A. The required sight distance that they are dealing with is where an automobile is — a vehicle is stopped and is looking down the track. For example, a truck is what they are dealing with there.

Q. Yes, and that requires — the sight distance is dependent on the train speed?

A. And a function of how fast the vehicle can proceed from a stop and move across the track.

Q. But it does say that the required sight distance is dependent on the train speed? That is a verbatim quote. Do you agree with it or not?

A. Yes.

Q. Sure.

Is it not true that if a motorist travelling south on County Road 400 East toward this crossing due to falling and blowing snow and poor sunlight and poor visibility could only see one track as he was going down County Road 400 East, then even if he saw or heard an approaching train, he would assume that that train was approaching on the track that he could see, isn't that a reasonable assumption?

A. You are saying that if he saw only one track, that the visibility was such that he could not see any other track —

Q. Right.

A. Tracks —

Q. Right.

A. And that then you also said — Read the second part of it.

Q. Even if he saw or heard an approaching train, wouldn't it be reasonable for him to assume that the train was approaching on the track he could see?

A. Yes.

Q. Sure. And then he would be making all of his decisions about how fast to go and what maneuvering his car ought to go through in making the decision on whether to try to pass the crossing or whether to stop on the assumption that he has got to deal with the train approaching on the tracks he can see?

A. Yes, but under those conditions, as you put it in the context of the track, that would be a very, very limited distance.

Q. But what I am saying was if there is no posted warning of a second track and he could only see one track and he heard a train whistle blowing or saw a train coming, isn't it reasonable to assume he would say, "There is a track, there is a train and I don't have to assume there is 15 other tracks behind it that I don't know about," right?

A. Yes, from what you are saying it is reasonable.

Q. Sure. Right. And then if the motorist clears that track and suddenly discovers the train was approaching him at high speed on a second track that was only a few feet away from him and that the train was only a few feet away from him, then the motorist would have a sudden emergency situation, wouldn't he?

A. Well, yes, from the question you asked.

Q. Now if a motorist at an intersection where two tracks intersect a road and where there is no warning of the presence of two tracks, crosses over one track and then looks down the second track in the opposite direction from which a train is actually really approaching on the second track and then he turns and looks and sees the train is almost upon him at high speed from the direction that he didn't first look at, wouldn't that driver also be in a sudden emergency situation?

A. Yes.

Q. Sure.

[H] I then moved for an admission from the witness that sudden peril can destroy all normal reaction times. It was a risk worth running, I decided, because the witness would either make the concession that destroyed most of his direct examination, or be pounded to pieces by my authorities and rebuttal experts:

Q. Isn't it a fact that sudden exposure to peril, to life-threatening situations, to emergency situations, can alter or even paralyze a motorist's ability to react?

A. Counsel, I wouldn't say it's a fact.

[I] Once I received that answer, I knew we were in for trench warfare. The jury had to be shown, quickly, that the witness was wrong:

Q. Are you familiar with the "Preliminary Investigation into a Physiological Assessment of Driving Stress" by Dr. T.J. Hunt published by the Division of Human Physiology, National Institute for Medical Research, Medical Research Council, London, England, 1968?

A. No, I am not.

Q. Would you agree or disagree with this statement from page 36 of that work:

> Records of journeys show that, as a result of exposure, a driver may continue in a state of apprehension and/or uncertainty for a minute — or even longer — following the actual incident which initiated the danger. Incorrect decision-making may therefore continue for some time after the unexpected incident, and any accident or error in driving occurring during that period may be occasioned by the continuing effects of startle, rather than as a direct result of the incident itself.

Would you agree with that statement or not?

A. Without being able to read it, I don't know what the surrounding study was.

Q. There is a second treatise on this very same point, on "Driver Reaction in Traffic" by G.M. Mackay of the University of Birmingham in the Dec.-Jan. 1967-1968 volume of New Zealand Road Safety.

Are you familiar with that work?

A. I am familiar with the New Zealand research work and I think I am familiar with the general publication that you are referencing. I am not familiar with the specific article, no.

Q. Do you consider that an authoritative work, the New Zealand Road Safety —

A. Yes, I would consider that authoritative.

Q. Would you agree or disagree with this language from page 18 of that work:

> In cases of extreme emotional stress, a pathological situation may arise in which the normal response to traffic may be suspended.

A. Here again, I don't know the context of the research. It sounds like they are talking about in the usual condition and when you talk about unusual emotional stress —

[J] By now the point was to let the jury hear what all this expert literature said, because the trial was in a jurisdiction where such literature can be used in cross-examination, but cannot be directly admitted into evidence. By bombarding the hostile expert with all of this literature, in one lump, I was violating my earlier decision to spread it out, but I was trying for a knock-out punch by now, and the constant drumroll of authorities was forcing the witness into a corner where he could either claim he was unfamiliar with the authorities, in which case he did not know what he was talking about, or he agreed with the authorities, in which case he destroyed his own direct testimony, or he disagreed with the authorities although he did not know anything about them except that they made him look bad. We proceeded:

Q. Are you familiar with the report "Psychology and Behavior of Drivers and the Causation of Accidents" by E.G. Poulton, Assistant Director of the Medical Research Counsel, Applied Psychology Research Unit, Cambridge, England, published in Volume 14, No. 4 of International Road Safety and Traffic Review?

A. Again, the International Road Safety and Traffic Review I have heard of but —

Q. Do you consider that to be competent?

A. Yes, I do.

Q. Would you agree or disagree with this statement from page 18 of that work:

> one of the most interesting pieces of experimental research carried out at the British Road Research Laboratory concerns overtaking on a two-lane road. The driver was following a car, and there was a car ahead coming in the opposite direction. At a given signal he had to decide whether or not to overtake. Decision times ranged from an average of about 1.0 second when the driver had four seconds to spare after overtaking, to about 2.0 seconds when the driver had no time to spare. Thus the decision times reflected the difficulty of the decisions. When the driver should have started to overtake at once if he was to do so at all, because he had little or no time to spare, his maneuver was delayed owing to the difficulty of deciding whether or not to overtake. Clearly drivers should not need to find themselves in such a difficult and dangerous situation.

[K] I then switched to another reason why the occupants in the car might not have been able to react to the train as quickly as the witness had testified they should have: the fact that the tracks extended both east and west of the approach road:

Q. If a motorist came to an intersection where the track goes across the road in two directions such as east and west as it does at the County Road 400 crossing, and the motorist looked down one way and thought he saw something but couldn't be sure what it was he saw, that he could reasonably be expected to look down the track long enough to tell what he was looking at, isn't that right?

A. To perceive it?

Q. Yes.

A. Yes.

Q. If a motorist came to an intersection like the one in this case with tracks east and west of the road and if there was obscure visibility from falling and blowing snow and from poor sunlight, then he might reasonably look first to the east to see if something was coming, right, instead of looking first to the west, right?

A. It depends on the person's habit.

Q. It could be either way, right?

A. Could be either way, right.

Q. And it might reasonably take him longer than .9 of a second just to check out the tracks to the east if there was poor visibility, right?

A. It could.

Q. Sure. And he could use more than .9 of a second before he even started to turn his head to look to the west, right?

A. Again yes, it would depend on where he is on the roadway.

[L] Having broken up the barrage of authorities, at least a little, we now returned to it:

Q. Dealing with reaction times, are you familiar with the National Cooperative Highway Research Program, Report No. 50, which is "Factors Influencing Safety, Highways, Railroad Grade Crossings," prepared by the Highway Research Board of the National Research Council, National Academy of Sciences and National Academy of Engineers?

A. Yes, you just referred to that a while ago.

Q. And you consider that competent?

A. Yes, I do.

Q. Do you agree with this statement from page 103 of that work:

> Response time to visual stimuli increases with an increasing complexity or number of the stimuli. The more complex the visual field, the more things one has to attend to; the longer it takes for any one thing to be reacted to. Response time also increases as the stimuli become less distinct and/or more ambiguous. Essen has shown reaction times to lights increase as the lights are placed further from the observer. The results suggest that reaction times obtained at near point must be increased if they are to be applied to the driver in motion, whose attention is diverted farther and farther down the road as his speed increases.
>
> Finally, response time increases with increasing angular displacement of the stimulus from the direct line of sight. A minimum glance to read a target outside of the 5° arc of clear vision requires from 0.6 to 1.0 seconds. This glance reading time will permit recognition (comprehension) of three to four short, familiar words. Perception of unfamiliar patterns, words, et cetera, will be less rapid.

Do you agree or disagree with that?

A. First of all what page was that?

Q. What page?

A. Yes.

Q. 84.

A. What were you quoting? I thought you said 103, excuse me.

Q. No, 84.

A. Yes. I would agree with that.

Q. Is it not true that a reaction time several times greater than .9 of a second could be necessary for an average motorist to perceive, recognize, and react to a train approaching his car at a sharp angle out of a snowstorm in obscured daylight such as dusk?

A. If he is looking straight ahead and has to respond to something out of his peripheral vision and turn to it.

Q. Isn't it possible —

A. Yes.

Q. — that reaction time could be greater than .9 of a second if he was looking straight ahead and couldn't tell what he was looking at?

A. Yes, because it would take time to look, you know, towards the light source.

Q. Are you familiar with the book Traffic Engineering by Matson, Smith, and Hurd?

A. Yes, I am.

Q. Do you consider that competent?

A. Yes.

Q. Are you familiar with the contents of P.I.E.V. in that book which I think you mentioned previously in your testimony to the railroad lawyer?

A. Yes.

Q. Now do you agree with the following language from that book at pages 20 and 21:

> Regardless of which sensory perceptions are involved, the road user's response to the stimulus of a particular traffic situation takes time. The time required for a response such as putting on the brake is taken up by the psychological processes of perception, intellection, emotion, and volition.
>
> "Perception" means the road user does not have a simple reflex response to the stimuli he encounters under most traffic conditions. In nearly every case, he must perceive a complex and involved situation before he can react, and as the complexity of the situation increases, the time required to perceive conditions increases.
>
> "Intellection" is the forming of new thoughts and ideas. The time required for comparing, regrouping and registering new sensations is the intellection time. "Emotion" means the emotion may vitally influence or affect the final message which is sent to the muscles to be carried out. Behavior growing out of fear or anger is not unusual in traffic accidents. "Volition" is the will to take some act.

Do you agree with that?
A. Yes, I do.

[M] I was now set to launch a detailed attack on the most important single statistic the witness had offered the jury on direct examination, that the people in the car should have seen, reacted to, and gotten out of the way of the train in 9/10 of a second, despite the snow, darkness, confusion, and sudden startle. The avenue of attack was to show how much longer than 9/10 of a second even uncomplicated traffic maneuvers made by people not suddenly confronting violent death will take:

Q. Do you agree or disagree with the following language on page 21 of that very same book:

> In his every act, the road user is dependent on perception, intellection, emotion, and volition. This process of P.I.E.V. requires a time ranging from as low as perhaps 0.5 seconds for simple problems to as much as 3 or 4 seconds for a more complex problem such as the decision to overtake and pass on a two-lane road.

Do you agree with that?
A. Yes, I do.
Q. Yes, you do say it can take three or four seconds for such a complex problem as deciding to pass on a two-lane road?
A. Yes.
Q. Are you familiar with the work of "A Policy on Geometric Design of Rural Highways" published in 1965 by the American Association of State Highway Officials?
A. Yes, I think you referenced that before, also.
Q. Do you consider it to be competent?
A. Yes.
Q. Do you agree or disagree with the following language from page 393 of that book:

> The minimum time in which deceleration can be started is the driver perception and reaction time which for intersection design can be assumed to be 2 seconds. An arbitrary minimum for the distance from an intersection where a driver can first see a vehicle approaching the intersection on the intersecting road is that traversed during 2 seconds driving for perception and reaction plus one additional second to actual braking or accelerating to regulate speed.

Do you agree or disagree with that statement?
A. Yes, I do.
Q. That is 3 seconds right there.
A. No, let's see —

Q. Isn't it?

A. I was trying to find where you were reading here.

Q. 393.

A. 393.

They are talking about the minimum time in which deceleration can be started.

Right. Okay. Three seconds.

Q. That is 3 seconds right there.

How much reaction time do you believe that a motorist travelling at 30 miles an hour on a straight well-surfaced road with perfect visibility would require to recognize and have to react to an intersection stop sign?

A. A stop sign?

Q. A stop sign.

A. It could take a second or longer depending on conditions.

Q. Could it take several seconds?

A. It could take — No.

Q. Could it take a lot more than .9 of a second?

A. To perceive a stop sign it is going to take, in fact, much shorter than a second, but to respond to it —

Q. The question I am asking you is how long would it take this motorist to recognize and react. Those are the words, recognize and react to an intersection stop sign.

What is your answer?

A. For a driver just to recognize it and respond to it, it could take anywhere from a few tenths of a second all the way up to several seconds depending on where he is relative to that stop sign.

Q. So that act of recognizing and reacting to a stop sign could take more, substantially more than .9 of a second, right?

A. It is going to depend — Yes, depending on where the vehicle is relative to the stop sign and what the driver is required to do.

Q. How much time do you think it would take a motorist to react, perceive and deal with a problem of passing another car on a two-lane road?

A. As was previously mentioned, and I agree to it, it can take several seconds again because of the complexity of the situation, evaluating all of the elements involved in a pass, the distance that the car is approaching, the driver's depth of field in perceiving the approaching velocity and the road conditions that he is facing in making the pass.

Q. Now in figuring and computing, how long it would take a motorist to start a car or stop a car or to accelerate in response to a traffic problem, you would have to allow for the necessary reaction time that it took him to perceive, understand and react to that problem, right?

A. Yes. Again with perception, with the reaction time, it depends on the stimulus that the driver is faced with.

Q. But the simple point is: Is it not true that the longer the time that the motorist requires to perceive and understand and react to the problem, the longer it will take him to start his car in response to it or stop his car in response to it or to accelerate his car in response to it?

A. Yes. The longer the reaction time, the longer it takes, right.

Q. Would you consider 4 or 5 seconds to be adequate warning time for a motorist at the County Road 400 East crossing to proceed and react to an approaching westbound train?

A. Would I consider 4 or 5 seconds reasonable time?

Q. Yes.

A. Yes, it can be.

Q. If visibility was impaired, would you consider 6.3 seconds to be adequate warning time for a motorist stopping at the cross buck to proceed, perceive and react to an approaching train?

A. Here again by referencing response time, you have to put it in the context of what the motorist is facing in terms of his own condition at the time.

Q. Let me ask you this —

A. What the motorist is facing while travelling in his vehicle.

Q. Are you aware of any authoritative publication anywhere in the United States or anywhere in the world that recommends .9 of a second normal reaction time as how much warning time a motorist at a crossing should be given of an approaching railroad train?

A. Five seconds?

Q. Five seconds.

A. I am not aware of 5 seconds. There are a number of different studies that they have come up with in different cities as criteria.

Q. Different amounts of warning time?

A. Different amounts of warning time, yes.

Q. Are you familiar with the Transportation and Traffic Engineering Handbook published in 1976 by the Institute of Traffic Engineers?

A. Yes.

Q. Do you consider that competent?

A. Yes, I do.

Q. Do you agree or disagree with this language from that work:

> When the grade crossing signal is operated automatically, tracks switches must be arranged so that the signal will operate for at least 20 seconds before the fastest train reaches the crossing.

Do you agree with that?

A. Yes.

[N] Having devoted substantial efforts to undermining the witnesses' claim to a normal 9/10 of a second reaction time by comparison with other, longer, known reaction times, the next stop was to undermine the basis for the 9/10 of a second figure by showing it was derived from tests on pre-warned subjects facing no stress or confusion, a completely different situation than the occupants of the car faced at the time of the crash.

Q. The article that you referred to in getting your .9 of a second driver reaction time, was that called Drivers Brake Reaction Time by authors named Johnson and Rumier?

A. Yes.

Q. Wasn't the reaction tested there simply how long it takes to step down on the brake after you hear a horn?

A. Yes.

Q. And the participants in that test knew about the test, and they knew what they were going to be asked to do, didn't they?

A. Well, only to the extent that they were advised that in driving along they would hear a horn and then respond to it but they didn't know where or —

Q. But they knew they were going to hear a horn?

A. I believe that was the perameter of that test, yes.

Q. Didn't some of those people have to be tested over and over and over again in that response? Weren't some of them tested repeatedly on just stepping down on the brake after they heard a horn?

A. No. I believe that was the observer who was treated to verify his response time in making the observations. The individual people themselves ran through it and responded as they were instructed but not knowing when the horn was going to be blown in their course of travel.

Q. I am asking you a very simple question and it really calls for a yes or no answer.

Weren't many of the people who were tested in that study where they simply had to step down on the brake when they heard a horn tested repeatedly over and over and over again to step down on the brake after they heard the horn?

A. No, not to my knowledge.

Q. Not to your knowledge.

In fact, weren't the first three tests discounted?

A. I don't know the specifics. I would have to read it again.

Q. Why don't you read it. Do you have it there?

A. Yes.

Q. Why don't you read it.

A. If you would point out where you are referencing —

Q. May I see it?

I call your attention to the very first page, paragraph No. 3, and I will ask you to read that aloud.

Read that out loud, please.

A. All right.

> This same small group was also tested several times in situations where the braking signal occurred completely unexpectedly. This provides measure of their BRT or braking reaction time in a surprise situation.

Q. So here are these people and they are in a surprise situation and all of the reaction that they are doing that is being tested is how long does it take them to step on the brake after they hear the horn and there they are tested several times?

A. Then in a driving situation.

Q. Yes, and they are pre-warned. They have done it several times, they know what is coming, right?

A. Yes. It is reported here they don't know when it is coming.

Q. But they know it is coming. Would you consider it to be more or less difficult to perceive a railroad train coming at you out of blowing snow, falling snow, in obscured light, at dusk, at an acute angle, do you consider that to be a more difficult decision than stepping down three or four times on a brake pedal after you hear a horn?

A. It may be that the train was going to be closer to the crossing when you are going to be able to see it, but once you see that train, you are going to, you know, you are going to respond to it.

Q. Once you see that train — now that assumes a lot, doesn't it? Incidentally, do you know what a median means? It means 50 percent, right?

A. That is right.

Q. That means you assumed that .9 of a second median reaction time, not normal reaction time but a median reaction time.

A. No, normal.

Q. You considered median to be normal? That means 50 percent of the people can't meet that reaction time, isn't that right?

A. Some were less, some were more.

Q. Median means 50 percent now, doesn't it?

A. Yes.

Q. Yes. So 50 percent, if you want to say 49 percent or higher or 49 percent, or lower, and here is the middle, one percent, .9 of a second, you have got .9 of a second reaction time that 50 percent of the people tested in that study don't meet, and what that study was surveying was stepping down on a brake when you hear a horn, right?

A. That is correct.

MR. KUHLMAN: I have no further questions of you.

CHAPTER 16

DEALING WITH EXPERTS

Science, not Communism or Capitalism, is the modern secular religion: it put a man on the moon, invented the computer, and will, hopefully, one day cure cancer. When science merges with the productive power of modern industry, it produces technology, whose pervasive flood of new products changes all aspects of society and many aspects of human nature. People today both fear and believe in science, as earlier chapters have documented. The point for this chapter is that science itself is mute: it can speak to us only through its artifacts and its high priests, the experts. For this reason, high technology litigation must center around the expert witness, whose ability to communicate with a jury, through the pitfalls of direct and cross-examination, will make the difference between success and failure in a technology-oriented trial.

In order for an expert witness to successfully communicate with a jury, an attorney must first successfully communicate with that expert. Technical litigation is a back alley brawl between competing teams, teams of lawyers and experts. The group of experts who best understand the legal issues and lawyers who best understand the technical issues will have the best prospects of winning. One impediment to this smooth interaction is that lawyers often treat experts too much like lawyers, assuming they understand the difference between legal and scientific causation, and can survive cross-examination without knowing what it is; while experts all too often treat the courtroom like a schoolroom, where no evidentiary or tactical obstacles will be placed in the path of their efforts to give the jury a lecture.

This final chapter is directed to both lawyers and experts, in an effort to give each a little better understanding of the other, to aid the essential flow of clear information to the jury without which litigation degenerates to a popularity contest and Democracy becomes a sham.

§ 16-1. When to Use Experts.

Transportation facility negligence situations usually hinge on competing expert testimony because only competent experts, usually engineers or policemen with special training, are qualified to attack or defend the facility at issue. Thus general techniques in the direct and cross-examination of expert witnesses often acquire specialized importance in these cases.

Expert testimony is appropriate in Illinois, under the general rule adopted in most jurisdictions where the subject matter is such that only persons of skill and experience in a particular field have the capacity to make correct judgments concerning facts connected therewith. *Nystrom v. Bub,* 36 Ill. App. 2d 333, 184 N.E.2d 273 (1962). The court had broad discretion on the issues of whether the subject matter, as an issue of law, is proper for expert testimony (*Freehill v. DeWitt County Serv. Co.,* 125 Ill. App. 2d 306, 261 N.E.2d 52 (1970)), and whether the proposed expert is qualified to testify on the subject. *Cannell v. State Farm Fire & Cas. Co.,* 25 Ill. App. 3d 907, 323 N.E.2d 418 (1975). The general standard is that expert testimony may be used when it will be "helpful" to the fact finder. It need not be "necessary" in the sense that the fact finder would have no way to decide the fact issues without input from the expert. Cleary and Graham, *Handbook of Illinois Evidence,* § 701.1, at 444 (4th ed. 1984).

Experts in most states can rely on nonadmissable evidence if it is of the kind such experts normally rely on for such opinions.

California Law: *Cohen v. Western Hotels, Inc.,* 276 F.2d 26 (9th Cir. 1960). California follows federal rules governing the admission of expert testimony.

Smith v. Lockheed Propulsion Co., 247 Cal. App. 2d 774, 56 Cal. Rptr. 128 (1967). The testimony of an expert is admissible for purposes of showing recognized accepted standards of practice in the professions.

Trust v. Arden Farms Co., 50 Cal. 2d 217, 324 P.2d 583 (1958). It must be shown that an expert is familiar with the standards required in order for the expert to qualify as a witness.

Chadock v. Cohn, 96 Cal. App. 3d 205, 157 Cal. Rptr. 640 (1979). The test to be applied for determining the foundation for expert testimony was whether the expert witness possessed special knowledge, skill, experience, training or education sufficient to qualify him as an expert on the subject to which his testimony related.

Kastner v. Los Angeles Metropolitan Transit Auth., 53 Cal. 2d 52, 403 P.2d 385, 45 Cal. Rptr. 129 (1965). Expert testimony is admissible or not dependent upon whether subject matter is within common experience or whether it is a special field where opinion of one of skill and experience would be greater than that of the ordinary juryman. If the case requires expert testimony, this is so not because the expert has witnessed the facts but because he is qualified by reason to form an opinion on facts while an ordinary juror is not.

Huffman v. Lindquist, 37 Cal. 2d 465, 234 P.2d 34 (1951). When it is shown that a medical expert is familiar with the standards required of physicians under similar circumstances then he qualifies as a witness.

Evans v. Ohanesian, 39 Cal. App. 3d 131, 112 Cal. Rptr. 236 (1974). Where licensed, practicing physician has gained knowledge of standard of care applicable to a speciality in which he is not directly engaged but to which he has an opinion based on education, experience, observation or association with that speciality, his opinion is competent. It is not critical whether a medical expert witness is a general practitioner or a specialist so long as he exhibits knowledge of the subject.

Hawke v. Burns, 14 Cal. App. 2d 158, 294 P.2d 1008 (1956). It was not error to admit into evidence portions of physician's testimony in reference to his prognosis as to plaintiff's lack of chances for complete recovery.

Vandermark v. Ford Motor Co., 61 Cal. 2d 256, 391 P.2d 168, 37 Cal. Rptr. 896 (1964). It was error to strike testimony of plaintiff's expert on operation of hydraulic automobile brakes as to possible causes of failure of brake master cylinder, where damage to automobile in collision precluded determination as to whether the master cylinder had been properly installed and adjusted before accident.

Naples Restaurant, Inc. v. Coberly Ford, 259 Cal. App. 2d 881, 66 Cal. Rptr. 835 (1968). Sources of expert opinion on value are not restricted to those who make its determination a full-time occupation. No special education or training is required to qualify witness to estimate values.

Culver Adjustment Bureau v. Hawkins Constr. Co., 217 Cal. App. 2d 143, 31 Cal. Rptr. 569 (1963). Evidence of a party testifying as to the value of his services and also the testimony of a qualified expert is not binding upon jury or trial court in final determination of the reasonable value of such services rendered.

Inskeep v. Busby, 207 Cal. App. 2d 848, 24 Cal. Rptr. 819 (1962). It is proper for medical expert to give his opinion whether a given substance might have produced particular result.

Physicians, who performed surgery on spine of plaintiff and who had seen herniated disc, were properly allowed in a personal injury action to testify about the herniated disc and the causal relationship between the herniated disc and the automobile crash.

In re Estate of Rowley, 247 Cal. App. 2d 324, 65 Cal. Rptr. 139 (1967). Expert medical witness may give his opinion reasoning from effect to cause as to means used to inflict a certain injury and the deduction being based on condition and appearance of the wound itself.

Niles v. City of San Rafael, 42 Cal. App. 2d 230, 116 Cal. Rptr. 733 (1974). Expert testimony may be used regarding assessment of future medical expenses as damages.

Bates v. Newman, 264 P.2d 197, 121 Cal. App. 2d 800 (1953). A medical expert may testify as to the nature of an injury, or to the ability or inability of a person to do certain acts.

Evans v. Ohanesian, 39 Cal. App. 3d 121, 112 Cal. Rptr. 236 (1974). Where an expert medical witness has disclosed sufficient knowledge of the subject to submit his opinion to the jury, the degree of his knowledge goes more to the weight of the evidence than its admissibility.

Jones v. Johnston Testers, Inc., 132 Cal. App. 2d 162, 281 P.2d 602 (1955). Expert testimony is proper and virtually indispensible in cases where relation between facts and results may be understood only by those with special skill or training.

Hart v. Wielt, 4 Cal. App. 3d 224, 84 Cal. Rptr. 220 (1970). Traffic officers are qualified experts and may properly testify concerning their opinions as to various factors involved in accidents based upon their own observations because their duties include investigations of auto accidents.

Florida Law: *McDonnell Douglas v. Holliday,* 397 So. 2d 366 (Fla. App. 1981). The trial court must determine the qualifications of an expert witness on the subject matter of his testimony; and the court's judgment will not be disturbed on appeal, absent a clear abuse of discretion.

Fred Howland, Inc. v. Morris, 196 So. 472, 143 Fla. 189 (1940). A witness with special knowledge or skill may state his inference from facts observed by him as to matters connected with his specialty.

Sontana Marine Serv., Inc. v. McHale, 346 F.2d 147 (5th Cir. 1965). One becomes qualified as an expert witness by practical experience and home study; professional education or degrees are not required.

Stempel v. Chrysler Corp., 495 F.2d 1247 (5th Cir. 1974). A registered engineer who was offered to give an opinion on automobile design and construction and who had investigated approximately 1,800 accidents involving vehicles was qualified to give opinion testimony on the design of padded dashboard, although the witness had no practical experience in the actual design of automobile dashboards.

Plastic surgeon, who was the plaintiff's treating physician, was qualified to give medical opinions about the effect that the dashboard's design had on the severity of the plaintiff's injuries. The surgeon had treated several hundred persons injured by auto dashboards and had examined the dashboards in question. The surgeon had no experience in the design of dashboards.

Horowitz v. American Motorist Ins. Co., 343 So. 2d 1305 (Fla. App. 1977). A state-licensed chiropractor who presents necessary credentials as to education and experience is qualified to to be an expert witness in relation to injuries that are within chiropractic discipline.

Buchman v. Seaboard Coast Line R.R., 381 So. 2d 229 (1980). Two elements must be considered when admitting expert testimony: (1) the subject must be beyond common understanding of average laymen; and (2) the witness must have such knowledge that will probably aid the trier of fact in the search for truth.

Perez v. American Mut. Liab. Ins. Co., 288 So. 2d 541 (Fla. App. 1973). In deciding what evidence is admissible in a suit to recover for loss of deceased child's prospective estate are the standard of living to which the child was likely to become accustomed and aspire; and the moral values and stability apparent in the home environment, the character training manifestly given him in other respects, and the habits and diligence of his parents or guardians in pursuing their own ambitions toward affluence.

Allapattah Community Ass'n v. City of Miami, 379 So. 2d 387 (Fla. App. 1980). Opinion of architect outside his field of expertise that rezoning was necessary to safeguard neighborhood from dangers of heavy traffic on street was a mere nonexpert conclusion which was devoid of any evidentiary value, particularly where only competent evidence in record, expert opinion of planning department, based upon county traffic department survey, was completely to the contrary.

Mathis v. O'Reilly, 400 So. 2d 795 (Fla. App. 1981). In vehicle crash case, the trial court's exclusion of plaintiff's expert testimony relating to comparison of speeds calculating was reversible error since testimony might have been used to impeach defendant's witness.

Sikes v. Seaboard Coast Line R.R., 429 So. 2d 1216 (Fla. App. 1983). An accident reconstruction expert for railroad, in action by estate of deceased truck driver arising out of train-truck collision, revealed the sources of information on which he based his opinion about how he believed accident might have occurred. They were types of information on which an expert normally would rely. His expert testimony which was based on deposition of truck driver's son, who observed accident, train personnel, statements of apparently disinterested witnesses, surveys of crash site, visits to site, and pictures of site, was admissible.

Chiles v. Beaudoin, 384 So. 2d 175 (Fla. App. 1980). In an action for injuries sustained in a rear-end collision, a physician's testimony that plaintiff might have suffered ruptured thoracic disc as a result of accident, was premised on assumption that plaintiff felt back pain immediately after accident. The opinion was inadmissible and jury should have been instructed to disregard it where plaintiff testified that he had not suffered back pain immediately after accident. Thus, facts must fit theory. Unfortunately, it is usually easier to change the latter than the former.

Redwing Carriers, Inc. v. Watson, 341 So. 2d 1049 (Fla. App. 1977). An accident reconstruction expert was properly permitted, in a suit arising out of head-on collision between two trucks, to give his expert opinion that one truck driver had been able to take evasive action so as to avoid accident. The facts contained in a hypothetical question propounded to the expert were properly based upon version of testimony of eyewitnesses which jury had right to accept. The expert's opinion did not improperly invade the province of jury, since it essentially concerned what physically could have been done under the circumstances, not what truck driver should have done.

Taylor v. Posey, 283 So. 2d 118 (Fla. App. 1973). Where plaintiff, in an auto crash case, laid the factual basis for a hypothetical question to be propounded to expert witness with regard to speed, on basis of skid marks, and tried to put into such basis all objections raised by defense counsel, the trial court refusing to permit the expert's testimony was error.

Quinn v. Millard, 358 So. 2d 1378 (Fla. App. 1978). Hypothetical questions were not required during examination of expert witness on non-hypothetical reconstruction of automobile collision. Although the expert did not see accident happen, he testified on the basis of his own physical findings at scene shortly after accident.

Trial court in personal injury action properly allowed examining psychiatrist to testify as to automobile accident victim's mental condition, although the witness was not a treating physician.

Tampa Transit Lines, Inc. v. Smith, 155 So. 2d 557 (Fla. App. 1963). The opinion of an orthopedic specialist, who was technically a treating physician, as to how long plaintiff's condition would last, was admissible in an action for neck injuries insofar as opinion related to pain, even though the opinion was based largely on subjective symptoms attested by plaintiff at time of trial.

Seaboard Coast Line R.R. v. Garrison, 336 So. 2d 423 (Fla. App. 1976). Expert testimony about future inflation was admitted to show estimated value of loss of future support for survivors of driver killed in train-car crash.

Hosbein v. Silverstein, 358 So. 2d 43 (Fla. App. 1978). In crash case, trial court erred in excluding expert testimony that went beyond what the eyewitnesses could testify about. The expert was prepared to testify about reaction time of the truck driver defendant, the point of impact, the angle of impact, and the speed of vehicles involved in the crash. The testimony of numerous eyewitnesses to the accident was contradictory, and hypothetical questions posed to the expert were based upon facts and inferences derived from testimony of witnesses. *NOTE:* This case again raises the issue of whether eyewitness testimony is more reliable than, and should bar, expert testimony on the same issues.

Kerr v. Caraway, 78 So. 2d 571 (Fla. 1955). In a crash case where automobile speed was an issue, the testimony of a police officer, who was qualified as an expert on stopping distances, braking distances, and skid marks was admissible.

Seaboard Air Line R.R. v. Gentry, 46 So. 2d 485 (Fla.), *cert. denied,* 340 U.S. 853 (1950). Courts generally trust to experts an engineering question such as whether ballast supporting railroad track was properly placed and preserved, so as to afford flagman a secure footing in attempting to board freight train caboose after throwing switch.

First Fed. Sav. & Loan Ass'n v. Wylie, 46 So. 2d 396 (Fla. 1950). Admitting in evidence anatomical charts and skeleton of an arm as demonstrative exhibits clarifying expert testimony on the nature and effects of plaintiff's injury was not abuse of discretion.

Indiana Law: No. 684 S 249 (6-22-84) 15 pp. On Petition To Transfer — Court of Appeals of Indiana No. 2-1281 A 418. Affirmed — Damages for personal injuries — Grant Superior Court No. II. Indiana State Police Trooper was qualified to state his opinion as to the speed of defendant's vehicle immediately prior to the accident by virtue of his training, experience, and general knowledge of vehicular speed. The witness' specific knowledge of scientific principles, formulas, and calculations was the proper subject of cross-examination.

Illinois Law: *Wilson v. Clark,* 84 Ill. 2d 186, 417 N.E.2d 1322 (1981), adopted Rules 703 and 705 of the Federal Rules of Evidence. Experts in Illinois can now base their opinions on hearsay, if the hearsay constitutes such facts as experts of this type reasonably rely on in forming opinions or inferences.

A. Cases following *Wilson v. Clark, supra,* have required some guarantee of the reliability of the hearsay facts the expert is relying on, and have also strictly construed the requirement that the hearsay relied on must really fall within the expert's area of expertise. Thus, in *Guerrero v. City of Chicago,* 117 Ill. App. 3d 348, 453 N.E.2d 767 (1983), where plaintiff sued defendant city for a fall allegedly in a hole in defendant's street, plaintiff's medical experts were not allowed to be cross-examined about hearsay statements in the medical records that plaintiff fell on glass in an alley. The court reasoned that the expert had not relied on these hearsay statements in forming opinions, and the hearsay did not concern medical matters within the expertise of the witness. Similarly, in *Bailey v. City of Chicago,* 116 Ill. App. 3d 862, 452 N.E.2d 680 (1983), the defendant was not allowed to cross-examine plaintiff's medical witness on hearsay statements in the medical records that did not concern medical matters and were not relied on by the witness. In *Johnson v. Commonwealth Edison Co.,* Cause 84-0612, the Illinois Appellate Court for the Second Division decided on April 2, 1985, that engineers should be allowed the same rights to rely upon professionally reliable hearsay that the medical profession had been allowed in *Wilson v. Clark, supra,* and cases following *Wilson.* In *Johnson,* an expert engineer was allowed to use depositions, accident reports, professional standards published by the National Safety Council, the Federal Register, and the Showing Institute, and his own work experience to substantiate an opinion that the

Defendant was employing an unsafe method for removing shoring towers from a turbine unit.

The *Johnson* case obviously applies directly to transportation negligence cases, which rely heavily upon engineering testimony. Beyond that, however, *Johnson* raises again the concept that in jurisdictions adopting Federal Rule of Evidence 703, eyewitness testimony to an accident or crash can be preserved without taking depositions by having the expert engineers interview the eyewitnesses. Such interviews would be equivalent to the depositions that the engineering expert was allowed to rely on in *Johnson.* The *Johnson* opinion was explicit on this point, stating:

> The facts or data upon which expert opinions are based may, under Rule 703, be derived from presentation of data to the expert outside of court and other than by his own perception. (Fed. R. Evid. 703, Advisory Committee Note.). . . . As explained in *Wilson v. Clark,* 84 Ill. 2d 186, 417 N.E.2d 1322, the key element in applying Federal Rule 703 is whether the information upon which the expert bases his opinion is of a type that is reliable. . . . Regarding the information relied upon by [Plaintiff's engineer] here, Defendant has failed to show why such information would be any less reliable then the inadmissible, unsworn statements of patients, pharmacists, doctors, etc. which are clearly contemplated by Rule 703. (*Hatfield v. Sandorf-Wander, Inc.* (1st Dist. 1984), 124 Ill. App. 3d 780, 788, 464 N.E.2d 1105.) See *Johnson v. Commonwealth Edison Co.,* see opinion, pp. 15-16.

If the expert does, however, rely on hearsay matters outside his normal area of expertise, he can be cross-examined in those areas. In *Montefelice v. Terminal R.R. Ass'n,* 100 Ill. App. 3d 858, 427 N.E.2d 370 (1981), a psychiatrist basing his opinion on the success or failure of a surgical procedure on the patient's back was cross-examined on his knowledge of that surgical technique.

The expert can also be cross-examined on matters that do fall within his normal area of expertise if those matters constitute reliable hearsay records the expert has never seen. *People v. Pitts,* 104 Ill. App. 3d 451, 432 N.E.2d 1062 (1982). Cross-examination of this type must, however, be limited to the portion of the hearsay records that such experts normally rely on.

The *Wilson v. Clark* decision, moreover, did not change the earlier rule that a proper foundation must be established before the hearsay records can be directly admitted as evidence. *Thompson v. Lietz,* 95 Ill. App. 3d 384, 420 N.E.2d 232 (1981).

B. Closely related to the aforementioned points is the issue concerning whether *Wilson v. Clark,* 84 Ill. 2d 186, 417 N.E.2d 1322 (1981), has allowed experts to be used as a new mechanism for the preservation of evidence. Rule 703 of the Federal Rules of Evidence allowed experts to base their opinions on hearsay or matters not in evidence, so long as those matters are "of a type reasonably relied upon by experts in the particular field in forming opinions or inferences upon the subject." Illinois has adopted virtually the same standard in *People v. Ward,* 61 Ill. 2d 559, 338 N.E.2d 171 (1975), where a medical witness was allowed to base medical opinions of the defendant's sanity on hearsay medical records not in evidence. The *Ward* court cited Federal Evidence Rule 703 to support its decision, and stated the new concept would "bring the judicial practice into line with the practice of the experts themselves when not in court." 338 N.E.2d at 176. Subsequent Illinois cases following *Ward* in allowing experts to rely on hearsay medical records include *Smith v. Williams,* 34 Ill. App. 3d 677, 339 N.E.2d 10 (1975); and *In re Germich,* 103 Ill. App. 3d 626, 431 N.E.2d 1092 (1981).

C. Experts may be permitted to testify on subjects of common knowledge if it would be difficult for the jury to understand the reasons for the commonly known matter without the expert. *Mack v. Davis,* 76 Ill. App. 2d 88, 221 N.E.2d 121 (1966); *Carlson v. Hudson,* 19 Ill. App. 3d 576, 312 N.E.2d 19 (1974).

D. Experts may give opinions on ultimate issues if the issues are beyond lay understanding or if the expert cannot otherwise express his opinion. Gary, *Illinois Evidence Manual,* § 7:13, p. 284; *Miller v. Pillsbury Co.,* 33 Ill. 2d 514, 211 N.E.2d 733 (1965); *Spiezio v. Commonwealth Edison Co.,* 91 Ill. App. 2d 392, 235 N.E.2d 323 (1968); *Boose v. Digate,* 107 Ill. App. 2d 418, 246 N.E.2d 50 (1969).

Thus an expert was allowed to testify on the "ultimate" issue of whether an accident was foreseeable in *Rucker v. Norfolk & W. Ry.,* 64 Ill. App. 3d 770, 381 N.E.2d 715 (1978).

Cases subsequent to the 1981 edition of this book have substantially established the ability of experts in Illinois courts to testify concerning "ultimate issues" such as negligence of a party. Thus, in *Perschall v. Metropolitan Life Ins. Co.,* 113 Ill. App. 3d 233, 446 N.E.2d 570 (1983), the court stated:

> It is now well established that an expert may directly express his opinion on an ultimate issue. (*Merchant's National Bank v. Elgin, Joliet & Eastern Ry. Co.* (1971), 49 Ill. 2d 118, 122, 273 N.E.2d 809, 811.) More recently, this court noted in *Binge v. J.J. Borders Construction Co.* (1981), 95 Ill. App. 3d 238, 50 Ill. Dec. 788, 419 N.E.2d 1237, that the modern standard for the admissibility of expert testimony is not whether the subject is beyond the understanding of the jury, but whether the testimony will aid the jury's understanding. No higher standard applies to opinion testimony on an ultimate issue. E. Cleary & M. Graham, Handbook of Illinois Evidence sec. 704.1, at 375-76 (3d ed. 1979); 2 Jones, Evidence sec. 418 at 789 (5th ed. 1958). 446 N.E.2d at 573.

Dodson v. Shaw, 113 Ill. App. 3d 1063, 448 N.E.2d 188 (1983), states:

> [T]he cases favor the permissive use of expert testimony in all types of cases where the jury would be aided in their understanding of the facts. Expert testimony will be admissible even when directed toward an ultimate issue since the jury is free to reject the testimony. [Citation omitted.] 448 N.E.2d at 195.

E. Reconstruction experts are discouraged from offering reconstruction testimony on matters covered by eyewitnesses. *Plank v. Holman,* 46 Ill. 2d 465, 264 N.E.2d 12 (1970); *Miller v. Pillsbury Co.,* 33 Ill. 2d 514, 211 N.E.2d 733 (1965).

However, reconstruction testimony should be proper on matters not covered by the eyewitnesses. *Adkins v. Chicago, Rock Island & Pac. R.R.,* 2 Ill. App. 3d 906, 274 N.E.2d 507 (1971), *rev'd on other grounds,* 54 Ill. 2d 511, 301 N.E.2d 729 (1973).

If there are witnesses to a crash, expert witnesses might not be allowed to reconstruct events the witnesses did see, but the experts should be allowed to reconstruct events the witnesses did not see.

Thus, in *Carlson v. Hudson, supra,* expert witnesses were allowed to reconstruct events that occurred moments before the arrival of the witnesses on the scene. Defense attorneys intending to present expert reconstruction evidence should therefore carefully cross-examine eyewitnesses introduced by the plaintiff to establish areas where the witnesses did not see particular events take place. One good and common example of this situation is where the eyewitnesses saw a vehicle go off the road into a ditch but do not know precisely where the vehicle left the road.

F. Experts in Illinois may be cross-examined on texts and authorities the experts did not themselves rely on in direct testimony so long as the authority of those texts is established by other qualified experts (presumably in the employ of the cross-examiner). This point was enunciated in *Darling v. Charleston Community Mem. Hosp.*, 33 Ill. 2d 326, 211 N.E.2d 253 (1965):

> The second major contention advanced by the defendant in this court is that it was prejudicial error to permit the cross-examination of its expert witnesses concerning the views of recognized authorities in their fields, upon the ground that the experts did not purport to base their opinions upon the views of these authorities. In support of this contention he relies upon *Ullrich v. Chicago City Ry.*, 265 Ill. 338, 106 N.E. 828, and *City of Bloomington v. Shrock*, 110 Ill. 219. Those cases hold that an expert witness can only be interrogated about those texts upon which he expressly bases his opinion. The appellate court held that the cross-examination in this case met that test. We do not consider that determination to ascertain whether every detail on cross-examination of each expert witness fits within the rule announced in those cases, for we are satisfied that the rule is not supported by sound reasons, and should no longer be adhered to.
>
> That rule has been criticized frequently by legal scholars. (6 Wigmore, Evidence, 3d ed. secs. 1690-1692; McCormick, Evidence, sec. 296, p. 620, n. 3.) It was rejected in the Uniform Rules of Evidence (see Rule 63(31) and comment), and in the Model Code of Evidence. (See Rule 529 and comment.) It has been rejected by the United States Supreme Court (*Reilly v. Pinkus* (1949), 338 U.S. 269, 70 S.Ct. 110, 94 L.Ed 63), and by other courts as well. (60 A.L.R.2d 77). It is supported by the considerations that support the hearsay rule, but the inapplicability of those considerations to scientific works has been convincingly demonstrated by Wigmore. 6 Wigmore, Evidence, 3rd ed. secs. 1691-92.
>
> The unsatisfactory quality of expert testimony has been the subject of frequent comment, and it has induced judicial action. (See *Opp v. Pryor*, 294 Ill. 538, 545, 128 N.E. 580; *Kemeny v. Skorch*, 22 Ill. App. 2d 160, 170, 159 N.E.2d 489; see also Supreme Court Rule

> 17-2, Ill. Rev. Stat. 1963, chap. 110, par. 101.17-2; Cleary, Handbook of Illinois Evidence, secs. 3.3, p. 41, 11.10, pp. 190-191.) An individual becomes an expert by studying and absorbing a body of knowledge. To prevent cross-examination upon the relevant body of knowledge serves only to protect the ignorant or unscrupulous expert witness. In our opinion expert testimony will be a more effective tool in the attainment of justice if cross-examination is permitted as to the views of recognized authorities, expressed in treatises or periodicals written for professional colleagues. (Cf. Model Code of Evidence, Rule 529.) The author's competence is established if the judge takes judicial notice of it, or if it is established by a witness expert in the subject. 211 N.E.2d at 258-59.

The direct examination of one's expert witnesses is, consequently, not only the usual time to establish the authorities upon which they rely, but it is also the time to establish the texts and literature from which one intends to cross-examine the hostile experts.

G. Always ask: Is the expert an expert on the things he is testifying about? The law loosely defines an expert as a person with "peculiar knowledge or experience, not common to the world, which renders their opinions founded on such knowledge or experience any aid to the court or the jury in determining the questions at issue." *Stanley v. Board of Educ.,* 9 Ill. App. 3d 963, 293 N.E.2d 417, 424 (1973). Thus defined, an expert could be anything or anyone with special relevant knowledge. In *Nowakowski v. Hoppe Tire Co.,* 39 Ill. App. 3d 155, 349 N.E.2d 578 (1976), a tire mechanic qualified as an expert on tire blowouts; but in *Hagerman v. National Food Stores, Inc.,* 5 Ill. App. 3d 439, 283 N.E.2d 321 (1972), a bubble gum machine filler was not qualified as an expert on the strength of glass in a bubble gum machine. If you are offering the expert, present his credentials as thoroughly as possible. Never stint on presenting your expert's pedigree. Since anyone, in the judge's discretion, can be an expert, the qualifying testimony is the best and sometimes the only way to make sure your expert stands out advantageously. Conversely, if the expert is hostile, examine his credentials (before trial) to determine if his expertise extends to the subject matter of his testimony. Thus a police officer may not give an opinion, based on skid marks, as to what lane an impact occurred (*Dauksch v. Chamness,* 11 Ill. App. 3d 346, 296 N.E.2d 592 (1973)), unless he has received special training qualifying him to make such an analysis. *Siebens v. Konicek,* 108 Ill. App. 2d 300, 247 N.E.2d 453 (1969).

H. Expert testimony in Illinois may be admitted into evidence to prove a custom or practice widely used in a particular field. *Clark v. Continental Ill. Nat'l Bank & Trust Co.,* 68 Ill. App. 2d 16, 215 N.E.2d 816 (1966). This may be particularly helpful for defendants in transportation facility negligence cases, for evidence that the defendant's alleged negligence conforms with industry customs, while not justifying negligence, if found, argues powerfully against the existence of negligence by "aid[ing] the jury in deciding what was feasible and what the defendant knew or should have known." *Darling v. Charleston Community Mem. Hosp., supra,* 211 N.E.2d at 257.

I. Experts can be cross-examined on their prejudice or bias (such as whether they are "hired guns" or whether their fees depend on the outcome). In *Sanchez v. Black Bros. Co.,* 98 Ill. App. 3d 264, 423 N.E.2d 1309 (1981), the plaintiff's counsel was allowed to cross-examine the defendants' expert about the following speech the expert had given to an engineering group: "Under direct examination, the jury understands everything that I say. Under cross examination, there are some things that I will allow the jury to understand and there are some things which I will not allow the jury to understand." 423 N.E.2d at 1320. The *Sanchez* court justified broad cross-examination on the bias of an expert thusly:

> The bias or prejudice of a witness is always relevant (81 Am.Jur.2d *Witnesses* § 547 (1976)), and evidence "elicited on cross-examination or offered as impeachment is admissible if it tends to show a witness' bias and lack of credibility. (*People v. Garth* (1975), 31 Ill. App. 3d 716, 719, 334 N.E.2d 359, 362.) 423 N.E.2d at 1320.

J. Before an expert in Illinois can use a new technique, test, or procedure, it must have some professional acceptance. Cleary and Graham, in their *Handbook of Illinois Evidence,* § 702-4, pp. 461-63 (4th ed. 1984), state the issue thusly:

> Expert testimony applying a particular scientific principle, technique, or test is admissible only if a sufficiently reliable field of scientific, technical, or other specialized knowledge has been developed. See *Heideman v. Kelsey,* 19 Ill. 2d 258, 166 N.E.2d 596 (1960), rejecting medical testimony claiming to determine competency of testator by appearance of signature; *People v. Driver,* 62 Ill. App. 3d 847, 20 Ill. Dec. 7, 379 N.E.2d 840 (1978), splatter characteristics of human blood indicated not to be a subject capable of expert evaluation; *People v. Perroni,* 14 Ill. 2d 381, 153 N.E.2d 578 (1958), expert testimony concerning matching of tool marks is proper on same basis as expert testimony relating to fingerprint identification; *People v. Lofton,* 45 Ill. App. 3d 157, 3 Ill. Dec. 859, 359 N.E.2d 498 (1977), the "dermal nitrate" or "paraffin" test's reliability is subject to serious question; *People v. Newell,* 77 Ill. App. 3d 577, 33 Ill. Dec. 66, 396 N.E.2d 291 (1979), expert may testify upon analysis of small amount of substance that entire contents was cannabis, the fact that only a portion was tested going to weight rather than admissibility. A neat illustration is afforded by comparing *People v. Berkman,* 307 Ill. 492, 139 N.E. 91 (1923), classifying ballistics identification as remarkable, absurd, preposterous, and inadmissible, with *People v. Fisher,* 340 Ill. 216, 172 N.E. 743 (1930), holding the same evidence admissible following a carefully laid testimo-

nial foundation of the techniques followed. . . . In determining whether a scientific principle, technique, or test is sufficiently reliable to be admitted, *People v. Baynes,* 88 Ill. 2d 225, 241, 58 Ill. Dec. 819, 430 N.E.2d 1070 (1981), provides that the test to be applied is that enunciated in *Frye v. United States,* 293 F. 1013, 1014 (D.C. Cir. 1923):

> Just when a scientific principle or discovery crosses the line between the experimental and demonstrable stages is difficult to define. Somewhere in this twilight zone the evidential force of the principle must be recognized, and while courts will go a long way in admitting expert testimony deducted from a well-recognized scientific principle or discovery, the thing from which the deduction is made must be sufficiently established to have gained general acceptance in the particular field in which it belongs.

Imposition of the Frye test serves to (1) ensure that a minimal reserve of experts exist who can critically examine the validity of a scientific determination in a particular case, (2) promote a degree of uniformity of decision, (3) avoid the interjection of a time-consuming and often misleading determination of the reliability of a scientific technique into the litigation; (4) assure that scientific evidence introduced will be reliable and thus relevant, (5) provide a preliminary screening to protect against the natural inclination of the jury to assign significant weight to scientific techniques presented under circumstances where the trier of fact is in a poor position to place an accurate evaluation upon reliability, in light of the fact that cross-examination by opposing counsel is unlikely to bring inaccuracies to the attention of the jury.

When offered into evidence for the first time, expert testimony as to the underlying scientific principle and as to the validity of the technique or test applying that principle will be received. On the basis of its evaluation of the conflicting expert testimony, the court must determine whether the scientific test is sufficiently reliable to be received into evidence. Application of the Frye standard calls for a judicial determination both that the court itself finds the scientific test

> reliable and that the test's reliability is generally accepted in the particular scientific field in which the test belongs. Newness alone is not a bar to admissibility, for every scientific technique that is eventually accepted must have its first day in court. Moreover, neither lack of absolute certainty nor lack of uniformity of expert opinion precludes a court from finding on the basis of expert witness testimony and other evidence admitted at trial that a scientific test is reliable and that the scientific test's reliability is, or clearly would be when brought to the attention of the appropriate experts, generally accepted in the particular scientific field in which the test belongs. . . . Once the particular scientific principle, technique, or test has been judicially determined after an evaluation of expert testimony to be reliable and to have received general acceptance by the appropriate scientific community as being reliable, the validity of the principle, technique, or test is either assumed in subsequent litigation or established through judicial notice.

K. Survey and opinion polls can be used as evidence in Illinois if you can show . . . "inherent reliability because the methods utilized are generally accepted in the scientific community to produce statistically accurate results." *Galindo v. Riddell, Inc.,* 107 Ill. App. 3d 139, 437 N.E.2d 376, 381 (1982); *Lawson v. G.D. Searle & Co.,* 64 Ill. 2d 543, 356 N.E.2d 779 (1976).

L. Generally, expert literature can be the basis of cross-examination, but is not directly admissible as evidence. *Walski v. Tiesenga,* 72 Ill. 2d 249, 258-59, 381 N.E.2d 279 (1978). However, in *Fornoff v. Parke Davis & Co.,* 105 Ill. App. 3d 681, 434 N.E.2d 793 (1982), the court held:

> Use of such evidence might be permitted where their exclusion would subject a plaintiff to serious hardship. Such might occur by a plaintiff's positive showing that securing medical testimony was impossible. In this case, plaintiffs produced ample medical testimony. Furthermore, refusing admission of the treatises to support plaintiffs' experts' opinion was not error. An

> expert witness may always state the basis for his opinion; however, admission of authoritative treatises are only for the purpose of impeaching that expert. The rule prohibiting introduction of medical treatises as substantive evidence is one of long-standing. (*Ullrich v. Chicago City Railway Co.* (1914), 265 Ill. 338, 341-342, 106 N.E.2d 790.) Because our supreme court's reluctance to overrule it (*Lawson v. G.D. Searle & Co.* (1976), 64 Ill.2d 543, 1 Ill. Dec. 497, 356 N.E.2d 779, *but cf. Wilson v. Clark* (1981), 84 Ill.2d 186, 191, 49 Ill. Dec. 308, 417 N.E.2d 1322), coupled with the availability and testimony of plaintiffs' experts, neither will we. (434 N.E.2d at 801.)

This language clearly suggests that expert literature might be admitted as evidence if a party had no other way to obtain such evidence.

Massachusetts Law: *Kapp v. Ballantine,* 380 Mass. 186, 402 N.E.2d 463 (1980). It is usually within the court's discretion whether an expert witness has been sufficiently qualified, and whether his opinions are admissible.

Garbincius v. Boston Edison Co., 621 F.2d 1171 (1st Cir. 1980). While the expert's work experience in traffic safety procedures during highway construction stopped many years ago, such background, plus his engineering training and study before trial, qualified the witness to give an opinion about warning devices on the road when plaintiff's intestate drove his automobile into an excavation.

Author's Note: The witness was found barely qualified, but he made it. Qualification is like pregnancy — you are or you aren't, period.

Carey v. General Motors Corp., 377 Mass. 736, 387 N.E.2d 583 (1979). In an action against an automobile manufacturer arising from an accident which plaintiff contended was caused by an accelerator pedal that stuck, there was adequate evidentiary support for the opinion of plaintiffs' expert that the pedal defect was one of the three defects resulting from negligent design that caused the accident, despite contrary opinions.

Bernier v. Boston Edison Co., 380 Mass. 372, 403 N.E.2d 391 (1980). An electric light pole was hit by a car, and then fell on plaintiff pedestrians, who sued the utility company for negligent design and placement of the pole. A structural engineer who was an expert witness as to the design of light poles was qualified to give an opinion about the speed of the car based on photographs of accident alone.

Henderson v. D'Annolfo, 446 N.E.2d 103 (Mass. App. 1983). An expert's testimony may be based on direct personal knowledge, evidence already in the record, or a combination of such sources.

Kerr v. Palmieri, 325 Mass. 554, 91 N.E.2d 754 (1950). Plaintiff's car collided with defendant's car on April 17, 1947. Plaintiff's dentist testified that he treated plaintiff in April 1947 for several loose, chipped teeth and that thereafter other teeth had to be extracted. There was testimony that this condition of plaintiff's teeth was due to a blow received in the collision. This was a sufficient basis for the dentist's opinion.

Nisbet v. Medaglis, 356 Mass. 580, 254 N.E.2d 782 (1970). It was error to allow an actuary to answer a hypothetical question based on the assumption that the plaintiff's earning capacity had been reduced by $35 per week from time of injury for his life expectancy. There was no evidence showing plaintiff had lost $35 weekly as a consequence of the accident, and the alleged diminution of earning power was not claimed to embrace his principle employment, but was confined to his ability to handle minor secondary jobs which were not terminated by the accident.

Standard Paper & Merchandise Co. v. City of Springfield, 356 Mass. 475, 253 N.E.2d 337 (1969). Lengthy hypothetical questions put to expert were not sufficiently objectionable to disqualify the expert witness from giving answers where factual basis for the questions was in evidence from various witnesses.

Gannon's Case, 352 Mass. 568, 227 N.E.2d 352 (1967). Expert witness may base his opinion upon facts assumed in hypothetical questions supported either by admissions or by prior testimony.

Lupia v. Marino, 353 Mass. 749, 231 N.E.2d 16 (1967). The credibility of experts and witnesses was properly left to jury.

LeBlanc v. Ford Motor Co., 346 Mass. 225, 191 N.E.2d 301 (1963). It was not error to admit hypothetical questions to an expert concerning technical matters, about which the jury would not have adequate knowledge, regarding the possible reasons for the engagement of an automobile clutch while in neutral position.

Burns v. Combined Ins. Co. of Am., 6 Mass. App. 86, 373 N.E.2d 1189 (1978). The trial judge did not abuse his discretion in allowing a doctor to give his expert medical opinion that the plaintiff was totally disabled beginning in November 1974, when insured was an eligible employee under terms of defendant's group policy.

Andrade v. Correia, 358 Mass. 786, 267 N.E.2d 503 (1971). A chiropractor was not incompetent to give expert testimony on the causal relationship between an accident and the present condition of the plaintiff. The court did not exceed its discretion in finding the chiropractor qualified to give expert testimony within the scope of his experience and within the limited scope of permissible practice of chiropractor.

Lovasco v. Parkhurst Marine Ry., 75 N.E.2d 924 (Mass. 1947). There is no set formula or rule for the admission of expert testimony. All that is necessary is that the subject matter be one about which special knowledge beyond that possessed by the ordinary jurymen will aid the jury in their deliberations, and that an expert possessing such knowledge gives opinions pertinent to such issues based upon facts which are in evidence, or which could warrantably be inferred from other evidence.

Bernier v. Boston Edison Co., 380 Mass. 372, 403 N.E.2d 391 (1980). An opinion attempted to estimate vehicle speeds from an interpretation of collision wreckage. Whether to admit the opinion was within the trial judge's discretion, especially as eyewitness accounts were confused.

Lucier v. Norcross, 310 Mass. 213, 37 N.E.2d 498 (1941). The distance at which automobile lights turned on low beam would pick up an object the size of an ordinary man was a proper subject of expert testimony.

Reardon v. Marston, 310 Mass. 461, 38 N.E.2d 644 (1942). The manner in which automobile brakes would operate if they were in good condition, including the effect that the brakes would have on the wheels, was a subject within the competent realm of an expert.

Harrington v. Travers, 288 Mass. 156, 192 N.E. 495 (1934). Expert testimony is competent to establish speed of motor vehicles.

Crowe v. Ward, 363 Mass. 85, 292 N.E.2d 716 (1973). In a two-vehicle crash case, a weather report which was an official record of facts made by public officials in performance of their duty established the weather at a reporting station seven and one quarter miles from the reporting station. Based on this report, an expert should have been allowed to state opinions about the chances of like or different weather at the place of the accident.

Venini v. Dias, 5 Mass. App. 695, 369 N.E.2d 1026 (1977). A service manager for an automobile dealership who did a lot of diagnostic work evaluating problems which customers might have on their automobiles should have been allowed to give an expert opinion about the noise which would have been produced by a broken bearing, and whether such a noise should have called the owner's attention to the problem before the rear wheel and axle assembly fell off the automobile, injuring persons in a following automobile.

Mohaghan v. Keith Oil Corp., 281 Mass. 129, 183 N.E. 252 (1932). Testimony of expert in automobile control and repair was held admissible as to manner in which tire marks had been made to show position of truck and effect on it of collision.

Michigan Law: *Gorelick v. Department of State Hwys.,* 127 Mich. App. 324, 339 N.W.2d 635 (1983). In an action against the state for injuries suffered from a crash allegedly caused by misplacement of a "pass with care" sign, the court acted properly in allowing an expert to go with the court to the crash scene, where the expert used various distance markers to demonstrate that objects in the passing lane were not visible at certain distances from the point where motorist pulled out to pass.

Syrowik v. City of Detroit, 119 Mich. App. 343, 326 N.W.2d 507 (1982). In order for expert testimony to be admitted, the witness must be an expert, there must be facts in evidence which require or are subject to examination and analysis by a competent expert, and the expert must have knowledge in a particular area that belongs more to the expert than to the common man.

Phardel v. State, 120 Mich. App. 806, 328 N.W.2d 108 (1982). Factors to be considered when determining a witness' qualifications as an expert are: learning, knowledge, and skill or practical experience.

The trial court properly allowed the administrator of decedent's estate to testify on the cause of decedent's death. The administrator was a licensed osteopathic surgeon whose practice involved accident or trauma surgery. He was able to diagnose presence of neurological and vascular conditions as aneurysm and subarachnoid hemorrhage. He had treated pathological and surgical problems involving the brain as a student, intern, and resident. He dealt with existing neurological problems and trauma to head.

Coles v. Galloway, 7 Mich. App. 93, 151 N.W.2d 229 (1967). Trial court did not err in permitting police officer, who had investigated accident and who had experience in training in accident investigation, to testify as to which automobile caused each pile of wreckage at the crash scene.

Snyder v. New York Cent. Transp. Co., 4 Mich. App. 38, 143 N.W.2d 791 (1966). A witness who was a professor of mechanical engineering, with a bachelor of science degree in aeronautical engineering and mathematics, a master of science in engineering mechanics, a doctorate in mechanical engineering, and who was also director of a transport research institute studying various safety factors of automobiles, was qualified to give opinions about vehicle speeds.

Brummitt v. Chaney, 18 Mich. App. 59, 170 N.W.2d 481 (1969). An experienced police officer who had proper qualifications and training could estimate the approximate speed of vehicles prior to a crash based upon skid marks, though the officer did not know coefficients of friction on the street, the efficiency of the automobiles, or whether the skid marks were made by front or rear tires. Those issues went to the weight of the evidence.

Keefer v. C.R. Bard, Inc., 110 Mich. App. 563, 313 N.W.2d 151 (1981). In order to admit expert testimony, the witness must be qualified as expert in his field; there must be facts which require expert's interpretation or analysis; and the expert's knowledge must be peculiar to experts rather than to lay persons.

Waatti v. Marquette Gen. Hosp., 329 N.W.2d 526 (Mich. App. 1982). Although a witness may qualify as an expert by virtue of experience, knowledge, skill, training, or education, he must in all cases state his familiarity with appropriate standards of care pertinent in a given situation.

Sarzynski v. Stern, 13 Mich. App. 158, 163 N.W.2d 641 (1968). Trial court did not err in allowing an orthopedic surgeon to testify that plaintiff had suffered a transverse fracture of his right femur and a complete disruption of two ligaments in his left knee and that there was very definite possibility of a progressing traumatic arthritis, together with proof of the costs anticipated for treatment, the expert established presently known facts and left it to the jury to set the future consequences of the injury.

Dudek v. Popp, 373 Mich. 300, 129 N.W.2d 393 (1964). A reconstruction expert may testify either from personal observation or from evidence in the record that, in his opinion, certain marks are skid marks and that they were made by a given motor vehicle and his reasons therefor, and may point only his opinion as to point of impact.

Goodman v. Stafford, 20 Mich. App. 631, 174 N.W.2d 593 (1969). It was a jury issue when medical testimony was in conflict about whether an auto crash caused plaintiff's injuries, and how long those injuries would last.

Elsasser v. American Motors Corp., 81 Mich. App. 379, 265 N.W.2d 339 (1978). Expert's testimony as to speed of vehicle involved in a crash was not barred by eyewitness lay testimony on the same point where lay testimony was subject to considerable doubt due to poor visibility conditions and the sudden short time available for observation before the crash.

Cook v. Kendrick, 16 Mich. App. 48, 167 N.W.2d 483 (1969). It was not error for the trial court not to allow a police officer to give opinions about the cause of an accident and an automobile's directions, when the proponent of the testimony did not lay a proper foundation concerning the accident and the officer's expertise before asking questions.

Rockey v. Pontiac Motor Div., 1 Mich. App. 100, 134 N.W.2d 371 (1965). Experiments in court must be done under circumstances similar to those existing at the time in issue. Where all eyewitnesses testified that steel was not being moved at time of the accident, an expert's opinion based on experiments done in miniature and not under conditions similar to those shown to have existed at time of accident that steel was being moved was excluded.

Hicks v. Bacon, 26 Mich. App. 487, 182 N.W.2d 620 (1970). Speed estimates based solely on opinions of force of impact are not admissible.

Tiffany v. Christman Co., 93 Mich. App. 267, 287 N.W.2d 199 (1979). Testimony of an economist who computed future wage loss by employing a six percent annual wage increase rate, a figure based on relevant economic data was properly admitted over the defendant's hearsay objections because the defendant could cross-examine the witness about his underlying data and assumptions.

Elsasser v. American Motors Corp., 81 Mich. App. 379, 265 N.W.2d 339 (1978). Expert's calculation of the speed of a vehicle involved in a crash was properly admitted despite the existence of eyewitness lay testimony on the same issues because the eyewitness testimony was doubtful on key issues due to poor weather conditions and sudden nature of collision.

Kujawski v. Cohen, 56 Mich. App. 533, 224 N.W.2d 908, *appeal after remand,* 268 N.W.2d 358 (1974). Trial court, in a crash case, properly allowed a crash reconstruction expert to testify.

O'Dowd v. Linehan, 385 Mich. 491, 189 N.W.2d 333 (1971). Where some of the expert's opinions in death action arising out of an auto crash were based on damages to the car that the expert saw for the first time four months after the crash at a location to which the car had been moved after the crash, the expert's opinions based on the damages he observed were properly stricken because crash photos did not show those damages, which may have been caused after the crash. The opinions were therefore lacking a proper foundation in relevant evidence.

LaFave v. Kroger Co., 5 Mich. App. 446, 146 N.W.2d 850 (1966). A crash investigation expert may testify either from personal observation or from evidence in the record that, in his opinion, certain marks are skid marks made by a given motor vehicle, and he may use those skid marks to establish a point of impact for a crash.

Cryderman v. Soo Line R.R., 78 Mich. App. 465, 260 N.W.2d 135 (1977). In a grade crossing crash case, a transportation safety expert was allowed to express an opinion embracing ultimate fact issues that prior to the crash a reasonably prudent railroad would have taken action to equip the crossing with flashing lights and would have petitioned the Public Service Commission for authority to erect flashing signals.

Green v. Federal Kemper Ins. Co., 88 Mich. App. 364, 276 N.W.2d 887 (1979). The trial court properly allowed registered nurses to testify that in their opinion private duty nurses were necessary for the care of an injured automobile passenger, since the nurses were familiar with nursing care, and knew from experience how much time was required to properly care for the injured passenger.

New York Law: *Sukiennik v. State,* 26 A.D.2d 769, 271 N.Y.S.2d 684, *on remand,* 56 Misc.2d 148, 288 N.Y.S.2d 766, *aff'd,* 29 A.D.2d 288 N.Y.S.2d 866 (1966). Whether the state could have achieved elevation of highway by some plan other than the one employed and thereby avoided loss of some or all of the driver access formerly enjoyed is a proper subject of expert proof.

Pontonero v. Da Prano, 24 A.D.2d 546, 261 N.Y.S.2d 425 (1965). In a crash case against a city and a town alleging negligent road construction and maintenance as a cause of the crash, conflicting expert testimony as to whether the relevant curve began in the town or in the city presented factual issue for jury.

Hileman v. Schmitt's Garage, Inc., 58 A.D.2d 1029, 397 N.Y.S.2d 501 (1977). This case points out that a witness' expertise must be relevant to his testimony. Here, the plaintiff's expert was a metallurgist specializing in the area of why metals fail. The trial court properly refused to allow this expert to express opinions about whether a guardrail pulled a wheel off plaintiff's vehicle, and as to what caused the wheel to fall off. The expertise of the witness was never made relevant to his opinions because the disengagement of the wheel was never connected in his testimony to a metal failure.

Stafford v. Mussers Potato Chips, Inc., 39 A.D.2d 831, 333 N.Y.S.2d 139 (1972). Investigating state trooper who visited crash scene was not allowed to express opinions about the point of crash impact where the trooper was not qualified as a reconstruction expert.

Feldsberg v. Nitschke, 49 N.Y.2d 636, 404 N.E.2d 1293, 427 N.Y.S.2d 751 (1980). In a crash case the defendant testified that there were no skid marks from his vehicle. The trial court therefore excluded expert testimony about the cause of skid marks from an investigator who had no knowledge of how the crash happened. There was no proper foundation for the expert's testimony, in that his testimony about skid marks was speculative.

Rodolitz v. Boston-Old Colony Ins. Co., 74 A.D.2d 821, 425 N.Y.S.2d 353 (1980). Expert's lack of direct knowledge concerning subject matter of his testimony is no bar to his testimony; in such cases the expert may base his opinion on facts proven by, or reasonably inferable from, testimony of other witnesses. The expert's lack of personal knowledge goes only to weight of his testimony.

Selkowitz v. County of Nassau, 45 N.Y.2d 97, 379 N.E.2d 1140, 408 N.Y.S.2d 10 (1978). Whether expert testimony is admissible on a particular point is a mixed question of law and fact left to the discretion of the trial court. Generally, an expert should testify about issues requiring professional or scientific knowledge, or skill not within the range of ordinary training or intelligence. For that reason expert testimony has been held to be admissible on complex medical and surgical issues, and also on a wide range of issues requiring the application of accepted professional standards.

Matott v. Ward, 48 N.Y.2d 455, 399 N.E.2d 532, 423 N.Y.S.2d 645 (1979). The usual basis for admitting expert testimony is that its subject matter concerns issues beyond the ordinary knowledge and experience of the trier of facts.

Feldsberg v. Nitschke, 49 N.Y.2d 636, 404 N.E.2d 1293, 427 N.Y.S.2d 751 (1980). In a crash case, the trial court properly excluded a transparent overlay allegedly depicting distances at the accident scene, because the measurements were made by pacing distances and did not represent accurate measurements for jury's consideration.

Larsen v. Vigliarolo Bros., 77 A.D.2d 562, 429 N.Y.S.2d 273 (1980). In a motorcycle crash case, a witness who saw the motorcycle only three or four seconds before the crash was not allowed to testify about the speed of the motorcycle for a second or less. The Court permitted the defendant's expert to give his opinion as to speed of the motorcycle based on other witness' testimony.

Washington v. Long Island R.R., 13 A.D.2d 710, 214 N.Y.S.2d 115 (1961). Evidence of experiments as to distances within which train could be stopped, under test conditions similar to conditions at time of accident, was admissible; a minor variation in circumstances affected weight of testimony rather than its admissibility. Note, however, that if the relevant circumstances become unduly dissimilar, the test will, in all likelihood, not be admitted.

Ohio Law: *Ishler v. Miller,* 56 Ohio St. 2d 447, 384 N.E.2d 296 (1978). The test of an expert's admissibility is whether the witness offered as an expert will aid the trier of fact in the search for the truth, not whether the expert witness is the best witness on the particular subject.

Shackelford v. Cortec, Inc., 8 Ohio App. 3d 418, 457 N.E.2d 876 (1982). Within the discretion of the trial court is the determination whether individual is qualified to give an expert opinion, and will not be reversed on appeal unless trial court clearly abused its discretion.

Tully v. Mahoning Exp. Co., 161 Ohio St. 457, 119 N.E.2d 831 (1954). There is no presumption that a witness is competent to give an opinion. The party offering expert testimony has the burden of showing that the witness possesses the necessary learning, knowledge, skill, or practical experience to allow him competently to give such testimony.

McManus v. Buskirk, 183 N.E.2d 473 (1962), *rev'd on other grounds,* 176 Ohio St. 75, 197 N.E.2d 560 (1964). Highway patrolman with 10 years of experience in investigating highway crashes, having thoroughly investigated a crash resulting in the death of an automobile passenger, was qualified to offer expert testimony based upon physical facts which he found at scene of the crash, about the speed at which an automobile was traveling before the driver lost control of it. Note, however, that most jurisdictions require the officer to show specific training in speed estimation and accident reconstruction before such testimony can be admitted.

Dibert v. Ross Pattern & Foundry Dev. Co., 105 Ohio App. 264, 152 N.E.2d 369 (1958). An experienced automobile mechanic who inspected the wreckage shortly after a crash and noted the location of damaged areas on the vehicles, was allowed to state opinions on the impact angle.

Mannino v. International Mfg. Co., 650 F.2d 846 (6th Cir. 1981). A biochemical engineer with an engineering PhD was allowed to give opinions on the design of auto seats for bodies based on the background facts that he had done research in automobile crashes, testing whiplash injuries to humans and had attended seminars on child restraint systems and had worked with orthopedic physicians studying injuries to the spine and neck.

Rouse v. Riverside Methodist Hosp., 9 Ohio App. 3d 206, 459 N.E.2d 593 (1983). Under Ohio law, a licensed practicing physician is competent to testify on medical issues, including the relationship of medical expenses to a particular injury; the fact that the physician may have a different specialty bears only upon the weight to be given evidence, not its admissibility.

Ragone v. Vitali & Beltrami, Jr., Inc., 42 Ohio St. 2d 161, 327 N.E.2d 645 (1975). In all issues involving scientific, mechanical, professional, or other matters requiring special study, experience or observation not within the common knowledge of laymen, expert opinion testimony is admissible to aid the court or jury in arriving at a correct determination of the litigated issue.

Johnson v. Knipp, 36 Ohio App. 2d 218, 304 N.E.2d 914 (1973). Generally the force of impact is a relevant issue, bearing on the extent of injury arising from vehicular collision.

Mayhorn v. Pavey, 8 Ohio App. 3d 189, 456 N.E.2d 1222 (1982). Facts assumed in a hypothetical question cannot be the basis of the expert witness' opinion unless evidence tending to establish them is admitted into evidence, either through other witnesses, or through the expert testifying upon his own personal knowledge.

One purpose for hypothetical questions given to an expert witness is to bring facts of which expert has no personal knowledge before him for his opinion, and to satisfy the requirement that matters upon which the expert bases his opinion are disclosed to the trier of facts. **Note:** The hypothetical question also makes a great mini closing argument summarizing all your helpful facts.

Burens v. Industrial Comm'n, 162 Ohio St. 549, 124 N.E.2d 724 (1955). Qualified expert witnesses can base their opinions on facts which are within their own personal knowledge, and also on assumed facts.

Hytha v. Schwendeman, 40 Ohio App. 2d 478, 320 N.E.2d 312 (1974). Where an expert's opinion is based upon a professional conclusion after examination of facts and the opinion is relevant to the issue being tried, the opinion is admissible.

Drayton v. Jiffee Chemical Corp., 591 F.2d 352 (6th Cir. 1978). In determining future earnings of an injured party and the present value thereof, it is proper to permit expert opinions about future variables, such as interest rates, amounts, returns on investments, earning values, existing rates of inflation or deflation, and changes in the purchasing power of the dollar. The economist can also give economic testimony concerning the past history of such variables as the increase of productivity of the average worker.

Moe Light, Inc. v. Foreman, 238 F.2d 817 (6th Cir. 1956). In a personal action, a medical expert's opinion that plaintiff would suffer a future loss of earning ability when he became unable to continue with present employment because of injury to first sacral nerve, which would probably become more painful and disabling over time, eventually causing a complete inability to work, was admissible, and was not mere speculation or conjecture.

Leichtamer v. American Motors Corp., 67 Ohio St. 2d 456, 424 N.E.2d 568 (1981). Testimony of neurosurgeon was properly admitted as bearing upon enhancement of personal injuries resulting from inadequacy of a roll bar on a vehicle.

Pennsylvania Law: *Reardon v. Meehan,* 424 Pa. 460, 227 A.2d 667 (1967). Qualified expert may be permitted to assert relevant fact known to him because of his special training and experience, but such special training and experience must be confined to technical knowledge beyond that of average men that would be of assistance in determining issues in case.

Collins v. Zediker, 421 Pa. 52, 218 A.2d 776 (1966). Admission of expert engineering testimony about the speed at which a pedestrian was walking when hit by an auto was reversible error, as speeds at which pedestrians walk was within the common knowledge and experience of jury and was not proper subject for expert testimony.

Rosato v. Nationwide Ins. Co., 263 Pa. Super. 340, 397 A.2d 1238 (1979). Investigating police officers are permitted to state their observations and measurements concerning automobile accident, but grossly speculative opinions are forbidden because of their tendency to taint verdict. A properly trained officer may, based upon skid measurements and his expertise, state approximate speed of car even though he was not present at accident. **Note:** The training must include speed or crash reconstruction in most jurisdictions.

Dougherty v. Fulton Ins. Co., 51 Berks 182 (Pa. Com. Pl. 1959). The report of a civil aeronautics investigator about a crash in which plaintiff's decedent was involved was excluded as an exhibit where the witness testified from his own recollection about the investigation; nor was the report rendered admissible under the Act of Congress, June 23, 1938, 49 U.S.C.A. § 425(d), which provides that such reports shall be competent evidence in state courts.

Vantell v. Black Top Paving Co., 80 D & C 54 (Pa. Com. Pl. 1952). In an action to recover for damages resulting from an automobile accident allegedly due to a recent application of top dressing on the highway by defendant, the defendant called the district construction engineer for the Department of Highways, who had general supervision over all the construction work in the district, and generally visited it weekly, at which time he discussed the progress of the work with a local inspector and examined the diary of the local inspector, a record that the inspector had to keep on every job. The construction engineer was allowed to authenticate and admit the diary.

In re Involuntary Termination of Parental Rights, 449 Pa. 543, 297 A.2d 117 (1972). An expert witness must state his qualifications and the source of his knowledge; witness must demonstrate special knowledge on the very question upon which he proposes to express his opinion.

Collins v. White, 68 York 110 (Pa. Com. Pl. 1954). A police officer may testify as to stopping distances where such testimony is made on his own knowledge and may use the manual on stopping distances prepared by the Government of Pennsylvania for use by police officers to support such testimony.

Lesher v. Henning, 302 Pa. Super. 508, 449 A.2d 32 (1982). In an auto crash case, the trial court erred in permitting state police trooper who did not witness the accident to express his opinion that plaintiff caused the crash by failing to stop at the sign. The opinion was not predicated upon facts determined after careful analysis of physical evidence at scene of the crash, was based on hearsay accounts of the accident given by two eyewitnesses, and should not have been admitted.

An investigating police officer who did not actually witness a crash is usually not competent at trial to render an opinion as to its cause. However, if the police officer can be properly qualified as an expert witness, and proper facts to support his opinions have been established in evidence, the officer may, like any expert witness, render an opinion on the question of causation.

Whistler Sportswear, Inc. v. Rullo, 289 Pa. Super. 230, 433 A.2d 40 (1981). A hypothetical question asked of expert witness need not be based upon evidence conclusively proven. The evidence supporting the hypothetical question need only tend to establish assumptions.

Bowles v. City of Pittsburgh, 343 Pa. 39, 20 A.2d 783 (1941). A court may, in the exercise of its sound discretion, permit an expert witness to express an opinion on a deferred portion of the testimony given in behalf of one of the parties and made known to him either by his reading or hearing it, which is not contradictory in itself, and the truth of which he expressly assumes for the purpose of his opinion. An expert witness should not be allowed to base opinions solely on statements of counsel as to what the facts are.

Houston v. Canon Bowl, Inc., 443 Pa. 383, 278 A.2d 908 (1971). An expert witness can express opinion about the cause of a crash based upon either his personal observations of the scene of the accident, or hypothetical questions based on certain assumptions founded in the evidence.

Kravinsky v. Glover, 263 Pa. Super. 8, 396 A.2d 1349 (1979). A clinical psychologist may be recognized as an expert qualified to testify on diagnosis, prognosis, and causation of emotional disturbance.

Simmons v. Mullen, 122 P.L.J. 75, *aff'd,* 231 Pa. Super. 179, 331 A.2d 892 (Pa. Com. Pl. 1973). Expert testimony of a psychologist as to emotional changes after a traumatic injury is permissible even though a psychologist cannot testify as to medical findings, he can testify to the result of damage to the brain.

Haines v. Reading Co., 178 F.2d 918 (3d Cir. 1950). A retired longtime railroad employee who had 37 years' experience with the railroad was qualified as an "expert" to testify as to certain rules of railroad relating to use of air brakes and placing of materials on top of cars.

Kuisis v. Baldwin-Lima Hamilton Corp., 457 Pa. 321, 319 A.2d 914 (1974). Engineer need not be registered as such in order to testify as expert if his education and experience so qualify him. If witness has any reasonable basis to claim specialized knowledge on the subject under investigation he may testify, and the weight to be given his evidence is for jury.

Fish v. Gosnell, 463 A.2d 1042 (Pa. Super. Ct. 1983). Either party in a negligence action is entitled to introduce expert or other evidence to establish actual expected future earnings capacity of plaintiff, but is not required to do so.

City of Philadelphia v. Shapiro, 416 Pa. 308, 206 A.2d 308 (1965). Testimony of plaintiff's doctors as to plaintiff's alleged pain was admissible as relevant and competent.

Texas Law: *Rogers v. Gonzales,* 654 S.W.2d 509 (Tex. Ct. App. 1983). It is almost impossible to form any definite guidelines for determining knowledge, skill, or experience required of a particular witness or in a particular case.

It is within the trial court's discretion to decide whether a particular witness is qualified to testify as an expert. That decision will not be disturbed on appeal unless a clear abuse of discretion is shown.

The difficulty in barring expert testimony when there is eyewitness testimony however biased or inaccurate or implausible, was shown in the Texas case of *Flores v. Clark,* at the Nuces County, 214th Judicial District Court, No. 81-2249-F, August 5, 1983, Reported at 27 A.T.L.A. L. Rep. 64. In that case although witnesses testified that the plaintiff's vehicle had run a red light, testimony by traffic engineers analyzing skid marks and other evidence, established that the light must have been green when plaintiff's vehicle entered the intersection.

The factual basis for opinions of an investigating highway patrolman concerning the pre-crash speed and evasive actions taken by a motorist, estimate of speed was based upon skid marks and statements of witnesses, though the patrolman did not detail other physical evidence relied on.

Adams v. Smith, 479 S.W.2d 390 (Tex. Civ. App. 1972). City traffic engineer was qualified to express opinion as to speed of vehicle. He was experienced in investigating and reconstructing crashes and had a degree in civil engineering and had considered road conditions, various photographs, terrain, law of conservation of momentum, weather conditions, direction of travel and other pertinent factors.

Texas Steel Co. v. Recer, 508 S.W.2d 889 (Tex. Civ. App. 1974). A professor of economics and a psychologist with 25 years experience were permitted to testify as experts on the issue of the plaintiff's future earning capacity.

Clark v. Cotten, 573 S.W.2d 886 (Tex. Civ. App. 1978). Evidence that a state trooper had been with the Department of Public Safety for eight and one-half years, had received 17 weeks of training, had investigated 350 accidents, had viewed marks on the highway at the scene of the accident indicating that one vehicle had gone into a skid or hydroplane, and had been trained that an automobile could "hydroplane" at 56 miles per hour when running through water was not sufficient to qualify the officer to testify that the accident was caused by excessive speed on the part of the vehicle which hydroplaned.

Missouri Pac. R.R. v. Rose, 385 S.W.2d 492 (Tex. Civ. App. 1964). The opinion of policemen, based on inspection of crash wreckage, as to the pre-crash speeds of the auto before a train hit it, was inadmissible without evidence that the policemen were qualified to give such an opinion.

Phoenix Refining Co. v. Powell, 251 S.W.2d 892 (Tex. Civ. App. 1952). Two trucks collided head-on, and there were no surviving eyewitnesses. A traffic and photographic expert testified, based on tire and rim marks and measurements and the position of the trucks after the collision, that a blowout or sudden deflation of the left-hand front tire had pulled one of the trucks to the left side of the highway. This testimony did not exceed the proper limitations of opinion testimony, nor could it be properly regarded as "no evidence."

Bufkin v. Texas Farm Bureau Mut. Ins. Co., 658 S.W.2d 317 (Tex. Ct. App. 1983). Factual basis upon which the expert reaches his conclusion goes to weight of testimony and not its admissibility.

Soriano v. Medina, 648 S.W.2d 426 (Tex. Ct. App. 1983). Testimony of an economist as to loss of wage-earning capacity of motorist injured in auto crash was admissible in view of fact that questions proposed to economist, although hypothetical, were based upon sufficient relevant facts established by evidence.

Adams v. Smith, 479 S.W.2d 390 (Tex. Civ. App. 1972). Objection to an expert witness' opinion concerning speed of one vehicle involved in a head-on collision went to weight rather than to admissibility where witness was qualified to give opinion and hypothetical questions proposed contained all essential elements and proper assumptions concerning particular occurrence.

MWJ Producing Co. v. Sparkman, 655 S.W.2d 286 (Tex. Ct. App. 1983). An expert is not limited to facts within his own knowledge in giving an opinion, and may properly base his opinion on hypothetical questions which embody facts in evidence.

O'Kelly v. Jackson, 516 S.W.2d 748 (Tex. Civ. App. 1974). Analysis and reconstruction of a crash by a qualified expert, including consideration of physical facts, photographs, diagrams, and depositions, will be accepted in evidence. This rule does not permit the formulation of evidence or calculations based upon facts assumed and not in evidence.

Southwestern Bell Tel. Co. v. Davis, 582 S.W.2d 919 (Tex. Civ. App. 1979). Qualified experts are commonly permitted to testify to such matters as braking time, and whether a crash would have happened had defendant's driver maintained proper lookout and applied his brakes in timely fashion.

Hooten v. Dunbar, 347 S.W.2d 775 (Tex. Civ. App. 1961). An expert could testify about the cause of a crash, even though there were eyewitnesses.

City of Denton v. Mathes, 528 S.W.2d 625 (Tex. Civ. App. 1975). The opinion of police officer, who was not witness to a crash, as to the cause of the crash was hearsay evidence; it was therefore not error for the court to refuse to admit portion of police report containing such opinion into evidence. Note: Flaws in the original source of evidence cannot be cured by transposing the evidence into another form, unless the Supreme Court overrules *Miranda.*

Finn v. Finn, 658 S.W.2d 735 (Tex. Ct. App. 1983). Oral testimony is hearsay when based on entries contained in written records without producing source of such information.

§ 16-2. Jury Can Disregard Experts.

An expert in offering sound technical testimony on the merits has taken the first, but not the only step necessary to have the jury accept his view of the case. For reasons they do not have to disclose, juries in virtually every state have the right to disregard the expert. (See *Wynn v. Cole,* 91 Mich. App. 517, 284 N.W.2d 144 (1979); *Dudley Sports Co. v. Schmitt,* 151 Ind. App. 217, 279 N.E.2d 266, 276 (1972).

Psychological research has established that the expert, like any other witness, may be discarded by juror who dislike his appearance, dress, or behavior. (See Laural, "Persuasion: A Tree of Courtroom Communication," in *Psychology: A Quarterly Journal of Human Behavior,* Vol. 19 (213) (1982)).

§ 16-3. Experts Can Testify on "Ultimate Issues."

Experts have, in most jurisdictions, always been able to give opinions within the realm of their competence. Thus, in a one vehicle off the road crash, a transportation engineer who examined skid marks, photos by a crack photographer, the police report, and other data, could usually give an estimate on how fast the vehicle was going when it left the pavement. Many jurisdictions, however, until recently, barred the expert from supposedly invading the province of the jury by testifying on the "ultimate issue" of whether a driver going at that speed was or was not negligent. The distinction between these two shades of opinion probably meant more to lawyers than anyone else, and served only to ensure the conclusion on "ultimate issues" such as negligence or its absence in technical cover were presented to the jury by the people in the courtroom generally least able to really understand what they were talking about: lawyers.

Fortunately, most jurisdictions have now allowed experts to testify on ultimate issues, leaving the jury to decide how much weight to give the ultimate opinion.

Florida Law: *Cromarty v. Ford Motor Co.,* 341 So. 2d 507 (Fla. 1976). Expert opinion may support jury verdict, so long as it is grounded in the evidence, even though it involves a conclusion as to ultimate causation.

Massachusetts Law: *Henderson v. D'Annolfo,* 446 N.E.2d 103 (Mass. App. Ct. 1983). It is not objectionable for expert to offer opinion testimony regarding issue which may be submitted to jury to decide.

Kennedy v. U-Haul Co., 360 Mass. 71, 271 N.E.2d 346 (1971). Although there was positive testimony that the brake system of a leased truck which ran over child was designed to last the life of the truck, and that there was no occasion to check bolts which hold on brake system cap. Jury could accept the opinion of plaintiff's expert witness that bolts should have been checked by defendant with a torque wrench, and they also could have accepted opinion that one of the bolts was broken before the accident and that a proper inspection would have disclosed a weakness in the brake system which could have been remedied.

Simon v. Solomon, 385 Mass. 91, 431 N.E.2d 556 (1982). Expert testimony on matters within witness' expertise is admissible whenever it will aid jury in reaching a decision, even if the expert's opinion touches on the ultimate issues which the jury must decide.

Michigan Law: *Garza v. Indiana & Mich. Elec. Co.,* 338 F.2d 623 (6th Cir. 1964). Hypothetical question is not rendered incompetent because it may involve ultimate fact.

New York Law: *Miller v. Food Fair Stores, Inc.,* 63 A.D.2d 766, 404 N.Y.S.2d 740 (1978). When ultimate issues of fact require technical testimony, expert is entitled to draw his conclusions, however, when the subject is one within the common knowledge of a jury an expert may not give such opinions.

Ohio Law: *McKay Mach. Co. v. Rodman,* 11 Ohio St. 2d 77, 278 N.E.2d 304 (1967). Expert testimony is admissible on ultimate fact issues without infringing upon the province of the jury where determination of facts requires application of expert knowledge not within common knowledge of jury.

Pennsylvania Law: *Morris v. Mass,* 290 Pa. Super. 587, 435 A.2d 184 (1981). In an action by a pedestrian to recover against driver of automobile which struck pedestrian, a policeman's estimate as to the speed at which automobile had been traveling was admitted over the objection that such testimony concerned an ultimate issue in the case. The policeman, who had taken seminars on traffic safety and traffic accidents and who, at time of accident, had been an officer for eight years, was qualified to give an estimate of speed.

Brydon v. Kimbob, Inc., 20 Cumb. 94 (Pa. Comm. Pl. 1970). A photograph showing a sign enacted during a previous change of traffic pattern is admissible as evidence of prior custom and usage, and is relevant on the issue of defendant's negligence.

Texas Law: *Connecticut Gen. Life Ins. Co. v. Tommie*, 619 S.W.2d 199 (Tex. Civ. App. 1981). An expert opinion on the ultimate facts will be received whenever it is given by a witness competent to do so, and if it is to be of appreciable aid to the jury in arriving at correct conclusions.

§ 16-4. Preparing the Direct Examination of Experts.

Experts tend to underestimate the damage attorneys can inflict upon them in their fields of expertise. Experts also tend to minimize the benefits friendly attorneys can confer on their testimony. Experts, in fact, often visualize the entire trial procedure as a flow of information from themselves to the fact finder without material input, for good or evil, from attorneys.

This attitude may make some experts sitting ducks, particularly if they are not "hired guns" who regularly testify in court. The "hired gun" professional witnesses, in turn, often have difficulty persuading juries that objectivity is compatible with their mercenary status.

§ 16-4(A). Establish a Viable Relationship.

The first essential element in preparing your experts for direct examination, therefore, is to make every effort to ensure that the expert is affording you the time and respect you will need to establish a viable working relationship. This problem is often particularly acute for defendants in transportation facility negligence situations because the amounts of money the defense team is allocated may not be sufficient to motivate the expert to give the case more than cursory attention.

§ 16-4(B). Coordinate Experts.

If more than one expert is employed, coordinate them by using one expert to verify and supplement another. In transportation facility negligence cases, this will be particularly helpful if the case can sustain both a practical engineer and an academic engineer. These two categories of experts naturally compliment each other in transportation cases — the practical engineer analyzing the facility with respect to sight distances and other basic features, and the broader spectrum academic engineer analyzing the facility in relation to crash reports and other safety criteria.

As a general rule, the practical engineer will be someone local, close to the scene of the crash, who can supply the academic engineer with surveys, blueprints, and other requested materials. The practical engineer will often also have knowledge of either the facility itself or other local people who may have such knowledge.

§ 16-4(C). Integrate Experts and Witnesses.

There is no reason to keep the experts isolated from the eyewitnesses before trial. In fact, the experts can rely on the testimony of the eyewitnesses in (among other things) formulating their opinions and illustrating the usefulness of getting the experts and witnesses together. Such coordination has the further salutary effect of helping the witnesses feel that they are on the same "team" with your experts.

§ 16-4(D). Monitor Technical Research.

Do not assume that your experts are willing or able to do all the required research on relevant state of the art technology. Find a good technical library in your area and use the experts to guide your research, which should be promptly forwarded to them for analysis. The simple fact is that such technical research is often the most vital issue in the case, and many experts lack either the time or the library access or both to produce a research product of requisite quality. Of course, coordinate research results between experts.

§ 16-4(E). Dry Run Questions.

Go over all possible question areas (and, if possible, all of your own questions verbatim) with the expert. Make sure that you and the expert are on the same wavelength before you begin direct examination. Before your expert is deposed or undergoes cross-examination at trial, put the expert through the toughest cross-examination you can think of. Duel with your expert: probe for what you consider the weak points in his position, attack his qualifications, point out his bias.

You can avoid countless problems at trial by ensuring that you and the expert agree on what each question means. Also be certain that the expert understands the difference between scientific cause and legal cause and that he has an opportunity to learn where the legal pitfalls are in his subject area.

§ 16-4(F). A Bad Deposition May Sometimes Be Survived.

Make sure your expert is at least reasonably prepared for his deposition, but do not be unduly dismayed if your opponent scores some points at the deposition. So long as the deposition does not totally destroy your expert (which can happen), a good cutting deposition administered by your opponent will (hopefully) outline to you many of the theories and tactical approaches your opponent will use at trial. In addition, the areas of difficulty your expert experiences on deposition can usually be largely mitigated by properly structured direct examination work that you and your expert have put in to correct the weaknesses exposed at the deposition.

§ 16-5. Preparing Your Expert for Cross-Examination.

§ 16-5(A). Anticipate Cross-Examination.

Go over with your expert the possible avenues of attack (indicated below) on cross-examination. Above all, make sure your expert reads his deposition before he testifies.

§ 16-5(B). Give Your Expert All Relevant Records.

It is crucial that your expert receive and review all relevant documents and records before his deposition. His opinions may change if he is presented with crucial facts he has not previously considered and, even if his opinions remain unaltered under such circumstances, they will lose a great deal of credibility.

In order to ensure production of all relevant documents and materials from the opposing party, vigorous discovery must be conducted. For documents and records the opposing party may destroy or alter if forewarned, recourse may be had through immediate production orders served contemporaneously with the summons, pursuant to Illinois Supreme Court Rule 201, Ill. Rev. Stat., ch. 110A, ¶ 201(d), which provides: "Time Discovery May Be Initiated. Prior to the time all defendants have appeared or are required to appear, no deposition or other discovery procedure shall be noticed or otherwise initiated without leave of court granted upon good cause shown."

§ 16-5(C). Explain Legal Causation to the Expert.

Most lawsuits involve crucial issues of causation, and that term means quite different things in science and in law. To the scientific expert, particularly one who has not done a great deal of testifying, causation is generally an area he will do poorly in without guidance from the attorney. The expert, within his own discipline, is accustomed to dealing with precise mathematical certainty and obviously, no expert who was not also an eyewitness can know with that kind of certainty what actually did cause a crash on even the most grossly deficient transportation facility. Such experts, without guidance from the attorney, consequently tend to be far stronger in testifying about negligence than in testifying about proximate cause.

Initially, it is helpful to point out to the expert that the crash need not have only one proximate cause, or even only one principal proximate cause. "[The] causes of an injury may be so commingled in a single act as to make the causes concurrent proximate causes." *Jones v. City of Rock Island,* 101 Ill. App. 2d 174, 242 N.E.2d 302, 305 (1968). See also *Millette v. Radosta,* 84 Ill. App. 3d 5, 404 N.E.2d 823 (1980); *Nelson v. Union Wire Rope Corp.,* 31 Ill. 2d 69, 199 N.E.2d 769 (1964). The law of virtually all other jurisdictions is similar.

The degree of certainty supporting the expert's opinion on causation should also be carefully reviewed. The stronger the expert is in contending that the defendant's negligence or the plaintiff's contributory negligence was a proximate cause of the crash, then the opportunities for cross-examination will be more restricted. The expert should, therefore, be sensitized to the vast differences, legally, that may follow the various ways he may phrase his opinions on causation.

In *Flifford-Jacobs Forging Co. v. Industrial Comm'n,* 19 Ill. 2d 236, 166 N.E.2d 582 (1960), it was held proper, and not unduly speculative, for an expert to testify that various conditions "could have" or "might have" caused death. An opinion on causation thus phrased, however, is obviously open to the immediate cross-examination that the conditions at issue "could not have" or "might not have" been the cause. Such an opinion on causation from your expert, then, is acceptable legally, but unacceptable tactically if the expert will give you anything stronger. For additional authority validating expert causation opinions couched as "could have" or "might have," see *Greim v. Sharpe Motor Lines,* 101 Ill. App. 2d 142, 242 N.E.2d 282 (1968).

Somewhat stronger was the expert opinion validated in *Beloit Foundry v. Industrial Comm'n,* 62 Ill. 2d 535, 343 N.E.2d 504 (1976), where the expert testified that the conditions at issue were "the most likely cause of injury, based on a statistical probability." This phraseology, which may not appear much different to your expert than the "might have" or "could have" answers discussed earlier, will obviously be much stronger on cross-examination than the weaker formulations. The attorney should make every effort to bring the expert to this level of certainty.

In *Johnson v. Ward,* 6 Ill. App. 3d 1015, 286 N.E.2d 637 (1972), the court accepted an expert opinion that certain defects "did cause" a crash. Obviously, this is the strongest and most desirable phraseology for the expert in giving his opinion on causation.

Whatever the phraseology used by your expert, make certain that you can withstand attack on every essential fact the expert opinion rests on. Standard cross-examination of such expert opinions begins by requesting the expert to list every essential fact he relies on and proceeds to launch a maximum attack on every listed fact.

§ 16-6. Preparing to Cross-Examine "Their" Expert.

Cross-examination of an expert witness involves your attempt to refute either the credibility or the competence, or both, of a person who knows virtually everything about a topic which you know virtually nothing about. It is a brutal, unforgiving war fought in the open arena before a jury which will decide whether your client wins or loses, and you must make the cross-examination at least reasonably understandable to the jury, although you may safely assume that the jury will know even less about what you are saying than you do. Not surprisingly, you will need every advantage you can give yourself.

Most successful cross-examinations are won before they begin. Extensive research into the background, writings, teachings, workings, and status of your target, done long before the trial begins, will usually prove far more useful areas for cross-examinations than scrawled notes and brainstorms you come up with during the expert's direct examination. The following is a partial listing, by no means intended to be exhaustive, of areas that may be fruitful for the pretrial preparations of expert witness cross-examination.

§ 16-6(A). The Retained Expert.

The jury will usually find it much easier to understand an attack on the expert witness' credibility than an attack on the merits of his opinion, which they may not understand anyway. His credibility may be attacked by establishing an apparent bias. Many experts are currently retained from expert referral services and their services are for sale to any bidder. Alternatively, many large defendants maintaining railroad crossings, roadways, and other transportation facilities have their own stable of "fast gun" experts, who often testify for few other clients. Some experts work for both plaintiffs and defendants, while some find it more profitable to work only one side of the street. Some plaintiffs' experts even require a percentage of the recovery!

These matters should be thoroughly pinned down, at the latest, during your pretrial deposition of the expert.

§ 16-6(B). Writings and Teachings of Expert.

If the adverse expert comes from an academic setting, obtain copies of the teaching texts he uses. Similarly, obtain copies of any writings he has published that may be relevant to the case. Obviously, these texts should be closely studied for statements inconsistent with positions the expert has taken in your case. If you can impeach the expert with his own words or with the materials he uses to teach his students, he will lose a great deal of credibility with the jury.

§ 16-6(C). Prepare for the Deposition.

The pretrial deposition of the hostile expert may well be the single most important factor in determining whether the trial cross-examination succeeds. The pretrial deposition is really your only chance before trial to pin the expert down on his opinions concerning the case, the knowledge he has of the case, and the reasons supporting his opinions. In order to accomplish each of these essential objectives, you must prepare for the deposition by studying the expert's background, the facts of the case, and the technical materials the deposition will cover. A hostile expert properly pinned down on deposition, particularly on the essential facts he does not know, although he already has formed his opinions, can be subjected to rather effective trial cross-examination, largely prepared before trial, based on the deposition transcript.

For these reasons, the depositions should be as thorough and exhaustive as possible. In fact, the depth and scope of examination at the deposition usually far exceeds that of the trial cross-examination, which should always be based on the strongest points from the deposition.

§ 16-6(D). Cross-Examine With Honey, Not Vinegar.

While cross-examining the hostile expert at trial from the transcript of the deposition and other materials (your scrawled notes which were made during the direct testimony of the expert should be least important if your deposition properly anticipated the direct), most of the old and oft-cited rules apply. Thus, questions should be tightly drafted, answered by as few words as possible (preferably "yes" or "no"), and you should know and be able to impeach with the deposition the answer to each question before it is asked. In addition, however, in order to maintain your credibility with the jury, be as polite as possible to the expert. Such an approach will also tend to lower his guard and relax his vigilance against the trick and trap questions. As the old saying goes, "You catch more flies with honey than with vinegar."

§ 16-6(E). Representative Citations on Cross-Examination of Experts.

Florida Law: *National Car Rental Sys. v. Holland,* 269 So. 2d 407 (Fla. App. 1972). Where non-expert witness' gratuitous statement of opinion that there was no way to avoid "it" was given, without objection, during cross-examination in action arising out of auto crash and objection was first raised during redirect examination directed toward clarification of opinion, objection came too late, and at that point, it was within the court's sound judicial discretion to permit redirect examination seeking clarification.

Wright v. Dade County, 216 So. 2d 494 (Fla. App. 1968), *cert. denied,* 396 U.S. 1008, 90 S. Ct. 565, 24 L.Ed.2d 500 (1969). Extent of cross-examination concerning qualifications of defendant's expert witness was within trial court's discretion.

Illinois Law: In *Sears v. Rutishauser,* 117 Ill. App. 3d 61, 453 N.E.2d 1 (1983), the Appellate Court of Illinois, Fourth District, the court affirmed a trial court ruling that the Defendant, in cross-examining the Plaintiff's medical expert, could ask *whether* he had received prior referrals from Plaintiff's counsel, but not *how numerous* those referrals had been. The Illinois Supreme Court, in cause 59196, reversed the Appellate Court, allowing experts to be cross-examined on their prior referral relationships with hiring attorneys. The highest Illinois Court reasoned: "It is virtually impossible to prosecute an expert witness for perjury. . . . The principal safeguard against errant expert testimony is cross-examination. Generally, opposing counsel may probe bias, partisanship or financial interest of an expert witness on cross-examination."

The new Illinois Supreme Court Rule 220 also now creates the category of "regular expert witnesses," who will be used at trial and who must be disclosed, "within 90 days after the substance of the experts opinion first becomes known, or at the first pre-trial conference, whichever is later." The rule also creates a second category of, "consulting expert," defined as people; "who have the same qualifications as an 'expert witness' but who are not called upon to testify, and need not be identified to the opponent unless there is a showing of 'exceptional circumstances.'"

Massachusetts Law: *O'Hare v. Gloag,* 221 Mass. 24, 108 N.E. 566 (1915). Question on cross-examination of a witness as to the ability of a person physically deficient, to operate an automobile safely held within the court's direction.

LeBlanc v. Ford Motor Co., 346 Mass. 225, 191 N.E.2d 301 (1963). Facts left out of a hypothetical question given to expert did not make question improper or require striking the answer where opposing counsel could point out on cross-examination any omitted facts and inquire whether such facts affected expert's opinion.

Michigan Law: *Williams v. Fiedlar,* 22 Mich. App. 179, 177 N.W.2d 461 (1970), *aff'd,* 386 Mich. 221, 191 N.W.2d 52 (1971). Permitting cross-examination of plaintiff's medical witness, who testified as expert, and who spent considerable time establishing his expertise, as to such witness' qualifications, credibility and professional ability was not abuse of discretion.

O'Dowd v. Linehan, 385 Mich. 491, 189 N.W.2d 333 (1971). A witness, on cross-examination, stated, in a crash case, that when he first observed southbound car involved in crash, he observed distances, speeds, time intervals, and that certain statements were made before the crash, namely, "My God, Carol, look at this guy coming at us!" It was proper for counsel to interrogate an expert as to length of southbound automobile and by use of stop watch have the expert announce the time it took counsel to repeat such a remark, and to have the expert compute closing time of the two autos.

Pennsylvania Law: *Jones v. Spidle,* 62 Lane Rev. 213, *remand from* 213 Pa. Super. 81, 245 A.2d 677 (1968), *aff'd,* 446 Pa. 103, 286 A.2d 366 (1971). Where plaintiffs were permitted to display an accident site diagram at the prior trial. Its inaccuracies were disclosed on cross-examination by the party who had prepared it and the court rejected its formal admission into evidence. The court sustained objection to its admission at the present trial for the reason that it could only have produced the recreation of the errors.

Texas Law: *Texas Employers Ins. Ass'n v. Hale,* 188 S.W.2d 899 (Tex. App. 1945), *aff'd,* 144 Tex. 432, 191 S.W.2d 472 (1946). A cross-examination is allowed a liberal range touching all matters testified to by an expert witness, and the scope of the cross-examination rests largely within the trial court's discretion.

Simms v. Southwest Tex. Methodist Hosp., 535 S.W.2d 192 (Tex. App. 1976). An expert witness may properly be cross-examined, for impeachment purposes, by reading to him excerpts from treatises, books, and scientific journals and asking him whether he agrees with the statements contained in such writings, but this use of documents is, in Texas, limited to publications which expert recognizes as authoritative.

§ 16-6(F). A Representative Expert Direct Examination.

The following exhibit is a reproduction of direct testimony from an engineer named Robert Lippman. It is broad spectrum direct testimony involving a head-on car crash on a negligently designed and maintained road curve. The testimony deals with inadequate sight distances, maintenance procedures, signing requirements, and the negligent failure to provide a necessary median barrier down the center of the road.

Exhibit

Direct Examination of Robert Lippman, Civil Engineer

ROBERT L. LIPPMAN, having been first duly sworn, testified as follows:

DIRECT EXAMINATION
BY MR. KUHLMAN:

Q. Mr. Lippman, would you tell the Court and Jury your name and address, please?

A. My name is Robert L. Lippman, and I live at 9025 Moraine Street, Dyer, Indiana.

Q. How long have you lived in Lake County, Indiana?

A. 39 years.

Q. How long have you lived in the State of Indiana?

A. 61 years.

Q. Who is your present employer?

A. I am self-employed.

Q. What is your profession or professions?

A. I'm a Civil Engineer, and a professional land surveyor.

Q. Would you explain to the Court and Jury what a Civil Engineer is?

A. A Civil Engineer is a person that takes mathematical theories and applies them to the solution of engineering problems. A Civil Engineer basically specializes in roads, highways, bridges, sewers, water lines, and structural designs of buildings and builds physical things.

Q. What is a surveyor?

A. A surveyor is basically a person trained in measurements in the field as a Civil Engineer, but he has the extra compensation or extra knowledge of writing legal descriptions and transferring land and marking out property.

Q. Now, you understand, Mr. Lippman, that in a court I can't just ask you to tell the Court and Jury everything you know about this road, we have to speak in questions and answers; right?

A. Yes.

Q. And you and I have discussed these questions and answers before; right?

A. That is true.

Q. So that hopefully I will know something about what I am talking about; right?

A. Right.

Q. And you are being compensated for your time here; is that right?

A. That is correct.

Q. What school are you a graduate of?

A. Graduate of Purdue University.

Q. What did you major in at Purdue?

A. Civil Engineering.

Q. Did you have a major in that?

A. Highways and structures.

Q. What field did you receive your degree in?

A. Civil Engineering.

Q. When did you receive that degree?

A. 1944.

Q. Are you a registered professional engineer in the State of Indiana?

A. Yes, I am.

Q. How does one become a registered professional engineer in Indiana?

A. Through education, experience and passing the licensing board.

Q. Are you a registered land surveyor in Indiana?

A. Yes, I am.

Q. How does one become a registered land surveyor in this State?

A. Same thing with a different board.

Q. How long have you been a registered professional engineer in this State?

A. Since 1952.

Q. How long have you been a registered land surveyor in this State?

A. Since 1954.

Q. Do you belong to any professional society?

A. Yes, I do.

Q. Which one?

A. National Society of Professional Engineers; Indiana Society of Professional Engineers; the American Society of Military Engineers; and I am a Fellow in the American Society, American Congress of Surveying and Mapping; I belong to the American Public Works Association.

Q. What qualifications are required to become a member of those Societies?

A. Some of them you've got to be an engineer; in Public Works you have to be a City Official interested in Public Works.

Q. Have you ever published any professional literature or legislation relating to roads or highways?

A. Yes, I did.

Q. What was that?

A. In 1952 I wrote the first subdivision control ordinance in the United States setting out standards of design for subdividers, when they are adding a subdivision to a municipality. Basically it was for the City of Hammond, but it was published in the American Public Works Magazine and I got nationwide publicity on it.

Q. What relationship did that publication have to roads and highways and highway safety?

A. It set up minimum standards for city streets, arterial highways, type of curbs, sight distances, sidewalks, street lights, everything that a city should require a subdivider to do before they accept a subdivision.

Q. To your knowledge, how widely has that been copied now in various updated versions throughout the United States?

A. I think that just about every City in the United States is using it now.

Q. First of all, have you ever made a survey?

A. Yes.

Q. Approximately how many surveys have you made?

A. Thousands.

Q. Have you ever surveyed an area of highway?

A. Yes, I have.

Q. Approximately how many areas of highway have you surveyed?

A. 500; 100 to 500; it's hard to say.

Q. What is a scale drawing?

A. Scale drawing is where you take a series of big measurements and draw them in proportion so that they fit on a piece of paper to a small scale.

Q. In connection with your work in engineering and surveying, did you yourself ever have to prepare any scale drawings?

A. Constantly.

Q. Approximately how many scale drawings have you prepared?

A. Thousands.

Q. Approximately how many scale drawings have you prepared in areas of highway?

A. Same, half of it.

Q. Over approximately how many years have you been preparing scale drawings of areas of highway?

A. About 40 years.

Q. Have you ever attended any seminars or courses in civil engineering or surveying?

A. I go to as many as I can when I have time. The Land Surveyors Association has seminars every year. In the early part of my career I went to the Purdue road schools and any extra courses that Purdue holds in Hammond; and I read all the literature that comes out now.

Q. Did you prepare that three-paneled drawing on easels?

A. Yes, I did.

Q. Is that a scale drawing?

A. That's a scale drawing.

Q. We'll talk about that later on.

Prior to graduating from Purdue University with a major in highways, what connection, if any, did you have with roads and highway operations and design?

A. Well, while I was a Senior in high school I took a job as a rod man working with the Highway Commission on Route 30. My Freshman year in college I worked on Route 20 as a rod man. Later out of school, at the end of my Sophomore year I went to work for the State Highway Commission as an inspector of paving and grading, and I then went with Kingsbury Ordnance plant construction as Assistant Party Chief, then I was a Party Chief in charge of laying out roads and highways. Then I went into the Army — wait a minute. Yes, then I went into the Army and the Army sent me back to Purdue and I graduated.

Q. What experience did you have in civil engineering and surveying between the time you graduated from Purdue and the year 1952?

A. I graduated from Purdue and I was assigned to Officer Candidate School at Ft. Sill and became a 1st Lieutenant in the Field Artillery. I was assigned to Ft. Sill Field Artillery School as a surveying instructor and I was there about a year teaching surveying to civilians who just became Army people, such as lawyers and so forth.

Then I went to Europe and I was in charge of fire control and surveying for the 394th Field Artillery Battalion until I was discharged.

Q. After you were discharged did you have any work?

A. After I was discharged I came back and worked for Sinclair Refining.

Q. Doing what?

A. In East Chicago, as a civil engineer in charge of layout of pipelines, roads, tunnels, buildings, and then in 1951 I signed a one-year contract with the Air Force to supervise the testing of atom bombs, the effect of atom bombs on highways and buildings, underground structures in Las Vegas and Amchitka in the Aleutian Islands.

Q. Did that work involve testing the effects of atomic bombs on roads and highways?

A. It did, and on airport runways, which is a little thicker than a highway but the same type.

Q. Will you tell the Court and Jury whose personal representative you were when you were studying those atomic bomb tests?

A. I was the direct representative of the Commanding General of the Air Force, including the contractor and the Research Department, make sure he got his money's worth.

Q. Have you ever held any employment positions with any governmental bodies in the State of Indiana?

A. I was City Engineer of Hammond, Indiana, from 1952 until 1956.

Q. What were your duties as the City Engineer of Hammond; let's refer only to the duties relating to roads and highways?

A. As City Engineer in Hammond, I set up the first Traffic Engineering Department in Hammond; I was in charge of maintenance of everything the City of Hammond owned, including roads; I was in charge of new construction of anything the City of Hammond built; I was in the charge of fixing alleys and pot holes; I was in charge of signing, marking, safety, location of speed signs, street lights, did anything else that the Mayor wanted me to do.

Q. Did you have any responsibilities toward the setting or supervising of speed limits?

A. Yes.

Q. As the Hammond City Engineer, did you learn, or prior to that time, did you learn what is meant by the term pavement markings?

A. Yes, I did.

Q. Will you tell the Court and Jury what that term means; what do you mean marking the street?

A. It means marking some information for the motorist on the street with paint, such as lane lines, crosswalks, painting stop, in other words marking information.

Q. Is that to be done with any kind of paint, house paint?

A. It's done with a reflectorized paint so that as the paint wears off the little glass beads will shine so that people can see it at night.

Q. Is that a special paint or a common average paint you can buy in a hardware store?

A. No, it's a special paint.

Q. As Hammond City Engineer, did you have responsibilities for pavement marking of streets, roads and highways in Hammond?

A. Yes.

Q. Approximately how many miles of streets, roads and highways were you responsible for marking or for maintaining the marking on?

A. The City of Hammond at the present time has 267 miles of street, and I think that we had about 250 then.

Q. That was all your baby?

A. Yes.

Q. What is meant by the term signing on a road?

A. That's the placement of signs to either give the motorist information or telling him what to do, such as turn, stop, yield.

Q. As Hammond City Engineer, did you have any responsibility for signing the streets of Hammond?

A. Yes, I did.

Q. Approximately how many street signs were you responsible for placing or properly maintaining in that position?

A. I didn't place any, the Traffic Assistant, Traffic Engineer and his crews placed them under my direction.

Q. How many signs were you responsible for directing the placement of?

A. I don't know, thousands.

Q. At that time did the State of Indiana have any authoritative standards, for engineers I am talking about, not for lawyers, did the State of Indiana at that time have any authoritative standards for engineers telling how the pavement marking and signing of State roads in Indiana was to be done?

A. Yes, the Uniform Traffic Safety Manual.

Q. Published by whom?

A. State of Indiana.

Q. What agency of the State of Indiana?
A. State Highway Commission.
Q. Now, to engineers, not to lawyers, I know you are not a lawyer, but to engineers how authoritative or non-authoritative were the standards for signing and marking state roads in those Indiana Uniform Manuals?
A. Marking State roads were mandatory.
Q. In the course of your career have you kept up-to-date with those Indiana Manuals since you were Hammond City Engineer?
A. Yes, I have.
Q. Are they still mandatory, or are they optional?
A. They are mandatory.
Q. Were there different rules in those Manuals, or are there today different rules, or have there ever been different rules in those Manuals for marking or signing different kinds of roads?
A. No.
Q. So that it's the same rule for all kinds of roads?
A. Yes.
Q. Big ones and little ones?
A. Right.
Q. Are you familiar with the Indiana State Manual Standards that were in effect for pavement marking and pavement signing of State roads between the years 1966 and 1970?
A. Yes.
Q. Where are those found?
A. They are in the Blue Books and the Red Books published by the American Association of Highway Officials.
Q. In which Indiana Manual are they in?
A. Which one now?
Q. Between the years 1966 and 1970?
A. What was the question?
Q. Are you familiar with the standards for marking and signing?
A. Marking and signing, yes.
Q. Of roads?
A. That's in the Uniform Traffic Manual.
Q. What year was that published?
A. 1968.
Q. As Hammond City Engineer, what involvement, if any, did you have with the analysis of roads and highway crashes?
A. When I first became City Engineer there was no Traffic Engineering Department in the City of Hammond. I set it up, we took the Traffic Sergeant, Larry Hoffman, and made him Assistant Traffic Engineer and took him out of the Police Department. We took two men from the street

department and assigned them to this section as the signing and painting crew. All accidents in the City of Hammond were brought to Mr. Hoffman's desk, it was right next to mine, so I could give him the engineering and he brought the expertise of a traffic policeman into it. We started sending traffic policemen to Northwestern, and all accidents in the City of Hammond came before me and we had a meeting once a week where we decided what we were going to do to eliminate them.

Q. What kind of things would you do at those meetings if you saw patterns of crashes developing in areas of roadway?

A. We would go out and try to find out why, and solve them. Sometimes it was a tree branch over a sign, or a bad sight distance. Whatever we could do engineering-wise to eliminate accidents in the City of Hammond we tried to do it.

Q. Did you ever consider it appropriate to ignore growing crash patterns on a particular area of highway?

A. No.

Q. Have you ever analyzed traffic crash reports?

A. Yes.

Q. Approximately how many traffic crash reports have you analyzed in your career?

A. Thousands.

Q. As Hammond City Engineer, did you have any responsibilities for locating and correcting very dangerous areas of road or highway?

A. Yes.

Q. And what were those responsibilities?

A. To engineer proper sight distance, divide traffic, or warn them, or whatever it took to make that location safer; prepare plans, find the money, try to get it done.

Q. Under reasonable engineering standards, did you consider the recommendations of engineers, qualified highway specialists who had previously analyzed an area of roadway to be relevant in the decision of whether it was dangerous and needed safety upgrading?

A. We always, I always made my own study of every accident, or every intersection I had to do.

Q. Approximately how many dangerous areas of road did you locate in your career as Hammond City Engineer?

A. Hammond is pretty flat, we didn't have too much trouble, about 50 or 60 places.

Q. Basically is there any working definition of what a road is. I know that sounds silly, but there are some things that people might consider to be a road that really aren't?

A. Fundamental definition of a road is a hard surface to keep you out of the mud, that you can drive over.

Q. Would that apply to any road no matter how big or how little?

A. Yes. You have different surfaces, but they are still —

Q. What experience, if any, have you had with road and highway design and sight distance analysis?

A. I studied it in school, I used it when I was the City of Hammond Engineer, and since then I have used it constantly in my profession.

Q. You have designed roads; is that correct?

A. That is correct.

Q. Have you ever designed bridges?

A. Yes, I have.

Q. Is there a relationship between bridge design on a road and the sight distance on the road coming to the bridge or going out of the bridge?

A. Normally a bridge is a bottleneck on the road and sight distance is more important on a bridge than it is on a highway. It's very important that motorists be forewarned that there should not be any difference in his driving habits going over a bridge than going over a road, therefore, the bridge has to be safer.

Q. What kind of roads have you designed in your career?

A. City streets or main arterial highways in Hammond; as a Consultant I haven't designed any highways, if that's what you're driving at.

Q. Do different kinds of roads have different design or sight distance principles?

A. No, they are all the same.

Q. So no matter how big or how small the road is, the road would have the same sight distance principles?

A. That's correct.

Q. And the road would have the same design principles?

A. That is correct.

Q. What experience in civil engineering and surveying have you had subsequent to being made Hammond City Engineer?

A. I started the Illiana Engineering Company and I designed subdivisions. Designed eight bridges in Porter County, one in Bellville, Illinois; I have investigated accidents and testified in court; surveyed many road intersections for attorneys; I have laid out parking lots; I have laid out roads around oil refineries and manufacturing plants; that's about it.

Q. Let me ask you this: About how many times have you calculated in your whole career the sight distances on curves and roads?

A. Four or 500 times probably.

Q. Is the analysis of road and highway design and construction and engineering the kind of work that laymen who are not trained in engineering can do for themselves?

A. No.

Q. Why not?

A. It takes mathematical principles to calculate the parabolas and the algebra that goes into calculating how far you can see around a curve.

Q. In your engineering consulting business — strike that.

Based on what you know of Mr. Edgman, could he have done this kind of work by himself?

A. I don't think so.

Q. In your engineering consulting business, have you analyzed vehicle crashes?

A. Yes, I have.

Q. Approximately how many?

A. Probably 100 to 150.

Q. In what geographic areas of Indiana?

A. Lake County, Porter County and LaPorte County.

Q. Have you had occasion in your consulting engineering work to analyze the design and sight distance of roads and highways?

A. Yes, each accident.

Q. Approximately how many such analyses have you made?

A. Say 100 to 150 altogether.

Q. Have you had occasion to analyze roads and highway signing?

A. Yes, I have.

Q. And markings?

A. Yes, I have.

Q. Approximately how many different occasions?

A. Each one of those accidents, 100 to 150.

Q. Who retained you to do this work?

A. Attorneys.

Q. Have you been retained to do this by plaintiffs' attorneys?

A. Yes.

Q. Have you been retained by defendants' attorneys?

A. Yes, I have.

Q. Approximately what percentage of your entire engineering business is related to litigation and lawyers?

A. About one or two percent.

Q. Have you ever been retained to investigate a crash or a road design and concluded that you could not reach conclusions favorable for the party retaining you?

A. Yes, I have.

Q. About how often was that?

A. About a third of the time.

Q. Have you ever previously before today qualified as an expert witness qualified to give expert opinions on due care and fault in a court of law in cases involving road signing, sight distance, road marking or appropriate safety protection?

A. Yes, I have.

Q. How many times?

A. I have been in court actually about 12 or 15 times.

Q. Have you ever been refused qualification as an expert ever before when you presented your qualifications to a court?

A. No, I haven't.

Q. From your work and study in engineering and mathematics, surveying and physics, have you learned of different kinds of curves that there are in a road?

A. Yes, I have.

Q. What are the different kinds of curves that there are in a road?

A. Horizontal curves and vertical curves.

Q. Would you explain to the Court and Jury what the difference is and what different kinds of curves are in each category?

A. A vertical curve is a curve that goes vertically up and down; a horizontal curve is a curve that goes to right or left.

Q. If a vertical curve goes up, what is it called?

A. It's called crest vertical curve.

Q. If it goes down, what is it called?

A. It's called a sag vertical curve.

Q. Approximately how many vertical curves and horizontal curves have you surveyed in areas of roadways?

A. Hundreds.

Q. How many vertical and horizontal curves have you analyzed for sight distances?

A. Hundreds.

Q. Do the same principles or different principles apply to the analysis of vertical and horizontal curves in big roads, medium size roads and small roads?

A. Same principles.

Q. What is the definition of a curve? We have used it in talking about it; what is it?

A. A curve is a line that is not straight.

Q. What is meant by the term degree of curvature?

A. The sharper the curve, the higher the degree of curvature.

Q. What is meant by the term length of curve?

A. That's the length around the axis of the curve, from the start of the curve to the end of the curve.

Q. What is meant by the term grade in a road?

A. Grade is the vertical, in simple language it's a hill up or down straight.

Q. In a simple vertical curve, one that's going up or down, how many different grades are there?

A. There's always two grades.

Q. Why is that?

A. If you went straight up, if you went straight down, you can get the car stuck up on the top of the road, so they smooth it off with a vertical curve.

Q. So that there is a grade going up and a grade going down?

A. And a vertical curve is what smoothes it off and gives the motorist sight distance.

Q. Okay, I'm going to ask you a little longer term, and I want you to explain to the Jury in simple layman's terms what it means: What is the algebraic difference in grades in a curve, what does that language mean?

A. If you have a grade going up and you subtract a grade going down which is minus, in algebra you subtract a minus number from a plus number, you add the two together. If you have one grade going up and another grade going up, both of them plus, then you will take the, subtract the second grade from the first one, because the algebra is exactly subtracting. It's kind of hard to explain if you haven't had algebra.

Q. What is meant by the term minimum stopping sight distance?

A. That is the distance a motorist needs to see in order to stop when he perceives something in front of him.

Q. What, if any, importance does that have to motorists' operation on road and highway?

A. Safety.

Q. What is design speed?

A. Design speed is a speed at which a highway or road should be designed for, in other words that should be the maximum safe speed that a person can drive it and still have minimum safe stopping sight distance.

Q. What is posted speed?

A. Posted speed is the speed that the operating department puts on a road, that's normally about 5 percent under the design speed, so that the dumb head that is going to exceed the speed limit doesn't kill himself on a road that it's not designed for.

Q. Should the posted speed ever be the design speed?

A. No.

Q. Why not?

A. Because normally a motorist knows that the police aren't going to arrest him within 10 percent of the posted speed, so most motorists will drive over the posted speed; unless there is a quota system going on then the police are out pretty hard.

Q. Should the posted speed ever be more than the design speed?

A. That would not be safe.

Q. Would the other one be safe either, where the posted speed was the design speed?

A. That would not be safe if you exceeded it.

Q. Is there any relationship between minimum stopping sight distance, the design speed of a road and crest vertical curves in roads?

A. Yes, all vertical curves should be designed to maintain the minimum safe stopping distance for a motorist going at the design speed.

Q. Is there any relationship between minimum stopping sight distance, the design speed, and the length or how long a crest vertical curve is?

A. There are standards set up by research based upon the height of the driver's eye, the height of the light that sets up tables that engineers use to determine how long to make the curve, based upon the algebraic difference of the grades and the speed of the vehicle.

Q. You just look it up in a table?

A. Yes, you can look it up in a table.

Q. During the years that you have been studying and practicing the profession of civil engineering and surveying, have you become personally familiar with the methods that engineers, surveyors use to calculate the minimum length that a crest or a sag vertical curve must have in order to give minimum stopping sight distance to a motorist at a given speed?

A. Yes, I have.

Q. How long have you been doing such calculations, looking up such tables?

A. 35 years; 30 years.

Q. During that period of time that you have been working as a surveyor and civil engineer, have there been any concepts or rules or formulas that have been promulgated to just tell people the minimum length of crest or sag vertical curve that is needed to give minimum stopping sight distance at a particular speed?

A. Yes, there have been.

Q. And who formulated those formulas?

A. Basically the books that all highway engineers use is the American Association of Highway Officials Red Book and Blue Book standards.

Q. Now, is there a short term for the American Association of State Highway officials?

A. AASHO I think they call it, yes.

Q. Called AASHO?

A. AASHO.

Q. How authoritative in the road and highway design and safety field is AASHO and the publications, and the Red Books and the Blue Books of AASHO?

A. Every State Highway Commission belongs to this association and they all use that as the Bible for designing roads.

Q. And how authoritative were the AASHO Tables on minimum stopping sight distances on roads from the year 1954 on to the present?

A. It's still the Bible, still used.

Q. In your engineering career you have actually calculated the minimum length of crest or sag vertical curve needed to give minimum stopping sight distance at a particular speed?

A. Yes, I have.

Q. About how long did you perform such calculations?

A. Hundreds.

Q. Over about how many years have you been doing this?

A. 30 or 40 years, I am not sure.

Q. Now, I want to ask you just a few general questions about this case, because you must qualify as an expert before I can ask you anything specific?

A. Okay.

Q. How long have you been working on this particular case, the Edgman crash?

A. Three years.

Q. Approximately how many documents on the Cline Avenue S-Curve or the area of Cline from Gary Avenue in the north to the Toll Road in the south have you reviewed?

A. Three or four hundred.

Q. Where have you examined them, where have you had to go to find these documents?

A. The Office of the Consulting Engineer.

Q. Who was that?

A. Consoer, Townsend.

Q. What connection did they have with this?

A. They were the Consulting Engineers that designed the road.

Q. Where else have you had to go to look for documents?

A. At the LaPorte District of the State Highway Commission, and the Indianapolis office of the State Highway Commission.

Q. Have you seen any evidence that anybody before you ever looked at all these documents and put them altogether?

A. No, I haven't.

Q. Have you seen any evidence in all these documents that anybody before you ever surveyed Cline Avenue from the Toll Road to Gary Avenue?

A. After it was constructed?

Q. Yes.

A. No, I didn't.

Q. Have you seen any evidence that anybody before you analyzed the sight distances on the various vertical curves at the Toll Road or the horizontal curves between the Toll Road and Gary Avenue after this road was completed?

A. No, I haven't.

Q. Approximately how many hours has it taken you to do all this work, investigation, drafting and analysis?

A. About 7 or 800.

Q. Why did it take so many hours?

A. Because I had to take the State Highway plans, analyze what was on the plans. I had to take a field party out and verify that they built it according to the plans, they surveyed the road. I had to read every document, every accident report I could find in the State of Indiana to analyze this section of road. And I have been working on it for three years.

Q. Have you seen any evidence that anybody besides you before you ever got together all the crashes that had occurred on Cline Avenue from Gary Avenue in the North to the Toll Road on the South between 1966 and July 27, 1970?

A. No, we could find no evidence that anybody ever looked at them.

Q. Did you ever see any spot maps or any evidence that somebody was keeping track?

A. I could find no map or anyone that said they had one.

Q. When you went to these various offices of the Highway Commission to look at documents, did they give you the document all neat with sub-files and jackets and labels and tags so that there was a reference number on every piece of paper and it would take you just a few minutes to look at them?

A. When we went to the State Highway Commission in Indianapolis, they gave us a room which had three tables in it piled high with boxes, boxes were on the floor, and they said here it is, start looking. So we started digging. There was nothing that was, each man had his own file and they were in different boxes. There was the Chief Engineer's file and the operating file, the traffic file, the right-of-way file and they weren't organized.

Q. If you hadn't done all this digging, organizing, surveying and drafting, would it have been possible for any human being to know the story of how the Cline Avenue S-Curve was built and what the problems with it are?

A. No.

Q. How much have you had to bill for this work and all this time you took?

A. $14,000.00.

Q. Have any local attorneys retained your professional expert services as an engineer in cases involving traffic crashes?

A. Yes, they have.

Q. Mr. Lippman, let me ask you this: Based on your researches on the Cline Avenue from Gary Avenue to the Toll Road, all right, what was the design speed of that road including the area from Gary Avenue in the north to the Toll Road in the south when it opened in 1966 as a four lane?

A. The plans say 70 miles an hour desirable.

Q. So was that a 70-mile an hour design speed road?

A. The word desirable usually isn't put on a set of plans, I believe that it meant get as close to 70 miles an hour as you could, but within the limits of your budget.

Q. Now, the data and information sheet on the construction project where they filled in all those blanks, what did that say?

A. The instructions to the Consulting Engineer stated design the road for 70 miles an hour.

Q. Now, was Cline Avenue, S.R. 912, a State road?

A. Yes, it was; yes, it is.

Q. Is the area that is on Cline between Gary Avenue in the north and the Toll Road in the south called the S-Curve?

A. Yes.

Q. Can you make a brief listing of the documents that you have examined in the course of your investigation of this particular road and this particular crash?

A. I examined the plans for the construction of the Toll Road structure which was built in 1955, and I examined the plans for the construction of the northern extension which started at the south end of the Toll Road structure and went north; I examined the instructions to the Consulting Engineer and all the correspondence that went back and forth between him and the State Highway Commission; I examined the documents from the Highway Commission to the Corps of Engineers establishing permission for their bridge; I examined traffic accidents; I examined newspaper articles; I examined correspondence between city officials and state representatives of the Highway Commission; I examined daily work logs; diaries, field notebooks, whatever I could get my hands on.

Q. Did you investigate police reports also?

A. Police reports; I said accident reports.

Q. Did you make any measurements of that area of Cline Avenue from the Toll Road to Gary Avenue?

A. Yes, I made a general survey from the Toll Road to north of Gary Avenue in which I checked out the horizontal curves and the distances, alignments, and I made a specific analysis of a horizontal curve, one between the Toll Road and the River Bridge.

Q. And about how many times have you previously made such surveys?

A. Never on that road.

Q. Surveys of roadway?

A. Hundreds.

Q. As you compare your survey with the plans as they built the road, by and large are they the same?

A. Yes.

Q. So that the road in 1966 was by and large the same as it was when you surveyed it; right?

A. Yes, once you pour a lot of concrete it stays there.

Q. Are these charts that Mr. Ortman is wrestling with the actual survey drawings?

A. I've got to see it.

MR. KUHLMAN: Mr. Ortman, would you bring these up to him?

WITNESS: A. Yes.

MR. KUHLMAN: Q. Will you tell the Court and jury something about how that survey was made, what a survey of Cline Avenue is and how you do it?

A. Well, first of all you couldn't afford a complete survey of everything out there, it takes the State Highway Commission to do it. Basically all I did is check the main curves and the distances between the main structures to see if they agreed with the construction plans.

Q. From your survey and from the blueprints and from the other documents that you examined, did you prepare any scale drawings of Cline Avenue from Gary Avenue in the north to the Toll Road in the south?

A. Yes, I did.

Q. All right.

A. These and that (Indicating).

Q. Now, with respect to that, what has been labeled as the three panels, Plaintiff's Exhibit 270, 271, and 272, I would ask you to step down with the pointer that Mr. Ortman will give you and explain to the Jury what that drawing is and how Cline Avenue runs both from up above and from the side between Gary Avenue in the north and the Toll Road in the south?

A. This is the Toll Road structure going north on Cline Avenue, you go through a vertical curve; there is another vertical curve; the sag curve; the horizontal curve; you cross the Grand Calumet River bridge; you continue on north up a grade through a vertical curve, up a grade through another vertical curve and continue on to East Chicago.

Q. Now, Mr. Lippman, there are two drawings of roads on that drawing, one on the top and one on the bottom. Would you tell the Jury the different views?

A. This is called a plan, this is pretending you are a bird looking straight down on it.

Q. Can everybody in the Jury see the drawing?

A. This is called a profile, this shows the vertical curves, this shows the horizontal curves.

Q. Now, you have labeled a vertical curve No. 1 on your drawing?

A. Yes.

Q. Is that a crest or a sag vertical curve?

A. That's a crest vertical curve.

Q. Is that north or south of the Toll Road?

A. That's south of the Toll Road structure.

Q. You have labeled the curve there Vertical Curve No. 2; can everybody see Vertical Curve No. 2?

Is that curve a crest or a sag vertical curve?

A. That's a crest vertical curve.

Q. You have indicated on your chart a Vertical Curve No. 3; is that a crest or a sag curve?

A. That is a sag curve.

Q. Is that going up or down?

A. Goes down into a valley.

Q. Can you speak up so that the jury can hear you?

A. It's going down into a valley.
Q. Is that curve north or south of the Toll Road structure?
A. It's north of the Toll Road structure.
Q. Now, you've got in the middle of that a structure indicated as the Grand Calumet River structure?
A. Right.
Q. Are there any horizontal curves between the Toll Road structure and the Grand Calumet River structure?
A. Horizontal Curve No. 1 between the two structures.
Q. Are there any other horizontal curves between the Toll Road structure and the Grand Calumet River structure?
A. No.
Q. Proceeding north of the Grand Calumet River structure you've got a curve indicated as Horizontal Curve, indicated as Horizontal Curve No. 2?
A. (Indicating).
Q. Now, Horizontal Curve No. 2 would be where on your second brown drawing showing the road from the side?
A. Starts right at the north end of the Grand Calumet River structure.
Q. Now, way at the north you've got a structure indicated as the Gary Avenue structure, and you've got Vertical Curve No. 5 indicated there?
A. (Indicating).
Q. Is that a crest or a sag vertical curve?
A. It is a crest.
Q. And which way is north on your drawing?
A. This way (Indicating).
Q. Towards me?
A. Yes.
Q. And which way is south?
A. Towards me.
Q. As a motorist was driving south on Cline Avenue approaching the Gary Avenue structure toward the river, would he or would he not go over a crest vertical curve?
A. Yes.
Q. As a motorist was driving north over the Toll Road toward the Grand Calumet River structure, would he or would he not go over a crest curve?
A. He would go over a crest curve, yes.
Q. Therefore, is it or is it not true to say that both the north and the southbound motorist going toward the Toll Road coming over Gary Avenue or coming over the Toll Road, would go over crest vertical curves

before he came to the horizontal curves around the Grand Calumet River?

A. That is correct.

Q. Would you please resume the stand.

Now, Mr. Lippman, approximately how far is the distance from the south end of the Toll Road structure to the north end of the Grand Calumet River structure?

A. Just a minute, I'll tell you exactly.

WITNESS: A. What was the question again?

Q. The question is approximately how far is the distance from the south end of the Toll Road structure to the north end of the Grand Calumet River structure?

A. 1,419.61 feet.

Q. Would that be roughly about a quarter of a mile?

A. Yes.

Q. Approximately how far is the distance from the north end of the Grand Calumet River structure to the north end of the Gary Avenue structure?

A. 1,497.32 feet.

Q. Would that also be roughly a quarter of a mile?

A. Right.

Q. Approximately how far is it from the start of the first crest curve, Crest Curve No. 1, to the south end of the Toll Road structure?

A. 321.43 feet.

Q. About how far is it from the south end of the Toll Road structure to the south end of the Calumet River bridge?

A. 974.81 feet.

Q. Approximately how far is it from the south end of the Toll Road structure to the north end of the Gary Avenue structure?

A. 2,916.93 feet, or .552 miles; about a half mile.

Q. From your studies what was the date when this four lane Cline Avenue, including the S-Curve, was opened to traffic?

A. In 1966, September.

Q. About how many months in 1966 was it opened?

A. About four.

Q. It was late September, wasn't it?

A. About the middle of September.

Q. Is there any relationship between minimum stopping sight distance and the length of a crest or a sag vertical curve?

A. Yes.

Q. What is that relationship?

A. The longer the curve, the better the sight distance.

Q. Were there any competent and authoritative criteria in effect when this area of Cline Avenue, including the S-Curve, was being designed and built establishing minimum lengths that crest or sag vertical curves were required to have in order to give minimum stopping sight distance at particular speeds to motorists?

A. Yes, there was.

Q. And what were those books and standards and criteria?

A. The 1954 Blue Book; the 1957 Red Book; the 1965 Blue Book, put out by the American Association of Highway Officials.

Q. Were the standards and criteria in the 1965 AASHO Blue Book known and published to engineers and traffic safety experts prior to its publication and at the time that this road was being designed and built?

A. It's common practice before one of these books are published that from two to three years before the research and thinking and voting that goes into these books are made available to engineers by publication in magazines, bulletins. Normally before a book comes out you know about it a couple of years in advance.

Q. Well, the particular standards in the 1965 Blue Book for minimum stopping sight distance, were they the same or were they different than the standards in the 1954 Blue Book and the 1957 Red Book?

A. The 1954 Blue Book was based on a car having a motorist's eye at about 4′6″ above the road, and around 1960 the cars were getting lower and the standards for the new book were based on 3′9″. Now they are thinking of lowering it again because the cars are still getting lower. In other words sight distance on a curve depends on how high your eye is above the road, so that you can see over the hill.

Q. So that the difference would be based on car height and the driver?

A. Yes.

Q. Now, were those 1965 standards known and published in the engineering and traffic engineering field at the time that they were designing this particular road?

A. Yes, they were.

Q. Now, I want to show you what has been marked as Plaintiff's Exhibit 264; it's a xerox copy.

Is that a true and correct copy of the 1954 AASHO Blue Book?

A. The title page says it is, yes. I believe it is.

Q. I show you what has been marked as Plaintiff's Exhibit No. 263; is this a true and correct copy of the 1957 AASHO Red Book?

A. Yes.

Q. I show you what has been marked as Plaintiff's Exhibit No. 265; is that a true and correct copy of the 1965 AASHO Blue Book?

A. Yes, this is the only one I can guarantee all the pages are —

Q. Mr. Lippman, let me ask you this: Were the standards that should have been used for the design and construction of Cline Avenue four-lane road, including the S-Curve Area, were they the minimum stopping sight distance standards in the 1954 Blue Book or the 1965 Blue Book?

A. In my opinion, they should have used the 1965 Book because it was common knowledge that the driver's eye was lower, and I believe the State in the Interrogatories said they used the 1954 Book.

Q. Let me ask you this: Under all these books, the 1954 Blue Book, the 1957 Red Book, and the 1965 Blue Book, are these minimum lengths of curve needed for minimum stopping sight distances, or are they optional?

A. They are basic minimum.

Q. Was it accepted engineering practice to build curves shorter than those indicated by the minimum charts in these books?

A. Minimum means as small as you can get them.

Q. I show you what has been marked as Plaintiff's Exhibit No. 268; is this a true and correct copy of the minimum stopping sight distance charts found in the 1954 AASHO Blue Book?

A. Yes.

Q. Do the curve lengths for design speeds in those charts set minimum or optional standards; under reasonable engineering standards can those curves be shorter than indicated there for a given speed?

A. This states minimum.

MR. KUHLMAN: Your Honor, at this time pursuant to discussion with counsel, I would ask that this chart from the — well, I move to introduce the 1954 Blue Book into evidence at this time to pass among the jury Chart 268, which is from the 1954 Blue Book.

THE COURT: The State's objection is overruled and Plaintiff's Exhibit No. 268 is now admitted and may be passed to the jury. I think that there was a request with respect to —

MR. KUHLMAN: Right, the Blue Book for 1964 and that is Plaintiff's Exhibit No. 264.

THE COURT: All right.

MR. KUHLMAN: I wouldn't pass that to the jury because it's not likely —

THE COURT: No.

DIRECT EXAMINATION (Continued)
BY MR. KUHLMAN:

Q. Mr. Lippman, do these tables deal with minimum lengths for both crest and sag vertical curves?

A. Yes.

Q. Now, once again, are these standards minimum or optional?

A. Minimum.

Q. Can they be deviated from and can curves be made shorter?

A. If they were, they wouldn't be safe.

MR. KUHLMAN: Now, your Honor, at this time I would also move for the introduction into evidence of Plaintiff's Exhibit No. 263, the 1957 AASHO Red Book which the State has also listed as one of their standards in the book, in the construction of this road; and the minimum charts on crest and sag vertical curves from that book which is Plaintiff's Exhibit No. 267.

DIRECT EXAMINATION (Continued)
BY MR. KUHLMAN:

Q. Mr. Lippman, before these charts are passed to the Jury from the 1957 Red Book, I'll ask you the same questions that I asked you before about the earlier charts; are these minimum lengths or are they optional?

A. Minimum lengths.

Q. Could reasonable due care be given by engineers who made the curves shorter than these indicated here for a given design speed?

A. It would not be safe.

MR. KUHLMAN: Ladies and gentlemen of the Jury, I now pass to you Plaintiff's Exhibit 267 from the 1957 AASHO Red Book which are the minimum safe stopping sight distance crest and vertical curve lengths.

Your Honor, I believe I did move for the admission of the 1957 Red Book previously.

THE COURT: Yes.

MR. KUHLMAN: And that was Plaintiff's Exhibit 263.

THE COURT: 263; that was admitted.

MR. KUHLMAN: Now, your Honor, at this time I move for the admission of Plaintiff's Exhibit No. 265, which is the 1965 AASHO Blue Book, and for permission to pass among the jury Chart 269, which is the minimum stopping sight distance chart for crest and sag vertical curves from the 1965 Blue Book.

DIRECT EXAMINATION (Continued)
BY MR. KUHLMAN:

Q. Now, Mr. Lippman, before we pass Chart 269 from the 1965 Blue Book to the Jury, I want to ask you the same questions that I asked you about the 1954 Blue Book Chart and the 1957 Red Book chart.

Are these truly minimum lengths that are required by AASHO for vertical curves at given speeds, or are they optional; can engineers make shorter curves than this for a given speed?

A. They are the minimum lengths of curve you design highways by.
Q. In other words, does minimum mean —
A. It means minimum.
Q. The minimum?
A. Yes, the smallest.
Q. Not optional?
A. Not optional.
Q. Not less?
A. Not less.

MR. KUHLMAN: Ladies and Gentlemen of the Jury, I now pass to you Plaintiff's Chart 269, which is the minimum stopping sight distance chart for crest and sag vertical curves from the 1965 AASHO Blue Book.

I believe your Honor has ruled on the objection, hasn't it?

THE COURT: Yes.

DIRECT EXAMINATION (Continued)
BY MR. KUHLMAN:

Q. Now, Mr. Lippman, just one more exhibit.

In the period of July 27, 1970, and going back from that period to the year 1968, I believe you referred to a standard in Indiana governing engineers and not lawyers in the painting and the marking and signing of state roads?

A. Yes, I did.
Q. And what was that standard?
A. Uniform Manual for Traffic Control.
Q. Now, I am not asking you as a lawyer because I know that you are not an attorney, but I am asking you as an engineer. As an engineer, how authoritative and binding were the standards in that Uniform Manual on the marking and signing of Indiana State roads in July, 1970?
A. They were the gospel.
Q. Could they be deviated from by engineers?
A. No.
Q. When an engineer would look for what he should do in marking or striping or signing of state roads, where would he look?
A. It's either in the book or he has to do so by an engineering study, something better than the book. But the book says exactly what he should do under certain conditions.
Q. And who published that book for the State?
A. Indiana State Highway Commission.
Q. I show you what has been marked as Plaintiff's Exhibit No. 266, and I ask you if that is a true and correct copy of the Indiana Uniform Manual on Traffic Control Devices published in 1968?

A. Yes, it is.

Q. Is this the book that was the guide and the authoritative standards you referred to for engineers in this State in July, 1970, for the rules on how to stripe and mark State roads?

A. Yes, it is.

MR. KUHLMAN: I now move for the introduction into evidence of the Indiana Uniform Manual on Uniform Traffic Control Devices for streets and highways, published by the Indiana State Highway Commission in the year 1968, as Plaintiff's Exhibit No. 266, and I ask to pass that to the Jury.

THE COURT: That exhibit has been admitted, and it may be passed to the jury.

DIRECT EXAMINATION (Continued)
BY MR. KUHLMAN:

Q. Mr. Lippman, are you familiar with the 1967 Yellow Book?

A. Yes, I am.

Q. Who publishes that?

A. The American Association of Highway Officials.

Q. How authoritative and competent is the 1967 Yellow Book?

A. Same as all the other ones.

Q. To Traffic Engineers and transportation safety —

A. To engineers and safety officials that's the gospel.

Q. I show you the xerox copy of the 1967 Yellow Book, and I ask you if that is a true and accurate copy thereof, and it has been marked as our Exhibit No. 273.

A. Yes.

MR. KUHLMAN: At this time I move for the introduction into evidence and ask it not be passed to the jury at this time, Plaintiff's Exhibit No. 273, the AASHO Yellow Book.

MR. HASSETT: I have no objection.

DIRECT EXAMINATION (Continued)
BY MR. KUHLMAN:

Q. Now, Mr. Lippman, we were talking before the break about minimum vertical curve lengths in the AASHO Blue and Red Books that applied to different given speeds to give minimum stopping sight distances; right?

A. That is correct.

Q. Now, do those minimum lengths apply to flat roads or down-grade roads, roads that are going down or roads that are going flat?

A. Flat roads you have all the sight distance you need, so this is for grades only.

Q. Now, do motorists have the same ability to see in front of their vehicles on a crest curve in both day and night?

A. No.

Q. Do they have more or less visibility in front of their cars on a crest curve at night?

A. They have less.

Q. Why is that?

A. Because the headlight is located approximately two feet off the pavement and doesn't have the range of a person's eye. So normally the sight distance is about 50 to 55 percent less than at night than it is in the daytime.

Q. On a crest curve?

A. On a crest curve.

Q. Are there any authoritative standards establishing that about 1/2 percent reduction?

A. The three books that you just passed out.

Q. I think one is 52 percent and one is 54?

A. One is 54.

Q. They are all around 1/2, aren't they?

A. Right.

Q. As a matter of fact, on an unlit road without fixed street lights, can a motorist see as far ahead of him at night on any kind of a road, straight, flat, up, down, as he can during the day?

A. No, he can't.

Q. Now, do those minimum stopping sight distances and those minimum curve lengths in the AASHO tables that we just passed out, do they assume daylight visibility or do they assume nighttime visibility?

A. They assume daylight visibility.

Q. So that actually would a motorist at night need more or less than the minimum curve length in those tables to have his minimum stopping sight distance at the same speed?

A. He would need more.

Q. So just to make the point clear, let me ask you this: If that table or one of those tables says that at a design speed of 30 miles an hour a motorist needed curve length on a crest curve of 100′, okay, that would be a daytime measurement; wouldn't it?

A. Yes, it would.

Q. At night would he need more or less than that curve length for the same speed, for minimum stopping sight distance?

A. The curve would have to be longer because his safe stopping sight distance would be 1/2 again as much as it is in the daytime.

Q. If a crest vertical curve under those AASHO Blue and Red Books had only minimum stopping sight distance during the day for speeds, design speeds up to 55 miles an hour, would it be acceptable to post a single speed effective both day and night of 55 miles an hour for that speed?

A. No, it wouldn't.

Q. Why not?

A. Because most motorists overdrive the posted speed.

Q. Now, if a crest or a sag curve was so short that you could only have your minimum stopping sight distance at speeds below 55, in other words 55 itself, wouldn't give you minimum stopping sight distance, then would it be acceptable to post that curve with a posted speed of 55 miles an hour?

A. No.

Q. Why not?

A. Because it would not be safe.

Q. Once again very briefly, what is the relationship between a posted speed, if there is a posted speed on a road, and minimum stopping sight distance?

A. Posted speed governs what the driver should drive and he should have more stopping sight distance than that, in other words, it should be designed for about 10 percent more than is posted.

Q. If a vertical curve, crest curve or a sag curve, would give minimum stopping sight distance at speeds up to 55, then it would not be acceptable to post it at 55; is that right?

A. It would be bad operating practice.

Q. Does that 1968 Indiana Uniform Manual that we introduced before the break which governs signing and which governs marking of roads, does that set minimum or maximum standards?

A. It's minimum standards.

Q. So that the State is free to do better than that; is that right?

A. Yes, that's correct.

Q. But can engineers as a matter of engineering do less than that?

A. No, they would break the law if they did.

Q. Now, and according to your measurements in July of 1970 that road had the same curves and the same proportions; is that right?

A. That's correct.

Q. So now and in July of 1970, as a motorist would approach the Toll Road on Cline Avenue from the south going north, he would encounter the first crest vertical curve; is that right?

A. That's right.

Q. And that's the one that is south of the Toll Road?

A. Right.
Q. All right, let's talk about that first crest curve for a moment. How long is it, what is the length of the curve?
A. Crest Curve 1 is a length of 300′.
Q. What is the algebraic difference in grades for that curve?
A. It goes uphill at a 4 percent grade and it has a plus .53% grade, so that the algebraic difference would be 3.47, which is the (a).
Q. On that first crest curve, under the 1954 Blue Book minimum length standards that we have passed to the jury, the 1954 standards that I think you said were lower than the 1965 Blue Book Standards, what is the minimum length that first crest curve must have to give a motorist minimum stopping sight distance during the day at a design speed of 70 miles an hour?
A. 780′.
Q. So at the design speed of 70 miles an hour under the 1954 Blue Book Standards, does Crest Curve 1 pass or fail?
A. It failed.
Q. What is the minimum length that that first crest curve must have under the 1965 Blue Book minimum stopping sight distance chart to give a motorist minimum stopping sight distance during the day at a design speed of 70 miles an hour?
A. Under the 1965 one?
Q. Yes.
A. 893′.
Q. So at a design speed of 70 miles an hour, does that first crest curve pass or fail under the 1965 Blue Book Standards which you said are the ones that should have been used?
A. It failed worse.
Q. How long would that first crest curve have to be to give minimum stopping sight distance during the day for a posted speed of 55 miles an hour under the 1954 Blue Book Standards?
A. 530′.
Q. So during the day under the 1954 Blue Book minimum standards, for minimum stopping sight distance, does the first crest curve pass or fail?
A. Fail.
Q. What is the minimum length the first crest curve would be required to have to give a motorist minimum stopping sight distance at night under the 1954 Blue Book Standards?
A. Under the 1954 book?
Q. 1954?
A. What speed?

Q. 55.
A. About a thousand feet.
Q. So at night under the Standards of the 1954 Blue Book for minimum stopping sight distance does Crest Curve 1 pass or fail at 55?
A. Fail.
Q. Now, under the 1965 Blue Book Standards that you said should have been used for the design on this road, what is the minimum length that that first crest curve should have had to give the motorist minimum stopping sight distance at a speed of 55 miles an hour during the day?
A. It would be about the same because the headlights don't change the formula that much.
Q. So during the day under the 1965 Blue Book Standards for minimum stopping sight distance would the first crest curve pass or fail?
A. Fail.
Q. Now, let's take it at night at 55 as a posted speed under the 1965 Blue Book Standards, how long would that first crest curve have to be as a minimum length to give minimum stopping sight distance to a motorist?
A. Curve 1 under the '65 Book if designed at 55?
Q. Right, at night.
A. 652′.
Q. So at night under the Standards of the 1965 Blue Book for minimum stopping sight distance at a speed of 55 miles an hour, does the first crest curve pass or fail?
A. Fails.
Q. Under every standard of the AASHO Blue and Red Books for minimum stopping sight distance in 1954 Blue Book, 1957 Red Book, 1965 Blue Book, and day and at night, at a design speed of 70, or at a posted speed of 55, does the first crest curve pass or fail?
A. Fails.
Q. Under the AASHO Blue and Red Books was it mandatory or optional that a road give a motorist minimum stopping sight distance at whatever speed they told them to go?
A. Mandatory.
Q. In your experience as the Hammond City Engineer, you have to sit and review speed limits on roads; is that right?
A. That is correct.
Q. Based on your experience as a Civil Engineer and the Hammond City Engineer, can you give us an idea on that first crest curve of about what is the highest speed a motorist could go, design speed, and still have his minimum stopping sight distance during the day under the 1954 Blue Book?

A. You can't really post one curve at a time, but that curve by itself at about 50 miles an hour would be safe.

Q. During the day?

A. During the day.

Q. How about at night?

A. Around 40.

Q. How about under the 1965 Blue Book during the day?

A. They don't change it that much. One figure is 50.85 and the other one is 50.125, so that it's 50 miles an hour round figures.

Q. Under any of the AASHO Standards from 1954, 1957, or 1965, would it be appropriate to post that first crest curve at 55 miles an hour?

A. No.

Q. Would it be competent engineering or traffic control to post that first crest curve day or night at 55?

A. No.

Q. Would it be worse to post it for a speed at night or during the day at 55?

A. Worse at night.

Q. Why?

A. Because you have less sight distance, you can't see hidden horizontal curves.

Q. Now, that's a design speed you were giving me?

A. That is correct.

Q. Would it be appropriate to post — in other words, 50 would be the highest theoretical speed you could go on that first curve and have minimum stopping sight distance?

A. That's correct.

Q. Would that be an appropriate speed to post on that curve, 50 miles an hour?

A. Should post about 45.

Q. Why?

A. Because most motorists drive faster than the speed limit.

Q. Now, assuming that first crest curve had the dimensions, and proportions established in your study of the blue prints and survey of the road on July 27, 1970; and assume that there was no lighting, no fixed street lighting on that roadway at that time. Do you have an opinion, based upon a reasonable degree of engineering and scientific certainty, as to whether that first crest curve could reasonably have been posted for a speed of 55 miles an hour for northbound motorists at night?

A. Yes; it shouldn't have been.

Q. Why not?

A. Didn't have safe sight distance.

Q. Would it make any difference to your opinion if that road on that night were not painted or striped and didn't have driver lane markings or outside edging or painted median curbs?

A. The tables in the book are based on flat roads, quick reactions, in other words, they figure about 2½ seconds to react and if you have, you can't see the lines or the road or the lights, you need more safe stopping sight distance than the book requires.

Q. Would it make any difference in your opinion if the road were not only unstriped and unlit, but was also dirty?

A. Yes.

Q. Why, how would that make a difference?

A. The curve would fail more and you would have to lower the speed limit for safe operation or clean it up.

Q. What effect, if any, can you tell the Court and jury does dirt on a road have if it is not striped and it is not lit on the ability of a motorist to see what the road is doing at night?

A. You can't see.

Q. Would it make any difference to your opinion if this road on the night of July 27, 1970, was not only not lit and not painted, and dirty, but it also had no warning signs?

A. It's the same problem as with sight distance whether it's signed or not. You are talking about a curve by itself right now.

Q. Well, if it didn't have all these other things would that make the motorist's problem better, worse, or leave it the same as it was?

A. It would make it worse.

Q. Now, let's move north from the first curve. You got over the Toll Road structure in the south what is marked as your Vertical Curve No. 2; is that a crest or a sag curve?

A. That is a crest curve.

Q. One that's right over the Toll Road structure?

A. That is correct.

Q. Do you know from your study of documents on this road how long was that second crest curve originally?

A. 550′.

Q. And were those first and second crest curves built before, during or after the S-Curve construction project?

A. Those two curves were built and approximately finished in 1955 when the Toll Road was built in Hammond.

Q. When they incorporated them into an allegedly 70-mile-an-hour design speed four-lane Cline Avenue, would those curves under competent engineering have to be 70-miles-an-hour design speed curves?

A. If the roads were 70-miles-an-hour design road, those should have been changed or the speed limit posted to compensate for the lack of sight distance.

Q. Now, what if anything, did the S-Curve construction project do to that second crest vertical curve?

A. They took a point on the north end of the bridge approximately 20′ out and they built in a sag vertical curve in order to get down into the Grand Calumet River, and they also put a horizontal curve in it.

Q. Now, I am referring to Plaintiff's Exhibits 270 and 271; is this the sag curve here I am indicating Vertical Curve No. 3 which you are talking about?

A. That is correct, they chopped off Vertical Curve No. 2 and installed Vertical Curve No. 3.

Q. And the horizontal curve you are referring to is this one here?

A. That is right.

Q. Marked on Exhibit 274, horizontal curve 1?

A. That is correct.

Q. So that is it your testimony then that they took Vertical 2 and chopped off part of the northern end and they put in the same sag curve, Vertical 3, and they put in a horizontal curve also at the same time, horizontal 1?

A. That is correct.

Q. Does Horizontal Curve 1 start in the sag curve or north of it or south of it?

A. Starts in the sag curve.

Q. So that at the point where the horizontal curve is starting in the sag curve, how many things is that road doing simultaneously at the same time?

A. It's dipping down and it is tilting sideways from super-elevation and it's turning to the right.

Q. It's going down like this —

A. Yes.

Q. And it's turning horizontally to the side; right?

A. Right.

Q. And it's tipping?

A. Right.

Q. Now, did the S-Curve construction project actually build this road and that part of the road in particular according to their design plans?

A. Yes and no.

Q. Will you explain that answer?

A. Well, the construction plans in the area of the sag Curve 3 are on the —

Q. It's Vertical Curve 3 on the chart.

A. The Vertical 3 are on two sets of plans, two pages in the plan. There is a gap between them. There was no reference on the State plans of Vertical Curves 1 and 2 which were shown on the Toll Road plans. So the Consulting Engineer picked a point at the north end of the bridge without studying what was in front of him and sort of independently started the rest of the road. Now, there was nothing on the plans to tell the project engineer how to get his super-elevation, the plans showed the Horizontal Curve No. 1 dimensions so he knew where to put that, but as far as the, he had to fudge in the super-elevation between the two bridges, because they didn't spend any money changing the Toll Road bridge except for adding a curb in the middle and widening it a little bit. But it was impossible to super-elevate that bridge without a big expense; they had the other bridge built at the other end, and so there's nothing on the plans, they left it up to the field engineer to work that section in between the two structures.

Q. Actually —

A. Go ahead, and finish.

Q. As actually built by the S-Curve construction project, how long is that sag curve which you labeled Vertical Curve 3?

A. Sag Curve 3, on the plans it shows 350′. But on the actual ground it measured about 171′.

Q. How long is what is remaining of Vertical Crest Curve 2?

A. Crest Curve 2, they chopped off — Crest Curve 2 is 387.77′ long.

Q. After they put in the sag?

A. After they put in the sag, yes, to the start of the sag, and it originally was 550′.

Q. Do the normal formulas for computing the minimum length of Crest Curve you need for minimum stopping sight distance apply to a combination of curves like Crest Curve 2 in the sag curve?

A. No, it's impossible to calculate.

Q. We know that they exist in the real world, but as a matter of mathematics, can such a combination theoretically exist?

A. It is not supposed to.

Q. As a matter of sound and competent road design, should it exist?

A. It is not supposed to.

Q. Can you tell the Court and jury why these things theoretically should not exist mathematically, theoretically can't exist, although they do, and as a matter of road design why they are not good road design?

A. Normally you finish one curve before you start another one. Where you have enough straight tangent, you don't get the bump when you go overhill and underhill too fast, and a curve should be a smooth parabola in order to work in these formulas and it isn't.

Q. Should that type of a situation involved here with Crest 2 in the sag have been apparent to the people designing and building the S-Curve project?

A. Just looking at it, it probably would have looked pretty good to the guys that there pouring concrete. It should have been apparent to the designers who had it on the table where they had the whole job.

Q. And how about to the people who approved it, this whole design, when they had it?

A. They couldn't tell because they didn't have the Toll Road plans.

Q. Should they?

A. Yes, when the State took this project and got Federal approval for it, they should have shown Vertical Curves 1 and 2 to the Federal Government so that somebody could have looked at the whole piece. In other words, they forgot what they built 10 years ago and just hooked onto it.

Q. But they should have remembered; isn't that right?

A. I think so, and I think the Consulting Engineer sent enough letters back and forth, he asked them should we change the grades, should we do something, and he got instructions not to change it.

Q. In fact from your studies do you know if the Consulting Engineer asked for lighting?

A. He asked for lighting, he asked for median guard rail.

Q. In the middle on the curve?

A. He asked to change the Toll Road bridge; he had a lot of requests in there.

Q. Were any of the requests put into the final S-Curve as built?

A. I didn't find any.

Q. Is it possible to calculate or plot in any way what minimum stopping sight distances a motorist will really have during the day and at night coming north over the Toll Road in July, 1970, over Crest Curve 2 in the sag?

A. Yes, it is.

Q. And have you performed such a calculation?

A. Yes, I have.

Q. And have you previously shown and explained this to counsel for the State?

A. Yes, I have.

Q. So that the jury can see this, we're going to hold the charts closer to the jurors so that Mr. Lippman can step down and explain.

Mr. Lippman, using the pointer, would you please explain to the Court and jury how the calculation of minimum stopping sight distance over the crest and the sag vertical curve under both the day and night standards of the 1954 and 1965 Blue Book was built, how you did it?

MR. KUHLMAN: Q. The first chart he will be speaking of will be Plaintiff's Exhibit 278.

A. The 1954 Blue Book puts the driver's eye 4½′ above the road. The 1965 Blue Book puts the driver's eye at 3′9″ above the road. So we plot the road in, the way we measured, we draw a line from the man's eye across the highest point of the road where he can see. And these lines are all touching the road right at the point where Vertical Curve 3 hits. Now, that tells me that if my eye were up here I can't see this area in the dip, but I can see the curve out in front of me. I also have on this exhibit the start of Horizontal Curve 1 and the middle of Horizontal Curve 1. So from either book standards, I can't see the start of Horizontal Curve 1 in that area. So that I am surprised as I come over the road, I don't have enough stopping sight distance to see that the road is turning or that there was something in the road I couldn't see.

Now, I have calculated from that point to where I can last see the curve, it's 313′, which gives you a maximum design speed of about 45 miles an hour.

Q. Now, summarizing just up to this point, is that day or night?

A. This is daytime.

Q. Under the 1954 Blue Book?

A. That is correct.

Q. Would that curve give a motorist minimum stopping sight distance under the 1954 Blue Book during the day, that combination of Crest Curve 2 in the sag at a design speed of 70 miles an hour?

A. No.

Q. Would it give a minimum stopping sight distance under the 1954 Blue Book during the day at a posted speed of 55?

A. No.

Q. Would it give him minimum stopping sight distance at night under the 1954 Blue Book at a design speed of 70?

A. No.

Q. Would it give the minimum stopping sight distance at night under the 1954 Blue Book at a posted speed of 55?

A. No.

Q. Proceed, please.

A. Now, here we have a nighttime study.

Q. That's chart, Exhibit 277, for the plaintiff.

A. Now, this takes the eye at 3′9″, but it puts the headlight at 2′ above the road, and it shows that the headlight, the man on top of the Toll Road is pointing out in front of him, normally the headlights are on 300′ or so, but I took it all the way, he's got his brights, and there's a little bit of light out in front of him.

Q. You are assuming bright lights?

A. Right.

Now, you draw a line from the bottom of the headlights to the road again, you find that from here down, which is about the start of the sag curve again, is in the shadow and you can't see it. When I was going down through there, but I don't have any lights on, so I have about 320′ of safe stopping sight distance at a speed of about 45 or 46 miles an hour from this point to the road.

Q. Under which Blue Book Standard?

A. This is 1965.

Q. Let me ask you these questions: Now, under the 1955 Blue Book Standards would that road give a motorist minimum stopping sight distance day or night at a design speed of 70?

A. No.

Q. Would it give —

WITNESS: A. Under all books it doesn't meet it.

DIRECT EXAMINATION (Continued)
BY MR. KUHLMAN:

Q. Under the 1965 Blue Book, at night or during the day at a design speed of 70 or posted speed of 55, does that curve pass or fail the combination of Crest 2 in the sag?

A. It failed.

Q. And incidentally, do the 1957 Red Book and the 1954 Blue Book have the same standards?

A. Yes, same standards.

Q. So we are really only talking two different standards?

A. That's correct.

Q. The 1954 and 1957 book have one, and the 1965 have another?

A. That's correct.

Q. Please proceed.

A. Now, I move the car north 50′ —

Q. Referring to Plaintiff's Exhibit No. 276.

A. And I tried the same. If you notice the difference, the light is beginning to point downhill, but I don't pick up much more of the curve and I still can't see the start of the horizontal. So when the car is at this point he only has 270′ of safe design stopping distance, and the safe design speed would be between 38 and 40 miles an hour. Now, after he moves another 50′ then his light is pointing down enough that he could see it. So there's a section in here for about 150′ to 200′ that he can't see anything. It happens pretty fast, but it's still invisible for that.

Q. Now, Mr. Lippman, you have been talking about design speed?

A. That is correct.

Q. All these speeds you have been giving us are design speeds?

A. That is correct.

Q. Should those speeds be the posted speeds on that combination of Crest 2 in the sag on the night of July 27, 1970?

A. Normally the posted speed should be 10 percent less than the design speed.

Q. So 55, should 55 miles an hour have been the posted speed on the combination of Crest 2 in the sag day or night under any Blue Book Standards on the night of July 27, 1970?

A. No, it shouldn't have been.

Q. What should the posted speed have been on Crest 2 in the sag for motorists under the 1954 Blue Book during the day?

A. Well, here it is not normal practice to post the speed, different speeds day and night on a curve where there is not too much difference, and this would be subject to designer review. My personal opinion, and I post it for 40 miles an hour all the time.

Q. Would your opinion be appreciably different under the 1965 Blue Book Standards?

A. It would be about the same because usually at night you are looking at headlights, you are not looking at a two-by-four that's on the road, and it's a fairly safe gamble, you don't try to post a highway at 35 miles an hour, nobody could get to work then. It should be in the range of 40 under anybody's standards.

Q. Mr. Lippman, let's do a little talking about that first horizontal curve that's labeled on your scale drawing. We talked about the three vertical curves before lunch.

According to your measurements as a motorist in July, 1970, came north at night over the Toll Road structure and over those vertical curves, could he see the start of the first horizontal curve in time to have minimum stopping sight distance at 55 miles an hour under either the 1954 or the 1965 Blue Book Standards?

MR. BLACKMUN: Objection, your Honor, the question has been asked and answered.

THE COURT: It has; objection sustained.

MR. KUHLMAN: Q. According to your measurements and calculations, if a motorist going northbound on Cline Avenue over the Toll Road towards Gary Avenue in the outer lane at 55 miles an hour at night in July, 1970, when this road had no lights, if he were doing that, where would his vehicle be when he could actually see the road then start to turn horizontally?

A. About at the north edge of the Toll Road structure.

Q. Does that assume the road were marked and striped?

A. That's when the curb was sticking up and it should be visible. If the curb were dirty or hidden in the sand, he couldn't see it until further in.

Q. What if it weren't painted at all?

A. Possibly he couldn't see it at all.

Q. Now, would this location of the vehicle when the motorist could first see the road was turning horizontally, have any relevance on the question of whether the road was safe to drive at night at 55 in July, 1970?

A. Yes.

Q. What would that relevance be?

A. The curve was originally designed as a 70-mile-an-hour curve and it was super-elevated almost for that. Any driving into the curve and then turning the wheel a little sharper will increase side friction factors and possibly cause the driver to skid. In other words, he has to be almost perfect on that curve by itself in order to make it at 70 miles an hour.

Q. In the 1960's and the 1970's, was it normal to design vertical curves for reduced night visibility?

A. No.

Q. In the 1960's and the 1970's, was it safe to post speeds on vertical curves greater than the speed that would give motorists minimum stopping sight distance at night?

A. No.

Q. In July of 1970 — strike that.

In July, 1970, under either the standards of the 1954 Blue or the 1965 Blue Book, would a northbound motorist doing 55 miles an hour at night have minimum stopping sight distance on the combination of Crest Curve 1, Crest Curve 2, the sag curve and the first horizontal curve?

A. No, he wouldn't.

Q. Why not?

A. He didn't have it.

Q. Would he have it during the day?

A. No.

Q. Now, where specifically does the first horizontal curve start in relation to the sag curve; we referred to that in general in the morning?

A. First horizontal curve starts 122½′ north of the start of Vertical Curve 3.

MR. BLACKMUN: Would you repeat that answer for me, please?

MR. KUHLMAN: I'll rephrase the question.

Q. Does the first horizontal curve start inside the sag curve?

A. Yes, it does.

Q. And I believe you testified this morning that the road is going down and tipping and turning horizontally at that point; is that right?

A. Yes, I did.

Q. Are there any authoritative road design standards that were in effect when the S-Curve construction was designed and built establishing whether it is good or bad road design to have an unlit road doing so many things simultaneously to a motorist?

A. Yes, there are.

Q. And what are those standards?

A. The Blue Books from 1954 and 1965, and the Yellow Book and the Red Book.

Q. And who publishes those?

A. The American Association of State Highway Officials.

Q. And is that an elementary or esoteric road design?

A. That's the gospel for engineers designing roads.

Q. What do those books say about having unlit roads simultaneously doing so many things in the dark?

A. It says it shouldn't be done and also the reaction time and stopping sight distance times are affected by that.

Q. What are the reasons why they say it shouldn't be done and why roads shouldn't simultaneously do so many things in the dark?

A. A motorist driving has to see something wrong, he has to think about what he is going to do, he has to do it, he has to react to what he is going to do, and then he's got to slam on his brakes if he's going to stop or he has to turn his wheels if he is going to turn. And the more things that you feed into your computer eye, the more time it takes you to sort out what you are going to do. Current studies now are talking about decision time and maneuver time and all these tables and books that you have been using are based on $2^1/_2$ seconds of thinking and reacting, and then slamming on the brakes. So the numbers in the 1978 transportation manual now are talking about 12 to 16 seconds for safety. So each year that a book comes out that they have increased the stopping sight distance on account of the studies all over the world showing that drivers take a little more time to react than your early tables showed. We are still having accidents even though we have roads designed under those standards.

Q. Let's talk for a minute about that $2^1/_2$ seconds. Does that $2^1/_2$ seconds include time for the driver to perceive the road situation?

A. In the old books which are obsolete, back in 1972 or 1973, they figured $2^1/_2$ seconds to perceive and react.

Q. Now, does that assume the driver can see the road and what it is doing?

A. He's got to see it instantly, that's from his last eye blink. If he blinks, he loses a half second.

Q. If the driver takes more than $2^1/_2$ seconds to perceive what the road is doing —

A. He's in trouble on these curves.

Q. And do those assumed numbers of $2^1/_2$ seconds mean anything at all?

A. That's most of his reaction time based on the sight distance that these tables give you.

Q. So that's assuming he can see what the road is doing?

A. He's got to see it otherwise he's in trouble.

Q. Now, if the road is unlit and unpainted and unmarked, and if it is doing several things in the dark, do those authoritative standards give any rules as to whether or not he could become disoriented?

A. He could get disoriented, he could freeze and panic, he could do a lot of things. It takes more time to think about what you are doing if you have to think about more than one thing at a time.

Q. Are there any authoritative road design standards that were in effect when the S-Curve was designed and built establishing whether it is good or bad road design to have vertical curves like Crest Curve 1 and Crest Curve 2 in the sag curve coming in front of horizontal curves like Horizontal 1?

A. All the books state that you should not hide a horizontal curve behind a crest curve.

Q. Why?

A. Because a motorist can't see it if it's hidden. It cuts down his reaction time; he is surprised. If you are surprised you could freeze and take more time.

Q. Would this situation of hiding the curve be more dangerous to a motorist during the day or night?

A. Dangerous both times, but at night it's very bad.

Q. Why, why is it worse at night?

A. Because —

MR. BLACKMUN: Your Honor, objection, the witness—

MR. KUHLMAN: I'll withdraw the word worse.

MR. BLACKMUN: The witness has made the answer to the question as to why it's more difficult to see at night numerous times.

THE COURT: I believe he has, Mr. Kuhlman.

MR. KUHLMAN: Your Honor, this is in another design context, but I'll withdraw the question.

THE COURT: All right.

DIRECT EXAMINATION (Continued)
BY MR. KUHLMAN:

Q. How many horizontal curves are there between the Toll Road and Gary Avenue?

A. Two.

Q. About how far south of the Toll Road would Cline Avenue appear straight to a driver?

A. There is a slight one-degree curve about a mile south but —

Q. You mean horizontal curve?

A. Horizontal curve, yes, but basically as you are driving it you don't turn your wheel enough to know that you are really going through curves.

Q. So how far south of the Toll Road would appear straight to a driver?

A. I would say approximately four miles, 4½.

Q. And approximately how far north of Gary Avenue would Cline Avenue appear straight to a driver?

A. Another couple of miles.

Q. In July, 1970, except for this area of Cline Avenue, was there any area of north-south Cline Avenue that would appear curving to a motorist?

A. This was the only noticeable curve.

Q. Are there any authoritativc road design standards that were in effect when the S-Curve was designed and built establishing whether these facts so that straight away south of the Toll Road and then straight away north of Gary Avenue would make these horizontal curves here anymore or less dangerous to drivers than if they were in a series of curves?

A. The Blue Book and the Red Books state that motorists should not be surprised by horizontal curves after driving on a fairly straight section of road.

Q. What does the term degree of curvature which we defined mean in a horizontal curve?

A. The sharper the degree of curvature, the sharper the turn you have to make.

Q. Now, I would like to ask you some questions about the first horizontal curve that you labeled on the chart. What is the degree of curvature in the first horizontal curve that you come to when you are going north from the Toll Road?

A. It's 3 degrees 30 minutes.

Q. Is the second horizontal curve the same degree of curvature?

A. The same degree of curvature.

Q. Were there any standards that you personally reviewed for the S-Curve construction project governing the degree of horizontal curvature to be used in horizontal curves?

A. Yes, on the standard super-elevation sheet attached to the construction plans it states that curves over 2 degrees 30 minutes shall not be used except under extraordinary circumstances.

Q. Now, are these horizontal curves here greater than 2 degrees 30 minutes?

A. Yes, they are.

Q. Under the standards of horizontal curvature that the S-Curve project was supposed to follow its own standards, would these then be considered sharp curves or not?

A. It's sharper than they planned for 70-mile-design road.

Q. What kind of circumstances would they have to have under their own standards to use 3 degree 30 minute horizontal curves?

A. Extraordinary.

Q. About how far is it from the start of the first horizontal to the bottom of the sag curve?

A. 27 1/2′.

Q. About how far is it from the start of the first horizontal to the top of Crest Curve No. 2?

A. 122 1/2′.

Q. Were there any authoritative road design standards in effect when the S-Curve was designed and built establishing whether it was good or bad road design to put horizontal curves with this degree of curvature that close to the top of a crest or the bottom of a sag?

A. Yes.

Q. And what are those standards?

A. The Blue Book and the Red Book and the Yellow Book.

Q. What do they say?

A. They say that horizontal curves shall not be constructed inside of a sag vertical curve near the bottom.

Q. What does the term run-on or super-elevation run-on of a horizontal curve mean; that's quite a mouthful, so will you explain that to me, please?

A. Every horizontal curve is banked or tilted —

Q. Or tipped?

A. Or tipped so that the centrifugal force of the car is balanced by the tip so that he doesn't get off the curve.

Q. Will you explain what centrifugal force is for the Court?

A. As you are going around a curve something is pushing you out towards the outside edge of the curve, that's the base sign of your velocity. All right, a run-on is the distance from the, where the road is flat to where it gets to about half of the tip required for the curve. And run-off is after you go through the curve and start tipping it back until it's level.

Q. What is a run-on of a horizontal curve supposed to do, if anything, for a motorist going through a horizontal curve?

A. It's supposed to alert him that he is beginning to turn, he can feel something in the road to tell him that there is a curve coming, and it's also to adjust his headlights so that as he gets into the curve the right headlight is also twisted down enough that he can see the curve. And it keeps sudden jerks from going from flat to maximum tilt. It's gradual.

Q. What is the run-off of a horizontal curve supposed to do for a motorist as he is driving?

A. It gets you back to level again.

Q. What is the relationship, if any, between the run-on, the run-off and the orientation of the driver?

A. Well, a smooth curve will start from nothing at the maximum tilt and go back to nothing smoothly, makes you navigate the curve easier.

Q. Did the run-on, run-off and the super-elevation of this first horizontal curve here meet the standards that the S-Curve construction project had established with the length of horizontal curves needed for that degree of curvature?

A. No, it didn't.

Q. Can you explain how it didn't?

A. In the standard sheets it tells them how much run-on and how much curve and how much run-off you need, and the fact that they had total structure already built means that they couldn't start the run-on until they got to the edge of the bridge. So they made it shorter.

Q. How long under their own standards was that first horizontal curve, if it was to be a 3-degree 30-minute curve, how long was it supposed to be from the start of the run-on to the end of the run-off at a minimum?

A. Should have been 845′ I believe, yes.

Q. How long actually was it from the start of the run-on to the end of the run-off?

A. 627′.

Q. Let's talk about the run-off itself, just that part of it. How long should the run-off have been?

A. Should have been about 280′.

Q. And how long was it?

A. 200.83, so that it was about 80′ short.

Q. Under the State's own standards used in this project for the length of a horizontal curve with a 3 degree 30-minute degree of curvature, does that first horizontal curve pass or fail?

A. It fails.

Q. And where does that defectively short run-off of the first horizontal curve end on your drawing?

A. Right at the bridge.

Q. Which edge of which bridge?

A. South edge of the Grand Calumet River structure.

Q. If I walk over to Plaintiff's Exhibit 271 and I put my finger here at the approximate south end of the Calumet River bridge, is that where approximate run-off of that first horizontal curve is stopping?

A. That is correct.

Q. As a northbound vehicle on Cline Avenue starts to run off out of the first horizontal curve, is it straight or is it tipping?

A. It's tipping.

Q. Which way is it tipping?

A. Tipping to the right or to the east.

Q. Is that vehicle supposed to straighten out at the end of the run-off?

A. Yes.

Q. Under the State's own standards for how long are run-offs supposed to be from horizontal curves of that degree of curvature, does that first horizontal curve give a motorist enough room to meet the standard, or enough time to meet the standards?

A. No.

Q. Now, Mr. Lippman, I would like you to make a calculation.

If an automobile were going 55 miles an hour, how long would it take it to travel from the end of the run-off of the first horizontal curve at the south edge of the Calumet River bridge to this spot marked with a red X on this photograph of the south edge of the Calumet River bridge?

First of all, based on your studies of the road, approximately how far is this red X from the south edge of the Calumet River bridge?

A. That's where the 10′ curb is; 10, 15′.

Q. How long would it take a motor vehicle traveling at 55 miles an hour to travel from the end of the run-off of the first horizontal at the south edge of the Calumet River bridge, to the approximate spot marked by that red X?

A. 1/8th of a second.

Q. Has your study of the photographs and blueprints and surveys of documents and correspondence and your other observations of Cline Avenue from Gary Avenue to the Toll Road in this case revealed any other optical or visual factors that could confuse motorists approaching the Toll Road from the south at night in July, 1970, assuming the road had no lights then, as to whether the road would be straight or curving as it went north of the Toll Road?

A. Yes.

Q. And what is that?

A. When they located the Grand Calumet River structure and put the first horizontal Curve 1 in, they moved the road over about 160′ parallel to old Cline Avenue. As you come up over the Toll Road structure, your headlights are pointing out into space, and as you look right in front of you, you see a row of power poles and down in front you see the old Cline Avenue, and you see the sign that says Gary Avenue, and you see lights ahead of you —

Q. Would you indicate to the jury on Plaintiff's Exhibit 232 where those lights —

A. First impression is that your road is going straight because this is in the shadow and you don't see it, you see the old Cline Avenue out in front of you, you see this row of poles coming right up alongside of you.

Q. Would that row of lights appear straight or curving?

A. It's dead straight, it's right even with it, because the Toll Road bridge is on the center line of old Cline Avenue.

Q. Now, how do you know that there were lights along the alignment of the old Cline Avenue?

A. Because there always has been lights down there as long as I have been in the area.

Q. Did you ever drive it with those lights there?

A. Yes, I have driven it.

Q. Would this illusion be any danger to a driver if he had driven the road before and was presumably from the local area?

A. No, it would just give you the feeling of security that the road is straight. Most of these structures are all built alike. As you drive by the handrail you can't tell whether you're on the Toll Road or Grand Calumet River or Gary Avenue at night because you can't see what's around you. So a motorist could get disoriented and with his lights shining out straight in front of him on top of a vertical Curve 2 and not seeing the horizontal Curve 1 for a split second, it could be just enough to louse him up.

Q. And would that be a danger even if the motorist had driven the road before?

A. Yes, right.

Q. If a motorist on that road was doing a steady 55 miles an hour in the dark on the night of July 27, 1970, and he suddenly realized that he was only a second or so instants away from hitting that center median curb at 55, are there any competent and authoritative standards for establishing what effect, if any, this situation would produce on his responses, his reaction time and his car control?

A. There are a lot of studies by psychologists, doctors.

Q. Is that just confined to the State of Indiana?

A. It's all over the world.

Q. All over the world?

A. And they are still working on new standards, every year they come out with more.

Q. Let's just talk about the old standards from the 1960's, were there standards back there in the 60's on this?

A. Yes, there were.

Q. And how widely distributed throughout the world were these?

A. Everyone involved in highway design knows that a motorist can freeze in unexpected situations and not react at all, or his reaction time can increase. The design factors in these tables are based on a wet road friction factor which is a little bit of safety factor in case he needs another split second, but anything that surprises a motorist can cause him to panic.

Q. Now, those friction factors you mentioned are based on wet roads; right?

A. In the tables of the Blue Book, Yellow Book and so forth friction factor of about 29, which is a wet road is what is used.

Q. What effect would dirt on the road have; what if the road wasn't wet but it was covered with filth?

A. If it were covered with the kind of sand we have around here, it's like rolling on marbles, it's probably worse than wet.

Q. So what effect, if any, would be produced on the driver reaction time that are built into a calculation of minimum stopping sight distances if the road geometrics, road angles, the absence to stripe or sign or warn or light, confused the motorist as he drove north from the Toll Road bridge in the dark on midnight, July 27, 1970?

A. You would need more stopping distance in order to react and turn.

Q. More than those tables we passed out to the jury?

A. More than the tables. The books that were out in the 1970's called for desirable stopping which is a great deal more than the minimum. These two books that we are using in this trial have been obsolete for years.

Q. Now, do those authoritative AASHO Standards comment on whether this kind of a combination of unlit road, and assume an unpainted road, and assume an unsigned road, and with these types of dimensions could disorient a motorist in the dark when it does several things to him?

A. Yes, it does.

Q. Let me ask you something: If I were to say to you a motorist who was going through all those situations in the dark should just have made that turn here, just following along with my pen on Plaintiff's Exhibits 270 and 271, and just going right on through, if he happened to hit anything there in the center median curb, it would be his own fault, even if the road was dirty and even if the road had no painting, and even if the road was not lit, and even if the road had no warning signs, and even if the road had no speed limit signs, and I ask you to assume all that, do you think that would be a fair assumption to make that whatever possible reason that it would be just the driver's fault and no other possibilities?

MR. BLACKMUN: Objection, your Honor, I think that invades the province of the jury.

MR. KUHLMAN: Your Honor, in Trial Briefs we established that an expert can give an ultimate opinion on an issue that goes to the question and the jury; that's why he's an expert.

THE COURT: I think so, I think that was established.

The jury will establish the weight to be given.

The objection is overruled.

WITNESS: A. It makes it tougher for the driver.

MR. KUHLMAN: Q. So there's other possible reasons besides the fact that he was negligent or suicidal?

A. Yes, sir.

MR. BLACKMUN: Excuse me, would you repeat that again, please.

MR. KUHLMAN: I said that if he hit the center curb under those circumstances, aren't there other possible explanations then that the driver going north was just negligent or suicidal?

WITNESS: A. I would say that road design could be one of the factors.

Q. Now, that could be; nobody is asking you to step into the actual head of the driver.

A. That's right, would be, could be, possibility.

Q. Now, have you examined Police Reports on crashes between the south end of the Toll Road structure and the north end of the Gary Avenue structure between 1966 and July of 1970?

A. Yes, I have.

Q. Do those Police Reports have any relevance to the question of whether drivers who were previously familiar with driving the S-Curve should be expected to avoid crossing the median or getting into crashes?

A. Most of the accident crashes that occurred in that area were local drivers.

Q. About what percentage of the drivers who crossed the median or who got into crashes on Cline Avenue from the Toll Road to Gary Avenue from 1966 to July of 1970 were local area drivers?

MR. BLACKMUN: Your Honor, I think he should limit that to cross-over accidents.

MR. KUHLMAN: Your Honor, I believe we have established in extensive discussions that — strike that, I'll withdraw the question.

Q. When an engineer looks at a road and looks at traffic crashes, does he confine his looking and inspection to one particular kind of crash, or does he look to the total number of crashes?

A. He looks to the total number of crashes.

Q. Why is that?

A. To an engineer all a crash means is that —

MR. BLACKMUN: Wait a minute — excuse me — could we approach the Bench?

THE COURT: Yes.

REPORTER: Q. "When an engineer looks at a road and looks at traffic crashes, does he confine his looking and inspection to one particular kind of crash, or does he look to the total number of crashes.

A. "He looks to the total number of crashes.

Q. "Why is that?

A. "To an engineer all a crash means is that —"

DIRECT EXAMINATION (Continued)
BY MR. KUHLMAN:

Q. As a transportation engineer, if you were going to consider traffic crashes at all relevant in looking for dangerous areas of highways, would you look for particular kinds of crashes or just a general number?

A. Just a general number, that triggers an engineering investigation.

Q. Would that require a particular analysis of each specific crash reported, or a look to see how many the total numbers were?

A. The first look would be just to see how bad it is, what's happening.

Q. Now, that's all I'm asking you here at this point.

Let me ask you this: What, if anything, does the fact that most of the drivers getting into cross median or other crashes on Cline from the Toll Road to Gary Avenue are from the local area, from 1966 to July of 1970, what, if anything, does that fact tell you about the road design and the other opinions you have given here about the sight distances?

A. That fact doesn't tell me anything about the road, but it does tell me that I should make an engineering study to find out what's wrong with the road.

Q. Would there be any significance to you as a traffic engineer about the fact that it was local people as opposed to foreigners or people from other areas getting involved in crashes out there?

A. Shouldn't make any difference, an accident is an accident caused by something.

Q. Does the fact that a high percentage of the people getting into crashes out there were local drivers have any relevance to the question of whether other drivers who were familiar with the S-Curve area should be expected to avoid accidents and crashes on it?

A. The fact that people familiar with the road were having the accidents would make me think that there's possibly something wrong with the design a little faster.

Q. Just briefly I would like to talk to you about bridge location.

Before this S-Curve project was built as a four-lane, was there an old Cline Avenue; I think you have referred to that?

A. Yes, there was.

Q. How many lanes was the old Cline?

A. About two.

Q. And where did it run?

A. Right straight up the South Shore line from the Toll Road to the mills.

Q. Did the old Cline Avenue have a bridge on the Grand Calumet River?

A. Yes it did.

Q. And where was that old Calumet River bridge located?

A. 160′ west of where it is now, or in a straight line with the Toll Road bridge, straight due north I mean.

Q. Did the S-Curve project use the location of the old Cline Avenue Grand Calumet River bridge?

A. They used it as a detour while they were building the new bridge.

Q. But is that old location built into the new, new one?

A. No.

Q. Did they build a new bridge?

A. Built a new bridge.

Q. What effect, if any, on the shape of the road or the sight distances in the road would have been produced by using the old location of the old Calumet River bridge?

A. We would have had a straight road, wouldn't have the horizontal curve 1 or 2 in it.

Q. When the S-Curve was being built, were there any requirements on how far above water level you had to build a bridge crossing this navigable stream, the Grand Calumet River?

A. Yes, there was.
Q. And who set those requirements?
A. The Congress of the United States.
Q. And how high was that supposed to be?
A. It was supposed to be, I think, 26′ above low water level.
Q. Did this new Grand Calumet River bridge meet that standard?
A. No, it didn't.
Q. Did it exceed that standard?
A. That one is lower than the standard.
Q. How much lower?
A. I think it's 5′ or 6′.
Q. What effect, if any, would have been produced on the sight distances and geometrics of this road if the new Grand Calumet River structure had met the old Federal standards?
A. We would have had possibly no vertical curve 3 and the sight distance would have been better over the Toll Road.
Q. Now, was there a waiver granted for the height given to the Grand Calumet bridge?
A. The height was approved on the condition that it was called a temporary structure and the State agreed to tear it out at such time as the river became a navigable canal.
Q. Have you seen any evidence in all the documents that you have reviewed that these sight distance configurations on Crest Curve 1, Crest Curve 2, the sag curve, and the first horizontal, were all presented and explained at the time that clearance was granted for the lowering of the bridge, the Grand Calumet River bridge?
A. No, it wasn't.
Q. According to the 1968 Indiana Manual on Uniform Traffic Control Devices, did they have a term in there called a speed zone?
A. Yes.
Q. Was the speed zone related to the lowering of the speed on part of a road?
A. Any time a speed is lower than the State limit, the Indiana Highway Commission has the authority to call for a speed zone.
Q. What made the speed zone effective under the Manual?
A. The placing of the signs after the resolution.
Q. Who was supposed to pass the resolution?
A. The State Highway Commission.
Q. If the Highway Commission passed a resolution lowering the speed on part of a road making a speed zone, would it be effective until the signs were actually physically put up?

A. It would not be effective until the signs were up according to the Manual.

Q. If in June of 1970 the area of Cline Avenue from a point 1500 feet north of Highway Avenue to the junction with U.S. 12, Columbus Drive, were promulgated by the Indiana Highway Commission as a 55 miles an hour speed zone, and the rest of Cline Avenue were not, would the S-Curve area be in that speed zone or out of it?

A. It would be in it.

Q. Are there any standards in the 1968 Indiana Manual for how frequently speed signs must be placed inside a speed zone?

A. Yes.

Q. What are the standards for how frequently speed signs must be placed inside a speed zone into the 1968 Manual?

A. In Urban streets I believe it's every block, definitely to be visible to traffic, I think is the word. If you've got the book, I think I can find it.

It's a long paragraph, it's hard to memorize.

"When a zone is long enough to require it, an intermediate sign, of the same size as the first, shall be placed at sufficiently frequent intervals to keep motorists informed and to secure obedience. In extreme Urban cases, this may require the use of these signs in every block, but as a rule they may be placed at intervals of two or three blocks."

Q. What if it's Rural?

A. "In Rural areas, the intermediate signs must be placed close enough together to be easily seen by cars in heavy traffic."

Q. Now, let's assume that a road must be interurban or rural, is that reasonable as an assumption?

A. Yes, if you are going to have a posted speed limit, you should be able to see the sign.

Q. Now, let's assume that Cline Avenue on the S-Curve here from the Toll Road to Gary Avenue was either an urban road or a rural road?

A. All right.

Q. How far is it approximately from the Toll Road at the south end to Gary Avenue structure at the north end?

A. I think 1200 feet or so.

Q. Is it about a half mile for the whole thing?

A. I think so; .55 I think I figured it.

Q. .55 of a mile?

A. Little bit over a half mile.

Q. Talk to an engineer and you get your .5.

But it's about a half mile; right?

A. Yes.

Q. Let me ask you this, under the standards of the 1968 Indiana Manual, if they had made a speed zone that included the S-Curve area, about how many speed signs would have to be posted in the area from the Toll Road here in the south to Gary Avenue here in the north, whether it was urban or rural, to conform with the manual standards for posting of speed signs inside speed zones?

A. At least five on each side, each way.

Q. Would they meet the standards if they have one sign only in that area?

A. There's so many curves that they would not be visible to traffic at all times unless you spot them about where you are going. You would need one in front of the Toll Road structure, you would need one in the horizontal curve, you would need one on the other side of the Grand Calumet River, you would need one going up Gary Avenue, and one on the far side, telling you that you are out of it.

Q. So if in June of 1970 this area of Cline Avenue here that I read to you, from a point 1500 feet north of Highway Avenue to the junction with U.S. 12, Columbus Drive, that was made a speed zone, then the S-Curve would be in it; right?

A. Yes.

Q. And then they would have to meet the manual standards on putting up speed signs at frequent intervals in a speed zone; right?

A. That's right.

Q. Would they conform with those standards if they didn't have any speed signs at all from the Toll Road to Gary Avenue?

A. No.

Q. If they only had one?

A. No.

Q. To engineers and traffic control specialists operating on State roads in June and July of 1970, was the Indiana 1968 Manual on Uniform Traffic Control Devices mandatory or optional?

A. Mandatory.

Q. And was that a State road?

A. That's a State road.

Q. Mr. Lippman, from your studies and your surveys of this road, and your observations of it, is it entirely within one city on both the east and west side of the road from the Toll Road to Gary Avenue?

A. From the north end of the Toll Road it's all in Gary.

Q. On the west or the east side?

A. East Chicago is on the east side, but the whole road is in Gary, because Cline Avenue is the city limits.

Q. Could any one city have lit both the east and the west side of Cline Avenue?

A. Because as you go south you are in Hammond and East Chicago would taunt you.

Q. What I'm asking you is this: Could any one city have lit the entire east and west side of Cline Avenue from the south edge of the Toll Road up to the north edge of Gary Avenue structure?

A. Not at the south edge of the Toll Road.

Q. Why is that?

A. It's a different city at the Toll Road.

Q. Let me ask you this: As a matter of road engineering design and traffic operation, if in July of 1970 Cline Avenue from the Toll Road to the Gary Avenue structure did not have median barriers, warning signs, edge lines, driver lane lines, a painted median curb, and if it had either no posted speed limit signs or a 55 mile-an-hour speed limit sign for both day and night, do you have an opinion based upon a reasonable degree of scientific and engineering certainty, as to whether that road would require lighting for safe operation, with all those other things missing?

A. Definitely would require lighting. That increases your night sight distance and brings back some of your factors of safety that you lost.

Q. I believe you have already testified that the 1968 Indiana Manual was the mandatory standard for State roads governing the marking and the painting of State roads in 1970; is that right?

A. That's correct.

Q. Now, Mr. Lippman, here on Plaintiff's Exhibit 231 I want to show you the outer edge line of the road; is that it?

A. That's it. (Indicating)

Q. Was it optional or mandatory under the 1968 Manual —

A. It was mandatory that that line be striped.

Q. So that in July of 1970, if that line was not striped, would the manual have been complied with?

A. No.

Q. Would the road have been marked with due engineering care?

A. No.

Q. I show you the middle of the road here on Plaintiff's Exhibit 231. In July of 1970, was it mandatory or optional to have a skip line or a painted line with that reflectorized paint you talked about down the center of the road so that motorists could see where the lane lines were?

A. It was mandatory.

Q. Now, if in July of 1970, the S-Curve area did not have that painting down the middle of the road to show the driver lane line, would the manual have been complied with?

A. No, it wouldn't.

Q. And would the road have been marked with due engineering care?

A. It would not have.

Q. Now, I show you the pavement that's right in front of the center median barrier here on the left side of the road on Exhibit 231. Under the 1968 Manual was it mandatory or optional that that pavement in front of the median be painted?

A. Mandatory.

Q. Now, if in July, 1970, they didn't have painting on the S-Curve on the pavement right in front of that median, would the manual have been complied with?

A. No, it wouldn't.

Q. Would the road have been marked with due engineering care?

A. No, it wouldn't.

Q. Now, I show you the median curb in the center of the roadway. Under the 1968 Manual was it mandatory or optional that that center median curb be painted?

A. Mandatory.

Q. If they didn't have the median painted on Cline Avenue from the Toll Road to Gary Avenue at midnight, in July, 1970, would they have complied with the Manual?

A. No, they wouldn't.

Q. Were they allowed to disregard it as an engineering matter?

A. As an engineering, no.

Q. Would they have painted the road with due care under their own standards if they didn't paint the median here on July of 1970?

A. No.

Q. I ask you this: If at midnight, July, 1970, there was no painting of the outer edge of that area of Cline, in the middle of Cline, on the pavement in front of the median barrier on Cline, on the median barrier itself, all that referring to the north lane, and if there was a similar failure to paint the outer edge line, the median curb, the pavement in front of the median curb, or the middle for the driver lane line on the south lane, and you have the same dimensions and measurements and sight distances on the road that you have surveyed, and there was no fixed lighting and no warning signs, would that be a dangerous area for a motorist going northbound over the Toll Road in the dark?

A. Yes, it would be.

Q. Now, are Police Crash Reports a tool that engineers and traffic planners use to review road design and the adequacy of road protection?

A. Yes, it is.

Q. Are there other tools as well?

A. Engineering study, sight distance, geometrics of the highway is the most important study to me.

Q. Are Police Reports the best tool that engineers have available to review the design and adequacy of protection on Cline Avenue from the Toll Road to Gary Avenue at midnight on July 27, 1970?

A. No.

Q. What better tools are available; first of all, let me ask you this, have you examined the recommendations of Consoer, Townsend?

A. Yes, I have.

Q. What did they recommend?

A. Lights, median barriers — you mean back when they first started designing this thing?

Q. Right.

Do you know whether the Indiana Highway Commission itself ever inspected this road in 1967?

A. Yes, there was a design review of the entire road which they recommended lights and median barriers.

Q. Have you examined the geometrics and the surveys of this road?

A. Yes, I have.

Q. And the sight distances?

A. Yes, I have.

Q. Would you consider those to be equal to, better than, or worse than the diagnostic tool of crash reports in evaluating the adequacy of protection of the Cline Avenue S-Curve at midnight, July 27, 1970?

A. Better than any crash report.

Q. Why is it?

A. Because it tells you why the crashes. Some of the crashes are driver error. All a crash does is to warrant an engineering study if you start getting a group of them. It's more important to find out why rather than how many.

Q. When Consoer, Townsend recommended lights and median barriers on that road before it opened, were they right?

A. Yes.

Q. When the Indiana Highway Commission's engineers inspected that roadway in 1967 and recommended median barriers, were they right?

A. Yes, but nobody recommended a lower speed, which should have been recommended too, because they are still hitting the barriers.

MR. BLACKMUN: Objection, your Honor, I request that the answer be stricken as not responsive to the question.

THE COURT: Sustained.

MR. BLACKUM: I ask that the jury be instructed to disregard the answer voluntarily made.

THE COURT: All right, that portion of Mr. Lippman's statement not responsive to the last question, the jury will disregard.

DIRECT EXAMINATION (Continued)
BY MR. KUHLMAN:

Q. Now, when did this road open again, what month and what year?

A. 1966; September.

Q. In 1967 AASHO published a book, we have already put into evidence called the 1967 Yellow Book?

A. Yes.

Q. Are you familiar with that book?

A. Yes.

Q. What, if anything, did that book have to say with the authority of AASHO about cross over median crashes?

A. It stated that divider or median barriers should be in when the divider is small and traffic is high, and it gave charts and tables. In other words —

Q. Under the standards in the 1967 Yellow Book, what, if anything, would the relevance be to the need for a median barrier on Cline Avenue from the Toll Road to Gary Avenue?

A. The curb there is only 4′ wide and the traffic count was more than 16,000 the day it opened, and at that time it was above 20,000, therefore, it needed a median barrier.

Q. I draw your attention to the year 1968, that's the very next year after the 1967 Yellow Book, and I show you what has been marked as Plaintiff's Exhibit 275.

Was this published in 1968?

A. Yes.

Q. Who published this in 1968?

A. Highway Research Board, the American Academy of Science and AASHO.

Q. How prestigious and authoritative in the traffic and transportation and road design field are the people who published this report and this chart in 1968?

A. The American Academy of Science is supposed to be the top brains in the country who are funded by the Federal Government to do research for the AASHO and states that require research in all fields of physics, chemistry, mathematics and highways and anything else along that line.

Q. Was this published and literature available to engineers throughout the United States in the year 1968?

A. Yes, it was.

Q. Would you explain to the jury and the Court — your Honor, I'll back it up like this so everybody can see it — what, if anything, this chart has to say about the need for a median barrier on Cline Avenue from the Toll Road to Gary Avenue?

A. The chart is a graph that shows where you need a median and based on the width at the bottom, and since our median is only 4′ wide you need a median. Everything above the line is median barrier required, everything to the right and below is median barrier not required.

Q. Can everybody see the chart?

A. In other words, you can build a median about 18′ wide at 20,000 traffic and you don't need a barrier.

Q. And this came out the very year after the 1967 Yellow Book?

A. Yes, I believe this is what they had as a warrant for finally putting it in in the late 70's.

Q. Now, do your own measurements, calculations, surveys, the expert's literature, that you have reviewed, and the tests that you have made on the physical design, proportions, dimensions, and layouts on Cline Avenue from the Toll Road to Gary Avenue have any relevance to the question lead you to an opinion as to whether or not you have a reasonable degree of scientific and engineering certainty as to whether Cline Avenue should have had a median barrier on the night of, and prior to the night of July 27, 1970, from the Toll Road to Gary Avenue?

A. Yes.

Q. And what is that opinion?

A. Should have had a median barrier.

Q. And what are the reasons for that opinion?

A. Due to the geometrics, or due to the number of cross-over crashes, due to the narrow width, closeness of opposing traffic, they all warrant a median barrier.

Q. Are you familiar with the Indiana Uniform Manual warrants on warning signs for state roads in 1968 Edition?

A. Yes.

Q. Did the warrants on warning signs have a mandatory or optional requirement for state roads in 1970?

A. It was mandatory after an engineering study showed that a warning sign was required.

Q. Do you have an opinion based upon a reasonable degree of scientific and engineering certainty, based upon your studies or observations and your measurements here, and all the documents and all the material that you have testified you examined, as to whether Cline Avenue should have had a warning sign from the Toll Road to Gary Avenue structure at midnight on July 27, 1970?

A. Yes, it should have.

Q. What is the reason for that opinion?

A. Because there is a hidden horizontal curve that's hidden by the vertical curves and there wasn't proper sight distance. Part of the duty of a transportation group is to not surprise the motorist.

Q. What kind of a warning sign do you think might have been appropriate for the S-Curve?

A. Personally I feel that you should have a speed limit, but there also should be a warning, an arrow or something to alert the driver who didn't have the striping and the delineators and everything else there to tell him that the road is turning. Possibly it doesn't warrant a curve sign.

Q. Why not?

A. Because the book sets up some minimum standards. It is not a curve according to the book.

Q. Because it doesn't pass a ball bank meter test?

A. That's correct.

Q. Would you tell the Court and jury what a ball bank meter test is?

A. It's like a carpenter's level, ball in a glass that's calibrated, you mount it in your car, as you drive fast around a curve, the ball swings out so many degrees and you tell how sharp the curve is.

Q. But even if it didn't pass the ball bank meter test there was no prohibition against putting a curve sign there, was there?

A. No, the State could have done it if they wanted to.

Q. Also were there other warning signs in the 1968 Indiana Manual for indicating a road that was not straight that didn't even require a ball bank meter test at all?

A. Yes, the main warrant was that after an engineering study if you felt something was needed, it could be done.

Q. How about the arrow sign?

A. That's what I stated originally, an arrow.

Q. Did you have any ball bank meter test requirement for an arrow?

A. Not for an arrow, or not for go slow.

Q. Just so the jury understands it, can you describe the difference between the arrow sign and the curve sign?

A. Page 63, it says: "An arrow sign is particularly useful at night to give notice of a sharp change of alignment such as at a curve or turn."

Q. May I have the book to show the arrow signs to the jury.

This is the large arrow sign, counsel, on Page 63, of the 1968 Indiana Manual.

Does that large arrow sign require any ball bank meter tests?

A. No, it doesn't.

Q. Can you all see it?

Now, would your opinion about the necessity for warning signs and median barriers on the night of July 27, 1970, on Cline Avenue from the Toll Road to Gary Avenue, be any stronger or weaker if this road were dirty?

MR. BLACKMUN: Objection, your Honor, the question has been asked and answered numerous times.

MR. KUHLMAN: I'll withdraw the question.

Q. Now, have your opinions so far and everything we have discussed about this road, and the need for warning signs, the need for painting, the need for median barriers, considered Police Reports and their numbers, or their quantities at all?

A. No, they haven't.

Q. Why not?

A. Because this is an engineering study not a study of the Police Reports.

Q. Let me ask you this: Based upon your surveys, tests, your observations, all the documents you have seen, all the measurements that you have made, all the evidence that you have seen, excluding the Police Reports, don't consider them at all, okay, do you have an opinion based upon a reasonable degree of scientific and engineering certainty, okay, just considering the AASHO 1967 Yellow Book, the Blue Books, the Red Books, that chart published by the National Academy of Sciences, the recommendations of Consoer, Townsend, and the other documents and surveys that you have made, and no Police Reports at all, as to whether it would be consistent with reasonable care for the state to wait three or four years from the opening of the Cline Avenue S-Curve before putting in a median barrier and just counting Police Reports?

A. It is not good practice.

Q. Why not?

A. You don't have to count Police Reports. If somebody would have flagged the, — Consoer, Townsend knew that they didn't have a 70 mile-an-hour bridge when they built that road, and someone in the State Highway Commission should have posted warning signs immediately at the time of construction. It's an engineering fact that those combination of curves just can't be driven at 70 miles an hour safely at all times.

Q. Could they be posted with reasonable engineering care at 55?

A. It's a gamble. That's why you have the crashes that you haven't referred to yet.

Q. Now, let me ask you this: I know you have refrained from crashes, but have you yourself ever analyzed any crashes?

A. Yes, I have.

Q. About how many crashes have you yourself analyzed, crash reports?

A. Between 500 and a thousand.

Q. Have you studied the crash reports on Cline Avenue from the south end of the Toll Road to the north end of Gary Avenue between the opening of the S-Curve and July 27, 1970?

A. Yes, I have.

Q. Do those crash reports now confirm or weaken your opinions which were formed on other bases entirely as to the need for striping, median barriers, and warning signs, and speed limit signs on Cline Avenue from the Toll Road to Gary Avenue at midnight, July 27, 1970?

A. They confirm and strengthen my convictions.

Q. Why is that?

A. Because a lot of the accidents, crashes were rear-enders; there were a great number of cross-overs, which are caused by the hidden curve, and the rear-enders are caused by sight distance problems, which the engineering study shows.

Q. Have you prepared any models or displays for the Court and jury of the information from those crash reports?

A. Yes.

MR. KUHLMAN: May be approach the Bench, your Honor?

THE COURT: Yes.

(SIDE BAR DISCUSSION OUT OF JURY'S PRESENCE)

DIRECT EXAMINATION (Continued)
BY MR. KUHLMAN:

Q. Mr. Lippman, very briefly, on Plaintiff's Exhibit No. 236, I believe you referred to the old Cline Avenue bridge being in line with the Toll Road bridge; is that right?

A. That's correct.

Q. Would you point out the old Cline Avenue bridge on this serial photo?

A. Straight on through here, and this is old Cline Avenue, kept on going (Indicating).

Q. Can everybody see that?

Directing your attention to Plaintiff's Exhibit 274, did you examine and collate the crash reports on the crashes on Cline Avenue only from the Toll Road to Gary Avenue in the years between the opening of the road in 1966 and prior to the Edgman crash in 1970?

A. Yes, I did.

Q. And did you do this yourself?

A. Yes, I did.

Q. Did you prepare this exhibit yourself?

A. Yes, I did.

Q. Now, the first page of this exhibit here is a drawing?

A. Is a drawing showing the road to scale in that area.

Q. And approximately how many such drawings have you prepared previously?

A. You mean of this road or any road?

Q. Of roads?

A. 100 to 150.

Q. And it only shows the crash reports in that area; is that correct?

A. It shows the crash reports that I could read in that area.

Q. Was there any problem with the microfilming at the Indiana State Police?

A. There were several tapes that were bad and any report that I couldn't get a definite clue as to where it was I didn't use. There's probably more than I've got here.

Q. Turning to the first acetate overlay, what does this depict?

A. This shows the crashes that occurred in 1966.

Q. In that area?

A. In that area.

Q. Turning to the second acetate overlay, what does that show?

A. Shows the crashes for 1967 in that area.

Q. And the previous ones from 1966?

A. 1966 that you can see there, yes.

Q. Turning to the next acetate overlay, what does that show?

A. All the crashes in 1968.

Q. Turning to the next acetate overlay, what does that show?

A. All the crashes in 1969.

Q. Turning to the next acetate overlay, what does that show?

A. Crashes in 1970 up to but not including the Edgman crash.

Q. Mr. Lippman, would it be a fair way to evaluate this road just to say 27,000 vehicles or more each day went over this road, and multiply that by the number of days from the opening of the road to the Edgman crash, and to get some gigantic astronomical number and to say this is the number of crashes more or less, therefore, almost everybody made it safely, therefore, the road is okay, there's no problem?

A. Those people didn't make it, and there is a problem.

Q. And would the geometrics that you testified to and the sight distance that you testified to have any —

A. This confirms the sight distance and geometric problem. It did the first year on the first nine accidents.

Q. Would your opinion be any different on the need for warning signs or lighting or median barriers or painting on Cline Avenue on the area from the Toll Road to the Gary Avenue structure on the night of July 27, 1970, if Mr. Edgman was the first person who was ever —

A. No, the design and geometrics are wrong whether they hurt anybody or not.

MR. KUHLMAN: Your Honor, at this time we would move for the introduction into evidence of Plaintiff's Exhibit No. 274.

DIRECT EXAMINATION (Continued)
BY MR. KUHLMAN:

Q. Mr. Lippman, just referring to Plaintiff's Exhibit 274, just as a question of notice, as Hammond City Engineer, or as traffic expert, as a civil engineering expert, would you expect to see that type of concentration of dots in the middle of the road where you have no side streets or side roads cutting out?

A. I wouldn't, no.

Q. Would it make any difference if it was a freeway or an expressway?

A. No.

Q. Or if it was a minor arterial street?

A. No.

Q. What's the difference between a freeway and an expressway?

A. An expressway has crossings at grade; a freeway has cloverleafs and ramps, traffic is separated, cross traffic.

Q. Just as a question of notice on these dots, why wouldn't you expect to see that type of concentration in a rural area or ordinary side streets?

A. If you don't have a lot of intersections you shouldn't have any accidents in the middle of blocks.

Q. And would your opinion matter whether that was an expressway or a freeway or a minor arterial road?

A. Too many accidents for that section from the first day.

Q. Would or would not that type of concentration have been a red flag to competent traffic engineers prior to July, 1970, prior to 1970, and prior to 1969, prior to 1968, to go out and look at the road?

A. It should have told them the first month that it was opened that they didn't have a 70 mile-an-hour road.

Q. I want you to assume Mr. Lippman, that on the night of July 27, 1970, that Cline Avenue between the Toll Road and Gary Avenue had the measurements and dimensions and proportions observed in your surveys and tests that you testified to; further assume that the road had a prior history of crashes that you see with that dot survey; further assume that all the the correspondence and documentation that you studied and observed about the area of road was written by the people who signed it and was received by the people that it was sent to, and that it was written on or about the time that the addresses on the letters, the dates on the letters have; I want you to assume that on that night there was no fixed lighting on Cline Avenue from Gary Avenue to the Toll Road, no street lighting; I want you to assume that the road has no painted edge lines in the north or south lanes at that night; no driver lane lines; no painted median curb, no delineators or reflectors in either the north lane or the south lane; no warning signs on Cline Avenue between the Toll Road and Gary Avenue that night.

Based on those assumptions, would it have been consistent with the exercise of due care by the state for northbound motorists on that road at night, or for any motorist under the applicable engineering and road design standards in effect at the time, for the state to have a posted speed both night and day of 55 miles an hour?

A. No.

Q. Why not?

A. It's not safe, it should be posted lower.

Q. Would it be consistent with due care for the state to have no posted speed signs?

MR. KUHLMAN: Q. I want you to add to your assumptions and your earlier statements these assumptions: Assume that at approximately midnight on the night of July 27, 1970, Robert Casillas drove a vehicle north over the Toll Road toward the Grand Calumet River, and about the same time James Edgman was driving a 1968 Ford Station Wagon with his wife, Lorene, inside as a passenger south toward the Grand Calumet River; assume that northbound Casillas had night visibility on that road as you have calculated in your studies; assume that on that night all the vertical and horizontal curves had these sight distances and proportions you measured; assume that Casillas hit the median curb in the center of the road about 10 or 20 feet south of the, north of the south end of the Calumet River Bridge; assume that the Casillas vehicle then went through the air after hitting the center curb, crossed over the inter [inner] lane of southbound traffic and struck the Edgman vehicle in the outer southbound lane after an air flight of about 20 or 30 feet, through the air north and hit the Edgman vehicle after flying 20 or 30 feet through the air.

Do you have an opinion, based upon reasonable degree of scientific and engineering certainty, as to whether the state's failure on that night at that time had a median barrier been placed on the center curb from the Toll Road to Gary Avenue on Cline Avenue was a substantial contributing factor in producing that crash?

A. Yes, I do.

Q. What is that opinion?

A. Median barrier, possibly would have deflected him enough that he wouldn't have hit Mr. Edgman to start with.

Q. So was the absence of a median barrier, in your opinion, a reasonable degree of engineering and scientific certainty a substantial contributing factor to the Casillas vehicle penetrating into the opposite lane of traffic and striking the Edgman vehicle?

MR. BLACKMUN: Objection, your Honor, he has just answered that question and he stated it was a possibility.

THE COURT: Perhaps we are arguing semantics, I believe that was the answer given.

MR. KUHLMAN: I want to make sure that he understands the question and I want to make sure we have an accurate answer.

MR. BLACKMUN: I think you have an accurate answer, it's just one you don't like.

MR. KUHLMAN: Well, I'm sorry, it's my question and I think I can—

MR. COHEN: What's wrong with the —

WITNESS: A. Median barriers are designed —

MR. BLACKMUN: Your Honor, I object, the witness has answered the question and Mr. Kuhlman has reasked the same question and I object to the same, to the question being reasked.

MR. KUHLMAN: It's not the same question. I am the one who has the right to object to responsiveness.

THE COURT: That's true.

Restate the question, Mr. Kuhlman.

MR. KUHLMAN: Q. Do you have an opinion, based upon a reasonable degree of scientific and engineering certainty as to whether the failure of the state to have a median barrier in place on Cline Avenue from the Toll Road to Gary Avenue was a substantial contributing factor in causing that Edgman-Casillas crash?

A. Yes.

DIRECT EXAMINATION (Continued)
BY MR. KUHLMAN:

Q. I want you to assume the same facts that we earlier stated, assume also that Mr. Casillas is driving in the outbound lane, in the outside lane, and I want you to assume that the road is dirty. On those assumptions, do you have an opinion, based upon a reasonable degree of scientific and engineering certainty, as to whether the state's failure to have a median barrier in place at the time and place was a substantial contributing factor to that crash?

A. Yes.

Q. What is your opinion?

A. Definitely median divider to prevent cross-over accidents due to the poor sight distance and the dirty road, lack of painting and everything else you've talked about all afternoon.

Q. Mr. Lippman, the state has challenged the plaintiffs in this case to show how and why Casillas went from the outer northbound lane and hit the center curb.

I want you to assume all the geometrics and proportions and correspondence and everything else you have assumed previously, assume that on the night of midnight, July 27, 1970, all those curves in the roadway of Cline Avenue from Gary Avenue to the Toll Road had the dimensions and proportions; assume Casillas is driving north around midnight over the Toll Road in the outer lane going north; assume the Edgman vehicle is traveling south from Gary Avenue in the outer lane; assume that the road at that time had no lights, no stripes, no warning signs, no delineators, no reflectors; assume there was dirt on the road; assume the sight distances and dimensions you testified to on the Crest Curve 1, Crest Curve 2, the sag curve, and the first horizontal; I want you to assume that Madrinan, Anthony Madrinan, is going south on the inside lane at about 70 to 80 miles an hour, and Madrinan at about the time of the crash is catching up on Edgman, but a little bit behind Edgman, when he sees oncoming lights coming at him from the direction of the Toll Road; I want you to assume that the Casillas vehicle hit the center median curb 10 to 20 feet north of the south edge of the Calumet River bridge; and assume that the Casillas vehicle then traveled through the air about 20 or 30 feet to the north and hit the Edgman vehicle.

Now, I know that there are many interpretations to this, I know you weren't in the car with Madrinan or Edgman or Casillas, but I want to ask you this: Do those facts that I have asked you to assume necessarily require the conclusion that Casillas was driving negligently?

A. No.

MR. KUHLMAN: Q. Is there a rational explanation that can be demonstrated by scientific and mathematical principles as to how these events could have happened to the Casillas vehicle that night without Casillas driving negligently?

A. Yes, there is.

Q. And have you prepared a mathematical graphic demonstrating this?

A. Yes, I have.

Q. And you are not claiming that this is absolutely the way it happened?

A. There's possibly 10 more solutions.

Q. Possibly he is out there trying to kill himself; right?

A. If he had done that, he might have probably done it at a different place.

MR. KUHLMAN: Can everyone in the jury see the exhibit?

Mr. Lippman, can you step down from the witness stand and explain this graphic?

WITNESS: A. Basically what have tried to do here is calculate the friction factor on the wheel of the car making maneuvers through the super-elevated curve. Now, most roads are designed for friction factor of about .3 for a wet pavement; a perfect pavement with perfect tires has a friction factor of .8, which you will see with the numbers in here.

Now, when a car goes around a curve centrifugal force is pushing him out. The super-elevation of the road is tending to hold him in. So taking the assumption that the driver of this car, Mr. Casillas, didn't see this curve until he was about half way in it, he turned his wheels slightly, came down here, he finally was heading off towards that edge of the road, he turned his wheel a little bit to the left and over-compensated due to the super-elevation working against him on this curve, and he hit here, and went over here and did all the other hitting in the assumptions.

Say if you were 65 miles an hour here, and you tried to turn, you have a coefficient of .58, almost .6, which in an average road should be .5. There is a possibility he could have skidded here and hit the middle and not had the accident down here. If he were asleep and driving straight ahead, he would have gone over here and would not have hit down here. So I was trying to get a pattern of something that would be even enough that you could see.

Now, at 65, like you start here, the friction factor is .58, over here it's .78, which means that the road had to be perfect and his tires had to be perfect or he would have skidded out over here. So he definitely was doing less than 65 or he would have bombed out over here.

Now, at 60, it becomes a twilight zone, he's at .67, he could have, he could not have. So about the best I can do from this diagram is say that he's doing someplace between 50 and 60 to make a maneuver and end up here. If he were going faster, he would have lost it here; if he were going slower, he would not have hit the other guy (Indicating).

MR. KUHLMAN: Q. Mr. Lippman, let me ask you just a few questions about this, and I know that the jury wants to get home this evening.

Under that series of events, would the lights of the car coming from the Toll Road appear to be coming straight at —

A. You've got to remember that this car was back here, and he saw these lights coming straight at him, and as he approached this approach, then the two vehicles looked like they were coming at him all the time (Indicating).

Q. So Madrinan would appear to have the lights coming straight at him?

A. This is Madrinan?

Q. Yes, the guy on the inside lane.

A. When he saw this guy coming, he thought he was coming right straight at him and he slammed on his brakes, and by the time he stopped this car was still coming at him. (Indicating).

Q. Let me ask you another question: How would that be affected if there was dirt on that road on that night?

A. It would make him slide at a lower speed. He could not have made this maneuver if the friction factor was .4 or .5; he would have lost it up here (Indicating).

Q. If Casillas came over the Toll Road in the outside lane going north with his wheels straight ahead of him and he never turned his wheels at all, could he have hit at the point that Madrinan marked that X about 10′ or 20′ —

A. He would have hit about here in the middle (Indicating).

Q. So in order for the Casillas car to hit where Madrinan put the X, he had to turn his wheel somewhere as he came over the Toll Road?

A. Right, and the sharper he turns the wheel, the more he has a chance of spinning out, so since he didn't spin out in this area, we know that he was working down in the 55 or 60 range. If he were doing 50 or 60, he could have spun out here because if the road was dirty, he might have spun out at 60 and he could have been doing 55. But definitely he's under 70 and he's under 65, or pretty close to it.

Q. Now, just so the jury understands, you are not saying that this is absolutely the way it happened?

A. No, you can come a little farther, turn a little sharper or start turning a little back, but he had to make two turns to end up over here where you wouldn't have said he hit.

Q. And even if Casillas was in fact doing something different from that, even if Casillas was out there driving negligently, or if he was drunk or if he was sleeping, or if he was suicidal, would that in any way alter any of the opinions you have stated as to the negligence of the State?

A. No.

Q. Would that in any way alter any of the opinions you have given as to the negligence of the State being a substantial contributing factor to this crash?

A. If he were driving straight through, he would have been here and hit somebody else —

(REPORTER REQUESTS WITNESS TO SPEAK UP)

WITNESS: A. If he drove straight through he would have hit somebody in the other lane about in the middle, if someone had been there. A divider would have kept him on his own side.

MR. KUHLMAN: Thank you very much, Mr. Lippman.

Your Honor, we have no more questions;

I note that it's 4:00 and I'm sure the jury would like to get home.

THE COURT: I'm certain they would too. Gentlemen, is there anything further for the record at this point?

MR. BLACKMUN: Is the plaintiff finished with the witness?

MR. COHEN: Yes.

MR. KUHLMAN: Just a minute, please.

We have a few more questions.

DIRECT EXAMINATION (Continued)
BY MR. KUHLMAN:

Q. Mr. Lippman, under the assumptions of what was out there on midnight of July 27, 1970, as to the absence of lighting, curbing dimensions and correspondence that you have seen, assume all the factors as to the path and direction of Edgman and Casillas in their vehicles, and where the Casillas vehicle hit, and how far it flew through the air, where it hit the Edgman vehicle, all that I have asked you, do you have an opinion, based upon a reasonable degree of scientific certainty as to whether the failure of the state to paint and mark and stripe the road that night, was a substantial contributing factor to that crash?

MR. BLACKMUN: Objection, your Honor.

THE COURT: For the same reason stated before?

MR. BLACKMUN: Yes.

THE COURT: The objection is overruled.

WITNESS: A. Yes.

MR. KUHLMAN: Q. And what is that opinion?

A. It would contribute to the crash.

Q. Do you have an opinion as to whether the failure of the State to have warning signs was a substantial contributing factor to that crash?

A. Yes.

Q. And what is that opinion?

A. There isn't; it contributed to the crash.

Q. What is the reason for those opinions?

A. They all make the reaction time, sight distance, the general geometrics of the road makes it a problem. Every little item by itself increases the danger as to whether one item could cause it or all of them. It's a combination.

Q. Do you have an opinion based upon a reasonable degree of scientific and engineering certainty as to whether the failure to have lighting on the road, assuming all the other conditions were also present, was a substantial contributing factor to the crash?

A. Yes.

Q. What is that opinion?

A. Same thing.

Q. What is the opinion?

A. It contributes to the problem?

Q. Why is that?

A. Because if lighting were there, he would have better nighttime sight distance, he might have anticipated, seen the curve a little sooner, he might not have had the accident.

Q. Assume all the other assumptions, and I'll ask you one last question, assume that the State at the time of the crash had either no speed signs or a 55-mile an hour speed sign for both day and nighttime driving on that area of Cline, do you have an opinion based upon a reasonable degree of scientific and engineering certainty as to whether either the failure to have any speed sign or 55-mile an hour speed signs would have been a substantial contributing factor to the crash?

A. Yes.

Q. What is that opinion?

A. Lack of a speed sign or a 55 would contribute because the geometrics of the road is not capable of safely handling 55 mile an hour —

MR. COHEN: Your Honor, the record does not show that the Uniform Manual has been admitted.

We move at this time to have it admitted.

MR. HASSETT: I believe it was admitted without objection.

MR. COHEN: The reporter doesn't have it; that was Exhibit No. 266.

THE COURT: All right, the Court will simply restate that Plaintiff's Exhibit 266 is admitted.

Will the record reflect a continuing objection to each of the matters about which Mr. Lippman testified, counsel.

MR. BLACKMUN: Yes, your Honor.

THE COURT: All right, the record will so reflect then as to each of those items to which Mr. Lippman testified, as to whether or not any were a substantial contributing factor, the defendant makes a continuing objection, overruled by the Court.

Anything further by the plaintiff?

MR. KUHLMAN: No, we excuse the witness.

CONCLUSION

Certain social forces dominate a society so thoroughly that they become the most characteristic example of that society. Slavery held that role in classic Greece and Rome. Technology performs that function for us today. This book has been about the impacts technology is having on one particular aspect of our society — the litigation system. It is from technology that the killer road systems were created, and it is only with knowledge of technology that those problems will be corrected by engineers in the field, by lawyers and jurors in the courtroom, and, ultimately, by voters who understand the issues and cast meaningful votes to provide the finds needed for a final solution of the problem. The unifying theme linking all these elements is that our social structure must function at several levels, each requiring knowledge of technology and how people react to it, if the killer roads are ever to pass from current events into the realm of history. If we cannot control our technology sufficiently to solve this problem, then there will be many other problems we will not be able to solve either. We will continue to pollute our own air and water, drown in our own garbage, mutate from our own chemicals, and watch helplessly as our legal and political systems become increasingly irrelevant to the common citizens who can neither understand nor operate them.

TABLE OF CASES

A

B

Bovsum v. Sanperi, 27 A.T.L.A. L. Rep. 0153 (1984) — § 5-2(F).
Bowen v. Riverton City, 656 P.2d 434 (Utah 1983) — ch. 4.
Bower, Campana v.
Bowles v. City of Pittsburgh, 343 Pa. 39, 20 A.2d 783 (1941) — § 16-1.
Bowman v. Columbia Tel. Co., 406 Pa. 455, 179 A.2d 197 (1962) — § 3-1(B).
Box v. California Date Growers Ass'n, 57 Cal. App. 3d 266, 129 Cal. Rptr. 146 (1976) — § 9-4.
Boyd v. McKeever, 384 Mich. 501, 185 N.W.2d 344 (1971) — § 8-4.
Boyer v. Tenn Tom Constructors, 702 F.2d 609 (5th Cir. 1983) — § 5-2(C).
Brackensick v. Chicago Motor Coach Co., 4 Ill. App. 2d 84, 123 N.E.2d 350 (1954) — § 7-2.
Bradley, MOMO v.
Bradshaw, MacGregor v.
Brazos County, Norton v.
Break, Gray v.
Brennan, Cunis v.
Briggs, Board of Comm'rs v.
Briggs v. State, 14 Cal. App. 3d 489, 92 Cal. Rptr. 433 (1971) — § 1-10(C); § 4; § 5-2(B).
Brinkman v. City of Indianapolis, 141 Ind. App. 662, 231 N.E.2d 169 (1967) — intro, n. 21.
Broderick v. City of New York, 255 A.D. 875, 7 N.Y.S.2d 809 (1938) — § 4-3(C)(3).
Broussard, Texas Hwy. Dep't v.
Brown, Bailey v.
Brown v. Blankenbaker, Cause No. 14707, Mason Sup. Ct., Wash. (Nov. 1983) — § 3-1(B).
Brown, Cadillac Motor Div., Gen. Motors Corp. v.
Brown v. City of Omaha, 183 Neb. 430, 160 N.W.2d 805 (1968) — intro, n. 21.
Brown Mfg. Co., Williams v.
Brummitt v. Chaney, 18 Mich. App. 59, 170 N.W.2d 481 (1969) — § 16-1.
Brush Racing Ass'n, Colorado Racing Comm'n v.
Brydon v. Kimbob, Inc., 20 Cumb. 94 (Pa. Comm. Pl. 1970) — § 16-3.
Bub, Nystrom v.
Buchman v. Seaboard Coast Line R.R., 381 So. 2d 229 (1980) — § 16-1.
Buckley Dickerson, Inc. v.
Buckley, Kelson v.
Buehler v. Whalen, 70 Ill. 2d 51, 374 N.E.2d 460 (1977) — § 6-2.
Bufkin v. Texas Farm Bureau Mut. Ins. Co., 658 S.W.2d 317 (Tex. Ct. App. 1983) — § 16-1.
Bunker v. City of Glendale, 111 Cal. App. 3d 325, 168 Cal. Rptr. 565 (1980) — § 1-10(A).
Burcroff v. County of Orleans, 114 Misc. 2d 16, 450 N.Y.S.2d 651 (1982) — § 5-1.
Burd, Sinn v.
Burdett, R. v.
Burens v. Industrial Comm'n, 162 Ohio St. 549, 124 N.E.2d 724 (1955) — § 16-1.
Burge, New Orleans & N.E.R.R. v.
Burleson, Beacon Nat'l Ins. Co. v.
Burlington N., Inc., Bak v.
Burlington N.R.R. v. JMC Transp., Inc., 567 F. Supp. 389 (N.D. Ill. 1983) — § 5-2(D).
Burlison, St. Louis-San Francisco Ry. v.
Burns v. Combined Ins. Co. of Am., 6 Mass. App. 86, 373 N.E.2d 1189 (1978) — § 16-1.
Burns, Hawke v.
Busby, Inskeep v.
Buschlen v. Ford Motor Co., 121 Mich. App. 113, 328 N.W.2d 592 (1982) — § 5-2(D).

G

L

M

O

S

U

V

Index

A

B

C

D

E

F

G

H

I

N

O

P

S